The Complexity of Computing

The Complexity
of Computing

John E. Savage
Brown University

A WILEY-INTERSCIENCE PUBLICATION

John Wiley & Sons, New York • London • Sydney • Toronto

Copyright © 1976 by John Wiley & Sons, Inc.

Library of Congress Cataloging in Publication Data:

Savage, John E   1939–
  The complexity of computing.

  "A Wiley-Interscience publication."
  Bibliography: p.
  Includes index.
  1. Machine theory. 2. Switching theory. 3. Com-
putational complexity. I. Title.
QA267.S28   001.6′4′0184   76-27733
ISBN 0–471–75517–6

Printed in the United States of America

10 9 8 7 6 5 4 3 2 1

To Patricia, Elizabeth, and Kevin, to my mother,
and to the memory of my father

Preface

The complexity of computing is one of the most important problems in computer science today. It represents an enormous challenge with which we must cope if we are to understand the complex programs and machines that we construct, and it is the principal motivation for the development of a science of computing.

There have been many responses to the complexity of computing, especially in the general area of programming. Ours is a different response. We explicitly measure the complexity of problems and then examine the resources, such as space and time, that are needed under the best possible conditions to compute functions of a given complexity on general-purpose computers. The results we derive concerning this topic are in the form of inequalities that state lower limits on possible space–time tradeoffs. The study of such tradeoffs is useful in developing intuition concerning the cost-effective use of computers.

This book serves two principal purposes. It develops the tradeoff results mentioned and gives an advanced treatment of important topics in switching and automata theory. In particular the book has two chapters (Chapters 2 and 3) on the size and depth of logic circuits and the size of formulas for Boolean functions. These chapters contain numerous interesting results, most of which are either very recent or are scattered throughout the Russian literature. The Bibliography contains an extensive list of works dealing with combinational complexity and related topics; these references are set off by asterisks.

Chapters 4 and 5 develop a number of classical topics in the theories of sequential machines and Turing machines, as well as some new results that are used to derive the tradeoff inequalities. The classical topics include reduced machines and regular expressions, universal Turing machines, unsolvability of the halting problem, and partial-recursive functions. The new topics include a product relation between the circuit size of a sequential machine, its computation time, and the circuit size of the function it is used to compute, as well as computational work and program complexity.

Chapter 6 gives an extensive treatment of the principal components of general-purpose computers, beginning with flip-flops and continuing through microprogramming to storage devices. These topics are examined from a complexity point of view. A number of interesting circuit algorithms are also given for arithmetic operations that have both small size and small depth. This chapter can serve as a good introduction to the organization of general-purpose computers.

Chapter 7 develops the computational inequalities that state lower limits on space–time tradeoffs. It also presents new results which show that the lower limits can be approached for many problems. Under the assumption that the lower limits can be achieved, we examine cost-effective operating points on the space–time boundaries under several different cost functions. We draw some interesting conclusions that are supportive of current practice.

Chapter 8 presents a sound introduction to three topics in the design and analysis of algorithms: sorting, matrix-multiplication and *NP*-complete problems. We examine a number of (nonadaptive) sorting networks as well as adaptive algorithms including Heapsort. The treatment of matrix multiplication includes the presentation of Strassen's matrix multiplication algorithm and a succinct derivation of the Fast Fourier transform algorithm. In the third section of Chapter 8, we examine a number of *NP*-complete problems as well as polynomial-time approximation algorithms for some of them. These three topics provide important results and examples of important problems that are used elsewhere in the book.

In the writing of this book I have been fortunate to have the assistance of many friends. They include Howard Elliott, Yeshoshua Imber, Roy Johnson, Edmund Lamagna, Joel Silverberg, Sowmitri Swamy, and Charles Wade, who are or recently were graduate students at Brown University and who have done a critical reading of most or much of the book. Other friends have read substantial portions of the book and/or have offered useful advice or input. They include Diedrich van Daalen, Andy van Dam, Larry Harper, Daniel Lehman, Clem McGowan, Ron Rivest, Bob Sedgewick, and Frances Yao. Many others have contributed, including my students in recent years.

The writing of the book began during my sabbatical leave in 1973–1974, which was spent in the Mathematics Department at the Technische Hogeschool Eindhoven (THE), The Netherlands. For the opportunity to spend my leave at this most hospitable institution in a most hospitable country, I thank Edsger Dijkstra and Jack van Lint. To Prof. Dr. Lunbeck I also express my thanks for a most attractive working environment.

The task of converting my jottings to typed form fell to E. E. F. M. Baselmans-Weijers, Hanny van Dongen-van Nisselrooij, Marèse van den Hurk, and H. K. van der Putten-Bosscher at THE, and to Linda and Sharon Trevitt, Joyce Oliver, and Claire Crockett at Brown. I give them my sincere thanks for their kind cooperation, speedy service, and terrific copy. My thanks are also due S. Lowes for her valuable help in chasing down references.

To Brown University, which supported a portion of my sabbatical leave as well as much of my time since then, and to the John Simon Guggenheim Memorial Foundation and the Netherlands–America Commission for Educational Exchange (NACEE) which also supported a portion of my sabbatical leave, I express my sincere appreciation. In particular, I wish to mention Wobbina Kwast, Executive Director of NACEE, who was most effective in making the Fulbright-Hays Scholars feel at home in the Netherlands. I also thank the National Science Foundation for the support of my research which has found its way into my book.

And finally, I express my sincere gratitude to my wife, Patricia, who has been a true source of support and encouragement and who has given generously of herself to facilitate the early completion of this book. I also remember our children, Elizabeth and Kevin, for their patience.

JOHN E. SAVAGE

Providence, Rhode Island
August 1976

Contents

The Complexity of Computing

Chapter 1

Introduction

. . . the world is waiting to hear the answers to such questions as
- *What measurements exist?*
- *What efficiencies do they indicate?*
- *How can operations be improved?*
- *And at what degree of predictability?*
To me this is the essence of science and engineering in any field of endeavor.

WALTER M. CARLSON
Reflections on Ljubljana
CACM, October 1971.

As we succeed in broadening and deepening our knowledge—theoretical and empirical—about computers, we shall discover that in large part their behavior is governed by simple general laws, that what appeared as complexity in the computer program was, to a considerable extent, complexity of the environment to which the program was seeking to adapt its behavior.

HERBERT A. SIMON
The Sciences of the Artificial
MIT Press, 1968.

Many important computing systems and programs are sufficiently complex that they tax our powers of comprehension, and yet we must attain some satisfactory understanding of these systems and programs before we can be reasonably confident that we are making efficient use of them. This book explicitly recognizes the complexity of computing and attempts to respond to the first question raised by Walter Carlson in the manner suggested by Herbert Simon, namely, by moving to the proper level of abstraction. At this level we examine computing systems and programs in terms of a few

1

macroscopic parameters such as space and time, and we make an effort to establish the fundamental relationships that exist between these parameters. For this purpose, we examine in detail a number of analytical tools that have a great deal of interest in their own right as well as for the role they play in the development of this new level of understanding.

1.1. COMPUTER SCIENCE AS A SCIENCE OF THE ARTIFICIAL

The handiwork of man, the artificial, is evident everywhere in our daily lives. It is seen in our clothing, the temperature of the air we breathe, the social and economic systems in which we participate, and in the composition of this book. Some of our artificial systems are fairly easy to understand and/or are not deserving of detailed analysis. Others, in particular, computer systems and programs, have such complexity and economic importance that they must be subjected to close analysis and comprehended at each of several levels.

Our purpose in this book is to lay the groundwork for such analysis and comprehension. But are we not doomed to failure? Isn't it impossible to develop a science of the artificial? These are questions that have attracted Herbert Simon in the context of management science, psychology, computer systems, and engineering education, and he offers convincing arguments that they will be settled in the negative. Speaking of natural science he says (Simon, 1969)

> The central task of a natural science is to make the wonderful commonplace:
> to show that complexity, correctly viewed, is only a mask for simplicity.

Should that not also be the objective of a science of the artificial?

If the need to understand complex man-made systems exists, where do we begin? Simon (1969) suggests an answer in his definition of an artifact, a man-made object or system:

> An artifact can be thought of as a meeting point—an "interface" in today's terms—between an inner environment, the substance and organization of the artifact itself, and an outer environment, the surroundings in which it operates.

Thus, the place to look for such an understanding is at the interface, at the point where the inner and outer environment meet, the point at which the stated goals of the system meet the internal constraints set by the inner environment.

In computing systems we suggest that one important interface is the point at which a computer program meets the physical computer. Here the physical limitations on space, time, and the capabilities of a central processor must live with the objective of the program, namely, to compute a specified function or complete some specified task. This is a profitable point at which to study programs and computers, as we see in Chapter 7.

But let us challenge this hypothesis in several ways before we accept it as a reasonable approach to the understanding of complex computer systems. We ask whether the multiplicity of computer organizations (Bell and Newell, 1971, have identified more than 1000 different such organizations) precludes the development of knowledge that is useful in studying the majority of these organizations. Despite the differentiation that has been observed in the above-mentioned taxonomy, there is a surprising degree of commonality among computer systems, and they can be grouped into a small number of classes of like systems. Thus, the interface is less complex than it would seem from this point of view. Then there is complexity in computer programs. Here we have learned recently (Dahl et al., 1972) of the importance of structured programs, programs that observe a hierarchical structure. Such programs are constructed with a few simple rules, and when approached this way they are much easier to design, understand, prove correct, and make efficient. Programs organized or viewed in this manner lose a great deal of their complexity at the interface, where they are characterized primarily by their goals. Again, it seems reasonable to examine programs and computers at this level of abstraction.

Given that it is reasonable to examine computing systems at the interface between their inner and outer environments, we ask how we might characterize the interface. A clue is found in the opinion voiced by Minsky (1970) in his Turing lecture.

> We have had misconceptions about the possible exchanges between time and memory, tradeoffs between time and program complexity, software and hardware, digital and analog circuits, serial and parallel computations, associative and addressed memory, and so on.

We are led to believe by this statement and personal programming experience that a most natural characterization of the interface is in terms of tradeoff relations. Minsky develops analogies with the natural sciences and argues that "the recognition of exchanges is often the conception of a science, if quantifying them is its birth." We are almost ready to accept this point of view, but further clarification is needed.

Computing systems are not only made by men, they are used by men. Therefore, if the interface is described by exchange relations of the equality variety, such as the conservation laws of physics, whatever invariants characterize the interface must be satisfied by all users. Because of the variety in the human race, it is unlikely that any such equality relation of any significance can hold. Thus, we are led to expect exchange relations of the inequality variety, such as the second law of thermodynamics or the Heisenberg uncertainty principle. Here the interface is characterized by inequalities that define lower limits on exchanges of space for time, for example, and explicitly permit users and programs to operate above the lower limits. One expects that the limits embody the essentials of the interface—they should be stated in terms of physical properties of computers, such as space and time, and they should reflect the nature of the program's objective. Such exchange relations are derived in Chapter 7, and the inner environment is reflected in the complexity of the program objective as measured in two different ways.

The development of computational inequalities that define the interface between programs and computers requires considerable preparation. We develop models to represent machines and computations, and we define and examine complexity measures. And finally we introduce some new concepts in the process of deriving our inequalities. The development of these ideas and tools is interesting in its own right and has occupied scholars for decades. We outline these methods and concepts in succeeding sections.

1.2. COMPUTATIONAL MODELS

To study programs and computers at their interface we must develop models for computation. In this section, we give a brief introduction to the three models we use and indicate the roles they play in modeling general-purpose computers. The three models are logic circuits, sequential machines, and Turing machines. We see that the first and last of these models play a second role, namely, providing a basis for measuring the complexity of functions.

A logic circuit, which we also call a combinational machine, is an assemblage of logic elements each of which realizes a Boolean function. (Precise definitions of circuits and functions are given in Chapter 2.) We assume that the reader has some familiarity with logic circuits and with the two-input Boolean functions of AND, OR, and NOT. (Readers not satisfying this condition can proceed directly to Chapter 2.) Denoting AND and OR by $\cdot$ and $+$, respectively, in a circuit and NOT by a small circle, we now illustrate the concept of a logic circuit by example. We do this for two problems which are instances of important problems studied later.

Given an undirected graph on four nodes, we ask whether it contains a subset of three nodes such that every pair of nodes in the subset is connected by an edge. In a graph of n nodes, a subset of k nodes that satisfies this property is called a k-clique. The "k-clique problem," which is to determine for arbitrary n and $k \leq n$ whether an arbitrary graph on n nodes has a k-clique, is very difficult and is an example of an NP-complete problem (see Chapter 8). These problems are all either of exponential or polynomial running time, but their best known algorithms are exponential. The Traveling Salesman problem and the 0-1 integer programming problem belong to this class.

The 3-clique problem on four nodes, as with the more general problem, can be characterized by a Boolean function, a function on 0-1 valued variables whose value is 0 or 1. Figure 1.2.1a shows a graph on four nodes with six edges labeled $y_1, y_2, \ldots, y_6$. Here y_i is a variable that has value 1 if the indicated edge is present and is equal to 0 otherwise. Thus, $(y_1, y_2, \ldots, y_6)$ is a binary 6-tuple that characterizes a graph on four nodes. Such a graph has a 3-clique if for one of the following sets of three nodes, every pair of nodes is connected by an edge: $\{a, b, c\}$, $\{b, c, d\}$, $\{c, d, a\}$, $\{d, a, b\}$. This condition holds for $\{a, b, c\}$ if $y_1 = y_2 = y_6 = 1$, that is, if $y_1 \cdot y_2 \cdot y_6 = 1$ where $\cdot$ denotes AND. Similar products can be formed for each set of three nodes, and if $f_{3-cl}(y_1, y_2, \ldots, y_6)$ is a Boolean function that has value 1 if and only if $(y_1, y_2, \ldots, y_6)$ characterizes a graph with a 3-clique, f_{3-cl} can be realized as the OR of these four products. Figure 1.2.1b shows a logic circuit that realizes this function. It is not known whether this circuit has a minimal number of elements or how many elements are needed in general for the k-clique problem.

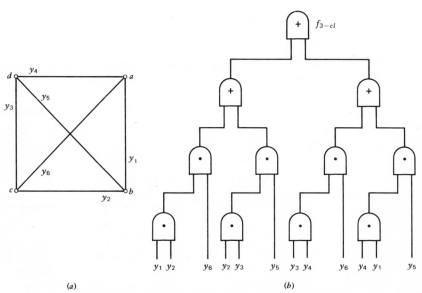

(a) (b)

Figure 1.2.1. Graph on four nodes and circuit for f_{3-cl}.

As a second example of problem and circuit consider whether $\mathbf{x} = (x_1, x_2)$ and $\mathbf{y} = (y_1, y_2)$, $x_i, y_i \in \{0, 1\}$, denoting integers $|\mathbf{x}| = x_1 \cdot 2 + x_0$ and $|\mathbf{y}| = y_1 \cdot 2 + y_0$ satisfy $|\mathbf{x}| > |\mathbf{y}|$. Let $f_{\text{COMP}}(\mathbf{x}, \mathbf{y})$ be the Boolean function defined as follows:

$$f_{\text{COMP}}(\mathbf{x}, \mathbf{y}) = \begin{cases} 1 & |\mathbf{x}| > |\mathbf{y}| \\ 0 & \text{otherwise} \end{cases}$$

This function is examined closely in Section 2.4.3. We observe that

$$f_{\text{COMP}}(\mathbf{x}, \mathbf{y}) = \begin{cases} 1 & \text{if } x_1 > y_1 \quad \text{or } x_1 = y_1 \quad \text{and } x_0 > y_0 \\ 0 & \text{otherwise} \end{cases}$$

Now if $^{-}$ denotes NOT in a formula, then $x_1 \cdot \bar{y}_1$ is 1 when $x_1 > y_1$, and $x_1 \cdot y_1 + \bar{x}_1 \bar{y}_1$ is 1 when $x_1 = y_1$. Thus, f_{COMP} can be realized by the circuit shown in Figure 1.2.2. We show in Section 2.4.3 that this circuit has a minimal number of AND's and OR's.

We turn now to the second computational model, the sequential machine. A sequential machine has memory and feedback, and at any one point in time it is in one of several states. It is given an input, then makes a state transition and produces an output. The successor state is determined

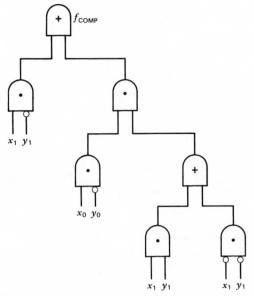

Figure 1.2.2. Circuit for f_{COMP}.

by the current state and input. Most sequential machines are clocked; that is, state transitions occur at time instants that are determined by a central clock. However, the definition of a sequential machine is not dependent on whether or not it is clocked. Sequential machines are the subject of Chapter 4.

Shown in Figure 1.2.3 are the state diagrams for two simple sequential machines. The states are numbered q_0, q_1, q_2, q_3, and the inputs are 0 and 1 for the first machine (*a*) and 0, 1, 2 for the second (*b*). The labels on arrows between states indicate the state transitions that are made on individual inputs; thus in state q_0 each machine moves to q_1 on an input of 1. The first machine produces an output of 0 in each state except q_3 in which an output of 1 is produced. If the initial state is q_0, the machine reaches this state only after receiving three 1's as input. Thus, it computes the threshold function of threshold 3.

The second machine in Figure 1.2.3 has three input symbols. Application of input 2 restores the machine to state q_0, which we take as the initial state. Otherwise the state advances on receipt of a 1, returning to q_0 on receiving a multiple of four 1's. Furthermore, the output associated with a state is a pair $\mathbf{a} = (a_1, a_0)$ which is the subscript of the state written in binary; that is, if $|\mathbf{a}| = a_1 2 + a_0$, then $\mathbf{a}$ is the output when the machine is in state $q_{|\mathbf{a}|}$. This sequential machine adds modulo 4 and can be used for three consecutive cycles and reset to q_0 in order to realize a Full Adder, a component in an adder for binary numbers (see Section 2.2).

An important point to be made here is that sequential machines compute functions, just as do logic circuits. However, since sequential

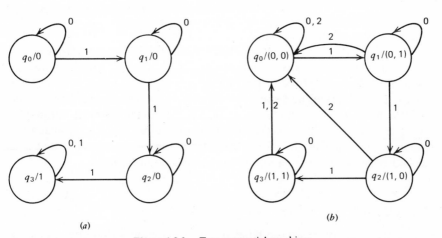

(*a*)   (*b*)

Figure 1.2.3. Two sequential machines.

machines use their memory to reuse their logic circuitry, they can realize functions with less circuitry than a no-memory machine but at the expense of time. This observation, which is elevated to the level of a theorem in Chapter 4, is one basis for the derivation of computational inequalities.

General-purpose computers come in many sizes and shapes, as indicated by the preceding. Nonetheless, they typically have the principal component shown in Figure 1.2.4. This consists of a central processing unit (CPU) and a random-access memory (RAM), the latter being a device holding an array of indexed words for which each word is accessible in one unit of time (the cycle of the RAM) by specifying its index or address. The CPU can address the RAM and store or fetch a word from it. It also executes instructions fetched from the RAM and has access to an outside world. The CPU typically can execute arithmetic operations and logical operations on words such as tests on the sign of a number, comparisons of numbers, and so forth. These operations are implemented in logic circuits, and the overall operation of the CPU and RAM can be modeled quite well as a pair of sequential machines. The component parts and functions of general-purpose computers are examined in considerable detail in Chapter 6.

Figure 1.2.4. Model of a general-purpose computer.

Our third computational model is the Turing machine. This consists of a Control, which is a sequential machine, and one or more potentially infinite tapes the heads of which are driven by the Control. It is not an especially good model for general-purpose computers, but it is a classical computational model that explicitly permits unlimited storage. In terms of the functions it can compute, no more general model has been found and yet it cannot solve some easily described problems. The Turing machine, which is described in Chapter 5, provides a complexity measure that is a second basis for the derivation of computational inequalities.

1.3. COMPLEXITY MEASURES

We make use of two basic types of complexity measures, one related to the size and depth of logic circuits, and another that is the length of a program for a Turing machine. Each is the measure of the complexity of a binary function $f: \{0, 1\}^n \rightarrow \{0, 1\}^m$ whose domain is the set of n-tuples over $\{0, 1\}$. We describe the former type of complexity measure first.

The *combinational complexity* of a function f relative to a basis Ω (set of Boolean functions such as AND, OR, and NOT), denoted $C_\Omega(f)$, is the minimum number of elements from Ω needed to realize f with a logic circuit. Although not necessary, some logic circuits have at most one edge directed away from each logic element. This is the case in Figure 1.2.2. Such circuits are said to have fan-out of 1. The minimal number of logic elements needed under this restriction is denoted $L_\Omega(f)$. This number is called *formula size* because each fan-out 1 circuit corresponds directly to a formula and the size of the circuit is the number of operators in the formula. The reader can verify this statement for f_{COMP}, whose circuit is shown in Figure 1.2.2, having the following corresponding formula: $x_1 \cdot \bar{y}_1 + (x_1 \cdot y_1 + \bar{x}_1 \cdot \bar{y}_1) \cdot x_0 \cdot \bar{y}_0$.

A combinational machine has a *depth* equal to the number of logic elements on the longest (directed) path from inputs to outputs. The *delay complexity* of f with respect to Ω, denoted $D_\Omega(f)$, is the depth of the smallest depth circuit over Ω for f. Delay complexity is proportional to the logarithm of formula size for $f: \{0, 1\}^n \rightarrow \{0, 1\}$ (Theorem 2.3.3). No other such tight relationship is known between delay complexity and combinational complexity or between formula size and combinational complexity. Combinational complexity, formula size, and delay complexity are examined in detail in Chapters 2 and 3.

In most combinational machines, the lengths of the several paths from inputs to a given logic element are different. Thus, simultaneously applied inputs arrive at the element at different times because of the differing amounts of delay introduced by elements on the several paths. Assume that each logic element introduces one unit of delay and prevent this phenomenon by introducing unit delay elements into a circuit, as necessary, to give each path to every element the same length. The resulting combinational machine is said to be *synchronous*. Then the *synchronous combinational complexity* of f relative to Ω, denoted $C_\Omega^s(f)$, is the minimum number of logic and delay elements in a synchronous combinational machine over the basis Ω. This measure is examined in Section 3.5.

Given a function f, one is often interested in finding a circuit of minimal size for it, that is, in computing its combinational complexity. One well-known tool that was introduced for this purpose is the Karnaugh map method whose generalization is the Quine–McClusky procedure (Booth, 1971). This method actually minimizes the size of a circuit that realizes functions from formulas in the sum-of-products form (see Section 2.1). This is a normal form realization, and we report a result by Lupanov which demonstrates that in this form, the simple *parity function*, which is 1 if the number of 1's among $x_1, x_2, \ldots, x_n$, $x_i \in \{0, 1\}$, is odd, has a circuit of exponential size (Theorem 2.1.2) while its minimal size circuit is linear in n. Similar results hold for other functions and other normal forms.

Combinational complexity is examined in Chapters 2 and 3, with the emphasis in Chapter 2 being on the development of lower bounds for bases Ω that are *complete*, that is, rich enough so that all functions $f: \{0, 1\}^n \to \{0, 1\}^m$ can be realized by circuits over Ω. (The basis $\Omega = \{\text{AND, OR, NOT}\}$ is complete.) Although most such functions have combinational complexity near $2^n/n$ when $m = 1$ and n is large (Section 3.4), the best lower bounds derived in Chapter 2 are linear in n. In Chapter 3 we consider an imcomplete basis $\Omega = \{\text{AND, OR}\}$ and show that binary sorting and Boolean matrix multiplication have a nonlinear combinational complexity over this basis. In fact, the standard matrix multiplication algorithm is shown to be optimal for Boolean matrix multiplication over this incomplete basis. If the basis is complete, Strassen's algorithm of Section 8.2.2 can be used to improve on the standard algorithm, thus showing the power of negation.

There are many important functions, especially addition, subtraction, multiplication, and division of binary numbers, whose combinational complexity is not known exactly. Numerous and important algorithms for these and other functions exist, and these are presented in Sections 3.1 and 6.3. These are primarily functions that find application in general-purpose computers.

Before turning to the other complexity measures, we note that in a few instances (Ehrenfeucht, 1972; Meyer, 1974; and Stockmeyer, 1974) exponential lower bounds have been derived on the combinational complexity of functions over complete bases. The method of proof of these results consists of showing that the computation of some one Boolean function on n variables amounts to the computation of all Boolean functions on k variables, where n is a polynomial in k. Because most of these have exponential combinational complexity, the result follows. These results are not treated elsewhere in the book.

Formula size is an important complexity measure in its own right as well as for the light it sheds on combinational complexity. In Section 3.4 it is shown to be near $2^n/\log_2 n$ for most functions $f: \{0, 1\}^n \to \{0, 1\}$ when n is large. It is much easier to derive nonlinear lower bounds to formula size over complete bases. The Krapchenko test (Section 3.3.1) applies to the basis $\{\text{AND, OR, NOT}\}$ and allows us to show that the parity function has formula size that is square in n over this basis. The Nechiporuk test (Section 3.3.2) applies to any complete basis and provides a lower bound that is nonlinear in n for many functions, but this lower bound is not larger than about n^2.

Synchronous combinational complexity is a new measure for which $n \log_2 n$ lower bounds can be derived for matrix multiplication and other functions. As with combinational complexity, there is some hope that this measure may be helpful in resolving the P vs NP question (Section 8.3).

The second type of complexity measure that plays an important role in this book is called *program complexity*. Defined relative to a Turing machine, it is the length of the shortest length program for a function f: $\{0, 1\}^n \rightarrow \{0, 1\}^m$ on the machine. Here a program is a fixed string whose entries are constants and variables; when the variables are evaluated, it provides a string that is placed on the nonblank portion of the input tape of the machine, and from this the function is computed. An example of such a program is a "prefix notation" for a formula. This is obtained by visiting the root node of the corresponding circuit and then visiting the left subtree and then the right subtree, applying the procedure recursively. The prefix notation for f_{COMP} as obtained from Figure 1.2.2 is $+ \cdot x_1$ $\urcorner y_1 \cdot \cdot x_0 \urcorner y_0 + \cdot x_1 y_1 \cdot \urcorner x_1 \urcorner y_1$ where $\urcorner$ denotes NOT. Because a Turing machine exists to compute f_{COMP} from this string, it represents a program. Clearly the variables must be evaluated before f_{COMP} can be computed.

The program complexity of f relative to U, a 1-tape universal Turing machine, is denoted $I_U(f)$ and is examined in Section 5.7. Unlike combinational complexity and related measures, the value of this measure on a function cannot be determined by enumeration. In fact there is no general procedure for this problem. Nonetheless, its value is known to within a small constant for many important functions f.

1.4. COMPUTATIONAL INEQUALITIES

Earlier in this chapter we argue that one useful way to characterize the interface between programs and computers is through exchange relations of the inequality variety. We now outline the development of these computational inequalities.

Exchange relations can be derived for any type of computer, as the reader will see. To illustrate the method of derivation, we examine in Chapter 7 a small set of representative machine types. In this section we limit our discussion to the general-purpose computer indicated schematically in Figure 1.2.4, namely, a machine with a CPU and an RAM.

We assume that the task or objective of a program is characterized by a function f: $\{0, 1\}^n \rightarrow \{0, 1\}^m$ and that the physical limitations on the machine are specified by T, the maximum number of cycles used to compute f on any point of its domain, and S, the storage capacity of the RAM measured in bits. We make no specific assumptions about the CPU except that its "size" increases slowly with S, the capacity of the RAM.

Inequalities of two kinds are derived, those of the "first kind," which make use of combinational complexity, and those of the "second kind," which make use of program complexity. The derivation of each kind of inequality uses the idea of simulation.

The starting point for the derivations is to characterize a general-purpose computer M by a *descriptor function* $G_{M,T}$ that maps the T external inputs M can receive and its initial state, which is the state of the CPU and of the RAM, onto the external outputs it generates. We assume that the external outputs contain the value of f. It follows that f can be obtained by programming M, that is, by fixing the variables of $G_{M,T}$ in some way. Indulging in a bit of poetic license, we say that

$$C_\Omega(f) \leq C_\Omega(G_{M,T})$$

$$I_U(f) \leq I_U(G_{M,T})$$

because, roughly speaking, f can be computed from a circuit for $G_{M,T}$ without additional logic elements and because it can be computed on the universal Turing machine U from a program for $G_{M,T}$ without an increase in its length. These inequalities are not quite correct, but are nearly so.

The next step is to derive upper bounds to $C_\Omega(G_{M,T})$ and $I_U(G_{M,T})$ in terms of the physical parameters of M. To bound the first quantity, we argue that M can be modeled as a sequential machine and bound $C_\Omega(G_{M,T})$ by the size of a logic circuit that computes $G_{M,T}$. Such a logic circuit can be constructed from approximately T copies of the equivalent logic circuit of M. If δ and λ map the input and state of M onto a successor state and output, respectively, then T copies of a circuit for δ, λ will compute $G_{M,T}$ because instead of feeding the successor state back to compute a new successor with δ, we can pass it forward to a second copy of a logic circuit for δ. It follows that

$$C_\Omega(G_{M,T}) \leq C_\Omega(\delta, \lambda)T$$

Again, we are indulging in a bit of poetic license as the reader can see by referring to Section 4.5 where this inequality is derived. Now $C_\Omega(\delta, \lambda)$ consists of two parts: the "size" of the CPU and the "size" of the RAM. In Chapter 6 the latter is shown to be proportional to S, so for large S we have

$$C_\Omega(f) \leq KST$$

where $K > 0$ is a constant.

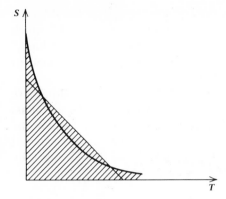

Figure 1.4.1. Space-time boundaries.

The upper bound to $I_U(G_{M,T})$ is derived by constructing a program on U for $G_{M,T}$. When S and T are large, the length of the program is dominated by the number of variables of $G_{M,T}$, and one can show that

$$I_U(G_{M,T}) \leq K^*(S + Tb)$$

where $K^* > 0$ is a constant. Here S is the amount of information that M has initially, Tb is the amount that it is supplied in T cycles in units of b bits per input word, and $I_U(G_{M,T})$ is the minimum amount of information that must be given to U to compute $G_{M,T}$.

These two inequalities apply to a general-purpose computer consisting of a CPU and an RAM of storage capacity S when S is large. They define lower limits on space-time exchanges as indicated in Figure 1.4.1. In Chapter 7 we show that under some circumstances we can come close to achieving these lower boundaries. That being the case, and in the absence of detailed knowledge of the achievable space-time curve for individual functions, we assume that we can operate on the lower boundaries to ascertain the implications of this assumption. We then examine and justify computing cost measures of the form $(\alpha + \beta S)T$ and $\alpha S + \beta T$ for non-negative constants α and β. We find that these costs are minimized when S is small and T large or vice versa or both. This strongly suggests that cost-effective computing occurs at the extremes of the space–time curves and tends to support multiprogramming and the use of minicomputers.

Chapter 2

Combinational
Complexity
of Functions

The origin of the study of the combinational complexity of binary functions can be traced to the thesis of Shannon (1938) in which he demonstrated the importance of Boolean algebra to the design and analysis of relay switching circuits. This was followed a short time later by the work of Riordan and Shannon (1942) on series-parallel networks, which gave further impetus to the study of switching circuits. Then in 1949 another paper by Shannon (1949) put the study of switching circuits on a proper footing and was particularly important in its impact on work in this area by Russian mathematicians. The very successful program of research carried on by this group has broadened the base of the field, has led to many refinements on Shannon's early work, and has resulted in studies of the complexities of many individual functions. Interest in combinational complexity has now become international, with many important contributions being made in all quarters. In addition, the overlap with the developing studies of the complexities of combinatorial and algebraic problems has become significant and important (Borodin, 1973).

In this and the following chapter, we give a broad review of contributions to the study of combinational complexity and survey those important results that are not developed in detail. This chapter develops normal form expansions of Boolean functions and defines chains, which are general representations for binary functions using functional composition. Complexity measures on chains are defined, and some relations between them are developed. A major portion of this chapter is concerned with methods for developing lower bounds to the value of one of these measures, combinational complexity. Chapter 3 continues the discussion of complexity measures on chains, primarily be examining many important types of functions.

2.1. BOOLEAN FUNCTIONS AND NORMAL FORMS

A *Boolean function* is a function f with domain $\{0, 1\}^n$ and range $\{0, 1\}$, for some integer n. Here $\{0, 1\}^n$ denotes the n-fold cartesian product of the set $\{0, 1\}$ with itself, that is, the set of binary n-tuples. This information about f is conveyed by the notation $f\colon \{0, 1\}^n \to \{0, 1\}$. Often a set of m Boolean functions $f_1, f_2, \ldots, f_m$ is under consideration where $f_i\colon \{0, 1\}^n \to \{0, 1\}$. In this case, it is convenient to represent this collection by a single function $f\colon \{0, 1\}^n \to \{0, 1\}^m$ whose range is a set of binary m-tuples. An arbitrary point in the domain $\{0, 1\}^n$ is denoted by $\mathbf{x} = (x_1, x_2, \ldots, x_n)$, and the value of f at this point is represented by $f(x_1, x_2, \ldots, x_n)$. We speak of x_i as a *variable* of f (more on this later).

A function $f\colon \{0, 1\}^n \to \{0, 1\}^m$ can be completely described by a table, as shown in Table 2.1.1 for the four functions $f_-, f_+, f_.,$ and $f_\oplus$. These are very important functions, and we shall encounter them often. They are called NEGATION (or Boolean complement), Boolean OR (or disjunction), Boolean AND (or conjunction), and EXCLUSIVE-OR (also equivalent to addition modulo 2), respectively. Simple enumeration demonstrates that there are four Boolean functions of one variable, namely, the identity mapping $f_I(x) = x$, f_-, and the two constant functions $f_0(x) = 0$ and $f_1(x) = 1$. Similarly, it can be shown that there are 2^{2^n} Boolean functions of n variables and 2^{m2^n} functions $f\colon \{0, 1\}^n \to \{0, 1\}^m$.

Tables do give complete descriptions of functions, but functions are often much more simply represented in other ways. One important method of representing functions, and the subject of this chapter, consists of the composition of functions from a basic set of functions. Through functional composition, a table can be described by logic circuits as well as by

Table 2.1.1. Tables of Four Important Boolean Functions

x_1	f_-		x_1	x_2	f_+		x_1	x_2	$f_.$		x_1	x_2	$f_\oplus$
0	1		0	0	0		0	0	0		0	0	0
1	0		0	1	1		0	1	0		0	1	1
			1	0	1		1	0	0		1	0	1
			1	1	1		1	1	1		1	1	0

formulas. In this section, we examine four types of formula expansions of functions which are called "normal forms." But first we introduce functional composition.

Definition 2.1.1. Given the functions g: $\{0, 1\}^p \to \{0, 1\}^m$ and h_i: $\{0, 1\}^n \to \{0, 1\}$, $1 \leq i \leq p$, the *composition* of g with $h_1, h_2, \ldots, h_p$, denoted $g(h_1, h_2, \ldots, h_p)$, defines a function f: $\{0, 1\}^n \to \{0, 1\}^m$ by the rule

$$f(\mathbf{x}) = g(h_1(\mathbf{x}), \ldots, h_p(\mathbf{x}))$$

for all $\mathbf{x} = (x_1, x_2, \ldots, x_n) \in \{0, 1\}^n$

Example 2.1.1. The function $f(x_1, x_2, x_3) = f.(f.(x_1, x_2), x_3)$ has value 1 only when x_1, x_2, and x_3 are all equal to 1.

The role of the functions $f_-, f_+, f_.,$ and $f_\oplus$ is so important in forming other functions by composition that we develop a few of their properties here. Before doing so, however, we note the existence of the important but trivial projection functions $\{ p_i(x_1, x_2, \ldots, x_n) = x_i \mid 1 \leq i \leq n \}$, which we henceforth call *variables* and denote simply as x_i, $1 \leq i \leq n$. The two constant functions are also denoted 0 and 1.

The functions $f_-, f_+, f_.,$ and $f_\oplus$ are used so frequently that the following shorthand exists for them:

$$f_-(x_1) = \bar{x}_1, \qquad f_+(x_1, x_2) = x_1 + x_2,$$

$$f.(x_1, x_2) = x_1 \cdot x_2, \qquad f_\oplus(x_1, x_2) = x_1 \oplus x_2$$

where occasionally $x_1 \cdot x_2$ is abbreviated to $x_1 x_2$ with the $\cdot$ removed. Some of the properties of these operators follow.

Theorem 2.1.1.
Associativity

$$x_1 + (x_2 + x_3) = (x_1 + x_2) + x_3$$

$$x_1 \cdot (x_2 \cdot x_3) = (x_1 \cdot x_2) \cdot x_3$$

$$x_1 \oplus (x_2 \oplus x_3) = (x_1 \oplus x_2) \oplus x_3$$

Commutativity

$$x_1 + x_2 = x_2 + x_1$$

$$x_1 \cdot x_2 = x_2 \cdot x_1$$

$$x_1 \oplus x_2 = x_2 \oplus x_1$$

Distributivity

$$x_1 \cdot (x_2 + x_3) = (x_1 \cdot x_2) + (x_1 \cdot x_3)$$

$$x_1 \cdot (x_2 \oplus x_3) = (x_1 \cdot x_2) \oplus (x_1 \cdot x_3)$$

$$x_1 + (x_2 \cdot x_3) = (x_1 + x_2) \cdot (x_1 + x_3)$$

DeMorgan's rules

$$\overline{(x_1 + x_2)} = \bar{x}_1 \cdot \bar{x}_2$$

$$\overline{(x_1 \cdot x_2)} = \bar{x}_1 + \bar{x}_2$$

Absorption rules

$$x_1 + \bar{x}_1 = 1$$

$$x_1 + x_1 = x_1$$

$$x_1 \cdot \bar{x}_1 = 0$$

$$x_1 \cdot x_1 = x_1$$

$$x_1 + x_1 \cdot x_2 = x_1 \cdot (x_1 + x_2) = x_1$$

Substitution of constants

$$x_1 + 0 = x_1$$
$$x_1 + 1 = 1$$
$$x_1 \cdot 0 = 0$$
$$x_1 \cdot 1 = x_1$$
$$x_1 \oplus 0 = x_1$$
$$x_1 \oplus 1 = \bar{x}_1$$

These properties are easily established, and their proofs are left as an exercise (Problem 2.1). Because of the commutativity laws, it is unnecessary to parenthesize repeated compositions of one of $+$, $\cdot$, or $\oplus$.

One important canonical representation of a Boolean function is the *disjunctive normal form* (DNF) which is formed by composition of the variables x_i with AND, OR, and NEGATION as follows. If $f: \{0, 1\}^n \to \{0, 1\}$ has value 1 on the point $(x_1, x_2, \ldots, x_n) = (c_1, c_2, \ldots, c_n)$ where

$c_i \in \{0, 1\}$, then we form the *minterm* function

$$m_{c_1}, \ldots, _{c_n}(x_1, \ldots, x_n) = x_1^{c_1} \cdot x_2^{c_2} \cdot \cdots \cdot x_n^{c_n}$$

where $x_i^1 = x_i$ and $x_i^0 = \bar{x}_i$. This function has value 1 only when $(x_1, x_2, \ldots, x_n) = (c_1, c_2, \ldots, c_n)$. Then, the DNF of f is given by

$$f(x_1, x_2, \ldots, x_n) = \sum_{\substack{c_1, c_2, \ldots, c_n \ni \\ f(c_1, c_2, \ldots, c_n) = 1}} m_{c_1, c_2, \ldots, c_n}(x_1, x_2, \ldots, x_n)$$

where Σ denotes the repeated Boolean OR and the sum is taken over all binary n-tuples.

Example 2.1.2. The function $f(x_1, x_2, x_3) = x_1 \oplus x_2 \oplus x_3$ has the DNF

$$x_1 \oplus x_2 \oplus x_3 = \bar{x}_1 \bar{x}_2 x_3 + \bar{x}_1 x_2 \bar{x}_3 + x_1 \bar{x}_2 \bar{x}_3 + x_1 x_2 x_3$$

From this demonstration of a canonical representation of Boolean functions we learn that

(1) Every function $f: \{0, 1\}^n \to \{0, 1\}^m$ can be realized by composition of functions from the *basis* $\{ +, \cdot, ^- \}$ when the variables $\{x_1, x_2, \ldots, x_n\}$ are available. We call a basis for which this is true a *complete basis*.

(2) Some "simple" functions such as $x_1 \oplus x_2 \oplus \cdots \oplus x_n$ have very "complex" DNFs. In fact the DNF of this function contains 2^{n-1} minterms since it has value 1 on 2^{n-1} points of its domain (see Theorem 2.1.2.).

The *conjunctive normal form* (CNF) of a Boolean function f is another canonical representation that is obtained from the negation of the DNF of $\bar{f}$ as follows. Let

$$s_{c_1, \ldots, c_n}(x_1, x_2, \ldots, x_n) = \left(x_1^{\bar{c}_1} + x_2^{\bar{c}_2} + \cdots + x_n^{\bar{c}_n} \right)$$

Then $s_{c_1, \ldots, c_n}(x_1, \ldots, x_n)$ has value 0 only when $x_i = c_i$, $1 \leq i \leq n$, and the CNF of f is given by

$$f(x_1, \ldots, x_n) = \prod_{\substack{c_1, \ldots, c_n \ni \\ f(c_1, \ldots, c_n) = 0}} s_{c_1, \ldots, c_n}(x_1, \ldots, x_n)$$

where $\prod$ denotes repeated application of Boolean AND and the product is taken over all binary n-tuples. It can be shown that this expansion follows from the application of DeMorgan's rules to the DNF of $\bar{f}$ (Problem 2.2), and $s_{c_1, \ldots, c_n}(x_1, \ldots, x_n)$ is the negation of the minterm $m_{c_1, \ldots, c_n}(x_1, \ldots, x_n)$.

Another important canonical representation is the *ring-sum expansion* (RSE) which is obtained from the DNF of a function f by use of the identity $\bar{x} = x \oplus 1$ and the observation that the OR in the DNF can be replaced by EXCLUSIVE-OR since only one minterm is nonzero on any given point $\mathbf{x}$ in the domain of f. Thus, a minterm $x_1\bar{x}_2\bar{x}_3$ can be expanded as

$$x_1\bar{x}_2\bar{x}_3 = x_1(x_2 \oplus 1)(x_3 \oplus 1) = x_1 \oplus x_1x_2 \oplus x_1x_3 \oplus x_1x_2x_3$$

so that f can be written in an RSE as

$$f(x_1, x_2, \ldots, x_n) = a_0 \oplus \sum_{j=1}^{n} \sum_{1 \leqslant i_1 < i_2 < \cdots < i_j \leqslant n} a_{i_1, \ldots, i_j} \cdot x_{i_1} \cdot \cdots \cdot x_{i_j}$$

where $a_0, a_{i_1, \ldots, i_j} \in \{0, 1\}$ and $\sum$ denotes addition mod 2 or repeated application of $\oplus$. It is left as an exercise (Problem 2.3) to show that there is a 1–1 correspondence between the coefficients in an RSE expansion and a function $f : \{0, 1\}^n \to \{0, 1\}$.

A fourth type of normal form is the *sum-of-products expansion* (SOPE) in which a Boolean function f is expanded as the Boolean OR of products of the form $x_{i_1}^{c_1} \cdot x_{i_2}^{c_2} \cdot \cdots \cdot x_{i_l}^{c_l}$ where $1 \leq l \leq n$. This expansion is encountered in almost every textbook on switching theory or logical design, and it is this expansion that is optimized by the well-known Quine–McCluskey algorithm (Miller, 1965; Harrison, 1965). In the DNF form of a function, two minterms such as $x_1\bar{x}_2\bar{x}_3$ and $x_1\bar{x}_2x_3$ may be combined into the product $x_1\bar{x}_2$, which permits a reduction in the number of binary operations. Thus, it is thought that the sum-of-products expansion may offer a considerable improvement over the DNF. In general this may be true, but we now show that our friendly function $f(x_1, x_2, \ldots, x_n) = x_1 \oplus x_2 \oplus \cdots \oplus x_n$ has a "best" SOPE that is identical with its DNF. This result is due to Lupanov (1961c) and demonstrates that the SOPE of some simple functions can have an exponential number of literals (a *literal* is a variable x_i or its complement $\bar{x}_i$).

Theorem 2.1.2. The sum-of-products expansion of the function $f(x_1, x_2, \ldots, x_n) = x_1 \oplus x_2 \oplus \cdots \oplus x_n$ with the fewest occurrences of literals is identical with the DNF of f and contains $n2^{n-1}$ literals.

Proof. The function f has value 1 on exactly 2^{n-1} points of its domain. Furthermore, its value is changed if any one of its variables is changed.
    Write f as

$$f = p_1 + p_2 + \cdots + p_k$$

where p_i is a product of literals. If p_i does not contain every variable or its complement (say x_l is missing), there exist $\mathbf{x}, \mathbf{y} \in \{0, 1\}^n$ differing in the value of one variable (x_l, say) such that $p_i(\mathbf{x}) = p_i(\mathbf{y}) = 1$. This contradicts the nature of f, so every product p_i is a minterm. The conclusion follows directly.   □

The normal forms presented above permit the representation of functions by formulas obtained from the constant functions 0, 1, and the variables $x_1, x_2, \ldots, x_n$ through functional composition of elements from a set of "basis" elements. These are not the most general representations of functions using composition nor are they the most compact. In fact, the number of terms in the SOPE of $x_1 \oplus x_2 \oplus \cdots \oplus x_n$ is exponential in n while the number of terms in its RSE is linear in n. The more general language for representing Boolean functions using just functional composition is the language of "computation chains," which is defined and examined in the next section.

2.2. COMPUTATION CHAINS AND COMBINATIONAL MACHINES

The computation chain, or simply *chain*, is a well-defined object that describes a data-independent sequence of steps for the evaluation of functions. The definition given here may be broadened in several ways and in fact may be used as a context in which to derive lower bounds on the number of multiplications required for such algebraic problems as matrix-vector multiplication and polynomial evaluation over rings and fields (Fiduccia, 1971; Winograd, 1970).

Definition 2.2.1. Given a set $\Omega = \{h_i | h_i: \{0, 1\}^{n_i} \to \{0, 1\}\}$ of Boolean functions, called the *basis*, and a *data set* $\Gamma = \{x_1, x_2, \ldots, x_n, 0, 1\}$ of the n variables $x_1, \ldots, x_n$ and the two constant functions, a k-step *chain* $\beta = (\beta_1, \beta_2, \ldots, \beta_k)$ is an ordered set of k steps $\beta_1, \beta_2, \ldots, \beta_k$ in which either $\beta_j \in \Gamma$ or

$$\beta_j = \left(h_i; \beta_{j_1}, \beta_{j_2}, \ldots, \beta_{j_{n_i}} \right)$$

in which case $1 \leq j_r < j$, $1 \leq r \leq n_i$, and $h_i \in \Omega$. Steps of the first type are called *data steps* and the others are called *computation steps*.

With each step is associated a function $\tilde{\beta}_j$ where $\tilde{\beta}_j = \beta_j$ if $\beta_j \in \Gamma$ and

$$\tilde{\beta}_j = h_i\left(\tilde{\beta}_{j_1}, \ldots, \tilde{\beta}_{j_{n_i}} \right)$$

otherwise. Clearly, composition is the only rule employed here. A chain β

is said to *compute* $f_1, f_2, \ldots, f_m$, where $f_i: \{0, 1\}^n \to \{0, 1\}$, if there exist m steps $\beta_{i_1}, \beta_{i_2}, \ldots, \beta_{i_m}$ such that $\tilde{\beta}_{i_r} = f_r$, $1 \leq r \leq m$.

A basis Ω is said to be *complete* if for every function $f: \{0, 1\}^n \to \{0, 1\}^m$ there exists a chain β with basis Ω over the data set Γ that computes f. The bases $\Omega_1 = \{+, \cdot, ^-\}$ and $\Omega_2 = \{\oplus, \cdot\}$ are complete.

It is often convenient to have a graphical representation of a chain. Such a *graph* of a chain β can be constructed by associating a labeled node with each step of β and by attaching a directed edge from node β_{j_r} to node β_j if step β_{j_r} is employed by step β_j. Nodes labeled with variables or constants are called *source nodes* and the others are called *computation nodes*. The graph of a chain is known as a *combinational machine* or a *logic circuit*, because an actual machine can be constructed by replacing the nodes by electrical or mechanical logic elements and the edges by wires. Note that there are no directed loops in a combinational machine.

Example 2.2.1. The function $x_1 \oplus x_2 \oplus \bar{x}_3$ is realized over the basis $\Omega = \{\oplus, \cdot, ^-\}$ by the chain $\beta = (\beta_1, \beta_2, \beta_3, \beta_4, \beta_5, \beta_6)$ where

$$\beta_1 = x_1, \qquad \beta_2 = x_2, \qquad \beta_3 = x_3, \qquad \beta_4 = (\oplus; \beta_1, \beta_2),$$

$$\beta_5 = (^-; \beta_3), \qquad \beta_6 = (\oplus; \beta_4, \beta_5)$$

and

$$\tilde{\beta}_4 = x_1 \oplus x_2, \qquad \tilde{\beta}_6 = x_1 \oplus x_2 \oplus \bar{x}_3$$

The graph of β is shown in Figure 2.2.1, where the nodes associated with steps β_4 and β_6 are given.

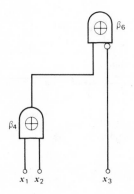

Figure 2.2.1. Graph of a chain for $x_1 \oplus x_2 \oplus \bar{x}_3$.

NOTE.   Nodes associated with NEGATION are shown as small circles; the other node labels are obvious. Although the graphs are directed, it is generally not necessary to show edge directions since they are obvious.

Example 2.2.2.   The two functions c_j and s_j given in terms of the variables c_{j-1}, x_j, and y_j describe a *Full Adder*, a component that may be used to realize binary addition.

$$s_j = c_{j-1} \oplus x_j \oplus y_j, \qquad c_j = c_{j-1} \cdot x_j + c_{j-1} \cdot y_j + x_j \cdot y_j$$

The graph of a chain for these two functions over the basis $\Omega = \{\oplus, +, \cdot\}$ is shown in Figure 2.2.2. The reader will want to show equivalence between the functions realized by the graph and the functions described by these equations.

NOTE.   To simplify a graph we often use many copies of source nodes.

The graph shown in Figure 2.2.2 has the property that one node has two edges directed away from it. A node is said to have *fan-out s* if it has s edges directed away from it, and the *fan-out of a chain* (and its associated combinational machine) is s if all nodes except source nodes have fan-out no larger than s. A basis Ω is said to have *fan-in r* if $n_i \le r$ for all basis elements

$$h_i \in \Omega, h_i : \{0, 1\}^{n_i} \to \{0, 1\}$$

and if $n_i = r$ for some i.

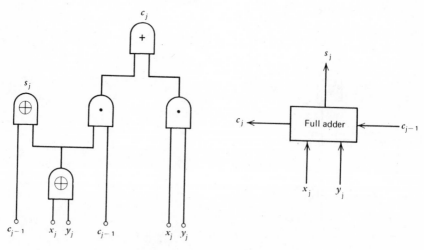

Figure 2.2.2.   Graph of a Full Adder.

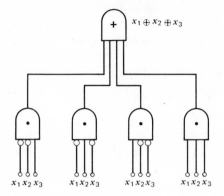

Figure 2.2.3. Disjunctive normal form of $x_1 \oplus x_2 \oplus x_3$.

A combinational machine with fan-out 1 is a tree or a collection of trees. Each tree in such a graph can be represented by a formula, as shown in Figure 2.2.3 for the DNF of $x_1 \oplus x_2 \oplus x_3$, when the basis consists of f_-, the three-input AND $f_.$ defined by $f_.(x_1, x_2, x_3) = x_1 \cdot x_2 \cdot x_3$, and the four-input OR f_+ defined by $f_+(x_1, x_2, x_3, x_4) = x_1 + x_2 + x_3 + x_4$. The DNF of $x_1 \oplus x_2 \oplus x_3$ is given in Example 2.1.2.

It is important to have a notion of the "depth" of a combinational machine. First, we observe that such a graph has nodes with no edges directed into them. These are called *source nodes* and are labeled with constants or variables and *terminal nodes*, which have no edges directed away from them. A *path* through the graph of a chain is a sequence of directed edges $e_1, e_2, \ldots, e_l$ where e_1 is directed away from a source node, e_l is directed toward a terminal node, e_i is directed toward some computation node, and e_{i+1} is directed away from that same node. Such a path is said to have *length l* and the graph of a chain is said to have *depth d* if its longest path has length d. For example, the graphs shown in Figures 2.2.1 and 2.2.2 have depth 2 and 3, respectively.

The depth of a combinational machine is an important measure of the time required to compute a function because in practice each logic element introduces a finite delay caused by its composition and size. If the delay introduced by each logic element is the same, then the depth of the machine measures the time required for inputs to propagate to the outputs, or the time required for the outputs to reach a steady-state condition.

2.3. COMBINATIONAL COMPLEXITY MEASURES

We now introduce the complexity measures that play such a large role in this chapter.

Definition 2.3.1. The *combinational complexity with fan-out s* of the function $f: \{0, 1\}^n \to \{0, 1\}^m$ over the basis Ω, denoted $C_{s, \Omega}(f)$, or $C_s(f)$ when Ω is understood, is the minimum number of computation steps required to compute f with a chain over Ω with fan-out s and with data set $\Gamma = \{x_1, x_2, \ldots, x_n, 0, 1\}$. If such a chain does not exist, $C_{s, \Omega}(f)$ is not defined.

NOTE. Source nodes are allowed to have unlimited fan-out.

Definition 2.3.2. The *delay complexity* of the function $f: \{0, 1\}^n \to \{0, 1\}^m$ over the basis Ω, denoted $D_\Omega(f)$, is the depth of the smallest depth chain for f over Ω with data set $\Gamma = \{x_1, x_2, \ldots, x_n, 0, 1\}$. If such a chain does not exist, $D_\Omega(f)$ is not defined.

We conclude immediately that

Theorem 2.3.1. Let Ω be a complete basis and let $f: \{0, 1\}^n \to \{0, 1\}^m$. Then $C_s(f)$ is defined for all integers $s \geq 1$ and

$$C_\infty(f) \leq C_{s+1}(f) \leq C_s(f) \leq C_1(f)$$

Proof. Since Ω is complete, there exists a chain for f. Given the graph of such a chain, a new graph with fan-out 1 can be constructed by replicating, repeatedly, all subgraphs of fan-out greater than 1 until a tree is constructed. (See, for example, Figure 2.2.2, in which the node labeled $\oplus$ and connected to x_j and y_j would be copied twice in such a process.) Having demonstrated the existence of a chain in which each node has fan-out at most s, we establish that $C_s(f)$ is defined for all $s \geq 1$.

Since a fan-out of $s + 1$ is less restrictive than a fan-out of s, the inequality $C_{s+1}(f) \leq C_s(f)$ follows. $\qquad \square$

The following result establishes that the complexity measures $C_\infty(f)$ and $C_s(f)$, $s \geq 2$, have about the same value on any $f: \{0, 1\}^n \to \{0, 1\}^m$ (reported in Johnson, Savage, and Welch, 1972).

Theorem 2.3.2. Let $f: \{0, 1\}^n \to \{0, 1\}^m$ and let Ω be a complete basis of fan-in r. There is a constant l_I peculiar to the basis with $1 \leq l_I \leq 2$, such that for $s \geq 2$

$$C_s(f) \leq \left(1 + l_I\left(\frac{r-1}{s-1}\right)\right)C_\infty(f) + \frac{ml_I}{s-1}$$

Proof. Let β be an optimal chain with unlimited fan-out for f. Number the $C_\infty(f)$ computation steps of this chain from 1 to $C_\infty(f)$ and let θ_i be the number of edges directed away from the ith computation node in the graph of this chain. Let the nodes numbered $C_\infty(f) - (m - 1), \ldots, C_\infty(f)$ be the terminal nodes associated with f that have $\theta_i = 0$. The number of edges in this graph is at least $\sum_i \theta_i$ and at most $rC_\infty(f)$ since each edge is directed into a computation node and there are at most r edges directed into any one computation node. It follows that

$$\sum_{i=1}^{C_\infty(f) - m} \theta_i \leq rC_\infty(f)$$

If $\theta_i > s$, where s is the desired fan-out, then a new subchain is formed to provide the θ_i output edges using fan-out at most s, but at the expense of a number of additional computation nodes. In constructing such a subchain, we assume the existence (shown later) of a chain that realizes the identity function $f_I(x) = x$ using l_I basis elements and that has fan-out 1 from the variable x.

If $s < \theta_i \leq 2s - 1$, reduce the fan-out from the ith computation nodes to s and use one of these edges as an input to a chain for f_I, the identity function. Let this chain have $\theta_i - s$ edges directed away from it. This construction can be used repeatedly so that if $s + (k - 1)(s - 1) < \theta_i \leq s + k(s - 1)$, then k copies of the chain for f_I may be used to generate the θ_i edges with a subchain of fan-out s. The number of computation steps added is kl_I, and this is bounded above by $l_I(\theta_i - 1)/(s - 1)$. Note that this bound is nonnegative even when $1 \leq \theta_i \leq s$. Therefore, the total number of computation steps in the modified chain is bounded above by

$$C_\infty(f) + l_I \sum_{i=1}^{C_\infty(f) - m} \frac{\theta_i - 1}{s - 1}$$

But from the earlier inequality this is further bounded by

$$C_\infty(f) + \frac{l_I}{s - 1}(rC_\infty(f) - C_\infty(f) + m)$$

Since the chain that has been constructed may not be an optimal chain of fan-out s, the inequality of the lemma follows.

We now show that every complete basis contains a basis element from which either x or $\bar{x}$ can be obtained by replacement of some of the variables with constants. Such an element realizes a nonmonotonic Boolean function. From it $f_I(x) = x$ can be realized with l_I elements, $1 \leq l_I \leq 2$.

Let $c_i, c_i' \in \{0, 1\}$ be ordered by the standard ordering relation $\leq$. Then $\mathbf{c}, \mathbf{c}' \in \{0, 1\}^p$ are ordered by $\leq$; that is, $\mathbf{c} \leq \mathbf{c}'$, if and only if $c_i \leq c_i'$ for all $1 \leq i \leq p$, where c_i and c_i' are the ith components of these two p-tuples. Then $g: \{0, 1\}^p \to \{0, 1\}$ is *monotone* if for all $\mathbf{c}, \mathbf{c}' \in \{0, 1\}^p$ with $\mathbf{c} \leq \mathbf{c}'$ we have $g(\mathbf{c}) \leq g(\mathbf{c}')$. Since the variables and constants are monotone, one can easily show that if every function in a basis Ω is monotone, then every function realized by a chain over that basis is also monotone. But since $\bar{x}$ is nonmonotone, every complete basis must contain a nonmonotone element.

Let $h: \{0, 1\}^p \to \{0, 1\}$ be such a nonmonotone element. For each $\mathbf{c} \in \{0, 1\}^p$ consider all $\mathbf{c}' \in \{0, 1\}^p$ with $\mathbf{c}' \geq \mathbf{c}$ and $\mathbf{c}'$ differing from $\mathbf{c}$ in one position. If for all such pairs $(\mathbf{c}, \mathbf{c}')$, $h(\mathbf{c}) \leq h(\mathbf{c}')$, then h is monotone. Therefore, there exists a pair such that $h(\mathbf{c}) > h(\mathbf{c}')$. Let such a $\mathbf{c}$ and $\mathbf{c}'$ differ in position j. Give the jth variable of h the name x and assign to its remaining variables the values of the corresponding components of $\mathbf{c}$. Then changing the value of x from 0 to 1 causes h to change from 1 to 0; that is, $\bar{x}$ is realized. From this $f_I(x) = x$ can be generated with at most two basis elements. $\qquad\square$

These two theorems demonstrate that the combinational complexity measures with fan-out s for $s \geq 2$ give the same order of magnitude estimate of the complexity of a function $f: \{0, 1\}^n \to \{0, 1\}^m$. However, we see later that the measures $C_1(f)$ and $C_\infty(f)$ can have markedly different values on particular functions. Therefore, from this point on we recognize and study only these two combinational complexity measures.

NOTATION. The *combinational complexity with fan-out* 1, namely, $C_1(f)$, is denoted $L_\Omega(f)$ and called *formula size*; the *combinational complexity with unlimited fan-out* is denoted $C_\Omega(f)$ and called simply the *combinational complexity* of f.

The remaining complexity measure, namely, delay complexity $D_\Omega(f)$, is not independent of these two measures. In fact, as shown in the following, given $L_\Omega(f)$, fairly tight bounds on $D_\Omega(f)$ can be derived. This type of result was first introduced by Spira (1971).

Theorem 2.3.3. Let $f: \{0, 1\}^n \to \{0, 1\}$ be a Boolean function and let Ω be a complete basis with fan-in r. Define the selection function by

$$\mathrm{sel}(x, y, z) = \begin{cases} y & x = 0 \\ z & x = 1 \end{cases}$$

Then

$$\log_r[(r - 1)L_\Omega(f) + 1] \leq D_\Omega(f) \leq K_r \log_r[(r - 1)L_\Omega(f) + 1]$$

where

$$K_r = \frac{D_\Omega(\text{sel}) + 1}{\log_r[(r + 1)/r]}$$

Proof. We first derive the lower bound. An optimal chain of fan-out 1 for a Boolean function has a single terminal node, and its graph is a single tree. If a tree of depth d has fan-in r, then it has at most $N = 1 + r + r^2 + \cdots + r^{d-1}$ nodes since it has one root, at most r ancestors of the root, at most r ancestors of ancestors, and so on. Since $rN - N = r^d - 1$, we have $N = (r^d - 1)/(r - 1)$. But $L_\Omega(f)$ nodes are required to compute $f: \{0, 1\}^n \to \{0, 1\}$ with a chain of fan-out 1 over Ω, so the best possible arrangement of these nodes leads to a tree with depth of at least d where d is the smallest integer satisfying

$$\frac{r^d - 1}{r - 1} \geq L_\Omega(f)$$

The lower bound follows immediately.

The upper bound is a little more difficult to derive. Our proof is by induction. We note that $0 < \log_r[(r + 1)/r] < 1$ and $K_r > 2$.

Basis. For $L_\Omega(f) = 1, 2$, $D_\Omega(f) \leq K_r \log_r[(r - 1)L_\Omega(f) + 1]$.

This follows directly from the observation that $D_\Omega(f) = L_\Omega(f)$ in these cases and from the knowledge that $K_r > 2$.

Induction Step. Suppose that $D_\Omega(f) \leq K_r \log_r[(r - 1)L_\Omega(f) + 1]$ for $L_\Omega(f) \leq L_0 - 1$. Show that is also holds for $L_\Omega(f) = L_0 \geq 3$.

Figure 2.3.1*a* shows schematically the tree corresponding to an optimal fan-out 1 chain for f of $L_\Omega(f)$ elements. The root node has fan-in k, $k \leq r$, and subtrees $T_1, T_2, \ldots, T_k$ with $t_1, t_2, \ldots, t_k$ computation

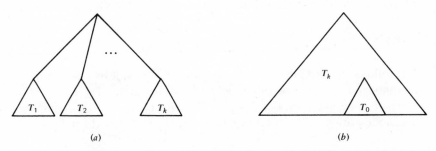

(a)   (b)

Figure 2.3.1. Schematic drawing of subtrees of graph of f.

nodes, respectively. Assume without loss of generality that $0 \leq t_1 \leq t_2 \leq \cdots \leq t_k$. (If $t_i = 0$, T_i consists of a single source node.) Obviously,

$$\sum_{i=1}^{k} t_i = L_\Omega(f) - 1$$

so it follows that

$$t_k \leq \sum_{i=1}^{k} t_i = L_\Omega(f) - 1$$

Since $2t_{k-1} \leq t_{k-1} + t_k$, it follows that

$$2t_{k-1} \leq \sum_{i=1}^{k} t_i = L_\Omega(f) - 1$$

or

$$t_{k-1} \leq \frac{L_\Omega(f) - 1}{2}$$

Also, we have

$$rt_k \geq kt_k \geq \sum_{i=1}^{k} t_i = L_\Omega(f) - 1$$

or

(A) $$t_k \geq \frac{L_\Omega(f) - 1}{r} \geq \frac{1}{r} > 0$$

From the tree T_k remove the smallest subtree T_0 of $t_0 \geq \lceil t_k/(r + 1)\rceil$ computation nodes* that is complete in the sense that all of its source nodes are source nodes of the tree T_k. (Subtrees could also be chosen whose source nodes are computation nodes.) We now show that

(B) $$t_0 \leq \frac{rt_k + 1}{r + 1}$$

It follows from (A) that $t_0 \geq 1$; therefore, T_0 has at least one computation node. Let the root node of T_0 have fan-in l, $1 \leq l \leq r$, with corresponding subtrees $T_{01}, T_{02}, \ldots, T_{0l}$ with $t_{01}, t_{02}, \ldots, t_{0l}$ computation nodes, respectively. It follows that $t_{0i} \leq \lceil t_k/(r + 1)\rceil - 1$ for $1 \leq i \leq l$,

---

* $\lceil x \rceil$ is the "ceiling" function which is the smallest integer greater than or equal to x.

because otherwise T_0 would not be the smallest complete subtree of T_k of size at least $\lceil t_k/(r + 1) \rceil$. Then we have

(C) $$t_0 \leq r\left(\left\lceil \frac{t_k}{r + 1} \right\rceil - 1\right) + 1$$

But $\lceil t_k/(r + 1) \rceil = (t_k + R)/(r + 1)$ for some integer R, $0 \leq R \leq r$. Consequently, $\lceil t_k/(r + 1) \rceil \leq (t_k + r)/(r + 1)$, which together with (C) implies (B).

Let h_i be the Boolean function computed by subtree T_i for $0 \leq i \leq k$. Let h_{k0} and h_{k1} be the Boolean functions computed by T_k from which T_0 has been removed and the root node of T_0 replaced by the constant functions 0, 1, respectively. Then h_k can be computed by computing h_{k0} and h_{k1} in parallel and by using h_0 to decide which is the correct value of h_k. This is obtained through composition with the selection function as follows:

(D) $$h_k = \text{sel}(h_0, h_{k0}, h_{k1})$$

Now apply the induction hypothesis. That it can be applied follows from the following upper bounds to the formula size of the various functions

$$L_\Omega(h_i) \leq t_i \leq t_{k-1} \leq \frac{L_\Omega(f) - 1}{2} < L_0, \qquad 1 \leq i \leq k - 1$$

(E) $$L_\Omega(h_0) \leq t_0 \leq \frac{rt_k + 1}{r + 1} \leq \frac{rL_\Omega(f) - (r - 1)}{r + 1} < L_0$$

$$L_\Omega(h_{kj}) \leq t_k - t_0 \leq \frac{r}{r + 1} t_k \leq \frac{r}{r + 1}(L_\Omega(f) - 1) < L_0, \qquad j = 0, 1$$

From equation (D) it follows that

$$D_\Omega(h_k) \leq D_\Omega(\text{sel}) + \max(D_\Omega(h_0), D_\Omega(h_{k0}), D_\Omega(h_{k1}))$$

In turn from (E) and the induction hypothesis this implies that

$$D_\Omega(h_k) \leq D_\Omega(\text{sel}) + K_r \log_r\left[(r - 1)\left(\frac{rL_\Omega(f) - (r - 1)}{r + 1}\right) + 1\right]$$

Again, from the construction of the graph of f from its subtrees $T_1, T_2, \ldots, T_k$, it follows that

$$D_\Omega(f) \leq 1 + \max_{1 \leq i \leq k}(D_\Omega(h_i))$$

and again from (E) this implies that

$$D_\Omega(f) \le (D_\Omega(\text{sel}) + 1) + K_r \log_r\left[(r-1)\left(\frac{rL_\Omega(f) - (r-1)}{r+1}\right) + 1\right]$$

Since

$$(r-1)\left(\frac{rL_\Omega(f) - (r-1)}{r+1}\right) + 1 \le \left(\frac{r}{r+1}\right)[(r-1)L_\Omega(f) + 1]$$

for $r \ge 2$, the conclusion of the theorem follows from the definition of K_r. $\square$

The size of the coefficient K_r in this theorem is an important measure of the tightness of the bounds. It is a function of the basis Ω. Two important bases are now considered.

Example 2.3.4.   Over the basis $\Omega = \{+, \cdot, ^-\}$, the function $\text{sel}(x, y, z)$ can be realized from the formula

$$\text{sel}(x, y, z) = \bar{x}y + x \cdot z$$

so that $D_\Omega(\text{sel}) \le 2$. With techniques to be introduced later it can be shown that $D_\Omega(\text{sel}) \ge 2$. Since Ω has fan-in $r = 2$, $K_r = 3/\log_2 \frac{3}{2} = 5.13$.

Example 2.3.5.   Over the basis $\Omega = \{h_i | h_i: \{0, 1\}^3 \to \{0, 1\}\}$, the function $\text{sel}(x, y, z)$ is a basis element. Therefore, $D_\Omega(\text{sel}) = 1$ and $K_r = 2/\log_3 \frac{4}{3} = 7.64$.

Theorem 2.3.3 may have value when upper bounds to formula size are desired and when an upper bound to delay complexity exists or vice versa. For example, a bound to $D_\Omega(f)$ for $f: \{0, 1\}^n \to \{0, 1\}$ such as $D_\Omega(f) \le a \log_r n$ implies that $L_\Omega(f) \le (n^a - 1)/(r - 1)$.

As the last results in this section we examine the effect of a change of basis on the combinational complexity, delay complexity, and formula size of a function.

Theorem 2.3.4.   Let $f: \{0, 1\}^n \to \{0, 1\}$ be a Boolean function and let Ω and Ω' be two complete bases of fan-in r and r', respectively. Furthermore, let C_0 and D_0 be two constants defined by

$$C_0 = \max_{h \in \Omega} C_{\Omega'}(h), \qquad D_0 = \max_{h \in \Omega} D_{\Omega'}(h)$$

Then

$$C_{\Omega'}(f) \le C_0 C_\Omega(f), \qquad D_{\Omega'}(f) \le D_0 D_\Omega(f)$$

and

$$L_{\Omega'}(f) \leq \frac{[(r-1)L_{\Omega}(f) + 1]^{\alpha} - 1}{r' - 1}$$

where

$$\alpha = D_0 K_r \log_r(r')$$

Proof. The first two inequalities follow from substituting into an optimal Ω-chain for f a subchain over Ω' for each basis element $h \in \Omega$ to produce an Ω'-chain for f. If the subchain for h has minimal combinational complexity over Ω', the first bound follows while the second results from use of a subchain for h with minimal delay complexity. The third inequality follows directly from an application of Theorem 2.3.3. $\square$

In Section 3.3, it is shown that $L_{\Omega}(f) = n - 1$ for $f(x_1, x_2, \ldots, x_n) = x_1 \oplus x_2 \oplus \cdots \oplus x_n$ over $\Omega = \{\oplus, \cdot, +, ^-\}$ but that $L_{\Omega'}(f)$ is on the order of n^2 over $\Omega' = \{\cdot, +, ^-\}$. Consequently, the exponent α cannot be smaller than 2, that is, $\alpha \geq 2$, for arbitrary Ω and Ω' of fan-in $r = r' = 2$.

In the next sections, techniques for lower bounding formula size and combinational complexity are derived.

2.4. LOWER BOUNDS TO COMBINATIONAL COMPLEXITY

The most important challange offered by the study of combinational complexity is the challenge to derive good lower bounds to the complexity of moderately complex functions. In this section we lay the foundation required for this problem. In reading this section, the reader should note, as shown in Section 3.4, that most Boolean functions $f: \{0, 1\}^n \rightarrow \{0, 1\}$ have $C_{\Omega}(f)$ on the order of $2^n/n$ for large n when the basis is $\Omega = \{+, \cdot, ^-\}$. Thus, it is a bit disappointing that the best techniques known for deriving lower bounds to the combinational complexity of individual Boolean functions all give bounds that are linear in the number of variables of these functions.

2.4.1. The Simple Linear Bound

In this subsection it is useful to introduce the modified combinational complexity measure $C_{\Omega}^*(f)$.

Definition 2.4.1.1. Let $f: \{0, 1\}^n \rightarrow \{0, 1\}^m$ and let Ω be a complete basis. Then $C_{\Omega}^*(f)$ is the combinational complexity of f not including the number of inversions ¯, when this operation is contained in Ω. Otherwise $C_\Omega^*(f) = C_\Omega(f)$.

An immediate consequence of this definition is the following:

Lemma 2.4.1.1. Let $f: \{0, 1\}^n \to \{0, 1\}^m$ and let Ω be a complete basis. Then

$$C_\Omega(f) \geq C_\Omega^*(f)$$

We now begin to classify functions by their properties. These classifications permit the derivation of several different lower bounds to the combinational complexity of functions so identified.

Definition 2.4.1.2. A Boolean function $f: \{0, 1\}^n \to \{0, 1\}$ is said to be *essentially dependent* on variable x_i, $1 \leq i \leq n$, if there exist values $c_j \in \{0, 1\}$ for $1 \leq j \leq n, j \neq i$, such that

$$f(c_1, c_2, \ldots, c_{i-1}, 0, c_{i+1}, \ldots, c_n) \neq f(c_1, c_2, \ldots, c_{i-1}, 1, c_{i+1}, \ldots, c_n)$$

This condition is enough to allow for the derivation of the first lower bound.

Theorem 2.4.1.1. Let $f: \{0, 1\}^n \to \{0, 1\}$ be essentially dependent on each of its variables and let Ω be any complete basis of fan-in r. Then

$$C_\Omega^*(f) \geq \left\lceil \frac{n-1}{r-1} \right\rceil$$

Also, for each r, there exist bases Ω, functions f, and infinitely many integers n such that the bound is met.

> **Proof.** Since f is essentially dependent on each of its variables, every chain for f must contain the data steps $x_1, x_2, \ldots, x_n$, and the graph of any such chain must contain at least one edge directed from each of the n source nodes. That is, the graph must contain at least n edges directed away from source nodes.
>
> Consider an optimal chain for f with k inversions and $C_\Omega^*(f)$ other basis elements. The graph of this chain has at least $n + k + C_\Omega^*(f) - 1$ edges directed away from nodes (note that the computation node associated with f has no edge directed away from it) and at most $k + rC_\Omega^*(f)$ edges directed into nodes. Therefore,
>
> $$k + rC_\Omega^*(f) \geq n + k + C_\Omega^*(f) - 1$$

and the desired bound follows.

To show that the bound can be achieved, consider the function $f_n(x_1, x_2, \ldots, x_n) = x_1 \cdot x_2 \cdot \cdots \cdot x_n$. This function obviously is essentially dependent on each of its variables. Consider a basis Ω that contains $\text{AND}(y_1, y_2, \ldots, y_r) = y_1 \cdot y_2 \cdot \cdots \cdot y_r$. Then, over this basis, we can write

$$f_r(x_1, x_2, \ldots, x_r) = \text{AND}(x_1, x_2, \ldots, x_r)$$

and when $n = l(r-1) + 1$, we can write

$$f_n(x_1, \ldots, x_n) = \text{AND}(f_{n-(r-1)}(x_1, \ldots, x_{n-(r-1)}), x_{n-r+2}, \ldots, x_n)$$

so that f_r is realized with one basis element and f_n by $l = \lceil (n-1)/(r-1) \rceil$, as can be seen by induction. $\qquad\square$

This test is useful in determining the combinational complexity of simple functions. This point is illustrated by an example.

Example 2.4.1.1. Let Ω be the set of all two-input Boolean functions in two or fewer variables. Then for n even the function

$$f_{\text{MATCH}}(x_1, x_2, \ldots, x_{n/2}, y_1, y_2, \ldots, y_{n/2})$$

$$= \begin{cases} 1 & x_i = y_i, \quad \text{all } 1 \leq i \leq n/2 \\ 0 & \text{otherwise} \end{cases}$$

has $C_\Omega(f_{\text{MATCH}}) = n - 1$. To show this, it is necessary to derive upper and lower bounds to $C_\Omega(f_{\text{MATCH}})$. The lower bound follows from Theorem 2.4.1.1, when it is shown that f_{MATCH} depends on each of its variables. To show that it depends on x_i, say, set all other variables equal to 0. Then, when $x_i = 0$, $f_{\text{MATCH}} = 1$ and it is zero otherwise. An upper bound is obtained by exhibiting a chain that computes f_{MATCH}. Let $\varphi \in \Omega$ be the function $\varphi(\zeta_1, \zeta_2) = \overline{\zeta_1 \oplus \zeta_2}$ which has value 1 only when $\zeta_1 = \zeta_2$. Then

$$f_{\text{MATCH}}(x_1, \ldots, x_{n/2}, y_1, \ldots, y_{n/2})$$

$$= \varphi(x_1, y_1) \cdot \varphi(x_2, y_2) \cdot \cdots \cdot \varphi(x_{n/2}, y_{n/2})$$

and this formula can be realized with $n - 1$ basis elements. This is the procedure that is followed in general to determine the combinational complexity of a function.

2.4.2. Extensions of the Simple Linear Bound

The test of Theorem 2.4.1.1 is simple and easy to apply, but it provides a lower bound that may be weak for some functions. We now generalize this test with the hope that substantially stronger lower bounds will result.

NOTATION.   Let J be a subset of $\{1, 2, \ldots, n\}$. Then the notation

$$f\Big|_{j \in J}^{x_j = c_j}$$

denotes the *subfunction* obtained from f by substituting the value $x_j = c_j \in \{0, 1\}$ for each integer $j \in J$. Also, $|J|$ is the number of elements in the set J.

Example 2.4.2.1.   Let $f(x_1, x_2, x_3) = (x_1 \oplus x_2) \cdot x_3$. Then, if $J = \{3\}$ and $c_3 = 0$,

$$f\Big|_{j \in J}^{x_j = c_j} = 0$$

and if $c_3 = 1$,

$$f\Big|_{j \in J}^{x_j = c_j} = x_1 \oplus x_2$$

It should now be apparent that $f \colon \{0, 1\}^n \to \{0, 1\}$ depends on each of its variables if and only if for all $J \subset \{1, 2, \ldots, n\}$ with $|J| = 1$,

$$\left\{ f\Big|_{j \in J}^{x_j = c_j} \,\big|\, c_j = 0, 1 \right\}$$

consists of two *distinct* functions. (Two functions over the same domain are distinct if there is a point in their common domain on which they have different values.)

The classes of Boolean functions $f \colon \{0, 1\}^n \to \{0, 1\}$ denoted $P_{p, q}^{(n)}$, where p and q are nonnegative integers, are now defined.

Definition 2.4.2.1.   The class of functions $P_{p, q}^{(n)}$ is defined as

$$P_{p, q}^{(n)} = \{\, f \colon \{0, 1\}^n \to \{0, 1\} |\ \text{for all } J \subset \{1, 2, \ldots, n\},\ |J| =$$
$$p,\ \text{there exist constants } c_j \in$$
$$\{0, 1\},\ j \in J,\ \text{such that there}$$
$$\text{are at least } q \text{ distinct subfunc-}$$
$$\text{tions } f\Big|_{j \in J}^{x_j = c_j} \,\}$$

The classes $P_{p, q}^{(n)}$, $p, q \geq 0$, have a number of interesting properties that are now given.

Property 1. $P_{p, 1}^{(n)} = P_{0, 1}^{(n)} = \{ f | f \colon \{0, 1\}^n \to \{0, 1\} \}$.

Property 2. $P_{1, 2}^{(n)} = \{ f | f \colon \{0, 1\}^n \to \{0, 1\}$ depends essentially on each of its variables$\}$.

Property 3. $P_{p, q}^{(n)} = \varnothing$ (the empty set) if $q > \min(2^p, 2^{2^{n-p}})$.

Proof. The number of distinct patterns of constants c_j for $j \in J$ and $|J| = p$ is 2^p, so the number of subfunctions

$$f \Big|_{j \in J}^{x_j = c_j}$$

cannot exceed 2^p. Furthermore, when p of the n variables are fixed, $n - p$ variables remain free, and there are at most $2^{2^{n-p}}$ distinct functions in a given set of $n - p$ free variables. The conclusion follows directly. $\square$

Property 4. $P_{p,q}^{(n)} \subset P_{p,q'}^{(n)}$ for $q' \leq q$.

Proof. If $f \in P_{p,q}^{(n)}$ then the number of distinct subfunctions

$$f \Big|_{j \in J}^{x_j = c_j}$$

for $|J| = p$ is greater than or equal to q' so f is also in $P_{p,q'}^{(n)}$. $\square$

Property 5. $P_{p,\,2^{l-1}+1}^{(n)} \subset P_{p-1,\,2^{l-2}+1}^{(n)}$ for $p \geq 2,\, l \geq 2$.

Proof. Let

$$f \in P_{p,\,2^{l-1}+1}^{(n)}$$

Assume that

$$f \notin P_{p-1,\,2^{l-2}+1}^{(n)}$$

and show that a contradiction results.

Since

$$f \notin P_{p-1,\,2^{l-2}+1}^{(n)}$$

there exists a set $J \subset \{1, 2, \ldots, n\}$ of size $p - 1$ such that there are at most 2^{l-2} subfunctions

$$f \Big|_{j \in J}^{x_j = c_j}$$

Consequently, augmenting J to J' by adding a new element of $\{1, 2, \ldots, n\}$ results in at most twice as many subfunctions

$$f \Big|_{j \in J'}^{x_j = c_j}$$

or at most 2^{l-1} subfunctions. Therefore

$$f \notin P_{p,\,2^{l-1}+1}^{(n)}$$

which contradicts our first assumption. $\square$

The classes $P_{1,2}^{(n)}$, $P_{2,3}^{(n)}$, $P_{3,5}^{(n)}$ and in general

$$P_{p,\,2^{p-1}+1}^{(n)}$$

are particularly interesting. By Property 5 they are nested sets, that is,

$$P_{1,2}^{(n)} \supset P_{2,3}^{(n)} \supset P_{3,5}^{(n)} \supset P_{p,\,2^{p-1}+1}^{(n)}$$

for $p \geq 3$, and $q = 2^{p-1} + 1$ is the smallest value such that $P_{p,q}^{(n)}$ is not (in general) empty but $P_{p-1,q}^{(n)}$ is empty. We now exhibit functions that are in $P_{2,3}^{(n)}$ and $P_{3,5}^{(n)}$.

Lemma 2.4.2.1.   For each $n \geq 3$, the function $h_n: \{0,1\}^n \to \{0,1\}$ defined as

$$h_3(x_1, x_2, x_3) = x_1 x_2 + \left(\overline{x_1 \oplus x_3} \right)$$

is in the class $P_{2,3}^{(n)}$, and for $n \geq 4$

$$h_n(x_1, \dots, x_n) = \begin{cases} x_n \cdot h_{n-1}(x_1, \dots, x_{n-1}) & n \text{ even} \\ x_n + h_{n-1}(x_1, \dots, x_{n-1}) & n \text{ odd} \end{cases}$$

Furthermore, $P_{2,3}^{(n)} = \varnothing$ for $n < 3$.

Proof.   See Appendix.   □

The graph of a chain for h_3 is shown in Figure 2.4.2.1. In Figure 2.4.2.2 is the graph of a chain for a function g_6 that is known to be in $P_{3,5}^{(6)}$ (Hsieh, 1974; see also Problem 2-14). It should be noted that over $\Omega = P_{0,1}^{(2)}$

$$C_\Omega(h_3) \leq 3 \qquad \text{and} \qquad C_\Omega(g_6) \leq 7$$

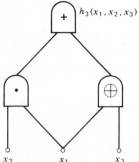

$h_3(x_1, x_2, x_3)$

x_2 x_1 x_3 **Figure 2.4.2.1.**   Graph of a chain for $h_3(x_1, x_2, x_3)$.

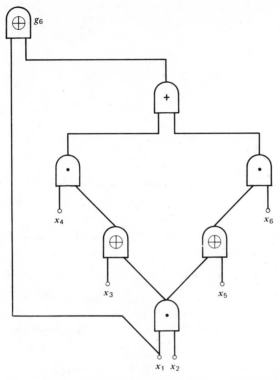

Figure 2.4.2.2. Graph of a chain for $g_6(x_1, x_2, x_3, x_4, x_5, x_6)$.

Table 2.4.2.1. All Subfunctions $h_3\big|_{j \in J}^{x_j = c_j}$ when $|J| = 2$

$h_3(x_1, x_2, x_3)$	$c_1 c_2$			
	0 0	0 1	1 0	1 1
$x_1 = c_1,\ x_2 = c_2$	$\bar{x}_3$	$\bar{x}_3$	x_3	1
$x_1 = c_1,\ x_3 = c_2$	1	0	x_2	1
$x_2 = c_1,\ x_3 = c_2$	$\bar{x}_1$	x_1	1	x_1

Table 2.4.2.2. All Subfunctions $h_3\big|^{x_j = c_j}$ when $j \in \{1, 2, 3\}$

$h_3(x_1, x_2, x_3)$	c_1	
	0	1
$x_1 = c_1$	$\bar{x}_3$	$x_2 + x_3$
$x_2 = c_1$	$x_1 \oplus \bar{x}_3$	$x_1 + \bar{x}_3$
$x_3 = c_1$	$\bar{x}_1 + x_2$	x_1

37

The following result due to Hsieh (1974) offers a method for generating, for infinitely many integers n, functions in $P_{3,5}^{(n)}$ from other such functions.

Lemma 2.4.2.2. Let

$$g \in P_{3,5}^{(n_1)}, \qquad h \in P_{3,5}^{(n_2)}, \qquad \text{and } g, h$$

such that for all sets J_1, J_2, $|J_1| \leq 2$, $|J_2| \leq 2$, none of the subfunctions

$$g\Big|_{j \in J_1}^{u_j = c_j}, \qquad h\Big|_{j \in J_2}^{v_j = d_j}$$

are constant. Then, if the variables of g and h are disjoint from one another and from the variable x, then the function f,

$$f = x \oplus g \cdot h$$

is in $P_{3,5}^{(n)}$, $n = n_1 + n_2 + 1$, and for all sets J, $|J| \leq 2$, none of the subfunctions $f\Big|_{j \in J}^{x_j = c_j}$ is constant.

Proof. See Appendix.   □

This lemma and the function g_6 described in Figure 2.4.2.2 are now used to generate an infinite set of functions in $P_{3,5}$ that have small combinational complexity (Hsieh, 1974; Harper, Hsieh, and Savage, 1975).

Lemma 2.4.2.3. The functions g_n: $\{0, 1\}^n \to \{0, 1\}$, $n = 7k + 6$ for k an integer $k \geq 0$, are in $P_{3,5}^{(n)}$ where

$$g_6(x_1, x_2, \ldots, x_6) = x_1 \oplus (x_4(x_3 \oplus x_1 x_2) + x_6(x_5 \oplus x_1 x_2))$$

and

$$g_{n+7} = x_{n+7} \oplus (g_6(x_{n+1}, \ldots, x_{n+6}) \cdot g_n)$$

Also, over $\Omega = P_{0,1}^{(2)}$,

$$C_\Omega(g_n) \leq \frac{9n - 5}{7}$$

Proof. It is left as an exercise for the reader to show that

$$g_6 \in P_{3,5}^{(6)}$$

and that

$$g_6\Big|_{j \in J}^{x_j = c_j}$$

is nonconstant for $|J| \leq 2$. (See Problem 2-14.) Then, from the preceding lemma, it follows that $g_n \in P_{3,5}^{(n)}$ for $n = 7k + 6$, $k \geq 0$. Let $C_\Omega(g_n) = \lambda_k$. Then, from $\lambda_0 \leq 7$ and recursive definition of g_n,

$$\lambda_k \leq 9 + \lambda_{k-1} \leq 9k + 7 = \frac{9n - 5}{7}. \qquad \square$$

Shortly, lower bounds to the combinational complexity of functions in the classes $P_{2,3}^{(n)}$ and $P_{3,5}^{(n)}$ are derived, and these last three lemmas give useful information on the tightness of these bounds.

Before these bounds are derived, it is desirable to digress and present another relation between combinational complexity measures. This relation justifies using the basis $\Omega = P_{1,2}^{(2)}$ in the succeeding theorem.

Theorem 2.4.2.1. Let $f: \{0, 1\}^n \rightarrow \{0, 1\}^m$ and let Ω be a complete basis. Then when $\Omega \subset P_{0,1}^{(r)}$, the set of all Boolean functions in r (or fewer) variables, the two measures $C_\Omega(f)$ and $C_\Omega^*(f)$ (inversions are not counted) are related as follows:

$$C_\Omega(f) \geq C_\Omega^*(f) \geq C_{P_{0,1}^{(r)}}^*(f) = C_{P_{0,1}^{(r)}}(f) = C_{P_{1,2}^{(r)}}(f)$$

Proof. The left-hand inequality was established in Lemma 2.4.1.1. The second inequality follows directly from the observation that Ω is a subset of $P_{0,1}^{(r)}$.

The left-hand equality relation is true because an optimal chain for f over $P_{0,1}^{(r)}$ does not contain isolated inversions, for if it did, these could be absorbed into other basis elements, reducing the number of elements and producing a contradiction.

The last equality relation is a consequence of the fact (to be established in Problem 2-16) that every function in $P_{0,1}^{(r)}$ can be obtained as a subfunction of a function in $P_{1,2}^{(r)}$. Therefore whenever an element of $P_{0,1}^{(r)}$ is needed that does not depend on all of its variables, it can be obtained from a single element of $P_{1,2}^{(r)}$ by fixing the values of some of its variables. $\qquad \square$

Let us now derive lower bounds to the combinational complexity of functions in the classes $P_{1,2}^{(n)}$, $P_{2,3}^{(n)}$, and $P_{3,5}^{(n)}$. These bounds apply to bases of fan-in 2, for which the best results are obtained. Early versions of the lower bounds in the following theorem are given by Harper and Savage (1973).

Theorem 2.4.2.2. Let $\Omega = P_{1,2}^{(2)}$ and let $C_p^{(n)}$ be the combinational complexity over Ω of the least complex Boolean function in

$$P_{p,\,2^{p-1}+1}^{(n)}$$

Then

$$C_1^{(n)} = n - 1, \qquad n \geq 1$$

$$C_2^{(n)} = n, \qquad n \geq 3$$

$$C_3^{(n)} \geq \left\lceil \frac{10n - 7}{9} \right\rceil, \qquad n \geq 5$$

$$C_3^{(n)} \leq \frac{9n - 5}{7}, \qquad n = 7k + 6, \qquad k \geq 0$$

Proof. The first result is a direct application of Theorem 2.4.1.1 when $r = 2$.

By virtue of Lemmas 2.4.2.1, 2.4.2.2, and 2.4.2.3, we have that $C_2^{(n)} \leq n$ for $n \geq 3$ and $C_3^{(n)} \leq (9n - 5)/7$ for $n = 7k + 6$, $k \geq 0$. It remains to derive the lower bounds $C_2^{(n)} \geq n$, $n \geq 3$, and $C_3^{(n)} \geq \lceil (10n - 7)/9 \rceil$, $n \geq 5$.

Both bounds are derived using essentially the same method. The bound to $C_2^{(n)}$ is shown as follows. Assume $f \in P_{2,3}^{(n)}$, then $f \in P_{1,2}^{(n)}$ and each source node (associated with variables $x_1, x_2, \ldots, x_n$) in any graph of f has at least one edge directed away from it. If $C_\Omega(f) < n$, then $C_\Omega(f) = n - 1$ (since $P_{2,3}^{(n)} \subset P_{1,2}^{(n)}$), and it follows from the proof of Theorem 2.4.1.1 that each source node has exactly one edge directed away from it. Furthermore, at least one computation node has edges directed into it from two source nodes (say x_i and x_j), for if not, the number of edges directed away from source nodes would not exceed $C_\Omega(f) < n$.

The one computation node v with inputs x_i and x_j is shown schematically in Figure 2.4.2.3 and when $x_i = c_i$, $x_j = c_j$, and c_i, c_j range over values in $\{0, 1\}$, the function $t(x_i, x_j)$ assumes at most two values. Since x_i and x_j do not affect other computation steps, f has at most two

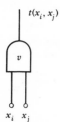

Figure 2.4.2.3. Component in a graph of f when $C_2^{(n)} < n$.

subfunctions

$$f\bigg|^{x_i = c_i,\ x_j = c_j}$$

so $f \notin P_{2,3}^{(n)}$, which contradicts the given and demonstrates that $C_2^{(n)} \geq n$.

The proof of a lower bound to $C_3^{(n)}$ is no longer but follows the same pattern. We show that a subchain of the type shown in Figure 2.4.2.4 occurs in every graph of f if $C_\Omega(f) < (10n - 7)/9$, where x_i, x_j, and x_k are source nodes of fan-out 1. When these variables are fixed, $t(v', x_i, x_j, x_k)$ is a function of one variable. Since there are only four functions of one variable, such a subchain cannot occur in the graph of f.

Let G be an optimal graph for a function $f \in P_{3,3}^{(n)}$. Transform G by removing all edges except those directed away from

1. Source nodes of fan-out 1.
2. Computation nodes of fan-out 1 whose one edge enters a node whose other edge is from a source node of fan-out 1.

The connected components of the transformed graph form cascades of the type shown in Figure 2.4.2.4 containing one or more nodes. Each node in a cascade has either no edges directed into it (in the figure, v' may be such a node); one edge directed into it, in which case the one edge is from a source node of fan-out 1; or two edges in which case one

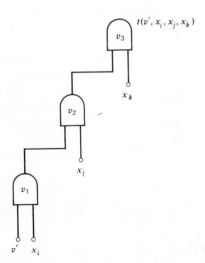

Figure 2.4.2.4. Component in a graph of f when $C_3^{(n)} < (10n - 7)/9$.

is from a source node of fan-out 1 and the other is from a computation node of fan-out 1.

If a cascade has more than two source node edges directed into it, as stated above, G is not a graph for f. Thus, if K is the number of cascades and S_1 is the number of source nodes of fan-out 1, then

$$S_1 \leq 2K$$

The number of cascades is equal to the number of nodes in the new graph without output edges. If W_1^* is the number of nodes described in 2., then

$$K = C - W_1^*$$

since G has C nodes. In turn, W_1^* is the number of source nodes of fan-out 1, S_1, minus the number S_1^* whose edges enter computation nodes whose other edge is from a source or computation node of fan-out greater than 1. Therefore, $W_1^* = S_1 - S_1^*$ and

$$K = C - S_1 + S_1^*$$

But S_1^* is no larger than the number of edges E directed away from nodes of fan-out greater than 1. Therefore, the following condition must be satisfied:

$$S_1 \leq 2(C - S_1) + 2E$$

If S_2 is the number of source nodes of fan-out greater than 1, $S_1 = n - S_2$, and the condition reduces to

$$3n \leq 2C + 3S_2 + 2E$$

It remains to relate n, C, S_2, and E.

Let e denote the excess number of edges in G, that is, the number over and above the number that G would have if every node except the terminal node had fan-out 1. It is easily shown that stand-alone inverters are not used in G, because of the nature of the basis, so that every computation node has fan-in 2. Therefore,

$$e = 2C - (C + n - 1) = C - n + 1$$

At most e nodes have fan-out greater than 1, so $S_2 \leq e$, and there are at most $2e$ edges directed away from these nodes, so $E \leq 2e$. Combining these results we have

$$3n \leq 2C + 7(C - n + 1)$$

or

$$C \geq \frac{10n - 7}{9} \qquad \qquad \square$$

As close as the bounds of this theorem are, they can be improved. Hsieh (1974) has announced a new upper bound and has presented a new lower bound using the weak duality theorem in linear programming. (See also Harper, Hsieh, and Savage, 1975.) These two bounds are stated in the following theorem. A proof of these results is not given here primarily because of the difficulty of establishing them. The lower bound requires the minimization of a linear functional under the constraints of 14 inequalities.

Theorem 2.4.2.3. The combinational complexity of the least complex function in $P_{3,5}^{(n)}$ over $\Omega = P_{1,2}^{(2)}$ satisfies

$$C_3^{(n)} \geq \left\lceil \frac{7n - 4}{6} \right\rceil, \qquad n \geq 5$$

$$\leq \frac{20n - 3}{17}, \qquad \text{infinitely many } n \geq 5$$

Now that lower bounds have been derived to the combinational complexity of functions in the classes $P_{1,2}^{(n)}$, $P_{2,3}^{(n)}$, and $P_{3,5}^{(n)}$, it would be desirable to present bounds for the classes

$$P_{p,\,2^{p-1}+1}^{(n)}$$

for $p \geq 4$. Unfortunately, such bounds are not known although it is anticipated that they will be derived.

The motivation for defining the function classes $P_{p,q}^{(n)}$ was the desire to derive nonlinear lower bounds to combinational complexity. Such a goal is not realizable for values of p up to about $n/\log_2 n$, as we now show by presenting a function similar to one introduced by Meyer and Paterson (personal communication, 1974).

Let $f^*: \{0, 1\}^n \to \{0, 1\}$ be a Boolean function for which $n = kb$, where k and b are integers. Let the variables of f^* be grouped into k blocks of b variables per block, namely, $B_0, B_1, \ldots, B_{k-1}$ where without loss of generality we let

$$B_i = \left\{ j \mid ib \leq j \leq ib + b - 1 \right\}$$

If $x_0, x_1, \ldots, x_{n-1}$ are the variables of f^*, we associate the binary function a_i with block B_i, $0 \leq i \leq k - 1$, as follows: Let $s_i = \sum_{j \in B_i} x_j$ where $\sum$

denotes integer addition. Then

$$a_i = \begin{cases} 1, & s_i \geq p + 1 \\ 0, & s_i \leq p \end{cases}$$

We define f^* by

$$f^*(x_0, x_1, \ldots, x_{n-1}) = x_l$$

where l is the integer represented by the binary string $(a_0, a_1, \ldots, a_{k-1})$; that is,

$$l = \left(a_0 + a_1 2 + a_2 2^2 + \cdots + a_{k-1} 2^{k-1}\right)$$

unless this sum exceeds $n - 1$, in which case $l = n - 1$.

We now show that under the following two conditions, the function f^* is in $P_{p, 2^p}^{(n)}$:

1. $k \geq \log_2 n$.
2. $p \leq \dfrac{b - 1}{2}$.

If $f^* \in P_{p, 2^p}^{(n)}$, it is also in

$$P_{p, 2^{p-1}+1}^{(n)}$$

by Property 4, so an upper bound to the combinational complexity of f^* over the basis $P_{1,2}^{(2)}$ is an upper bound to $C_p^{(n)}$.

Let J be a subset of p variables of f^*. These p variables fall into one or more of the k blocks $B_0, \ldots, B_{k-1}$, but not more than p fall into any one block. Thus, regardless of what values are given to these p variables, when the value given to each of the remaining variables is 0, each $a_i = 0$.

By condition 2, there are at least $2p + 1$ variables in each block; at most p of these are in the set J. In each block choose a set of $p + 1$ variables not in J and set the remaining variables equal to 0. When the chosen variables in the ith block are 0, the associated sum $\sum_{j \in B_i} x_j$ lies between 0 and p and $a_i = 0$. When the chosen variables are equal to 1, the associated sum lies between $p + 1$ and $2p + 1$ and $a_i = 1$. Thus, the value of each function a_i can be controlled even when the values of the p variables in J are given arbitrary values. We conclude that for each subfunction

$$f^*\Big|_{\substack{x_j = c_j \\ j \in J}}$$

of f^* with $|J| = p$, under condition 2, by assigning values to the $n - p$ remaining variables we can control the values given to $a_0, a_1, \ldots, a_{k-1}$ and to l.

From this last observation and from condition 1, it follows that we can give l any value in the range of 0 to $n - 1$. Since $f^*(x_0, x_1, \ldots, x_{n-1}) = x_l$, it follows that the values given to the variables $x_j, j \in J$, in the subfunction

$$f^* \Big|_{\substack{x_j = c_j \\ j \in J}}$$

can be determined by assigning the appropriate values to the remaining variables. Therefore, there is a 1–1 correspondence between values given to the set of variables indexed by J and subfunctions, or there are 2^p subfunctions and $f^* \in P_{p,2^p}^{(n)}$.

Theorem 2.4.2.4. The function $f^*: \{0, 1\}^n \to \{0, 1\}$ defined in the preceding, where $n = kb$ and

1. $b = \left\lfloor \dfrac{2^k}{k} \right\rfloor$

2. $p \leq \dfrac{b - 1}{2}$

is in $P_{p,2^p}^{(n)}$. Furthermore, $p \leq [(n/\log_2 n) - 1]/2$, and over the basis $\Omega = P_{1,2}^{(n)}$, there exists a constant $\kappa > 0$ such that

$$C_\Omega(f^*) \leq \kappa n$$

for all $k \geq 1$.

Proof. The first statement has been established in the preceding discussion, and the upper bound on p is a direct consequence of the two conditions.

The linear bound to the combinational complexity of f^* is established with the aid of results in Chapter 3. The functions $a_0, a_1, \ldots, a_{k-1}$ are each threshold functions of the same type and, as shown in Section 3.1, they have a linear combinational complexity, linear in b. Therefore, the set of k functions has a combinational complexity that is linear in $n = kb$.

From $a_0, a_1, \ldots, a_{k-1}$, the binary-to-positional transformer of Section 3.1 may be used to generate 2^k outputs only one of which has value 1, namely, that with the index $|a| = a_0 + a_1 2 + \cdots + a_{k-1} 2^{k-1}$. The number of computation steps required to realize this transformer is linear in 2^k. If $y_0, y_1, \ldots, y_{2^k - 1}$ are the components of the positional representation of $|a|$, we OR $y_{n-1}, y_n, \ldots, y_{2^k - 1}$ to form y_{n-1}^*. Then, $(y_0, y_1, \ldots, y_{n-2}, y_{n-1}^*)$ forms the positional representation of l since $y_{n-1}^* = 1$ only when $|a| \geq n - 1$ and $l = n - 1$. We then form the following functions:

$$x_0 \cdot y_0, \ x_1 \cdot y_1, \ \ldots, \ x_{n-2} \cdot y_{n-2}, \ x_{n-1} \cdot y_{n-1}^*$$

and OR them to form x_l. The construction of y_{n-1}^* and x_l require an additional $2^k - n + 2n - 2 = 2^k + n - 2$ computation steps. Thus, as long as 2^k is linear in n, the combinational complexity of f^* is linear in n. But we have chosen b such that $n = kb \leq 2^k$ and $n \geq 2^k - k$.   □

The function classes $P_{p,\,2^{p-1}+1}^{(n)}$ may admit large lower bounds to the combinational complexity measure $C_p^{(n)}$ but, as the last result indicates, these larger bounds are only likely to result when p grows fairly rapidly with n.

In general, stronger conditions on functions imply stronger lower bounds to their complexity. The next result, which is due to Schnorr (1974), illustrates this point.

Definition 2.4.2.2.   Let $Q_{2,3}^{(n)}$, $n \geq 3$, be the class of Boolean functions of n variables defined by

$$Q_{2,3}^{(3)} = P_{2,3}^{(3)}$$

$$Q_{2,3}^{(n)} = \{ f \in P_{2,3}^{(n)} | \text{for all } 1 \leq j \leq n, \text{ there exists } c_j \in \{0, 1\}$$

$$\text{such that } f|^{x_j = c_j} \in Q_{2,3}^{(n-1)}\}, \qquad \text{for } n \geq 4$$

Lemma 2.4.2.4.   The Boolean function $f_{\text{mod }3}^c : \{0, 1\}^n \to \{0, 1\}$ defined by

$$f_{\text{mod }3}^c (x_1, \ldots, x_n) = \left(\left(\sum_{i=1}^{n} x_i + c \right) \text{mod } 3 \right) \text{mod } 2$$

is in $Q_{2,3}^{(n)}$ for each $c \in \{0, 1, 2\}$ and for $n \geq 3$, where Σ and $+$ denote integer addition.[†]

Proof.   First we demonstrate that $f_{\text{mod }3}^c$, $c = 0, 1, 2$, are distinct for $n \geq 1$. Let y denote $(\sum_{i=1}^{n} x_i) \text{mod } 3$. Clearly,

$$f_{\text{mod }3}^c (x_1, \ldots, x_n) = ((y + c) \text{ mod } 3) \text{ mod } 2$$

and it follows that $f_{\text{mod }3}^0$, $f_{\text{mod }3}^1$, and $f_{\text{mod }3}^2$ are distinct functions for $n \geq 2$ because they have value 1 only when $y = 1, 0,$ and 2, respectively, and y can assume each of these three values if $n \geq 2$. For $n = 1$, $f_{\text{mod }3}^0(x_1) = x_1$, $f_{\text{mod }3}^1(x_1) = \bar{x}_1$, and $f_{\text{mod }3}^2(x_1) = 0$, and they are also distinct. It is now very easy to show that $f_{\text{mod }3}^c \in P_{2,3}^{(n)}$ for $n \geq 3$. Choose

[†] If y is a nonnegative integer, $y \text{ mod } p$ is the remainder after dividing y by p.

$J \subset \{1, 2, \ldots, n\}$, $|J| = 2$. Then we can write

$$f^c_{\mathrm{mod}\ 3}\Big|^{x_j = c_j}_{j \in J} = \big[(y^* + c^*) \bmod 3\big] \bmod 2$$

where

$$y^* = \sum_{j \notin J} x_j \quad \text{and} \quad c^* = \left(c + \sum_{j \in J} c_j\right) \bmod 3$$

If $n \geq 3$, then c^* ranges over $\{0, 1, 2\}$ as c_j ranges over $\{0, 1\}$ for $j \in J$. Clearly, $f^c_{\mathrm{mod}\ 3} \in P^{(n)}_{2,3}$. This same argument applied to

$$f^c_{\mathrm{mod}\ 3}\Big|^{x_j = c_j}_{j \in J''}, \quad J' \subset \{1, 2, \ldots, n\}, \quad 0 \leq |J'| \leq n - 3$$

demonstrates that it is in $P^{(n - |J'|)}_{2,3}$. If in the definition we choose $c_j = 0$, it follows that $f^c_{\mathrm{mod}\ 3} \in Q^{(n)}_{2,3}$.   ☐

Theorem 2.4.2.5. Let $\Omega = P^{(2)}_{1,2}$. Then, if $f \in Q^{(n)}_{2,3}$, $n \geq 3$,

$$C_\Omega(f) \geq 2n - 3$$

Proof. Consider an optimal chain for $f \in Q^{(n)}_{2,3}$ over Ω, and let G be the graph of this chain. As stated in Theorem 2.4.2.1, $C_\Omega(f) = C^*_\Omega(f)$ so that every computation node of G has fan-in of 2; G does not contain inverters, and constants are not used in G (otherwise, the operations using constants would be either the identity function or inversions). Then the inputs to each computation node of G are (1) both computation nodes, (2) both from variable source nodes, or (3) one from a computation node and one from a variable source node. If case (2) does not occur, the graph G can easily be shown to contain a directed loop that contradicts the definition of a chain.

Consider a computation node both of whose inputs are from source nodes. These nodes must be distinct else the computation node can be absorbed into other nodes, contradicting the assumption that the chain is optimal. Let x_i, x_j be the variables associated with this computation node. At least one of these, say x_i, must have fan-out greater than or equal to 2. Otherwise we can fix x_i and x_j, and there will be at most two resulting subfunctions. But this would contradict the assumption that $f \in Q^{(n)}_{2,3}$. Fixing x_i eliminates at least two computation nodes, because the resulting functions at these nodes depend on at most one variable and can be absorbed into other computation nodes of G. Therefore,

$$C_\Omega(f) \geq 2 + C_\Omega\big(f\big|^{x_i = c_i}\big)$$

But $f\big|^{x_i=c_i}$ is in $Q_{2,3}^{(n-1)}$, so in general

$$C_\Omega(f) \geq 2|J| + C_\Omega\left(f\big|_{j\in J}^{x_j=c_j}\right)$$

for $1 \leq |J| \leq n - 3$. Choosing $|J| = n - 3$, noting that $f\big|_{j\in J}^{x_j=c_j} \in P_{2,3}^{(3)}$, and using the lower bound of Theorem 2.4.2.2, we have

$$C_\Omega(f) \geq 2(n - 3) + 3 = 2n - 3$$

which completes the proof.   □

In Section 3.1 we examine the class of Boolean symmetric functions of which $f_{\text{mod }3}^c$ is one and show that the combinational complexity of each such function over $\Omega = P_{1,2}^{(2)}$ is bounded above by a quantity that is asymptotic to $6.5n$ for $n = 2^l - 1$ and l large. Thus, the lower bound given above is fairly good.

The reader is asked to show (Problem 2-18) that the function $f(x_1, \ldots, x_n) = (x_1 \oplus x_2 \oplus \cdots \oplus x_{n-1}) \cdot (x_2 + \cdots + x_n)$ is also in $Q_{2,3}^{(n)}$ for $n \geq 3$ and that $C_\Omega(f) = 2n - 3$ over $\Omega = P_{1,2}^{(2)}$. This establishes that the lower bound given in the above theorem for functions in $Q_{2,3}^{(n)}$ cannot be improved.

The bounds derived in this section apply to the largest basis with fan-in of 2. As would be expected, stronger lower bounds can be derived for certain functions when the basis is restricted. Such results are presented in the next subsection.

Before going on to the next topic, we take note of a new result by Paul (1975). He exhibits a function $f: \{0, 1\}^n \rightarrow \{0, 1\}$ for which he obtains a lower bound of $2.5n - 2$ over the basis $P_{1,2}^{(2)}$. This is the strongest bound yet obtained over this full basis.

2.4.3. Some Special Linear Lower Bounds

In this subsection, methods are illustrated for computing linear lower bounds that are better than those derived above. These bounds are derived for three functions, addition modulo 2, f_{MATCH} given in Example 2.4.1.1, and f_{COMP}, the integer comparison function. The bases considered are $\Omega_0 = \{+, \cdot, \bar{\ }\}$ and subsets of Ω_0, and the measure chosen is $C_\Omega^*(f)$. We also state bounds derived elsewhere for $C_\Omega(f)$. The following theorem expresses a relationship between these two measures.

Theorem 2.4.3.1. Let Ω be a subset of $\Omega_0 = \{+, \cdot, \bar{\ }\}$ and let $f: \{0, 1\}^n \rightarrow \{0, 1\}^m$. Then

$$C_\Omega^*(f) \leq C_\Omega(f) \leq 2C_\Omega^*(f) + n - 1$$

Proof. In an optimal chain for f over Ω, optimal with respect to $C_\Omega^*(f)$, we want to count the number of inverters. The output of each node, a computation node of fan-in 2 or a data node, may or may not be inverted. Thus, the chain has at most $C_\Omega^*(f) + n - 1$ inversions (at least one node of the graph is a terminal node of fan-out 0, else the chain is not optimal or it contains a directed loop) and a total of at most $2C_\Omega^*(f) + n - 1$ basis elements. $\qquad\square$

The first special result, due to Schnorr (1974), concerns addition modulo 2, which is easily shown to have combinational complexity of $n - 1$ over the basis $P_{1,2}^{(2)}$.

Theorem 2.4.3.2. Let $f_\oplus^c \colon \{0, 1\}^n \to \{0, 1\}$ for $c \in \{0, 1\}$ be the following Boolean function:

$$f_\oplus^c (x_1, \ldots, x_n) = x_1 \oplus x_2 \oplus \cdots \oplus x_n \oplus c$$

Then

$$C_{\Omega_0}^*(f_\oplus^c) = 3(n - 1)$$

Proof. As shown in Figure 2.4.3.1a and b, the functions $f_\oplus^0$ and $f_\oplus^1$ with $n = 2$ can each be realized with three binary operations. Furthermore, for $n \geq 3$ we can write

$$f_\oplus^c (x_1, \ldots, x_n) = f_\oplus^0 (x_1, x_2, \ldots, x_{n-2}, f_\oplus^c (x_{n-1}, x_n))$$

so that we have

$$C_{\Omega_0}^*(f_\oplus^c) \leq 3(n - 1)$$

by induction on n. To complete the proof, we need only show that $C_{\Omega_0}^*(f_\oplus^c) \geq 3(n - 1)$. Note that the subfunction $f_\oplus^c \big|_{j \in J}^{x_j = c_j}$, for $J \subset \{1, 2, \ldots, n\}$, is equal to $f_\oplus^{c^*} \colon \{0, 1\}^{n - |J|} \to \{0, 1\}$ where $c^* = c \oplus \boxtimes_{j \in J} c_j$ and $\boxtimes$ denotes addition modulo 2.

Consider a chain optimal with respect to $C_\Omega^*(f)$ for $f_\oplus^c$ and let G be its graph. Paralleling the argument given in the proof of Theorem 2.4.2.5, there must exist a computation node with two inputs both of which are variables or the Boolean complement of variables. Let x_i and x_j be these variables, $i \neq j$. Suppose that the graph contains only one literal of $\{x_i, \bar{x}_i\}$ and one of $\{x_j, \bar{x}_j\}$. The operation at the given computation node is either AND or OR; therefore a value can be given to x_i so that the output of this node is a constant independent of the value of x_j, the

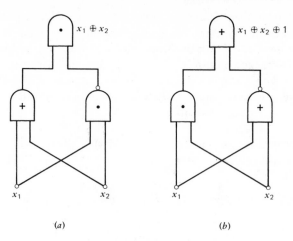

Figure 2.4.3.1.   Chains for (a) $f_{\oplus}^{0}$ and (b) $f_{\oplus}^{1}$.

other variable.[†] Thus, $f_{\oplus}^{c}\big|^{x_i = c_i}$ does not depend on x_j for some value c_i. But this plainly contradicts the definition of $f_{\oplus}^{c}$. Consequently, at least two instances of the literals in each set $\{x_i, \bar{x}_i\}$, $\{x_j, \bar{x}_j\}$ must occur in the graph G.

Let v_1 be a computation node of G whose inputs are from x_i and x_j (perhaps through inverters). Let v_2 be a node of G with fan-in 2 one of whose inputs is the output of v_1 (with or without inversion), as shown in Figure 2.4.3.2. Clearly such a node exists. The input x_i has fan-out of at least 2, so let v_3 be one of the nodes of fan-in 2 that receives x_i or its complement. Figure 2.4.3.2(a) shows the case when $v_3 \neq v_2$, and (b) the case when $v_3 = v_2$. In case (a), assign x_i a value c_i that sets the output of v_1 to a constant value. Then the inputs to v_2 and v_3 are constant, and they along with v_1 can be removed to form an optimal chain for $f_{\oplus}^{c}\big|^{x_i = c_i}$.

Similarly, in case (b), choose x_i to set the output of v_2 to a constant. In either case, at least three computation nodes of fan-in 2 can be removed so that

$$C_{\Omega_0}^{*}(f_{\oplus}^{c}) \geq 3 + C_{\Omega_0}^{*}\left(f_{\oplus}^{c}\big|^{x_i = c_i}\right)$$

and using induction leads to

$$C_{\Omega}^{*}(f_{\oplus}^{c}) \geq 3(n-1)$$ $\square$

[†] Note: $x + c = \begin{cases} x, & c = 0 \\ 1, & c = 1 \end{cases}$ and $x \cdot c = \begin{cases} 0, & c = 0 \\ x, & c = 1 \end{cases}$.

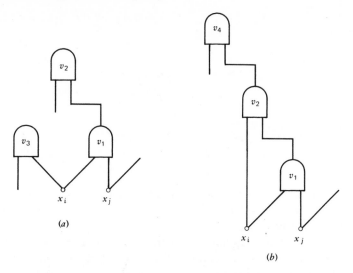

Figure 2.4.3.2. Chains occurring in proof of Theorem 2.3.4.2.

The critical step in the derivation of the lower bound in this theorem involves showing that no variable *obstructs* any other variable; that is, it is not possible to assign a value to one variable so that the function does not depend on the other variable. This notion of obstruction is used to derive the remaining results of this subsection. It can be shown (Problem 2-19) that there are exactly two functions f which are such that no subset of fewer than n variables of $f: \{0, 1\}^n \rightarrow \{0, 1\}$ obstructs any of the remaining variables.

Red'kin (1973) has established the following stronger results for the measure $C_\Omega(f)$.

Theorem 2.4.3.3. Over the basis Ω_0,

$$C_{\Omega_0}(f_\oplus^c) = 4(n - 1)$$

and over the bases $\Omega_1 = \{+, \,^-\}$, $\Omega_2 = \{\cdot, \,^-\}$,

$$C_{\Omega_1}(f_\oplus^c) = C_{\Omega_2}(f_\oplus^c) = 7(n - 1)$$

This theorem is considerable more difficult to prove than the previous theorem because of the many cases that must be considered. The reader interested in a proof of this theorem should see the appropriate reference.

The next result concerns the function f_{MATCH} first seen in Example 2.4.1.1. Over the basis $P_{1,2}^{(2)}$, it has a combinational complexity of $n - 1$.

Theorem 2.4.3.4. Let $f_{\text{MATCH}}: \{0, 1\}^n \to \{0, 1\}$ be the Boolean function defined by

$$f_{\text{MATCH}}(x_1, \ldots, x_{n/2}, y_1, \ldots, y_{n/2}) = \begin{cases} 1, & x_i = y_i, \quad 1 \le i \le \dfrac{n}{2} \\ 0, & \text{otherwise} \end{cases}$$

when n is even. Then

$$C_{\Omega_0}^*(f_{\text{MATCH}}) = 2n - 1$$

Proof. The upper bound follows directly from the expansion of f_{MATCH} given in Example 2.4.1.1 and from the fact that $C_{\Omega_0}^*(x_1 \oplus x_2) = 3$ as shown in Theorem 2.4.3.2.

The lower bound argument parallels that of Theorem 2.4.3.2. As stated in that proof, a $C_{\Omega_0}^*$-optimal chain for a function must contain a computation node of fan-in 2 whose inputs are from distinct variables (perhaps through inverters). If the distinct variables happen to be (a) x_i and x_j, or (b) x_i and y_j, $j \ne i$, or (c) y_i and y_j, then, since no variable in such a pair obstructs the other, a value can be assigned to one of them so that at least three computation nodes can be removed. This follows directly from the proof of Theorem 2.4.3.2. The remaining case to consider, in which the two variables are x_i and y_i for some $1 \le i \le n/2$, is treated later.

Again suppose that case (a), (b) or (c) occurs. We now show that at least one more computation node can be removed by fixing a second variable. Let the variable that is fixed above in order to eliminate three computation nodes be from the match pair $\{x_l, y_l\}$ and let ζ be the other variable in this pair. If, for example, $\zeta = y_l$ then giving it the same value that has been given to x_l will allow us to remove at least one more node. This is clearly true if neither ζ nor $\bar{\zeta}$ is an input to a node in the subchains of Figure 2.4.3.2. If one occurs as an input to such a subchain, the node to which it is input cannot be an output node; otherwise ζ obstructs all variables. Giving ζ a fixed value fixes the output of that node which allows for the removal of a successor node. After ζ has been fixed so that $x_l = y_l$, at last four nodes can be removed to produce a graph for f'_{MATCH}, which is the original function on two fewer variables. It follows that

$$C_{\Omega}^*(f_{\text{MATCH}}) \ge 4 + C_{\Omega}^*(f'_{\text{MATCH}})$$

The last case to consider is that in which the two variables entering a common node are x_i and y_i. Again neither x_i nor y_i obstructs the other, so they each must have fan-out of at least 2. Let v_1 be a node with input from both x_i and y_i and let x_i also have an edge to v_2 and y_i an edge to v_3, perhaps through inverters.

There are several cases to consider. Indicated schematically in Figure 2.4.3.3 are the cases that occur when $v_2 \neq v_3$. In (a) the output of v_1 is input to v_4 which is distinct from v_2 and v_3. Note that v_1 is not the terminal node, else x_i and y_i would obstruct all other variables. In (b) one of v_2 and v_3 is identical with v_4. We have shown the case when $v_4 = v_3$. Clearly, v_3 is not the terminal node. In the first case, choose x_i to fix the output of v_1 and set y_i to the same value. In the second case $v_5 \neq v_2$; otherwise x_i could obstruct y_i. Thus, set y_i so that the output of v_3 is constant and equate it with x_i. In each case, four computation nodes of fan-in 2 can be removed and f'_{MATCH} realized.

When $v_2 = v_3$, the graphs of Figure 2.4.3.4 have to be considered. In case (a), $v_3 \neq v_4$ and, when $x_i = y_i = c_i$ are chosen, the outputs of v_1 and v_2 are constant, and v_1, v_2, v_3, and v_4 can be absorbed to produce a chain for f'_{MATCH}. In case (b), $v_3 = v_4$ and the outputs of v_1, v_2, and v_3 are constant for $x_i = y_i = c_i$, and again four elements can be removed. In every case considered,

$$C_{\Omega_0}^*(f_{MATCH}) \geq 4 + C_{\Omega_0}^*(f'_{MATCH})$$

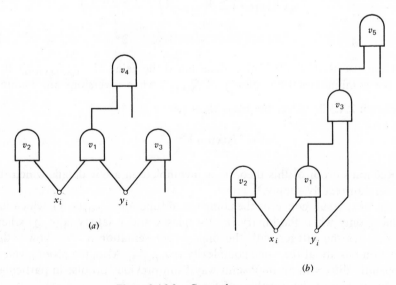

Figure 2.4.3.3. Cases when $v_2 \neq v_3$.

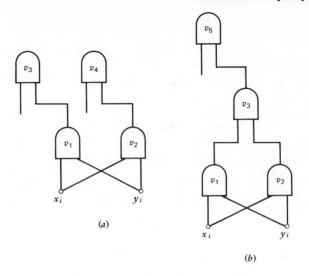

Figure 2.4.3.4.   Cases when $v_2 = v_3$.

where f'_{MATCH} is f_{MATCH} on $n - 2$ variables. Since f_{MATCH} on $n = 2$ variables is identical with $f^1_\oplus$ on 2 variables, $C_\Omega(f_{\text{MATCH}}) = 3$ when $n = 2$ and it follows that

$$C^*_\Omega(f_{\text{MATCH}}) \geq 4\left(\frac{n}{2} - 1\right) + 3 = 2n - 1$$

□

Here also Red'kin (1973) has determined the value of $C_{\Omega_0}(f_{\text{MATCH}})$, that is, the combinational complexity of f_{MATCH} when inversions are counted.

Theorem 2.4.3.5.   Over the basis $\Omega_0 = \{ +, \cdot, ^- \}$,

$$C_{\Omega_0}(f_{\text{MATCH}}) = \tfrac{5}{2}n - 1$$

Red'kin's proof of this theorem is incomplete in a few details which the reader can readily supply.

The next result concerns the comparison function $f_{\text{COMP}}(\mathbf{x}, \mathbf{y})$, which has value 1 only when the binary $(n/2)$-tuples $\mathbf{x}$ and $\mathbf{y}$ satisfy $|\mathbf{x}| < |\mathbf{y}|$ where $|\mathbf{x}|$ denotes the integer with the binary representation $\mathbf{x}$. As shown, this function has about the same complexity as f_{MATCH}. Also, the proof given in Appendix differs in an important way from previous proofs; in particular, we fix on two of the variables of f_{COMP}.

Theorem 2.4.3.6. Let f_{COMP}: $\{0, 1\}^n \rightarrow \{0, 1\}$ be defined by

$$f_{COMP}(x_1, \ldots, x_{n/2}, y_1, \ldots, y_{n/2}) = \begin{cases} 1 & |\mathbf{x}| < |\mathbf{y}| \\ 0 & \text{otherwise} \end{cases}$$

when n is even, where $|\mathbf{x}| = x_1 2^0 + x_2 2^1 + \cdots + x_{n/2} 2^{n/2-1}$ and $+$ denotes integer addition. Then

$$C_{\Omega_0}^*(f_{COMP}) = 2n - 3$$

Proof. See Appendix. □

The Red'kin (1973) result for the measure C_{Ω_0} on f_{COMP} is given by the following theorem.

Theorem 2.4.3.7. Over the basis Ω_0,

$$C_{\Omega_0}(f_{COMP}) = \tfrac{5}{2}n - 3$$

Soprunenko (1965) studied the two functions $x_1 \cdot x_2 \cdot \cdots \cdot x_n$ and $x_1 + x_2 + \cdots + x_n$ over the complete basis Ω consisting of the single element $\overline{x \cdot y}$ known as the NAND operator. His results, which have not yet been translated from the original Russian, are that the combinational complexity of these functions over this basis are $2(n - 1)$ and $3(n - 1)$, respectively.

The bounds derived in this subsection all have used the notion of "obstruction." A different technique, which holds some promise for producing better than linear lower bounds, is now described. To date, however, the best bounds derived with this method are linear. This method is due to Schnorr (1974).

Consider an optimal chain over a basis of fan-in 2 for a Boolean function f: $\{0, 1\}^n \rightarrow \{0, 1\}$. This chain contains a step both of whose inputs are variables or the complements of variables. Let these variables be x_i and x_j, $i \neq j$. Remove this step and replace with a new variable to create a function f_1. If no other step makes use of one of the variables x_i, x_j, then f_1 does not depend on that variable. We write $f \rightarrow f_1$ and say that f has been *reduced* to f_1. This process can be repeated to produce a sequence of functions $f_1, f_2, \ldots, f_q$ where $f_q = x_q$, a variable that is not a variable of f or of $f_1, f_2, \ldots, f_{q-1}$. Then we write

$$f \rightarrow f_1 \rightarrow f_2 \rightarrow \cdots \rightarrow f_q = x_q$$

Suppose there is a *step-counting measure* μ that is a mapping from

Boolean functions to the integers with the following properties:

1. $\mu(x_q) = 0$.
2. If $f_i \rightarrow f_{i+1}$ then $\mu(f_{i+1}) \geq \mu(f_i) - 1$.

Then, at every step in a reduction sequence $f \rightarrow f_1 \rightarrow \cdots \rightarrow f_q$, $\mu(f_i)$ decreases by at most one, which implies that $\mu(f) \leq q$. But each step of the reduction process eliminates one step of an optimal chain for f. Therefore, $C_\Omega(f) = q$, and we have

Theorem 2.4.3.8. Let μ be a step-counting measure. Then, for $f: \{0, 1\}^n \rightarrow \{0, 1\}$ and Ω a complete basis of fan-in 2,

$$C_\Omega^*(f) \geq \mu(f)$$

A step-counting measure is a generalization of the combinational complexity measure. Schnorr has made use of such a measure based on the number of "prime implicants" of a function to derive a lower bound to $C_\Omega(f)$ when $\Omega = \{+, {}^-\}$. Since the Schnorr method has only produced a bound of $2n - 1$ for a special Boolean function, at this point in time we limit ourselves to a definition of prime implicants and a description of the result. The interested reader can see the appropriate reference.

Definition 2.4.3.1. A product $t(x_1, \ldots, x_n)$ (Boolean AND) of *literals* from $\{x_1, \bar{x}_1, x_2, \bar{x}_2, \ldots, \bar{x}_n\}$ is an *implicant* of $f: \{0, 1\}^n \rightarrow \{0, 1\}$ if for every $(x_1, x_2, \ldots, x_n) \in \{0, 1\}^n$ for which $t(x_1, \ldots, x_n) = 1$, $f(x_1, \ldots, x_n) = 1$ also. An implicant t of f is *prime* if there is no other implicant t^* of f with fewer literals such that $t^* = 1$ implies $t = 1$.

Example 2.4.3.1. The function $f(x_1, x_2, x_3, x_4) = x_4 \cdot (x_2 \oplus x_3) + \bar{x}_1 \cdot x_3 \cdot \bar{x}_4$ has the minterms (minterms are defined in Section 2.1)

$$\bar{x}_1 \bar{x}_2 x_3 x_4, \quad \bar{x}_1 x_2 x_3 \bar{x}_4, \quad \bar{x}_1 x_2 \bar{x}_3 x_4, \quad \bar{x}_1 \bar{x}_2 x_3 \bar{x}_4, \quad x_1 x_2 \bar{x}_3 x_4, \quad x_1 \bar{x}_2 x_3 x_4$$

which are shown in Table 2.4.3.1. Such a table is called a Karnaugh map (Harrison, 1965). Using the absorption rules of Theorem 2.1.1, we can combine minterms to form implicants. Clearly, each of the minterms is an implicant and, if two or more minterms can be combined into a single product, this product is also an implicant. In fact, this is the only way in which implicants can be formed. The Karnaugh map is a useful tool for forming prime implicants for functions of five or fewer variables. The following three of the four prime implicants of f are circled in the table:

$$x_2 \bar{x}_3 x_4, \quad \bar{x}_2 x_3 x_4, \quad \bar{x}_1 x_3 \bar{x}_4$$

as the reader can readily verify.

Table 2.4.3.1.   Karnaugh Map of $f(x_1, x_2, x_3, x_4) = x_4(x_2 \oplus x_3) + \bar{x}_1 x_3 \bar{x}_4$

$x_1 x_2$ \\ $x_3 x_4$	0 0	0 1	1 1	1 0
0 0			1	1
0 1		1		1
1 1		1		
1 0			1	

Let t be a product of literals of f and let $|t|$ be the number of literals in t. Also, let $\mathrm{gcn}(t_1, t_2)$ be the common number of literals in the products t_1 and t_2. Schnorr (1974) has shown that

$$\#(f) = \max_{t_1, t_2}\left(|t_1| + |t_2| - \mathrm{gcn}(t_1, t_2) - 1\right)$$

where t_1 and t_2 are prime implicants of f, is a step-counting measure for $\Omega = \{+, {}^-\}$. Therefore,

Theorem 2.4.3.9.   Over the basis $\Omega = \{+, {}^-\}$, the function $f: \{0, 1\}^n \to \{0, 1\}$ has

$$C_\Omega^*(f) \geq \#(f)$$

The reader is asked (Problem 2-21) to use this theorem to prove the following result:

Theorem 2.4.3.10.   Over the basis $\Omega = \{+, {}^-\}$, the function

$$f(x_1, \ldots, x_n) = x_1 x_2 \cdots x_n + \bar{x}_1 \bar{x}_2 \cdots \bar{x}_n$$

has combinational complexity

$$C_\Omega^*(f) = 2n - 1$$

This completes the discussion of special linear lower bounds. We now turn to deriving bounds to the combinational complexity of a *set* of Boolean functions.

2.4.4.   The Combinational Complexity of a Set of Functions

All of the lower bounds derived above apply *only* to individual Boolean functions. Often, however, it is desirable to have lower bounds for the combinational complexity of a set of Boolean functions.

Theorem 2.4.4.1. Let Ω be any basis and let f_j: $\{0, 1\}^n \to \{0, 1\}$, $1 \leq j \leq m$. Then

$$C_\Omega^*(f_1, f_2, \ldots, f_m) \geq \max_j C_\Omega^*(f_j)$$

This result is obvious. The next, reported by Lamagna and Savage (1973), is a little less so.

Theorem 2.4.4.2. Let Ω be any basis, let f_j: $\{0, 1\}^n \to \{0, 1\}$, $1 \leq j \leq m$, be such that no one function is equal to another or to the inverse of another, and let $C_\Omega^*(f_j) \geq 1$ for all $1 \leq j \leq m$. Then

$$C_\Omega^*(f_1, \ldots, f_m) \geq m - 1 + \min_j C_\Omega^*(f_j)$$

Proof. Let β be an C_Ω^*-optimal chain for $f_1, f_2, \ldots, f_m$ over Ω. In β, a step β_k is a *descendant* of step β_l if there is a directed path from β_l to β_k. Let $\beta^{(j)}$ be the subchain of β obtained by removing all steps that are descendants of f_j. Let $|\beta^{(j)}|$ be the number of computation steps of fan-in greater than or equal to 2 in $\beta^{(j)}$. Let t be such that

$$|\beta^{(t)}| = \min_{1 \leq j \leq m} |\beta^{(j)}|$$

Then, if $j \neq t$, neither f_j nor $\bar{f}_j$ is computed by the terminal step of $\beta^{(t)}$ or by its input nodes if this step is an inversion step. Also, f_j is not computed by any subchain of $\beta^{(t)}$ because this would require that $|\beta^{(j)}| < |\beta^{(t)}|$. Furthermore, in β but not in $\beta^{(t)}$, there must be one distinct step (with fan-in greater than or equal to 2) for each f_j, $1 \leq j \leq m$, $j \neq t$, since $f_j \neq f_l$ and $f_j \neq \bar{f}_l$ for $j \neq l$. Consequently,

$$C_\Omega^*(f_1, \ldots, f_m) \geq m - 1 + |\beta^{(t)}|$$

from which the conclusion follows. $\square$

The next two examples present functions for which the two bounds are exact and for which the second dominates the first.

Example 2.4.4.1. Define the set of m functions $f_1, \ldots, f_m$ by

$$f_1 = x_1 \cdot x_2$$

$$f_j = f_{j-1} \cdot x_{j+1}, \qquad 2 \leq j \leq m$$

Then, over $\Omega = \{+, \cdot, ^-\}$, we have

$$C_\Omega^*(f_1, \ldots, f_m) \geq C_\Omega^*(f_m) \geq m$$

by applying Theorems 2.4.4.1 and 2.4.1.1 (f_m depends on each of its $m + 1$ variables). But the functions also satisfy the conditions of Theorem 2.4.4.2, so the same lower bound results from its application. It follows by construction that all the functions can be realized with m two-input operations; therefore, they have combinational complexity of m.

Example 2.4.4.2. Let g_l: $\{0, 1\}^n \to \{0, 1\}$, $0 \leq l \leq 2^n - 1$, defined by

$$g_l(x_1, \ldots, x_n) = \begin{cases} 1, & x_1 \cdot 2^0 + x_2 \cdot 2^1 + \cdots + x_n \cdot 2^{n-1} = l \\ 0, & \text{otherwise} \end{cases}$$

where $+$ denotes integer addition. Then, from Theorem 2.4.4.1,

$$C_\Omega^*(g_0, \ldots, g_{2^n-1}) \geq n - 1$$

whereas from Theorem 2.4.4.2,

$$C_\Omega^*(g_0, \ldots, g_{2^n-1}) \geq 2^n + n - 2$$

when $\Omega = \{+, \cdot, ^-\}$. The first result follows because $g_l(x_1, \ldots, x_n)$ is the product of n literals. For example, when $n = 4$ and $l = 3$, $g(x_1, x_2, x_3, x_4) = x_1 x_2 \bar{x}_3 \bar{x}_4$. In Section 3.1 we show that this complexity can be upper-bounded by an expression that approaches 2^n when n is large.

Appendix

This appendix gives the proofs of two lemmas and one theroem of Chapter 2.

Lemma 2.4.2.1. For each $n \geq 3$, the function h_n: $\{0, 1\}^n \to \{0, 1\}$ defined as

$$h_3(x_1, x_2, x_3) = x_1 x_2 + \left(\overline{x_1 \oplus x_3} \right)$$

is in the class $P_{2,3}^{(n)}$, and for $n \geq 4$,

$$h_n(x_1, \ldots, x_n) = \begin{cases} x_n \cdot h_{n-1}(x_1, \ldots, x_{n-1}), & n \text{ even} \\ x_n + h_{n-1}(x_1, \ldots, x_{n-1}), & n \text{ odd} \end{cases}$$

Furthermore, $P_{2,3}^{(n)} = \varnothing$ for $n < 3$.

Proof. That $P_{2,3}^{(n)}$ is empty for $n = 1, 2$ follows directly from Property 3. Table 2.4.2.1 shows $h_3\big|_{j \in J}^{x_j = c_j}$ for all sets $J \subset \{1, 2, 3\}$ such that $|J| = 2$

and all values of c_j. Clearly, $h_3 \in P_{2,3}^{(3)}$. Table 2.4.2.2 shows $h_3\big|^{x_j = c_j}$ for all values of $j \in \{1, 2, 3\}$ and all values of c_j. From this it follows that $h_3\big|^{x_j = c_j}$ is nonconstant.

To show that $h_l \in P_{2,3}^{(l)}$, choose any two variables x_i and x_j with $i < j$ and show that there are at least three distinct subfunctions $h_l\big|^{x_i = c_i, x_j = c_j}$. Suppose the hypothesis is true for $3 \leq l \leq n - 1$; we show that it is also true for $l = n$.

Before proceeding, let us establish another result, namely, that $h_l\big|^{x_i = c_i} \neq 1$ (the constant function) when l is even and $\neq 0$ when l is odd for $l \leq n - 1$. From Table 2.4.2.2, the result holds when $l = 3$. Assume that $h_l \in P_{2,3}^{(l)}$ for $3 \leq l \leq n - 1$. By Property 5, $h_l \in P_{1,2}^{(l)}$ for $3 \leq l \leq n - 1$. Then

$$h_l\big|^{x_j = c_j} = \begin{cases} x_l \circ h_{l-1}\big|^{x_j = c_j}, & j \leq l - 1 \\ c_j \circ h_{l-1}, & j = l \end{cases}$$

where $\circ$ denotes $\cdot$ when l is even and $+$ when l is odd. Clearly, when $j \leq l - 1$ the hypothesis holds, because the assumption that $h_l\big|^{x_j = c_j} = 1$ for l even is contradicted by setting $x_l = 0$ and similarly for l odd. For $j = l$,

$$h_l\big|^{x_l = c_l} = \begin{cases} 0, & c_l = 0, \\ & \quad\quad\quad l \text{ even} \\ h_{l-1}, & c_l = 1, \\ h_{l-1}, & c_l = 0, \\ & \quad\quad\quad l \text{ odd} \\ 1, & c_l = 1, \end{cases}$$

and since h_{l-1} is nonconstant (it is in $P_{1,2}^{(l-1)}$), the desired conclusion follows. The conclusion also follows for $l = n$ once it has been established that $h_n \in P_{2,3}^{(n)}$.

Now let $h_l \in P_{2,3}^{(l)}$ for $3 \leq l \leq n - 1$. Consider the subfunction $h_n\big|^{x_i = c_i, x_j = c_j}$ and let $i < j$. When $j \leq n - 1$,

$$h_n\big|^{x_i = c_i, x_j = c_j} = x_n \circ h_{n-1}\big|^{x_i = c_i, x_j = c_j}$$

and the inductive hypothesis establishes that there are at least three such distinct subfunctions.

When $j = n$,

$$h_n\big|^{x_i = c_i, x_n = c_n} = c_n \circ h_{n-1}\big|^{x_i = c_i}$$

and there are two cases to consider, n even and n odd.

Case 1, n *even.*

$$h_n\Big|^{x_i = c_i,\, x_n = c_n} = \begin{cases} 0, & c_n = 0 \\ h_{n-1}\Big|^{x_i = c_i}, & c_n = 1 \end{cases}$$

But $h_{n-1}\big|^{x_i = 0} \neq h_{n-1}\big|^{x_i = 1}$ since $h_{n-1} \in P_{1,2}^{(n-1)}$ and $h_{n-1}\big|^{x_i = c_i} \neq 0$, as established above, because $n - 1$ is odd. Therefore, the inductive hypothesis applies here.

Case 2, n *odd.*

$$h_n\Big|^{x_i = c_i,\, x_n = c_n} = \begin{cases} h_{n-1}\Big|^{x_i = c_i}, & c_n = 0 \\ 1, & c_n = 1 \end{cases}$$

By a similar reasoning, the inductive assertion holds and the desired result is shown. $\qquad\square$

Lemma 2.4.2.2. Let

$$g \in P_{3,5}^{(n_1)}, \qquad h \in P_{3,5}^{(n_2)} \qquad \text{and} \qquad g, h$$

such that for all sets $J_1, J_2, |J_1| \leq 2, |J_2| \leq 2$, none of the subfunctions

$$g\Big|^{u_j = c_j}_{j \in J_1}, \qquad h\Big|^{v_j = d_j}_{j \in J_2}$$

are constant. Then, if the variables of g and h are disjoint from one another and from the variable x, then the function f,

$$f = x \oplus g \cdot h$$

is in $P_{3,5}^{(n)}$, $n = n_1 + n_2 + 1$, and for all sets $J, |J| \leq 2$, none of the subfunctions $f\big|^{x_j = c_j}_{j \in J}$ is constant.

Proof. The last statement is established first. We note that if subfunctions obtained by fixing two variables are nonconstant, then the same is true of the original function and of subfunctions obtained by fixing one variable. Thus, it is sufficient to prove the last statement when $|J| = 2$. We also note that the function $x \oplus q$ is nonconstant when q is any function, constant or nonconstant, whose variables do not include x. Also, $x \oplus q = x \oplus q'$ if and only if $q = q'$.

To prove that $f\big|^{x_j = c_j}_{j \in J}, |J| = 2$, is nonconstant, consider the following two cases:

(a) x is indexed in J; (b) x is not indexed in J.

(a) $\quad f\big|^{x = 0} = g \cdot h, \qquad f\big|^{x = 1} = \overline{g \cdot h}$

The remaining variable to be indexed in J is a variable of g or h but not of both. Without loss of generality, let it be u, a variable of g. The resulting subfunction is either $g\big|^{u=c_j}\cdot h$ or $\bar{g}\big|^{u=c_j} + \bar{h}$. Since h is nonconstant, neither of these functions is constant and the result is established.

(b) $f\big|^{x_j=c_j}_{j\in J} = x \oplus (g\cdot h)\big|^{x_j=c_j}_{j\in J}$

This function is nonconstant, as observed in the preceding paragraph.

To show that $f \in P^{(n)}_{3,5}$, we need the fact that the functions

$$g\bigg|^{u_j=c_j}_{j\in J_1}\cdot h\bigg|^{v_j=d_j}_{j\in J_2} \quad \text{and} \quad \bar{g}\bigg|^{u_j=c'_j}_{j\in J_1} + \bar{h}\bigg|^{v_j=d'_j}_{j\in J_2}$$

are unequal when $|J_1|, |J_2| \leq 2$ and the constants $c_j, c'_j, j \in J_1$, and d_j, d'_j, $j \in J_2$ are not all equal. This fact is derived by noting that all of the subfunctions shown are nonconstant. Thus, choose the values of the remaining variables of $g\big|^{u_j=c_j}_{j\in J_1}$ so that it equals 0. Then $\bar{g}\big|^{u_j=c'_j}_{j\in J_1}$ with the remaining variables fixed as indicated is a constant, which if 1, proves that the two original functions are not equal. If the constant is 0, the two original functions are equal only if $\bar{h}\big|^{v_j=d'_j}_{j\in J_2}$ is equal to 0. This contradicts the assumption that it is nonconstant. Now let us show that $f \in P^{(n)}_{3,5}$. We want to show that there are at least five subfunctions $f\big|^{x_j=c_j}_{j\in J}$ for $|J| = 3$. There are again two cases to consider: (a) x is indexed in J and (b) it is not indexed in J.

(a) Consider the subfunctions obtained when $x = 0$, that is, the subfunctions $(g\cdot h)\big|^{x_j=c_j}_{j\in J'}$, $|J'| = 2$. If both variables indexed in J' are variables of g, there are at least three such functions since $g \in P^{(n_1)}_{2,3}$; the same is true for h. If one variable is a variable of g, the other variable of h, then there are four subfunctions since $g \in P^{(n_1)}_{1,2}$ and $h \in P^{(n_2)}_{1,2}$. The same arguments hold when $x = 1$.

From this and the earlier observation, there are at least three subfunctions of f with $x = 0$ and at least three distinct such subfunctions of f when $x = 1$. Clearly, $f \in P^{(n)}_{3,5}$ when x is indexed in J.

(b) $f\big|^{x_j=c_j}_{j\in J} = x \oplus (g\cdot h)\big|^{x_j=c_j}_{j\in J}$ and there are at least five such subfunctions if there are at least five functions $(g\cdot h)\big|^{x_j=c_j}_{j\in J}$. This clearly is true when the variables indexed by J are variables of g or h but not both, since g and h are nonconstant and $g \in P^{(n_1)}_{3,3}$, $h \in P^{(n_2)}_{3,3}$. Thus, without loss of generality, let two of the indexed variables be variables of g. Since $g \in P^{(n_1)}_{2,3}$ and none of the subfunctions are constant, the reader can show that there are at least six such subfunctions. $\square$

Theorem 2.4.3.6. Let $f_{\text{COMP}}: \{0, 1\}^n \to \{0, 1\}$ be defined by

$$f_{\text{COMP}}(x_1, \ldots, x_{n/2}, y_1, \ldots, y_{n/2}) = \begin{cases} 1, & |\mathbf{x}| < |\mathbf{y}| \\ 0, & \text{otherwise} \end{cases}$$

when n is even, where $|\mathbf{x}| = x_1 2^0 + x_2 2^1 + \cdots + x_{n/2} 2^{(n/2)-1}$ and $+$ denotes integer addition. Then

$$C_{\Omega_0}^*(f_{\text{COMP}}) = 2n - 3$$

Proof. Let f'_{COMP} be f_{COMP} defined on $n - 2$ variables. Then

$$f_{\text{COMP}} = \bar{x}_{n/2} \cdot y_{n/2} + (\bar{x}_{n/2} + y_{n/2}) \cdot f'_{\text{COMP}}$$

since

$$f_{\text{COMP}} = \begin{cases} 1, & x_{n/2} = 0, y_{n/2} = 1 \\ 0, & x_{n/2} = 1, y_{n/2} = 0 \\ f'_{\text{COMP}} & x_{n/2} = y_{n/2} \end{cases}$$

Also, when $n = 2$, $f_{\text{COMP}} = \bar{x}_1 \cdot y_1$. Therefore, it follows directly that

$$C_{\Omega_0}^*(f_{\text{COMP}}) \leq 2n - 3$$

The lower bound is a little more difficult to derive. It is obtained by considering the various cases that can occur. Let t_x and t_y be the number of occurrences of the literals $\{x_{n/2}, \bar{x}_{n/2}\}$ and $\{y_{n/2}, \bar{y}_{n/2}\}$, respectively, in a $C_{\Omega_0}^*$-optimal graph of f_{COMP}. Denote a literal in $\{\zeta, \bar{\zeta}\}$ by $\tilde{\zeta}$. In the following, a node always has fan-in 2. Inverters are suppressed.

(a) $t_x = 1$, $t_y = 1$. See Figure 2.A.1.

$v_1 = v_2$. This implies that $x_{n/2}$ obstructs $y_{n/2}$. Contradiction.

$v_1 \neq v_2$. Since neither v_1 nor v_2 is a terminal node, there exist nodes v_3 or v_4. Assume that v_3 exists (a similar argument applies to v_4).

Clearly, $v_3 \neq v_2$ since otherwise $y_{n/2}$ would obstruct $x_{n/2}$.

(i) Subgraph G_1 of G realizing φ_1 does not contain v_2; φ_1 is a nonconstant function depending on some of $\{x_1, \ldots, x_{n/2-1}, y_1, \ldots, y_{n/2-1}\}$. Then these variables obstruct $x_{n/2}$. Contradiction.

(ii) G_1 contains v_2. The subgraph G_2 realizing φ_2 does not contain v_1, so φ_2 depends on some of $\{x_1, \ldots, x_{n/2-1}, y_1, \ldots, y_{n/2-1}\}$, and they obstruct $y_{n/2}$. Contradiction.

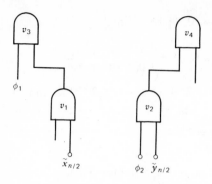

Figure 2.A.1. Cases when $t_x = 1$, $t_y = 1$.

We conclude that this case leads to a contradiction.

(b) $t_x = 1$, $t_y \geq 2$. See Figure 2.A.2.

Let v_1 be the two-input node to which $\tilde{x}_{n/2}$ is directed and let v_2 and v_3 be similar nodes for $\tilde{y}_{n/2}$. If $v_2 = v_3$, the chain is not optimal. If $v_1 = v_2$ or $v_1 = v_3$, then $y_{n/2}$ obstructs $x_{n/2}$. Therefore, v_1, v_2, and v_3 are distinct. Since v_1, v_2, and v_3 are not terminal nodes and since there are no directed loops in a chain, there must exist a node v_4 that is connected to an output of one of v_1, v_2, or v_3 and that is distinct from these. Without loss of generality, let v_4 be the output of v_2. Then set $\tilde{y}_{n/2}$ to fix the output of v_2 and set $x_{n/2} = y_{n/2}$ so that at least four two-input nodes can be eliminated to produce a chain for f'_{COMP}.

(c) $t_x \geq 2$, $t_y = 1$. Same as (b).

(d) $t_x \geq 2$, $t_y \geq 2$. See Figure 2.A.3.

Let v_1, v_2 be two of the two-input computation nodes associated with $\tilde{x}_{n/2}$ as input and let v_3, v_4 be the same for $\tilde{y}_{n/2}$. Clearly, $v_1 \neq v_2$ and $v_3 \neq v_4$ since the graph is optimal.

    (i) Two distinct elements in $\{v_1, v_2, v_3, v_4\}$.

        Let $v_1 = v_3$ and $v_2 = v_4$, as in Figure 2.A.3(a). Then neither

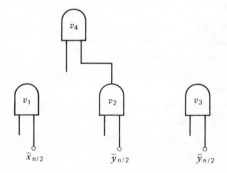

Figure 2.A.2. Cases when $t_x = 1$, $t_y \geq 2$.

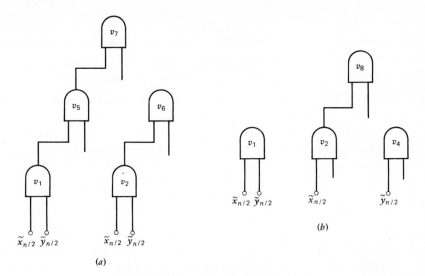

Figure 2.A.3. Cases when $t_x \geq 2$, $t_y \geq 2$.

v_1 nor v_2 is a terminal node. If $v_5 = v_6$, setting $x_n = y_n$ causes the output of v_1, v_2, and v_5 to be constant; therefore, v_5 is not a terminal node and there exists another node v_7. Under these conditions, v_1, v_2, v_5, and v_7 can be eliminated. If $v_5 \neq v_6$, setting $x_{n/2} = y_{n/2}$ allows v_1, v_2, v_5, and v_6 to be eliminated.

(ii) Three distinct elements in $\{v_1, v_2, v_3, v_4\}$.

Let $v_1 = v_3$ as in Figure 2.A.3(b). Then none of $\{v_1, v_2, v_3, v_4\}$ is a terminal node, and no directed loops exist. Thus, there must exist some node v_8 that is an output of v_1, v_2, v_4 but is distinct from them. Without loss of generality, let v_8 be an output of v_2; set $\tilde{x}_{n/2}$ to fix the output of v_2, and the input to v_8. Set $y_{n/2} = x_{n/2}$ so that at least four two-input elements can be removed to form a chain for f'_{COMP}.

(iii) All elements of $\{v_1, v_2, v_3, v_4\}$ are distinct.

Set $x_{n/2} = y_{n/2} = 0$ to eliminate four elements and produce a chain for f'_{COMP}.

After consideration of all cases, we find that

$$C^*_{\Omega_0}(f_{\text{COMP}}) \geq 4 + C^*_{\Omega_0}(f'_{\text{COMP}})$$

and since $C^*_{\Omega_0}(f_{\text{COMP}}) \geq 1$ for $n = 2$, the conclusion of the theorem follows. $\square$

Problems

2-1. Prove Theorem 2.1.1 by establishing each of the stated properties for the Boolean functions AND, OR, NOT, and EXCLUSIVE OR.

2-2. Using DeMorgan's rules, show that the conjunctive normal form (CNF) of a Boolean function f can be derived from the disjunctive normal formal (DNF) of $\bar{f}$.

2-3. Show that each Boolean function has a unique ring sum expansion (RSE).

2-4. Find the DNF, CNF, and RSE of the following Boolean functions:
   (a) $x_1 \cdot x_2 + \bar{x}_3$.
   (b) $x_1 + x_2 + \cdots + x_n$.
   (c) $x_1 \cdot x_2 \cdot \cdots \cdot x_n$.

2-5. Show that $\Omega = \{\oplus, \cdot\}$ is a complete basis. Is it complete when the data set does not contain the constant functions 0 and 1?

2-6. Show that the basis $\Omega = \{+, \cdot\}$ is not complete.
   Hint. Is there a nonmonotone function that cannot be realized with a chain over this basis. (See the proof of Theorem 2.3.2 for a definition of monotone function.)

2-7. The Boolean functions s_j and c_j of Example 2.2.2 are defined by

$$s_j = c_{j-1} \oplus x_j \oplus y_j, \qquad c_j = c_{j-1} \cdot x_j + c_{j-1} \cdot y_j + x_j \cdot y_j$$

   Show that the combinational machine of Figure 2.2.2 realizes these two functions.

2-8. Show that every $f: \{0, 1\}^n \to \{0, 1\}$ can be expanded as follows:

$$f(x_1, x_2, \ldots, x_n) = x_1 \cdot f(1, x_2, \ldots, x_n) + \bar{x}_1 \cdot f(0, x_2, \ldots, x_n)$$

   where $+$ and $\cdot$ denote OR and AND. Apply this expansion repeatedly to each variable of $f(x_1, x_2, x_3) = x_1 \cdot \bar{x}_2 + x_2 x_3$ to obtain its DNF.

2-9. Apply DeMorgan's rules to obtain the dual of the expansion of Problem 2-8.

2-10. Show the existence of a circuit of fan-out 1 for $f(x_1, \ldots, x_n) = x_1 \cdot x_2 \cdot \cdots \cdot x_n$, $n = 2^k$, which has the minimum number of elements and minimum depth simultaneously. Show that the lower bound of Theorem 2.3.3 is achieved.

2-11. Determine $C_\Omega^*(f_1)$ and $C_\Omega^*(f_2)$ for the following functions when $\Omega = \{+, \cdot, ^-, \oplus\}$:

$$f_1(x_1, \ldots, x_n, y_1, \ldots, y_n) = \begin{cases} 1 & x_i = 1 \text{ or } y_i = 1 \text{ or both for } 1 \le i \le n \\ 0 & \text{otherwise} \end{cases}$$

$$f_2(x_1, \ldots, x_n, y_1, \ldots, y_n) = \begin{cases} 1 & x_i \ne y_i, \quad 1 \le i \le n \\ 0 & \text{otherwise} \end{cases}$$

2-12. Obtain good upper and lower bounds to the combinational complexity (without counting inversions) and delay complexity of the function $f: \{0, 1\}^{(n+1)b} \to \{0, 1\}$ defined by

$$f(\mathbf{x}_1, \mathbf{x}_2, \ldots, \mathbf{x}_n, \mathbf{y}) = \begin{cases} 1 & \mathbf{x}_i = \mathbf{y} \quad \text{some } 1 \le i \le n \\ 0 & \text{otherwise} \end{cases}$$

over $\Omega = \{+, \cdot, ^-, \oplus\}$ where $\mathbf{x}_i, \mathbf{y} \in \{0, 1\}^b$ and $\mathbf{x}_i = \mathbf{y}$ if and only if they agree in every component.

2-13. Let $N_{1,2}^{(n)}$ be the number of distinct functions in the set $P_{1,2}^{(n)}$ (functions that depend on each of their variables). Show that $N_{1,2}^{(n)}$ satisfies the equation

$$2^{2^n} = \sum_{j=0}^{n} N_{1,2}^{(j)} \binom{n}{j}$$

where $\binom{n}{j}$ is the binomial coefficient $n!/j!(n-j)!$ and we define $N_{1,2}^{(0)} = 2$. Solve the equation for $N_{1,2}^{(n)}$ and determine its value explicitly for $n = 4$; compare with 2^{2^n}.

2-14. Show that the function $g_6: \{0, 1\}^6 \to \{0, 1\}$ is in $P_{3,5}^{(6)}$ where

$$g_6(x_1, x_2, \ldots, x_6) = x_1 \oplus (x_4(x_3 \oplus x_1 x_2) + x_6(x_5 \oplus x_1 x_2))$$

Also, demonstrate that none of the subfunctions $g_6\big|_{j \in J}^{x_j = c_j}$, where $J \in \{1, 2, \ldots, 6\}, |J| \le 2$, are the constant functions.

2-15. Show that the functions h_n, $n \ge 3$, defined in Lemma 2.4.2.1 are not in $P_{3,5}^{(n)}$ for any n.

2-16. Show that every function Q in $P_{0,1}^{(n)}$ is a subfunction of some function Q^* in $P_{1,2}^{(n)}$.

2-17. Show that if f is in the class

$$R_{2,3}^{(n)} = \left\{ f \in P_{2,3}^{(n)} | c_1, \ldots, c_n \in \{0, 1\} \right.$$

such that for all $J \subset \{1, 2, \ldots, n\}$,

$$1 \leq |J| \leq n - 3, f\Big|_{j \in J}^{x_j = c_j} \in P_{2,3}^{(n-|J|)} \Big\}$$

then $C_\Omega(f) \geq 2n - 3$ if $\Omega = P_{1,2}^{(2)}$.

2-18. Show that

$$f(x_1, \ldots, x_n) = (x_1 \oplus x_2 \oplus \cdots \oplus x_{n-1}) \cdot (x_2 + \cdots + x_n)$$

is in $Q_{2,3}^{(n)}$.

2-19. A set of variables $\{x_i\}$ of $f: \{0, 1\}^n \to \{0, 1\}$ obstructs a variable x_j if values can be assigned to variables in $\{x_i\}$ so that f does not depend on x_j. Find the two functions which are such that no subset of fewer than n variables obstructs any of the remaining variables.

2-20. Represent 0 with the pair (0, 1) and 1 with the pair (1, 0). An inverter in this representation system is a pair of twisted wires. How are AND and OR realized in this system? Show that every function f: $\{0, 1\}^n \to \{0, 1\}^m$ can be realized by a circuit of AND's and OR's in which inverters are used only on the variables.

2-21. Prove Theorem 2.4.3.10 by applying Theorem 2.4.3.9 to the function

$$f(x_1, \ldots, x_n) = x_1 x_2 \cdots x_n + \bar{x}_1 \bar{x}_2 \cdots \bar{x}_n$$

2-22. Let Σ and $+$ denote integer addition. Define $f_4: \{0, 1\}^n \to \{0, 1\}$ and $f_5: \{0, 1\}^n \to \{0, 1\}$ by

$$f_4(x_1, \ldots, x_n) = \left(\left(\sum_{i=1}^{m} x_i + 2 \right) \bmod 4 \right) \bmod 2$$

$$f_5(x_1, \ldots, x_n) = \left(\left(\sum_{i=1}^{n} x_i + 2 \right) \bmod 5 \right) \bmod 2$$

Determine good lower bounds to the combinational complexity of these two functions over $\Omega = P_{1,2}^{(2)}$.

Chapter 3

Combinational Complexity and Formula Size

In Chapter 2, combinational complexity and formula size were introduced, and methods for lower bounding the combinational complexity of functions were developed. In this chapter, we continue our study of these two measures. We examine a number of important arithmetic and logical functions as well as symmetric functions and develop upper bounds to their combinational complexities over complete bases. Monotone functions can be computed by chains over the incomplete basis of AND and OR, and we show that nonlinear lower bounds to combinational complexity can be derived for some important monotone functions.

In this chapter, we also present important methods for deriving lower bounds to the formula size of Boolean functions. The chapter closes with the development of asymptotic bounds to combinational complexity and formula size and with the introduction of synchronous combinational complexity.

3.1. FUNCTIONS OVER COMPLETE BASES

This section is devoted primarily to deriving upper bounds to the combinational complexity of important functions over complete bases.

We examine some logical and arithmetic operations as well as symmetric functions. Our treatment of arithmetic functions here is cursory, since a more detailed study is found in Chapter 6, "General-Purpose Computers."

3.1.1. Logical and Arithmetic Operations

A most important logical function, and one that occurs frequently in the construction of chains, is the *binary-to-positional transformer* $f_T^{(n)}: \{0, 1\}^n \to \{0, 1\}^{2^n}$. It is defined by

$$f_T^{(n)}(x_0, \ldots, x_{n-1}) = (y_0, \ldots, y_{2^n-1})$$

and for $1 \leq i \leq 2^n$

$$y_i = \begin{cases} 1, & \text{if } x_{n-1} \cdot 2^{n-1} + \cdots + x_1 2^1 + x_0 = i \\ 0, & \text{otherwise} \end{cases}$$

where $+$ denotes integer addition. Then only one component of $(y_0, y_1, \ldots, y_{2^n-1})$ is 1 on any input, and it is that component which corresponds to the integer $|\mathbf{x}| = x_{n-1} 2^{n-1} + \cdots + x_1 2^1 + x_0$.

The astute reader will note that y_i is the minterm function of $x_0, \ldots, x_{n-1}$ defined by

$$y_i(x_0, \ldots, x_{n-1}) = m_{c_0 \cdots c_{n-1}}(x_0, \ldots, x_{n-1}) = x_0^{c_0 \bullet} \cdots \bullet x_{n-1}^{c_{n-1}}$$

where $(c_0, c_1, \ldots, c_{n-1})$ is the binary expansion of i and $x^0 = \bar{x}, x^1 = x$. For example, when $i = 3$, $y_3(x_0, x_1, x_2, x_3) = x_0 x_1 \bar{x}_2 \bar{x}_3$.

Suppose that n is even and the two functions $f_T^{(n/2)}(x_0, x_1, \ldots, x_{n/2-1})$ and $f_T^{(n/2)}(x_{n/2}, \ldots, x_{n-1})$ have been realized with chains. Then all minterms

$$x_0^{c_0} x_1^{c_1} \cdots x_{n/2-1}^{c_{n/2-1}} \quad \text{and} \quad x_{n/2}^{c_{n/2}} \cdots x_{n-1}^{c_{n-1}}$$

have been realized, and all 2^n minterms in $x_0, x_1, \ldots, x_{n-1}$ can be computed by AND'ing the minterms of the two functions in all possible pairs. Thus, if $C_\Omega^*(f_T^{(n)})$ is the combinational complexity of f_T over $\Omega = \{ +, \cdot, ^- \}$ where NOT has zero cost, it follows that

$$C_\Omega^*(f_T^{(n)}) \leq 2^n + 2C_\Omega^*(f_T^{(n/2)})$$

A direct realization of $f_T^{(n)}$ uses $n2^n - 1$ AND's and OR's, so we have

$$C_\Omega^*(f_T^{(n)}) \leq 2^n + n2^{n/2} - 2$$

for n even. For n odd, we group the variables into sets of size $(n + 1)/2$ and $(n - 1)/2$, and the second term is bounded by $n2^{(n+1)/2} - 2$.

Theorem 3.1.1.1. Over the basis $\Omega = \{ +, \cdot, ^- \}$, the binary-to-positional transformer has combinational complexity $C_\Omega^*(f_T^{(n)})$ where

$$2^n + n - 2 \leq C_\Omega^*(f_T^{(n)}) \leq 2^n + n2^{\lceil n/2 \rceil} - 2$$

The lower bound was derived in Example 2.4.4.2. We see that for any $\varepsilon > 0$ the upper bound can be replaced by $2^n(1 + \varepsilon)$ for n large.

Integer addition is obviously very important, especially when integers are represented in the standard binary representation. This representation for addition is characterized by the function $f_A^{(n)}: \{0, 1\}^n \to \{0, 1\}^{n/2+1}$ for n even, where $(x_0, x_1, \ldots, x_{n/2-1})$ and $(y_0, y_1, \ldots, y_{n/2-1})$ represent the integers $|\mathbf{x}|$ and $|\mathbf{y}|$ where

$$|\mathbf{x}| = \sum_{j=0}^{(n/2)-1} x_j 2^j, \qquad |\mathbf{y}| = \sum_{j=0}^{(n/2)-1} y_j 2^j$$

and

$$f_A^{(n)}(x_0, \ldots, x_{n/2-1}, y_0, \ldots, y_{n/2-1}) = (s_0, s_1, \ldots, s_{n/2-1}, c_{n/2})$$

Here $(s_0, s_1, \ldots, s_{n/2-1}, c_{n/2})$ is the binary representation of $|\mathbf{s}|$ where

$$|\mathbf{s}| = c_{n/2} 2^{n/2} + \sum_{j=0}^{(n/2)-1} s_j 2^j = |\mathbf{x}| + |\mathbf{y}|$$

and where Σ and $+$ denote integer addition.

The function $f_A^{(n)}$ can be realized by a chain consisting of a cascade of Full Adders, as shown in Figure 3.1.1.1, where the Full Adder was defined in Example 2.2.2 and Figure 2.2.2. Since for each j, the sum and carry digits s_j and c_{j+1} can be realized from c_j and x_j, y_j with five elements from $\Omega = \{+, \cdot, ^-, \oplus\}$, and with two elements for $j = 0$, it follows that

Theorem 3.1.1.2. Over the basis $\Omega = \{+, \cdot, ^-, \oplus\}$, the binary integer addition function satisfies

$$n - 1 \leq C_{\Omega}^*\left(f_A^{(n)}\right) \leq \tfrac{5}{2}n - 3$$

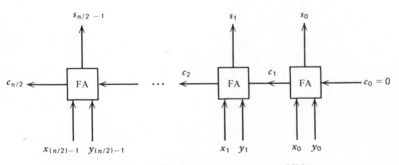

Figure 3.1.1.1. Full Adder chain for integer addition.

The lower bound applies to $c_{n/2}$ alone and follows from Theorem 2.4.1.1.

Integer multiplication is another basic arithmetic operation which we illustrate here with a simple but decidedly nonoptimal chain. Let $f_M^{(n)}$: $\{0, 1\}^n \to \{0, 1\}^n$, $n \geq 4$, characterize integer multiplication when integers $|\mathbf{x}|$ and $|\mathbf{y}|$ are given the standard binary representations $(x_0, \ldots, x_{n/2-1})$, $(y_0, \ldots, y_{n/2-1})$. Then

$$f_M^{(n)}(x_0, \ldots, x_{n/2-1}, y_0, \ldots, y_{n/2-1}) = (p_0, p_1, \ldots, p_{n-1})$$

where

$$|\mathbf{p}| = \sum_{j=0}^{n-1} p_j 2^j = |\mathbf{x}| * |\mathbf{y}| = \sum_{j=0}^{n/2-1} \left(x_j 2^j \right) * |\mathbf{y}|$$

and $*$ denotes integer multiplication. In this expansion of $|\mathbf{p}|$, the product $2^j * |\mathbf{y}|$ corresponds to a shifting operation that produces $(0, 0, \ldots, 0, y_0, y_1, \ldots, y_{n/2-1})$, where j zeros precede the other digits. Furthermore, $(x_j 2^j) * |\mathbf{y}|$ can be realized with $n/2$ AND's for each $0 \leq j \leq n/2 - 1$, and $f_M^{(n)}$ can be computed by summing the terms in the above sum or by using $n/2 - 1$ copies of the integer addition function $f_A^{(2(n-1))}$.

Theorem 3.1.1.3. Over the basis $\Omega = \{ +, \cdot, ^-, \oplus \}$, the integer multiplication function $f_M^{(n)}$ satisfies

$$n - 1 \leq C_\Omega^* (f_M^{(n)}) \leq \tfrac{11}{4} n^2 - 9n + 8$$

The upper bound can be considerably improved as stated in Chapter 6. With this improvement, we shall also have a bound on the complexity of the following *shifting functions*:

Let $\mathbf{a} = (a_0, a_1, \ldots, a_{\lceil \log_2 n \rceil - 1})$ denote the integer $0 \leq |\mathbf{a}| \leq 2^{\lceil \log_2 n \rceil} - 1$ and let $\mathbf{x} = (x_0, x_1, \ldots, x_{n-1})$.

SHIFT-RIGHT LOGICAL

$$f_{SR}(\mathbf{a}, \mathbf{x}) = (y_0, y_1, \ldots, y_{n-1})$$

$$y_i = \begin{cases} x_{i-|\mathbf{a}|}, & i - |\mathbf{a}| \geq 0 \\ 0, & i - |\mathbf{a}| < 0 \end{cases}$$

SHIFT-LEFT LOGICAL

$$f_{SL}(\mathbf{a}, \mathbf{x}) = (z_0, z_1, \ldots, z_{n-1})$$

$$z_i = \begin{cases} x_{i+|\mathbf{a}|}, & i + |\mathbf{a}| \leq n - 1 \\ 0, & i + |\mathbf{a}| > n - 1 \end{cases}$$

The second function can be obtained from the first by reversing the digits in **x** and **y**. Furthermore, f_{SR} can be realized with a multiplier since **y** is the result of multiplying $|\mathbf{x}|$ by $2^{|\mathbf{a}|}$ and keeping the n least significant bits. The mapping from **a** to a binary representation of $2^{|\mathbf{a}|}$ can be done with the function $f_T^{(\lceil \log_2 n \rceil)}$ so that f_{SR} is realizable from $f_M^{(2n)}(f_T^{(\lceil \log_2 n \rceil)}(\mathbf{a}), \mathbf{x})$ by suppressing all but the n least significant digits of the result. Therefore,

$$C_\Omega^* (f_{SR}) \leq C_\Omega^* (f_T^{(\lceil \log_2 n \rceil)}) + C_\Omega^* (f_M^{(2n)})$$

Since $C_\Omega^*(f_T^{(\lceil \log_2 n \rceil)})$ is linear in n, a nonlinear lower bound to the complexity of f_{SR} or a linear upper bound to the complexity of $f_M^{(2n)}$ would provide valuable information about these functions.

The next function treated here, the *binary sorting function* $f_s^{(n)}$: $\{0, 1\}^n \to \{0, 1\}^n$, is very important because of the role it plays in the study of symmetric functions, the subject of the next subsection. It is defined as

$$f_s(x_1, x_2, \ldots, x_n) = (\tau_1, \tau_2, \ldots, \tau_n)$$

$$\tau_t = \begin{cases} 1, & \sum_{j=1}^{n} x_j \geq t \\ \\ 0, & \text{otherwise} \end{cases}$$

where Σ denotes integer addition. Thus, f_s rearranges the zeros and ones in $(x_1, x_2, \ldots, x_n)$ so that ones precede zeros. Over the basis $\Omega_m = \{+, \cdot\}$, every chain for f_s requires at least on the order of $n \log_2 n$ computation steps, as shown in Section 3.2. However, over a complete basis, the number required is linear in n, as we now show. This result is due to Muller and Preparata (1975) although it is implicit in the work of Lupanov (1961b).

The basic idea involved is to "count" the number of ones among $x_1, x_2, \ldots, x_n$, represent the result in a binary $\lceil \log_2 (n + 1) \rceil$-tuple, and then use the binary-to-positional transformer together with a few additional computation steps to produce the desired result. Let $f_c^{(n)}$: $\{0, 1\}^n \to \{0, 1\}^{\lceil \log_2 n + 1 \rceil}$ be the function that counts the number of ones. Let $n = 2^k - 1$. Then

$$f_c^{(n)}(x_1, x_2, \ldots, x_n) = (a_0, a_1, \ldots, a_{k-1})$$

$$|\mathbf{a}| = \sum_{j=0}^{k-1} a_j 2^j = \sum_{i=1}^{n} x_i$$

where Σ denotes integer addition. We find an iterative realization of $f_c^{(n)}$.

Construct a chain for f_c on $x_1, x_2, \ldots, x_{n_1}$ and another for f_c on $x_{n_1+1}, \ldots, x_{n-1}$ where $n_1 = 2^{k-1} - 1$. Recall that we have chosen $n = 2^k - 1$. Then $n - 1 - n_1 = n_1 = 2^{k-1} - 1$ also. If $\mathbf{a}^1 = (a_0^1, a_1^1, \ldots, a_{k-2}^1)$ are the outputs of the first chain and $\mathbf{a}^2 = (a_0^2, a_1^2, \ldots, a_{k-2}^2)$ are the outputs of the second, the number of ones among $x_1, \ldots, x_{n-1}$ can be found by adding $\mathbf{a}^1$ and $\mathbf{a}^2$ in the Full Adder chain shown in Figure 3.1.1.1. The additional variable is applied to the c_0 input, that is, $c_0 = x_n$, and $f_c^{(n)}$ is realized. Since the Full Adder may be implemented with five elements from $\Omega = \{+, \cdot, ^-, \oplus\}$, it follows that

$$C_\Omega^*\left(f_c^{(n)}\right) \leq 5(k - 1) + 2C_\Omega^*\left(f_c^{(n_1)}\right)$$

where $n = 2^k - 1$ and $n_1 = 2^{k-1} - 1$. Also, $C_\Omega^*(f_c^{(1)}) = 0$, so that by induction on k, we have

$$C_\Omega^*\left(f_c^{(n)}\right) \leq 5(2^k - k - 1)$$

for $n = 2^k - 1$. For $2^{k-1} - 1 < n \leq 2^k - 1$, $f_c^{(n)}$ is obtained from $f_c^{(n^*)}$, $n^* = 2^k - 1$, by assigning the value zero to unchosen variables. Thus, the upper bound applies in general with $k = \lceil \log_2(n + 1) \rceil$.

Again, when $n = 2^k - 1$, define the function $f_E^{(n)}: \{0, 1\}^n \to \{0, 1\}^{n+1}$ by the composition

$$f_E^{(n)}(x_1, x_2, \ldots, x_n) = f_T^{(k)}\left(f_c^{(n)}(x_1, x_2, \ldots, x_n)\right)$$

$$= (\sigma_0, \sigma_1, \sigma_2, \ldots, \sigma_n)$$

so that $\sigma_t: \{0, 1\}^n \to \{0, 1\}$ and

$$\sigma_t(x_1, x_2, \ldots, x_n) = \begin{cases} 1, & \sum_{j=1}^{n} x_j = t \\ 0, & \text{otherwise} \end{cases}$$

where Σ denotes integer addition. The functions $\sigma_0, \sigma_1, \ldots, \sigma_n$, called the *elementary symmetric functions*, play an important role in the next subsection. From the above bounds, it is immediately apparent that over $\Omega = \{+, \cdot, ^-, \oplus\}$,

$$C_\Omega^*\left(f_E^{(n)}\right) \leq 6 \cdot 2^k + k\left(2^{\lceil k/2 \rceil} - 5\right) - 7$$

when $n = 2^k - 1$. For $2^{k-1} - 1 < n \leq 2^k - 1$, choose $k = \lceil \log_2(n + 1) \rceil$.

The *threshold functions* $\tau_1, \tau_2, \ldots, \tau_n$ are related to the elementary symmetric functions as follows:

$$\tau_n = \sigma_n$$

$$\tau_{n-j} = \tau_{n-j+1} + \sigma_{n-j}, \qquad 1 \leq j \leq n - 1$$

Here $+$ denotes OR. Since $f_s(x_1, \ldots, x_n) = (\tau_1, \ldots, \tau_n)$, we have

Theorem 3.1.1.4. Over the basis $\Omega\{+, \cdot, ^-, \oplus\}$, the combinational complexity of the binary sorting function $f_s^{(n)}: \{0, 1\}^n \to \{0, 1\}^n$ satisfies

$$2(n - 1) \leq C_\Omega^*(f_s^{(n)}) \leq 6 \cdot 2^k + k(2^{\lceil k/2 \rceil} - 5) + n - 8$$

for $k = \lceil \log_2(n + 1) \rceil$.

The lower bound is derived by using Theorem 2.4.4.2 and Theorem 2.4.1.1 and using the fact that each of the threshold functions depends on each of the n variables.

3.1.2. Symmetric Functions

Symmetric functions are encountered many times in this book. For example, addition modulo 2, AND, OR, and the threshold functions are all symmetric. Before defining the symmetric functions, we remind the reader that a *permutation* $\pi = (\pi(1), \pi(2), \ldots, \pi(n))$ is a rearrangement of the elements of the set $\{1, 2, \ldots, n\}$; that is, $\pi(i) \in \{1, 2, \ldots, n\}$ for $1 \leq i \leq n$, and $\pi(i) \neq \pi(j)$ for $i \neq j$.

Definition 3.1.2.1. A function $f: \{0, 1\}^n \to \{0, 1\}^m$ is *symmetric* if for all $\mathbf{c} \in \{0, 1\}^n$, $\mathbf{c} = (c_1, c_2, \ldots, c_n)$, and for all permutations π of $\{1, 2, \ldots, n\}$,

$$f(c_1, c_2, \ldots, c_n) = f(c_{\pi(1)}, c_{\pi(2)}, \ldots, c_{\pi(n)})$$

Example 3.1.2.1. The following are symmetric functions:

1. *Addition modulo 3*, $S_{\mathrm{mod}\,3}^c: \{0, 1\}^n \to \{0, 1\}^2$
   Let $s = (\sum_{i=1}^n x_i + c) \bmod 3$ where Σ denotes integer addition. Then

$$S_{\mathrm{mod}\,3}^c(x_1, x_2, \ldots, x_n) = (s_0, s_1)$$

   where (s_0, s_1) is the binary expansion of s. The function $s_0 = f_{\mathrm{mod}\,3}^c$ is the subject of Theorem 2.4.2.5.

2. *Threshold functions* $\tau_t: \{0, 1\}^n \to \{0, 1\}$, $0 \leq t \leq n$,

$$\tau_t(x_1, x_2, \ldots, x_n) = \begin{cases} 1, & \sum_{i=1}^n x_i \geq t \\ 0, & \text{otherwise} \end{cases}$$

   where Σ denotes integer addition.

Let $g_j: \{0, 1\}^n \to \{0, 1\}$, $1 \leq j \leq m$, be Boolean functions. Then it should be obvious that $f = (g_1, g_2, \ldots, g_m)$ is symmetric if and only if each of the Boolean functions $g_1, g_2, \ldots, g_m$ is symmetric.

If a Boolean function $f: \{0, 1\}^n \to \{0, 1\}$ is symmetric, then it has the same value on all binary n-tuples containing the same number of 1's, that is, which have the same *weight*. If f has value a_i, $a_i \in \{0, 1\}$ on n-tuples of weight i for $1 \leq i \leq n$, then f can be expanded as

$$f(x_1, x_2, \ldots, x_n) = a_0 \cdot \sigma_0(x_1, \ldots, x_n) + \cdots + a_n \cdot \sigma_n(x_1, \ldots, x_n)$$

where $\cdot$ and $+$ denote AND and OR, and $\sigma_t: \{0, 1\}^n \to \{0, 1\}$ is the *elementary symmetric function*

$$\sigma_t(x_1, x_2, \ldots, x_n) = \begin{cases} 1, & \sum_{i=1}^{n} x_i = t \\ 0, & \text{otherwise} \end{cases}$$

defined in the preceding subsection. Here Σ denotes integer addition.

This expansion is unique in the sense that two symmetric Boolean functions $f: \{0, 1\}^n \to \{0, 1\}$ and $h: \{0, 1\}^n \to \{0, 1\}$ are functionally equal if and only if the binary $(n + 1)$-tuple of values $(a_0, a_1, \ldots, a_n)$ (called the *weight vector*) for the two functions are equal. Thus, it is immediately obvious that there are 2^{n+1} symmetric Boolean functions in n variables.

Theorem 3.1.2.1. Over the basis $\Omega = \{+, \cdot, {}^-, \oplus\}$, the combinational complexity of every symmetric function $f: \{0, 1\}^n \to \{0, 1\}^m$ is bounded by

$$C_\Omega^*(f) \leq \frac{m(n-1)}{2} + 6 \cdot 2^k + k(2^{\lceil k/2 \rceil} - 5) - 8$$

where $k = \lceil \log_2(n + 1) \rceil$.

Proof. The function $f_E^{(n)}$ described in the previous subsection generates all elementary symmetric functions in n variables when $n = 2^k - 1$. If $2^{k-1} - 1 < n \leq 2^k - 1$, the function may be used with $k = \lceil \log_2(n + 1) \rceil$ by assigning 0 to the $2^k - 1 - n$ unchosen variables.

Let g_j be the jth Boolean function in the representation of $f = (g_1, g_2, \ldots, g_m)$. If $\mathbf{a} = (a_0, a_1, \ldots, a_n)$ is the weight vector of g_j and if it has l 1's, then g_j may be formed from f_E with $l - 1$ additional OR's. But g_j can also be realized as the Boolean inverse of the function g_j^* with weight vector $\mathbf{a} = (\bar{a}_0, \bar{a}_1, \ldots, \bar{a}_n)$, that is, $g_j = \bar{g}_j^*$. If $l \leq (n + 1)/2$ realize g_j directly as indicated above; otherwise, that is, when $l \geq (n + 1)/2 + 1$, realize g_j from g_j^*. The first case requires at most $(n - 1)/2$ OR's, and the second requires at most $(n - 1)/2 - 2$ OR's and one NOT. In either case, at most $(n - 1)/2$ additional computation steps are required to realize g_j from f_E. $\qquad\square$

As indicated in the previous subsection, there exist symmetric functions $f: \{0, 1\}^n \to \{0, 1\}^m$ for $m = n$ whose combinational complexity is much less than this upper bound. One such function is the binary sorting function whose complexity is linear in n.

3.1.3. The Determinant Function

The determinant function examined here is an important and useful function whose combinational complexity is not known except to within rather large bounds. This function is one that we shall encounter again in later sections.

Let $\mathbf{A} = (a_{ij})$ be an $m \times m$ matrix of Boolean variables, $m \geq 2$; then $f: \{0, 1\}^{m^2} \to \{0, 1\}$ is the determinant function defined by

$$f(a_{11}, a_{12}, \ldots, a_{1m}, \ldots, a_{m1}, \ldots, a_{mm}) = \det \mathbf{A}$$

$$= \sum_{\sigma} a_{1\sigma(1)} \cdot a_{2\sigma(2)} \cdot \cdots \cdot a_{m\sigma(m)}$$

where $\sum$ denotes addition modulo 2 and the sum ranges over all permutations σ of $\{1, 2, \ldots, m\}$.

The function $\det \mathbf{A}$ is Boolean and is essentially dependent on each of its m variables, as we show. Given i and j, $1 \leq i, j \leq m$, to show that $\det \mathbf{A}$ depends on a_{ij}, pick some permutation σ such that $\sigma(i) = j$; set all variables $a_{l\sigma(l)} = 1$ for $l \neq i$ and set all other variables to 0. Then

$$\det \mathbf{A} = a_{ij}$$

and the value of the function is clearly determined by the value of a_{ij}.

In the next theorem we state bounds on the combinational complexity of $\det \mathbf{A}$. The lower bound follows directly from Theorem 2.4.1.1 and the proof that $\det \mathbf{A}$ is essentially dependent on each of its variables. The upper bound is established in the proof of the theorem.

Theorem 3.1.3.1. Over the basis $\Omega = P_{1, 2}^{(2)}$, the function $\det \mathbf{A}: \{0, 1\}^{m^2} \to \{0, 1\}$ has a combinational complexity bounded by

$$m^2 - 1 \leq C_{\Omega}^*(\det \mathbf{A}) \leq \tfrac{10}{3}m^3 + 3m^2 - \tfrac{7}{3}m - 4 \leq 4m^3$$

for $m \geq 2$.

Proof. The upper bound follows by exhibiting a chain for f. The chain exhibited implements a modified form of the Gaussian elimination algorithm (MacLane and Birkhoff, 1967). We note that $\det \mathbf{A} = 1$ if and only if $\mathbf{A}$ is nonsingular.

Let $\mathbf{a}_i = (a_{i1}, a_{i2}, \ldots, a_{im})$ denote the ith row of $\mathbf{A} = (a_{ij})$ and let $\mathbf{c}_j$ denote its jth column. The algorithm is defined as follows.

ALGORITHM.

1. If $\mathbf{c}_j = \mathbf{0}$ for some $1 \leq j \leq m$, set $f = 0$.
2. Find the first row such that $a_{i1} = 1$. (This step is empty if there is no such row.) Add $\mathbf{v} = \mathbf{a}_i$ term-by-term and modulo 2 to every row $\mathbf{a}_j$ for which $a_{j1} = 1$. Call the new rows $\mathbf{a}'_1, \mathbf{a}'_2, \ldots, \mathbf{a}'_m$ and let $\mathbf{A}'$ be the corresponding matrix.
3. Remove the ith row and first column of $\mathbf{A}$ to form a matrix $\mathbf{A}^{(1)}$ and repeat steps 1 and 2 to form matrices $\mathbf{A}^{(2)}, \ldots, \mathbf{A}^{(m-1)}$ until $\mathbf{A}^{(m-1)}$ with a single element is produced. If this element is not zero and if f has not previously been set to zero, then $f = 1$; otherwise, $f = 0$.

To see that the algorithm is correct, observe that $\det \mathbf{A} = 0$ if $\mathbf{c}_j = \mathbf{0}$ for some $1 \leq j \leq m$ and that $\det \mathbf{A} = \det \mathbf{A}' = \det \mathbf{A}^{(1)}$ otherwise. By induction, $\det \mathbf{A} \neq 0$ only if $\mathbf{c}_j \neq \mathbf{0}$ for all j and $\det \mathbf{A}^{(l)} \neq 0$ for $1 \leq l \leq m - 1$. A chain realizing this algorithm is now constructed.

Let $\zeta_1(a_{11}, a_{12}, \ldots, a_{mm})$ be a Boolean function that has value 1 if any column of $\mathbf{A}$ is zero. Then

$$\zeta_1(a_{11}, a_{12}, \ldots, a_{mm}) = \left(\overline{a_{11} + a_{21} + \cdots + a_{m1}} \right) + \cdots$$

$$+ \left(\overline{a_{1m} + a_{2m} + \cdots + a_{mm}} \right)$$

and this can be realized with $m^2 - 1$ operations from $P_{1,2}^{(2)}$. Let $s_i(a_{11}, a_{12}, \ldots, a_{mm})$ be 1 if the ith row is the first row containing $a_{i1} = 1$. Then

$$s_i = \begin{cases} a_{i1}, & i = 1 \\ \left(\overline{a_{11} + a_{21} + \cdots + a_{i-1,1}} \right) \cdot a_{i1}, & 2 \leq i \leq m \end{cases}$$

and all these functions can be realized with $2m - 3$ operations.

Calculate row $\mathbf{v}$ which is to be added to rows for which $a_{i1} = 1$ as follows:

$$v_j = \sum_{i=1}^{m} s_i \cdot a_{ij}, \qquad 1 \leq j \leq m$$

where Σ denotes Boolean OR. Here $\mathbf{v}$ can be realized with $(2m - 1)m$ binary operations. The rows $\mathbf{a}'_i$ of the new matrix $\mathbf{A}'$ are then formed from the formula

$$a'_{ij} = \overline{a_{i1}} \cdot a_{ij} + a_{i1} \cdot (v_j \oplus a_{ij}) = \begin{cases} a_{ij}, & a_{i1} = 0 \\ v_j \oplus a_{ij}, & a_{i1} = 1 \end{cases}$$

for $1 \le i, j \le m$. For each pair (i, j) only four binary operations are necessary, so a total of $4m^2$ additional binary operations are sufficient.

Up to this point $7m^2 + m - 4$ binary operations have been used to compute ζ_1 and the $m \times m$ matrix $\mathbf{A}'$ from the matrix $\mathbf{A}$.

A new $(m - 1) \times (m - 1)$ matrix $\mathbf{A}^{(1)}$ is formed by eliminating the first column of $\mathbf{A}'$ and the row $\mathbf{a}'_i$ for which $s_i = 1$. We do this by shifting the last $m - 1$ digits of row $\mathbf{a}'_i$ up one place if $s_i = 1$ for any $i \le l$ and omitting the ith row if $s_i = 1$. If $\mathbf{b}_i$ is the row formed by the last $m - 1$ positions of $\mathbf{a}'_i$ and $\mathbf{a}_i^{(1)}$ is the ith row of $\mathbf{A}^{(1)}$, then

$$\mathbf{a}_i^{(1)} = \mathbf{b}_i \cdot (\overline{t_{i+1}}) + \mathbf{b}_{i+1} \cdot t_{i+1}, \qquad 1 \le i \le m - 1$$

where t_i is 0 if no row above i is selected and 1 otherwise; that is, $t_1 = 0$ for $i \ge 2$

$$t_i = t_{i-1} + s_{i-1}$$

All the functions t_i, $2 \le i \le m$, can be realized with a total of $m - 2$ operations, each $\mathbf{a}_i^{(1)}$ can be realized with $3(m - 1)^2$ additional operations, and the creation of $\mathbf{A}^{(1)}$ from the $\mathbf{a}'_i$ can be realized with a total of $3m^2 - 5m + 1$ operations.

At this point ζ_1 and $\mathbf{A}^{(1)}$ have been realized with a total of $\alpha(m) = 10m^2 - 4m - 3$ binary operations, and $\mathbf{A}^{(1)}$ is an $(m - 1) \times (m - 1)$ matrix. This process is repeated to produce ζ_2 and $\mathbf{A}^{(2)}$ with $\alpha(m - 1)$ operations and continued until ζ_{m-1} and $\mathbf{A}^{(m-1)}$ are formed where $\mathbf{A}^{(m-1)}$ contains a single element $a^{(m-1)}$. Then $f = \det \mathbf{A}$ can be written as

$$f = (\overline{\zeta_1 + \zeta_2 + \cdots + \zeta_{m-1} + \overline{a}^{(m-1)}})$$

because $f = 0$ if, at any step including the last, $\det \mathbf{A}^{(i)} = 0$.

A chain realizing the algorithm has been completely described and it uses a total of $N(m)$ operations where

$$N(m) = m - 1 + \sum_{l=2}^{m} \alpha(l) = \tfrac{10}{3}m^3 + 3m^2 - \tfrac{7}{3}m - 4$$

(In computing this expression, use has been made of the identities given in Problem 3-1.) A little elementary calculus will demonstrate that $N(m) \le 4m^3$ for $m \ge 2$, to complete the proof. $\qquad\square$

3.2. FUNCTIONS OVER INCOMPLETE BASES

In earlier sections, we have examined the combinational complexity, formula size, and delay complexity of binary functions over complete bases. It was demonstrated that $C_\Omega(f)$ and $D_\Omega(f)$ are affected by at most multiplicative factors when the basis Ω is replaced by another complete basis, while $L_\Omega(f)$ may be exponentiated by an exponent that depends on the two bases (Theorem 2.3.4).

In this section, we demonstrate that the combinational complexity of some functions over incomplete bases is much larger than over complete bases. A similar result is shown for formula size. The functions studied include the binary sorting function and matrix multiplication.

3.2.1. Monotone Functions

All the functions under study in Section 3.2 are monotone and can be realized over the *monotone basis* $\Omega_m = \{+, \cdot\}$, that is, without negation.

Definition 3.2.1.1. Let $\mathbf{x} = (x_1, x_2, \ldots, x_n)$ and $\mathbf{y} = (y_1, y_2, \ldots, y_n)$ be binary n-tuples and let the relation $\leq$ on pairs $\mathbf{x}$ and $\mathbf{y}$ in $\{0, 1\}^n$ be defined by $\mathbf{x} \leq \mathbf{y}$ if and only if $x_i \leq y_i$, $1 \leq i \leq n$. Then a function f: $\{0, 1\}^n \to \{0, 1\}^m$ is *monotone* (increasing) if for all $\mathbf{x}, \mathbf{y} \in \{0, 1\}^n$ such that $\mathbf{x} \leq \mathbf{y}, f(\mathbf{x}) \leq f(\mathbf{y})$.

Example 3.2.1.1. The following are monotone functions:

$$\text{(a)} \quad f(x_1, x_2) = (x_1 + x_2, x_1 \cdot x_2)$$

$$\text{(b)} \quad f(x_1, x_2, x_3) = x_1 \cdot x_2 + x_1 \cdot x_3 + x_2 \cdot x_3$$

Let $g_1, g_2, \ldots, g_m$ be m Boolean functions over $\{0, 1\}^n$. Then they can be represented by the single binary function $f = (g_1, g_2, \ldots, g_m)$ where f: $\{0, 1\}^n \to \{0, 1\}^m$. Now it can easily be shown that f is monotone if and only if each of the functions $g_1, g_2, \ldots, g_m$ is monotone.

Definition 3.2.1.2. Let f: $\{0, 1\}^n \to \{0, 1\}$ and g: $\{0, 1\}^n \to \{0, 1\}$ be monotone. Then g is in the relation $g \subseteq f$ to f if $g(x_1, \ldots, x_n) = 1$ *implies* that $f(x_1, \ldots, x_n) = 1$. A product (AND) p of uncomplemented variables of f is a *monotone implicant* of f if $p \subseteq f$. A *monotone prime implicant* of f is a monotone implicant p of f such that for no other monotone implicant g of f is $g \subseteq p$.

Example 3.2.1.2. Function (b) of the above example has $x_1 x_2 x_3$ as a monotone implicant. Its prime implicants are $x_1 x_2$, $x_1 x_3$, $x_2 x_3$.

Lemma 3.2.1.1. Every monotone Boolean function has a unique expansion as the sum (OR) of its monotone prime implicants.

Proof. Let $p_1, p_2, \ldots, p_l$ be the monotone prime implicants of f: $\{0, 1\}^n \to \{0, 1\}$. We claim that f can be written as

$$f = p_1 + p_2 + \cdots + p_l$$

Certainly if p_i is 1 for some $\mathbf{x} \in \{0, 1\}^n$, f is 1. Suppose that $f = 1$ on $\mathbf{x} \in \{0, 1\}^n$ but for no p_i is $p_i(\mathbf{x}) = 1$. Form q which is the AND of the variables of f that correspond to 1's in $\mathbf{x}$. Then $q(\mathbf{x}) = 1$ and q is a monotone implicant of f. If it is not prime, there is a prime implicant p such that $p \subseteq q$. But this contradicts the assumption that $\{p_1, \ldots, p_l\}$ contains all of the prime implicants of f. Therefore, the above expansion is an expansion for f.

If there is some other sum of monotone prime implicants of f, say

$$f = p_1' + p_2' + \cdots + p_{l'}'$$

then, since $p_i' \subseteq f$, $p_i' \subseteq p_j$ for some j which implies that $p_j = p_i'$ and $l = l'$. Therefore, the expansion is unique. $\qquad\square$

Definition 3.2.1.3. The expansion of a monotone Boolean function as the sum (OR) of its monotone prime implicants is called its *monotone disjunctive normal form* (MDNF).

Lemma 3.2.1.2. Every monotone Boolean function can be realized by a chain over the monotone basis $\Omega_m = \{ +, \cdot \}$. Furthermore, the functions associated with every step of a chain over Ω_m are monotone.

Proof. The first half of the theorem follows from the MDNF of monotone functions.

The second half of the theorem is easily established. The functions associated with data steps are from the following set of monotone functions: $\{x_1, x_2, \ldots, x_n, 0, 1\}$. Furthermore, if g_1 and g_2 are monotone Boolean functions, then so are $g_1 + g_2$ and $g_1 \cdot g_2$. It follows by induction on the size of chains that each function associated with a step of a chain over Ω_m is monotone. $\qquad\square$

3.2.2. Binary Sorting

The *binary sorting function* f_s: $\{0, 1\}^n \to \{0, 1\}^n$ that rearranges 0's and 1's so that 1's precede 0's is our first candidate for a function whose combinational complexity over Ω_m is much larger than it is over a complete basis. It is defined by $f_s = (\tau_1, \ldots, \tau_n)$ where $\tau_t \colon \{0, 1\}^n \to \{0, 1\}$ and

$$\tau_t(x_1, \ldots, x_n) = \begin{cases} 1, & \sum_{i=1}^{n} x_i \geq t \\ 0, & \text{otherwise} \end{cases}$$

and Σ denotes integer addition. Thus, τ_t is a monotone *threshold* function of threshold t. The following lower bound is due to Lamagna and Savage (1974), while the upper bound follows from results in Section 8.1.1.

Theorem 3.2.2.1. The binary sorting function f_s has combinational complexity $C_{\Omega_m}(f_s)$ over Ω_m that satisfies

$$n\lceil \log_2 n \rceil - 2^{\lceil \log_2 n \rceil} + 2 \leq C_{\Omega_m}(f_s) \leq n(\lceil \log_2 n \rceil^2 + 4)$$

for $n \geq 2$.

Proof. The source nodes labeled $x_1, x_2, \ldots, x_n$ each have at least one directed path from them to the node associated with the function τ_1, since τ_1 depends on each of its variables. In the graph of an optimal chain β over Ω_m for f_s, remove all nodes and edges not on the shortest paths from nodes labeled $x_1, \ldots, x_n$ to τ_1. The computation nodes remaining have at most two input edges directed into them. If l is the length (number of edges) on the longest path in the truncated graph, at most 2^l source nodes can be reached. Thus, we must have $2^l \geq n$ or $l \geq \lceil \log_2 n \rceil$ and there must exist a source node, say x_i, such that *every* path from this node to τ_1 has length at least $\lceil \log_2 n \rceil$. We shall show that setting $x_i = 1$ allows the removal of at least $\lceil \log_2 n \rceil$ elements to form a chain that realizes f_s', the binary sorting function on the remaining variables.

Set $\mathbf{x} = \mathbf{0}$ and observe that the value of the functions associated with nodes of β is 0. This follows because these functions are monotone (Lemma 3.2.1.2), and if 1 on $\mathbf{x} = \mathbf{0}$, they are constant functions; but $y + 1 = 1$ and $y \cdot 1 = y$ which means that such nodes can be removed from β and that it is nonoptimal. This would contradict the assumed optimality of β.

Now let $x_i = 1$ and $x_j = 0$, $j \neq i$. Traversing every path from source nodes to τ_1, replace the first node encountered whose function has value 0 with the constant 0 and remove the node in question. Note that only nodes on paths from x_i to τ_1 can have functions valued 1. If on every path from x_i to τ_1 there is a node with value 0, then in the truncated graph every path from a new source node to τ_1 starts with a 0 source node. By the monotonicity of τ_1 and the absence of constant 1 nodes in the original graph, the value of τ_1 must be 0. But this contradicts the definition of τ_1. Therefore, there must exist a path from x_i to τ_1 with value 1 at the output of every node. The functions at these nodes are monotone and have value 1 on any x for which $x_i = 1$. Remove them and replace by the constant 1.

This removal process reduces the number of computation nodes in β by at least $\lceil \log_2 n \rceil$, and the function f_s with $x_i = 1$ reduces to $f_s' = (\tau_2', \ldots, \tau_n')$ where τ_t' is τ_t with $x_i = 1$ or τ_t' is τ_{t-1} on the remaining variables. Thus, f_s' is the binary sorting function of the $n-1$ remaining variables. Let $\lambda(n) = C_{\Omega_m}(f_s)$. Then

$$\lambda(n) \geq \lceil \log_2 n \rceil + \lambda(n-1)$$

and $\lambda(2) = 2$. It follows that

$$\lambda(n) \geq \left(\sum_{j=3}^{n} \lceil \log_2 j \rceil \right) + 2.$$

However, $\lceil \log_2 j \rceil = l$ for $2^{l-1} < j \leq 2^l$, that is, for 2^{l-1} values of j. Letting k be such that $2^{k-1} < n \leq 2^k$, we have

$$\lambda(n) \geq (n - 2^{k-1})k + \left(\sum_{l=2}^{k-1} l2^{l-1} \right) + 2$$

But it can be shown by induction that the sum equals $(k/2 - 1)2^k$ for $k \geq 3$; consequently,

$$\lambda(n) \geq n\lceil \log_2 n \rceil - 2^{\lceil \log_2 n \rceil} + 2 \quad \text{for } n \geq 2.$$

This concludes the derivation of the lower bound.

The upper bound follows from Batcher's construction of a sorting network that uses $[k(k-1) + 4]2^{k-2} - 1$ comparators to sort 2^k numbers (see Section 8.1.1). A comparator has two inputs and two outputs, the outputs being the maximum and minimum of the inputs. But they can be realized with $+$ and $\cdot$, respectively. If $2^{k-1} < n \leq 2^k$, fill out the $2^k - n$ places with 0's and use $k = \lceil \log_2 n \rceil$ to obtain the upper bound. $\square$

As shown in Section 3.1.1, f_s can be realized by a chain over $\Omega = \{+, \cdot, ^-\}$ using a number of elements linear in n. Thus, addition of a single operation, negation, to the monotone basis Ω_m greatly reduces the number of computation steps required to realize f_s. Of course, this suggests that the number of elements required in general sorting networks might be considerably reduced by using more than just comparators.

The lower bound of this theorem has been improved by Lamagna (1975). He has demonstrated that the lower bound cited above holds independently for the number of OR's and for the number of AND's.

3.2.3. The Computation of Monotone Bilinear Forms

An important class of monotone functions, and the one considered in this subsection, is the class of disjoint monotone bilinear forms. A set of m functions $g_1, \ldots, g_m$ in n distinct variables $x_1, \ldots, x_p, y_1, \ldots, y_q$, $p + q = n$, is said to be a set of monotone bilinear forms if each function g_k, $1 \leq k \leq m$, can be expressed in its MDNF as

$$g_k = \sum x_r \cdot y_s \qquad (r, s) \in P_k$$

where $\sum$ denotes repeated Boolean OR, and P_k is a set of pairs of indices where $1 \leq r \leq p$ and $1 \leq s \leq q$. A pair (r, s) is *valid* if it is in P_k for some k.

Let R_k be the set of first components of pairs in P_k, and S_k the set of second components. With each valid pair (r, s) associate a set of .valid pairs V_{rs} with the property that $(r, s) \in V_{rs}$, and if the pair $(r', s') \in V_{rs}$, then so is every valid pair (r', s'') and (r'', s'). A set of monotone bilinear forms is *disjoint* if the following conditions are satisfied:

C1. The sets P_k, $1 \leq k \leq m$ are disjoint.
C2. For each $1 \leq k \leq m$, for each $1 \leq r \leq p$, there is at most one s, $1 \leq s \leq q$, such that $(r, s) \in P_k$ and vice versa.
C3. For each valid pair (r, s) and each $1 \leq k \leq m$, there is at most one pair in $V_{rs} \cap P_k$.

These conditions are useful in this form for determining the number of AND's and OR's necessary to realize disjoint monotone bilinear forms. It is often convenient to represent such forms by a matrix-vector product:

$$\begin{bmatrix} g_1 \\ g_2 \\ \cdot \\ \cdot \\ \cdot \\ g_m \end{bmatrix} = \mathbf{M}_x \begin{bmatrix} y_1 \\ y_2 \\ \cdot \\ \cdot \\ \cdot \\ y_q \end{bmatrix}$$

Conditions C1 and C2 require that the entries of $\mathbf{M}_x$ be 0 or single variables from $\{x_1, x_2, \ldots, x_p\}$ and that no two nonzero entries in any row or column of $\mathbf{M}_x$ be equal.

Boolean matrix-matrix multiplication (multiplication is AND, addition is OR) of a $u \times t$ matrix **B** with a $t \times v$ matrix **C**, resulting in a $u \times v$ matrix $[f_{ij}]$, can be represented as a matrix-vector product:

$$
\begin{bmatrix} f_{11} \\ f_{21} \\ \vdots \\ f_{u1} \\ f_{12} \\ \vdots \\ f_{uv} \end{bmatrix}
=
\begin{bmatrix} \mathbf{B} & & & \\ & \mathbf{B} & \mathbf{0} & \\ & & \ddots & \\ \mathbf{0} & & & \mathbf{B} \end{bmatrix}
\begin{bmatrix} c_{11} \\ c_{21} \\ \vdots \\ c_{t1} \\ c_{12} \\ \vdots \\ c_{tv} \end{bmatrix}
$$

One can easily verify that all three conditions for disjointness are satisfied. The same is true for the following multiplication of a triangular matrix by an m-vector:

$$
\begin{bmatrix} g_1 \\ g_2 \\ \vdots \\ g_m \end{bmatrix}
=
\begin{bmatrix} x_1 & x_2 & \cdots & & x_m \\ x_{m+1} & \cdots & x_{2m-1} & \cdots & 0 \\ \vdots & & 0 & & \vdots \\ x_p & 0 & \cdots & & 0 \end{bmatrix}
\begin{bmatrix} y_1 \\ y_2 \\ \vdots \\ y_m \end{bmatrix}
$$

Here $p = m(m + 1)/2$.

The following theorem establishes bounds on the number of AND and OR's required to compute disjoint monotone bilinear forms with chains over the monotone basis $\Omega_m = \{+, \cdot\}$.

Theorem 3.2.3.1. Let $g_1, g_2, \ldots, g_m$ be m disjoint monotone bilinear forms in the distinct Boolean variables $x_1, x_2, \ldots, x_p$ and $y_1, y_2, \ldots, y_q$. Then the minimum number of AND nodes, N_M, and the minimum number of OR nodes, N_S, required to compute these function with chains over Ω_m satisfy

$$
N_M = \sum_{k=1}^{m} |P_k|
$$

$$
N_S = N_M - m
$$

Here $|P_k|$ is the number of distinct pairs in P_k and $\Sigma|P_k|$ is the number of valid pairs.

It is clear that the obvious chain for $g_1, g_2, \ldots, g_m$ is optimal.

The proof of this theorem depends on a number of replacement rules which permit the elimination of certain computation nodes. Associated with every node of a chain is a function, and in a chain over Ω_m, if the MDNF of such a function contains a term (product) that is not in the MDNF of an output function, then that term could be eliminated without affecting the functions computed.

Theorem 3.2.3.1 is a generalization of a result obtained independently in 1974 by Melhorn (1974) and Paterson (1975) for matrix–matrix multiplication. Theirs is an extension of an earlier result by Pratt (1975). The proof that we present is patterned after that of Paterson.

Let g and h be two monotone Boolean functions with a common domain $\{0, 1\}^n$. We use the notation

$$g \subseteq h$$

to indicate that for each $\mathbf{x} \in \{0, 1\}^n$ for which $g(\mathbf{x}) = 1$, we also have $h(\mathbf{x}) = 1$. We say that g is contained in h. For example,

$$x_r y_s \subseteq x_r + y_s \not\subseteq y_s$$

Therefore, $x_r y_s$ is contained in x_r, in y_s, and in $x_r + y_s$, but $x_r + y_s$ is not contained in y_s since $x_r + y_s = 1$ when $x_r = 1$ and $y_s = 0$.

To determine whether $g \subseteq h$, it is sufficient to show that every product in the MDNF of g is contained in some product in the MDNF of h.

Let U denote the set of variables $\{x_1, x_2, \ldots, x_p, y_1, y_2, \ldots, y_q\}$ and let $z, z_1, z_2, \ldots$, denote arbitrary elements of U. In this section, let $f, f', f_1, f_2, \ldots$, denote monotone functions. The following two elementary properties of monotone functions are stated without proof (see Problem 3-15).

P1. If $x_1 x_2 \subseteq f_1 + f_2$, then $x_1 x_2 \subseteq f_1$ or $x_1 x_2 \subseteq f_2$ or both.

P2. If $f_1 \cdot f_2 \subseteq x_1 + x_2 + \cdots + x_k$, then $f_1 \subseteq x_1 + \cdots + x_k$ or $f_2 \subseteq x_1 + \cdots + x_k$ or both.

Many products of pairs of variables of U do not occur in any output function. The following is the MDNF of a function containing all such products:

$$f_{\text{dross}} = \sum_{\substack{r, r' \\ r \neq r'}} x_r x_{r'} + \sum_{\substack{s, s' \\ s \neq s'}} y_s y_{s'} + \sum_{\substack{r, s \\ (r, s) \notin P_k \\ \text{for any } k}} x_r y_s$$

Here $\sum$ denotes Boolean OR.

Pairs (r, s) such that $(r, s) \in P_k$ for some k are called *valid pairs*. The last sum of f_{dross} is over pairs that are not valid.

Let f be a monotone Boolean function computed by some node of a chain for $g_1, g_2, \ldots, g_m$ such that for some $x \in U$ (see Problem 3-16)

$$x \subseteq f \subseteq x + f_{\text{dross}}$$

The f can be replaced by the variable x without changing the output functions computed by the chain. We have the following replacement rule.

R1. If for some $x \in U$, $x \subseteq f \subseteq x + f_{\text{dross}}$, replace f by x.

To develop the next set of replacement rules, we introduce a partition of the valid pairs into disjoint sets $V_1, V_2, \ldots, V_L$. Each pair falls into some set and each set has the following two properties:

Q_1. If $(r, s) \in V_i$, then so is every valid pair (r, s') and (r', s).
Q_2. For each k, $1 \leq k \leq m$, V_i contains at most one pair from P_k.

If two sets V_i and V_j have a pair in common, then by the first property they are identical. Therefore, they are disjoint. Q_2 is a restatement of C3.

Let the sets λ_i and ρ_i be the left and right components of pairs in V_i. That is,

$$\lambda_i = \{ r | (r, s) \in V_i \}, \qquad \rho_i = \{ s | (r, s) \in V_i \}$$

The set of left and right components of pairs in P_k are R_k and S_k. If $|\lambda_i \cap R_k| \geq 2$ or $|\rho_i \cap S_k| \geq 2$, then V_i and P_k have two or more pairs in common in violation of Q_2, so

$$|\lambda_i \cap R_k| \leq 1, \qquad |\rho_i \cap S_k| \leq 1$$

The following lemma derives a result that leads to several additional replacement rules.

Lemma 3.2.3.1. Let $r, r' \in \lambda_i$, and $s, s' \in \rho_i$, with $r \neq r'$ and $s \neq s'$. Then, for all monotone functions f, if for some monotone bilinear form g_l, $g_l = f(U, x_r y_s + x_{r'} y_{s'})$, then $g_l = f(U, 1)$.

Proof. Suppose that $g_l \neq f(U, 1)$. By the monotonicity of $x_r y_s + x_{r'} y_{s'}$, there exist values for variables such that

$$g_l = f(U, x_r y_s + x_{r'} y_{s'}) = 0, \qquad f(U, 1) = 1$$

where $x_r y_s + x_{r'} y_{s'} = 0$. However, increasing one of the variables in each product will cause this sum to increase to 1. Without loss of generality, let $x_r = 0$, $y_s = 1$, so that increasing x_r causes the sum to increase. This causes g_l to increase so that g_l depends on x_r and $r \in R_l$. Among the variables $x_{r'}, y_{s'}$, one is 0 and the other 1. If $x_{r'} = 0$, the above argument establishes that $r' \in R_l$. Since r, $r' \in \lambda_i$, and $|\lambda_i \cap R_l| \leq 1$, we have a contradiction.

Consider the remaining case in which $y_{s'} = 0$. Since $r \in R_l$, by condition C2 there exists a unique $s^* \in S_l$ such that $(r, s^*) \in P_l$. Furthermore, $y_{s^*} = 1$ (because increasing x_r causes g_l to increase), so $s^* \neq s'$. By the definition of V_i, $(r, s^*) \in V_i$ and $s^* \in \rho_i$. Therefore, $s^* \in \rho_i \cap S_l$. But increasing $y_{s'}$ causes g_l to change, so $s' \in S_l$. Since s' is also in ρ_i, $s' \in \rho_i \cap S_l$ and $s' = s^*$ because $|\rho_i \cap S_l| \leq 1$. This contradicts $s' \neq s^*$, and we conclude that $g_l = f(U, 1)$. □

Corollary 3.2.3.1. Let r, $r' \in \lambda_i$, and s, $s' \in \rho_i$, with $r \neq r'$ and $s \neq s'$. Then, if $g_l = f(U, f')$ where $x_r y_s + x_{r'} y_{s'} \subseteq f'$, then $g_l = f(U, 1)$.

Proof. By the monotonicity of f,

$$f(U, x_r y_s + x_{r'} y_{s'}) \subseteq f(U, f') \subseteq f(U, 1)$$

and the left- and right-hand terms equal g_l. □

This result, with f' taking the forms $x_r + x_{r'}$, $y_s + y_{s'}$, $x_r + y_{s'}$, and $x_{r'} + y_s$, leads to the following replacement rules:
If r, $r' \in \lambda_i$, and s, $s' \in \rho_i$, with $r \neq r'$, $s \neq s'$,

R2. If $x_r + x_{r'} \subseteq f$, replace f by 1.
R3. If $y_s + y_{s'} \subseteq f$, replace f by 1.
R4. If $x_r + y_{s'} \subseteq f$, replace f by 1.
R5. If $x_{r'} + y_s \subseteq f$, replace f by 1.

We now present the proof of the main result.

Proof (of Theorem 3.2.3.1). Consider a chain for $g_1, g_2, \ldots, g_m$ with the fewest total number of computation nodes. For pairs $(r, s) \in V_1$, consider nodes with the property that their output functions f satisfy the following condition:

$$A_{rs}: x_r y_s \subseteq f, \qquad x_r \not\subseteq f, \qquad y_s \not\subseteq f$$

Condition A_{rs} requires that $x_r y_s$ be a product in the MDNF of f. This condition is satisfied by the output function g_k where k is such that $(r, s) \in P_k$, but it is not satisfied by any source node. Therefore, there are *initial nodes* $I(A_{rs})$ whose output functions satisfy A_{rs} but neither of whose input functions does.

Consider a node $\beta \in I(A_{rs})$. Let f, f_1, and f_2 be its output and input functions. If β is an OR, then $x_r \not\subseteq f_1$ and $y_s \not\subseteq f_1$, else, if $x_r \subseteq f_1$, say, then $x_r \subseteq f$, contradicting the fact that f satisfies A_{rs}. Since the same is true of f_2, both f_1 and f_2 satisfy

$$x_r y_s \not\subseteq f_i$$

because both violate A_{rs}, and by property P1, $x_r y_s \not\subseteq f$ which violates A_{rs}. Therefore, β is an AND node. If follows that $x_r \subseteq f_1$ and $y_s \subseteq f_2$, or vice versa. Therefore, setting $x_r = 1$ allows β to be eliminated.

We now show that $I(A_{rs})$ and $I(A_{r's'})$ are disjoint for $(r, s) \neq (r', s')$ so that at least $|V_1|$ AND nodes can be eliminated by setting $x_r = 1$ for r such that $(r, s) \in V_1$.

Suppose that β is in $I(A_{rs}) \cap I(A_{r's'})$. Then $x_r + x_{r'} \subseteq f_1$ and $y_s + y_{s'} \subseteq f_2$, or vice versa, or $x_r + y_{s'} \subseteq f_1$ and $x_{r'} + y_s \subseteq f_2$, or vice versa. Since $(r, s) \neq (r', s')$, replacement rules R_2, R_3, R_4, and R_5 can be used to replace at least one of f_1 and f_2 by 1 and eliminate β. Therefore, $I(A_{rs})$ and $I(A_{r's'})$ are disjoint.

Now identify nodes whose output functions f satisfy the following condition for $(r, s) \neq (r', s') \in V_1$:

$$B_{rs}: x_r y_s \subseteq f \subseteq h_k + y_s \qquad \text{and} \qquad f \not\subseteq y_s$$

where

$$h_k = \sum_{\substack{r^* \in R_k \\ r^* \neq r}} x_{r^*}$$

Here Σ denotes OR, and k is the unique integer such that $(r, s) \in P_k$. The output function g_k satisfies B_{rs} if $|P_k| \geq 2$ but none of the source nodes do, so if $|P_k| \geq 2$, there exist *initial nodes* $I(B_{rs})$ whose output functions satisfy B_{rs} but whose input functions do not. We show that nodes in $I(B_{rs})$ are OR nodes, that the sets are disjoint, and that the nodes can be eliminated by setting $y_s = 0$. We consider only sets $I(B_{rs})$ for which $(r, s) \in P_k$ and $|P_k| \geq 2$.

Suppose that $\beta \in I(B_{rs})$ is an AND node with output function f and input functions f_1 and f_2. We have that $f \not\subseteq y_s$. If $f_1 \subseteq y_s$ or $f_2 \subseteq y_s$, then $f \subseteq y_s$. Consequently, $f_1 \not\subseteq y_s$ and $f_2 \not\subseteq y_s$. Also, if $x_r y_s \not\subseteq f_i$ for $i = 1$ or 2, then it is possible to assign values to variables so that $x_r y_s = 1$ but $f_i = 0$, implying that $f = 0$. But $x_r y_s \subseteq f$, so $x_r y_s \subseteq f_1$ and $x_r y_s \subseteq f_2$. Since f_1 and f_2 violate B_{rs}, $f_1 \not\subseteq h_k + y_s$ and $f_2 \not\subseteq h_k + y_s$, and from property P2, $f \not\subseteq h_k + y_s$, contradicting the assumption that f satisfies B_{rs}. Therefore, β is an OR node.

Since $\beta \in I(B_{rs})$ is an OR node, both $f_i \subseteq h_k + y_s$, $i = 1$ and 2, for otherwise $f \not\subseteq h_k + y_s$. By P1, at least one of f_1 and f_2, say f_1, satisfies $x_r y_s \subseteq f_1$, so $f_1 \subseteq y_s$ because f_1 violates B_{rs}. Thus, setting $y_s = 0$ sets

$f_1 = 0$ and the OR node β can be eliminated. If $f_2 \subseteq y_s$, then $f \subseteq y_s$ and f violates β_{rs}. We conclude that $f_2 \not\subseteq y_s$.

Suppose that β is in $I(B_{rs}) \cap I(B_{r's'})$ for $(r, s) \neq (r', s')$. Then $f_1 \subseteq y_s$, as shown above, and $f_1 \subseteq h_{k'} + y_{s'}$ where k' is such that $(r', s') \in P_{k'}$, that is, $f_1 \subseteq y_s(h_{k'} + y_{s'})$. We have shown that $x_r y_s \subseteq f_1$ so that either $x_r \subseteq h_{k'}$ or $s = s'$. But $x_r \not\subseteq h_{k'}$ because if not, r' and $r \in R_{k'}$ where $r, r' \in \lambda_i$, $r \neq r'$. This implies that $|\lambda_1 \cap R_{k'}| \geq 2$, contradicting the definition of V_1. This means that $s = s'$ and $f_1 \subseteq y_s(h_{k'} + y_s) = y_s$. Because f_2 violates $B_{r's}$ and $f_2 \not\subseteq y_s$ (from above), it follows that $x_{r'} y_s \not\subseteq f_2$. But one of f_1, f_2 must contain $x_{r'} y_s$, so $x_{r'} y_s \subseteq f_1$. Hence, $x_{r'} y_s$ and $x_r y_s$ are contained in f_1 or $x_{r'} y_s + x_r y_s \subseteq f_1 \subseteq y_s$. However, $(r, s) \neq (r', s')$, so $r \neq r'$. Since this reduces to $(x_{r'} + x_r) y_s \subseteq f_1 \subseteq y_s$, by replacement rule R2 we can replace f_1 by y_s. Also,

$$y_s \subseteq f_1 + f_2 \subseteq (h_k + y_s) \cdot (h_{k'} + y_s)$$

$$\subseteq y_s + f_{\text{dross}}$$

since $h_k y_s$ and $h_{k'} y_s$ contain only terms in f_{dross} because by C2, for each s there exists a unique r (if any) for which $(r, s) \in P_k$. But by R1, $f_1 + f_2$ can be replaced by y_s and the computation nodes is superfluous, contradicting the optimality of the chain. Therefore, $I(B_{rs})$ and $I(B_{r's'})$ are disjoint.

If we fix $x_r = 1$, $y_s = 0$ for all r, s such that $(r, s) \in V_1$, then all computation nodes in $I(A_{rs})$ and $I(B_{rs})$ can be eliminated. The number of AND's so eliminated is $|V_1|$ and the number of OR's is $|V_1| - v$ where v is the number of k's in V_1 such that $|P_k| = 1$. By the construction of V_1, all instances of x_r and y_s in $g_1, \ldots, g_m$ are eliminated by this reduction. Thus, the new set of functions $g'_1, \ldots, g'_{m'}$ are also disjoint monotone bilinear forms. This process can be repeated until all functions are 0. Since P'_k, the set P_k after the reduction, has at most one fewer pair, this process eliminates $\sum_{k=1}^{m} |P_k|$ AND's and $(\sum_{k=1}^{m} |P_k|) - m$ OR's.   □

Theorem 3.2.3.1 only holds over the incomplete monotone basis Ω_m. When the basis is enlarged to a complete basis, perhaps by adding negation, a considerable reduction in the number of required operations is possible, as we now show for Boolean matrix-matrix multiplication.

As has been noted by Fischer and Meyer (1971), the Strassen matrix-matrix multiplication algorithm, which is described in Chapter 8, can be used to compute the Boolean matrix-matrix product. To see this, observe that when Σ is interpreted as integer addition and $\cdot$ as integer multiplication,

$$c_{ij} = \sum_{r=1}^{t} a_{ir} \cdot b_{rj}$$

is zero only when the corresponding term is zero and when Σ is interpreted as OR and $\cdot$ as AND. Also, $c_{ij} > 0$ otherwise. Therefore, Strassen's algorithm may be applied. It uses no more than 4.7 $t^{\log_2 7}$ integer additions and multiplications for square $t \times t$ matrices, and since $c_{ij} \leq t$, the additions and multiplications can be done modulo 2^k, $k = \lceil \log_2(t + 1) \rceil$. In Problem 3-12, we show that the number of elements required to realize these operations in chains over $\Omega = \{ +, \cdot, {}^- \}$ grows no faster than $(\log_2 t)^2$ for any $\varepsilon > 0$. Since the number of variables in two $t \times t$ matrices is $n = 2t^2$, it follows that

Theorem 3.2.3.2. Let Ω be a complete basis and let $f: \{0, 1\}^n \to \{0, 1\}^{n/2}$ represent square Boolean matrix-matrix multiplication. Then, given $N > 0$, there exists a constant $K(N) > 0$ such that

$$C_{\Omega}(f) \leq K(N) n^{(\log_2 7)/2} (\log_2 n)^2$$

for $n \geq N$.

Thus, we have exhibited another problem for which the gap between combinational complexity over complete and incomplete bases is large.

3.3. BOUNDING METHODS FOR FORMULA SIZE

In this section, we present a number of general methods for deriving lower bounds to the formula size of Boolean functions. The Krapchenko bound of Section 3.3.1 applies to functions realized over the AND, OR, NOT basis, whereas the Nechiporuk bound of Section 3.3.2 applies to functions over any complete basis. These lower bounds are stated in terms of explicit properties of functions, and functions are exhibited that achieve or come close to achieving the lower bounds. In Section 3.3.3, a lower bound to the formula size of threshold functions is derived for formulas over the AND, OR basis.

3.3.1. The Krapchenko Lower Bound

The formula size of a function $f: \{0, 1\}^n \to \{0, 1\}^m$ with respect to a basis Ω, $L_{\Omega}(f)$, is defined in Section 2.3 as the combinational complexity of f

over Ω when the graph of f has *fan-out* 1. Such a graph consists of m *trees*, as illustrated by the following example.

Example 3.3.1.1.   Consider f: $\{0, 1\}^3 \rightarrow \{0, 1\}^2$ defined by $f(x_1, x_2, x_3) = (f_1, f_2)$ where

$$f_1(x_1, x_2, x_3) = (x_1 \oplus x_2) \cdot (\bar{x}_1 \oplus x_3)$$

$$f_2(x_1, x_2, x_3) = \overline{x_1 \cdot x_2} + \bar{x}_1 \cdot x_3 + x_2 \cdot x_3$$

A graph of f is shown in Figure 3.3.1.1, where $\Omega = \{ \oplus, +, \cdot, {}^- \}$. Note the repetition of source nodes.

There are several important observations to be made concerning the fan-out 1 graphs, that is, trees, representing functions.

OBSERVATIONS

1. There is a 1-1 correspondence between each computation node of the tree and an operation in a formula for the function.
2. In general, the fan-out from source nodes exceeds 1.
3. Over a basis of fan-in 2, the number of *binary* computation nodes in a single tree is one less than the total fan-out of source nodes that are input to that tree. This follows directly from the proof of Theorem 2.4.1.1.

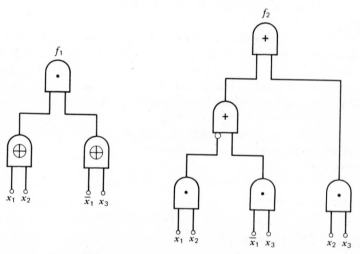

Figure 3.3.1.1.   Tree realization of (f_1, f_2).

In this section, we are concerned with bases Ω that are complete.

The first lower bounding method to be presented here is a method due to Krapchenko (1971a, 1971b), for Boolean functions over the basis $\Omega_0 = \{+, \cdot, ^-\}$. His results were originally stated for contact networks but have been translated here into results for chains. He has used his technique to demonstrate that the formula size of $x_1 \oplus \cdots \oplus x_n$ is quadratic in n over this basis, although, as is obvious, its formula size is $n - 1$ if $\oplus$ is included in the basis.[†]

The derivation of the Krapchenko result is simplified by considering the measure $L^*_{\Omega_0}(f)$ over $\Omega_0 = \{+, \cdot, ^-\}$ which is defined to be $L_{\Omega_0}(f)$ minus the number of Boolean inversions. It can be readily shown that an L_{Ω_0}-optimal graph for f cannot have a computation node with two or more of its inputs and outputs inverted; otherwise, DeMorgan's rules (Theorem 2.1.1) could be used to reduce the number of inversions without affecting the number of binary operations. From this observation, it follows that

Theorem 3.3.1.1. Let Ω be a subset of $\Omega_0 = \{+, \cdot, ^-\}$ and let f: $\{0, 1\}^n \to \{0, 1\}^m$. Then

$$L^*_\Omega(f) \leq L_\Omega(f) \leq 2L^*_\Omega(f)$$

Now consider a formula over Ω_0 for a Boolean function f: $\{0, 1\}^n \to \{0, 1\}$. If this formula contains inversions other than inversions of variables, as is the case for the formula for f_2 given above, the formula can be modified without changing the number of binary operations or the function that it represents so that in the resulting formula the only inversions are those applied directly to variables. This is done by using DeMorgan's rules. For example, the formula given above for f_2 can be modified as follows:

$$f_2 = \overline{x_1 \cdot x_2} + \bar{x}_1 \cdot x_3 + x_2 \cdot x_3 = \bar{x}_1 + \bar{x}_2 + \bar{x}_1 \cdot x_3 + x_2 \cdot x_3$$

Its tree is shown in Figure 3.3.1.2.

The Krapchenko bound is derived for the measure $L^*_{\Omega_0}(f)$, f Boolean, so we shall assume without loss of generality that any inversions used to realize f are applied only to variables.

In a tree for f in which inversions are applied only to variables, there may be one or more occurrences of each of the variables x_l or their complements $\bar{x}_l$, $1 \leq l \leq n$. Let m_l be the number of occurrences of elements from the set $\{x_l, \bar{x}_l\}$ and assign each occurrence a distinct labeled

[†] Subbotovskaya (1961) preceded Krapchenko by deriving an $n^{3/2}$ lower bound to the formula size of this function over the same basis.

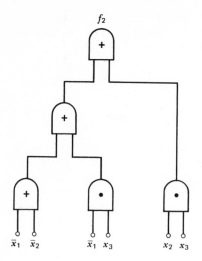

f_2

$\bar{x}_1$ $\bar{x}_2$ $\bar{x}_1$ x_3 x_2 x_3 **Figure 3.3.1.2.** Modified tree for f_2.

variable $\tilde{x}_{l1}, \tilde{x}_{l2}, \ldots, \tilde{x}_{l, m_l}$. For example, in Figure 3.3.1.2, the function f_2 has $m_1 = 2$, $m_2 = 2$, $m_3 = 2$.

The graph with inputs labeled $\tilde{x}_{1, 1}, \tilde{x}_{1, 2}, \ldots, \tilde{x}_{n, m_n}$ has computation nodes labeled with $+$ and $\cdot$. Thus, the output of the graph as a function in these variables is monotone.

A 1-*set* A of a formula for f is a subset of the set of *literals* $\{\tilde{x}_{1, 1}, \tilde{x}_{1, 2}, \ldots, \tilde{x}_{1, m_1}, \ldots, \tilde{x}_{n, m_n}\}$ of that formula such that if $\tilde{x}_{l, k} = 1$ for all $\tilde{x}_{l, k} \in A$, then $f = 1$ for all values of the remaining literals. By the comment above, there exists such a set unless f is identically 0. For example, the second instance of x_2 and of x_3 in Figure 3.3.1.2 form a 1-set of the corresponding formula for f_2. A *minimal* 1-*set* is a 1-set none of whose proper subsets is a 1-set.

A 0-*set* B of a formula for f is a subset of the literals $\{\tilde{x}_{1, 1}, \tilde{x}_{1, 2}, \ldots, \tilde{x}_{n, m_n}\}$ of that formula such that if $\tilde{x}_{l, k} = 0$ for all $\tilde{x}_{l, k} \in B$, then $f = 0$ for all values of the remaining literals. Again, by the comment, such a set exists unless f is identically 1. For example, a 0-set of the formula represented in Figure 3.3.1.2 consists of both instances of $\bar{x}_1$ and the instances of x_2 and $\bar{x}_2$. A *minimal* 0-*set* is a 0-set none of whose proper subsets is a 0-set.

Lemma 3.3.1.1. Let G be a tree for f: $\{0, 1\}^n \to \{0, 1\}$ over $\Omega_0 = \{+, \cdot, ^-\}$ in which inversions occur only on source nodes. Then the intersection of a minimal 1-set and a minimal 0-set is a single literal.

Proof. The proof is by induction on the number Q of literals in $\{\tilde{x}_{1,1}, \ldots, \tilde{x}_{1,m_1}, \ldots, \tilde{x}_{n,m_n}\}$. When $Q = 1$, the statement is obviously true.

Suppose the result has been shown for $Q \leq q - 1$; we show that it is also true for $Q = q$. Let G have q literals, let it represent the formula φ, and consider the case where the terminal node of G is labeled $\cdot$, the AND. Then $f = 1$ only when both inputs to the terminal node are also 1. Let the formula associated with these inputs be h and g. Then a 1-set of φ includes a 1-set for h and a 1-set for g; otherwise h and g cannot both be fixed at 1 for all values of literals outside the 1-set. A set that is a 0-set of h or a 0-set of g is a 0-set of φ since $f = 0$ if $h = 0$ or $g = 0$; and a set that is not a 0-set of either h or g cannot be a 0-set of φ. Then a minimal 0-set of φ is a minimal 0-set of h or g but not both. Suppose it is a 0-set of h. Then its intersection with a 1-set of φ is the intersection with a 1-set of h which by the induction hypothesis is a singleton. A similar argument applies when the terminal node of g is labeled $+$. $\qquad\square$

A graph G for $f: \{0, 1\}^n \to \{0, 1\}$ of the type mentioned in Lemma 3.3.1.1 has

$$\sum_{l=1}^{n} m_l - 1$$

computation nodes. This follows from Observation 3. The Krapchenko result follows from a lower bound to the sum. The result is stated for Boolean functions that in general may be *incompletely specified*; that is, the function is total, but its value is known only over a portion of its domain. In effect, then, an incompletely specified function represents a class of functions.

It is useful to have the concept of adjacent elements of $\{0, 1\}^n$. Two points $\mathbf{b}_1$ and $\mathbf{b}_2$ of $\{0, 1\}^n$ are *adjacent* if $\mathbf{b}$ and $\mathbf{b}_2$ differ in exactly one place.

Theorem 3.3.1.2. Let $f: \{0, 1\}^n \to \{0, 1\}$ have value 1 on points $B_1 \subset \{0, 1\}^n$ and value 0 on points $B_0 \subset \{0, 1\}^n$ where $B_1 \cap B_0 = \varnothing$ and $B_1 \cup B_0 \subset \{0, 1\}^n$. Let A be the set of pairs of adjacent points, one from B_0 and the other from B_1. If $|B|$ is the cardinality of the set B, then

$$L_{\Omega_0}^*(f) \geq \frac{|A|^2}{|B_0|\,|B_1|} - 1$$

Proof. Let x_l^σ denote x_l when $\sigma = 1$ and $\bar{x}_l$ when $\sigma = 0$. Then $f(\mathbf{b}) = 1$

for $\mathbf{b} \in B_1$, and only the literals labeled $x_1^{b_1}, x_2^{b_2}, \ldots, x_n^{b_n}$ can have value 1 on the n-tuple $\mathbf{b}$. Those literals of this type that exist in a graph G of f form a 1-set of f. Let $s_1(\mathbf{b})$ denote a minimal 1-set contained within this 1-set.

Similarly, $f(\mathbf{b}) = 0$ for $\mathbf{b} \in B_0$, and only the literals labeled $x_1^{\bar{b}_1}$, $x_2^{\bar{b}_2}, \ldots, x_n^{\bar{b}_n}$ can have value 0 on the n-tuple $\mathbf{b}$. Those literals of this type that exist in the graph of f form a 0-set of f. Let $s_0(\mathbf{b})$ denote a minimal 0-set contained within this 0-set.

Let $\mathbf{b}^0 \in B_0$ and $\mathbf{b}^1 \in B_1$ be *adjacent* and let them disagree in their lth positions. Then, from the two preceding paragraphs, it follows that $s_0(\mathbf{b}^0)$ and $s_1(\mathbf{b}^1)$ can only agree in a literal in x_l. Let $s_0(\mathbf{b}^0) \cap s_1(\mathbf{b}^1) = \{\tilde{x}_{l,k}\}$. As $(\mathbf{b}^0, \mathbf{b}^1)$ ranges over adjacent pairs, let $p_{l,k}$ be the number of times $\tilde{x}_{l,k}$ occurs in $s_0(\mathbf{b}^0) \cap s_1(\mathbf{b}^1)$. Then

$$\sum_{k=1}^{m_l} p_{l,k} = a_l$$

where a_l is the number of pairs in A that disagree in the lth coordinate. Also,

$$\sum_{l=1}^{n} a_l = |A|$$

Form Tables I and II of size $|B_0| \times n$ and $|B_1| \times n$, respectively, as follows. The rows of Table I correspond to the n-tuples of B_0, and the columns correspond to potentially adjacent n-tuples. Thus, column l is identified with the n-tuple $\mathbf{b}^0 \oplus \mathbf{e}_l$ which disagrees in the lth coordinate with the row n-tuple $\mathbf{b}^0$. In this proof $\oplus$ denotes term-by-term addition modulo 2, and $\mathbf{e}_l$ is the binary n-tuple with 1 in the lth coordinate. The entry corresponding to row $\mathbf{b}^0$ and column l, denoted $\alpha(\mathbf{b}^0, l)$, is undefined if $\{\mathbf{b}^0, \mathbf{b}^0 \oplus \mathbf{e}_l\} \notin A$, and is $s_0(\mathbf{b}^0) \cap s_1(\mathbf{b}^0 \oplus \mathbf{e}_l)$ otherwise. Similarly, Table II is formed, and the entry $\beta(\mathbf{b}^1, l)$ for $\mathbf{b}^1 \in B_1$ is undefined if $\{\mathbf{b}^1, \mathbf{b}^2 \oplus \mathbf{e}_l\} \notin A$, and is $s_1(\mathbf{b}^1) \cap s_0(\mathbf{b}^1 \oplus \mathbf{e}_l)$ otherwise.

Clearly, $\tilde{x}_{l,k}$ occurs only in the lth column of either table, and it occurs $p_{l,k}$ times in each table. Also, a row from Table I can agree in its defined entries with a row from Table II in at most one place. Otherwise, a 0-set $s_0(\mathbf{b}^0)$ and a 1-set $s_1(\mathbf{b}^1)$ would have at least two elements in common, contradicting Lemma 3.3.1.1. (All entries of row $\mathbf{b}^0$ of Table I are contained in $s_0(\mathbf{b}^0)$. A similar statement applies to Table II.)

Form Table III with $|B_0||B_1|$ rows and n columns by associating a row with each pair $(\mathbf{b}^0, \mathbf{b}^1)$, $\mathbf{b}^0 \in B_0$, $\mathbf{b}^1 \in B_1$; let the entry corresponding to row $(\mathbf{b}^0, \mathbf{b}^1)$ and column l be $(\alpha(\mathbf{b}^0, l), \beta(\mathbf{b}^1, l))$. Consider the entries that are defined and for which $\alpha(\mathbf{b}^0, l) = \beta(\mathbf{b}^1, l)$. By the comment in the last paragraph, there is at most one such symmetric pair per row.

The number of pairs for which $\alpha(\mathbf{b}^0, l) = \beta(\mathbf{b}^1, l) = \tilde{x}_{l,k}$ is $p_{l,k}^2$ by construction. Therefore, the number of symmetric pairs is $\sum_{l=1}^n \sum_{k=1}^{m_l} p_{l,k}^2$. By the observation that there is at most one such symmetric pair per row, we have

$$\sum_{l=1}^n \sum_{k=1}^{m_l} p_{l,k}^2 \leq |B_0||B_1|$$

From this and the two previous equations, we derive the lower bound to formula size.

From the Schwarz inequality (Problem 3-19), it follows that

$$\left(\sum_{k=1}^{m_l} p_{l,k}\right)^2 \leq m_l \left(\sum_{k=1}^{m_l} p_{l,k}^2\right)$$

and from the previously derived identities,

$$\sum_{l=1}^n \frac{1}{m_l} a_l^2 \leq \sum_{l=1}^n \sum_{k=1}^n p_{l,k}^2 \leq |B_0||B_1|$$

where the left-hand sum is over indices l for which $m_l > 0$. Again, applying the Schwarz inequality to $|A| = \sum_l a_l$, we have

$$\left(\sum_{l=1}^n a_l\right)^2 \leq \left[\sum_{l=1}^n \left(\frac{a_l}{\sqrt{m_l}}\right)^2\right]\left[\sum_{l=1}^n \left(\sqrt{m_l}\right)^2\right]$$

from which it follows that

$$|A|^2 \leq |B_0||B_1|\left(\sum_{l=1}^n m_l\right)$$

Therefore, in any tree for f over Ω_0 in which the only inversions are those applied to source nodes,

$$\sum_{l=1}^n m_l \geq \frac{|A|^2}{|B_0||B_1|}$$

and the number of binary nodes is $\sum_l m_l - 1$. Since every Boolean function has an $L_{\Omega_0}^*$-optimal tree of this type, the theorem follows. □

This bounding method is illustrated by applying it to several important functions.

Theorem 3.3.1.3. Over the basis $\Omega_0 = \{+, \cdot, \bar{\ }\}$, the functions

$$f_{\oplus}^c (x_1, \ldots, x_n) = x_1 \oplus x_2 \oplus \cdots \oplus x_n \oplus c$$

where $c \in \{0, 1\}$ have formula size

$$n^2 - 1 \leq L_{\Omega_0}^*(f_{\oplus}^c) \leq (2^{\lceil \log_2 n \rceil})^2 - 1$$

and the lower bound is achieved when n is a power of 2.

Proof. Since functions $f_{\oplus}^0$ and $f_{\oplus}^1$ are Boolean complements of one another, $L_{\Omega_0}^*(f_{\oplus}^0) = L_{\Omega_0}^*(f_{\oplus}^1)$.

Consider $f_{\oplus}^0$. It has value 1 on n-tuples with odd weight (number of 1's) and value 0 on those of even weight. Thus, $|B_0| = |B_1| = \frac{1}{2}2^n$. Let $\mathbf{b}^0 \in B_0$ and $\mathbf{b}^1 \in B_1$ be adjacent pairs. Then, for some $1 \leq l \leq n$, we can write $\mathbf{b}^1 = \mathbf{b}^0 \oplus \mathbf{e}_l$ where in this paragraph $\oplus$ denotes term-by-term addition modulo 2 and $\mathbf{e}_l$ is a binary vector with a single 1 in position l. Clearly, $\mathbf{b}^0 \oplus \mathbf{e}_1$, $\mathbf{b}^0 \oplus \mathbf{e}_2$, $\ldots$, $\mathbf{b}^0 \oplus \mathbf{e}_n$ are all distinct and of odd weight; they are also the only members of B_1 adjacent to $\mathbf{b}^0$. Since there are 2^{n-1} elements in B_0, there are exactly $|A| = n \cdot 2^{n-1}$ adjacent pairs. The lower bound follows directly from Theorem 3.3.1.2.

In Figure 3.3.1.3 is shown a tree for $f_{\oplus}^0(x_1, x_2)$.

Note that each variable is repeated twice. Let $\lambda(n)$ be the value of $L_{\Omega_0}^*(f_{\oplus}^0)$ where $f_{\oplus}^0: \{0, 1\}^n \to \{0, 1\}$. Then, writing

$$f_{\oplus}^0 (x_1, \ldots, x_n) = f_{\oplus}^0 \left(f_{\oplus}^0 (x_1, \ldots, x_m), f_{\oplus}^0 (x_{m+1}, \ldots, x_n) \right)$$

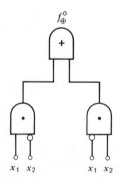

Figure 3.3.1.3.

we deduce that

$$\lambda(n) \leq 3 + 2\lambda(m) + 2\lambda(n - m)$$

Consider the case $n = 2^k$. Then choose $m = n/2$ and observe that

$$\lambda(n) \leq 3 + 4\lambda\left(\frac{n}{2}\right)$$

Applying this inequality recursively and noting that $\lambda(2) = 3$, we demonstrate that

$$\lambda(n) \leq 3(4^0 + 4^1 + 4^2 + \cdots + 4^{k-1}) = 4^k - 1 = n^2 - 1$$

for $n = 2^k$. If $2^{k-1} < n \leq 2^k$, realize $f_\oplus^0$ with the function defined on 2^k variables with $2^k - n$ of these variables replaced by the constant 0. Then the same bound can be used with $k = \lceil \log_2 n \rceil$.

Stronger bounds can be obtained with more elaborate arguments. $\square$

The function det $\mathbf{A}$ defined on the $m \times m$ matrix $\mathbf{A} = (a_{ij})$ of Boolean variables with addition modulo 2 was defined in Section 3.1.3. It is our next candidate for a lower bound.

Theorem 3.3.1.4. Over the basis $\Omega_0 = \{+, \cdot, ^-\}$, the function $f: \{0, 1\}^{m^2} \to \{0, 1\}$,

$$f(a_{11}, \ldots, a_{mm}) = \det \mathbf{A}$$

has formula size

$$L_{\Omega_0}^*(f) \geq \tfrac{1}{12} m^4 - 1$$

for $m \geq 2$.

Proof. Let us determine the number of nonsingular $m \times m$ binary matrices $\mathbf{A}$. There are $2^m - 1$ nonzero m-tuples that could be chosen as the first row of $\mathbf{A}$ such that det $\mathbf{A}$ is nonzero. The second row must not equal the first or be zero, and it can be chosen from any one of $2^m - 2$ m-tuples. The third must not be a linear combination of the first two, and since there are four such linear combinations, it can be chosen from a set of $2^m - 4$ elements. Proceeding in this manner, it can be shown that there are

$$M = (2^m - 1)(2^m - 2)(2^m - 4) \cdots (2^m - 2^{m-1})$$

$m \times m$ binary nonsingular matrices. Therefore, $f = \det \mathbf{A}$ has value 1 on

$|B_1| = M$ points and value 0 on $|B_0| = 2^m - M$ points. But

$$M = \alpha_m 2^{m^2}$$

where

$$\alpha_m = \prod_{l=1}^{m} (1 - 2^{-l})$$

and $\alpha_m \leq 1$. Using the identity $(1 - a_1)(1 - a_2) \geq 1 - a_1 - a_2$ for $a_1, a_2 \geq 0$ on the second through mth terms, we have

$$\alpha_m \geq \tfrac{1}{2}\left(1 - \sum_{l=2}^{m} 2^{-l}\right) = \tfrac{1}{2}\left(\frac{1}{2} + \frac{1}{2^m}\right) \geq \frac{1}{4}$$

for $m \geq 2$. Thus, $\tfrac{1}{4} \leq \alpha_m \leq 1$, and α_m approaches a limit with increasing m.

To determine the number of adjacent pairs, consider two constant matrices differing in the value assigned to a_{11}, as indicated. Since the addition rule is addition modulo 2, it is clear that

$$\det\begin{bmatrix} 0 & c_{12} & \cdots & c_{1m} \\ c_{21} & c_{22} & \cdots & c_{2m}. \\ \vdots & & & \\ c_{m1} & c_{m2} & \cdots & c_{mm} \end{bmatrix} \neq \det\begin{bmatrix} 1 & c_{12} & \cdots & c_{1m} \\ c_{21} & c_{22} & \cdots & c_{2m}. \\ \vdots & & & \\ c_{m1} & c_{m2} & \cdots & c_{mm} \end{bmatrix}$$

if and only if

$$\det\begin{pmatrix} c_{22} & \cdots & c_{2m} \\ \cdot & \cdots & \cdot \\ c_{m2} & \cdots & c_{mm} \end{pmatrix} \neq 0$$

There are $\alpha_{m-1}2^{(m-1)^2}$ such submatrices and $2^{2(m-1)}$ ways to choose $c_{12}, \ldots, c_{1m}, c_{21}, \ldots, c_{m1}$ or $\alpha_{m-1}2^{(m-1)^2}2^{2(m-1)}$ adjacent pairs that disagree in the value assigned to x_{11}. By symmetry, this argument applies to each of the m variables so that

$$|A| = m^2 \frac{\alpha_{m-1}}{2} 2^{m^2}$$

It follows that

$$L_{\Omega_0}^*(\det \mathbf{A}) \geq \frac{(\alpha_{m-1})^2}{4\alpha_m(1 - \alpha_m)} m^4 - 1$$

Since $\alpha_{m-1} \geq \alpha_m$ and $\alpha_m \geq \frac{1}{4}$ for $m \geq 2$, it also follows that

$$L_{\Omega_0}^*(\det \mathbf{A}) \geq \frac{\alpha_m}{4(1 - \alpha_m)} \, m^4 - 1 \geq \tfrac{1}{12} m^4 - 1$$

for $m \geq 2$. $\qquad\qquad\qquad\qquad\qquad\qquad\qquad\qquad\qquad\qquad\qquad\qquad$ □

An upper bound of $4m^3$ to the combinational complexity of $\det \mathbf{A}$ is derived in Theorem 3.1.3.1 by constructing a chain for $\det \mathbf{A}$. This chain has fan-out greater than 1, and it is not known whether the lower bound to the formula size of $\det \mathbf{A}$ given here can be achieved even approximately.

A close examination of the Krapchenko lower bound reveals that $|A|$, the number of adjacent pairs, one from B_0, the other from B_1, cannot exceed the minimum of $n|B_0|$ and $n|B_1|$ for a function of n variables because there are at most n n-tuples adjacent to a given n-tuple. Therefore, the Krapchenko lower bound cannot be larger than $n^2 - 1$. As shown, this maximum value is achieved with addition modulo 2, and the lower bound for $\det \mathbf{A}$ also grows linearly with the square of the number of variables.

3.3.2 The Nechiporuk Lower Bound

The Krapchenko result applies only to the AND, OR, NOT basis, and as we have seen with $f_\oplus^c$, a change of basis can produce approximately a squaring of formula size. The next result, due to Nechiporuk (1966), is a test that may give almost square lower bounds, but it applies to all complete bases.

Theorem 3.3.2.1. Let $f: \{0, 1\}^n \to \{0, 1\}$ and let $A_1, A_2, \ldots, A_p$ be a partition of $\{1, 2, \ldots, n\}$. Then $A_i \subset \{1, 2, \ldots, n\}$, $A_i \cap A_j = \varnothing$, $i \neq j$, and $\cup_{i=1}^p A_i = \{1, 2, \ldots, n\}$. Let F_i be the number of subfunctions

$$f \Big|_{\substack{x_j = c_j \\ j \in A_i^c}}$$

where A_i^c denotes the complement of the set A_i with respect to $\{1, 2, \ldots, n\}$. Then the formula size of f, not counting inversions, satisfies

$$L_\Omega^*(f) \geq \left(\frac{1}{r' - 1} \right) \left(\frac{1}{2(r' - 1)} \sum_{i=1}^p \log_2 F_i - 1 \right)$$

for *any complete basis* Ω where $r' = \max(3, r)$ and r is the fan-in of Ω.

Proof. To the basis Ω adjoin the function $\eta \cdot x \oplus \gamma$ to form the basis Ω' of fan-in r'. Clearly, $L_\Omega^*(f) \geq L_{\Omega'}^*(f)$.

Let β be an optimal fan-out 1 chain over Ω' for f. Let t_i be the fan-out from all source nodes in A_i and let $t = \sum_i t_i$ be the total fan-out from all source nodes. From a simple extension of Theorem 2.4.1.1, we have

$$L_{\Omega'}^*(f) \geq C_{\Omega'}^*(f) \geq \frac{t-1}{r'-1}$$

Consider β as a chain for

$$f \Big|_{\substack{x_j = c_j \\ j \in A_i^c}}$$

by setting $x_j, j \in A_i^c$, to constants (call them *free constants*). Then β may be far from optimal, and the following operations will, in general, reduce the number of operations: (*a*) If a subtree of the graph of β has only constant or free-constant inputs, replace that tree by a new node representing a new free-constant. (*b*) If a subtree has exactly one variable input, replace it with the basis element computing $\eta \cdot x \oplus \gamma$, where η and γ are chosen as new free constants. This element has the property that each of the four distinct Boolean functions in the variable x can be obtained by suitable choice of free constants η and γ.

Denote with β_i the chain obtained from β by these transformations. Clearly, β_i computes each of the F_i subfunctions

$$f \Big|_{\substack{x_j = c_j \\ j \in A_i^c}}$$

by suitable choice of the free constants. Also, β_i has t_i variable inputs.

Every computation node of β_i is the root of a tree. Those trees containing a single node have at least one variable input and larger trees have at least two. Let d_1 and d_2 denote the number of computation nodes that are the roots of trees having one and more than one variable input, respectively. By induction on the size of d_2, it is easy to show that $t_i \geq d_2 + 1$. Also, the number of computation nodes in β_i, L_0, is given by $L_0 = d_1 + d_2$. Finally, each of the t_i inputs can be followed by at most one computation node with a single variable, so $t_i \geq d_1$. It follows that $L_0 \leq 2t_i - 1$.

By another application of Theorem 2.4.1.1,

$$L_0 \geq \frac{h-1}{r'-1}$$

where h is the number of free constants in β_i. But since β_i can compute any one of F_i subfunctions, $h \geq \log_2 F_i$.

Putting all of these inequalities together, we have

$$L_\Omega(f) \geq \frac{t-1}{r'-1} \geq \frac{\sum_{i=1}^{p} t_i - 1}{r'-1}$$

$$\geq \left(\frac{1}{r'-1}\right)\left(\sum_{i=1}^{p} \frac{1}{2}\left(\frac{\log_2 F_i - 1}{r'-1} + 1\right) - 1\right)$$

$$\geq \left(\frac{1}{r'-1}\right)\left(\sum_{i=1}^{p} \frac{\log_2 F_i}{2(r'-1)} - 1\right)$$

and this completes the proof. $\qquad\square$

The Nechiporuk lower bound cannot grow faster than n^2 because $F_i \leq 2^{n-n_i}$, where $n - n_i$ is the number of free constants in A_i^c and

$$\sum_{i=1}^{p} \log_2 F_i \leq \sum_{i=1}^{p} (n - n_i) = np - n \leq n(n-1)$$

As the next theorem shows, the function $N(\mathbf{X})$ introduced by Nechiporuk has a formula size that grows almost with the square of n over any complete basis. The Nechiporuk test has also been applied to the Marriage Problem (Harper and Savage, 1972).

Theorem 3.3.2.2. Consider a positive integer n; let $m = [\log_2 n] + 2$ and let $\mathbf{X}$ be an $[n/m] \times m$ matrix of independent Boolean variables, x_{ij}. Also, let $\sigma = (\sigma_{ij})$ be an $[n/m] \times m$ matrix of distinct m-tuples σ_{ij} over $\{0, 1\}$, each containing at least two 1's. Then the function $N(\mathbf{X})$ is defined by

$$N(\mathbf{X}) = \sum_{ij} x_{ij} \sum_{\substack{k=1 \\ (k \neq i)}}^{\lceil n/m \rceil} \prod_{\sigma_{ij}(l)=1} x_{kl}$$

where $\boxtimes$ denotes repeated addition modulo 2. It has a formula size bounded by

$$\left(\frac{1}{r'-1}\right)\left[\frac{n^2}{4(r'-1)(\log_2 n)} - 1\right] \leq L_\Omega(N) \leq Kn^2$$

when Ω is complete of fan-in r, $r' = \max(3, r)$, and K is a constant dependent on the basis Ω.

Proof.   The lower bound is derived by choosing the rows of $\mathbf{X}$ as blocks $\{A_s\}$ of the partition. Fixing s, let $\{c_{ij}\}$ and $\{c'_{ij}\}$ be assignments of constants to rows of $\mathbf{X}$ other than the sth. Let i_0, j_0 be such that $c_{i_0 j_0} \neq c'_{i_0 j_0}$ and $i_0 \neq s$. Then

$$N(\mathbf{X})\Big|_{\substack{x_{ij}=c_{ij}\\ i,j\in A_s^c}} \neq N(\mathbf{X})\Big|_{\substack{x_{ij}=c'_{ij}\\ i,j\in A_s^c}}$$

since only one contains the product

$$\prod_{\sigma_{i_0 j_0}(l)=1} x_{sl}$$

of at *least two variables* from the sth row (products of two or more variables from a given row only occur in the inside product), and by Problem 2-3 for the ring-sum expansion of Boolean functions, they must be distinct functions of the variables in A_s, the sth row of $\mathbf{X}$.

Thus, for every two distinct assignments of constants to the entries of $\mathbf{X}$ outside of A_s, the subfunctions of $N(\mathbf{X})$ are distinct. But, since there are $(\lceil n/m \rceil - 1)m$ such entries,

$$F_s = 2^{m(\lceil n/m \rceil - 1)}$$

for each $1 \leq s \leq p$, $p = \lceil n/m \rceil$, and

$$L_\Omega^*(N) \geq \left(\frac{1}{r'-1}\right)\left(\frac{m}{2(r'-1)}\left\lceil\frac{n}{m}\right\rceil\left(\left\lceil\frac{n}{m}\right\rceil-1\right)-1\right)$$

This expression is simplified with the aid of the inequalities

$$\left\lceil\frac{n}{m}\right\rceil \geq \frac{n}{m}$$

$$\frac{n}{m} - 1 \geq \frac{n}{2m} \qquad \text{for } n \geq 16$$

$$m = 2 + \lceil \log_2 n \rceil \leq 3 + \log_2 n$$

from which we deduce that

$$L_\Omega^*(N) \geq \left(\frac{1}{r'-1}\right)\left[\frac{n^2}{4(r'-1)(\log_2 n + 3)} - 1\right]$$

The upper bound is easily derived by counting the number of AND's and OR's employed in the defining formula for $N(\mathbf{X})$. At most $m-1$

AND's are used for each inner product, and there are $m\lceil n/m\rceil(\lceil n/m\rceil - 1)$ such distinct inner products for a total of $m(m - 1)\lceil n/m\rceil(\lceil n/m\rceil - 1)$ operations. The inner sum and outer product require $\lceil n/m\rceil - 1$ additional operations for each value of i and j, $1 \le i \le \lceil n/m\rceil$, $1 \le j \le m$, or $m\lceil n/m\rceil(\lceil n/m\rceil - 1)$ operations. Finally, the outer sum uses $m\lceil n/m\rceil - 1$ additions. Thus, $N(\mathbf{X})$ can be realized from its defining formula with

$$\left(m\left\lceil \frac{n}{m} \right\rceil\right)^2 - m(m - 1)\left\lceil \frac{n}{m} \right\rceil - 1 \le \left(m\left\lceil \frac{n}{m} \right\rceil\right)^2 \le (n + \log_2 n + 3)^2$$

binary operations. The upper bound follows directly.

Before closing this subject, let's verify that the values of n and m are such that $m\lceil n/m\rceil$ distinct vectors $\boldsymbol{\sigma}_{ij}$ of weight two or more exist. Each vector is an m-tuple, and there are $2^m - m - 1$ binary m-tuples of weight two or more. If

$$2^m - m - 1 \ge m\left\lceil \frac{n}{m} \right\rceil$$

then we are done. This is easily verified by using the relation $x \le \lceil x\rceil < x + 1$. $\qquad\square$

As a second illustration of the Nechiporuk test, we again consider the determinant function. In this case, however, the lower bound that is derived grows only as $n^{3/2}$, although the bound applies to any complete basis. Kloss (1966) is the author of this result.

Theorem 3.3.2.3. Let $\mathbf{A}$ be an $m \times m$ matrix of independent Boolean variables $\{x_{ij}\}$. Then $\det \mathbf{A}$ has a formula size bounded by

$$L_\Omega^*(\det \mathbf{A}) \ge \left(\frac{1}{r' - 1} \right)\left(\frac{m^3}{6(r' - 1)} - 1 \right)$$

when $m \ge 3$, where Ω is a complete basis of fan-in r and $r' = \max(3, r)$.

Proof. Let the blocks of the partition $A_1, A_2, \ldots, A_m$ be the main diagonal, the diagonal below the main diagonal plus the $(1, m)$ element, and so forth. By symmetry, the number of subfunctions

$$\det \mathbf{A}\bigg|_{\substack{x_{ij} = c_{ij} \\ i,j \in A_s^c}}$$

is the same for each block.

A lower bound to F_s, the number of such subfunctions, is obtained as follows. Consider the function

$$
\Theta_{\mathbf{C}}(y_1, y_2, \ldots, y_m) = \det
\begin{bmatrix}
y_1 & c_{12} & c_{13} & \cdots & c_{1m} \\
1 & y_2 & c_{23} & \cdots & c_{2m} \\
0 & 1 & y_3 & \cdots & c_{3m} \\
\hdotsfor{5} \\
0 & 0 & 0 & \cdots & 1 \quad y_m
\end{bmatrix}
$$

where $\mathbf{C}$ is the triangular matrix of Boolean constants shown. It is easy to show directly that $\Theta_{\mathbf{C}}$ and $\Theta_{\mathbf{C}'}$ are distinct if $\mathbf{C} \neq \mathbf{C}'$ when $m = 2, 3$. Let us now demonstrate by induction on the size of m that this property holds in general.

Since the determinant is unchanged by adding a multiple of one row of a matrix to another, multiply the second row of the matrix by y_1 and add to the first

$\Theta_{\mathbf{C}}(y_1, \ldots, y_m)$

$$
= \det
\begin{bmatrix}
0 & y_1 y_2 \oplus c_{12} & y_1 c_{23} \oplus c_{13} & \cdots & y_1 c_{2m} \oplus c_{1m} \\
1 & y_2 & c_{23} & \cdots & c_{2m} \\
0 & 1 & y_3 & \cdots & c_{3m} \\
\hdotsfor{5} \\
0 & 0 & & \cdots & 1 \quad y_m
\end{bmatrix}
$$

Expanding this determinant on the first column, we have

$\Theta_{\mathbf{C}}(y_1, \ldots, y_m)$

$$
= \det
\begin{bmatrix}
y_1 y_2 \oplus c_{12} & y_1 c_{23} \oplus c_{13} & \cdots & \cdots & y_1 c_{2m} \oplus c_{1m} \\
1 & y_3 & \cdots & \cdots & c_{3m} \\
0 & 1 & y_4 & \cdots & c_{4m} \\
\hdotsfor{5} \\
0 & 0 & \cdots & 1 & y_m
\end{bmatrix}
$$

This is the determinant of an $(m - 1) \times (m - 1)$ matrix, and if $y_1 = 1$, $\Theta_{\mathbf{C}}(1, y_2, \ldots, y_m)$ is a function of the desired type in the $m - 1$ variables $y_2 \oplus c_{12}, y_3, \ldots, y_m$. Therefore, by the induction hypothesis, any two triangular matrices $\mathbf{C}$ and $\mathbf{C}'$ that differ in positions of their third through $(m - 1)$st rows must correspond to distinct functions $\Theta_{\mathbf{C}}(y_1, \ldots, y_m)$.

This same argument can be applied to columns by adding y_m times the $(m - 1)$st column to the mth column. We conclude that if $\mathbf{C}$ and $\mathbf{C}'$

differ in any position other than $(1, m-1)$, $(1, m)$, $(2, m-1)$, and $(2, m)$, then they correspond to distinct functions Θ.

Consider the case where $\mathbf{C}$ and $\mathbf{C}'$ agree in every position but these four positions.

(a) $c_{1,m-1} \oplus c_{2,m-1} \neq c'_{1,m-1} \oplus c'_{2,m-1}$ or $c_{1,m} \oplus c_{2,m} \neq c'_{1,m} \oplus c'_{2,m}$, or both. Then $\Theta_{\mathbf{C}}(1, y_2, \ldots, y_m)$ and $\Theta_{\mathbf{C}'}(1, y_2, \ldots, y_m)$ are determinants of two distinct $(m-1) \times (m-1)$ matrices of the desired type, and by the inductive hypothesis, must be distinct functions. This is true also of $\Theta_{\mathbf{C}}$ and $\Theta_{\mathbf{C}'}$.

(b) $c_{1,m-1} \oplus c_{2,m-1} = c'_{1,m-1} \oplus c'_{2,m-1}$ and $c_{1,m} \oplus c_{2,m} = c'_{1,m} \oplus c'_{2,m}$,

but $\mathbf{C} \neq \mathbf{C}'$, so one of the following three subcases holds:

  (i) $(c_{1,m-1}, c_{2,m-1}) \neq (c'_{1,m-1}, c'_{2,m-1})$.
      This implies that $c_{2,m-1} \neq c'_{2,m-1}$.
  (ii) $(c_{1,m}, c_{2,m}) \neq (c'_{1,m}, c'_{2,m})$.
      This implies that $c_{2,m-1} \neq c'_{2,m-1}$.
  (iii) Both of these.
      This implies that $c_{2,m-1} \neq c'_{2,m-1}$ and $c_{2,m} \neq c'_{2,m}$.

Let $\mathbf{V}$ be an $n \times n$ matrix over a field with rows $\mathbf{v}_1, \mathbf{v}_2, \ldots, \mathbf{v}_n$ and let $d(\mathbf{v}_1, \ldots, \mathbf{v}_n)$ be the the determinant of $\mathbf{V}$. It is easily demonstrated (Herstein, 1964) that

$$d(\mathbf{v}_1, \ldots, \mathbf{v}_{i-1}, \mathbf{u}_i {}^{``}+{}^{\prime\prime} \mathbf{v}_i, \mathbf{v}_{i+1}, \ldots, \mathbf{v}_n)$$

$$= d(\mathbf{v}_1, \ldots, \mathbf{v}_{i-1}, \mathbf{v}_i, \mathbf{v}_{i+1}, \ldots, \mathbf{v}_n) + d(\mathbf{v}_1, \ldots, \mathbf{v}_{i-1}, \mathbf{u}_i, \mathbf{v}_{i+1}, \ldots, \mathbf{v}_n)$$

where $\mathbf{u}_i$ is another potential row of $\mathbf{V}$, "+" denotes vector addition, and $+$ denotes field addition. (Note that $\{0, 1\}$ with addition $\oplus$ and multiplication $\cdot$ is a field.)

In subcase (i) we have

$$\Theta_{\mathbf{C}}(0, y_2, \ldots, y_m) \oplus \Theta_{\mathbf{C}'}(0, y_2, \ldots, y_m)$$

$$= \det \begin{bmatrix} 0 & 0 & \cdots & 1 & 0 \\ 1 & y_3 & \cdots & c_{3m-1} & c_{3m} \\ 0 & 1 & y_4 & \cdots & c_{4m} \\ \hdotsfor{5} \\ 0 & 0 & \cdots & 1 & y_m \end{bmatrix} = y_m.$$

Similarly, it can be shown that the function given above has value 1 in subcase (ii) and value $y_m \oplus 1$ in the subcase (iii).

Thus, we have established that $\Theta_{\mathbf{C}} \neq \Theta_{\mathbf{C}'}$ if $\mathbf{C} \neq \mathbf{C}'$. Since $\mathbf{C}$ has $(m^2 - m)/2$ entries, there are $2^{(m^2-m)/2}$ such functions and at least that many subfunctions of det $\mathbf{A}$ with respect to each block in the partition.

Applying the Nechiporuk lower bound, we have

$$L_\Omega^*(\det A) \geq \frac{1}{r'-1}\left(\frac{1}{2(r'-1)} \cdot m\left(\frac{m^2-m}{2}\right) - 1\right)$$

But $(m^2 - m)/2 \geq m^2/3$ for $m \geq 3$, from which the theorem follows. □

Paul (1975) has exhibited a function $f:\{0, 1\}^n \to \{0, 1\}$ that has combinational complexity linear in n over the full basis $P_{1,2}^{(2)}$ but has formula size at least on the order of $n^2/\log_2 n$ over the same basis. A similar result holds for $x_1 \oplus x_2 \oplus \cdots \oplus x_n$, as was demonstrated in the preceding section but only for the restricted basis $\{+, \cdot, ^-\}$. The Paul function is given in Problem 3-22.

There is another technique, due to Specker (1967), for measuring the formula size of Boolean functions. It amounts to a condition that formulas for functions of n variables must satisfy if the functions are to have formula size less than $c \cdot n - 1$ for a constant $c > 0$. If the condition is not satisfied, there is no constant $c > 0$ such that the formula size is less than $cn - 1$, so it must grow faster than linearly in n. At best, this method gives a weak lower bound. For this reason, we are content to merely state Specker's Theorem.

Theorem 3.3.2.4. Let Ω be the set of all Boolean functions in two or fewer variables and let $\{f_n | f_n: \{0, 1\}^n \to \{0, 1\}\}$ be an infinite sequence of Boolean functions. There exists a number theoretic function $G(w, z)$ such that given any integers $c, p \geq 0$, then for all $n \geq G(p, c)$, if

$$L_\Omega^*(f_n) \leq cn - 1$$

then there exist p distinct integers $k_1, \ldots, k_p$ from $\{1, 2, \ldots, n\}$ and three constants $b_0, b_1\, b_2 \in \{0, 1\}$ such that

$$f\Big|_{\substack{x_j=0\\ j \notin \{k_1, \ldots, k_p\}}} = b_0 \oplus b_1 \cdot \left(\prod_{i=1}^{p} \bar{x}_{k_i}\right) \oplus b_2 \cdot \left(x_{k_1} \oplus \cdots \oplus x_{k_p}\right)$$

Furthermore, if the f_n are realized with formulas over only $\{+, \cdot, ^-\}$, then we can take $b_2 = 0$.

Hodes (1970) has used this theorem in his study of the logical complexity of geometric properties in the plane.

3.3.3. Formula Size of Threshold Functions

The threshold functions, defined in Section 3.1.2, are additional examples of monotone Boolean functions. We recall the definition of the threshold function $\tau_t^{(n)}$: $\{0, 1\}^n \to \{0, 1\}$ of threshold t:

$$\tau_t^{(n)}(x_1, x_2, \ldots, x_n) = \begin{cases} 1, & \sum_1^n {}^* x_i \geq t \\ 0, & \text{otherwise} \end{cases}$$

Here Σ^* denotes integer addition. We develop lower bounds to the formula size of these functions over $\Omega = \{+, \cdot, {}^-\}$ that are on the order of $n \log_2 n$. In this connection, we make use of some of the bounding arguments of Krichevskii (1963) and Hansel (1964). We also present or mention various upper bounds to formula size of threshold functions over $\Omega_m = \{+, \cdot\}$.

The MDNF of $\tau_t^{(n)}$ is given by

$$\tau_t^{(n)}(x_1, \ldots, x_n) = \sum_{i_1} \cdots \sum_{i_t} x_{i_1} x_{i_2} \cdots x_{i_t}$$

where

$$1 \leq i_1 < \cdots < i_t \leq n$$

and Σ denotes OR. The function $\tau_1^{(n)}$ is the OR of n variables and $L_{\Omega_m}(\tau_1^{(n)}) = n - 1$. The function $\tau_2^{(n)}$ can be realized recursively from the following formula when n is even:

$$\tau_2^{(n)}(x_1, \ldots, x_n) = \tau_1^{(n/2)}(x_1, \ldots, x_{n/2}) \cdot \tau_1^{(n/2)}(x_{n/2+1}, \ldots, x_n)$$

$$+ \tau_2^{(n/2)}(x_1, \ldots, x_{n/2}) + \tau_2^{(n/2)}(x_{n/2+1}, \ldots, x_n)$$

where $+$ denotes OR. It follows that for even n,

$$L_{\Omega_m}(\tau_2^{(n)}) \leq n + 1 + 2L_{\Omega_m}(\tau_2^{(n/2)})$$

If $n = 2^k$, this reduces to

$$L_{\Omega_m}(\tau_2^{(n)}) \leq n \log_2 n - 1$$

as the reader can demonstrate by solving the implied recurrence relation.

The following upper bound is due to Khasin (1969a).

Theorem 3.3.3.1. There exists a constant $K > 0$ such that for all $n \geq t \geq 1$,

$$L_{\Omega_m}(\tau_t^{(n)}) \leq K 2^{1/4(\log_2 t)^2(1+\gamma_t)} n \log_2 n$$

where $\gamma_t \to 0$ as $t \to \infty$.

This bound demonstrates that for fixed t, the threshold function $\tau_t^{(n)}$ has formula size that grows no faster than $n \log n$. The method that Khasin uses to establish this result is noncontructive; he demonstrates the existence of a formula for $\tau_t^{(n)}$ of this size without exhibiting such a formula.

An $n \log n$ lower bound is developed to the formula size of $\tau_2^{(n)}$ over $\{+, \cdot, {}^-\}$, and this is later applied to the other threshold functions. The lower bound to the formula size of $\tau_2^{(n)}$ is derived by first showing that an optimal formula for it exists that has only AND's and OR's.

Let $g: \{0, 1\}^n \to \{0, 1\}$ be a function with the property

P1. $g(x_1, x_2, \ldots, x_n) = 0$ when $\Sigma^* x_i = 1$.

Consider the class $M(g)$ of functions $h: \{0, 1\}^n \to \{0, 1\}$ defined by the following properties:

P2. If $h \in M(g)$, then h satisfies P1.
P3. $h(x_1, \ldots, x_n) \geq g(x_1, \ldots, x_n)$ if $\Sigma^* x_i \neq 0$.
P4. The formula size of all functions in $M(g)$ is the smallest of all functions satisfying P2 and P3.

The set $M(g)$ is nonempty.

Lemma 3.3.3.1. For every $g: \{0, 1\}^n \to \{0, 1\}$ with the property P1, there exists a function in $M(g)$ one of whose minimal formulas over $\{+, \cdot, {}^-\}$ has the following *Krichevskii normal form:*

$$\sum_{i=1}^{k} s_{i1} \cdot s_{i2}$$

where Σ denotes OR. Here s_{i1} and s_{i2} are sums (OR) of disjoint uncomplemented variables from $\{x_1, x_2, \ldots, x_n\}$.

> **Proof.** By repeated application of DeMorgan's rules, every formula over $\{+, \cdot, {}^-\}$ can be transformed without changing its size so that no subformula, except perhaps individual variables, appears complemented. We consider only such formulas for $h \in M(g)$.
>
> If $g \doteq 0$, for $\Sigma^* x_i \geq 1$, then we can choose, $h = 0$ and satisfy P2, P3, and P4; $h \in M(g)$ can then be realized by a formula without NOT's. Suppose, then, that g satisfies P5.
>
> P5. $g(x_1, \ldots, x_n) = 1$ for some $x_1, \ldots, x_n \ni \Sigma^* x_i \geq 2$. Then h satisfies P1 and P5 and requires at least one AND. Furthermore, $n \geq 2$.
>
> We show by induction on the number of AND's required, that for every g satisfying P1 and P2, there exists an $h \in M(g)$ that can be

realized by an optimal formula in the Krichevskii normal form. Consider g such that $h \in M(g)$ requires one AND. Then a formula ϕ for h can be written in the form

$$\phi(x_1, \ldots, x_n) = \phi_0(x_1, \ldots, x_n) + \phi_1(x_1, \ldots, x_n) \cdot \phi_2(x_1, \ldots, x_n)$$

where ϕ_0, ϕ_1, and ϕ_2 are sums (OR) of variables with or without complementation. Both ϕ_0 and $\phi_1 \cdot \phi_2$ must satisfy P1. Since $n \geq 2$, this implies that $\phi_0 = 0$. We conclude that $\phi_1 \cdot \phi_2$ satisfies P1 and P5.

We show that any formula of the form $\phi_1 \cdot \phi_2$ that satisfies P1 and P5 and where ϕ_1 and ϕ_2 are sums of variables with or without complementation must have the property that the variables are uncomplemented. We establish this result by showing first that the variables of ϕ_1 and ϕ_2 are disjoint.

Suppose that the variables of ϕ_1 and ϕ_2 are not disjoint. Then, for some variables x_j that (a) both contain x_j or (b) both contain $\bar{x}_j$ or (c) one contains x_j and the other contains $\bar{x}_j$. If (a) holds, $\phi_1 \cdot \phi_2$ violates P1. If (b) holds, $\phi_1 \cdot \phi_2$ violates P1 because $n \geq 2$ and we can set $x_j = 0$. Consider the remaining case and without loss of generality let $\phi_1 = x_j + s_1$, $\phi_2 = \bar{x}_j + s_2$, where s_1 and s_2 are possibly empty sums of complemented or uncomplemented variables. If $s_1 = 0$, then $\phi_1 \phi_2$ is equivalent to $x_j s_2$ which has a smaller formula size than $\phi_1 \phi_2$ in contradiction to P4. A similar argument applies to s_2, so $s_1 \neq 0$ and $s_2 \neq 0$.

Now let y and z be literals in s_1 and s_2, respectively, so that $y = x_l$ or $\bar{x}_l$ and $z = x_k$ or $\bar{x}_k$ for variables x_l and x_k. (It is possible that $l = k$ but $l \neq j$ and $k \neq j$.) If $y = x_l$, set $x_l = 1$ and $x_j = 0$ and P1 is violated. Therefore, $y = \bar{x}_l$. If $n \geq 3$, set $x_l = x_j = 0$ and some one other variable to 1 and again P1 is violated. The last case to consider is that for which $n = 2$ and

$$\phi_1 \phi_2 = (x_j + \bar{x}_l)(\bar{x}_j + z)$$

where $z = x_l$ or $\bar{x}_l$. If $z = x_l$, $\phi_1 \phi_2$ is equivalent to $x_j x_l$ for $\Sigma^* x_i \geq 1$, so $\phi_1 \phi_2$ is not an optimim formula and P4 is violated. If $z = \bar{x}_l$, set $x_j = 1$, $x_l = 0$ in violation of P1.

From the above arguments, we conclude that the variables of ϕ_1 and ϕ_2 are disjoint. If one of the variables of ϕ_1 or ϕ_2 is complemented, all the variables of both must be complemented or P1 is violated. But if they are all complemented and $n \geq 3$, P1 is violated. If $n = 2$, $\phi_1 \phi_2 = \bar{x}_i \cdot \bar{x}_j$ and this does not satisfy P5. Consequently, the variables of ϕ_1 and ϕ_2 are uncomplemented and disjoint.

Our inductive hypothesis is that if $h \in M(g)$ has an optimal formula with $k - 1$ or fewer AND's, then there exists $h' \in M(g)$ (h' possibly equal to h) that has an optimal formula in the Krichevshii normal form.

Let g satisfy P5 and suppose that some $h \in M(g)$ requires k AND's in an optimal formula ϕ. Such a formula can be expressed as

$$\phi(x_1, \ldots, x_n) = \sum_{i=1}^{p} \phi_{i1}(x_1, \ldots, x_n) \cdot \phi_{i2}(x_1, \ldots, x_n)$$

where Σ denotes OR, $p \leq k$, at least one AND of ϕ is explicit, and ϕ and ϕ_{i2} are nonzero. Both ϕ_{i1} and ϕ_{i2} cannot be constant, else $\phi_{i1} \cdot \phi_{i2} = 1$ and $\phi = 1$, contradicting P1. All ϕ_{ij} have $k - 1$ or fewer AND's.

Without loss of generality, we can write

$$\phi_{i1} \cdot \phi_{i2} = (s_1 + t_1)(s_2 + t_2)$$

where s_1 and s_2 are sums (OR) of variables, complemented or uncomplemented, and both t_1 and t_2 satisfy P1. If t_1 or t_2 violate P5, it can be removed without violating P1 or P3 but in violation of P4. Thus, t_1 and t_2 are either 0 or satisfy P1 and P5 and, by the inductive hypothesis, have a Krichevskii normal form.

Note that $s_1 \cdot s_2$ satisfies P1 because if not, then $\phi_{i1} \cdot \phi_{i2}$ violates P1, a contradiction. Also,

$$\phi_{i1} \cdot \phi_{i2} \leq s_1 s_2 + t_1 + t_2$$

and this new expression can be used to replace $\phi_{i1} \cdot \phi_{i2}$ without violating P1 or P3 and without changing the number of AND's or OR's used. This replacement may result in the replacement of h by some other function h' in $M(g)$. If $s_1 \cdot s_2$ violates P5, then it can be removed without violating P1 and P3 but in contradiction to the assumed optimality of ϕ. Thus, each of s_1 and s_2 contains at least one variable and, by the argument given above for the case of a single AND, s_1 and s_2 consist of sets of disjoint, uncomplemented variables.

We conclude that for g satisfying P1 there exists an $h \in M(g)$ whose optimal formula over $\{+, \cdot, {}^-\}$ has the Krichevskii normal form.   □

Corollary 3.3.3.1. The function $\tau_2^{(n)}$ has an optimal formula over $\{+, \cdot, {}^-\}$ that has the Krichevskii normal form.

Proof. If $h \in M(\tau_2^{(n)})$, then $h = \tau_2^{(n)}$ or $h = \tau_2^{(n)} + \bar{x}_1 \cdot \bar{x}_2 \cdot \cdots \cdot \bar{x}_n$. Of the two only the first, which is monotone, has a Krichevskii normal form.   □

We now establish the main result.

Theorem 3.3.3.1. Over the basis $\Omega = \{+, \cdot, ^-\}$,

$$L_\Omega(\tau_2^{(n)}) \geq n \log_2 n - 1$$

Proof. In the Krichevskii normal form, no two sums s_{ij} are equal because otherwise the absorption rule $ab + ac = a(b + c)$ could be used to simplify the formula.

Expand $\tau_2^{(n)}$ in an optimal formula ϕ:

$$\phi(x_1, \ldots, x_n) = \sum_{i=1}^{p} S_{i1} \cdot S_{i2}$$

There are $2p$ sums s_{ij}, and if we form a set of p such sums, one from each product, and set all variables in each sum to 0, $\tau_2^{(n)} = 0$. These sets are called *break sets*. There are 2^p break sets.

In the above optimal formula for $\tau_2^{(n)}$, let p_j be the number of products for which $x_j \notin s_{i1}$, $x_j \notin s_{i2}$. In the remaining $p - p_j$ products, x_j is contained in exactly one sum. Therefore, there are 2^{p_j} break sets that do not contain x_j. Furthermore, the break sets not containing x_j are disjoint from those not containing x_i, $i \neq j$, because, if not, we can set all sums of such a break set to 0 and have $\tau_2^{(n)} = 0$ even when $x_i = x_j = 1$. Therefore, they are disjoint and $2^p \geq \sum_{j=1}^{n} 2^{p_j}$.

The number of occurrences of x_j in the optimal formula for $\tau_2^{(n)}$ is $p - p_j$. The formula size is one less than the number of literals, so

$$L_\Omega(\tau_2^{(n)}) = \sum_{j=1}^{n} (p - p_j) - 1 = np - \sum_{1}^{n} p_j - 1$$

$$\geq n \log_2 \left(\sum_{1}^{n} 2^{p_j} \right) - \left(\sum_{1}^{n} p_j \right) - 1$$

From the inequality between the arithmetic and geometric means (see Problem 3-23), namely, for $a_i \geq 0$,

$$\frac{1}{n} \sum_{1}^{n} a_i \geq \left(\prod_{1}^{n} a_i \right)^{1/n}$$

where Σ and $\prod$ denote integer addition and multiplication. With $a_i = 2^{p_i}$, we have

$$L_\Omega(\tau_2^{(n)}) \geq n \log_2 n - 1 \qquad \square$$

This lower bound is achieved, as demonstrated above, when n is a power of 2. In Problem 3-24, the reader is asked to improve this lower bound to $n[\log_2 n] - 2$ when n is not a power of 2. Problem 3-25 asks the reader to show that $\tau_2^{(n)}$ can be realized with formula size of no more than $n[\log_2 n] - 2$ over $\{+, \cdot\}$ when n is not a power of 2.

Given $\tau_t^{(n)}$, $\tau_{t-1}^{(n-1)}$ can be obtained by setting any one variable of $\tau_t^{(n)}$ to 1. Following the arguments of Section 2.4.3, it is possible to show that some variable, say x_j, has fan-out of at least 2 in any optimal formula for $\tau_t^{(n)}$. Setting $x_j = 1$ eliminates at least two binary operations. Thus, over $\Omega = \{+, \cdot, ^-\}$,

$$L_\Omega(\tau_t^{(n)}) \geq L_\Omega(\tau_{t-1}^{(n-1)}) + 2 \geq L_\Omega(\tau_2^{(n-t+2)}) + 2(t - 2)$$

$$\geq (n - t + 2)\log_2(n - t + 2) + 2(t - 2) - 1$$

for $t \leq n$. This can be improved to the following:

$$L_\Omega(\tau_t^{(n)}) \geq t(n - t + 1) - 1$$

by using Krapchenko's lower bound (see Problem 3-20), when t is large by comparison to $\log_2 n$.

3.4. ASYMPTOTIC BOUNDS

There are 2^{2^n} Boolean functions of n variables, so many in fact, that most of them have very large combinational complexity and very large formula size. In this section, we establish this by showing that the number of circuits and formulas of small size is insufficient to realize all Boolean functions $f : \{0, 1\}^n \to \{0, 1\}$. We also exhibit circuits and formulas for each such function whose size is near the minimal size required for most such functions.

Let us count the number of combinational machines over the basis $\{+, \cdot, ^-\}$ with input variables from the set $\{x_1, x_2, \ldots, x_n\}$ that have at most C two-input logic elements. Consider a circuit with c two-input gates and d inverters (NOT's). We can assume that at most one of the two inputs to an AND or OR is inverted because otherwise we can apply DeMorgan's rule (Theorem 2.1.1) and replace the two inverters with one on the output by exchanging an AND for an OR, or vice versa. Thus, we can assume that $d \leq c$. We count by first upper bounding the number of combinational machines without inverters and multiplying this by the number of ways in which inverters can be added.

Each of the inputs to a logic element could conceivably be a constant (0 or 1), one of the n variables or one of the outputs of the $c - 1$ remaining two-input logic elements. Thus, each input could take on one of at most $c + n + 1$ values, and a circuit of c two-input, unlabeled elements could be constructed in at most $(c + n + 1)^{2c}$ ways. An element could have neither input inverted or one inverted, which means that any one of three conditions could apply to the inputs of a two-input logic element. Furthermore, since each two-input logic element can be one of two functions, there are at most 6^c circuits with a given interconnection pattern between the two-input elements. Thus, there are at most $(c + n + 1)^{2c} 6^c$ circuits with c two-input elements and they compute at most $N/c!$ different sets of functions because there are $c!$ different permutations of computation nodes which compute the same set of functions. Since $c! \geq c^c e^{-c}$ (which can be obtained by lower bounding $\ln(c!)$ by an integral), it follows that 1)$(C + (n + 1)(n + 3))^C (6e)^C \leq ((6e)x)^x$ distinct sets of functions computed by circuits with c elements where $0 \leq c \leq C$ and $x = C + (n + 1)(n + 3)$.

Theorem 3.4.1 Let $0 < \delta < 1$. Then a fraction $F \geq 1 - 2^{-\delta 2^n}$ of the Boolean functions $f : \{0, 1\}^n \to \{0, 1\}$ have

$$C^*_\Omega(f) \geq \frac{2^n(1 - \delta)}{n + \log_2[6e(1 - \delta)]} - (n + 1)(n + 3) + 1$$

over $\Omega = \{ +, \cdot, {}^- \}$ when $n \geq -\log_2(3e(1 - \delta))$.

Proof. Choose x so that $(6ex)^x = 2^{2^n(1 - \delta)}$. Then, a fraction of at most $2^{-\delta 2^n}$ of the functions have $C^*_\Omega(f) \leq C$ where C is the solution implied by this equation (since $x = C + (n + 1)(n + 3)$). The solution x satisfies

$$(6ex)\log_2(6ex) = 6e2^n(1 - \delta)$$

and since $y \log_2 y = A$ implies $y \geq A/\log_2 A$ for $A \geq 2$, we have

$$x \geq 2^n(1 - \delta)/\log_2(6e2^n(1 - \delta))$$

for $n \geq -\log_2(3e(1 - \delta))$ which completes the proof. $\square$

We now derive a similar result for formula size over the same basis. For this purpose, we refer the reader to Section 5.7, where we demonstrate that a formula can be uniquely characterized by a prefix notation. If a formula has c two-input operators and d inverters, it has $c + 1$ occurrences of variables or constants, and the corresponding prefix notation has $2c + d + 1$ characters corresponding directly to the operators and inputs. From a preceding argument, $d \leq c$. There are at most

$$\begin{pmatrix} 2c + d + 1 \\ c, c + 1, d \end{pmatrix}$$

(this is a trinomial coefficient) ways to choose positions in prefix notations for unary and binary operators. Since this is the coefficient of $x^c y^{c+1} z^d$ in the expansion of $(x + y + z)^{2c+d+1}$, there are no more than 3^{2c+d+1} ways to choose these positions. When these positions are fixed, there are at most 2^c ways to assign the two-input operators AND and OR, and $(n + 2)^{c+1}$ ways to assign the inputs from the set $\{x_1, x_2, \ldots, x_n, 0, 1\}$. Thus, there are at most $3^{2c+d+1} 2^c (n + 2)^{c+1}$ prefix notations for formulas over $\{+, \cdot, ^-\}$ containing c AND's or OR's and d NOT's. Summing over $0 \leq d \leq c$ and then over $0 \leq c \leq L$, we find that there are at most $\phi(L)$ formulas where

$$\phi(L) \leq \sum_{c=0}^{L} 3^{2c+1} 2^c (n + 2)^{c+1} \sum_{d=0}^{c} 3^d$$

$$\leq \sum_{c=0}^{L} 3^{2c+1} 2^c (n + 2)^{c+1} \frac{3}{2}^{c+1} \leq \frac{(4.5)(n + 2)}{54(n + 2) - 1} \left[54(n + 2) \right]^{L+1}$$

$$\leq \left[54(n + 2) \right]^{L+1}$$

Theorem 3.4.2. Let $0 < \delta < 1$. Then a fraction $F \geq 1 - 2^{-\delta 2^n}$ of the Boolean function $f:\{0, 1\}^n \to \{0, 1\}$ have

$$L_{\Omega}^*(f) \geq \frac{2^n(1 - \delta)}{\log_2 \left[54(n + 2) \right]}$$

over $\Omega = \{+, \cdot, ^-\}$ when $n \geq 1$ and NOT's are not counted.

Proof. Equate the bound to $\phi(L)$ with $2^{2^n(1-\delta)}$ and observe that a fraction of at most $2^{-\delta 2^n}$ functions have $L_{\Omega}^*(f) \leq L$. □

Our next task is to develop upper bounds to the combinational complexity and formula size of arbitrary Boolean functions $f:\{0, 1\}^n \to \{0, 1\}$. The basis for these bounds is an expansion of Boolean functions which is due to Lupanov (1958). Given a function $f:\{0, 1\}^n \to \{0, 1\}$, we construct a table of the type shown in Figure 3.4.1.

The 2^k rows of this table are divided into p groups $A_1, A_2, \ldots, A_p$ where the first $p - 1$ each contain s consecutive rows and the last contains the

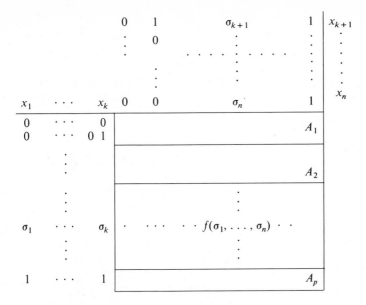

Figure 3.4.1. A tabular representation of a Boolean function.

last s' consecutive rows where $1 \leq s' \leq s$. Also,

$$p = \left\lceil \frac{2^k}{s} \right\rceil \leq \frac{2^k}{s} + 1$$

Define $f_i : \{0, 1\}^n \to \{0, 1\}$ by

$$f_i(x_1, \ldots, x_n) = \begin{cases} f(x_1, \ldots, x_n), & \text{if } (x_1, \ldots, x_k) \in A_i \\ 0 & \text{otherwise} \end{cases}$$

Shown in Figure 3.4.2 is the tabular description of sample function f_i. Let $B_{i,\mathbf{v}}$ be the columns of such a table which, when intersected with A_i, are the s-tuple $\mathbf{v}$. For example, in Figure 3.4.2, $B_{2,(1,1,0)} = \{(0, 0, 0), (0, 1, 0)\}$ and $B_{2,(0,1,0)} = \{(1, 0, 0), (0, 1, 1)\}$. We further define $f_{i,\mathbf{v}} : \{0, 1\}^n \to \{0, 1\}$ by

$$f_{i,\mathbf{v}} = \begin{cases} f_i(x_1, \ldots, x_n), & \text{if } (x_{k+1}, \ldots, x_n) \in B_{i,\mathbf{v}} \\ 0, & \text{otherwise} \end{cases}$$

The full tabular definition of $f_{i,\mathbf{v}}$ contains columns that are (*a*) all zero or (*b*) are 0 except where they intersect A_i, where they have value $\mathbf{v}$. Thus, we can write $f_{i,\mathbf{v}}$ as the AND of two functions on disjoint subsets of the

			0	1	0	1				1	
			0	0	1	1	·	·	·	1	
			0	0	0	0				1	
0	0	0	0	0	0	0	0	0	0	0	
0	0	1	0	0	0	0	0	0	0	0	A_1
0	1	0	0	0	0	0	0	0	0	0	
		·	1	0	1	0	1	0	0	1	
		·	1	1	1	0	0	0	1	1	A_2
		·	0	0	0	0	0	1	0	1	
			0	0	0	0	0	0	0	0	
1	1	1	0	0	0	0	0	0	0	0	A_3

Figure 3.4.2. Tabular description of f_2.

variables:

$$f_{i,\mathbf{v}} = f_{i,\mathbf{v}}^{(r)}(x_1, \ldots, x_k) \cdot f_{i,\mathbf{v}}^{(c)}(x_{k+1}, \ldots, x_n)$$

Here,

$$f_{i,\mathbf{v}}^{(r)}(x_1, \ldots, x_k) = \begin{cases} 1, & \text{if}(x_1, \ldots, x_k)\text{corresponds to a 1 in } \mathbf{v} \text{ in } A_i \\ 0, & \text{otherwise} \end{cases}$$

$$f_{i,\mathbf{v}}^{(c)}(x_{k+1}, \ldots, x_n) = \begin{cases} 1, & \text{if}(x_{k+1}, \ldots, x_n) \in B_{i,\mathbf{v}} \\ 0, & \text{otherwise} \end{cases}$$

Two observations are important here:

1. $f_{i,\mathbf{v}}^{(r)}$ has value 1 on at most s points in its domain $\{0, 1\}^k$.
2. $B_{i,\mathbf{v}} \cap B_{i,\mathbf{v}'} = \phi$ if $\mathbf{v} \neq \mathbf{v}'$.

Now we can write

$$f(x_1, \ldots, x_n) = \sum_{i=1}^{p} f_i(x_1, \ldots, x_n) = \sum_{i=1}^{p} \sum_{\mathbf{v} \neq \mathbf{0}} f_{i,\mathbf{v}}^{(r)} \cdot f_{i,\mathbf{v}}^{(c)}$$

where Σ denotes OR. This is the (k, s)-*Lupanov representation* of $f:\{0, 1\}^n \rightarrow \{0, 1\}$.

We now develop an upper bound to the combinational complexity of f over $\Omega = \{+, \cdot, ^-\}$. We generate all minterms in $x_1, \ldots, x_k$ and $x_{k+1}, \ldots, x_n$ by using the binary-to-positional transformers $f_T^{(k)}(x_1, \ldots, x_k)$ and $f_T^{(n-k)}(x_{k+1}, \ldots, x_n)$ of Section 3.1.1. If k and $n - k$

are large, they can be realized with $2^k(1 + \varepsilon)$ and $2^{n-k}(1 + \varepsilon)$ elements, respectively, for some $\varepsilon > 0$. To realize $f_{i,\mathbf{v}}^{(r)}$ requires at most an additional $s - 1$ ($s' - 1$ if $i = p$) OR's to combine its minterms (see observation 1) and to realize all $f_{i,\mathbf{v}}^{(r)}$, $1 \leq i \leq p - 1$, $\mathbf{v} \in \{0, 1\}^s$, and $\mathbf{v} \in \{0, 1\}^{s'}$ for $i = p$ requires at most $[(p - 1)(s - 1) + s' - 1]2^s$ OR's for a total of at most 2^{k+s} OR's.

The function $f_{i,\mathbf{v}}^{(c)}(x_{k+1}, \ldots, x_n)$ is a sum of minterms corresponding to columns in $B_{i,\mathbf{v}}$. By observation 2, these sets are disjoint. They contain 2^{n-k} columns together, so that to form $f_{i,\mathbf{v}}^{(c)}$ for all $\mathbf{v}$ requires no more than 2^{n-k} OR's, and for $1 \leq i \leq p$, the number is at most $p2^{n-k}$.

Once $f_{i,\mathbf{v}}^{(r)} \cdot f_{i,\mathbf{v}}^{(c)}$ has been formed for all $1 \leq i \leq p$ and all $\mathbf{v}$ using at most $p \cdot 2^s$ AND's, f can be formed with $2^s - 2$ OR's for $1 \leq i \leq p - 1$ and $2^{s'} - 2$ OR's for $i = p$, for a total of at most $p2^s$ OR's.

The total number of elements that is sufficient to realize f from a (k, s)-Lupanov representation, $C(k, s)$, satisfies

$$C(k, s) \leq (2^k + 2^{n-k})(1 + \varepsilon) + 2^{k+s} + p(2^{n-k} + 2^{s+1})$$

$$\leq (2^k + 2^{n-k})(1 + \varepsilon) + 2^{k+s} + \left(\frac{2^k}{s} + 1\right)(2^{n-k} + 2^{s+1})$$

$$\leq (2^k + 2 \cdot 2^{n-k} + 2^{s+1})(1 + \varepsilon) + 2^{k+s}\left(1 + \frac{2}{s}\right) + \frac{2^n}{s}$$

Now choose $k = \lceil 3 \log_2 n \rceil$ and $s = \lceil n - 5 \cdot \log_2 n \rceil$. Then $k + s \leq n - \log_2(n^2) + 2$ and $n - k \leq n - \log_2(n^3)$, so all terms in the bound are small by comparison to the last when n is large. The latter is bounded above by $2^n/(n - 5 \log_2 n)$.

Theorem 3.4.3. For $0 < \varepsilon < 1$ there exists $N(\varepsilon) \geq 1$ such that for $n \geq N(\varepsilon)$ all $f : \{0, 1\}^n \to \{0, 1\}$ have

$$C_\Omega^*(f) \leq \frac{2^n}{n}(1 + \varepsilon)$$

where $\Omega = \{+, \cdot, ^-\}$.

The ratio of this upper bound to the "almost all" lower bound of Theorem 3.4.1 is asymptotically 1. We now develop an analogous upper bound for formula size.

Let $L^*(r, n)$ be the formula size over $\Omega = \{+, \cdot, ^-\}$ of the most complex function $f : \{0, 1\}^n \to \{0, 1\}$ that has value 1 on r points of its domain. The number of NOT's is not included in $L^*(r, n)$. Clearly,

$$L^*(r, n) \leq rn - 1$$

because each of the r minterms can be formed with $n - 1$ AND's and combined with $r - 1$ OR's. We have the following result due to Finikov (1957):

Lemma 3.4.1. $L^*(r, n) \leq 2n - 1 + r2^{r-1}$.

Proof. Given $f: \{0, 1\}^n \to \{0, 1\}$ with value 1 on r points of its domain, form a matrix of r rows and n columns:

$$
\begin{matrix}
1 & 1 & 1 & 1 & 1 & 1 \\
0 & 1 & 0 & 1 & 0 & 1 \\
1 & 0 & 1 & 0 & 0 & 0 \\
0 & 1 & 0 & 1 & 1 & 1
\end{matrix}
$$

where the rows correspond to the n-tuples on which f has value 1.

One row can be chosen to be 1 without affecting $L^*_\Omega(f)$ by replacing some variables of f by their complements. Now group together those

$$
\begin{matrix}
1 & 1 & 1 & 1 & 1 & 1 \\
0 & 0 & 1 & 1 & 1 & 0 \\
1 & 1 & 0 & 0 & 0 & 0 \\
0 & 0 & 1 & 1 & 1 & 1
\end{matrix}
$$

columns of the matrix into blocks that correspond to the same r-tuple: (We interchange the second with the third column and the fifth with the sixth.) This involves a relabeling of the variables. Assume that columns from left to right correspond to $x_1, \ldots, x_n$.

Now let

$$
f_1(x_1, \ldots, x_n) = \prod_{i=1}^{l} \left[\left(\prod_{p=n_{i-1}+1}^{n_i} x_p \right) + \left(\prod_{p=n_{i-1}+1}^{n_i} \bar{x}_p \right) \right]
$$

where Π denotes AND, $n_0 = 0$, and $x_{n_{i-1}+1}$ is the first variable in the ith block of columns and x_{n_i} is the last. Also, l is the number of distinct blocks of columns and $l \leq 2^{r-1}$, since each block corresponds to an r-tuple with first component 1. Let

$$
f_2(x_1, \ldots, x_n) = \sum_{q=1}^{r} \prod_{i=1}^{l} x_{n_i}^{\sigma_{q,n_i}}
$$

where Σ denotes OR and σ_{q,n_i} is the value of x_{n_i} in the qth row of the matrix. Then, with the convention $x^1 = x$, $x^0 = \bar{x}$, $x_{n_i}^{\sigma_{q,n_i}} = 1$ when $x_{n_i} = \sigma_{q,n_i}$, and the qth product is 1 whenever $(x_1, \ldots, x_n)$ is the qth row of the matrix. Furthermore, a straightforward expansion of $f_1 \cdot f_2$ shows that it is 1 exactly when $(x_1, \ldots, x_n)$ is a row of the above matrix; thus, we can write

$$f = f_1 \cdot f_2$$

It follows that

$$L_\Omega^*(f) \leq L_\Omega^*(f_1) + L_\Omega^*(f_2) + 1$$

Also,

$$L_\Omega^*(f_1) \leq l - 1 + 2 \sum_{i=1}^{l} (n_i - n_{i-1} - 1) + l$$

$$= 2l - 1 + 2(n_l - l) = 2n_l - 1 = 2n - 1$$

and

$$L_\Omega^*(f_2) \leq r - 1 + r(l - 1) = rl - 1 \leq r2^{r-1} - 1$$

from which the conclusion follows. ☐

Lemma 3.4.2. Let $r \geq (\log_2 n)^2$. Then there is a real-valued function $\psi(n)$ with the property that $\psi(n) \to 0$ as $n \to \infty$ such that

$$L^*(r, n) \leq \frac{2nr}{\log_2 n} (1 + \psi(n))$$

Proof. Partition the r points on which a function $f: \{0, 1\}^n \to \{0, 1\}$ has value 1 into $\lfloor r/r_0 \rfloor$ blocks of r_0 points and one block of $r_1 = r - r_0 \lfloor r/r_0 \rfloor$ points. Then apply the upper bound of Lemma 3.4.1 to each block and combine the blocks with $\lfloor r/r_0 \rfloor$ OR's. It follows that

$$L^*(r, n) \leq \left(2n - 1 + r_0 2^{r_0 - 1}\right) \left\lfloor \frac{r}{r_0} \right\rfloor$$

$$+ \left(2n - 1 + r_1 2^{r_1 - 1}\right) + \left\lfloor \frac{r}{r_0} \right\rfloor$$

Note that $r_1 \leq r_0$ and choose $r_0 = \lceil \log_2(n/(\log_2 n)^2) \rceil$. For n large, $r_0 \ll r$ and the conclusion follows from easy algebraic manipulations. ☐

We are now prepared to derive an upper bound to the formula size of an arbitrary Boolean function $f: \{0, 1\}^n \to \{0, 1\}$. Returning to the (k, s)-Lupanov representation for f, we have

$$L_\Omega^*(f) \leq \sum_{i=1}^{p} \sum_{\mathbf{v} \neq 0} \left(L_\Omega^*(f_{i,\mathbf{v}}^{(r)}) + L_\Omega^*(f_{i,\mathbf{v}}^{(c)})\right) + 2p2^s + p - 1$$

Given i, the sum over $\mathbf{v} \neq 0$ is the sum over s-tuples $\mathbf{v}$ such that f has this set of values for $(x_1, \ldots, x_k) \in A_i$. Let $q_i(r)$ be the number of these s-tuples $\mathbf{v}$ that occur r times in the columns of the table of Figure 3.4.1. Then $\sum_r q_i(r) \leq 2^s$ and $\sum_r r q_i(r) = 2^{n-k}$.

The contribution of $f_{i,\mathbf{v}}^{(r)}$ to the bound on $L_\Omega^*(f)$ is bounded by

$$\sum_{i=1}^{p} \sum_{\mathbf{v} \neq 0} L_\Omega^*(f_{i,\mathbf{v}}^{(r)}) < pks2^s$$

The contribution of $f_{i,\mathbf{v}}^{(c)}$ is bounded by the following expressions where $m = n - k$:

$$\sum_{i=1}^{p} \sum_{\mathbf{v} \neq 0} L_\Omega^*(f_{i,\mathbf{v}}^{(c)}) \leq \sum_{i=1}^{p} \sum_{r} L^*(r, m)q_i(r)$$

$$\leq \sum_i \sum_{r < (\log_2 m)^2} L^*(r, m)q_i(r) + \sum_i \sum_{r \geqslant (\log_2 m)^2} L^*(r, m)q_i(r)$$

$$\leq \sum_i \sum_{r < (\log_2 m)^2} (rm - 1)q_i(r) + \sum_i \sum_{r \geqslant (\log_2 m)^2} \frac{2rm}{\log_2 m}(1 + \psi(m))q_i(r)$$

$$\leq \sum_i \sum_r q_i(r)m(\log_2 m)^2 + \sum_i \sum_r \frac{2m}{\log_2 m}(1 + \psi(m))rq_i(r)$$

$$\leq p2^s m(\log_2 m)^2 + p\frac{2m2^m}{\log_2 m}(1 + \psi(m))$$

Therefore,

$$L_\Omega^*(f) \leq pks2^s + p2^s m(\log_2 m)^2 + p\frac{2m2^m}{\log_2 m}(1 + \psi(m)) + 2p2^s + p - 1$$

Now choose $k = \lceil 2\log_2 n \rceil$, $s = \lceil n - 3\log_2 n \rceil$. Recognizing that

$$p \leq \left(\frac{2^k}{s} + 1\right)$$

we have the following:

Theorem 3.4.4. For $0 < \varepsilon < 1$ there exists $N(\varepsilon) \geq 1$ such that for $n \geq N(\varepsilon)$ all $f:\{0, 1\}^n \to \{0, 1\}$ have

$$L_\Omega^*(f) \leq \frac{2^{n+1}}{\log_2 n}(1 + \varepsilon)$$

where $\Omega = \{+, \cdot, ^-\}$.

This completes our bounds on combinational complexity and formula size. We see that almost all $f:\{0, 1\}^n \to \{0, 1\}$ have combinational complexity that is within a small factor of $(2^n/n)(1 + \varepsilon)$ and formula size that is within a factor of 2 of $[2^n/(\log_2 n)](1 + \varepsilon)$. The "almost all" lower bounds on formula size and combinational complexity are due originally to Riordan and Shannon (1942) and Shannon (1949), respectively. The upper bounds are due to Lupanov (1958), but the first upper bound on combinational complexity is due to Shannon (1949), who had a slightly weaker coefficient.

3.5. SYNCHRONOUS COMBINATIONAL COMPLEXITY

In this section, we examine an important complexity measure that is closely related to combinational complexity and for which nonlinear lower bounds can be obtained. The measure was introduced by Harper (1975b) and is called synchronous combinational complexity.

Shown in Figure 3.5.1a) is a circuit with three inputs and two logic elements. If each logic element introduces one unit of delay, then when all three inputs are simultaneously applied, the second logic element does not receive all of its inputs at the same time. In Figure 3.5.1b is shown the same circuit with a unit delay element introduced so that signals arrive at the same time at each logic element. The second circuit is called *synchronous*. In general, a synchronous combinational machine is a logic circuit that contains delay elements for which a *rank function* can be defined such that the input nodes have rank 0 and elements (logic or delay) at rank $j \geq 1$ receive inputs only from elements at rank $j - 1$.

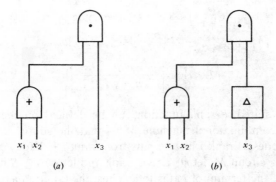

Figure 3.5.1. Combinational machine (a) and its synchronous equivalent (b).

A *race condition* is said to occur in a logic circuit if it is not synchronous, because the circuit outputs may change several times before settling down to their final values. For this reason alone, it is desirable to have synchronous circuits.

Definition 3.5.1. Let Ω be a set of Boolean functions. Then the *synchronous combinational complexity* of $f:\{0, 1\}^n \to \{0, 1\}^m$ relative to Ω, denoted $C_\Omega^s(f)$, is the minimum number of delay elements and elements from Ω needed to realize f with a synchronous combinational machine.

We develop a method for lower bounding the synchronous combinational complexity of functions $f:\{0, 1\}^n \to \{0, 1\}^m$. This work is reported in Harper and Savage (1976) and extends the results of Harper (1975b). In the latter paper, it is shown that if $f:\{0, 1\}^n \to \{0, 1\}$ is in $P_{p,q}^{(n)}$ (see Section 2.4.2) where $q = 2^{\alpha p}$, $0 < \alpha \leq 1$ and $p \geq n - n^c$, $0 < c < 1$, then $C_\Omega^s(f) \geq \alpha(1 - c)n \log_2 n$ when Ω has fan-in of 2. Harper (1975a) has shown that for $0 < \tau < \frac{1}{2}$, almost all $f: \{0, 1\}^n \to \{0, 1\}$ are in $P_{p,\,\tau p}^{(n)}$ for p a solution of $p2^p = 2^n$ and n sufficiently large, that is, for $p \approx n - \log_2 n$. Thus, there are many functions for which $C_\Omega^s(f)$ is nonlinear in the number of variables.

We extend the class of functions $P_{p,q}^{(n)}$ and derive a lower bound to the synchronous combinational complexity of functions in the new class.

Definition 3.5.2. The class of functions $P_{p,q}^{(n,m)}(\varepsilon)$, $0 < \varepsilon < 1$, is defined as $P_{p,q}^{(n,m)} = \{ f: \{0, 1\}^n \to \{0, 1\}^m |$ for all but a fraction ε of the subsets $J \subset \{1, 2, \ldots, n\}$, $|J| = p$; there exist $c_j \in \{0, 1\}, j \in J$, such that there are at least q distinct subfunctions $f \big|_{\substack{x_j = c_j \\ j \in J}} \}$.

The lower bound is stated in the following theorem, the proof of which depends on two succeeding lemmas.

Theorem 3.5.1. Let Ω have fan-in 2 and let $f \in P_{p,\,q}^{(n,m)}(\varepsilon)$. Then

$$C_\Omega^s(f) \geq (1 - \varepsilon)(L - 2)\log_2 q$$

where $L \leq D_\Omega(f)$ and

$$L < \log_2 \left[\frac{p}{2(n - p) + 1} \right]$$

As already stated, a rank function can be defined on the nodes of a synchronous combinational machine M so that the source nodes S have rank 0 and nodes at rank j have inputs from rank $j - 1$ for $j \geq 1$. If v is a node of such a circuit M, let $r(v)$ be its rank and let $s(v) \subseteq S$ be the source nodes that are the termini of paths to v. Thus, the function associated with v could depend on all the source nodes in $s(v)$.

Let N_l be the nodes in a synchronous combinational machine M at rank l, let $n_l = |N_l|$, and let $\bar{}_l F : \{0, 1\}^n \to \{0, 1\}^{n_l}$ be the function that maps the $n_0 = n$ inputs onto the n_l nodes at rank l in M. Let $\bar{}_l^+ F : \{0, 1\}_l^n \to \{0, 1\}^m$ be the function that maps the outputs of nodes at rank l onto the circuit outputs. Then

$$f = {}_l^+ F \circ {}_l^- F$$

where $\circ$ denotes functional composition. It is easy to show that if $f \in P_{p,q}^{(n,m)}(\varepsilon)$, then ${}_l^- F \in P_{p,q}^{(n,n_l)}(\varepsilon)$.

Lemma 3.5.1. Let M be a synchronous combinational machine for $f \in P_{p,q}^{(n,m)}(\varepsilon)$ and let $J \subset \{1, 2, \ldots, n\}$, $|J| = p$. For all but a fraction ε of such subsets J,

$$\sum_{\substack{v \in M \\ r(v) = l}} \min\{i(v), 2^{j(v)}\} \geq \log_2 q$$

for $0 \leq l \leq d$ where d is the rank of the outputs and

$$i(v) = |J \cap s(v)|$$

$$j(v) = |J^c \cap s(v)|$$

where $J^c = \{1, 2, \ldots, n\} - J$.

Proof. Consider the nodes $v \in N_l$. By fixing J, we can fix the variables in $J \cap s(v)$ of the function associated with v. The number of subfunctions of this function is clearly at most $2^{i(v)}$. Also, this function has at most $j(v)$ remaining variables, so the number of its subfunctions is at most $2^{2^{j(v)}}$. Finally, the number of subfunctions of ${}_l^- F$ obtained by fixing the variables in J is at most

$$\prod_{v \in N_l} \min\{2^{i(v)}, 2^{2^{j(v)}}\}$$

where $\prod$ denotes integer multiplication. Taking logarithms and noting that ${}_l^- F \in P_{p,q}^{(n,n_l)}(\varepsilon)$, we have the desired result. $\qquad\square$

From this lemma we conclude that

$$\log_2 q \leq \sum_{v \in N_l} 2^{|J^c \cap s(v)|}$$

for all but a fraction ε of the sets J of size p. The next lemma derives an upper bound to the sum that applies to a fraction of greater than ε of the sets J. Thus, there is some set J to which both the upper and lower bounds apply. In the proof of this lemma we use some simple ideas from probability theory.

Lemma 3.5.2. Let M be a synchronous combinational machine for $f:\{0, 1\}^n \to \{0, 1\}^m$ over Ω of fan-in 2. Let $0 < \varepsilon < 1$ and let $J \subset \{1, 2, \ldots, n\}$, $|J| = p$. For a fraction greater than ε of these sets and for all $v \in N_l$,

$$\sum_{v \in N_l} 2^{|J^c \cap s(v)|} \leq \frac{n_l}{(1 - \varepsilon)\{1 - (2(n - p)2^l)/(p - 2^l)\}}$$

if $2(n - p)2^l < p - 2^l$.

Proof. Since v has rank l and Ω has fan-in 2, $|s(v)| \leq 2^l$. Let $e = 2^l$ and consider the random variable

$$\chi_E(J^c) = 2^{|J^c \cap E|}$$

where J is given a uniform distribution and $|J| = p$. The set E denotes a set $s(v)$ for some v and $|E| \leq e$. We derive an upper bound to $\chi_E(J^c)$ that holds for a fraction greater than ε of the sets J, so we may assume that $|E| = e$ and further over bound the value of this random variable.

The mean of χ_E, namely μ_E, is given by

$$\mu_E = \frac{1}{\binom{n}{n - p}} \sum_k \binom{e}{k}\binom{n - e}{n - p - k}2^k$$

where k is such that $0 \leq k \leq e$ and $0 \leq n - p - k \leq n - e$. The ratio of two consecutive binomial coefficients is

$$\frac{\binom{a}{j + 1}}{\binom{a}{j}} = \frac{a - j}{j + 1}$$

and the ratio of two consecutive terms in μ_E is

$$R_k = \frac{e - k}{k + 1} \frac{(n - p - k)}{(p - e + k + 1)} 2$$

This ratio is largest at $k = 0$. Also,

$$R_0 = \frac{2e(n-p)}{p-e+1} < \frac{2e(n-p)}{p-e} = \alpha$$

Therefore, if $\alpha < 1$

$$\mu_E \leq \frac{\binom{n-e}{n-p}}{\binom{n}{n-p}} \sum_{k=0}^{\infty} \alpha^k$$

$$\leq \frac{1}{1-\alpha}$$

By the linearity of $\sum_{|E|=e} \chi_E(J^c)$, the average of this expression, μ_Σ, satisfies

$$\mu_\Sigma \leq \frac{n_l}{1 - \dfrac{2(n-p)e}{p-e}} = \bar{\mu}_\Sigma$$

Finally, we employ Markov's inequality, which states that

$$P_r[y \geq y_0] \leq \frac{\mu_y}{y_0}$$

for y a positive random variable and μ_y the average of the random variable y.

Now choose y to be $\sum \chi_E(J^c)$ and $y_0 = \bar{\mu}_\Sigma/(1-\varepsilon)$. Then

$$P_r\left[\sum_{\substack{E \\ |E|=e}} 2^{|J^c \cap E|} < \frac{n_l}{(1-\varepsilon)\left(1 - \dfrac{2(n-p)e}{p-e}\right)} \right] > \varepsilon$$

where $e = 2^l$. $\qquad\square$

Combining the two lemmas, we find that there exists $J \subset \{1, 2, \ldots, n\}$, $|J| = p$, such that

$$n_l \geq b_l = (1-\varepsilon)\left[1 - \frac{2(n-p)2^l}{p-2^l} \right] \log_2 q$$

Now let M be an optimal synchronous combinational machine for f. Then

$$C_\Omega^s (f) \geq \sum_{l=1}^{d} n_l \geq \sum_{l=1}^{L} n_l$$

where $L \leq d$, the depth of M and

$$L < \log_2\left[\frac{p}{2(n - p) + 1} \right]$$

Also,

$$b_l \geq (1 - \varepsilon)\left[1 - \frac{2(n - p)2^l}{p - 2^L} \right]\log_2 q$$

for $1 \leq l \leq L$, and we have

$$C_\Omega^s (f) \geq (1 - \varepsilon)(L - 2)\log_2 q$$

by the definition of L. This completes the proof of Theorem 3.5.1.

We now apply Theorem 3.5.1 to Boolean matrix multiplication of $r \times r$ matrices with addition that is EXCLUSIVE OR and multiplication that is AND. Let A and B be $r \times r$ matrices and let D be the product AB. This defines a function $f_{MM}^{(r)}:\{0, 1\}^{2r^2} \to \{0, 1\}^{r^2}$.

Theorem 3.5.2. $f_{MM}^{(r)} \in P_{p,q}^{(2r^2, r^2)}(\varepsilon)$ for $p = 2r^2 - [(2r - 1 + 1/r)(k + \ln 2r)]$, $q = 2^p$, and $\varepsilon = e^{-k}$ for $k > 0$.

Proof. Let $J \subset \{1, 2, \ldots, n\}$, $|J| = p$, be such that J^c intersects every column of A and every row of B. Let

$$f_{MM}\Big|_{j \in J}^{x_j = c_j} \quad \text{and} \quad f_{MM}\Big|_{j \in J}^{x_j = c'_j}$$

be two subfunctions where $c_j \neq c'_j$ for some $j \in J$. We show that the subfunctions are unequal. Assume that $c_j \neq c'_j$ for j in the kth row and lth column of B. Then the kth column of A contains a variable, say a_{ik}, and in one subfunction a_{ik} appears in the (i, l) position while in the other it is missing. By the uniqueness of the ring-sum expansion of a function (Problem 2-3), the two subfunctions are different. A similar argument applies to constants in A.

We now show that a fraction of at most ε of the subsets $J \subset \{1, 2, \ldots, n\}$, $|J| = p$, are such that J^c does not intersect every column of A and every row of B.

Let the sets J be given a uniform probability distribution and let a_k and b_l be the events that J^c does not intersect the kth column of A and the lth row of B, respectively. Then

$$Q = P_r\left[\bigcup_{k=1}^{r} a_k \cup \bigcup_{l=1}^{r} b_l\right] \leq \sum_{k=1}^{r} P_r(a_k) + \sum_{l=1}^{r} P_r(b_l)$$

and

$$P_r(a_k) = P_r(b_l) = \frac{\displaystyle\binom{2r^2 - r}{p^c}}{\displaystyle\binom{2r^2}{p^c}} < \left(1 - \frac{p^c}{(2r^2 - r + 1)}\right)^r$$

where $p^c = 2r^2 - p = |J^c|$. It follows from $(1 - a) \leq e^{-a}$, $a < 1$, that

$$Q < 2re^{-p^c r/(2r^2 - r + 1)} \leq e^{-k} = \varepsilon.$$

Corollary 3.5.1.   Let Ω have fan-in 2. Then

$$C_\Omega^s\left(f_{MM}^{(r)}\right) \geq (1 - \delta(r))2r^2\log_2 r$$

where $0 < \delta(r)$ and $\delta(r) \to 0$ as $r \to \infty$.

Proof.   Let $k = k(r) \to \infty$ slowly as r increases. $\square$

It is of interest to note that Strassen's algorithm for matrix multiplication, which is given in Section 8.2.2, applies to matrix multiplication as defined here. Furthermore, this algorithm can be realized in a synchronous combinational machine with on the order of $n^{\log_2 7}$ elements, about the same number of elements as used in a standard combinational machine. A similar lower bound can be derived for the determinant function (Problem 3-27).

Problems

3-1. Let $S_l(n) = \sum_{j=1}^{n} j^l$ where Σ denotes the integer summation operator. Show that the following identities hold:

(a) $S_1(n) = \dfrac{n(n + 1)}{2}$.

(b) $S_2(n) = \dfrac{n^3}{3} + \dfrac{n^2}{2} + \dfrac{n}{6}$.

(c) $S_3(n) = \dfrac{n^4}{4} + \dfrac{n^3}{2} + \dfrac{n^2}{4}$.

3-2. Improve on the bound of Theorem 3.1.1.3 to the number of two-input logic elements needed to implement integer multiplication by shifting and adding. Use the results of Problem 1, if necessary.

3-3. Construct a circuit over $P_{1,2}^{(2)}$ for shifting $x_0, x_1, \ldots, x_{n-1}$ by either 0 or k places. Show that the function $f_{SR}(\mathbf{a}, x_0, \ldots, x_{n-1})$ which shifts $x_0, \ldots, x_{n-1}$ right logically by an amount indicated by the binary number $\mathbf{a}$ has a combinational complexity over $P_{1,2}^{(2)}$ that is bounded above by $Kn \log_2 n$ for some constant $K > 0$.

3-4. Let $f_c^{(n)}:\{0, 1\}^n \to \{0, 1\}^k$, $k = [\log_2(n + 1)]$, be the *counting function* where

$$f_c(x_1, x_2, \ldots, x_n) = (y_{k-1}, y_{k-2}, \ldots, y_0) = \mathbf{y}$$

and $\mathbf{y}$ is the standard binary representation for the number of 1's among $x_1, x_2, \ldots, x_n$. Show that over the basis $\Omega = P_{1,2}^{(2)}$, $C_\Omega(f_c^{(n)}) \leq 5(n - 1)$ for all $n \geq 1$.

3-5. Show that the counting function $f_c^{(n)}$ has

$$D_\Omega(f_c^{(n)}) \leq 4\lceil \log_2(n + 1)\rceil - 5$$

over the basis $\Omega = \{+, \cdot, \oplus, ^-\}$.

Hint. Use the construction of Section 3.1.1 where the Full Adder circuit has been organized as shown in Figure 2.2.2. Show by induction that

$$D_\Omega(c_{i+1}^{(k)}) \leq 2(k + i) - 3, \qquad D_\Omega(s_i^{(k)}) \leq 2(k + i) - 4$$

for $1 \leq i \leq k - 1$ on the Full Adder chain that combines the value of the counting function on the first and second sets of $2^{k-1} - 1$ variables and x_n.

3-6. Use the results of Problem 5 to derive a good upper bound to the delay complexity of an arbitrary symmetric function.

3-7. Show that the first threshold function $\tau_1^{(n)}:\{0, 1\}^n \to \{0, 1\}$ can be written as

$$\tau_1(x_1, \ldots, x_n) = x_1 + \cdots + x_n$$

where $+$ denotes OR and the second threshold function $\tau_2^{(n)}:\{0, 1\}^n \to \{0, 1\}$ can be realized from the following expression when n is even:

$$\tau_2^{(n)}(x_1, \ldots, x_n) = \tau_1^{(n/2)}(x_1, \ldots, x_{n/2}) \cdot \tau_1^{(n/2)}(x_{n/2+1}, \ldots, x_n)$$

$$+ \tau_2^{(n/2)}(x_1, \ldots, x_{n/2}) + \tau_2^{(n/2)}(x_{n/2+1}, \ldots, x_n)$$

When $n = 2^k$, show that

$$C_\Omega(\tau_2^{(n)}) \leq 3n - 5$$

where $\Omega = \{+, \cdot\}$.

3-8. Demonstrate that every monotone Boolean functuon $f:\{0, 1\}^n \to \{0, 1\}$ can be expanded about its first variable in either of the following ways:

$$f(x_1, \ldots, x_n) = x_1 f(1, x_2, \ldots, x_n) + f(0, x_2, \ldots, x_n)$$

$$f(x_1, \ldots, x_n) = f(1, x_2, \ldots, x_n) \cdot (x_1 + f(0, x_2, \ldots, x_n))$$

3-9. Let $f:\{0, 1\}^n \to \{0, 1\}$ and $g:\{0, 1\}^n \to \{0, 1\}$ be monotone Boolean functions defined on *disjoint* variables. Show that an optimal AND, OR circuit for computing (f, g) consists of two disjoint circuits.

3-10. Derive a lower bound to the combinational complexity over $\Omega_m = \{+, \cdot\}$ of the function $f:\{0, 1\}^n \to \{0, 1\}^{n/2}$ define by $f(x_1, \ldots, x_n) = (\tau_1, \ldots, \tau_{n/2})$ where n is even and τ_j is the threshold function of threshold j.

3-11 Find the MDNF of the following functions:
(a) $(x_1 + x_4)(x_2 + x_3 + x_4)$.
(b) The threshold function $\tau_t^{(n)}:\{0, 1\}^n \to \{0, 1\}$.

3-12. (a) Show that Boolean matrix multiplication of a $u \times t$ matrix by a $t \times v$ matrix satisfies the three conditions on disjoint monotone bilinear forms.
(b) Do the same for the triangular matrix-vector multiplication problem of Section 3.2.3.

3-13. Show that Boolean matrix-vector multiplication by the $n \times n$ matrix

$$T = \begin{bmatrix} x_1 & x_2 & 0 & 0 & 0 & \cdots & 0 & 0 & 0 \\ x_3 & x_4 & x_5 & 0 & 0 & \cdots & 0 & 0 & 0 \\ 0 & x_6 & x_7 & x_8 & 0 & \cdots & 0 & 0 & 0 \\ & & & & \vdots & & & & \\ 0 & 0 & 0 & 0 & 0 & \cdots & 0 & x_{3n-3} & x_{3n-2} \end{bmatrix}$$

has a combinational complexity of $5n - 4$ over the monotone basis $\Omega_m = \{+, \cdot\}$.

3-14. Let $g:\{0, 1\}^n \to \{0, 1\}$ and $h:\{0, 1\}^n \to \{0, 1\}$ be monotone Boolean functions. Shown that $g \subseteq h(g$ implies $h)$ if and only if every product in the MDNF of g implies some product in the MDNF of h.

3-15. Establish the following two properties stated in Section 3.2.3, where $x_1, \ldots, x_k$ are variables and f_1 and f_2 are monotone Boolean functions:

P1. If $x_1 x_2 \subseteq f_1 + f_2$, then $x_1 x_2 \subseteq f_1$ or $x_1 x_2 \subseteq f_2$, or both.

P2. If $f_1 \cdot f_2 \subseteq x_1 + \cdots + x_k$, then $f_1 \subseteq x_1 + \cdots + x_k$ or $f_2 \subseteq x_1 + \cdots + x_k$, or both.

3-16. Consider a monotone circuit for the monotone Boolean functions $g_1, \ldots, g_m$ and let x be a variable of one or more of these functions. Assume that f is a (monotone) function computed by some node of this circuit and that f satisfies

$$x \subseteq f \subseteq x + f_{\text{dross}}$$

where f_{dross} is a monotone Boolean function with the property that none of the products in its MDNF implies g_1 or g_2 or $\cdots$ or g_m. Show that f can be replaced by x without changing the output functions $g_1, \ldots, g_m$.

3-17. (Lamagna, 1975.) Let $(S, +, \cdot)$ be an algebraic system with binary addition and multiplication operations denoted by $+$ and $\cdot$, respectively, over a finite set S. Suppose that:

(1) S is closed under $+$ and $\cdot$.

(2) There exists a unique element 0 in S such that for all a in S,
   (a) $0 + a = a + 0 = a$,
   (b) $0 \cdot a = a \cdot 0 = 0$.

(3) For all a and b in S,
   (a) $a + b \neq 0$ unless a and b are both 0,
   (b) $a \cdot b \neq 0$ unless either a, b, or both are 0.

Such an algebraic system is said to be *monotone mappable* since we can define a mapping θ from systems of this type onto the monotone Boolean algebra $(\{0, 1\}, \text{OR}, \text{AND})$ as follows:

$$\theta: (S, +, \cdot) \rightarrow (\{0, 1\}, \text{OR}, \text{AND})$$

where

(1) For the unique 0 in S, $\theta(0) = 0$.

(2) For all $a \neq 0$ in S, $\theta(a) = 1$.

This mapping is *homomorphic* because for all a and b in S,

$$\theta(a + b) = \theta(a) \text{ OR } \theta(b) \qquad \text{and} \qquad \theta(a \cdot b) = \theta(a) \text{ AND } \theta(b)$$

(a) Give two examples of algebraic systems that are monotone mappable.

(b) Let $f: S^n \to S^m$ be a function realized by a chain over $\{+, \cdot\}$ with constants and variables defined over S. Let $g:\{0, 1\}^n \to \{0, 1\}^m$ be the function obtained from f by applying the homomorphism θ. Show that the combinational complexity of f with respect to $\{+, \cdot\}$, $C_{\{+, \cdot\}}(f)$, is bounded below by the combinational complexity of g with respect to $\{OR, AND\}$, $C_{\{OR, AND\}}(g)$.

3-18. Show that addition and multiplication modulo 2^k can be realized by logic circuits with at most Kk^2 elements for some constant $K > 0$.

3-19 Let $r_j, s_j \geq 0$ for $1 \leq j \leq k$. Establish the Schwarz inequality, which states that

$$\left(\sum_{j=1}^{k} r_j s_j \right)^2 \leq \left(\sum_{j=1}^{k} r_j^2 \right) \left(\sum_{j=1}^{k} s_j^2 \right)$$

Hint. Use $\sum_{j=1}^{k}(a_j - b_j)^2 \geq 0$ and an appropriate substitution for a_j and b_j.

3-20. Derive a lower bound to the formula size over $\Omega_0 = \{+, \cdot, {}^-\}$ of

$$f(x_1, \ldots, x_n) = \begin{cases} 1 & \sum_{l=1}^{n} x_l = k \\ 0 & \sum_{l=1}^{n} x_l = k - 1 \end{cases}$$

where Σ denotes the integer sum. An example of such a function is a symmetric monotone threshold function of threshold k.

3-21. (Lamagna, 1975.) Let $f: \{0, 1\}^p \to \{0, 1\}$ be the monotone function defined as follows, where $p = n + \sqrt{n}(\sqrt{n} - 1)/2$ and n is a square. Derive good upper and lower bounds to its formula size over $\{+, \cdot, {}^-\}$.

Let the variables of f be $x_1, x_2, \ldots, x_n$ and $y_1, y_2, \ldots, y_q$ where $q = \sqrt{n}(\sqrt{n} - 1)/2$. Block the variables $x_1, \ldots, x_n$ into $\sqrt{n}$ equal size blocks of $\sqrt{n}$ variables where $B_i = \{x_{(i-1)\sqrt{n}+1}, \ldots, x_{i\sqrt{n}}\}$ for $1 \leq i \leq \sqrt{n}$. Let $h_j(x_1, \ldots, x_{\sqrt{n}})$, $1 \leq j \leq \sqrt{n}(\sqrt{n} - 1)/2$, be the set of Boolean functions on B_1 that are all the products (AND) of pairs of variables on B_1. For example, when $n = 9$, $\sqrt{n} = 3$, and

$$h_1 = x_1 x_2, \qquad h_2 = x_1 x_3, \qquad h_3 = x_2 x_3$$

then f is formed as follows:

$$f(x_1, \ldots, x_n, y_1, \ldots, y_q) = h_1(x_1, \ldots, x_{\sqrt{n}}) \cdot h_1(x_{\sqrt{n}+1}, \ldots, x_{2\sqrt{n}})$$

$$\cdot \cdots \cdot h_1(\cdots x_n) \cdot y_1$$

$$+ h_2(x_1, \ldots, x_{\sqrt{n}}) \cdot h_2(x_{\sqrt{n}+1}, \ldots, x_{2\sqrt{n}})$$

$$\cdot \cdots \cdot h_2(\cdots x_n) \cdot y_2$$

$$\vdots$$

$$+ h_q(x_1, \ldots, x_{\sqrt{n}}) \cdot h_q(x_{\sqrt{n}+1}, \ldots, x_{2\sqrt{n}})$$

$$\cdot \cdots \cdot h_q(\cdots x_n) \cdot y_q$$

Here $+$ denotes OR.

3-22. (Paul, 1975.) Consider the function $f_p: \{0, 1\}^n \to \{0, 1\}$ defined as follows:

$$s = 2^{2^l}, \quad l \text{ an integer}$$

$$n = \log_2 s - \log_2 \log_2 s + 2s$$

$$\mathbf{a} = (a_{k-1}, a_{k-2}, \ldots, a_0), \quad k = \log_2 s - \log_2 \log_2 s$$

$$\mathbf{x} = (x_1, x_2, \ldots, x_s), \quad \mathbf{y} = (y_0, y_1, \ldots, y_{s-1})$$

$$f_p(\mathbf{a}, \mathbf{x}, \mathbf{y}) = y_{|\mathbf{b}|}$$

where

$$|\mathbf{c}| = c_{p-1} 2^{p-1} + c_{p-2} 2^{p-2} + \cdots + c_0$$

for $\mathbf{c} = (c_{p-1}, \ldots, c_0)$ and

$$\mathbf{b} = (x_{|\mathbf{a}| \log_2 s + 1}, \ldots, x_{|\mathbf{a}| \log_2 s + \log_2 s})$$

(a) Show that

$$L_\Omega(f_p) \geq \tfrac{1}{2}\left(\tfrac{1}{4} \frac{s^2}{\log_2 s} - 1 \right) \cong \frac{1}{32} \frac{n^2}{\log_2 n} \quad \text{when } \Omega = P_{1,2}^{(2)}.$$

Hint. Block the variables of f_p in such a way that the variables $\mathbf{x}$ are blocked in a "natural" way.

(b) Show that f_p can be realized from the composition of functions

$$f_Q^{(k)}: \{0, 1\}^{k+2^k} \to \{0, 1\}$$

where

$$f_Q^{(k)}(c_{k-1}, \ldots, c_0, z_0, \ldots, z_{2^k-1}) = z_{|c|}, \qquad k = \log_2 s - \log_2 \log_2 s$$

Hint. Compute $f_Q^{(k)}(\mathbf{a}, x_l, x_{\log_2 s+l}, \ldots, x_{s-\log_2 s+l})$ for $1 \le l \le \log_2 s$ and apply the results to

$$f_Q^{(\log_2 s)}(d_{\log_2 s-1}, \ldots, d_0, \mathbf{y})$$

Use this to show that the combinational complexity of f_p over $P_{1,2}^{(2)}$ is linear in n.

3-23. Let $a_i \ge 0$. Show that the inequality

$$\frac{1}{n} \sum_{i=1}^{n} a_i \ge \prod_{i=1}^{n} a_i^{1/n}$$

holds between the arithmetic and geometric means. Here Σ and Π denote integer addition and multiplication.
Hint. Show that $\lambda + (1 - \lambda)c \ge c^{1-\lambda}$ for $c \ge 0$, $0 \le \lambda \le 1$.

3-24. Improve the lower bound of Theorem 3.3.3.1 to

$$L_\Omega(\tau_2^{(n)}) \ge n\lceil \log_2 n \rceil - 2$$

where n is not a power of 2 and $\Omega = \{+, \cdot, \bar{\ }\}$.
Hint. Show that $\lceil a + b \rceil \ge \lceil a \rceil + \lceil b \rceil - 1$.

3-25. Show that $L_\Omega(\tau_2^{(n)}) \le n\lceil \log_2 n \rceil - 2$ if $\Omega = \{+, \cdot\}$ and n is not a power of 2.

3-26. Derive "almost all" lower bounds to the combinational complexity and formula size of functions $f: \{0, 1\}^n \to \{0, 1\}^m$. Also derive upper bounds to these complexity measures for these functions and determine conditions on m and n such that the upper and lower bounds are close for large n.

3-27. Apply Theorem 3.5.1 to the determinant function of a Boolean matrix when addition is EXCLUSIVE OR and multiplication is AND.

Chapter 4

Sequential Machines

The sequential machine is a mathematical model for the digital machines with memory which we know how to build. Our excursion through the subject of sequential machines is brief and finishes with the derivation of a computational inequality which demonstrates that these machines are natural extensions of combinational machines, that is, logic circuits or graphs of chains. The reader interested in subjects that are not treated here, such as experiments on sequential machines and machine decomposition, is advised to see other sources such as Booth (1967), Harrison (1965), and Hennie (1968).

4.1. FINITE–STATE MACHINE MODEL

To some, a *sequential machine* S is a 5-tuple $S = \langle S, I, \delta, \lambda, O \rangle$ where S is a finite *state set*, I is the *input alphabet*, O is the *output alphabet*, and δ: $S \times I \to S$ and λ: $S \to O$ are the *transition and output functions*, respectively. That is, δ maps the current state and the input into a successor state, and λ maps the current state into the output. The time required to perform these maps is called a *cycle*. Others prefer to think of a sequential machine in terms of the units shown schematically in Figure 4.1.1. Here M is the *memory unit* which holds the current state, and L is the *logic unit* which maps the current state and input into the successor state and output. To us, this diagram *represents* the mathematical object defined in the first sentence of this paragraph; namely, L represents the simultaneous computation of the transition and output functions δ and λ, and M holds the current state.

The sequential machines defined are called *Moore machines* (Moore, 1956). *Mealy machines* (Mealy, 1955) differ from these in that the output function λ is potentially a function of the current input as well as of the current state, that is, λ: $S \times I \to O$. Although these machines appear to be

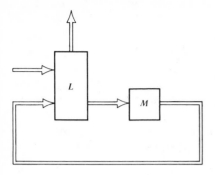

Figure 4.1.1. Schematic diagram of a sequential machine.

different (in particular, it may appear that Mealy machines are more general), it can be shown that for every Mealy machine there is an equivalent (in the sense defined in the next section) Moore machine, and vice versa.

It is often useful and convenient to have another representation of a sequential machine, namely, the *state diagram*. As shown in Figure 4.1.2, the diagram consists of circles and directed edges, with the edges labeled with input letters and the circles labeled with a state name, q_j, and an output letter. In this example, the states are numbered q_0, q_1, q_2 and represent the result of adding Boolean variables modulo 3. Thus, the machine state advances from q_0 to q_1, q_1 to q_2, or q_2 to q_0 when the input is 1, and the state remains unchanged when the input is 0. The output

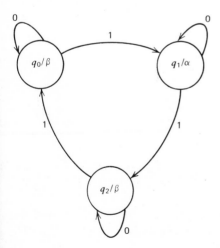

Figure 4.1.2. State diagram of a sequential machine.

alphabet $O = \{\alpha, \beta\}$, and the output is α if and only if the state is q_1. If the initial state is q_0, then the output is α if and only if the current sum of the inputs taken modulo 3 and then modulo 2 is 1. Thus, the function $f_{\text{mod } 3}^0$, introduced in Section 2.4, is "computed" by this machine with memory.

The information that is contained in such a state diagram can also be recorded in transition and output tables. A *transition table* is a tabular description of a transition function $\delta: S \times I \to S$, and an *output table* is a similar description of the output function $\lambda: S \to O$. For example, the sequential machine of Figure 4.1.2 is described by the Table 4.1.1.

Table 4.1.1. Transition and Output Tables of a Sequential Machine Where $S = \{q_0, q_1, q_2\}$, $I = \{0, 1\}$, and $O = \{\alpha, \beta\}$

	u	$\delta(q, u)$				q	$\lambda(q)$
	q	0	1				
δ	q_0	q_0	q_1		λ	q_0	β
	q_1	q_1	q_2			q_1	α
	q_2	q_2	q_0			q_2	β

The static descriptions of sequential machines shown in Table 4.1.1 provide the information required to determine their dynamic behavior. These descriptions can also be used to determine the results of a number of cycles of computation. If a sequential machine S executes T cycles of computation with q as its initial state and $u_1, u_2, \ldots, u_T$ as the inputs, then the $T + 1$ outputs $v_0, v_1, \ldots, v_T$ that are produced are defined by

$$v_0 = \lambda(q)$$

$$v_1 = \lambda(\delta(q, u_1))$$

$$v_j = \lambda\big(\delta^{(j)}(q, u_1, \ldots, u_j)\big)$$

where

$$\delta^{(1)} = \delta$$

and

$$\delta^{(j)}(q, u_1, \ldots, u_j) = \delta\big(\delta^{(j-1)}(q, u_1, \ldots, u_{j-1}), u_j\big)$$

That is, $\delta^{(j)}: S \times I^j \to S$ returns as value the state into which the machine enters after executing j cycles with initial state q and inputs $u_1, \ldots, u_j$. The function that maps $(q, u_1, \ldots, u_T)$ into $(v_0, \ldots, v_T)$ for the machine S is called the *descriptor function* (or more simply the *descriptor*) $G_{S,T}: S \times I^T \to O^{T+1}$. For the example shown in Figure 4.1.2, the descriptor function is

$$G_{S,T} = \left(c \bmod 2, f^{c,1}_{\bmod 3}, f^{c,2}_{\bmod 3}, \ldots, f^{c,T}_{\bmod 3} \right)$$

where

$$f^{c,n}_{\bmod 3} = \left(\left(\sum_{i=1}^{n} x_i + c \right) \bmod 3 \right) \bmod 2$$

the initial state is q_c, x_i is the value of the ith input, and α is identified with 1 and β with 0. Here Σ and $+$ denote integer addition.

The descriptor functions, simple though they may be, prove to be very important in this chapter and later chapters in the derivation of computational inequalities. The descriptors focus attention on sequential machines at a level of abstraction at which it is possible to extract certain fundamental relations between parameters of computation such as storage space and time.

The transition and output tables of Table 4.1.2 define a sequential machine of great importance. Here we have used a shorthand in which state q_i is replaced by the integer $i \in \{0, 1, 2, 3\}$. Then $S = \{q_0, q_1, q_2, q_3\}$, $I = \{0, 1, 2, 3\}$, and $O = \{0, 1\}$. The reader can readily verify that, with the normal binary encoding for inputs [e.g., 3 denotes $(1, 1)$] and states [e.g., q_2 denotes $(1, 0)$], the transition table represents a Full Adder for binary addition of integers (see Section 2.2). Here an input u represents a pair of binary digits (x_j, y_j), a state represents the previous sum and carry (s_{j-1}, c_{j-1}), and the successor state is the new sum and carry (s_j, c_j). Also, the output function maps the state (s_j, c_j) onto the sum digit s_j.

Table 4.1.2. Defining Tables for a Full Adder

	u		$\delta(q, u)$					q	$\lambda(q)$
q		0	1	2	3				
	0	0	2	2	1			0	0
	1	2	1	1	3			1	0
δ	2	0	2	2	1		λ	2	1
	3	2	1	1	3			3	1

With this explanation, it should be apparent that, if the initial state is q_0 and if the inputs $(x_0, y_0), (x_1, y_1), \ldots, (x_{n-1}, y_{n-1})$ are suitably encoded, then the n outputs are $s_0, s_1, \ldots, s_{n-1}$, that is, the digits in the binary encoding of the sum of the binary numbers $(x_0, x_1, \ldots, x_{n-1})$ and $(y_0, y_1, \ldots, y_{n-1})$ after disregarding the overflow bit c_n. Thus, from the descriptor, we have $G_{S,n}(q_0, (x_0, y_1), \ldots, (x_{n-1}, y_{n-1})) = (0, s_0, s_1, \ldots, s_{n-1})$.

We turn now to the issue of sequential machine equivalence and to the problem of finding a machine with fewest states that is equivalent to a given machine.

4.2 REDUCED MACHINES AND MACHINE EQUIVALENCE

Given two sequential machines $S_1 = \langle S_1, I_1, \delta_1, \lambda_1, O_1 \rangle$ and $S_2 = \langle S_2, I_2, \delta_2, \lambda_2, O_2 \rangle$, we might ask whether they are "equivalent" in the sense that as "black boxes" they exhibit the same input-output behavior. To answer such a question, a formal notion of machine equivalence is necessary.

Definition 4.2.1. Sequential machines S_1 and S_2 are *equivalent* if both of the following are true:

1. $I_1 = I_2$.
2. For each state $q \in S_1$, there exists a state $q' \in S_2$ such that for all $T \geq 1$ and all $u_i \in I_1$,

$$G_{S_1, T}(q, u_1, \ldots, u_T) = G_{S_2, T}(q', u_1, \ldots, u_T)$$

and vice versa.

Clearly this definition can be extended to machines for which $I_1 \neq I_2$ but in which they have the same size so that a 1-1 correspondence between the two input alphabets can be established.

It is infrequent in practice that two machines are tested for equivalence, primarily because a designer defines machines in such a way that their intended functions are well defined and it is clear whether two machines are equivalent or not. Also, machines of more than moderate size have so many states that comparing them for equivalence by using their transition and output functions is a task that often is beyond the power of our computing machines. For example, a 32-bit shift register has about 4×10^9 states, and to test each in one microsecond per test would require more than one hour. Also, a typical sequential machine has many shift-registers and other more complicated subunits.

Nevertheless, it is useful to examine one particular aspect of machine equivalence, namely, that of finding a reduced machine for a given machine. A *reduced sequential machine* is a machine for which no other equivalent machine has fewer states. We now present a procedure for constructing a reduced machine $r(S)$ equivalent to a given sequential machine S. This procedure requires on the order of $|S|^2$ computations to find $r(S)$. If a reduced machine is actually to be constructed, the procedure introduced by Hopcroft (1971), which uses on the order of $|S| \log_2 |S|$ computations, is of interest.

Definition 4.2.2. A *partition* Π of a set S is a disjoint set of subsets (or classes) of S that exhaust S. That is,

$$S = \bigcup_{j=1}^{p} s_j, \qquad s_i \cap s_j = \phi$$

A partition Π of S defines an *equivalence relation* on S in which σ and $\sigma' \in S$ are said to be *equivalent*, written $\sigma \Pi \sigma'$, if and only if they are members of the same *equivalence class* or subset of S. We write $\sigma \not\!\Pi \sigma'$ if σ and σ' are not equivalent under the equivalence relation Π.

The procedure that we present for determining a reduced machine (there may be many) for a sequential machine $S = \langle S, I, \delta, \lambda, O \rangle$ invokes equivalence relations $\Pi_1, \Pi_2, \ldots$, on the state set S. The relation Π_0 is defined by

$$q \Pi_0 q' \Leftrightarrow \lambda(q) = \lambda(q')$$

(Here $\Leftrightarrow$ denotes "if and only if".) And Π_j, $j \geq 1$, is defined by

$$q \Pi_j q' \Leftrightarrow q \Pi_{j-1} q' \quad \text{and} \quad \delta(q, u) \Pi_{j-1} \delta(q', u) \qquad \text{for all } u \in I$$

Clearly, $q \Pi_1 q'$ if and only if $G_{S,1}(q, u) = G_{S,1}(q', u)$ for all $u \in I$. Similarly, $q \Pi_j q'$ if and only if $G_{S,j}(q, u_1, u_2, \ldots, u_j) = G_{S,j}(q', u_1, u_2, \ldots, u_j)$ for all $u_1, \ldots, u_j \in I$. This implies that q and q' cannot be distinguished by j or fewer inputs to S and that they cannot be distinguished in the absence of input. States equivalent under Π_j are called *j-equivalent*.

Note that Π_j is a refinement of Π_{j-1}; that is, $q \Pi_j q'$ implies that $q \Pi_{j-1} q'$. Thus, the subsets of Π_j are each contained in the subsets of Π_{j-1}. It follows that the number of equivalence classes of Π_j, denoted $|\Pi_j|$, satisfies

$$|\Pi_{j-1}| \leq |\Pi_j| \leq |S|$$

where $|S|$ is the cardinality of the state set S. The latter inequality is a consequence of the fact that no partition can separate S into more than $|S|$ disjoint subsets.

Since $|\Pi_1| \leq |\Pi_2| \leq \cdots \leq |\Pi_j| \leq |\Pi_{j+1}| \leq |S|$, it follows that there exists an integer k such that $|\Pi_{k+1}| = |\Pi_k|$, and since Π_{k+1} refines Π_k, we have that

$$\Pi_{k+1} = \Pi_k$$

We now show that $\Pi_j = \Pi_k$ for all $j \geq k$.

Lemma 4.2.1. Let Π_j, $j \geq 1$, be the equivalence relation defined above on the sequential machine $S = \langle S, I, \delta, \lambda, O \rangle$. There exists an integer k such that $\Pi_j = \Pi_k$ for all $j \geq k$.

Proof. The proof is by induction. We wish to show that $\Pi_{j+1} = \Pi_j$ implies that $\Pi_{j+2} = \Pi_{j+1}$. To prove this, we assume that $\Pi_{j+2} \neq \Pi_{j+1}$ and demonstrate that a contradiction results.

If $\Pi_{j+2} \neq \Pi_{j+1}$, since Π_{j+2} is a refinement of Π_{j+1}, there exist states q, q' such that $q\Pi_{j+1}q'$ and $q\rlap{/}{\Pi}_{j+2}q'$. From the definition of the equivalence relations, this implies that $\delta(q, u)\rlap{/}{\Pi}_{j+1}\delta(q', u)$ for some $u \in I$. Since $\Pi_{j+1} = \Pi_j$, this also means that $\delta(q, u)\rlap{/}{\Pi}_j\delta(q', u)$ for some $u \in I$.

On the other hand, $q\Pi_{j+1}q'$, and we have

$$q\Pi_{j+1}q' \Leftrightarrow q\Pi_j q' \qquad \text{and} \qquad \delta(q, u)\Pi_j\delta(q', u) \qquad \text{for all } u \in I$$

Since $\Pi_{j+1} = \Pi_j$, it follows that $\delta(q, u)\Pi_j\delta(q', u)$ for all $u \in I$, in contradiction to the conclusion reached above. Since $\Pi_{k+1} = \Pi_k$, we conclude that $\Pi_j = \Pi_k$, $j \geq k$. $\qquad\qquad\square$

The partition Π_k of S such that $\Pi_k = \Pi_{k+1}$ defines a reduced machine $r(S)$. Let $s_1, s_2, \ldots, s_p$ be the equivalence classes of Π_k. Then it follows from the definition of Π_k that for each $1 \leq j \leq p$ and any two states q, $q' \in s_j$, and for all $u \in I$, $\delta(q, u)$ and $\delta(q', u)$ are in the same equivalence class. Thus, we can unambiguously define the transition function

$$\delta_r: \{s_1, s_2, \ldots, s_p\} \times I \to \{s_1, s_2, \ldots, s_p\}$$

by $\delta_r(s_j, u) = s_i$, where s_i is such that $\delta(q, u) \in s_i$ for all $q \in s_j$. Similarly, since Π_k refines Π_0, we can unambiguously define the output function

$$\lambda_r: \{s_1, s_2, \ldots, s_p\} \to O$$

by $\lambda_r(s_j) = \lambda(q)$ for all $q \in s_j$.

Theorem 4.2.1. The reduced sequential machine $r(S) = \langle \{s_1, \ldots, s_p\}, I, \delta_r, \lambda_r, O \rangle$ is equivalent to $S = \langle S, I, \delta, \lambda, O \rangle$, and no other machine equivalent to S has fewer states.

Proof. To show that $r(S)$ and S are equivalent, choose any state $q \in S$. We show that the state s_j or $r(S)$ that, as a subset of S, contains q is such that

$$\lambda(q) = \lambda_r(s_j)$$

and for all $T \geq 1$ and all $u_i \in I$,

$$G_{S,T}(q, u_1, \ldots, u_T) = G_{r(S),T}(s_j, u_1, \ldots, u_T)$$

The first statement follows from the definition of λ_r and the fact that Π_k refines Π_0. The second follows from the fact that for all $T \geq 1$ and all $u_i \in I$,

$$G_{S,T}(q, u_1, \ldots, u_T) = G_{S,T}(q', u_1, \ldots, u_T)$$

for any two states q, q' such that $q\Pi_k q'$.

Also, for any $s_j \in r(S)$, choose a $q \in S$ such that $q \in s_j$ and the above properties also clearly hold. Therefore, S and $r(S)$ are equivalent.

Let M be another sequential machine equivalent to S. Clearly, M and $r(S)$ are also equivalent. Assume that M has fewer states than $r(S)$. Then, by the pigeonhole principle,[†] two states s_i and s_j of $r(S)$ are equivalent to some one state of M. Thus, s_i and s_j are equivalent states of $r(S)$, and the states of S in s_i and s_j are equivalent states of S. But if that is true, the states in s_i and s_j are equivalent under Π_k, in contradiction to the definition of Π_k. $\qquad\square$

To illustrate the preceding procedure for computing the reduced machine of a sequential machine S, consider the following example.

Example 4.2.1. Consider the sequential machine whose state diagram is given in Figure 4.2.1. It has state set $S = \{q_1, q_2, \ldots, q_9\}$, input alphabet $I = \{0, 1\}$, and output alphabet $O = \{0, 1, 2\}$. If the first five inputs are labeled x, a_3, a_2, a_1, a_0, and the initial state is q_0, then the sixth output is 1 when $x = 0$ and $a_0 = 1$ or $x = 1$ and $a_3 \oplus a_2 \oplus a_1 \oplus a_0 = 1$. Thus, it computes $a_3 x^3 \oplus a_2 x^2 \oplus a_1 x \oplus a_0$ where $x^i = x$, $i \geq 1$.

Clearly,

$$\Pi_0 = \{(q_5, q_8), (q_6, q_9), (q_0, q_1, q_2, q_3, q_4, q_7)\}$$

[†] The *pigeonhole principle* states that if $n + 1$ or more pigeons are put into n pigeonholes, then some hole has at least two pigeons.

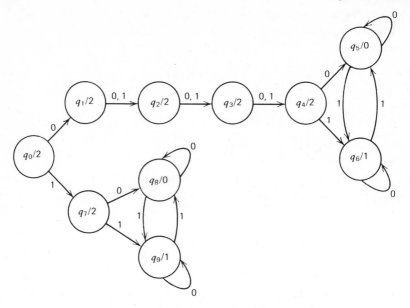

Figure 4.2.1. A sequential machine state diagram.

It follows that

$$\Pi_1 = \{(q_5, q_8), (q_6, q_9), (q_0, q_1, q_2, q_3), (q_4, q_7)\}$$

$$\Pi_2 = \{(q_5, q_8), (q_6, q_9), (q_0), (q_1, q_2), (q_3), (q_4, q_7)\}$$

$$\Pi_3 = \{(q_5, q_8), (q_6, q_9), (q_0), (q_1), (q_2), (q_3), (q_4, q_7)\}$$

$$\Pi_4 = \Pi_3$$

so that in $r(S)$, states q_4 and q_7 are identified, as are states q_5, q_8 and q_6, q_9. Thus, $r(S)$ has seven states.

This method for constructing reduced machines was introduced by Huffman (1954) and Moore (1956).

This completes our discussion of machine equivalence and reduced machines. We turn now to a characterization of machines in terms of the language of regular expressions.

4.3. REGULAR EXPRESSIONS AND SEQUENTIAL MACHINES

The language of regular expressions developed in this section provides another way of describing the computations that can be carried out by sequential machines. Regular expressions are especially useful for stating recognition tasks which can then be translated into sequential machines that act as recognizers of strings. For example, the set $R = (0, 1)^*(101)(0, 1)^* \cap \overline{((0, 1)^*(11))}$ is a regular expression that describes those binary strings which contain the substring 101 but which do not end in 11. In Section 4.3.3, a six-state sequential machine is derived that generates an output of 1 if such a string is given to it and an output of 0 otherwise.

Kleene (1956) introduced regular expressions and demonstrated the correspondence between regular expressions and sequential machines. Our demonstration of this correspondence makes use of derivatives of regular expressions and follows the development of Brzozowski (1964).

4.3.1. Regular Expressions and Their Derivatives

Let I be a finite set (which corresponds to the input alphabet of a sequential machine). A regular expression over I describes a finite or infinite set of strings over the set I. Such sets of strings are described by the application of three different types of operations on sets, namely, concatenation, star operation, and Boolean functions.

To define these operations, we introduce the *empty set* $\emptyset$, the *empty string* λ,[†] and *string concatenation*. The empty set $\emptyset$ contains no elements, and λ is the string over I containing no characters. The concatenation of two strings **p** and **q** over I, denoted **pq**, is the string of characters over I consisting of those of **p** followed by those of **q**. The empty string λ has the property that for any string **p** (including the empty string), $\lambda \mathbf{p} = \mathbf{p}\lambda = \mathbf{p}$.

If P and Q are two sets of strings over I, then the three types of operations are defined as follows:

Concatenation. $P \cdot Q = \{s \mid s = \mathbf{pq}, \ \mathbf{p} \in P, \ \mathbf{q} \in Q\}$.

Star Operation. $\cdot P^* = \bigcup_{n=0}^{\infty} P^n$ where $P^n = P \cdot P^{n-1}$, $P^0 = (\lambda)$ (the set containing the empty string), and $\cup$ denotes set union.

Set Operations. Let $\cap$, $\cup$ denote set intersection and union, and let $^-$ denote set complementation with respect to I^*, the set of all strings over I. Then $\overline{P}$ is the set of strings over I that are not in P.

[†] The reader should not confuse this use of λ with its use in preceding sections. There it was used to denote a transition function.

The • which denotes concatenation may be omitted for convenience. Note that this operation is associative but that it is not commutative. Also, the star operation P^* defines an infinite set if P contains a string of finite but nonzero length. Also, $P \cdot \emptyset = \emptyset$.

We are now prepared to define regular expressions.[†]

Definition 4.3.1.1. *Regular expressions* are defined recursively by the following rules:

1. Sets consisting of the individual elements of I and the sets $\emptyset$ and (λ) are regular expressions.
2. If P and Q are regular expressions, then so are $P \cdot Q$, P^*, $P \cap Q$, $P \cup Q$, and $\bar{P}$.
3. There are no other regular expressions except those that result from a finite number of applications of the first two rules.

Example 4.3.1.1. The example given in the opening paragraph of Section 4.3, namely, $R = (0, 1)^*(101)(0, 1)^* \cap \overline{((0, 1)^*(11))}$, is a regular expression over $I = (0, 1)$ that consists of those strings in $P = I^*(101)I^*$ that are not in $Q = I^*(11)$. These are the strings containing the substring 101 but not ending in the substring 11.

Later a procedure is given to construct sequential machines that correspond to regular expressions. This procedure makes use of derivatives of regular expressions, which are relatively simple objects defined as follows:

Definition 4.3.1.2. Let s be a string over I. The *derivative* D_sR *of the regular expression* R *with respect to* s is defined by

$$D_sR = \{\, t \mid st \in R \,\}$$

That is, D_sR is the set of suffixes of strings in R that have s as their prefix.

To develop some of the properties of derivatives, we now make the following:[‡]

Definition 4.3.1.3. If R is a subset of I^*, then $\delta(R)$ is defined by

$$\delta(R) = \begin{cases} (\lambda), & \text{if } \lambda \in R \\ \emptyset, & \text{if } \lambda \notin R \end{cases}$$

[†] Strictly speaking, regular expressions are formulas that describe sets called *regular sets*. Since this distinction is not important for our purposes, we shall refer to regular sets by the expressions that define them.

[‡] The reader should also note this use of δ, which differs from its use in preceding sections. Context always determines the proper interpretation of δ and λ.

It is apparent that if u is any element in I, then $\delta((u)) = \varnothing$. Also, $\delta((\lambda)) = (\lambda)$, $\delta(\varnothing) = \varnothing$, $\delta(P^*) = (\lambda)$, and $\delta(P \cdot Q) = \delta(P) \cap \delta(Q)$. It is also easily demonstrated that

$$\delta(P \cup Q) = \delta(P) \cup \delta(Q)$$

$$\delta(P \cap Q) = \delta(P) \cap \delta(Q)$$

$$\delta(\overline{P}) = \begin{cases} (\lambda), & \text{if } \delta(P) = \varnothing \\ \varnothing, & \text{if } \delta(P) = (\lambda) \end{cases}$$

With the aid of the function δ, we are prepared to develop properties of the derivative operator.

Theorem 4.3.1.1. Let $u \in I$ and let P, Q be subsets of I^*. Then

$$D_u(u) = (\lambda)$$

$$D_u(u') = \varnothing \text{ for } u' = \varnothing \text{ or } (\lambda) \text{ or } u' = (b), b \in I, b \neq u$$

$$D_u(P \cup Q) = D_u(P) \cup D_u(Q)$$

$$D_u(P \cap Q) = D_u(P) \cap D_u(Q)$$

$$D_u(\overline{P}) = \overline{D_u(P)}$$

$$D_u(P \cdot Q) = (D_u P) \cdot Q \cup \delta(P) \cdot D_u(Q)$$

$$D_u(P^*) = (D_u P) \cdot P^*$$

Proof. The first two results follow directly from the definition of derivatives. The next two are easy consequences of the definitions. Consider, then, the relation

$$D_u(\overline{P}) = \overline{D_u(P)}$$

This is a consequence of the following results:

$$(D_u P) \cup (D_u \overline{P}) = D_u(P \cup \overline{P}) = D_u(I^*) = I^*$$

$$(D_u P) \cap (D_u \overline{P}) = D_u(P \cap \overline{P}) = D_u(\varnothing) = \varnothing$$

Therefore, the union of $D_u P$ and $D_u \overline{P}$ is I^*, but they are nonintersecting, or $D_u P$ is the complement of $D_u \overline{P}$.

Consider next $D_u(P \cdot Q)$. Any string in PQ that begins with u is a string $\mathbf{pq}$ with $\mathbf{p} \in P$, $\mathbf{q} \in Q$, and $\mathbf{p}$ begins with u or $\mathbf{q}$ begins with u if $\mathbf{p} = \boldsymbol{\lambda}$. The fourth equation then follows.

Concerning the last equation of Theorem 4.3.1.1, we observe that the derivative of a countable union of sets is the countable union of the derivatives of the sets. It follows that

$$D_u P^* = D_u \left(\bigcup_{n=0}^{\infty} P^n \right) = \bigcup_{n=0}^{\infty} D_u(P^n)$$

$$D_u(\lambda) = \varnothing$$

$$D_u P^n = D_u(P \cdot P^{n-1}) = (D_u P)P^{n-1} \cup \delta(P)D_u(P^{n-1})$$

If $\delta(P) = \varnothing$, the second term is absorbed in the first. If $\delta(P) = (\lambda)$, the second term is equal to $D_u(P^{n-1})$, which is the preceding term in the countable union. It follows that

$$D_u P^* = \bigcup_{n=1}^{\infty} (D_u P^n) = \bigcup_{n=1}^{\infty} (D_u P)P^{n-1} = (D_u P)P^* \qquad \square$$

This theorem develops the properties of derivatives of regular expressions with respect to strings of single elements of I. The next theorem demonstrates that derivatives with respect to strings of more than one character can be obtained directly from derivatives with respect to individual characters.

Theorem 4.3.1.2. Let $s = a_1 a_2 \cdots a_r$ be a string over I and let R be a regular expression over I. Then

$$D_s R = D_{a_r}(D_{a_1 \cdots a_{r-1}} R) = D_{a_r}(D_{a_{r-1}}(\cdots (D_{a_1} R) \cdots))$$

If $s = \lambda$, then $D_s R = D_\lambda R = R$.

The proof of this theorem is an immediate consequence of the definition of a derivative and is not given here. To illustrate these two theorems, consider the regular expression already introduced.

Example 4.3.1.2. Consider the regular expression $R = P \cap \overline{Q}$, $P = I^*(101)I^*$, $Q = I^*(11)$, which was discussed in the preceding example.

$$D_s R = D_s P \cap \overline{D_s Q}$$

This and the other properties of derivatives are used to construct the following list, which contains all the distinct derivatives of R.

$$D_\lambda R = R$$

$$*D_0 R = (D_0 P) \cap (\overline{D_0 Q}) = P \cap (\overline{Q}) = D_\lambda R = R$$

$$D_1 R = (I^*(101)I^* \cup 01I^*) \cap (\overline{I^*(11) \cup 1})$$

$$D_{10} R = D_0(D_1 R) = (I^*(101)I^* \cup 1I^*) \cap (\overline{I^*(11)})$$

$$D_{11} R = D_1(D_1 R) = (I^*(101)I^* \cup 01I^*) \cap (\overline{I^*(11) \cup 1 \cup \lambda})$$

$$*D_{100} R = D_0(D_{10} R) = (I^*(101)I^*) \cap (\overline{I^*(11)}) = D_\lambda R = R$$

$$D_{101} R = D_1(D_{10} R) = (I^*(101)I^* \cup 01I^* \cup I^*) \cap (\overline{I^*(11) \cup 1})$$

$$*D_{110} R = D_0(D_{11} R) = (I^*(101)I^* \cup 1I^*) \cap (\overline{I^*(11)}) = D_{10} R$$

$$*D_{111} R = D_1(D_{11} R) = (I^*(101)I^* \cup 01I^*) \cap (\overline{I^*(11) \cup 1 \cup \lambda}) = D_{11} R$$

$$D_{1010} R = D_0(D_{101} R) = (I^*(101)I^* \cup 1I^* \cup I^*) \cap (\overline{I^*(11)})$$

$$D_{1011} R = D_1(D_{101} R) = (I^*(101)I^* \cup 01I^* \cup I^*) \cap (\overline{I^*(11) \cup 1 \cup \lambda})$$

$$D_{10100} R = D_0(D_{1010} R) = (I^*(101)I^* \cup I^*) \cap (\overline{I^*(11)})$$

$$*D_{10101} R = D_1(D_{1010} R) = (I^*(101)I^* \cup 01I^* \cup I^*) \cap (\overline{I^*(11) \cup 1})$$

$$= D_{101} R$$

$$*D_{10110} R = D_0(D_{1011} R) = (I^*(101)I^* \cup 1I^* \cup I^*) \cap (\overline{I^*(11)}) = D_{1010} R$$

$$*D_{10111} R = D_1(D_{1011} R) = (I^*(101)I^* \cup 01I^* \cup I^*) \cap (\overline{I^*(11) \cup 1 \cup \lambda})$$

$$= D_{1011} R$$

$$*D_{101000} R = D_0(D_{10100} R) = (I^*(101)I^* \cup I^*) \cap (\overline{I^*(11)}) = D_{10100} R$$

$$*D_{101001} R = D_1(D_{10100} R) = (I^*(101)I^* \cup 01I^* \cup I^*) \cap (\overline{I^*(11) \cup 1})$$

$$= D_{101} R$$

The asterisks mark the derivatives that are equal to derivatives with respect to shorter strings.

The last property of derivatives that we need to develop is that there are at most a finite number of distinct derivatives of each regular expression. This property is illustrated by the preceding example. Before we proceed, however, the reader should note that Theorem 4.3.1.1 establishes that $D_u R$ is a regular expression for $u \in I$ when R is a regular expression and that by induction on the length of strings, $D_s R$ is regular for any string s over I.

Theorem 4.3.1.3. Every regular expression R has a finite number of distinct derivatives d_R. These distinct derivatives must occur among derivatives of R with respect to strings of length $d_R - 1$ or less.

Proof. We prove the second statement first by assuming that its converse is true and establishing a contradiction. Given any sequence $s = a_1 \cdots a_p$, $p \geq k = d_R - 1$, form the d_R derivatives $D_\lambda R, D_{a_1} R, D_{a_1 a_2} R, \ldots, D_{a_1 \cdots a_k} R$. By assumption, they are not all distinct. Therefore, there exist t, r with $t < r \leq k$ such that $D_{a_1 \cdots a_t} R = D_{a_1 \cdots a_r} R$. It follows that $D_s R = D_{s'} R$ where $s' = a_1 \cdots a_t a_{r+1} \cdots a_p$ (if $p = r$, $s' = a_1 \cdots a_t$). If the length of s' is greater than k, this process can be repeated on s' to show that $D_{s'} R$ is equal to the derivative of R with respect to a shorter sequence. We conclude that every derivative of R is equal to a derivative with respect to a sequence of length $d_R - 1$ or less. But this contradicts the assumption that such derivatives do not exhaust the set of derivatives.

To show that every regular expression has a finite number of distinct derivatives, we proceed by induction on the number N of operators.

Basis Step (N = 0).   The sets ϕ, (λ), and (u), $u \in I$, clearly have a finite number of distinct derivatives. In fact, $d_\phi = 1$, $d_{(\lambda)} = 2$, and $d_{(u)} = 3$.

Induction Step (N $\geq$ 1).   Assume that each regular expression X with N or fewer operators has a finite number d_X of derivatives. If R is a regular expression with $N + 1$ operators, we show that it too has a finite number of distinct derivatives.

Case 1. Set Operations.   From the last two theorems it is clear that $D_s(P \cup Q) = D_s P \cup D_s Q$, $D_s(P \cap Q) = (D_s P) \cap (D_s Q)$ and $D_s \overline{P} = \overline{D_s P}$ for any string s over I. It follows that if $R = P \cup Q$ or $P \cap Q$, then $d_R \leq d_P d_Q$ since there are at most $d_P d_Q$ pairs of derivatives $(D_s P, D_s Q)$. Also, $d_R = d_P$ if $R = \overline{P}$.

Case 2. $R = P \cdot Q$. Let $s = a_1 a_2 \cdots a_r$. Then $D_s R = (D_s P)Q \cup \delta(D_{a_1 \cdots a_{r-1}} P)D_{a_r} Q \cup \cdots \cup \delta(D_{a_1} P)D_{a_2 \cdots a_r} Q \cup \delta(P)D_s Q$, which contains two types of terms, $(D_s P)Q$ and the union of a subset of the derivatives of Q. If Q has d_Q distinct derivatives, the number of distinct unions of them that can be formed is at most 2^{d_Q}. For each of these, $(D_s P)Q$ can have at most d_P values so that $d_R \leq d_P 2^{d_Q}$.

Case 3. $R = P^*$. Observe that

$$D_{a_1} P^* = (D_{a_1} P) P^*$$

$$D_{a_1 a_2} P^* = ((D_{a_1 a_2} P) \cup \delta (D_{a_1} P) D_{a_2} P) P^*$$

both of which consist of the union of derivatives of P concatenated with P^*. This is true of all derivatives of P^*. Since P has d_P distinct derivatives, there are 2^{d_P} distinct unions of these distinct derivatives. Since the empty union is not formed above, $d_R \leq 2^{d_P} - 1$.

We conclude, by induction on N, that each regular expression has a finite number of distinct derivatives. □

This completes our discussion of regular expressions and their derivatives. We now turn to the application of these ideas to the characterization of sequential machines.

4.3.2. Regular Expressions from Sequential Machines

In this section we demonstrate that regular expressions arise naturally in the description of sequential machines. In fact, they can be used to describe the strings of inputs that take a sequential machine from one state to another or that result in some particular output from the machine.

Consider the sequential machine S shown in Figure 4.3.2.1. The initial state is assumed fixed at q_0 (which is indicated by the edge labeled λ), and the set of input strings that takes S from q_0 back to q_0 is called E_0. That which takes S from q_0 to q_1 is called E_1. The set E_0 contains λ since S is taken from q_0 to q_0 on no input and E_0 also contains 0, 00, 11, 101, 01001, and so forth. Clearly, a string is in E_0 if and only if it contains an even number of 1's. Since E_1 is the set of strings over $I = \{0, 1\}$ that are not in E_0 (a string takes S either from q_0 to q_0 or from q_0 to q_1), $E_1 = \bar{E}_0$, and E_1 contains those strings with an odd number of 1's. Thus, this machine recognizes the parity of the input strings.

Equations can be written that define E_0 and E_1 recursively:

$$E_0 = E_0 (0) \cup E_1 (1) \cup (\lambda)$$

$$E_1 = E_0 (1) \cup E_1 (0)$$

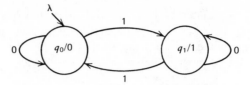

Figure 4.3.2.1. The "Parity" sequential machine.

The first equation states that a string is in E_0 if and only if it is the empty string, a string that takes q_0 to q_0 followed by 0, or a string that takes q_0 to q_1 followed by 1. The second can be given a similar interpretation.

Equations of this type can be written as

$$X = XA \cup B$$

and if $\lambda \notin A$, a straightforward substituting of $X = BA^*$ and equating terms of equal length shows this to be the unique solution to this recursive equation. Equations of this type always lead to sets A that do not contain λ. It should be clear that the solutions to such defining equations are all regular sets described by regular expressions.

Let us now solve this set of equations:

$$E_0 = E_0(0) \cup E_1(1) \cup (\lambda)$$

implies that

$$E_0 = (E_1(1) \cup (\lambda))(0)^*$$

and

$$E_1 = E_1(0) \cup E_0(1) = E_1(0) \cup ((E_1(1) \cup (\lambda))(0)^*)(1)$$
$$= E_1((0) \cup (1)(0)^*(1)) \cup (\lambda)(0)^*(1)$$

This has the solution[†]

$$E_1 = (0^*1)(0 \cup 10^*1)^*$$

and

$$E_0 = ((0^*1)(0 \cup 10^*1)^*1 \cup (\lambda))0^*$$

[†] Unless confusion is likely, from this point on we show strings that are members of sets without parentheses. For example, $((0)^*)(1)$ is shown as 0^*1.

These solutions were obtained by solving for E_0 first and then solving for E_1. If the order is reversed, the solutions obtained are

$$E_0 = (0 \cup 10^*1)^*, \quad E_1 (0 \cup 10^*1)^*10^*$$

which define the same regular sets as do the regular expressions given above. This example illustrates that it is not always possible to see immediately that two different expressions define equivalent regular sets.

In general, it cannot be assumed that the initial state of a sequential machine is fixed. To reflect this fact, in the defining recursive equation for the ith state, we add σ_i, which is later given the value (λ) if this is chosen as the initial state and is otherwise given the value ϕ.

Example 4.3.2.1. Consider the sequential machine of Figure 4.1.2. Its defining equations are

$$E_0 = E_0 0 \cup E_2 1 \cup \sigma_0$$

$$E_1 = E_0 1 \cup E_1 0 \cup \sigma_1$$

$$E_2 = E_1 1 \cup E_2 0 \cup \sigma_2$$

Solving the equations in the order given, we have

$$E_0 = (E_2 1 \cup \sigma_0)0^*$$

$$E_1 = (E_2 10^*1 \cup \sigma_0 0^*1 \cup \sigma_1)0^*$$

$$E_2 = (\sigma_0 0^* 10^*1 \cup \sigma_1 0^*1 \cup \sigma_2)(0 \cup 10^* 10^*1)^*$$

The last solution has this interpretation: If q_0 is the initial state, strings in 0^*10^*1 take the machine to q_2 for the first time, and strings in $(0 \cup 10^*10^*1)^*$ take q_2 back to itself. Similar interpretations can be given to $\sigma_1 0^*1$ and σ_2.

It should be clear now that the strings taking a machine from an initial state to a given state can be described by regular expressions. The strings resulting in a given output can also be described this way; one simply forms the union of all regular expressions associated with states having that given output. For example, the strings that result in output β from the machine in Figure 4.1.2 are described by

$$E_0 \cup E_2 = (\sigma_0 0^* 10^*1 \cup \sigma_1 0^*1 \cup \sigma_2)(0 \cup 10^*10^*1)^*(\lambda \cup 10^*) \cup \sigma_0 0^*$$

We turn now to the construction of sequential machines from regular expressions.

4.3.3.   Sequential Machines from Regular Expressions

As stated in the preceding section, regular expressions are especially well suited for the description of recognition tasks. In this case, a regular expression R is given and a machine is desired that reports whether a given input string is in R or not. This idea can be generalized somewhat to the case in which several regular expressions $R_1, R_2, \ldots, R_k$ are given that define nonintersecting sets of strings and a machine is desired that reports which set an input string is in, if any. The reader can verify that this is only a weak generalization, because from individual recognizing machines for $R_1, R_2, \ldots, R_k$, we can construct, using a few logic elements, one sequential machine for the more general task. Thus, we concentrate on the simple recognition problem.

Our objective is to construct a sequential machine S that recognizes strings over I defined by a regular expression R. Thus, we let the output alphabet of S be $\{0, 1\}$ and we ask that S produce an output 1 after the last digit of $\mathbf{s}$ if $\mathbf{s} \in R$ and an output 0 if $\mathbf{s} \notin R$. To simplify matters, we let the initial state of S be fixed.

If $q_j \in S$, we say that a string $\mathbf{s}$ is *recognized* by q_j if and only if the last output produced by S with input $\mathbf{s}$ and with initial state q_j is 1. Let R_j be the set of strings recognized by q_j and include λ if the output of S in q_j is 1. Then two states q_i and q_j of S are indistinguishable on the basis of inputs and outputs if and only if $R_i = R_j$.

Let the initial state of S be q_0. Then the regular expression R defines the set of input strings to S with initial state q_0 that result in output 1. If $\mathbf{s}$ is an input string that takes q_0 to state q_i, then the strings in R with prefix $\mathbf{s}$ are those strings that take S from q_0 to q_i and then result in an output of 1, either on reaching q_i or after receiving subsequent inputs. That is, if the initial state of S were q_i, then the input strings in $D_{\mathbf{s}}R$ would result in an output of 1. This implies that q_i and any other state q_j reached from q_0 by an input string $\mathbf{s}'$ are indistinguishable if and only if $D_{\mathbf{s}}R = D_{\mathbf{s}'}R$. We conclude that the states of S correspond to derivatives of R and that there must be at least one state for each distinct derivative. (If there is one state for each distinct derivative, S is reduced.)

Let $D_{\mathbf{s}}R$ be the derivative associated with q_i. Then, if $q_{j_1}, q_{j_2}, \ldots, q_{j_{|I|}}$ are the states associated with the $|I|$ derivatives $D_{su_1}R, D_{su_2}R, \ldots, D_{su_{|I|}}R$, where $u_1, \ldots, u_{|I|}$ are the distinct elements of I, then the successor states of q_i under these inputs are $q_{j_1}, q_{j_2}, \ldots, q_{j_{|I|}}$. A state q_i has an output 1 associated with it if and only if it is reached from q_0 by an input string $\mathbf{s}$ in R, that is, if and only if λ is contained in $D_{\mathbf{s}}R$ where $\mathbf{s}$ is such that q_i is associated with $D_{\mathbf{s}}R$.

This information accumulated on the sequential machine S that recognizes R is sufficient to construct S from the derivatives of R. This point is illustrated for the regular expression R whose derivatives are given in Example 4.3.1.2.

Example 4.3.3.1. Consider the following regular expression $R = (I^*(101)I^*) \cap \overline{(I^*(11))}$ over $I = \{0, 1\}$. The distinct derivatives of R are contained among the entries that are not marked with asterisks in Example 4.3.1.2. (This list contains several derivatives that define the same regular set.) We associate states with each of these derivatives:

q		u — 0	1		q	$\lambda(q)$
$q_0 \leftrightarrow D_\lambda R$		q_0 q_0	q_1		q_0	0
$q_1 \leftrightarrow D_1 R$		q_1 q_2	q_3		q_1	0
$q_2 \leftrightarrow D_{10} R$		q_2 q_0	q_4		q_2	0
$q_3 \leftrightarrow D_{11} R$	δ	q_3 q_2	q_3	λ	q_3	0
$q_4 \leftrightarrow D_{101} R$		q_4 q_5	q_6		q_4	1
$q_5 \leftrightarrow D_{1010} R$		q_5 q_7	q_4		q_5	1
$q_6 \leftrightarrow D_{1011} R$		q_6 q_5	q_6		q_6	0
$q_7 \leftrightarrow D_{10100} R$		q_7 q_7	q_4		q_7	1

The transition function is determined as already indicated, and a state has an output of 1 if and only if λ is in its associated derivative. A reduced equivalent to this machine can be found by invoking the procedure of Section 4.2. The equivalence relations generated by this procedure are given below. (Here i is shorthand for state q_i, $0 \leq i \leq 7$.)

$$\Pi_0 = \{(0, 1, 2, 3, 6), (4, 5, 7)\}$$

$$\Pi_1 = \{(0, 1, 3), (2), (6), (4), (5, 7)\}$$

$$\Pi_2 = \{(0), (1, 3), (2), (4), (6), (5, 7)\}$$

$$\Pi_3 = \Pi_2$$

Thus, it is clear that states q_1 and q_3 are equivalent, as are states q_5 and q_7. Therefore, the derivatives associated with q_1 and q_3 define the same regular set as do those for q_5 and q_7. The reduced machine that is determined by Π_2 is the sequential machine with fewest states and with input and output alphabets $\{0, 1\}$ that recognize R.

As the last topic of Section 4.3, we present a property of regular expressions that is often sufficient to show that a set of strings is not a regular set.

4.3.4. The Pumping Theorem for Regular Sets

We have shown that the sets of input strings that take a sequential machine from an initial state to some particular state as well as those that result in some particular output are regular sets describable by regular expressions. Conversely, every regular set is recognized by some sequential machine. Thus, the behavior of finite-state sequential machines is describable by regular expressions, and regular expressions describe the behavior only of finite-state sequential machines. We ask, "What sets of strings are not recognizable by sequential machines?" The next theorem helps to answer this question. It is called the *pumping theorem* because if R contains one sufficiently long string, this string can be "pumped up" to generate longer strings in R.

Theorem 4.3.4.1. Let R be a regular expression over I and let $S = \langle S, I, \delta, \lambda, O \rangle$ be a reduced sequential machine that recognizes R. Then, if S has $n = |S|$ states and if R contains a string of length n or greater, it contains an infinite set of strings. In fact, if $\mathbf{s} \in R$ has length $k = |\mathbf{s}|$ and $k \geq n$, then $\mathbf{s}$ can be written as the concatenation $\mathbf{s} = \mathbf{s}_1\mathbf{s}_2\mathbf{s}_3$, $|\mathbf{s}_2| \geq 1$, such that

$$\mathbf{s}' = \mathbf{s}_1(\mathbf{s}_2)^l\mathbf{s}_3$$

is also in R for any integer $l \geq 0$. [Here $(\mathbf{s}_2)^l$ is the l-fold concatenation of $\mathbf{s}_2$ with itself, e.g., $(\mathbf{s}_2)^3 = (\mathbf{s}_2\mathbf{s}_2\mathbf{s}_2)$.]

> *Proof.* The second statement is established, from which the first follows directly.
>
> Let R contain $\mathbf{s}$ where $k = |\mathbf{s}| \geq n$. Let $\mathbf{s} = a_1a_2 \cdots a_k$ and let $q^{(0)}$ be the initial state of S. Then $q^{(1)}, q^{(2)}, \ldots, q^{(k)}$ are the successor states under the inputs $a_1, a_2, \ldots, a_k$ where $q^{(j)} = \delta(q^{(j-1)}, a_j)$. Since $k \geq n$ and S has n states, by the pigeonhole principle, at least two of the $k + 1$ states $q^{(0)}, q^{(1)}, \ldots, q^{(k)}$ are identical; that is, for some r and t, $r < t$, $q^{(r)} = q^{(t)}$. This implies that the input sequence $a_{r+1} \cdots a_t$ takes S from state $q^{(r)}$ back to $q^{(r)}$. Let $\mathbf{s}_1 = a_1a_2 \cdots a_r$, $\mathbf{s}_2 = a_{r+1} \cdots a_t$ and $\mathbf{s}_3 = a_{t+1} \cdots a_k$. Then, since $\mathbf{s} = \mathbf{s}_1\mathbf{s}_2\mathbf{s}_3$ is recognized by S and is in R, it follows that the same is true for $\mathbf{s}_1(\mathbf{s}_2)^2\mathbf{s}_3$ and in general for $\mathbf{s}_1(\mathbf{s}_2)^l\mathbf{s}_3$ for $l \geq 1$. The same is true for $\mathbf{s}_1\mathbf{s}_3$. ☐

As the following applications of this theorem indicate, finite-state sequential machines cannot count beyond a limit imposed by their numbers of states.

Example 4.3.4.1. The set P of strings consisting of a number of zeros that are the square of an integer, namely, $P = \{0, 0^4, 0^9, 0^{16}, 0^{25}, \ldots\}$, is not a regular set. To show this, assume that it is regular and demonstrate that a contradiction results. Let P be recognized by an n-state sequential machine and let m be such that $m^2 \geq n$. Then $s = 0^{m^2} = s_1s_2s_3$ is in P, as is $s_1(s_2)^l s_3$ for $l \geq 1$. Let $k_1 = |s_1|$, $k_2 = |s_2|$, $k_3 = |s_3|$; then $p_l = k_1 + lk_2 + k_3$ must be a square by the definition of P for each $l \geq 1$. Therefore, the difference between two successive squares defined in this way is $p_l - p_{l-1} = k_2$. But for large l, this is a contradiction because the difference between two successive squares is $m^2 - (m-1)^2 = 2m - 1$, which grows without limit.

Example 4.3.4.2. The set $Q = \{0^m 1^m | m \geq 1\}$ is not a regular set. If it is regular, there is an integer n such that, for $2m \geq n$, $s = 0^m 1^m = s_1s_2s_3$ is in Q as well as $s_1(s_2)^l s_3$ for all $l \geq 1$. But if $s_2 = 0^k$ or $s_2 = 1^k$, then $s_1(s_2)^2 s_3 = 0^{m+k} 1^m$ or $0^m 1^{m+k}$, which are clearly not in Q. Also, if $s_2 = 0^{k_1} 1^{k_2}$ for k_1, $k_2 \geq 1$, then $s_1(s_2)^2 s_3 = 0^m 1^{k_2} 0^{k_1} 1^m$, which is also not in Q. Since there are not other cases for s_2, Q is not regular.

The pumping theorem for sequential machines was derived by Rabin and Scott (1959).

4.4. BOUNDS ON THE COMPLEXITIES OF DESCRIPTOR FUNCTIONS

From the preceding discussion we might be inclined to view the sequential machine exclusively as a mathematical object and to examine it for its mathematical, as opposed to engineering, properties. However, it is more than a mathematical object, it is a model for a physical object constructed from physical components. As such, and in common with other physical objects, it imposes constraints on its use. These constraints, which are generally hidden from us, are very important to the efficient use of computing machines. In the following section we determine two such constraints which are stated in the form of inequalities and which make use of two previously introduced complexity measures, combinational complexity and delay complexity. This section lays the foundation for these results.

The starting point for our discussion is the descriptor function $G_{S,T}$: $S \times I^T \to O^{T+1}$ for a sequential machine S that describes the input-output behavior of S over T cycles of computation. (S has an initial output that is determined by its initial state and produces T additional outputs in response to T inputs.) An example of such a descriptor function was given in Section 4.1 for the sequential machine that determines the sum of its binary inputs modulo 3 and then modulo 2. As another example, consider the sequential machine of Figure 4.4.1. This machine receives inputs of

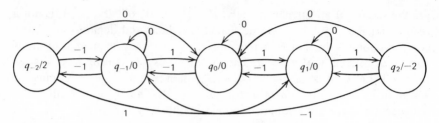

Figure 4.4.1. A "Controller".

-1, 0, $+1$, and if the sum of the inputs reaches $+2$, the output of -2 is produced and the sum is effectively reduced to 0. If the sum reaches -2, the output of $+2$ is produced to effectively increase the sum to 0. Thus, if the input is viewed as the discrete derivative of a "signal" and the output is viewed as an additive correction to the "signal," this machine could be viewed as the discrete equivalent of a control unit or as a "controller."

The descriptor for this machine captures the control aspect of this machine. The "signal" at the end of the kth cycle, $\sigma(k)$, is the sum of the initial signal i if the initial state is q_i, $-2 \leq i \leq 2$, and the first k inputs, $u_1, u_2, \ldots, u_k$, that is

$$\sigma(k) = i + \sum_{j=1}^{k} u_j$$

If the outputs produced are $v_0, v_1, \ldots, v_k$, the correction to this signal is $c(k)$, where

$$c(k) = \sum_{j=0}^{k} v_j$$

The corrected signal then is $\Delta(k) = \sigma(k) + c(k)$, and the $(k + 1)$st output v_{k+1} is determined by $u_{k+1} + \Delta(k)$. Then the descriptor is given by

$$G_{S,T}(q_i, u_1, u_2, \ldots, u_T) = (v_0, v_1, \ldots, v_T)$$

where

$$v_{k+1} = \begin{cases} -2, & u_{k+1} + \Delta(k) = 2 \\ 0, & -1 \leq u_{k+1} + \Delta(k) \leq 1 \\ +2, & u_{k+1} + \Delta(k) = -2 \end{cases}$$

for $k \geq 0$, and v_0 is the output associated with the initial state. The "controller" described by this function is a machine that incorporates "branching" as it is normally conceived in a programming context. Nonetheless, as a sequential machine, its state diagram is no different, in general, from that of other sequential machines.

These two examples are "special-purpose" sequential machines. It should be apparent, however, that a descriptor can also be associated with each of those machines that we call "general-purpose." In Chapter 7, descriptors of general-purpose computers are used to derive important computational inequalities for these machines.

Let us now derive upper bounds to the combinational complexity and delay complexity of $G_{S,\,T}$ for a sequential machine S. We suppose that the sets S, I, and O are binary sets and are represented as binary tuples over $\{0, 1\}^s$, $\{0, 1\}^a$, $\{0, 1\}^c$, respectively, where s, a, and c are positive integers.[†] (If S, I, and O were not represented this way, suitable encodings of them could be found. These encodings could conceivably be chosen to minimize the complexity of $G_{S,\,T}$, as measured below.) We make this assumption because machines are realized this way and because we want the combinational and delay complexities of $G_{S,\,T}$ to be well defined. We now derive upper bounds to $C_\Omega(G_{S,\,T})$ and $D_\Omega(G_{S,\,T})$.

Theorem 4.4.1. Given a sequential machine S, its associated descriptor $G_{S,\,T}\colon \{0, 1\}^{s+Ta} \to \{0, 1\}^{(T+1)c}$ has a combinational complexity and a delay complexity bounded above by

$$C_\Omega(G_{S,\,T}) \le C_\Omega(\delta, \lambda)T + C_\Omega(\lambda)$$

$$D_\Omega(G_{S,\,T}) \le D_\Omega(\delta)T + D_\Omega(\lambda)$$

Here $\delta\colon \{0, 1\}^{s+a} \to \{0, 1\}^s$ and $\lambda\colon \{0, 1\}^s \to \{0, 1\}^c$ are the transition and output functions, respectively of S. Also, Ω is assumed to be a complete basis.

Proof. Let $\mathbf{q}, \mathbf{u}_1, \ldots, \mathbf{u}_T$ denote the initial state and T inputs to S, as binary tuples, and let $\mathbf{v}_0, \ldots, \mathbf{v}_T$ denote the $T+1$ output tuples of S. Then the combinational machine in Figure 4.4.2 computes $G_{S,\,T}$.

This combinational machine uses T copies of a chain that computes δ and λ and one additional copy of a chain that computes λ. Since δ and λ can be computed by a common chain, the first inequality follows. This machine is obtained effectively by unwinding the machine diagramed in Figure 4.1.1.

[†] Note that s denotes an integer here and not a string. This use of s continues throughout the remainder of the text.

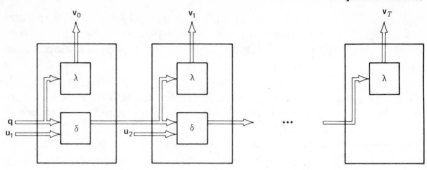

Figure 4.4.2. A combinational machine computing $G_{S,T}$.

The reader can readily verify that

$$D_\Omega(f, g) = \max(D_\Omega(f), D_\Omega(g))$$

for two binary functions f and g. It follows that the length of the longest path through the machine given in Figure 4.4.2 has length of at most $D_\Omega(\delta)T + D_\Omega(\lambda)$ and that this is an upper bound to $D_\Omega(G_{S,T})$. This establishes the second inequality. ☐

This result can be extended to a machine that is the interconnection of a number of distinct sequential machines. As an example of such a set of machines, consider the pair of machines shown in Figure 4.4.3 in which the length of one cycle on S_1 is τ_1 seconds and on S_2 is τ_2 seconds where $\tau_2 = 2\tau_1$. The output of S_1 is a binary 4-tuple while that of S_2 is a binary triple, and each has an input that is a binary triple. Some of the output digits of S_1 are inputs to S_2, and vice versa. Binary inputs and outputs that are received from and directed to the external environment are called *external inputs and external outputs*. Each machine shown in Figure 4.4.3 has three external binary outputs, S_1 has two external inputs, and S_2 has one.

We now make some realistic assumptions that are necessary when several machines are interconnected.

1. Each sequential machine is *clocked* (the cycle lengths are fixed).
2. State transitions in each machine are instantaneous.
3. State transitions occur at the end of cycles.
4. A state is determined by the state in the preceding cycle and the input to the machine just before the start of that cycle.
5. Machine outputs remain constant over a machine cycle.
6. No machine uses its own output as input.

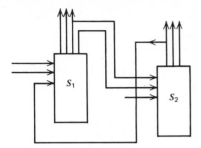

Figure 4.4.3. An interconnected pair of sequential machines.

Note that the fourth assumption implies that one full cycle is required for an input to affect the state of a machine. In the example of Figure 4.4.3, this means that S_2 uses every other pair of outputs from S_1 to determine successive states since $\tau_2 = 2\tau_1$.

Let $S_1, S_2, \ldots, S_L$ be a set of L sequential machines with binary input and output alphabets and state sets and let them have cycle lengths $\tau_1, \tau_2, \ldots, \tau_L$. Let this collection of machines together with an interconnection pattern be called S. (The reader can verify that S is a sequential machine, but in general, the duration of a cycle is not fixed; see Problem 4-13.) Let the machines execute $T_1, T_2, \ldots, T_L$ cycles, respectively. Then, just as for a single sequential machine, a descriptor function $G_{S, T_1, \ldots, T_L}$ can be defined for S that maps the initial states and external inputs onto external outputs, and a theorem such as Theorem 4.4.1 can be derived. The procedure used is the same; namely, the feedback loops between logic and memory are opened, and $T_j + 1$ copies of the logic unit of S_j are cascaded for $1 \leq j \leq L$. This is illustrated in Figure 4.4.4 for the machine of Figure 4.4.3.

NOTE. The outputs for the second copy of the logic unit of S_1 are not used as inputs to the first copy of the logic unit of S_2, while an output of the latter copy is used as input to the first two copies of the logic unit of S_1. This interconnection pattern is dictated by the duration of the cycles of S_1 and S_2 and the way in which they use inputs. The reader can readily demonstrate that this combinational machine contains no directed loops.

Before we state the generalization of Theorem 4.4.1, we note that a sequential machine may have a state from which it does not exit. Such a state is a "halting" state, and after a machine enters such a state, its output remains constant. In the preceding, we have assumed that the number of cycles executed by each machine in a collection is fixed. This could mean that the machines with differing cycle lengths finish computing at the same

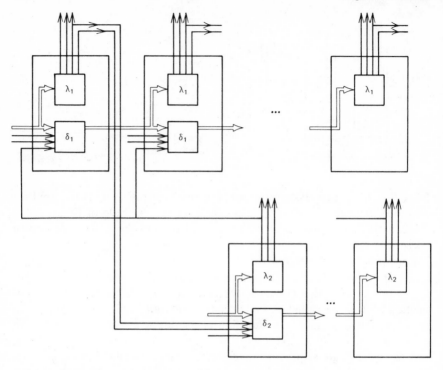

Figure 4.4.4. Cascade realization of combinational machine for G_{S, T_1, T_2}.

time or it could mean that some machines enter halting states before the overall computation is completed.

Theorem 4.4.2. Let S be a sequential machine obtained from an interconnection of $S_1, S_2, \ldots, S_L$, where $S_j = \langle S_j, I_j, \delta_j, \lambda_j, O_j \rangle$ for $1 \leq j \leq L$. Let S_j have a cycle length of τ_j seconds, execute T_j cycles, and let $S_j, I_j,$ and O_j be sets of binary tuples. Then the descriptor function $G_{S, T_1, \ldots, T_L} = G$ for this machine satisfies the inequalities

$$C_\Omega(G) \leq \sum_{j=1}^{L} \left\{ C_\Omega(\delta_j, \lambda_j) T_j + C_\Omega(\lambda_j) \right\}$$

$$D_\Omega(G) \leq \left(\max_i \frac{D_\Omega(\delta_i, \lambda_i)}{\tau_i} \right) \left(\max_j T_j \tau_j \right)$$

where Ω is a complete basis.

Proof. The first inequality is obvious. The second is much less so, but follows from upper bounding the length of the longest path through the cascade realization of a combinational machine for $G_{S, T_1, \ldots, T_L}$.

Let P be the longest path through this combinational machine and suppose that it passes consecutively through several copies of the logic circuits of $S_{l_1}, S_{l_2}, \ldots, S_{l_N}$. Here l_i and l_{i+1} must differ. Let P enter the circuits of S_{l_j} at an input given to S_{l_j} at the end of its M_{l_j}th cycle and exit at an output produced by a state reached at the end of its N_{l_j}th cycle. Then clearly $0 \leq M_{l_j} \leq N_{l_j} - 1$. Also, since $S_{l_{j+1}}$ can act on an input from S_{l_j} only after it has received that input, it follows that $N_{l_j}\tau_{l_j} < M_{l_{j+1}}\tau_{l_{j+1}}$.

The length of the portion of P passing through the circuits of S_{l_j} is no more than $(N_{l_j} - M_{l_j} - 1)D_\Omega(\delta_{l_j}) + D_\Omega(\lambda_{l_j})$, which is no more than $(N_{l_j} - M_{l_j})D_\Omega(\delta_{l_j}, \lambda_{l_j})$. It follows that the length of P is bounded by

$$\Lambda(P) \leq \sum_{j=1}^{N} (N_{l_j} - M_{l_j})\tau_{l_j} \frac{D_\Omega(\delta_{l_j}, \lambda_{l_j})}{\tau_{l_j}}$$

Let

$$R = \max_{1 \leq i \leq L} \frac{D_\Omega(\delta_i, \lambda_i)}{\tau_i}$$

Then

$$\Lambda(P) \leq R \sum_{j=1}^{N} (N_{l_j} - M_{l_j})\tau_{l_j}$$

But the path P defines N nonoverlapping time intervals of duration, at least $(N_{l_j} - M_{l_j})\tau_{l_j}$ for $1 \leq j \leq N$, and the total length of these intervals is at most t seconds where $t = \max_i(T_i\tau_i)$ is the maximum running time of any one of the machines; that is,

$$\sum_{j=1}^{N} (N_{l_j} - M_{l_j})\tau_{l_j} \leq t$$

It follows directly that the length of the longest path P through a cascade realization of a combinational machine for $G_{S, T_1, \ldots, T_L}$ satisfies

$$\Lambda(P) \leq Rt$$

and this is an upper bound to the delay complexity of this function. $\square$

These two inequalities are applied later to important sequential machines, namely, general-purpose computers. They are very useful in developing information on storage–time tradeoffs.

4.5. COMPUTATIONAL WORK AND EFFICIENCY

In this section we derive two types of computational inequality that relate the combinational complexity and delay complexity of a function to the running time, size, and delay of sequential machines used to compute the function. We make use of the bounds to the complexities of descriptors of sequential machines that were derived in the preceding section. One of our inequalities suggests natural measures of computational work and efficiency.

Let $f: \{0, 1\}^n \to \{0, 1\}^m$ be a function that is to be computed on a sequential machine or a collection of interconnected sequential machines. The machine or machines are supplied inputs consisting of data and instructions (if necessary) and produce outputs. Conventions must be adopted for input and output formats to

1. prevent the value of f being given as data,
2. clearly specify those outputs of the machines that are associated with the value of f, and which
3. determine the order in which these outputs are combined to form the value of f.

The first condition is necessary to preclude the precomputation of f. The second is important because we must know where the results of the computation are to be found. Once they are found, the third condition states the obvious fact that the ordering of these outputs is important.

There are many ways in which outputs can be generated by machines while computing functions. Several examples are:

(a) S is a single sequential machine that computes f by executing exactly T cycles and generates the value of f as its last output word.
(b) S is as given in (a) and the value of f is the *valid portion* (all but the first bit) of the only output word whose first bit is 1. (Such words are called *valid words*.)
(c) S is as given in (a) and the value of f is the concatenation of the valid portions of the r valid outputs, $r \leq T + 1$.
(d) Same as in (c) except that the correct order of the r valid outputs is data dependent and determined by indices carried in the valid portions of the r words. These indices specify the correct position of the corresponding valid output.

(e) S is a collection of sequential machines for which the valid outputs are generated at one machine (the output machine) according to one of the formats given above, or outputs are generated by several machines.

As these examples indicate, there are very many different ways to produce the results of computations.

Suppose that $f: \{0, 1\}^n \to \{0, 1\}^m$ is "computed" by a single sequential machine that executes T cycles on every point of the domain of f and suppose that the value of f is the concatenation of the valid portions of r valid words whose *positions in time are data independent*. (Note that we have not yet completely specified what it means for a sequential machine to compute a function. We do so shortly.) Then any combinational machine for $G_{S,T}$, the descriptor function of S, can be used by deleting nonvalid outputs to produce a combinational machine for f. Therefore, in this case, the combinational complexity of f is no more than that of $G_{S,T}$, or

$$C_\Omega(f) \leq C_\Omega(G_{S,T}) \leq C_\Omega(\delta, \lambda)T + C_\Omega(\lambda)$$

Also,

$$D_\Omega(f) \leq D_\Omega(G_{S,T}) \leq D_\Omega(\delta)T + D_\Omega(\lambda)$$

These are the prototypes for more general computational inequalities to be derived.

The first inequality has several important interpretations. First, if a function f with a large combinational complexity is computed by a machine S with a small combinational complexity $C_\Omega(\delta, \lambda)$, then the machine must execute enough cycles so that the *equivalent number of logical operations* $C_\Omega(\delta, \lambda)T + C_\Omega(\lambda)$ is no smaller than $C_\Omega(f)$. Clearly, then, f can be computed by S with few equivalent logic elements only if logic elements have been traded for time in a manner that does not violate this computational inequality.

Second, $C_\Omega(\delta, \lambda)$ and $C_\Omega(\lambda)$ are "equivalent numbers of logic elements in S" because these functions could actually be realized in S with elements from a different basis Ω' and they may not necessarily be realized with these minimum numbers of elements.

Third and fourth interpretations follow from the observations that power consumption in a machine should be roughly proportional to $C_\Omega(\delta, \lambda)$, as should be the cost of the machine. Therefore, $C_\Omega(\delta, \lambda)T$ is a rough measure of the energy consumption of S in T cycles, and if the machine has a fixed lifetime, customers should be charged for each unit of time an amount proportional to the cost of S, or roughly $C_\Omega(\delta, \lambda)$, so that the cost of T units of time on S should be roughly proportional to $C_\Omega(\delta, \lambda)T$ also.

There are many ways to generalize the computational inequalities given above. We choose one of these to illustrate the method, and the reader can see how other generalizations can be made. We assume that $f: \{0, 1\}^n \to \{0, 1\}^m$ is computed by a collection of sequential machines, one of which is designated as the output machine. We assume that the value of f is obtained by concatenating the valid portions of the valid words produced by the output machine in the order in which the machine generates them [see (b), (c), and (e)].

Definition 4.5.1. Let S be a collection of L interconnected sequential machines $S_1, \ldots, S_L$ whose state sets and input and output alphabets are collections of binary tuples. Let a_j and s_j denote the numbers of external binary inputs[†] and binary digits in the state of S_j, respectively, and let $\mathbf{u}_{jr}$ and $\mathbf{q}_j$ denote the rth external input a_j-tuple (in time) and initial state of S_j, respectviely. Then a $T_1, T_2, \ldots, T_L$ *program* for $f: \{0, 1\}^n \to \{0, 1\}^m$ on S is a string $\boldsymbol{\sigma}$ of length $l = \sum_{j=1}^L (s_j + T_j a_j)$ over $\{0, 1\} \cup \{x_1, x_2, \ldots, x_n\}$ such that the value of f is produced, as indicated above, by S with input

$$(\mathbf{q}_1 \mathbf{u}_{11} \mathbf{u}_{12} \cdots \mathbf{u}_{1T_1} \cdots \mathbf{q}_j \mathbf{u}_{j1} \cdots \mathbf{u}_{jT_j} \cdots \mathbf{u}_{LT_L}) = \boldsymbol{\sigma}$$

That is, for each

$$(x_1, x_2, \ldots, x_n) \in \{0, 1\}^n, f(x_1, x_2, \ldots, x_n)$$

is obtained by concatenating the valid portions of the valid words generated by the output machine of S with input $\boldsymbol{\sigma}$. We say that f is *computed* by S if there exists a $T_1, T_2, \ldots, T_L$ program for f on S for some integers $T_1, T_2, \ldots, T_L$.

This definition of a program legitimates a large spectrum of different methods of computing with sequential machines. *The definition allows the initial states to be fixed or to be program dependent and in fact to depend on some of the variables of* f.

Theorem 4.5.1. Let S be an interconnected set of L sequential machines, $S_1, S_2, \ldots, S_L$, that compute $f: \{0, 1\}^n \to \{0, 1\}^m$. Let S_l be the output machine with c_l external binary digits per output word. We assume that $c_l - 1$ divides m and observe that S_l must generate $m/(c_l - 1)$ valid output words. Then, for every set of nonnegative integers $T_1, T_2, \ldots, T_L$ such

---

[†] Note: $a_j = 0$ if S_j has no external binary inputs.

that a $T_1, T_2, \ldots, T_L$ program for f on S exists, the following computational inequalities must be satisfied:

$$C_\Omega(f) \leq \sum_{j=1}^{L} \{ C_\Omega(\delta_j, \lambda_j) T_j + C_\Omega(\lambda_j) \} + C_\Omega(V)$$

$$D_\Omega(f) \leq \left(\max_i \frac{D_\Omega(\delta_i, \lambda_i)}{\tau_i} \right) \left(\max_j T_j \tau_j \right) + D_\Omega(V)$$

Here Ω is any complete basis and V: $\{0, 1\}^{(T_l + 1)c_l} \to \{0, 1\}^m$ is the function that maps the $T_l + 1$ external output words onto the $m/(c_l - 1)$ words, of $c_l - 1$ bits each, that form the value of f. If for a $T_1, T_2, \ldots, T_L$ program for f the positions, in time, of the valid words of S_l are fixed and data independent, then the additive terms involving V can be eliminated. Over the basis $\Omega_1 = \{ +, \cdot, \oplus, {}^- \}$, we have

$$C_{\Omega_1}^*(V) \leq 5mT_l$$

$$D_{\Omega_1}(V) \leq 5 \lceil \log_2(T_l + 1) \rceil$$

Proof. Given any combinational machine for $G_{S, T_1, \ldots, T_L}$ a combinational machine for f can be constructed directly if the positions of valid words are data independent. One merely deletes outputs that are not in valid words and provides as input to $G_{S, T_1, \ldots, T_L}$ a program for f. It follows that $C_\Omega(f) \leq C_\Omega(G_{S, T_1, \ldots, T_L})$. However, if the positions of the valid words are data dependent, then the function V must be applied to the $T_l + 1$ output words of the output machine S_l, namely, $v_0, v_1, \ldots, v_{T_l}$ to select the valid portions of the $m/(c_l - 1)$ valid words and concatenate them to form the m-tuple that is the value of f. The same argument holds for D_Ω.

A chain for V is constructed as follows: Let the jth output word v_j of S be represented as $v_j = (v_{j0}, \ldots, v_{j, c_l - 1})$. Let $\theta_j = v_{j0}$ and $z_j = (v_{j, 1}, \ldots, v_{j, c_l - 1})$. Then, if $r = m/(c_l - 1)$,

$$V(v_0, v_1, \ldots, v_{T_l}) = \omega_1 \omega_2 \cdots \omega_r$$

where $\omega_i \in \{0, 1\}^{c_l - 1}$ and ω_i is the ith word that has $\theta_j = 1$, if any, and $\mathbf{0}$ otherwise. Let $\gamma_j^{(i)}$, $0 \leq j \leq T_l$, be 1 if and only if v_j is the ith word with $\theta_j = 1$. Then, outside the range $i - 1 \leq j \leq T_l - r + i$, $\gamma_j^{(i)}$ is identically zero because the ith word with $\theta_j = 1$ cannot occur among the first $i - 1$ or among the last $r - i$ words. (This range contains $T_l - r + 2$ integers.)

It follows that ω_i is obtained from

$$\omega_i = \gamma_0^{(i)} \cdot z_0 + \cdots + \gamma_{T_l}^{(i)} z_{T_l}$$

where $\cdot$ denotes vector AND (of $c_l - 1$ components) and $+$ denotes vector OR (of $c_l - 1$ tuples). A total of $2m(T_l - r + 2) - m$ binary operations from Ω_1 is sufficient for this task, as the reader can show, and they can be done with circuits of delay complexity $\lceil \log_2(T_l - r + 2) \rceil + 1$ given that $\{\gamma_j^{(i)}\}$ is available.

Consider the functions $\psi_j^{(i)}$, $i - 1 \leq j$, where $\psi_j^{(i)} = \gamma_{i-1}^{(i)} + \cdots + \gamma_j^{(i)}$. Then $\psi_j^{(i)}$ is 1 if and only if the ith valid word occurs in one of the positions $i - 1, i, \ldots, j$. We can now write

$$\gamma_j^{(i)} = \begin{cases} \theta_{i-1} \cdot \psi_{i-2}^{(i-1)}, & j = i - 1 \\ \theta_j \cdot \overline{\left(\psi_{j-1}^{(i)}\right)} \cdot \psi_{j-1}^{(i-1)}, & i \leq j \leq T_l - r + i \end{cases}$$

if we let $\gamma_j^{(0)} = \psi_j^{(0)} = 1$ for all j, as the reader can demonstrate. The reader is asked to show that $b = (T_l - r + 2)(3r - 1)$ binary operations from Ω_1 suffice to realize $\gamma_j^{(i)}$ for all i and j. Therefore, a total of $(T_l - r + 2)(2m + 3r - 1)$ operations from Ω_1 suffices to realize V (see Problem 4-14). The bound follows directly when $r \geq 2$ because $r \leq m$ and $m \geq 1$. When $r = 1$, it is again easy to verify that it holds.

The function $\gamma_j^{(i)}$ can also be written as

$$\gamma_j^{(i)} = \theta_j \cdot \sigma_{i-1}(\theta_0, \theta_1, \ldots, \theta_{j-1})$$

where σ_{i-1} is an elementary symmetric function. From Problem 4-15, we have that

$$D_{\Omega_1}(\gamma_j^{(i)}) \leq 5\lceil \log_2(j + 1) \rceil - 5$$

for $0 \leq j \leq T$, from which it follows that V can be realized with a delay of at most $5\lceil \log_2(T_l + 1) \rceil$. $\qquad\square$

The combinational and delay complexity of V is negligible if m is small by comparison with $C_\Omega(\delta_l, \lambda_l)$ and $D_\Omega(\delta_l)$, the combinational and delay complexity of the output machine. In practical applications, we would expect this to be the case unless the number of outputs that must be generated to compute $f: \{0, 1\}^n \to \{0, 1\}^m$ is very large. It is quite apparent what must be done to derive computational inequalities of this type when other output conventions are employed: find an output function analogous to V.

The first inequality of Theorem 4.5.1 suggests a measure of computational work and a measure of efficiency. If the use of one equivalent logic element represents one unit of work, then we have the following definition.

Definition 4.5.2. If S, as described in Theorem 4.5.1, computes f, the *computational work* W that is done is given by

$$W = \sum_{j=1}^{L} \left\{ C_\Omega(\delta_j, \lambda_j) T_j + C_\Omega(\lambda_j) \right\} + C_\Omega(V)$$

Theorem 4.5.1 requires that the computational work done to compute f be no less than its combinational complexity. Furthermore, part of this work ($C_\Omega(V)$) is done outside of S and part is done by S itself. Also, at least $C_\Omega(f)$ equivalent logical operations must be performed whether the function f is realized by combinational (or no-memory) machines or by sequential machines. .

A natural measure of efficiency is the following.

Definition 4.5.3. If S, as described in Theorem 4.5.1, computes f, the *efficiency* E of the computation is given by

$$E = \frac{C_\Omega(f)}{W}$$

This measure is interesting because (1) $E \leq 1$, and (2) [if $C_\Omega(V)$ is small] W is a crude measure of the physical energy expended by S to compute f and is a crude measure of the cost of the hardware (and memory) to compute f when hardware has a fixed lifetime (for accounting purposes). Thus, E is normalized, and minimizing W maximizes E.

The reader should observe that very few restrictions are placed on the way S may be used to compute f. In particular, although the computational inequalities are derived by "simulating" $G_{S, T_1, \ldots, T_L}$ with combinational machines (graphs of straight-line algorithms or chains), we do not require that f be realized by straight-line algorithms on S. Also, in the definition of E, the combinational complexity of f only plays the role of a normalizing coefficient.

To illustrate the use of computational inequalities and the new measure of efficiency, consider the function $f^c_{\text{mod } 3}(x_1, \ldots, x_n)$, which is defined in Section 2.4.2 and discussed in Section 4.1. A sequential machine is given in Section 4.1 that computes this function in $T = n$ cycles by producing its value as the last output. It follows that

$$C_\Omega(f^c_{\text{mod } 3}) \leq C_\Omega(\delta, \lambda) T + C_\Omega(\lambda)$$

Let the states in the machine given in Figure 4.1.2 be encoded as

$$
\begin{array}{ccc}
q \leftrightarrow (\sigma_0, \sigma_1) & & \\
q_0 & 0 & 0 \\
q_1 & 0 & 1 \\
q_2 & 1 & 0
\end{array}
$$

Then the output function $\lambda(q) = \sigma_1$, and if the successor state $\delta(q, u) = (\sigma_0', \sigma_1')$, then we can write

$$
\sigma_1' = \overline{\sigma_0} \cdot (\sigma_1 \oplus u)
$$

$$
\sigma_0' = \overline{\sigma_1'} \cdot (\sigma_0 \oplus u)
$$

and it follows that over $\Omega = P_{1,2}^{(2)}$, $C_\Omega(\delta, \lambda) \leq 4$ and $C_\Omega(\lambda) = 0$. Therefore,

$$
C_\Omega(f_{\text{mod }3}^c) \leq 4T = W
$$

But from Theorem 2.4.2.5, $C_\Omega(f_{\text{mod }3}^c) \geq 2T - 3$ for $T = n$. Consequently, the efficiency of the computation on this machine is

$$
E = \frac{C_\Omega(f)}{W} \geq \frac{(2T - 3)}{4T}
$$

which approaches $\frac{1}{2}$ with increasing T. Note that E is generally a function of the basis Ω as well as of the structure of the sequential machine. This is a very high efficiency which is not likely to be achieved for many functions on many machines.

Problems

4-1. Design a two-state sequential machine that computes $f_{\text{COMP}}^{(n)}: \{0, 1\}^n \to \{0, 1\}$ where n is even,

$$
f_{\text{COMP}}^{(n)}(x_1, \ldots, x_{n/2}, y_1, \ldots, y_{n/2}) = \begin{cases} 1 & |\mathbf{x}| < |\mathbf{y}| \\ 0 & \text{otherwise} \end{cases}
$$

and $|\mathbf{x}| = x_1 \cdot 1 + x_2 \cdot 2 + x_3 \cdot 2^2 + \cdots + x_{n/2} 2^{n/2 - 1}$. Assume that the inputs are given as pairs $(x_1, y_1), (x_2, y_2), \ldots, (x_{n/2}, y_{n/2})$. Show that the descriptors compute $f_{\text{COMP}}^{(1)}, f_{\text{COMP}}^{(2)}, \ldots, f_{\text{COMP}}^{(n)}$.

4-2. Find a reduced sequential machine equivalent to the machine

q \ u	$\delta(q, u)$ 0	1
q_0	q_0	q_1
q_1	q_2	q_3
q_2	q_4	q_1
q_3	q_5	q_3
q_4	q_4	q_6
q_5	q_4	q_6
q_6	q_5	q_3

δ

q	$\lambda(q)$
q_0	0
q_1	0
q_2	0
q_3	1
q_4	0
q_5	0
q_6	0

λ

4-3. (a) Given an n-state sequential machine S, derive an upper bound on the smallest value of k such that $\Pi_k = \Pi_{k+1}$ where Π_j is the equivalence relation that defines j-equivalent states of S.

(b) Determine the value of k defined in (a) for the sequential machine $S = \langle (q_1, q_2, \ldots, q_{n-1}), \{1\}, \delta, \lambda, \{0, 1\} \rangle$ that counts modulo p where

$$\delta(q_i) = \begin{cases} q_{i+1}, & 0 \le i \le n - 1 \\ q_1, & i = n \end{cases}$$

$$\lambda(q_i) = \begin{cases} 0, & i \ne n \\ 1, & i = n \end{cases}$$

4-4. Let S_1 and S_2 be two machines with identical input alphabets that are to be tested for equivalence. Let $S_1 + S_2$ be the direct sum of S_1 and S_2 formed by concatenating the transition and output tables of S_1 and S_2. Show that equivalence or nonequivalence of S_1 and S_2 can be determined by an examination of $r(S_1 + S_2)$, the reduced machine equivalent to $S_1 + S_2$. If k is the integer defined in Problem 3a for $S_1 + S_2$, show that S_1 is not equivalent to S_2 if $k \ge \min(|S_1|, |S_2|)$, where $|S_i|$ is the number of states in S_i.

4-5. Show that for every Moore machine there is an equivalent Mealy machine, and vice versa. Ignore the output of the Moore machine from its initial state.

4-6. Give a regular expression describing those strings over $I = \{0, 1\}$ that contain 11 or 100 and end in 11. Compute all the distinct derivatives of this expression.

4-7. In the following machine let q_0 be the initial state. Find a regular expression for the input strings that results in an output of 1.

δ	u q	0	1
	q_0	q_0	q_1
	q_1	q_0	q_2
	q_2	q_0	q_2

λ	q	$\lambda(q)$
	q_0	0
	q_1	0
	q_2	1

Is this regular expression equivalent to $I*11$?

4-8. A regular expression over the set $\Sigma = \{0, 1, 2, 3\}$ is given by $E = (0, 2, 3)*1 \cup (0, 1, 3)*$. Find a sequential machine that recognizes E.

4-9. Generalize the pumping theorem of Section 4.3.4 by demonstrating that if a regular set R is recognized by a sequential machine with n states and $\mathbf{s} \in R$, $|s| \geq n$, then we can write $\mathbf{s} = \omega_1 \mathbf{z} \omega_2$ where $|\mathbf{z}| = n$, $\mathbf{z} = \mathbf{s}_1 \mathbf{s}_2 \mathbf{s}_3$, $|\mathbf{s}_2| \geq 1$ so that $\mathbf{s}' = \omega_1 \mathbf{s}_1 (\mathbf{s}_2)^l \mathbf{s}_3 \omega_2 \in R$ also for all $l \geq 0$.

4-10. Show that the set of strings $\{\omega \omega^R | \omega \in \{0, 1\}^*$, ω^R is the reverse of $\omega\}$ is not a regular set.

4-11. (a) Show that $\{0^m 1^n | m, n \geq 1\}$ is a regular set.
    (b) Exhibit a subset of this set that is not regular.

4-12. Let the sequential machine S be used to compute $f: \{0, 1\}^n \to \{0, 1\}^m$ in T cycles and let the input-output convention of Section 4.5 apply. If the positions of the valid output words are data independent, the following computational inequality holds, as is shown in Section 4.5:

$$D_\Omega(f) \leq D_\Omega(G_{S, T}) \leq D_\Omega(\delta) T + D_\Omega(\lambda)$$

Here δ and λ are the transition and output functions, respectively, of S. Using a technique similar to that of Theorem 2.3.3 and the binary-to-positional transformer, show that under the same conditions

$$D_\Omega(f) \leq D_\Omega(G_{S, T}) \leq D_\Omega(\delta, \lambda) + D_\Omega(\lambda) + \lceil \log_2 T \rceil (s + 1 + \lceil \log_2 s \rceil)$$

where the state set $S = \{0, 1\}^s$, a set of binary s-tuples.

4-13. Demonstrate that a set of clocked sequential machines and an interconnection pattern that meet the conditions of Section 4.4.3 form a sequential machine. In general, this sequential machine is not clocked.

4-14. Let $\{\theta_j, \psi_j^{(i)}, \gamma_j^{(i)} | i - 1 \leq j \leq T - r + i, \ 1 \leq i \leq r\}$ be Boolean variables with the following properties:

$$\gamma_j^{(0)} = \psi_j^{(0)} = 1 \qquad \text{for all } j$$

$$\psi_j^{(i)} = \gamma_{i-1}^{(i)} + \cdots + \gamma_j^{(i)}$$

$$\gamma_j^{(i)} = \begin{cases} \theta_{i-1} \cdot \psi_{i-2}^{(i-1)}, & j = i - 1 \\ \theta_j \cdot \overline{\left(\psi_{j-1}^{(i)}\right)} \cdot \psi_{j-1}^{(i-1)}, & i \leq j \leq T - r + i \end{cases}$$

These relationships are defined in the proof of Theorem 4.5.1. Show that the functions $\{\gamma_j^{(i)}\}$ can be realized by chains over $\{+, \cdot, ^-\}$ with at most $(T - r + 2)(3r - 1) - (2r - 1)$ binary operations.

4-15. Use Problem 3-5 to show that each of the elementary symmetric functions of n variables, $\sigma_i^{(n)}: \{0, 1\}^n \to \{0, 1\}$, can be realized with a delay of

$$D_\Omega(\sigma_i) \leq 5\lceil \log_2(n + 1) \rceil - 6$$

over the basis $\Omega = \{+, \cdot, \oplus, ^-\}$.

4-16. Compute the efficiency of the machine designed in Problem 4-1.

4-17. Consider a machine that accepts two integers in binary notation (of potentially unlimited size) and that produces their product, also represented in binary. For concreteness, assume that the numbers are $\mathbf{x} = (x_0, x_1, x_2, \ldots)$, $\mathbf{y} = (y_0, y_1, y_2, \ldots)$ and that in each cycle the machine requires a pair (x_i, y_i), $0 \leq i$. Let the output be $\mathbf{z} = (a, a, \ldots, a, z_0, z_1, z_2, \ldots)$ where $a, \ldots, a$ is a fixed finite sequence of unspecified outputs that represents a delay and $z_0, z_1, z_2, \ldots$, are the digits in the binary expansion of the product $|\mathbf{x}| \times |\mathbf{y}|$. Show that the machine cannot be a finite-state sequential machine.

Hint. Consider the result of multiplying 2^k by 2^k for a large integer k.

Chapter 5

Turing Machines

In this chapter, we introduce and examine a class of machines that have access to a potentially unlimited source of storage capacity in the form of storage tapes. These machines are called *Turing Machines* in honor of A. M. Turing, who introduced them in his well-known 1936 paper (Turing, 1936). The computational procedures that these machines define are very powerful, in accord with intuitive notions of procedures, and to date no one has discovered or introduced procedures that are not equivalent to these. Thus, the thesis postulated by Church, namely, that any procedure introduced by man can be realized on a Turing machine, is most plausible.

We define the Turing machine and show equivalence of its several forms to the one-tape, semiinfinite tape version. Universal Turing machines, which are capable of simulating arbitrary Turing machines, are discussed and an unsolvable problem presented. Then the partial recursive functions on the integers are defined using the conditional expression "if then else" in the McCarthy formalism. Also in this chapter, we develop a complexity measure on functions of finite domain called *program complexity* that is used in Chapter 7 to derive computational inequalities of the second kind. These inequalities are different from those derived in the preceding chapter but are similar in that they put limits on the exchange of computational resources.

5.1. THE BASIC TURING MACHINE

Our treatment of Turing machines begins with the discussion of the basic model, shown in Figure 5.1.1, which consists of a semiinfinite *tape* ruled into cells, a *tape head*, and a *control* which is a finite-state sequential machine. In the next section, other Turing machine models are examined that are formally different from the basic model, but they are shown to be computationally equivalent.

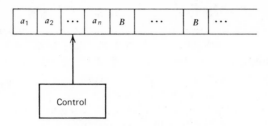

Figure 5.1.1. The basic Turing machine.

In the basic Turing machine, each cell contains one symbol from Σ, the (finite) *tape alphabet*, and the tape head, which is under the direction of the Control, can move left or right one cell or not at all in any one cycle of the Control. Before each computation on this machine, the tape is blank, that is, a reserved symbol B (the *blank*) is stored in every cell of the tape, and a finite-length nonblank string [i.e., a string over $\Sigma - (B)$] is written left adjusted on the tape. A computation begins by placing the tape head over some cell, usually the leftmost, whereupon the contents of the cell is read as an input to the Control, which then produces a pair of outputs, namely, a new symbol to be written under the head, and a command to move the head left, right, or not at all. The Control then makes an internal state transision and is prepared to begin another cycle. The machine will have *halting states* which are states of the Control which, when entered, end all motion of the tape head and prevent additional state transitions. Some of the halting states are designated as *accepting states* which, when entered, signify that the original nonblank string on the tape is accepted. Non-accepting halting states are called *rejecting states*. For our purposes, a halting state is a *self-looping state*; that is, if q is a halting state, $\delta(q, u) = (q, u, N)$ for all $u \in \Sigma$ (these quantities are defined below).

Formally, a (basic) *Turing machine* T is a 5-tuple $T = \langle S, \Sigma, \delta, F, q_0 \rangle$ where S is the finite state set of the Control, Σ is the finite tape alphabet, $\delta : S \times \Sigma \to S \times \Sigma \times \{L, N, R\}$ is the *transition function* of the Control, $F \subseteq S$ is a set of halting accepting states, and $q_0 \in S$ is the initial state of the Control. The transition function δ maps the current state of the Control and the symbol under the tape head into a potentially new state of the Control, a potentially new symbol under the head, a move left (L), right (R), or no move (N). It is understood that the tape head does not move left off the end of the tape. As a convenience and to assure this, we introduce a new cell at the left-hand end of the tape that permanently contains $\#$, a symbol not in Σ that acts as an end marker. We also require that for all $q \in S$, $\delta(q, \#) = (q', \#, X)$ where $q' \in S$ and $X \neq L$.

A (basic) Turing machine is said to *accept* a string **s** over $\Sigma - (B)$ if the machine eventually enters an accepting halting state when its tape is initialized with **s**, left-adjusted, and with the tape head over the leftmost symbol in **s**. It is said to *accept* a subset P of $(\Sigma - (B))^*$ if it accepts every string in P and no others. Note that a string is rejected if the machine enters a rejecting halting state or if it never halts.

To illustrate this definition, as well as computations on a Turing machine, we present a machine that accepts the set $\{\mathbf{w}\mathbf{w}^R | \mathbf{w} \in \{0, 1\}^*, \mathbf{w}^R$ is the reverse of $\mathbf{w}\}$ of even-length "palindromes". Its transition function is shown in Table 5.1, where the dashes identify "don't care" conditions, which are never reached. In the initial state q_0, this machine immediately accepts the string (and enters the accepting state q_A) if it encounters a blank since $\lambda = \mathbf{w}\mathbf{w}^R$ is in the set. (Here the empty string λ is recorded as the blank string.) Otherwise, it stores the symbol under the head in its control by entering q_a or q_b, and it erases the tape symbol. It then moves right. If it immediately encounters the blank symbol, the string is not of the form $\mathbf{w}\mathbf{w}^R$ and it is rejected (by entering the reject state q_R). To follow the action of the machine, assume that the leftmost tape symbol is 0. Then q_a is entered to record the presence of 0 and to test in one move that the tape contains at least one other symbol. If it does, q_{aa} is entered, the machine loops back to q_{aa}, and the head moves right without changing symbols until a blank is found. It then enters q_{aaa} and moves left. In this state, it examines the rightmost nonblank symbol on the tape and rejects the tape if it is not 0. If 0, it is erased, the head is moved left, and q_T is entered. If the symbol examined is blank, all nonblank symbols have been erased after checking left-and rightmost symbols for equality, and the string is accepted since it is of the form $\mathbf{w}\mathbf{w}^R$. If the symbol examined while in q_T is not blank, q_{TT} is entered for the purpose of moving left until the

Table 5.1.1. A Turing Machine that Accepts $\{\mathbf{w}\mathbf{w}^R | \mathbf{w} \in \{0, 1\}^*\}$

q \ u	#	B	0	1	
q_0	—	q_A, B, N	q_a, B, R	q_b, B, R	
q_a	—	q_R, B, N	$q_{aa}, 0, R$	$q_{aa}, 1, R$	
q_{aa}	—	q_{aaa}, B, L	$q_{aa}, 0, R$	$q_{aa}, 1, R$	
q_{aaa}	—	—	q_T, B, L	$q_R, 1, N$	
q_b	—	q_R, B, N	$q_{bb}, 0, R$	$q_{bb}, 1, R$	
q_{bb}	—	q_{bbb}, B, L	$q_{bb}, 0, R$	$q_{bb}, 1, N$	
q_{bbb}	—	—	$q_R, 0, N$	q_T, B, L	
q_T	—	q_A, B, N	$q_{TT}, 0, L$	$q_{TT}, 1, L$	
q_{TT}	—	q_0, B, R	$q_{TT}, 0, L$	$q_{TT}, 1, L$	
q_R	—	q_R, B, N	$q_R, 0, N$	$q_R, 1, N$	rejecting state
q_A	—	q_A, B, N	$q_A, 0, N$	$q_A, 1, N$	accepting state

first blank is encountered. The machine then moves right and enters q_0 to repeat the process since, after stripping off equal left-and rightmost symbols from **s**, the resulting string is of the form $\mathbf{ww}^R$ only if **s** is. The reader is advised to follow these steps through on the string 0 1 1 1 1 0 which is accepted and on 0 1 1 1 0 which is not accepted.

This machine demonstrates that a Turing machine can *store in the Control* some information that is on its tape. In particular q_a, q_{aa}, and q_{aaa} record that the leftmost symbol is 0 while q_b, q_{bb}, and q_{bbb} are associated with 1. It also demonstrates that a Turing machine can *shift its head across a string* until a particular symbol is found. A less obvious but equally important task that this machine performs is *recursion*. Starting in state q_0 on a string **s**, it strips off the left-and rightmost symbols, if possible, and if the resulting string is not empty (if empty it is accepted), it returns to q_0 to examine **s** with its equal outside symbols removed.

The computational power available to a Turing machine is a direct consequence of its ability to write on its tape and thus extend its memory. This is shown by considering Turing machines that do not write on their tapes. Such machines, which can only move their tape heads from left to right, advancing one cell per cycle, are clearly equivalent to sequential machines. While it is not so obvious, it can be shown (see Rabin and Scott, 1959, and Shepherdson, 1959) that every read-only Turing machine, including those that can move both ways on their tapes, is equivalent to some finite-state sequential machine for the purpose of accepting sets of strings.

5.2. EXTENSIONS OF THE BASIC MACHINE

Turing machines may take several other forms; the single tape may be extended to make it doubly infinite, and one or more additional tapes may be added. Also, the storage medium may be the plane ruled into squares or an n-dimensional space ruled into n-dimensional cubes. We demonstrate or at least sketch a proof showing that each of these extensions of the basic machine is equivalent to it in the sense that a basic machine can be constructed that "simulates" the behavior of an extended machine. We also demonstrate that a machine consisting of a Control and two "pushdown stacks" is equivalent to the basic Turing machine.

Consider first a Turing machine T_1 with a doubly infinite tape, as shown in Figure 5.2.1. Shown in the same figure is a semiinfinite tape ruled into two tracks with the lower track containing the symbols in the right half of the doubly infinite tape and the upper track containing those in the left half. One cell of the two-track tape contains an entry from each track. The

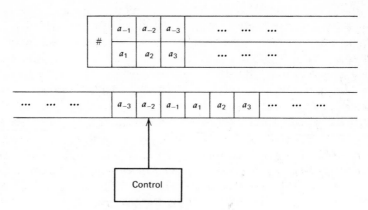

Figure 5.2.1. Turing machine with doubly infinite tape.

two tracks are simulated by choosing for a tape alphabet the alphabet $\Sigma' = \Sigma \times \Sigma$ which is the cartesian product of the tape alphabet Σ of the doubly infinite tape machine with itself. Thus, every cell of the semiinfinite tape is viewed as containing a pair $(u, v) \in \Sigma \times \Sigma$ where u is on the lower track and v on the upper.

A basic machine T_B that simulates T_1 can now be constructed. Given the representation of the tape of T_1 on the tape of T_B, T_B moves on its lower track without changing entries on its upper track in exact correspondence to T_1 as long as T_1 is on cells labeled a_i, $1 \leq i$. When T_1 moves left off of a_1, T_B encounters the end marker and then reverses the direction of its head moving on the upper track in reverse direction to moves of T_1 on cells labeled a_{-i}, $1 \leq i$. During this action, cells on the lower track remain unchanged.

A complete description of T_B requires that we specify its transition function, as we now do. If q_i is a state of T_1, then T_B has two corresponding states q_i^U and q_i^L that correspond to q_i when T_B is on its upper and lower tracks, respectively. If on T_1, $\delta_1(q_i, a) = (q_j, b, M)$ where $b \in \Sigma$, $M \in \{L, N, R\}$, then $\delta_B(q_i^L, (u, v)) = (q_j^L, (b, v), M)$ when $u = a$, and $\delta_B(q_i^U, (u, v)) = (q_j^U, (u, b), M^+)$ when $v = a$, where $M^+ = N$ when $M = N$ and $M^+ = L$ or R when $M = R$ or L, respectively. Thus, q_i^U and q_i^L result in the correct motion on corresponding tracks of T_B's tape. At the end marker #, $\delta_B(q_i^L, \#) = (q_i^U, \#, R)$ and $\delta_B(q_i^U, \#) = (q_i^L, \#, R)$ so that a move left from the lower track or from the upper track results in a reversal of the roles of q_i^U and q_i^L.

This example illustrates in detail the simulation of one machine by another and the use of fictional tape tracks. A further use of tape tracks is now made to demonstrate that *multitape Turing machines* are equivalent to machines of the basic type. It is clear from the preceding argument that we need only consider machines with several semiinfinite tapes. Figure 5.2.2 shows such a machine with two tapes. The two tape heads are capable of independent movement and are under the direction of the Control, which is now defined by a transition function $\delta : S \times \Sigma_1 \times \Sigma_2 \to S \times \Sigma_1 \times \Sigma_2 \times \{L, N, R\}^2$ which maps its current state and the entries under the two heads into new entries, head movements, and a new state for the Control.

Figure 5.2.3 shows a single semiinfinite tape that has two tracks for each of the tapes shown above, one to record the entries on a tape and the other to record the head position on that tape. The one-tape machine simulates the two-tape machine by alternating between the two simulated tapes, moving the checks to record the correct head positions, and making the correct entries into the cells on the corresponding tracks.

The simulation of the two tapes is potentially quite costly to the one-tape machine because its head must move up and down the tape searching for the checks that identify head positions on the two tapes. Since the two heads are allowed to move independently, there is no upper

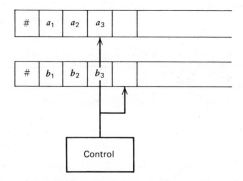

Figure 5.2.2. Multitape Turing machine.

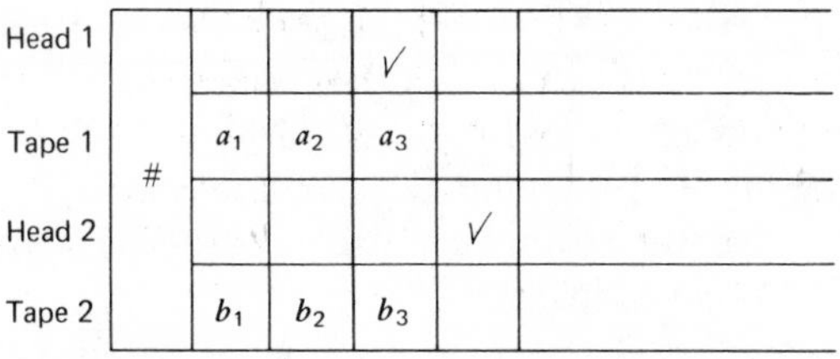

Figure 5.2.3. One-tape simulation of two tapes.

bound on the separation of checks on the single tape. This point is made clearer by considering the problem of recognition of strings over $\{0, 1\}$ that are in $\{0^n 1^n | n = 1, 2, \ldots \}$. On a one-tape machine, the time to verify that a binary string is of the form $0^n 1^n$ is on the order[†] of n^2. However, on a two-tape machine, a copy of the leading 0's can be recorded on the second tape, and when a 1 is reached, the head on this tape is reversed, checking off 0's against 1's in the first tape. Thus, the recognition time measured in cycles on the two-tape machine is at most the length of the input string.

The simulation of a multitape Turing machine by a single-tape machine illustrates the use of symbols to *check off* positions in a multitrack tape. We also observe that each demonstration of the equivalence of one machine with another involves the encoding of a multidimensional storage space onto a one-dimensional, semiinfinite string over a finite set. This can always be done as long as the space has a countable number of regions and each region contains one of a finite number of symbols. In particular, this is true of a storage space consisting of the plane ruled into squares or the n-dimensional space ruled into n-cubes.

The *push-down stack* is a storage space familiar to those who frequent cafeterias. This is a container that holds trays in a stack; trays can only be inserted or removed from the top. When a tray is inserted, all trays are pushed down one position, and when one is removed, all trays move up one position. A stack in which each tray is allowed to contain one of a finite number of symbols, is a push-down stack. Again, operations are allowed only at the top of the stack, and these operations are "push A" and "pop," where the first results in the new entry being pushed down onto the stack and the second results in the reading and removing of the top item.

Push-down stores are usually implemented on general-purpose computers, so it is interesting to observe that every computation that can be carried out on a Turing machine can also be done on a machine consisting of a Control and two push-down, stacks, and vice versa. The simulation of a single doubly infinite-tape Turing machine by a two-stack machine is easily sketched, and the general conclusion follows from this. As the tape head moves on the tape of the Turing machine, let the stack machine pop from one stack and push onto the other, changing the pushed item if necessary, to simulate left-to-right motion. Motion in the other direction is simulated by poping and pushing on the two stacks in reverse order. Finally, it should be quite obvious that a two-stack machine can be simulated by a Turing machine.

[†] A proof of this result uses "crossing sequences," which are introduced in Hennie (1965).

5.3.   COMPUTATIONS ON TURING MACHINES

As stated earlier in this chapter, Church's plausible thesis argues that any computational procedure that might be invented is a procedure that could be implemented on a Turing machine. To this point, we have seen that Turing machines can carry out simple tasks such as scanning a list for an item and checking off items in a list; one can imagine a machine that moves or interchanges blocks of items in a list. Turing machines can also loop from state to state or from item to item in a list and can execute conditional or unconditional jumps from state to state or from item to item, as was seen in the simulation of two tapes with one tape. We have also seen that Turing machines can execute recursively defined procedures, as in the recognition of binary strings that are in $\{ww^R\}$.

Although it is perhaps not apparent, some Turing machines do not halt on all inputs; that is, some inputs cause some machines to loop. Any computational process defined by Turing machine, whether it halts on all inputs or not, is called a *procedure*. Procedures that result in halting on all inputs are given a special name: *algorithms*. Corresponding to this classification of processes and Turing machines is a classification of sets. A set p of strings over the finite set A is called *recursively enumerable* if there exists a procedure that accepts exactly the strings in P (perhaps not halting on strings over A that are not in P), and P is called *recursive* if there is an algorithm that accepts P (and halts on all strings over A). Later we exhibit a set that is recursively enumerable but not recursive.

Recognition problems define functions whose range is binary and whose two elements correspond to acceptance and rejection. These functions fall into two classes, functions defined at all points of their domain, called *total functions*, and functions that are not so defined, *partial functions*. The class of functions computable by Turing machines contains functions whose domains and ranges are finite and infinite (but countable) sets, and in each case, the functions are either partial or total.

Every total function f of finite domain D has a finite range R, $f\colon D \to R$, and is computable by a Turing machine, given some encoding of D and R into the tape alphabet of the machine. If $D = \{d_1, d_2, \ldots, d_k\}$ and $R = \{r_1, r_2, \ldots, r_l\}$, then f is computed in one cycle by the machine with tape alphabet $\Sigma = D \cup R \cup \{B\}$ which has a single state q_0 and transition function defined by

$$\delta(q_0, d_i) = (q_0, f(d_i), N)$$

$$\delta(q_0, u) = \text{``don't care''} \qquad \text{for } u \in \Sigma - D$$

An element $d \in D$ is placed in the leftmost square of the tape of a basic Turing machine and in one cycle, the value of f at d is returned in that cell.

The computation of functions on Turing machines becomes interesting primarily when finite functions are computed on machines of finite size or when the functions to be computed have infinite domain. The first case is considered in Section 5.7, and we concentrate on the latter case here. Functions of infinite domain computable on Turing machines must have a countable domain; otherwise, not all points in such domains could be inscribed on the tape or tapes of such machines. Therefore, the domains and ranges of Turing machine–computable functions can be mapped into $N = \{0, 1, 2, 3, \ldots\}$ or subsets of N and without loss of generality we consider functions $f : N \to N$.

To compute a function $f : N \to N$, some representation must be given of points in N. As our standard representation, we denote $n \in N$ by the unary notation 1^{n+1} where $1 \in \Sigma$, the tape alphabet of the machine in question. Other representations are acceptable, such as the standard binary notation, if they are obtainable by a Turing machine computation from the standard representation. As the standard input and output formats, we ask that 1^{n+1} be placed left-adjusted on the otherwise blank portion of the tape of a basic Turing machine with the head over the leftmost cell and that the head and the result $1^{f(n)+1}$ be similarly placed at the end of the computation if f is defined on n. Other formats are acceptable if they are obtainable from the standard format by a Turing machine computation.

If a function $f : N \to N$ is obtainable from a Turing machine computation for each point of the domain where it is defined with an acceptable representation of N and acceptable formats, then it is said to be *computable*. It is called a *recursive function* if it is total, and a *partial recursive function* if it is not. The function $f_{\text{PRIME}} : N \to N$ which has as its value on n $f_{\text{PRIME}}(n)$, the nth prime integer, is recursive, while the function f_p which has value 1 when $n \in P$ and 0 otherwise, where P is a recursively enumerable but not recursive set, is a partial recursive function. Such a set is given in Section 5.5.

5.4. UNIVERSAL TURING MACHINES

There are Turing machines that can simulate the computations of arbitrary Turing machines, as we demonstrate in this section. Such machines are called *universal machines*. As the reader will soon see, conventional general-purpose computers, when provided with potentially unlimited storage capacity, are universal machines.

To simulate a (basic) machine $T = \langle S, \Sigma, \delta, F, q_0 \rangle$, it is necessary that some way be found to compute the transition function $\delta : S \times \Sigma \to S \times \Sigma \times \{L, N, R\}$ and to record the contents of T's tape and the position of its head. In turn, this requires an encoding of states in S and symbols in Σ into the tape alphabet Σ_U of the simulating universal machine U. For simplicity, let $0, 1 \in \Sigma_U$ and let the states in S be numbered $q_0, q_1, \ldots, q_k$. Then $q_j \in S$ can be encoded into the string $\mathbf{q}_j = 1^{j+1}0^{k-j}$. Also, for the purpose of illustration, let $\Sigma = \{0, 1\}$, an assumption that is examined later. Then, if $\mathbf{s}_\delta$ is a string over Σ_U describing δ, the tape shown in Figure 5.4.1 contains enough information to simulate T. Here $a_1, a_2, \ldots,$ are the symbols on T's tape; $A_i = \alpha$ if $a_i = 0$ and $A_i = \beta$ if $a_i = 1$. The new symbols α and β mark the position of T's head.

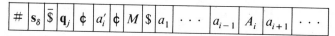

Figure 5.4.1. Tape of a universal machine.

A universal machine U that can use this information to simulate T has two submachines U_{TR} and U_{TA} where U_{TR} takes $\mathbf{q}_j$ and a_i, computes $\delta(q_j, a_i)$, and stores the result (q', a', M) between $\bar{\$}$ and $\$$. Then control is given to U_{TA} (by making the halting state of U_{TR} the initial state of U_{TA}), which changes A_i to a' and moves the head position according to the instruction M. Submachine U_{TA} then transfers control to U_{TR} which repeats the process. Shown in Table 5.4.1 is a tabular description of U_{TA} where $\bar{\$}$, $\$$, ϕ, 0, 1, α, β, L, N, and R are symbols in Σ_U. If Σ_U has other symbols, the other entries in this table are "don't cares" (which are indicated by a dash).

The machine U_{TA} is initially in state q_0 with the head over $\bar{\$}$, and it moves right in state q_0 until it finds a_i'. (The entries MR and ML mean that the machine moves right or left, respectively, one cell without changing state or the tape entry.) It records the value of a_i' in its state with q_2 and q_3 being associated with 0 and 1, respectively, and then moves right until α or β is found. If in state q_2, this entry is set to α (corresponding to 0) and if in q_3, it is set to β (corresponding to 1). Then U_{TA} enters q_4, which takes the head back to the cell marked M which contains the directions for T's head movement. This is recorded in states q_L and q_R (if $M = N$, q_6 is entered), and U_{TA} then moves its head right until α or β are found. These are then changed to 0 or 1, and an adjacent cell is marked with α or β; U_{TA} then enters q_6, which repositions its head over $\bar{\$}$.

If $\Sigma \neq \{0, 1\}$, then symbols in Σ can be recorded as strings over $\{0, 1\}$. For example, symbols in $\{0, 1, B\}$ can be encoded as $\{100, 110, 111\}$.

Table 5.4.1. Transition Table for U_{TA}

q \ u	$\bar{\$}$	$\$$	¢	0	1	α	β	L	N	R	Comments
q_0	MR	—	$q_1, ¢, R$	MR	MR	—	—	—	—	—	Positions head over a_i'
q_1	—	—	—	$q_2, 0, R$	$q_3, 1, R$	—	—	—	—	—	Records a_i'
q_2	—	MR	MR	MR	MR	$q_4, α, L$	$q_4, α, L$	MR	MR	MR	Moves right to A_i and changes to a_i'
q_3	—	MR	MR	MR	MR	$q_4, β, L$	$q_4, β, L$	MR	MR	MR	The same
q_4	—	$q_5, \$, L$	—	ML	ML	—	—	—	—	—	Positions head over M
q_5	—	—	—	—	—	—	—	q_L, L, R	q_6, N, L	q_R, R, R	Records M
q_6	HALT	ML	ML	ML	ML	—	—	ML	ML	ML	Positions head over $\bar{\$}$
q_L	—	MR	—	MR	MR	$q_{LL}, 0, L$	$q_{LL}, 1, L$	—	—	—	Changes α, β to 0, 1 and moves left
q_{LL}	—	—	—	$q_6, α, L$	$q_6, β, L$	—	—	—	—	—	Changes 0, 1 to α, β and moves left
q_R	—	MR	—	MR	MR	$q_{RR}, 0, R$	$q_{RR}, 1, R$	—	—	—	Changes α, β to 0, 1 and moves right
q_{RR}	—	—	—	$q_6, α, L$	$q_6, β, L$	—	—	—	—	—	Changes 0, 1 to α, β and moves left.

184

Then, since U does not know, a priori, the size of the tape alphabet that it is simulating, it must use the number of characters between ¢ and ¢ on its tape to determine the number of tape characters to alter in each move to T. This can be done by making a fairly straightforward change in the description of U_{TA}.

There are many ways to realize U_{TR}, the submachine that computes δ. One of the more obvious but least efficient ways to compute δ is to generate a string that records its tabular description, from which the value of $\delta(q, a)$ can be found by "table look-up." We know from our treatment of binary functions that most, if not all, interesting functions can be described by straight-line programs (or chains) much more efficiently than they can this way.[†] Nevertheless, to demonstrate the existence of universal machines we consider just such a description of transition functions.

The following is a string $\mathbf{s}_\delta$ for a machine with two states and three tape symbols:

$$\overline{C}q', a', m'Cq'', a'', m''Cq''', a''', m'''\overline{C}\tilde{q}', \tilde{a}', \tilde{m}'C\tilde{q}'', \tilde{a}'', \tilde{m}''C\tilde{q}''', \tilde{a}''', \tilde{m}'''\overline{C}\$$$

The entries between pairs of $\overline{C}$'s describe one row in the table of δ, and in one row, entries for each of the three tape symbols are separated by C. Thus, if the states of T are q_0 and q_1 and its tape symbols are 0 1, and B, then $\delta(q_1, 0) = (\tilde{q}', \tilde{a}', \tilde{M}')$ where $\tilde{q}' \in \{q_0, q_1\}$, $\tilde{a}' \in \{0, 1, B\}$, and $\tilde{M}' \in \{L, N, R\}$. This string could be placed on the lower track of a two-track tape, and the upper track could be used to place checks to locate the row entries being sought.

To compute $\delta(q, a)$, U_{TR} will place a check on the leftmost $\overline{C}$ and move it right until it is over the $\overline{C}$ preceding the row corresponding to the state q. It can do this by "counting down" on q which is located between $\overline{\$}$ and $\$$. For each 1 in q, U_{TR} advances to the next $\overline{C}$ on the right. It then examines a and places a check in front of the block containing the value of $\delta(q, a)$ which can then be transported to the region between $\overline{\$}$ and $\$$.

This completes our discussion of universal machines. We now turn to a discussion of unsolvable problems.

5.5. UNSOLVABILITY OF THE HALTING PROBLEM

Will a given (arbitrary) Turing machine with a given (arbitrary) initial tape string halt on that string or will it not? The problem this question poses is known as the *halting problem*. We shall see that this is an *unsolvable problem*, meaning that no algorithm (or halting procedure) exists for solving this problem for all machines and all inputs.

[†] The construction of Turing machine programs for functions of finite domain is discussed in Section 5.7.

The halting problem is shown to be unsolvable by demonstrating that a restricted version of the problem is unsolvable. This problem is loosely defined by the question, "Will a Turing machine T halt when given as its initial string a description of itself?" To pose the problem correctly, we must define "descriptions" of Turing machines. For this we recall the arguments of the preceding section and observe that a string $\mathbf{w} = \mathbf{s}_\delta \overline{\mathbf{S}} \mathbf{q}_j \mathbf{¢} a_i' \mathbf{¢} M \$$, as shown in Figure 5.4.1, contains enough information to simulate and hence describe a Turing machine T with transition function δ. Such strings are over the tape alphabet Σ_U of the universal machine U, and Σ_U may contain more symbols than does the tape alphabet of T. Consequently, encode symbols of Σ_U into distinct binary strings (over $\{0, 1\}$) of length $l = \lceil \log_2 |\Sigma_U| \rceil$. Let d_T be the encoded version of $\mathbf{w}$.

Clearly, a universal Turing machine U_B exists with a tape alphabet $\{0, 1\}$ that simulates U by treating blocks of l of its tape cells as single cells of U. Since d_T is a complete description of T on U_B, we call d_T the U_B-*descriptor* of T on U_B. By renaming 0 and 1, we can regard d_T as written in the tape alphabet of T. We are now prepared to demonstrate the unsolvability of the restricted version of the halting problem.

Theorem 5.5.1. There is no algorithm that can determine from the U_B-descriptor d_T of an arbitrary Turing machine T whether or not T halts on the input d_T.

Proof. (By contradiction). Assume that H is a machine for the restricted halting problem that, given d_T, can determine whether T halts on d_T or not. The machine H has two halting states which are associated with the two conclusions (Yes and No), and for each T it reaches one of these conclusions.

Given H, construct a new machine L with two additional states, q_1', q_2'. When H enters its Yes halting state, transfer to the first of the two new states of L, q_1'. Let $\delta(q_1', u) = (q_2', u, R)$ and $\delta(q_2', u) = (q_1', u, L)$ for all $u \in \Sigma_L$, the tape alphabet of L. Clearly, when H enters its Yes halting state, L enters a looping mode in which its head oscillates between two adjacent tape squares. Let L otherwise be identical with H.

Now, if H declares that T halts on d_T, then L does not halt on d_T, and if H declares that T does not halt on d_T, then L does halt. Thus, L on d_T halts if and only if T on d_T does not halt. But now let $T = L$. We then conclude (by assuming the existence of H) that L halts on d_L if and only if L does not halt on d_L. This contradicts the assumed existence of H. $\square$

If an algorithm for the halting problem existed, it could be used to solve the restricted halting problem, which is shown to be unsolvable.

Corollary 5.5.1. There is no algorithm that can determine from the U_B-descriptor d_T of an arbitrary Turing machine T whether or not T halts on the initial and arbitrary tape string t.

A set of strings P over an alphabet A is recursively enumerable but not recursive if there exists a procedure that accepts every string in P (by halting) but, for every such procedure, there are strings over A not in P such that the procedure never halts on them. The restricted halting problem also provides us with an example of a set that is recursively enumerable but not recursive. Let $P = \{d_T | d_T$ is a U_B-descriptor of T and T halts on input $d_T\}$. Then P is well defined and not empty because it contains the (basic) machine E which erases its tape and halts. (E has two states q_0 and q_1 and $\delta(q_0, u) = (q_0, B, R)$ if $u \neq B$ and $\delta(q_0, B) = (q_1, B, N)$, $\delta(q_1, u) = (q_1, u, N)$ for all u. Started in q_0 on the left-hand edge of its tape, it erases every input string and halts). There exists a machine D that given $d_T \in P$, halts and accepts d_T. This machine constructs a second copy of d_T so that $d_T d_T$ lies on its tape. It then transfers control to U_B which simulates T on d_T and by definition halts. But D recognizes halting and then enters a special halting state designating acceptance. Thus, P is recursively enumerable. It is not recursive because if it were, an algorithm would exist to determine membership in P, which means that for all U_B-descriptors d_T, a machine would exist that halts entering the accepting state for $d_T \in P$ and a nonaccepting halting state for $d_T \notin P$. But this is exactly an algorithm for the restricted halting problem, which has been shown above to be an unsolvable problem.

Theorem 5.5.2. The class of binary strings P defined by

$$P = \{d_T | d_T \text{ is a } U_B\text{-descriptor of } T \text{ and } T \text{ halts on } d_T\}$$

is a set that is recursively enumerable but not recursive.

In the course of proving this theorem, we have used the fact that a set which is recursively enumerable and whose complement is recursively enumerable is recursive. Since the set P defined above is recursively enumerable but not recursive, we conclude that the complement of P relative to $\{0, 1\}^*$ is not recursively enumerable.

5.6. PARTIAL RECURSIVE FUNCTIONS—THE McCARTHY FORMALISM

The Turing machine is a conceptually simple device for the mechanical realization of procedures, but it is a less than satisfactory instrument for the description of the functions it can compute. The latter purpose is more effectively served by a language that makes explicit reference to primitive functions and to operations, and methods for managing the flow of control of a computation. In this section, we describe such a language, which was presented by McCarthy (1963) and which makes use of functional composition, the "if then else" flow of control primitive of ALGOL 60 (Dijkstra, 1962), and three simple functions. It can be shown (Minsky, 1967) that every Turing Machine computation can be expressed in this language.

The language to be described is a language for expressing functions $f : N^k \rightarrow N$ for some integer k, where $N = \{0, 1, 2, 3, \dots \}$ is the set of natural numbers. The *zero function*, denoted 0, has the value 0 on all points of its domain. The *successor function*, $S : N \rightarrow N$, maps $n \in N$ to $n + 1$, the next largest integer, $S(n) = n + 1$. We also use the shorthand $n^+ = S(n)$. Clearly, all of the integers can now be constructed using *functional composition*. For example, $4 = ((((0)^+)^+)^+)^+$. The *equality function*, equ $: N^2 \rightarrow \{0, 1\}$, is a function of two variables where $equ(n_1, n_2) = 1$ if and only if n_1 and n_2 are equal integers. (Functions whose range is $\{0, 1\}$ are called *predicates*.) We often use the shorthand $n_1 = n_2$ for $equ(n_1, n_2)$ when it is clearly understood that this is to be interpreted as a predicate whose value is 1 when n_1 and n_2 are equal and 0 otherwise.

The *conditional expression*

$$f : = \textbf{if } p \textbf{ then } e_1 \textbf{ else } e_2 \textbf{ fi}$$

defines a procedure that has a meaning only when p is a predicate and e_1 and e_2 are expressions defining functions over N. The interpretation of the conditional expression is that if $p = 1$ (that is, if it is TRUE), then e_1 is computed and f has result e_1, else (that is, if p is FALSE) e_2 is computed and f has result e_2. It is important to note that the conditional expression defines a procedure and not a function. In the latter case, p, e_1, and e_2 would have to be evaluated before the expression is evaluated, but it may be true that e_2 defines a nonhalting computation when p is TRUE and when e_1 defines a halting computation. Thus, evaluating f as a function may lead to nontermination whereas the specified order of evaluation of e_1 and e_2 would not. The conditional expression f is *undefined* (it describes a nonterminating computation) if p is undefined, or if p is defined and TRUE but e_1 is not, or if p is FALSE and e_2 is not defined.

The conditional expression can be used in two ways: for self-referencing or for nonself-referencing. The first case occurs when the "name" f appears in either of the expressions e_1 or e_2; the second case occurs when it does not. When self-referencing occurs, the conditional expression describes what is commonly called a *recursive procedure*, in the parlance of programming languages, because it is recursively defined.

The *predecessor function* **pred**: $N \to N$ (not defined for $n = 0$) is defined in terms of the procedure **pred 2** below and illustrates one use of self-referencing.

$$\mathbf{pred}\ (n) := \mathbf{pred\ 2}\ (n, 0)$$

$$\mathbf{pred\ 2}\ (n, m) := \textbf{if}\ m^+ = n\ \textbf{then}\ m\ \textbf{else pred 2}\ (n, m^+)\ \textbf{fi}$$

For $n \neq 0$, **pred** $(n) = n - 1$. We introduce the shorthand n^- for it. Let's carry out the sequence of operations that are dictated by this recursively defined procedure for $n = 4$.

pred 2 $(4, 0) := \textbf{if}\ 1 = 4\ \textbf{then}\ 0\ \textbf{else pred 2}\ (4, 1)\ \textbf{fi}$

pred 2 $(4, 1) := \textbf{if}\ 2 = 4\ \textbf{then}\ 1\ \textbf{else pred 2}\ (4, 2)\ \textbf{fi}$

pred 2 $(4, 2) := \textbf{if}\ 3 = 4\ \textbf{then}\ 2\ \textbf{else pred 2}\ (4, 3)\ \textbf{fi}$

pred 2 $(4, 3) := \textbf{if}\ 4 = 4\ \textbf{then}\ ③\ \textbf{else pred 2}\ (4, 4)\ \textbf{fi}$

Each time except the last, the predicate $m^+ = n$ is FALSE and **pred 2** calls itself. When it does, we recopy the entire description of the procedure, giving each of its variables their potentially new values (this is called the *copy rule*) and then execute that copy. We can think of **pred 2** (4, 0), **pred 2** (4, 1), **pred 2** (4, 2), and **pred 2** (4, 3) as the locations containing the values of the corresponding instances of **pred 2**. In this case, when **pred 2** (4, 3) is evaluated (its value is circled), the result is passed back to **pred 2** (4, 2), and so forth, until the value of **pred 2** (4, 0) is computed. The use of the copy rule and this method of addressing can be implemented on a Turing machine to realize this recursively defined procedure and any such procedure that *does not* invoke another recursively defined procedure.

Frequently it is desirable to define a procedure recursively in terms of one or more recursively defined procedures. For example, the procedure **pred**, which returns **pred** $(n) = n - 1$ when $n \neq 0$ and is undefined otherwise, is used below to define **par**: $N \to \{0, 1\}$, which returns **par** (n) which is the remainder of n after division by 2; that is, **par** (n) is 1 if n is odd and 0 if n is even.

$$\mathbf{par}\ (n) := \textbf{if}\ n = 0\ \textbf{then}\ 0\ \textbf{else}\ (\textbf{if}\ n = 1\ \textbf{then}\ 1\ \textbf{else par}\ (n^{--})\ \textbf{fi})\ \textbf{fi}$$

In this situation, it is not immediately apparent how to *correctly interpret* this statement. If, for example, $n = 1$ and we evaluate the innermost argument first, namely, $n^{--} = 1^{--} = 0^{-}$, we immediately encounter a function that is undefined. The (recursively defined) rules we shall always follow for interpreting recursively defined procedures are the following:

1. Evaluate conditional expressions from left to right, as indicated in the preceding.
2. Evaluate other expressions consisting of predicates, functions, or procedures from outside to inside.
3. Evaluate directly any functions that do not require the evaluation of procedures.
4. Evaluate procedures by applying the copy rule and returning to 1.

These rules define the *semantics* of the McCarthy formalism.

We illustrate these rules on the computation of **pred (pred (3)) = 1**.

pred (pred (3)): = pred 2 (pred (3), 0)

    pred 2 (pred (3), 0): = if 0^{+} = pred (3) then 0 else pred 2 (pred (3), 0^{+}) fi

      pred (3): = pred 2 (3, 0)

        pred 2 (3, 0): = if 1 = 3 then 0 else pred 2 (3, 1) fi

        pred 2 (3, 1): = if 2 = 3 then 1 else pred 2 (3, 2) fi

        pred 2 (3, 2): = if 3 = 3 then ② else pred 2 (3, 3) fi

pred 2 (pred (3), 0^{+}): = if 0^{++} = pred (3) then ①

                           else pred 2 (pred (3), 0^{++}) fi

      pred (3): = pred 2 (3, 0)

        pred 2 (3, 0): = if 1 = 3 then 0 else pred 2 (3, 1) fi

        pred 2 (3, 1): = if 2 = 3 then 1 else pred 2 (3, 2) fi

        pred 2 (3, 2): = if 3 = 3 then ② else pred 2 (3, 3) fi

We see that **pred** calls **pred 2**, which is copied with the appropriate arguments, one of which is **pred** (3). (0^+ is evaluated directly since it is the value of a primitive function.) In turn, **pred** is called and it generates the sequence of calls and executions resulting in the computation of **pred** (3) = 2 which is circled. The predicate 0^+ = **pred** (3) is then evaluated and found to be FALSE, which causes branching to the "else clause." This involves a procedure call that again leads to evaluations of **pred** (3) in order to determine the value of the predicate in the conditional expression. It is TRUE, and **pred 2** (**pred** (3), 0^+) is given the value 1 which is passed back until **pred** (**pred** (3)) is assigned the value 1.

The correct interpretation of the procedure **par** involves the interpretation of **pred** (**pred** ( )) and each execution of **par** (n) involves a computation like that illustrated for **pred** (**pred** (m)). To see that **par** (n) is indeed the parity of n, observe that each call of **par** (n) subtracts 2 from n unless n is 0 or 1. Thus, each call of **par** subtracts 2 from n *until* n is 0 or 1; that is, **par** computes the remainder of n after division by 2.

It should be quite apparent now that the three simple functions $0, n^+$, and equ can be realized by Turing machines, as can composition, the conditional expression, and any finite, well-formed expression that makes use of these primitives. (The conditional expression without self-referencing is a simple branching operation.) As mentioned above, one can demonstrate that every Turing machine computation can be described in this language, which means, of course, that all functions computable with Turing machines are describable in this simple language.

To suggest the power of expression of this language, we now present programs for a number of interesting functions. The following expressions define the sum

$$m + n = \textbf{sum } (m, n) := \textbf{if } n = 0 \textbf{ then } m \textbf{ else sum } (m^+, n^-) \textbf{ fi}$$

the product

$$mn = \textbf{prod } (m, n) := \textbf{if } n = 0 \textbf{ then } 0 \textbf{ else sum } (m, \textbf{prod } (m, n^-)) \textbf{ fi}$$

and the difference

$$m - n = \textbf{diff } (m, n) := \textbf{if } n = 0 \textbf{ then } m \textbf{ else diff } (m^-, n^-) \textbf{ fi}$$

which is defined only for $m \geq n$. Each procedure is recursively defined, and the procedure **prod** invokes the procedure **sum** so that **prod** is defined by two levels of recursion. Also, in each definition an *invariant relation* holds (e.g., $m + n = m^+ + n^-$ if $n \neq 0$, $mn = m + mn^-$ if $n \neq 0$, and $m - n = m^- - n^-$ if $m \geq n$ and $n \neq 0$), and each application of the procedure drives the predicate being tested, namely, equ (n, 0), closer to being satisfied.

If A and B are predicates, the Boolean operations of *complement* $\sim A$, *conjunction* (AND) $A \wedge B$ and *disjunction* (OR) $A \vee B$ are very useful and are defined using the conditional expressions without the self-referencing given in the following:

$\sim A$: = **if** $A = 1$ **then** 0 **else** 1 **fi**

$A \wedge B$: = **if** $A = 1$ **then**

if $B = 1$ **then** 1 **else** 0 **fi**

else 0 **fi**

$A \vee B$: = $\sim ((\sim A) \wedge (\sim B))$

The inequality predicate $m \leq n$ and strict inequality predicate $m < n$ are defined recursively by

$m \leq n =$ **ineq** (m, n): = **if** $m = 0$ **then** 1 **else**

if $n = 0$ **then** 0 **else ineq** (m^{-}, n^{-}) **fi fi**

$n < n =$ **sineq** (m, n): = **ineq** $(m, n) \wedge (\sim$ equ $(m, n))$

and are also useful in constructing more complex functions.

The divisibility of a number n by a number m, denoted $m|n$, is defined by the predicate

$m|n$: = **if** $n = 0$ **then** 1 **else if** $m \leq n$ **then** $m|(n - m)$ **else** 0 **fi fi**

and is useful in determining whether as integer n is prime. We also define the predicate **prime** (n) by

prime (n): = **if** $n \geq 2$ **then prime** 2 $(n, 2)$ **else if** $n = 1$ **then** 1 **else** 0 **fi fi**

where

prime 2 (m, n): = **if** $m = n$ **then** 1 **else if** $n|m$ **then** 0

else **prime** 2 (m, n^{+}) **fi fi**

Thus, **prime** (n) is 1 (TRUE) when n is a prime number and is 0 (FALSE) otherwise.

As a further illustration of the power of recursion, consider Ackerman's function defined by the procedure **ack**:

ack (m, n): = **if** $m = 0$ **then** $n + 1$ **else if** $n = 0$ **then ack** $(m - 1, 1)$

else **ack** $(m - 1,$ **ack** $(m, n - 1))$ **fi fi**

It can be shown that **ack** is defined for all $m, n \geq 0$. Let $A(n) = $ **ack** (n, n). Then $A(0) = 1$, $A(1) = 3$, $A(2) = 7$, $A(3) = 61$, and $A(4) = 2^{2^{2^{2^{16}}}} - 3$, which is a pretty big number.

5.7. PROGRAM COMPLEXITY OF FINITE FUNCTIONS

Combinational complexity plays a central role in the computational inequalities of Section 4.4. Program complexity plays a similar role in the computational inequalities of the "second kind" which are derived in Chapter 7. Combinational complexity and program complexity are both measures of the complexities of functions $f : \{0, 1\}^n \rightarrow \{0, 1\}^m$. The former is the minimum number of operators in a straight-line algorithm for a function f, whereas the latter is the minimum amount of information (including data) that must be given to a universal Turing machine U in order to compute f. Thus, the first measure is defined relative to a restricted class of algorithms, while in the second case the class of computational procedures is unrestricted.

In this section, program complexity is defined and a number of its properties are developed. We begin with an exercise that initially may appear to be tangential to this topic; we develop the prefix notations of Boolean formulas. It is not tangential, howver, because these notations serve as basic examples of Turing machine programs for finite functions. In fact, we present a relatively simple Turing machine that can read and execute prefix notations.

Shown in Figure 5.7.1 are the graphs of two formulas for Boolean functions $f_1 : \{0, 1\}^4 \rightarrow \{0, 1\}$ and $f_2 : \{0, 1\}^3 \rightarrow \{0, 1\}$. (Note that a small circle denotes NOT.) Together they define a function $f = (f_1, f_2)$ where $f : \{0, 1\}^4 \rightarrow \{0, 1\}^2$. The prefix notation for a formula is determined by a traversal of the corresponding tree. A *preorder traversal* of a tree is defined recursively as follows:

> Visit the root of the tree (with k subtrees)
> Do a preorder traversal of 1st subtree (on the left)
> .   .
> .   .
> .   .
> Do a preorder traversal of kth subtree

In Figure 5.7.1, the tree for f_1 has three nodes with fan-in 2, one (the NOT) with fan-in 1, and four with fan-in 0. A preorder traversal of its nodes generates the following set of node labels:

$$+ \cdot {}^{-} x_1 \oplus x_2 x_3 x_4$$

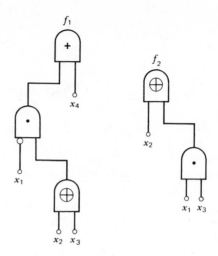

Figure 5.7.1. Graphs of two formulas.

in the order encountered. A preorder traversal of the tree for f_2 generates the node labels

$$\oplus\ x_2 \cdot x_1 x_3$$

These are known as *prefix notations* for the corresponding formulas.

It is relatively straightforward to compute a Boolean function from one of its prefex notations. One simply reads such a string from right to left until an operator is encountered, determines its fan-in, and moves right to find this many arguments which are then "erased" and used to compute the value of the operator that replaces the operator symbol in the string. This process is then repeated until the left-hand end of the string has been reached. If we denote an erased digit in the string by underscoring it, that is, replacing 0, 1 by 0,1, then, after computing the value of $\oplus$ in the first string given above, this procedure generates the following string:

$$+ \ \cdot \ ^- \ 1 \ 0 \ \underline{1} \ \underline{1} \ 0$$

when $(x_1, x_2, x_3, x_4) = (1, 1, 1, 0)$. After computing $^-$, the string becomes

$$+ \ \cdot \ \underset{*}{\underline{0}} \ \underline{1} \ 0 \ \underline{1} \ \underline{1} \ 0$$

and the next step is to move left (from the position of the asterisk) to the next operator symbol, namely, $\cdot$, and then move right to find the two unerased symbols on its immediate right (there are three to its right), erase them, and then evaluate $\cdot$ and replace it by its value.

This procedure works equally well when two or more prefix notations are concatenated. Concatenating the two prefix notations for f_1 and f_2, we have

$$+ \cdot {}^- x_1 \oplus x_2 x_3 x_4 \oplus x_2 \cdot x_1 x_3$$

which after evaluation on $(x_1, x_2, x_3, x_4) = (1, 1, 0, 1)$ gives

$$1 \; \underline{0} \; \underline{0} \; 1 \; 1 \; 1 \; \underline{0} \; 1 \; 1 \; 1 \; \underline{0} \; 1 \; \underline{0}$$

which has two unerased entries corresponding to the values of f_1 and f_2, in that order.

The basic Turing machine F whose control is defined by Table 5.7.1 executes these procedures on strings that are in the concatenations of prefix notations. Moreover, after completing this computation, it shifts all unerased symbols left into one block of unerased symbols and replaces all other entries with the blank B.

A computation of F is carried out as follows. A string is placed left-adjusted on the nonblank portion of the tape, the head is placed over the first cell (to the right of #), F is placed in state q_0, and the right-hand end of the tape is found. In q_1, the operator symbol on the left is found and the appropriate state is entered. If there is no such symbol, namely, # is encountered, then q_2 is entered for the purpose of bringing all unerased symbols together in a block and then blanking the rest of the tape. In a state such as q_+, F picks up the first and then the second unerased digit on its right and proceeds to evaluate + and erase these two digits. *ML* and *MR* cause the head to move left or right, respectively, without changing the symbol under the head. The table is incomplete, and it is left to the reader to use 12 additional rows to complete it. The completed machine will have 33 states (not including the HALT state) and a tape alphabet of 10 symbols.

The strings that are concatenations of prefix notations over the basis $\Omega = \{ +, \cdot, \oplus, {}^- \}$ are "programs" for the Turing machine F. However, F cannot execute programs because the variables are not in its tape alphabet. It can only execute "valuations" of programs. We are now prepared to define "programs" and "program complexity".

Definition 5.7.1. Let T be a universal basic Turing machine with tape alphabet Σ that contains a single blank B as well as 0 and 1. Let $\tilde{\mathbf{x}} = (x_1, x_2, \ldots, x_n)$ denote the variables of $f : \{0, 1\}^n \to \{0, 1\}^m$ where each x_i, $1 \le i \le n$, is a distinct symbol not in Σ. Then a *program for f on T* is a string $s(\tilde{\mathbf{x}})$ over $(\Sigma - \{B\}) \cup \{x_1, \ldots, x_n\}$ with the property that, for each $\mathbf{x} \in \{0, 1\}^n$, the valuation $s(\mathbf{x})$ of this string, when placed left-adjusted on the nonblank portion of the tape of T, results in a halting

Table 5.7.1. Transition Table for Machine F

	0	1	$\underline{0}$	$\underline{1}$	+	·	⊕	−	B	#
q_0	MR	MR	—	—	MR	MR	MR	MR	q_1, B, L	—
q_1	ML	ML	—	—	q_+, +, R	$q_\cdot$, ·, R	$q_\oplus$, ⊕, R	q_-, −, R	—	—
q_2	q_3, 0, R	q_3, 1, R	—	—	—	—	—	—	—	q_2, #, R
q_3	q_4, $\underline{0}$, L	q_6, $\underline{1}$, L	MR	MR	—	—	—	—	q_8, B, L	—
q_4	q_5, 0, R	q_5, 1, R	ML	ML	—	—	—	—	—	—
q_5	—	—	q_3, 0, R	q_3, 0, R	—	—	—	—	—	—
q_6	q_7, 0, R	q_7, 1, R	ML	ML	—	—	—	—	—	—
q_7	HALT	HALT	q_3, 1, R	q_3, 1, R	—	—	—	—	—	—
q_8	q_-^0, $\underline{0}$, L	q_-^1, $\underline{1}$, L	q_8, B, L	q_8, B, L	—	—	—	—	—	—
q_-	—	—	—	—	—	—	—	—	—	—
q_-^0	—	—	—	—	—	—	—	q_1, 1, L	—	—
q_-^1	—	—	—	—	—	—	—	q_1, 0, L	—	—
q_+	q_+^0, $\underline{0}$, R	q_+^1, $\underline{1}$, R	MR	MR	—	—	—	—	—	—
q_+^0	q_+^{00}, $\underline{0}$, L	q_+^{01}, $\underline{1}$, L	MR	MR	—	—	—	—	—	—
q_+^1	q_+^{10}, $\underline{0}$, L	q_+^{11}, $\underline{1}$, L	MR	MR	—	—	—	—	—	—
q_+^{00}	—	—	ML	ML	q_1, 0, L	—	—	—	—	—
q_+^{01}	—	—	ML	ML	q_1, 1, L	—	—	—	—	—
q_+^{10}	—	—	ML	ML	q_1, 1, L	—	—	—	—	—
q_+^{11}	—	—	ML	ML	q_1, 1, L	—	—	—	—	—
$q_\oplus$	$q_\oplus^0$, $\underline{0}$, R	$q_\oplus^1$, $\underline{1}$, R	MR	MR	—	—	—	—	—	—
⋯					⋯				⋯	
$q_\cdot^{11}$	—	—	ML	ML	—	q_1, 1, L	—	—	—	—

computation and the printing of $f(\mathbf{x})$ left-adjusted on the nonblank portion of its tape.

Definition 5.7.2. The *length* of a T-program $s(\tilde{\mathbf{x}})$ is the number of characters that it contains. The *program complexity* of $f : \{0, 1\}^n \to \{0, 1\}^m$ on U, a universal basic Turing machine, denoted $I_U(f)$, is the length of the shortest length U-program for f.

Our detour through prefix notations for formulas has given us concrete examples of Turing machine programs that make these definitions more comprehensible. It also has prepared us to prove the following theorem, which establishes an interesting relationship between program complexity and formula size.

Theorem 5.7.1. Let $f : \{0, 1\}^n \to \{0, 1\}^m$ be given and let Ω be a basis of fan-in r. Let $L_\Omega(f)$ be the sum of the formula sizes of the m Boolean functions associated with f. Then there exists a universal basic machine U with tape alphabet of size $|\Omega| + 6$ such that for all such functions f,

$$I_U(f) \leq rL_\Omega(f) + m$$

Proof. The existence of universal Turing machines has been argued in Section 5.4, and, as is stated in Problem 5-4, there exist such machines with a binary tape alphabet. Let U^* be one such machine. The machine U of this theorem is designed to respond as follows. If the first symbol on its tape is not an operator symbol, it enters the initial state of U^*. Otherwise, it enters the initial state of a machine F^* that computes functions from prefix notations of their formulas. Such a machine, namely F, is given above for $\Omega = \{+, \cdot, \oplus, {}^-\}$ and, in general, can be constructed for any basis. Clearly, U can be used either as a universal machine U^* or as a special purpose machine F^*, depending on the value of its first tape symbol. To derive the upper bound, U is used as F^*.

Let f_i be one of the m Boolean functions associated with f. Let $L_\Omega(f_i)$ be its formula size and let V_i be the number of input nodes to a tree with $L_\Omega(f_i)$ internal nodes. Also, let l_j be the number of internal nodes with fan-in j, $1 \leq j \leq r$. Then

$$L_\Omega(f_i) = \sum_{j=1}^{r} l_j$$

and the graph has $L_\Omega(f_i) + V_i - 1$ edges directed away from nodes (the single terminal node has no edges directed away from it). This must equal the number of edges directed into nodes, or

$$\sum_{j=1}^{r} l_j + V_i - 1 = \sum_{j=1}^{r} j l_j$$

from which we have that

$$V_i = 1 + \sum_{j=2}^{r} (j - 1)l_j \leq 1 + (r - 1)L_\Omega(f_i)$$

But the prefix notation for a tree of $L_\Omega(f_i)$ internal nodes and V_i input nodes has $L_\Omega(f_i) + V_i$ characters in it, from which it follows that this number is at most $rL_\Omega(f_i) + 1$. Since f consists of m Boolean functions, the bound follows directly. $\qquad\square$

We return to this result later, but now let us go on to develop other properties of the program complexity measure.

Theorem 5.7.2. Let U and U' be two universal basic Turing machines. Then there exist integers $K_1, K_2 \geq 0$ such that, for all $n, m \geq 1$ and all $f : \{0, 1\}^n \to \{0, 1\}^m$,

$$I_U(f) \leq K_1 I_{U'}(f) + K_2$$

Proof. This result follows directly from the construction of Section 5.4. U simulates U' from a fixed-length description of U' (plus working space) and a record of the tape of U' which is constructed using a fixed number of cells of U for each cell of U'. $\qquad\square$

This result demonstrates that a change in the basis (universal machine) for measuring program complexity has at most a multiplicative effect. It shares this property with combinational complexity.

Theorem 5.7.3. Let f be obtained by restricting the domain of $g : \{0, 1\}^n \to \{0, 1\}^m$; that is, $f = g \big|_{j \in J}^{x_j = c_j}$, $J \subset \{1, 2, \ldots, n\}$ and $c_j \in \{0, 1\}$. Then

$$I_U(f) \leq I_U(g)$$

Proof. Any program for g can be used as a program for f by fixing each variable x_j such that $j \in J$ to c_j. $\qquad\square$

The next result states the obvious, that each variable of $f : \{0, 1\}^n \to \{0, 1\}^m$ must occur in every program of f if f depends on each, that is, if each variable can influence the value of f.

Theorem 5.7.4. Let $f : \{0, 1\}^n \to \{0, 1\}^m$ depend on each of its variables. Then

$$I_U(f) \geq n$$

Not only can we use formulas to construct Turing machine programs, we can use straight-line algorithms or chains, as the next theorem states.

Theorem 5.7.5. Let $f : \{0, 1\}^n \to \{0, 1\}^m$ and let Ω be a basis of fan-in r. Given a universal basic machine U, there exist nonnegative constants K_1, K_2 that are dependent on Ω, r, and U but independent of f, n, and m such that

$$I_U(f) \leq K_1\left[C_\Omega(f)(r\lceil \log_2(C_\Omega(f) + n + 2)\rceil] + \lceil \log_2|\Omega|\rceil) + n + 2 \right] + K_2$$

Proof. This result follows from a straightforward construction of a special Turing machine S that computes functions f from their chains. A U-program for f is then obtained by simulating S on U.

Let $\beta = (\beta_1, \beta_2, \ldots, \beta_K)$ be an optimal chain for f over Ω. Without loss of generality, we assume that each variable of f and each of the two constants occur at most once. Then $K \leq n + 2 + C_\Omega(f)$. Let $\beta_j = (h_i; \beta_{j_1}, \ldots, \beta_{j_{r_i}})$ be a computation step where $h_i \in \Omega$, $j_l < j$, and r_i is the fan-in of h_i. Then it can be represented by a string of $\lceil \log_2|\Omega| + r_i\lceil \log_2(K - 1)\rceil]$ binary digits since h_i is in Ω and $j_l < K$. To separate the encodings of h_i and β_{j_l} for $1 \leq l \leq r_i$, the leading character in each can be given special labels. For example, the leading character of h_i can be labeled A or B, depending on whether it is 0 or 1, whereas that of β_{j_l} can be labeled α or β. If β_j is a data step, it can be given a special label depending on which of the values 0 or 1 it is given.

Clearly, a machine S can be constructed that (knowing Ω) interprets such encodings of programs and computes the associated function. The number of characters in such a program is at most

$$n + 2 + C_\Omega(f)(\lceil \log_2|\Omega|\rceil + r\lceil \log_2(C_\Omega(f) + n + 1)\rceil])$$

from which the theorem follows from a straightforward simulation of S on U. $\qquad \Box$

This result is similar to that of Theorem 5.7.1, which relates program complexity to formula size. The bound that it provides is sometimes weaker than that provided by formula size and sometimes stronger. For example, when $f = x_1 \oplus x_2 \oplus \cdots \oplus x_n$ and $\Omega = \{ +, \cdot, \oplus, ^- \}$, $L_\Omega(f) = C_\Omega(f) = n - 1$ and Theorem 5.7.1 is the stronger bound. However, when $\Omega = \{ +, \cdot, ^- \}$, $L_\Omega(f)$ is square in n (see Theorem 3.3.1.3) while $C_\Omega(f) = 3(n - 1)$ (see Theorem 2.4.3.2) so that Theorem 5.7.5 presents the stronger result.

Theorem 5.7.6. There exists a universal basic Turing machine U with tape alphabet Σ of size 9 such that for all $f : \{0, 1\}^n \to \{0, 1\}^m$

$$I_U(f) \leq m \left[\frac{2^{n+2}}{\log_2 n} (1 + \varepsilon(n)) + 1 \right]$$

where $\varepsilon(n) > 0$ and $\varepsilon(n) \to 0$ as $n \to \infty$. Furthermore, given $0 < \delta < 1$, the fraction of the functions $f : \{0, 1\}^n \to \{0, 1\}^m$ for which

$$I_U(f) \geq \frac{m2^n(1 - \delta)}{\log_2(n + 8)}$$

approaches 1 with increasing n.

Proof. The first half of the proof follows from Theorem 5.7.1 and the fact that every Boolean function $f : \{0, 1\}^n \to \{0, 1\}$ can be realized over $\Omega = \{ +, \cdot, {}^- \}$ with formula size of at most $\{2^{n+1}/(\log_2(n))\} (1 + \varepsilon(n))$ (see Section 3.4).

The second half follows from a counting argument assuming the machine U of Theorem 5.7.1 with tape alphabet of size $|\Sigma| = |\Omega| + 6 = 9$. A program for a function $f : \{0, 1\}^n \to \{0, 1\}^m$ is a string $s(\tilde{x})$ over $(\Sigma - \{B\}) \cup \{x_1, \ldots, x_n\}$. There are at most $(n + |\Sigma| - 1)^l = a^l$ such strings of length l where $a = n + 8$, and at most $N(k) = a + a^2 + \cdots + a^k$, of length k or less that are programs for functions $f : \{0, 1\}^n \to \{0, 1\}^m$. (It is easy to demonstrate that $N(k) = (a^k - 1)/(a - 1) \leq a^{k+1}$ for $a \geq 2$.) There are 2^{m2^n} functions $f : \{0, 1\}^n \to \{0, 1\}^m$, so we set

$$a^{k+1} = 2^{m2^n(1-\delta)}$$

and observe that at most this many such functions have program complexity less than or equal to k. But this is a fraction $2^{-\delta m2^n}$ that approaches 0 with increasing n. Therefore, most functions have program complexity greater than or equal to $k + 1$, and solving for it, we have

$$I_U(f) \geq \frac{m2^n(1 - \delta)}{\log_2(n + 8)} \qquad \square$$

It is now clear that most functions $f : \{0, 1\}^n \to \{0, 1\}^m$ have a program complexity that is linear in m and exponential in n with respect to any universal machine U (apply Theorem 5.7.2). Furthermore, for most functions, formula size provides a good bound to program complexity.

The reader who has been sensitized by the discussions of unsolvable problems may wonder whether a procedure exists for determining, for arbitrary n and m and arbitrary $f :\{0, 1\}^n \to \{0, 1\}^m$, the program complexity $I_U(f)$. As the following theorem demonstrates, no such procedure exists. In practice, this is not a problem because most functions that we want to compute have $I_U(f)$ linear in n and the coefficient can be determined quite accurately. Nonetheless, program complexity does contrast in this property with combinational complexity.

Theorem 5.7.7. Given U, there does not exist a Turing machine that, for arbitrary n, m, and $f :\{0, 1\}^n \to \{0, 1\}^m$ computes $I_U(f)$, the program complexity of f relative to U.

Proof. We prove the result for Boolean functions $f :\{0, 1\}^n \to \{0, 1\}$, from which the general result holds.

Suppose that such a machine T exists. Design a machine M that uses T to find a Boolean function on $n, n \geq N$, variables, g_n, for which $I_U(g_n) \geq n^2$. (Such functions exist if N is chosen so that n^2 is less than the lower bound of Theorem 5.7.6 for $n \geq N$.) Then M can find such a function by examining all $f :\{0, 1\}^n \to \{0, 1\}$ in lexicographical order (on the 2^n-tuples of values of f). Thus, M can be used to construct another machine P that, for each $n \geq N$, computes $g_n : \{0, 1\}^n \to \{0, 1\}$. (Here n is determined by the length of the string on P's tape.) Let P compute $g_n = 0$ for $1 \leq n \leq N$. Then P computes a total function $g : \{0, 1\}^* \to \{0, 1\}$. However, P can be simulated by U so that there exist constants $K_1, K_2 > 0$ such that for each $n \geq 1$, g_n can be computed on U with a program of length $K_1 n + K_2$. But this contradicts the construction based on T and denies the existence of T. □

The argument that has been employed here is interesting and differs from the argument given in Section 5.4 for demonstrating the unsolvability of the halting problem. This completes our discussion of program complexity in this chapter. The subject is taken up again in Chapter 7, where we derive computational inequalities of the second type. Program complexity and its various properties were introduced and developed by Savage (1973). Program complexity represents an extension of the Chaitin–Kolmogorov–Solomonoff measure of the randomness of strings (Solomonoff, 1964; Kolmogorov, 1965; Chaitin, 1966), which is the program complexity of a nullary function whose single value is a string **x**.

5.8. A COMPUTATIONAL INEQUALITY FOR TURING MACHINES

We now derive a computational inequality for Turing machines that is analogous to that derived for sequential machines in Section 4.5. It is derived by the same method, namely, the construction of a logic circuit that simulates the computation by the Turing machine. The first inequality of this kind was derived by Savage (1972). It states that if $f : \{0, 1\}^n \rightarrow \{0, 1\}^m$ is computed in T cycles, then $C_\Omega(f) \leq KT^2$ for some constant $K > 0$. Fischer and Pippenger (1973) improved the upper bound to KT log T where K is a constant linear in the "size" of the Control. Schnorr (1975) improved this to KT log S where S is the storage capacity of the tape; our derivation improves on this by considerably weakening the dependence of the bound on the size of the Control.

Consider a one-tape Turing machine with a doubly infinite tape, as shown in Figure 5.8.1. We exhibit an efficient logic circuit that simulates T cycles of computation by this machine, from which extension to multitape machines will become apparent. We assume that at most $2k + 1$ b-bit tape squares are used to compute $f : \{0, 1\}^n \rightarrow \{0, 1\}^m$ and that the head is initially located at the center of the tape. If it is located anywhere else in this region, we at most double k so that the head does start at the center.

Figure 5.8.1 shows a circuit for such a one-tape machine in which the contents of each tape square, $\mathbf{a}_i \in \{0, 1\}^b$, is augmented by a one-bit status indicator, s_i, which is 1 if the head is residing over that square and 0 otherwise. Here the Control is simulated by a logic circuit that receives the

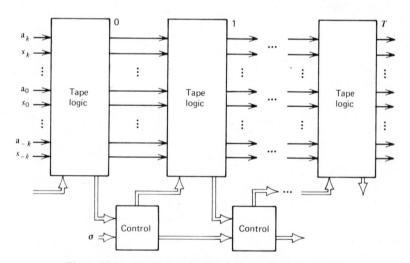

Figure 5.8.1. Circuit that simulates a one-tape Turing machine.

current state and the contents of the sequence under the head, say, a_i, as input. The circuit produces a next state as well as a pair of outputs $(\mathbf{w}, \mathbf{c})$ where $\mathbf{w} \in \{0, 1\}^b$ is the replacement for a_i and $\mathbf{c} \in \{0, 1\}^3$ represents a command to move the head left (L), right (R), or not at all (N). For concreteness, assume the encoding shown in Table 7.2.2.1 for these commands. In the above circuit, the initial status input is $s_0 = 1$, $s_i = 0$, $i \neq 0$. After l moves, the head can be over squares labeled $-l, -(l - 1), \ldots, 0, 1, \ldots, l$ so that a straightforward realization of this circuit would use on the order of T^2 elements and be about equivalent with the earlier bound.

Table 5.8.1. Encoding for Head Commands

Command	(c_1, c_2, c_3)
L	100
N	010
R	001

To improve on the circuit of Figure 5.8.1, we follow the head movement and *cyclically* shift a central portion of the tape every so often to place squares that contain the head near the center of the tape. Subsequently, a reverse cyclic shift is necessary to return the tape to its initial condition. This will result in a simulating circuit for the *tape* whose size is on the order of $T \log S$.

Consider a network of $p + 2q$ input lines that simulates q moves of the head and in which the initial head position is any one of the middle p positions. Call this an $N(p, q)$ network. It will have a b-bit tape symbol and a status bit on each input line, and it will produce q outputs to and receive q inputs from a Control equivalent logic circuit.

Shown in Figure 5.8.2 is the portion of an $N(3, 1)$ circuit that produces the contents of the square under the head, that is, the square for which $s_i = 1$. This circuit has $5b$ AND's and $4b$ two-input OR's, for a total of $9b$ elements. Such a subcircuit with r input lines has $(2r - 1)b$ elements. A subcircuit that replaces the contents of the square under the head and changes the head location is shown in Figure 5.8.3. Observe that s_i' is 1 if s_{i+1} is 1 and the head moves right, s_i is 1 and there is no move, or s_{i-1} is 1 and it moves left. To compute the new status and new contents of one square requires a maximum of $3b + 5$ elements. Therefore, at most $9b + 5(3b + 5) = 24b + 25$ elements are necessary for $N(3, 1)$ and at most $5b + 3 \cdot (3b + 5) = 14b + 15$ are required for $N(1, 1)$ since each simulates one move of the head. We are now prepared to derive an efficient circuit to simulate a Turing machine.

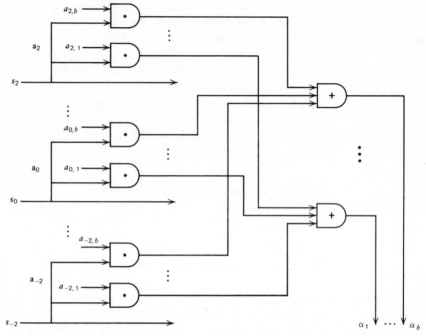

Figure 5.8.2. Subcircuit that reads a square.

A circuit to simulate $2q$ moves of the head when the head is initially at the center of the tape, $N(1, 2q)$, can be realized from the composition of an $N(1, q)$ circuit and an $N(2q + 1, q)$ circuit, as shown in Figure 5.8.4. If $C(p, q)$ is the combinational complexity of $N(p, q)$, then

$$C(1, 2q) \leq C(1, q) + C(2q + 1, q)$$

We now present a recursive realization of an $N(2q + 1, q)$ circuit that allows us to bound its complexity as well as that of $C(1, T)$, which is our principal objective.

Shown in Figure 5.8.5 is a circuit that realizes $N(4q + 1, 2q)$ from two q-centering circuits, two q-correction circuits, and two $N(2q + 1, q)$ circuits. The q-centering circuit has $8q + 1$ input lines, each carrying a b-bit word and a status bit, and a like number of output lines plus a centering line c. If the lines $-1, -2, \ldots, -2q$ contain the head position, that is, if $s_{-2q} + s_{-2q+1} + \cdots + s_{-1}$ is 1, where $+$ denotes OR, all $8q + 1$ lines are shifted *cyclically* up q places; that is, (a_{q-1}, s_{q-1}) is replaced by (a_{-1}, s_{-1}) and (a_{-q}, s_{-q}) is replaced by (a_{-2q}, s_{-2q}). Thus, if the head is in one of the positions $-1, -2, \ldots, -2q$, the q-centering

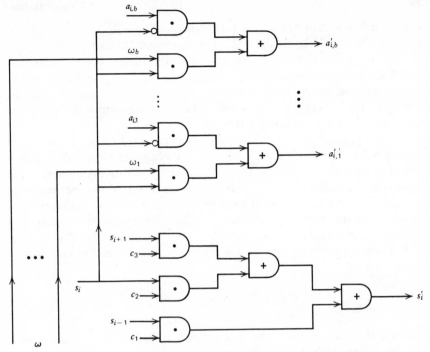

Figure 5.8.3. Subcircuit to change contents and status of a square.

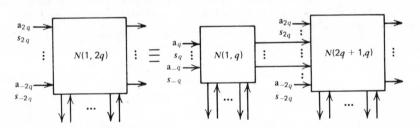

Figure 5.8.4. Simulation of $N(1, 2q)$.

circuit moves it into one of the positions $q - 1, q - 2, \ldots, - q$. Then q steps can be simulated by an $N(2q + 1, q)$ circuit. Similarly, if $s_{2q} + s_{2q-1} + \cdots + s_0$ is 1, all $8q + 1$ lines are shifted cyclically down q places so that if the head is in any one of positions $2q, 2q - 1, \ldots, 0$, then it will be placed into one of positions $q, q - 1, \ldots, - q$ and q steps can again be simulated by an $N(2q + 1, q)$ circuit. The centering output is $c = 1$ if the cyclic shift is down and $c = 0$ if it is up.

In the circuit of Figure 5.8.5, the head is assumed to be in one of the positions $2q, \ldots, 0, \ldots, - 2q$ so that the centering circuit puts it into one of the positions $+q, \ldots, 0, \ldots, - q$. After simulating q steps, it can be in one of positions $+2q, \ldots, 0, \ldots, - 2q$ again, so another centering is done, followed by another q steps of simulation and two restoring steps in which the first two cyclic shifts are undone. Clearly, such a circuit is an $N(4p + 1, 2p)$ circuit.

A q-centering circuit can be realized from a q-correction circuit with input $\bar{c}$ where

$$\bar{c} = s_{-2q} + s_{-2q+1} + \cdots + s_{-1}$$

because the head can only be in positions $-2q, \ldots, 0, \ldots, 2q$. Also, $\bar{c}$ can be realized with $2q - 1$ elements. In a q-correction circuit, each of the $b + 1$ bits on a line is shifted into one of two places depending on the value of c. This can be done with three elements per bit (see Section 6.3.2) so that a q-correction circuit requires at most $(8q + 1)3(b + 1)$ elements. Thus, the two q-centering and q-correction circuits can be realized with $2(2q - 1) + 4[(8q + 1)3(b + 1)] = 4q(24b + 25) + (12b + 10)$ elements.

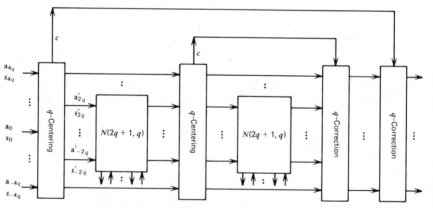

Figure 5.8.5. Realization of an $N(4q + 1, 2q)$ circuit.

From the above construction, it follows that

$$C(4q + 1, 2q) \leq 2C(2q + 1, q) + q(96b + 100) + (12b + 10)$$

If it is known that the head never moves beyond the positions $-r, -r + 1, \ldots, 0, \ldots, r - 1, r$, this inequality can be improved. Let $N_r(p, q)$ be an $N(p, q)$ simulating circuit in which the head does not move outside of these positions. Then an $N_r(4q + 1, 2q)$ circuit can be realized from two $N_r(2q + 1, q)$ circuits and centering and correction circuits, as in Figure 5.8.5, except that these latter circuits need not test the head position outside of $-r, \ldots, 0, \ldots, r$ or shift the region outside of $-2r, \ldots, 0, \ldots, 2r$. (Actually, it need not shift the region outside of $-r, \ldots, 0, \ldots, r$, but the former condition simplifies the analysis.) Thus, if $2q \geq r$, we can replace the q-centering and q-correction circuits by $\lceil r/2 \rceil$-centering and $\lceil r/2 \rceil$-correction circuits:

Repeating the above bounding arguments for $N_r(p, q)$ circuits, we have for the complexity of such circuits, $C^r(p, q)$, the following bounds:

$$C^r(1, 2q) \leq C^r(1, q) + C^r(2q + 1, q)$$

$$C^r(4q + 1, 2q) \leq 2C^r(2q + 1, q) + \min\left(q, \left\lceil \frac{r}{2} \right\rceil\right)(96b + 100) + (12b + 10)$$

Let

$$\sigma(2^k) = C^r(1, 2^k)$$

$$\lambda(2^k) = C^r(2 \cdot 2^k + 1, 2^k)$$

Then the two inequalities become

$$\sigma(2^{k+1}) \leq \sigma(2^k) + \lambda(2^k)$$

$$\lambda(2^{k+1}) \leq 2 \cdot \lambda(2^k) + \alpha \cdot \min\left(2^k, \left\lceil \frac{r}{2} \right\rceil\right) + \beta$$

where $\alpha = 96b + 100$ and $\beta = 12b + 10$. The reader can verify (see Problem 5-13) that the solution to the second of these inequalities satisfies

$$\lambda(2^k) \leq 2^k \left[\lambda(1) + \beta + \frac{\alpha}{2} \min(k, l)\right] - \beta$$
$$+ \max(2^{k-l} - 1, 0)\alpha \left\lceil \frac{r}{2} \right\rceil$$

where l is the smallest integer for which

$$2^{-l} \left\lceil \frac{r}{2} \right\rceil \le 1$$

that is, $l = \lceil \log_2 \lceil r/2 \rceil \rceil$. Combining these inequalities, the reader can demonstrate that (see Problem 5-13)

$$\sigma(2^k) \le \sigma(1) + 2^k \left[\lambda(1) + \alpha + \beta + \frac{\alpha}{2} \min(k, l) \right]$$

Theorem 5.8.1. Let $\Omega = P_{1,2}^{(2)}$. Let $f : \{0, 1\}^n \to \{0, 1\}^m$ be computed by a multitape Turing machine with p tapes in a maxiumum of T cycles. Let each tape have an alphabet of size 2^b and let at most M squares of any one tape be used in any computation of f. Also, let the Control of the machine contain s states. Then the following relation must hold between these parameters of computation:

$$C_\Omega(f) \le \left[C_{\text{CONT}} + 100p(b + 1)(3 + \log_2 M) \right] T + 15p(b + 1)$$

Here C_{CONT} is the combinational complexity of the transition and output function of the Control and

$$C_{\text{CONT}} \le \left(1 + \frac{3p}{a} \right) 2^a (1 + \varepsilon)$$

where

$$a = \lceil \log_2 s \rceil + pb$$

and $\varepsilon \to 0$ as $a \to \infty$.

Proof. We recall that $\lambda(1) = C^r(3, 1) \le 24b + 25$, $\sigma(1) = C^r(1, 1) \le 14b + 15$, $\alpha = 96b + 100$, and $\beta = 12b + 10$.

If at most M squares are used on any one tape, it must be possible to visit each from the initial square in T cycles. A best placement permits each to be visited in at most $\lceil (M - 1)/2 \rceil$ steps from the initial square, so $T \ge \lceil (M - 1)/2 \rceil$.

Choose k such that $2^{k-1} < T \le 2^k$ or $k = \lceil \log_2 T \rceil$.

If at most M squares are used on any tape, they could consist of the initial square plus $M - 1$ squares to one side. Thus, we can choose $r = M - 1$ and limit each tape to squares labeled $-2r, \ldots, 0, \ldots, 2r$.

The number of logic elements needed to simulate T steps of computation by one tape, $\sigma(T) = C^r(1, T)$, is bounded by $\sigma(2^k)$ and

$$\sigma(T) \le \sigma(2^k)$$

$$\le (14b + 15) + 2T\left[132b + 135 + (48b + 50)\left[\log_2 \min\left(T, \left\lceil \frac{M-1}{2} \right\rceil\right)\right]\right]$$

But $T \ge \lceil(M-1)/2\rceil$ and $\lceil\log_2\lceil r/2\rceil\rceil \le \log_2(r+1)$, so we have

$$\sigma(T) \le 15(b+1) + 100(b+1)(3 + \log_2 M)T$$

for the number of equivalent logic elements to simulate one tape. There are p tapes and a Control that can be simulated with $C_{\text{CONT}}T$ elements from which the principal result follows.

The Control is characterized by a function δ that maps the state (there are s), and the contents of cells under the p heads (each represented by b bits) to a new state and p pairs of outputs consisting of a new cell entry (b bits) and a command (3 bits). Thus, δ is a function $\delta : \{0, 1\}^{\lceil\log_2 s\rceil + pb} \to \{0, 1\}^{\lceil\log_2 s\rceil + p(b+3)}$ that can be viewed as $\lceil\log_2 s\rceil + p(b+3)$ Boolean functions. But in Section 3.4 we have derived a bound to the combinational complexity of every Boolean function on n variables. Applying this result, we see that the second inequality follows directly. $\square$

The extent to which this inequaltiy can be satisfied is illustrated by the following argument. Write a straight-line program for $f : \{0, 1\}^n \to \{0, 1\}^m$ on a universal machine U, as is done for Theorem 5.7.5. The length of the program is roughly proportional to $C_\Omega(f) \log C_\Omega(f)$. The reader can verify that f can be computed from such a program with about this much storage and with time proportional to the square of this length by a one-tape universal Turing machine.

Theorem 5.8.2. Let $f : \{0, 1\}^n \to \{0, 1\}^m$, $\Omega = P_{1,2}^{(2)}$, and $C_\Omega(f) \ge n - 1$. Then there exist constants $K_1, K_2 \ge 0$ such that all such functions can be computed on a universal one-tape Turing machine U for which

$$C_\Omega(f) \le \left[C_{\text{CONT}} + 100(b+1)(3 + \log_2 M)\right]T + 15(b+1)$$

$$\le K_1 C_\Omega^2(f)(\log_2 C_\Omega(f))^3 + K_2$$

where the tape alphabet has size 2^k, $k \ge 1$.

This theorem provides a rough measure of the strength or weakness of the improved inequality for Turing machines.

In testing the strength of an inequality, it is important to know precisely the conditions under which it applies. We observe that the improved inequality for Turing machines holds under any initialization of the p tapes and also holds when the Control is permitted to receive external inputs in each cycle. The latter condition means that the size of the input tape need not be included in M if the head on this tape moves in an *oblivious* manner, that is, in a manner that is data independent.

Problems

5-1. Consider a one-tape Turing machine in which the head can move $0, 1, 2, \ldots, k$ cells to the left or right of the cell under the head in one move. If k is fixed, show that this Turing machine is equivalent to a basic Turing machine.

5-2. Describe a basic Turing machine that accepts palindromes of even and odd length.

5-3. Given a Turing machine with a doubly infinite tape over the tape alphabet Σ, show that an equivalent Turing machine exists with a semiinfinite tape and the same tape alphabet.

5-4. Show the existence of a universal Turing machine with a tape alphabet containing two symbols.

5-5. Show the existence of a universal Turing machine containing two states.

5-6. Show that there does not exist a Turing machine that, given an arbitrary (one-tape, semiinfinite tape) Turing machine and input string for that machine, can determine whether this machine ever prints the symbol S on its tape.

Hint. All of the halting states of every such Turing Machine are given as part of the description of the machine.

5-7. By exhibiting invariance relations, demonstrate that the procedures **ineq**, $m|n$ and **prime** defined in Section 5.6 are correct.

5-8. Construct procedures for the following functions on the natural numbers:

(a) x^y.

(b) $\lceil \sqrt{x} \rceil$.

(c) $\phi(n)$ = the number of divisors of n including 1 and n.

5-9. In the McCarthy formalism, procedures are given only for functions $f : N \to N$ where N is the set of natural numbers. Thus, to represent strings over a finite set requires a numbering (arithmetization) of the strings so that there is a 1-1 correspondence between a string and an integer in N.

(a) Give an arithmetization of the strings over $\{1, 2, 3\}$.

(b) Define a procedure on N that returns the value 1 on integer n if and only if n corresponds to a string $1^k 2^k 3^k$ for some $k \geq 1$.

5-10. Compute the value of $\mathbf{ack}(m, n)$ for $m = 0, 1, 2, 3, 4$.

5-11. A *postorder* traversal of a tree is defined recursively as follows:

> Do a postorder traversal of 1st subtree (on the left)
>
> $\vdots \qquad \vdots$
>
> Do a postorder traversal of kth subtree
> Visit the root of the tree   (with k subtrees)

Show that postorder traversals of trees corresponding to formulas for functions f yield unique (postfix) notations. Show that the postfix notations yield programs for these functions on suitably defined Turing machines.

5-12. Let U be a universal one-tape Turing machine, let n be large, and let $f : \{0, 1\}^n \to \{0, 1\}$. For most such functions, determine whether or not their prefix notations are nearly optimal programs on U.

5-13. Solve the following two recursion inequalities using a parameter l that satisfies $l = \lceil \log_2 \lceil \frac{r}{2} \rceil \rceil$:

(a) $\sigma(2^{k+1}) \leq \sigma(2^k) + \lambda(2^k)$

(b) $\lambda(2^{k+1}) \leq 2 \cdot \lambda(2^k) + \alpha \cdot \min(2^k, \lceil \frac{r}{2} \rceil) + \beta$.

Here α, β, and r are positive integers.

Chapter 6

General-Purpose Computers

In a recent book, Bell and Newell (1971) catalogue and describe a large number of distinct general-purpose computers (GPCs). They also mention that (as of 1971) about 1000 distinct computer organizations can be identified. While this is a remarkably large number, what is surprising is that there is so much similarity between these machines. We acknowledge this strong similarity in this chapter by presenting an introduction to the principal functions and components of general-purpose computers. Our objective is to examine these functions from a point of view that facilitates the development of computational inequalities in the following chapter. This chapter begins with a discussion of the general organizations of GPCs and continues with a description of storage organizations, arithmetic and logical functions, and the organization of a central processing unit.

6.1. ORGANIZATION OF GENERAL–PURPOSE COMPUTERS

As indicated above, general-purpose computers come in many shapes and forms. Each, however, contains at a minimum a memory and a central processing unit (CPU) as indicated schematically in Figure 6.1.1. The memory contains instructions and data, and the CPU carries out these instructions and makes use of this data.

In the simple example shown, the output explicitly exercises no control over the input. Furthermore, all inputs to the computer, that is, instructions and data, reach it through the single input port. This organization is typical of many early machines where the input was read directly from cards or paper tape into memory, the program was run, and on completion, the output was printed on paper or punched onto cards or paper tape.

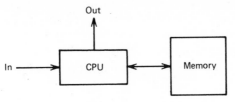

Figure 6.1.1. Simple general purpose computer.

We call this *dumping and running*. It is not an efficient strategy for use of computers.

For various reasons, including efficiency and ease of use and access, the organization of general-purpose computers has become quite complex. Today computers have many peripheral devices, as shown in Figure 6.1.2, and often they contain more than one CPU. A large machine usually has a main memory and one or more CPUs as well as many peripherals such as multiple card readers and punches; line printers; drum, disk, and tape storage units; many teletypewriters; and graphics terminals. In machines of low cost and complexity, access to input/output devices (I/O) is handled directly by the CPU while in other general-purpose machines a small computer (called Controller in the preceding) is available to handle the routing of I/O and the scheduling of accesses to peripheral devices for which access is not instantaneous.

It is common for graphics terminals as well as for some keyboards and teletypewriters to have a small memory and a small CPU. In addition, some machines have small but very high-speed memories (called cache memories) as part of the main memory. The task of controlling all of the

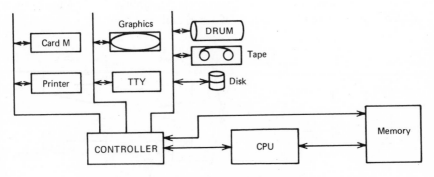

Figure 6.1.2. Typical general purpose computer.

many activities of such complex hardware systems is enormous and requires very complex software systems (called *operating systems*). Our purpose in this chapter is to describe the important hardware components at a level that will permit the development of the trade-off inequalities that must apply to computation on these machines regardless of what operating systems are used.

6.2. STORAGE MEDIA

In this section, we describe a number of models for storage media, ranging from registers to associative (or content-addressable) memories. Each of these models is a sequential machine and for each we describe the transition and output functions. We also bound the combinational complexity of these functions.

6.2.1. Flip-Flops and Registers

Registers are ubiquitous in computing systems. They are found in CPUs and at the input and output of every storage and peripheral device. Registers are simple objects, consisting of a number of binary memory cells, and they provide storage for individual computer words. With the addition of logic elements, they can be transformed into counters, adders, and other useful circuits.

Registers are constructed from flip-flops which are two state sequential machines. These in turn are realized from logic elements which have a finite response time. Shown in Figure 6.2.1.1 is an *S-R* (set-reset) *flip-flop* which has been realized from two NOR elements (the Boolean complement of OR). It is shown symbolically and as realized from elements with finite delay (of Δ seconds). The *S-R* flip-flop has an indeterminate state when both S and R are 1, so we assume that this condition never occurs. If $S = R = 0$, the reader can verify that no change occurs in z and the output labeled $\bar{z}$ does indeed have value 1 if $z = 0$ and 0 if $z = 1$.

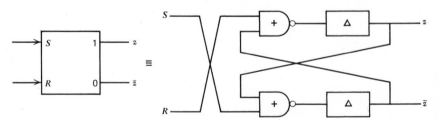

Figure 6.2.1.1. *S-R* flip-flop and its schematic representation.

We assume that $S = R = 0$ except during those time intervals when an input is given to the flip-flop. Since we do not allow $S = 1$ and $R = 1$ simultaneously, an input is given by setting $S = 0$, $R = 1$ or $S = 1$, $R = 0$; that is, the flip-flop is given one of two different types of inputs. If $S = 0$, $R = 1$ is the input at time t, and $z(t) = 0$, the input causes no change in z. However, if $z(t) = 1$, the reader can verify that after a delay of 2Δ seconds $z = 0$. Similarly, if $S = 1$, $R = 0$ is the input at time t, and $z(t) = 0$, z changes to 1 after a delay of 2Δ seconds; if $z(t) = 1$, no change occurs. To *summarize*,

1. No change in the state of the flip-flop occurs if $S = R = 0$.
2. If $S = 0$ and $R = 1$, then z is set at 0, if it is not already 0, after a delay of 2Δ seconds.
3. If $S = 1$ and $R = 0$, then z is set at 1, if it is not already 1, after a delay of 2Δ seconds.

Clearly, the proper functioning of an S-R flip-flop requires that an input ($S = 0$, $R = 1$ or $S = 1$, $R = 0$) be maintained long enough for the proper transitions to occur.

In most computers, it is desirable that transitions in the states of the flip-flops occur during a given time interval. For this purpose a central clock is constructed (the details of which are not discussed here) that generates a pulse once every τ seconds. The clock signal is then applied through AND gates to both S and R inputs of an S-R flip-flop to produce a *clocked* S-R *flip-flop*, as shown schematically in Figure 6.2.1.2. The duration of a clock pulse is at least 2Δ, the time required for the flip-flop to change state. The S and R inputs to the unclocked flip-flop are both 0 except during the clock pulse.

The *J-K flip-flop* is another useful flip-flop which responds to inputs just as does the clocked S-R flip-flop except that both the J and K inputs, corresponding to S and R, are allowed to have value 1. In this case, that is, when $J = K = 1$, the clock input causes the state of the flip-flop to change (*toggle*) from 0 to 1 or from 1 to 0. A circuit diagram and schematic

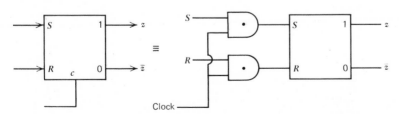

Figure 6.2.1.2.   Clocked S-R flip-flop and its schematic representation.

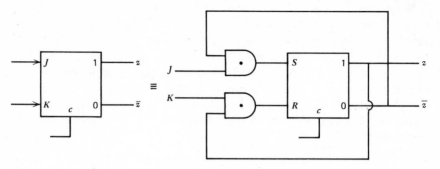

Figure 6.2.1.3. J-K flip-flop and its schematic representation.

representation of the J-K flip-flop, as realized from a clocked S-R flip-flop, is shown in Figure 6.2.1.3. The feedback from the output to the input insures that S and R are not simultaneously 1.

The clocked S-R flip-flop and the J-K flip-flop are sequential machines characterized by states and transition and output functions, namely, δ_{SR}, λ_{SR} and δ_{JK}, λ_{JK}. In both cases, the state is the output z and $\lambda_{SR}(z) = (z, \bar{z})$, $\lambda_{JK}(z) = (z, \bar{z})$. Table 6.2.1.1 shows the transition functions when z is the initial state and z' is its successor. Dashes indicate "don't cares" and identify state and input configurations that do not occur. Formulas can be written for the successor states of the two flip-flops. For the S-R flip-flop, we can write

$$z' = (z + S) \cdot \bar{R}$$

and for the J-K flip-flop,

$$z' = \bar{z} \cdot J + z \cdot \bar{K}$$

Table 6.2.1.1.   Transition Functions for S-R and J-K Flip-Flops

z	S	R	z'		z	J	K	z'
0	0	0	0		0	0	0	0
0	0	1	0		0	0	1	0
0	1	0	1		0	1	0	1
0	1	1	—		0	1	1	1
1	0	0	1		1	0	0	1
1	0	1	0		1	0	1	0
1	1	0	1		1	1	0	1
1	1	1	—		1	1	1	0

We are now prepared to determine the combinational complexity of the transition and output functions of these two simple sequential machines. We use the C_Ω^* measure which does not count the number of inversions and we use the basis $\Omega = P_{1,2}^{(2)}$ which consists of all Boolean functions on two variables.

Theorem 6.2.1.1. For the S-R and J-K flip flops,

$$C_\Omega^*(\delta_{SR}, \lambda_{SR}) = 2, \qquad C_\Omega^*(\delta_{JK}, \lambda_{JK}) = 3$$

$$D_\Omega(\delta_{SR}, \lambda_{SR}) = 2, \qquad D_\Omega(\delta_{JK}, \lambda_{JK}) = 2$$

when $\Omega = P_{1,2}^{(2)}$.

Proof. The reader can verify directly that $\delta_{SR}(z, (S, R)) = z'$ is in $P_{1,2}^{(3)}$ and $\delta_{JK}(z, J, K) = z'$ is in $P_{2,3}^{(3)}$ (see Section 2.4.2 and Theorem 2.4.2.2). Therefore, $C_\Omega^*(\delta_{SR}, \lambda_{SR}) \geq 2$ and $C_\Omega^*(\delta_{JK}, \lambda_{JK}) \geq 3$. But from the above formulas and the fact that NEGATIONS are not counted, the lower bounds can be achieved. Similarly, $L_\Omega^*(f) \geq C_\Omega^*(f)$ and from Theorem 2.3.3, the delay complexities are at least 2 and these limits can be achieved. $\qquad\square$

It is interesting to observe that the S-R and J-K flip-flops can be realized with these numbers of binary operations plus the number of elements (two) required for clocking.

The flip-flop is the basic element in registers and counters. Shown in Figure 6.2.1.4 is a *shift-register* which receives one input per clock cycle and which shifts the current entries right one stage in each cycle, dropping the rightmost entry. The R input of the first flip-flop is fixed at $\bar{S}$ by use of an *inverter* (triangle with a circle). It is assumed that the S and R inputs to a clocked S-R flip-flop remain constant during a clock cycle. This can be achieved in the shift-register with the use of "master-slave flip-flops" which do not change their outputs until a clock pulse terminates (see Booth, 1971, Chapter 8).

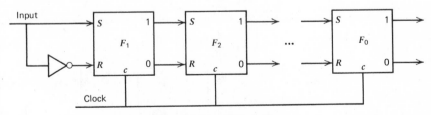

Figure 6.2.1.4. Shift-register.

In general, a *register* is a collection of flip-flops. Shown in Figure 6.2.1.5 is a register that can receive an input from an external source during clocking or from a second register depending on whether the gating signal g is 1 or 0. This is an example of a parallel *transfer operation* obtained by *gating* of signals. Such transfers and gatings are a very important part of the design of general-purpose computers.

There are two types of counters of particular importance in computers, the *modulo* 2^k *counter* and the *ring counter*. The first can be realized by the array of *J-K* flip-flops and logic shown in Figure 6.2.1.6. When the reset input is 1, a clock pulse causes all stages to be set to a $z = 0$. When the reset is 0, a clock pulse causes F_0 to toggle (change its state) while F_i toggles if the state of all previous stages is 1. Otherwise, the state of F_i is unchanged. Let $\mathbf{z} = (z_0, z_1, \ldots, z_{k-1})$ be the state of $F_0, F_1, \ldots, F_{k-1}$. Let $|\mathbf{z}|$ be the integer $z_0 + z_1 2 + z_2 2^2 + \cdots + z_{k-1} 2^{k-1}$ with this binary representation. Then a clock pulse causes $|\mathbf{z}|$ to be increased by 1, and if F_i toggles, it is because a carry is propagated through this stage. When the count reaches $2^k - 1$ [corresponding to $(1, 1, 1, \ldots, 1)$] an additional clock pulse causes the count to fall to 0 [corresponding to $(0, 0, \ldots, 0)$].

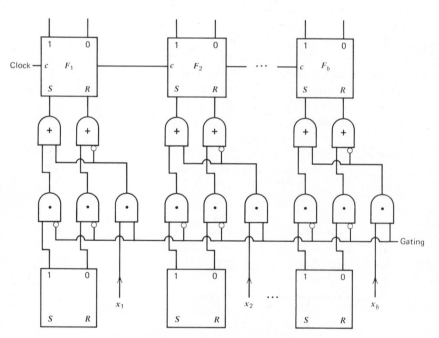

Figure 6.2.1.5.   Transfer operations with gating.

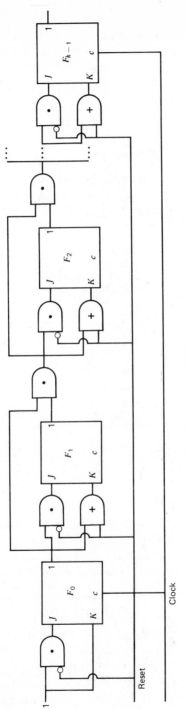

Figure 6.2.1.6. Modulo 2^k counter.

NOTE. We assume that the output of a flip-flop remains constant during a clock pulse. This can be achieved through the use of master-slave flip-flops.

A *ring counter* is a cyclic shift-register that contains a single 1. When the counter is reset, the 1 is put into the left-hand register and during each clock cycle the 1 moves right one stage, cycling back to the first stage upon reaching the right-hand stage. The reader is encouraged to design such a counter from gates and S-R flip-flops.

Theorem 6.2.1.2. Let δ, λ be transition and output functions of a b-stage shift-register, modulo 2^b counter, b-stage ring counter, or b-stage register with parallel transfer for input from another register. Then the combinational complexity $C_\Omega^*(\delta, \lambda)$ over the basis $\Omega = P_{1,2}^{(2)}$ is linear in b and

$$C_\Omega^*(\delta, \lambda) \leq 9b$$

Furthermore, $C_\Omega^*(\delta, \lambda)$ is a constant independent of b, except for the modulo 2^b counter where it is linear in b.

Proof. The reader can verify from the constructions that $C_\Omega^*(\delta, \lambda) \leq 9b$ (see Problem 6-3 for the ring counter). The transition function δ has value $(z_1', z_2', \ldots, z_b')$ where z_i' is the state of the ith stage. For each sequential machine, z_i' is a function of at least two variables, and no two z_i''s are equal to one another or to the complement of the other. Therefore, at least b elements are required to realize δ (see Theorem 2.4.4.2).

Except for the modulo 2^b counter, the function z_i' depends on a finite number of other variables, so its delay complexity is independent of b. In the case of the counter, z_i' has delay linear in i. $\square$

6.2.2. Random Access Memory

A *random access memory* is a storage medium containing a number of binary words of equal length such that any one word is accessible for reading or replacement during any given unit time interval. These unit time intervals, called *cycles*, are measures of the time it takes for physical devices to respond to excitation. We let τ be the length in seconds of such a cycle.

The most common type of large random access memory is the core storage unit realized from three-dimensional arrays of small ferrite cores. Very high-speed random access memories are often realized from arrays of semiconductor registers together with addressing logic. These semiconductor memories were initially of small storage capacity, but capacities increase with improvements in technology. We now sketch the functioning of the random access memory and follow this with the definition of its transition and output function.

The random access memory is shown schematically in Figure 6.2.2.1. It has M storage words of b bits apiece and one output word $\mathbf{w}_M$ of the same size. The control receives an input $(\mathbf{s}, \mathbf{a}, \mathbf{w}^*)$ where $\mathbf{s}$ denotes a command with the meaning

$$\mathbf{s} = \begin{cases} (0, 0) & \text{state unchanged} \\ (0, 1) & \text{"fetch" word } \mathbf{w}_a \\ (1, 0) & \text{"store" } w^* \text{ at location } a \\ (1, 1) & \text{undefined} \end{cases}$$

Also, $\mathbf{a}$ is the binary representation of the integer $a \in \{0, 1, 2, \ldots, M - 1\}$, and $\mathbf{w}^*$ is a b-bit input word.

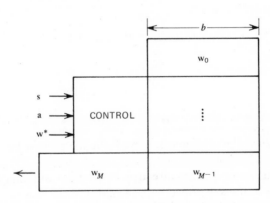

Figure 6.2.2.1. Schematic representation of random access memory.

Definition 6.2.2.1. An (M, b) *random access memory* (RAM) is a sequential machine $S_{ra} = \langle S_{ra}, I_{ra}, \delta_{ra}, \lambda_{ra}, O_{ra} \rangle$ where $S_{ra} = \{(\mathbf{w}_0, \mathbf{w}_1, \ldots, \mathbf{w}_M)\} = \{0, 1\}^{(M+1)b}$ is the state set, $I_{ra} = \{(\mathbf{s}, \mathbf{a}, \mathbf{w}^*)\} \subseteq \{0, 1\}^{2+m+b}$ is the input alphabet (and where $m = \lceil \log_2 M \rceil$ is the length of $\mathbf{a}$), and $O_{ra} = \{\mathbf{w}_M\} = \{0, 1\}^b$ is the output alphabet. The output function $\lambda_{ra}: S_{ra} \to O_{ra}$ is a simple projection operator defined by

$$\lambda_{ra}(\mathbf{w}_0, \mathbf{w}_1, \ldots, \mathbf{w}_M) = \mathbf{w}_M$$

The transition function $\delta_{ra}: S_{ra} \times I_{ra} \to S_{ra}$ is defined by

$$\delta_{ra}((w_0, w_1, \ldots, w_M), (s, a, w^*))$$

$$= \begin{cases} (w_0, \ldots, w_{M-1}, w_M), & s = (0, 0) \\ (w_0, \ldots, w_{M-1}, w_a), & s = (0, 1) \\ (w_0, \ldots, w_{a-1}, w^*, w_{a+1}, \ldots, w_M), & s = (1, 0) \\ \text{undefined}, & s = (1, 1) \end{cases}$$

A "fetch" operation moves w_a into the last position while a "store" operation changes w_a to w^*. Note that a fetch is a nondestructive read operation.

We now proceed to bound the combinational complexity and delay complexity of the transition and output function of this sequential machine.

Theorem 6.2.2.1. Let $\Omega = P_{1,2}^{(2)}$. Then, for the (M, b) random access memory with $M = 2^m$,

$$C_\Omega(\lambda_{ra}) = D_\Omega(\lambda_{ra}) = 0$$

and

$$S \leq C_\Omega(\delta_{ra}, \lambda_{ra}) \leq 5S\left(1 + \frac{1}{b}\right) + 2(b - 1)$$

$$\log_2 M \leq D_\Omega(\delta_{ra}, \lambda_{ra}) \leq \log_2 M + \lceil \log_2 \log_2 M \rceil + 3$$

where $S = Mb$ is the storage capacity of the memory in bits.

Proof. The lower bounds are developed first and that for combinational complexity is obtained with the aid of the following technique. Let $f: \{0, 1\}^n \to \{0, 1\}^m$, $g: \{0, 1\}^m \to \{0, 1\}$, and let $g(f): \{0, 1\}^n \to \{0, 1\}$ be the function obtained by composing f with g. Since $g(f)$ can be obtained by concatenating circuits for f and g, it follows that

$$C_\Omega(g(f)) \leq C_\Omega(f) + C_\Omega(g)$$

If $C_\Omega(g)$ is known, a lower bound to $C_\Omega(f)$ can be derived. This method can be used for functions that are binary but not Boolean to permit the use of lower bounding methods for Boolean functions.

Let $(w_0', w_1', \ldots, w_M')$ be the successor state to $(w_0, w_1, \ldots, w_M)$ when the input is (s, a, w^*). Let the function g defined in the preceding paragraph be the OR of the b bits of w_M', so that

$$g(\delta_{ra}((w_0, \ldots, w_M), (s, a, w^*))) = w_{M, 1}' + w_{M, 2}' + \cdots + w_{M, b}'$$

where $w'_{M,i}$ is the ith component of $\mathbf{w}'_M$. If we set $\mathbf{s} = (0, 1)$, $g(\delta_{\mathrm{ra}})$ has the value $w_{a,1} + w_{a,2} + \cdots + w_{a,b}$ which is the OR of the b components of $\mathbf{w}_a$. Since a can take any value in $\{0, 1, 2, \ldots, M - 1\}$, it is clear that $g(\delta_{\mathrm{ra}})$ is a Boolean function that depends on the Mb variables of $\mathbf{w}_0, \mathbf{w}_1, \ldots, \mathbf{w}_{M-1}$. With $\mathbf{s} = (0, 0)$, $g(\delta_{\mathrm{ra}})$ has value $w_{M,1} + w_{M,2} + \cdots + w_{M,b}$, so it depends on at least $(m + 1)b$ variables. It follows from the simple linear lower bound (Theorem 2.4.1.1) that

$$C_\Omega(\delta_{\mathrm{ra}}, \lambda_{\mathrm{ra}}) \geq (M + 1)b - 1 - C_\Omega(g) = Mb$$

since $C_\Omega(g) = b - 1$. Also, since $w'_{M,j}$ defines a Boolean function that depends on at least M variables, $L_\Omega(w'_{M,j}) \geq M - 1$, and from Theorem 2.3.3,

$$D_\Omega(\delta_{\mathrm{ra}}, \lambda_{\mathrm{ra}}) \geq D_\Omega(w'_{M,j}) \geq \log_2 M$$

We now turn to the derivation of upper bounds.

Upper bounds are derived by constructing circuits or chains for the function δ_{ra}. (λ_{ra} is a simple projection operator.) Let the address $\mathbf{a}$ be used as input to a circuit for the binary-to-positional transformer $f_T^{(m)}$: $\{0, 1\}^m \rightarrow \{0, 1\}^{2^m}$ discussed in Section 3.1.1. The outputs are ordered so that the ith output of this circuit, y_i, is 1 if and only if $\mathbf{a}$ is the binary representation of the integer $a = i$; that is,

$$y_i = \begin{cases} 1, & a = i \\ 0, & a \neq i \end{cases}$$

Let $\mathbf{s} = (s_1, s_2)$ and let $w'_{i,j}$ be the jth component of the b-tuple $\mathbf{w}'_i$ in the successor state. If

$$h_i = y_i \cdot s_1$$

then h_i is 1 only if $a = i$ and a "store" operation is performed. Therefore,

$$w'_{i,j} = \bar{h}_i \cdot w_{i,j} + h_i \cdot w_j^*$$

correctly computes the components $w'_{i,j}$, $1 \leq j \leq b$, $0 \leq i \leq M - 1$, of the successor state. The component $w'_{M,j}$ is obtained from

$$w'_{M,j} = \left(\sum_{i=0}^{M-1} y_i \cdot w_{i,j} \right) \cdot s_2 + \left(w_{M,j} \cdot \bar{s}_2 \right)$$

for $1 \leq j \leq b$ where Σ denotes M-fold OR.

The y_i's are computed from $f_T^{(m)}$ and from Theorem 3.1.1.1 with $C_\Omega(f_T^{(m)}) \leq 2^m + m2^{(m+1)/2} - 2$. Also, the h_i's are computed with M

additional operations and the $w'_{i,j}$'s with $3Mb$ more. Finally, $\mathbf{w}'_M$ is realized with $2(M + 1)b$ operations. Since $M = 2^m$, it follows that

$$C_\Omega(\delta_{ra}) \leq 5Mb + 2M + \sqrt{2M} \ \log_2 M + 2(b - 1)$$

However, $2M + \sqrt{2M} \ \log_2 M \leq 5M$ for $M \geq 1$, so

$$C_\Omega(\delta_{ra}, \lambda_{ra}) = C_\Omega(\delta_{ra}) \leq 5S\left(1 + \frac{1}{b}\right) + 2(b - 1)$$

for all $M \geq 1$.

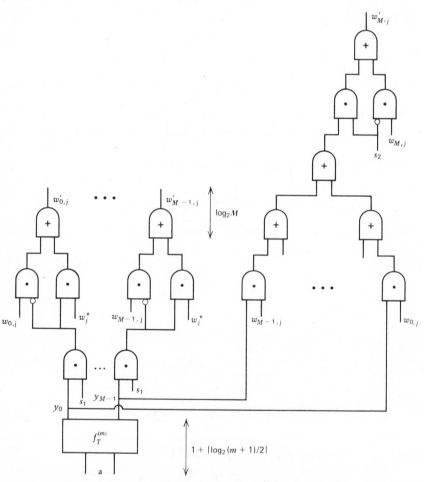

Figure 6.2.2.2. Transition and output function for RAM.

The upper bound to $D_\Omega(\delta_{ra})$ is also easy to derive. Since y_i is a minterm in m variables, it can be realized with delay $\lceil \log_2 m \rceil$. In addition, h_i introduces one unit of delay, so $w'_{i,j}$, $0 \leq i \leq M - 1$, $1 \leq j \leq b$, can be realized with delay of at most $\lceil \log_2 m \rceil + 3$. On the other hand, $w'_{M,j}$, $1 \leq j \leq b$, is realized with the preceding formula with delay $\lceil \log_2 M \rceil + \lceil \log_2 m \rceil + 3$, which dominates the above delay for all $M \geq 1$ and is the upper bound we desire. $\qquad \square$

The upper bounds are quite tight and show that the combinational complexity for the RAM is linear in storage capacity whereas delay complexity is logarithmic in the number of words. Also, the delay complexity is almost exclusively caused by the delay encountered in generating the components of the output word w'_M. The constant multiplier 5, which appears in the upper bound to combinational complexity, is attributable to the particular choice of basis Ω and, in general, changes with a change in basis.

6.2.3. Tape Memory

Tape memories were encountered in our treatment of Turing machines. The model that we adopt here for study is finite in size and contains M storage cells with b binary digits per cell. It has a head and a control that directs the movement of the head, records the head position with $\mathbf{p}$, the binary representation of the integer $p \in \{0, 1, 2, \ldots, M - 1\}$, and has a register to hold the output word w_M. Such a machine is shown schematically in Figure 6.2.3.1.

The memory receives an input $(\mathbf{s}, \mathbf{a}, \mathbf{w}^*)$ that has the same meaning as for the random access memory. However, for the tape memory, once an

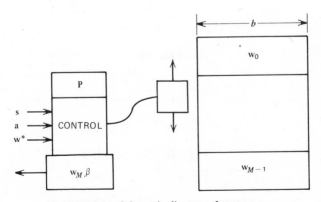

Figure 6.2.3.1. Schematic diagram of tape memory.

action command (a "store" or a "fetch") is issued, no further inputs are accepted until the first request is satisfied. This requires that the head position be incremented or decremented one position per cycle until $p = a$.

Definition 6.2.3.1. An (M, b) *tape memory* (TAM) is a sequential machine $S_t = \langle S_t, I_t, \delta_t, \lambda_t, O_t \rangle$ where $S_t = \{(\mathbf{W}, \beta, \mathbf{D}, \mathbf{p})\} \subseteq \{0, 1\}^{(M+2)b + 2m + 3}$ is the state set,

$$\mathbf{W} = (\mathbf{w}_0, \mathbf{w}_1, \dots, \mathbf{w}_M), \qquad \mathbf{w}_i \in \{0, 1\}^b$$

holds the M memory words and the output word $\mathbf{w}_M$, β records the status of the TAM ($\beta = 1$ means that it is ready to receive another request), and

$$\mathbf{D} = (\sigma, \alpha, \mathbf{v}^*)$$

is the input presented when β was last 1. Here $\alpha \in \{0, 1\}^m$, $m = \lceil \log_2 M \rceil$. The input alphabet is $I_t = \{(\mathbf{s}, \mathbf{a}, \mathbf{w}^*)\} \subseteq \{0, 1\}^{m + b + 2}$, and the output alphabet is $O_t = \{(\mathbf{w}_M, \beta)\} = \{0, 1\}^{b+1}$. The output function λ_t: $S_t \to O_t$ is a simple projection operator whose value is $(\mathbf{w}_M, \beta)$. The transition function δ_t: $S_t \times I_t \to S_t$ is defined by

$$\delta_t((\mathbf{W}, \beta, \mathbf{D}, \mathbf{p}), (\mathbf{s}, \mathbf{a}, \mathbf{w}^*)) = (\mathbf{W}', \beta', \mathbf{D}', \mathbf{p}')$$

where

$$p' = \begin{cases} p + 1, & \alpha > p \text{ or } \alpha = p, \quad \mathbf{s} \neq (0, 0), \quad \text{and } a > p \\ p, & \text{otherwise} \\ p - 1, & \alpha < p \text{ or } \alpha = p, \quad \mathbf{s} \neq (0, 0), \quad \text{and } a < p \end{cases}$$

that is, if necessary, the head moves to satisfy the last request, and

$$\mathbf{D}' = (\sigma', \alpha', \mathbf{v}'^*) = \begin{cases} (\mathbf{s}, \mathbf{a}, \mathbf{w}^*), & \beta = 1 \\ \mathbf{D}, & \beta = 0 \end{cases}$$

records the value of the last input requiring service. Also,

$$\beta' = \begin{cases} 1, & p' = \alpha' \\ 0, & p' \neq \alpha' \end{cases}$$

and

$$\mathbf{W}' = \begin{cases} \delta_{\mathrm{ra}}(\mathbf{W}, \mathbf{D}'), & \beta' = 1 \\ \mathbf{W}, & \beta' = 0 \end{cases}$$

that is, $\beta' = 1$ if and only if the head finishes at the target position α'.

Also, $\mathbf{W}'$ is changed to the value that the state of the RAM would have in this case.

As defined, the TAM responds to commands to fetch and store individual words. However, in practice, tape units are frequently designed to produce as output a block of words of some preset size, the first word of which is at the address specified. The reader should have little difficulty in augmenting this model to accommodate this feature. We now turn to the derivation of bounds to the combinational and delay complexities of this machine.

Theorem 6.2.3.1. Let $\Omega = P_{1,2}^{(2)}$. Then, for the (M, b) tape memory with $M = 2^m$,

$$C_\Omega(\lambda_t) = D_\Omega(\lambda_t) = 0$$

and

$$S \leq C_\Omega(\delta_t, \lambda_t) \leq 5S\left(1 + \frac{1}{b}\right) + 5b + 23 \log_2 M - 1$$

$$\log_2 M \leq D_\Omega(\delta_t, \lambda_t) \leq \log_2 M + 7.17\lceil \log_2 \log_2 M \rceil + 20.34$$

where $S = Mb$ is the storage capacity of the memory in bits.

Proof. The lower bounds follow directly from the definition of $\mathbf{W}'$ and the bounds for the RAM. The derivation of the upper bounds also makes use of the RAM results.

The quantity $\mathbf{D}'$ is easily computed from the formulas

$$\sigma_i' = s_i \cdot \beta + \sigma_i \cdot \overline{\beta}, \qquad 1 \leq i \leq 2$$

$$\alpha_i' = a_i \cdot \beta + \alpha_i \cdot \overline{\beta}, \qquad 1 \leq i \leq m$$

$$v_i'^* = w_i^* \cdot \beta + v_i^* \cdot \overline{\beta}, \qquad 1 \leq i \leq b$$

and $C_\Omega(\mathbf{D}') \leq 3(m + b + 2)$, $D_\Omega(\mathbf{D}') = 2$.

The quantity β' is easily computed from $\mathbf{p}'$ and α' and

$$\beta' = f_{\text{MATCH}}(\mathbf{p}', \alpha')$$

where $f_{\text{MATCH}}: \{0, 1\}^{2m} \to \{0, 1\}$ is 1 if and only if the corresponding components of $\mathbf{p}'$ and α' are equal. Clearly, $C_\Omega(\beta') = 2m - 1$ and $D_\Omega(\beta') = \lceil \log_2 m \rceil + 1$.

To form $\mathbf{W}'$, observe that

$$\delta_{\mathrm{ra}}(\mathbf{W}, \mathbf{D}') = \mathbf{W}$$

if σ', the first component of $\mathbf{D}'$, is $\sigma' = (0, 0)$. Therefore, replace σ' by σ'' where

$$\sigma_i'' = \sigma_i' \cdot \beta', \qquad 1 \leq i \leq 2$$

and let $\mathbf{D}'' = (\sigma'', \alpha', \mathbf{v}^*)$. Then $\mathbf{W}'$ can be written as

$$\mathbf{W}' = \delta_{\mathrm{ra}}(\mathbf{W}, \mathbf{D}'')$$

and $C_\Omega(\mathbf{W}') \leq C_\Omega(\delta_{\mathrm{ra}}) + 2$ and $D_\Omega(\mathbf{W}') \leq D_\Omega(\delta_{\mathrm{ra}}) + 1$ when β' and $\mathbf{D}'$ are given.

The final task is to realize $\mathbf{p}'$. Let t_1 and t_2 be the Boolean functions

$$t_1 = \begin{cases} 1, & \alpha > p \quad \text{or} \quad (\alpha = p, \mathbf{s} \neq (0, 0), \text{ and } a > p) \\ 0, & \text{otherwise} \end{cases}$$

$$t_2 = \begin{cases} 1, & \alpha < p \quad \text{or} \quad (\alpha = p, \mathbf{s} \neq (0, 0), \text{ and } a < p) \\ 0, & \text{otherwise} \end{cases}$$

Then, if $\mathbf{s} = (s_1, s_2)$,

$$t_1 = f_{\mathrm{COMP}}(\mathbf{p}, \alpha) + f_{\mathrm{MATCH}}(\mathbf{p}, \alpha) \cdot (s_1 + s_2) \cdot f_{\mathrm{COMP}}(\mathbf{p}, \mathbf{a})$$

$$t_2 = f_{\mathrm{COMP}}(\alpha, \mathbf{p}) + f_{\mathrm{MATCH}}(\mathbf{p}, \alpha) \cdot (s_1 + s_2) \cdot f_{\mathrm{COMP}}(\mathbf{a}, \mathbf{p})$$

Here $f_{\mathrm{COMP}}: \{0, 1\}^{2m} \to \{0, 1\}$ is the comparison function of Theorem 2.4.3.6 and $C_\Omega(f_{\mathrm{COMP}}) \leq 4m - 3$. This bound is realized by a formula so that Theorem 2.3.3 and Example 2.3.4 can be used to show that

$$D_\Omega(f_{\mathrm{COMP}}) \leq 5.17 \log_2 (4m - 2).$$

Since $f_{\mathrm{COMP}}(\alpha, \mathbf{p}) = \overline{f_{\mathrm{COMP}}(\mathbf{p}, \alpha)} \cdot \overline{f_{\mathrm{MATCH}}(\mathbf{p}, \alpha)}$, both t_1 and t_2 can be realized with $C_\Omega(t_1, t_2) \leq 12m$ elements and delay complexity $D_\Omega(t_1, t_2) \leq D_\Omega(f_{\mathrm{COMP}}) + 2 \leq 2 + 5.17 \log_2(4m - 2)$. Here we have used the fact that $C_\Omega(f_{\mathrm{MATCH}}) = 2m - 1$ and $D_\Omega(f_{\mathrm{MATCH}}) = \lceil \log_2 m \rceil + 1$ since $f_{\mathrm{MATCH}}: \{0, 1\}^{2m} \to \{0, 1\}$.

If $t_1 = 1$, p is incremented by 1. Let $\mathbf{p} = (p_{m-1}, \ldots, p_1, p_0)$. Then incrementing p by 1 causes a carry c_j into position j only if $p_{j-1} = \cdots = p_1 = p_0 = 1$, that is,

$$c_j = p_{j-1} \cdot \cdots \cdot p_0, \qquad 1 \leq j \leq m - 1$$

$$c_0 = 1$$

If $c_j = 1$, $p'_j = p_j \oplus c_j$; that is, the value of p_j is changed. If $t_2 = 1$, p is decremented by 1. This will cause a deficit d_j from position p_j only if $p_{j-1} = \cdots = p_0 = 0$, that is

$$d_j = \bar{p}_{j-1} \cdot \cdots \cdot \bar{p}_0, \qquad 1 \le j \le m - 1$$

$$d_0 = 1$$

If $d_j = 1$, $p'_j = p_j \oplus d_j$; that is, the value of p_j is changed. These observations can now be combined to compute $\mathbf{p}'$ from $\mathbf{p}$ under all stated conditions. Let

$$n_j = c_j \cdot t_1 + d_j \cdot t_2$$

Then

$$p'_j = p_j \oplus n_j$$

and $p'_j = p_j$ if $t_1 = t_2 = 0$; otherwise p is appropriately incremented or decremented. It follows that $C_\Omega(\mathbf{p}') \le 6(m - 1)$ and $D_\Omega(\mathbf{p}') \le \lceil \log_2 m \rceil + 3$, given t_1 and t_2 without delay. Including t_1 and t_2, the delay is $D_\Omega(\mathbf{p}') \le 5 + 5.17 \log_2(4m - 2)$.

Combining these results, we observe that

$$C_\Omega(\delta_t, \lambda_t) \le 3(m + b + 2) + 2m - 1 + C_\Omega(\delta_{\mathrm{ra}}) + 2 + 12m + 6(m - 1)$$

$$= C_\Omega(\delta_{\mathrm{ra}}) + 23m + 3b + 1$$

from which the first bound follows. By examining Figure 6.2.3.2, the reader can verify that the longest delay is encountered in the successive computation of $\mathbf{p}'$, β', $\mathbf{D}''$, and $\mathbf{W}'$ and that the total delay is bounded by

$$D_\Omega(\delta_t, \lambda_t) \le 5 + 5.17 \log_2(4m - 2) + \lceil \log_2 m \rceil + 1 + D_\Omega(\delta_{\mathrm{ra}}) + 1$$

$$\le D_\Omega(\delta_{\mathrm{ra}}) + 6.17 \lceil \log_2 m \rceil + 17.34$$

from which the last bound follows. $\qquad\qquad\qquad\qquad\qquad\qquad\square$

These bounds are also quite tight, basis dependent, and very close to those for the RAM. This suggests that there are problems that could be solved in equal numbers of cycles by both a RAM and a TAM doing approximately equal amounts of computational work. This is certainly true of a task that requires fetching words in sequence from memory, because then the RAM is used exactly as a TAM.

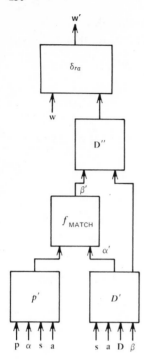

Figure 6.2.3.2. Transition and output function for TAM.

6.2.4. Drum and Disk Memories

Drum and disk memories are other types of storage of large capacity that usually serve as auxiliary bulk storage media on general-purpose computers. These two types of devices, which are logically equivalent but functionally different, are illustrated pictorially in Figure 6.2.4.1.

The drum rotates at constant speed, and its surface is ruled into M tracks with each track carrying K words of b bits apiece. A reading head sits over each track, and in one cycle, one of the b-bit words on one track can be read. Since each track contains K words, the total storage capacity of the memory is KMb bits. An input $(\mathbf{s}, \mathbf{a}, \mathbf{w}^*)$ has essentially the same meaning as for the TAM except that $\mathbf{a} = (a_1, a_2)$, where $a_1 \in \{0, 1, \ldots, M - 1\}$ is the track number and $a_2 \in \{0, 1, \ldots, K - 1\}$ is the position of the word to be accessed on the track. If $\beta = 1$, the drum is ready for a new input, and if $\beta = 0$, it is waiting for the word specified by the last input to appear under the head.

The disk memory is logically identical with the drum, but physically it is quite different. It has b platters which rotate at constant speed and a

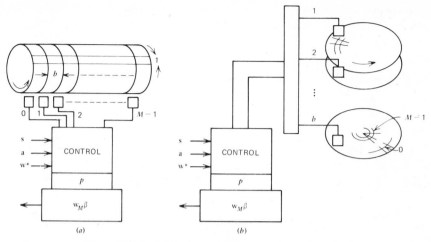

Figure 6.2.4.1. Two storage media, (a) drum and (b) disk.

"comb" on which rests b reading heads.[†] Each head can read a single bit so that b-bits are available under the b heads on the comb. The b annuli defined by the comb position are called collectively a *cylinder*, and this corresponds to a track on the drum. We let K be the number of bits on one annulus so that a cylinder contains K b-bit words. Each comb position defines a cylinder, and we let M be the number of distinct cylinders on the disk unit.

The disk unit receives the same inputs as does the drum, and they have the same interpretation. Clearly, they are logically equivalent. The big difference between them is that it takes many milliseconds to change cylinders, because to do so requires movement of the comb. With the drum, only one cycle is required to change tracks since the switching is done electronically. There is no physical reason why moving-head drums or fixed-head disks cannot be constructed, in which case the disk and drum would model the drum and disk, respectively, as we have described them. In fact, such devices do exist.

We limit our formal presentation to the drum and encourage the reader to develop the formal model for the moving-head disk. The only difference in the two models is that a change in the cylinder number can occur only after a number of cycles proportional to the magnitude of the change in the number.

[†] Frequently, a pair of platters consists of opposite sides of the same physical platter.

Definition 6.2.4.1. A (K, M, b) *drum memory* (DRUM) is a sequential machine $S_d = \langle S_d, I_d, \delta_d, \lambda_d, O_d \rangle$ where the state set $S_d = \{(\mathbf{W}, \beta, \mathbf{D}, \mathbf{p})\}$ $= \subseteq \{0, 1\}^{(KM+2)b + 2k + m + 3}$ and

$$H\mathbf{W} = (\mathbf{W}_0, \mathbf{W}_1, \ldots, \mathbf{W}_{K-1}, \mathbf{w}_M), \qquad \mathbf{W}_t = (\mathbf{w}_{t,0}, \mathbf{w}_{t,1}, \ldots, \mathbf{w}_{t,M-1})$$

$$\mathbf{w}_{ti} \in \{0, 1\}^b, \qquad \mathbf{w}_M \in \{0, 1\}^b$$

holds the KM words on the M tracks and the output word $\mathbf{w}_M$. Here $m = \lceil \log_2 M \rceil$ and $k = \lceil \log_2 K \rceil$. Also, β records the status of the DRUM ($\beta = 1$ if and only if it is ready to accept a new input), and

$$\mathbf{D} = (\sigma, \alpha_1, \alpha_2, \mathbf{v}^*)$$

is the input when β was last 1. The input alphabet is $I_d = \{(\mathbf{s}, \mathbf{a}_1, \mathbf{a}_2, \mathbf{w}^*)\}$ $\subseteq \{0, 1\}^{m+k+b+2}$ where $\mathbf{a}_1$ and $\mathbf{a}_2$ are binary representations of $a_1 \in \{0, 1, \ldots, M-1\}$ and $a_2 \in \{0, 1, \ldots, K-1\}$, and the output alphabet is $O_d = \{(\mathbf{w}_M, \beta)\} = \{0, 1\}^{b+1}$. The output function $\lambda_d: S_d \to O_d$ is a simple projection operator, and the transition function $\delta_d: S_d \times I_d \to S_d$ is defined by

$$\delta_d((\mathbf{W}, \beta, \mathbf{D}, \mathbf{p}), (\mathbf{s}, \mathbf{a}_1, \mathbf{a}_2, \mathbf{w}^*)) = (\mathbf{W}', \beta', \mathbf{D}', \mathbf{p}')$$

where $\mathbf{p}$ is the binary representation of $p \in \{0, 1, \ldots, K-1\}$, the position of the heads, and $p' = (p + 1)$ modulo K. (The DRUM rotates at constant speed.) Also,

$$\mathbf{D}' = (\sigma', \alpha_1', \alpha_2', \mathbf{v}'^*) = \begin{cases} (\mathbf{s}, \mathbf{a}_1, \mathbf{a}_2, \mathbf{w}^*), & \beta = 1 \\ \mathbf{D}, & \beta = 0 \end{cases}$$

and

$$\beta' = \begin{cases} 1, & p' = \alpha_2' \\ 0, & p' \neq \alpha_2' \end{cases}$$

At each instant of time $\mathbf{W}_0$ is the Mb-bit word under the head and $\mathbf{W}_t$ is the word removed from $\mathbf{W}_0$ by t cycles. The contents of $\mathbf{W}_t$, $t \neq 0$, after one cycle is the adjacent word, that is,

$$\mathbf{W}_t' = \mathbf{W}_{(t+1) \bmod K}, \qquad 1 \leq t \leq K - 1$$

Also, $\mathbf{W}_0$ is modified and $\mathbf{w}'_M$ is computed as follows:

$$(\mathbf{W}'_0, \mathbf{w}'_M) = \begin{cases} \delta_{\text{ra}}((\mathbf{W}_{K-1}, \mathbf{w}_M), (\sigma', \alpha'_1, \mathbf{v}'^*)), & \beta' = 1 \\ (\mathbf{W}_{K-1}, \mathbf{w}_M), & \beta' = 0 \end{cases}$$

Thus, p records the relative angular position of the DRUM, and words rotate on the drum with access to a word available only when it arrives under the heads.

Theorem 6.2.4.1. Let $\Omega = P_{1,2}^{(2)}$. Then, for the (K, M, b) drum memory with $M = 2^m$, $K = 2^k$,

$$C_\Omega(\lambda_d) = D_\Omega(\lambda_d) = 0$$

and for $K \geq 8$,

$$Mb \leq C_\Omega(\delta_d, \lambda_d) \leq 5Mb\left(1 + \frac{1}{b}\right) + 5b + 3 \log_2 M + 7 \log_2 K + 2$$

$$\log_2 M \leq D_\Omega(\delta_d, \lambda_d) \leq \log_2 M + \lceil \log_2 \log_2 M \rceil + 2\lceil \log_2 \log_2 K \rceil + 6$$

where KMb is the storage capacity of the memory in bits.

Proof. The lower bounds follow from the definition of $(\mathbf{W}'_0, \mathbf{w}'_M)$ and Theorem 6.2.2.1. The upper bounds follow by construction.

From the construction in the proof of Theroem 6.2.3.1, it is clear that $\mathbf{p}' = (p'_{k-1}, p'_{k-2}, \ldots, p'_0)$ can be formed from $\mathbf{p}$ with $C_\Omega(\mathbf{p}') \leq 2k - 3$, $D_\Omega(\mathbf{p}') \leq \lceil \log_2(k - 1) \rceil + 1$. Also, $\mathbf{D}'$ requires at most $C_\Omega(\mathbf{D}') \leq 3(m + k + b + 2)$ elements and $D_\Omega(\mathbf{D}') = 2$. Furthermore, β' is the value of the function $f_{\text{MATCH}}(\mathbf{p}', \alpha'_2)$ and $C_\Omega(\beta') = 2k - 1$, $D_\Omega(\beta') = \lceil \log_2 k \rceil + 1$ when $\mathbf{p}'$ and α'_2 are available.

The words $\mathbf{W}'_1, \mathbf{W}'_2, \ldots, \mathbf{W}'_{K-1}$ are computed without logic elements while $(\mathbf{W}'_0, \mathbf{w}'_M)$ can be computed by the scheme given for the TAM [note that $(\mathbf{W}'_0, \mathbf{w}'_M)$ is equivalent to $\mathbf{W}'$ in this case], and

$$C_\Omega((\mathbf{W}'_0, \mathbf{w}'_M)) \leq C_\Omega(\delta_{\text{ra}}) + 2$$

$$D_\Omega((\mathbf{W}'_0, \mathbf{w}'_M)) \leq D_\Omega(\delta_{\text{ra}}) + 1$$

when β' and $\mathbf{D}'$ are available.

It follows that

$$C_\Omega(\delta_d, \lambda_d) \leq 2k - 3 + 3(m + k + b + 2) + 2k - 1$$

$$+ 5Mb\left(1 + \frac{1}{b}\right) + 2(b - 1) + 2$$

$$= 5Mb\left(1 + \frac{1}{b}\right) + 5b + 7k + 3m + 2$$

Also,

$$D_\Omega(\delta_d, \lambda_d) \leq \lceil \log_2(k - 1) \rceil + 1 + \lceil \log_2 k \rceil + 1 + D_\Omega(\delta_{ra}) + 1$$

$$\leq \log_2 M + \lceil \log_2 \log_2 M \rceil + 2\lceil \log_2 \log_2 K \rceil + 6$$

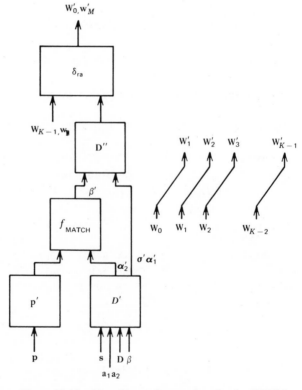

Figure 6.2.4.2. Transition and output function for DRUM.

since the longest path occurs in computing $\mathbf{p}'$, β', and $(\mathbf{W}'_0, \mathbf{w}'_M)$ when $k \geq 3$ or $K \geq 8$, as seen in Figure 6.2.4.2. □

The DRUM has KM b-bit words, or K times as many words as the RAM and TAM. Nevertheless, the combinational complexity of δ_d and λ_d differs principally by an additive term of only $7 \log_2 K$. That is, $C_\Omega(\delta_d, \lambda_d)$ is not linear in the storage capacity KMb. The delay complexities also differ by a relatively small additive term of $2\lceil \log_2 \log_2 K \rceil$. These differences reflect the severe limitations on access of words imposed by the rotational nature of the drum memory.

6.2.5. Associative Memory

An associative memory allows us to access a word by some portion of the content of the word rather than by its physical location. This is useful in those cases where a table of items is to be accessed or updated and each item contains a unique identifier as part of its content. This occurs in an inventory of parts in which a data item contains the part number along with other information such as the location and numbers of such parts, the number on order, and so forth.

An associative memory is also said to be "content-addressable." A subword is specified as part of the input, and all words in the memory that contain the subword are available for reading or updating. The *content-addressable memory* (CAM) holds M data words $\mathbf{w}_0, \mathbf{w}_1, \ldots, \mathbf{w}_{M-1}$ of b bits apiece and an output $\mathbf{w}_M$ of equal length. An input is a triple $(\mathbf{s}, \mathbf{c}, \mathbf{w}^*)$ where $\mathbf{s} \in \{0, 1\}^2$ is a command with the interpretation given for the RAM, $\mathbf{c} \in \{0, 1\}^r$ is an r-bit word used to address the CAM, and $\mathbf{w}^*$ is an input word. If $\mathbf{s} = (0, 1)$ denotes a "fetch," $\mathbf{w}_M$ is replaced by the "vector OR" of all data words that agree with $\mathbf{c}$ in their leftmost r positions. If $\mathbf{s} = (1, 0)$ denotes a "store," every data word so agreeing with $\mathbf{c}$ is replaced by $\mathbf{w}^*$. When it is possible to access all M words, clearly $2^r \geq M$. The reader is invited to contribute a formal definition of the (M, b, r) CAM sequential machine so described and of its transition and output functions δ_{CAM} and λ_{CAM}, respectively.

Theorem 6.2.5.1. Let $\Omega = P_{1,2}^{(2)}$. Then, for the (M, b, r) associative memory (CAM) with $M = 2^m$,

$$C_\Omega(\lambda_{\text{CAM}}) = D_\Omega(\lambda_{\text{CAM}}) = 0$$

and

$$S \leq C_\Omega(\delta_{CAM}, \lambda_{CAM}) \leq 5S\left(1 + \frac{(2r)}{5b}\right) + 2b$$

$$\log_2 M \leq D_\Omega(\delta_{CAM}, \lambda_{CAM}) \leq \log_2 M + \lceil \log_2 r \rceil + 4$$

where $S = Mb$ is the storage capacity of the memory in bits.

Proof. The lower bounds are derived by the methods of Theorem 6.2.2.1 and follow from the fact that $\mathbf{w}'_M$, the value of $\mathbf{w}_M$ in the successor state, can be any one of the M words in the memory.

The upper bounds are derived following the pattern of Theorem 6.2.2.1 and using the same circuits, with the exception that the binary-to-positional transformer is replaced by a new function. The functions y_i, $0 \leq i \leq M - 1$, of this transformer are replaced by functions z_i, $0 \leq i \leq M - 1$, which select the ith word $\mathbf{w}_i$ if the first r digits of $\mathbf{w}_i$ match $\mathbf{c}$; that is,

$$z_i = f_{MATCH}((w_{i1}, w_{i2}, \ldots, w_{ir}), \mathbf{c})$$

This is a function of $2r$ variables with combinational complexity $2r - 1$ and delay complexity $\lceil \log_2 r \rceil + 1$. Hence, $\{z_i | 0 \leq i \leq M - 1\}$ has combinational complexity $M(2r - 1)$ and the same delay complexity.

Since the rest of the circuit for $(\delta_{CAM}, \lambda_{CAM})$ is identical with that for $(\delta_{ra}, \lambda_{ra})$, the upper bounds follow.   □

The associative memory described in the preceding has about the same combinational complexity and delay complexity as the random access memory. This implies that the cost of constructing each out of semiconductors should be approximately the same.

The associative memory is very good for accessing items by their internal labels. For this reason, it is difficult to replace items in memory unless their key words are known. To overcome this, a memory with the features of both the CAM and the RAM can be constructed. One need only realize both the function y_i and the function z_i for $0 \leq i \leq M - 1$, and choose between them with a Boolean variable. The reader can verify that the additional cost of adding the CAM feature to the RAM or vice versa is minuscule in its effect on either complexity measure (see Problem 6-6).

6.3. ARITHMETIC AND LOGICAL FUNCTIONS

In this section, we take up and study in greater detail a subject discussed in Section 3.1.1: the set of arithmetic and logical functions that play a principal role in central processing units. We examine vector operations, shifting, tests on integers, and the four arithmetic operations. These we examine in some detail, and we present or discuss optimal or best known straight-line algorithms as measured by combinational complexity and delay complexity.

6.3.1. Vector Operations

A *vector operation* on a pair of words x_1, $x_2 \in \{0, 1\}^b$ is a function that returns a result $y \in \{0, 1\}^b$ where y_j is a function of x_{1j} and x_{2j}, the jth components of the corresponding words. That is, for some Boolean function $h: \{0, 1\}^2 \to \{0, 1\}$,

$$y_j = h(x_{1j}, x_{2j})$$

We recognize the vector OR, AND, and EXCLUSIVE OR in which $h = +$, $\cdot$, and $\oplus$, respectively. Another important *vector operation* maps $x \in \{0, 1\}^b$ into y where $y_j = \bar{x}_j$, the Boolean complement of x_j.

Clearly, each of these operations has a combinational complexity over any complete basis of fan-in 2 that is at most linear in b and a delay complexity independent of b.

Vector operations have many important applications. For example, vector AND is useful for masking out a portion of a word, and vector EXCLUSIVE OR is Galois field addition for fields of characteristic 2, which is used in coding and decoding of error-correcting codes. Also, the vector NOT is used in subtraction of binary numbers using either 1's or 2's complement arithmetic.

6.3.2. Shifting

Shifting is discussed in Section 3.1.1 and shown to have a combinational complexity that is at most square in the size of the word to be shifted. Here give improved bounds on this complexity and develop bounds on the delay complexity of the shifting function.

Let $a = (a_0, a_1, \ldots, a_{\lceil \log_2 b \rceil - 1})$ represent an integer $|a| \in \{0, 1, 2, \ldots, b - 1\}$ and let $x = (x_0, x_1, \ldots, x_{b-1})$. Then we recall from Section 3.1.1 the definitions of the *shift-right logical function* f_{SR} and the *shift-left logical function* f_{SL}.

$$f_{SR}(\mathbf{x}, \mathbf{a}) = (y_0, y_1, \ldots, y_{b-1})$$

$$y_i = \begin{cases} x_{i-|\mathbf{a}|}, & i - |\mathbf{a}| \geq 0 \\ 0, & i - |\mathbf{a}| < 0 \end{cases}$$

$$f_{SL}(\mathbf{x}, \mathbf{a}) = (y_0, y_1, \ldots, y_{b-1})$$

$$y_i = \begin{cases} x_{i+|\mathbf{a}|}, & i + |\mathbf{a}| \leq b - 1 \\ 0, & i + |\mathbf{a}| > b - 1 \end{cases}$$

We also introduce the (right) *cyclic shift function* f_{CS} defined by

$$f_{CS}(\mathbf{x}, \mathbf{a}) = (y_0, y_1, \ldots, y_{b-1})$$

$$y_i = x_{(i-|\mathbf{a}|) \bmod b}$$

The first two functions permit the shifting of $\mathbf{x}$ to the right or left with deletions, while the third permits cyclic shifting of $\mathbf{x}$ to the right.

Frequently, these functions are realized from shifting functions that shift at most one position right or left, either cyclically or logically. Each of these functions has a linear combinational complexity and a delay complexity independent of word size. These statements are also true of the function $f_{CSk}: \{0, 1\}^{b+1} \rightarrow \{0, 1\}^b$ which permits right cyclic shifting by either 0 or k positions.

$$f_{CSk}(\mathbf{x}, t) = (y_0, y_1, \ldots, y_{b-1})$$

$$y_i = \begin{cases} x_i, & t = 0 \\ x_{(i-k) \bmod b}, & t = 1 \end{cases}$$

The function y_i can be realized by the formula

$$y_i = x_i \cdot \bar{t} + x_{(i-k) \bmod b} \cdot t$$

and it follows that

$$C^*_{\Omega_0}(f_{CSk}) \leq 3b, \qquad D_\Omega(f_{CSk}) = 2$$

when $\Omega_0 = \{+, \cdot, {}^-\}$, the basis consisting of OR, AND, and NOT. These bounds also apply to logical shifting by 0 or k positions since some of the functions y_i have value x_i or 0 depending on whether $t = 0$ or 1.

It is now easy to construct a chain to realize f_{CS} using f_{CS2^j}, $0 \leq j \leq \lceil \log_2 b \rceil - 1$. Let $l = \lceil \log_2 b \rceil - 1$. Then $\mathbf{x}$ is shifted by an amount $|\mathbf{a}| = a_0 + a_1 2 + \cdots + a_l 2^l$ if we first shift it by either 0 or 2^l, shift the result by either 0 or $2^{l-1}, \ldots$, and finally shift the result by either 0 or 1. This leads immediately to the following expression for f_{CS}:

$$f_{CS}(\mathbf{x}, \mathbf{a}) = f_{CS1}(f_{CS2}(f_{CS4}(\cdots (f_{CS2^l}(\mathbf{x}, a_l) \cdots), a_2), a_1), a_0)$$

(This is a standard construction; the origin of which is unknown.)

Theorem 6.3.2.1. Let $\Omega_0 = \{ +, \cdot, {}^- \}$. Then, for each of the functions $f \in \{ f_{CS}, f_{SR}, f_{SL} \}$,

$$b \leq C^*_{\Omega_0}(f) \leq 3b \lceil \log_2 b \rceil$$

$$\lceil \log_2(b + \lceil \log_2 b \rceil) \rceil \leq D_{\Omega_0}(f) \leq 2 \lceil \log_2 b \rceil$$

Proof. The upper bounds follow directly from the preceding construction for f_{CS} and the observation that the other functions can be obtained from f_{CS} by deleting logic elements and permuting inputs and outputs.

The lower bound to delay complexity uses the fact that for each function at least one output (namely, y_0 for f_{SL}, y_{b-1} for f_{SR}, and all outputs for f_{CS}) depends on all inputs. The lower bound to combinational complexity follows from Theorem 2.4.4.2 and the observation that each output for every y_i depends on at least two variables. □

The upper bounds to combinational complexity are considerable improvements on the bounds of Section 3.3.1. We observe that a nonlinear lower bound to the combinational complexity of f_{SL} or f_{SR} will yield a nonlinear lower bound to the combinational complexity of integer multiplication, as discussed in Section 3.1.1.

6.3.3. Comparison Tests

The comparison tests $\{ \geq, >, =, <, \leq \}$ on the integers are very useful in their own right and as machine instructions because they facilitate conditional branching. When the integers are given the standard binary representation, the functions "greater than, $>$" and "less than, $<$" are both realized by the function $f_{COMP}: \{0, 1\}^{2b} \to \{0, 1\}$ presented in Section 2.4.3. We have

$$f_{COMP}(x_0, x_1, \ldots, x_{b-1}, y_0, \ldots, y_{b-1}) = \begin{cases} 1, & |\mathbf{x}| < |\mathbf{y}| \\ 0, & \text{otherwise} \end{cases}$$

and from Theorem 2.4.3.6, $C^*_{\Omega_0}(f_{\text{COMP}}) = 4b - 3$ over the basis $\Omega_0 = \{+, \cdot, ^-\}$.

Also, the realization of f_{COMP} given in that theorem is a formula; therefore, we can use Theorem 2.3.3 to bound the delay complexity by

$$\lceil \log_2(4b - 2) \rceil \leq D_{\Omega_0}(f_{\text{COMP}}) \leq 5.17 \log_2(4b - 2)$$

The coefficient of the upper bound is computed in Example 2.3.4.

The equality function "=" for integers in binary is realized by f_{MATCH}: $\{0, 1\}^{2b} \to \{0, 1\}$ where

$$f_{\text{MATCH}}(x_0, \ldots, x_{b-1}, y_0, \ldots, y_{b-1}) = \begin{cases} 1, & x_i = y_i, \quad 0 \leq i \leq b - 1 \\ 0, & \text{otherwise} \end{cases}$$

and from Theorem 2.4.3.4, $C^*_{\Omega_0}(f_{\text{MATCH}}) = 4b - 1$ while over the full basis $\Omega_1 = P^{(2)}_{1,2}$ of all nontrivial functions of two variables, $C^*_{\Omega_1}(f_{\text{MATCH}}) = 2b - 1$. Over Ω_1, $D_{\Omega_1}(f_{\text{MATCH}}) = \lceil \log_2 2b \rceil$ since we can write

$$f_{\text{MATCH}}(x_0, \ldots, y_{b-1}) = \overline{(x_0 \oplus y_0)} \cdot \overline{(x_1 \oplus y_1)} \cdot \cdots \cdot \overline{(x_{b-1} \oplus y_{b-1})}$$

which can be realized with this delay, and this delay is necessary to reach all inputs. Over Ω_0, $D_{\Omega_0}(f_{\text{MATCH}}) \leq \lceil \log_2 2b \rceil + 1$ since $\oplus$ can be realized with two units of delay over this basis.

The functions "greater than or equal, $\geq$" and "less than or equal, $\leq$" for integers in binary can also be obtained from f_{COMP} using NEGATION:

$$\overline{f}_{\text{COMP}}(x_0, \ldots, x_{b-1}, y_0, \ldots, y_{b-1}) = \begin{cases} 1, & |\mathbf{x}| \geq |\mathbf{y}| \\ 0, & \text{otherwise} \end{cases}$$

It is often important to compare a binary number $\mathbf{x}$ with 0. Equality with 0 is realized by $\bar{x}_0 \cdot \bar{x}_1 \cdot \cdots \cdot \bar{x}_{b-1}$, and greater than 0 is realized by $x_0 + x_1 + \cdots + x_{b-1}$, which are trivial functions.

These results are summarized in the following theorem.

Theorem 6.3.3.1. With the standard binary representation of integers as b-tuples, the functions $>$ and $<$ are represented by f_{COMP}: $\{0, 1\}^{2b} \to \{0, 1\}$, the functions $\geq$ and $\leq$ are represented by $\overline{f}_{\text{COMP}}$, and the function $=$ is represented by f_{MATCH}: $\{0, 1\}^{2b} \to \{0, 1\}$. Over the basis $\Omega_0 = \{+, \cdot, ^-\}$,

$$C^*_{\Omega_0}(f_{\text{COMP}}) = 4b - 3, \qquad C^*_{\Omega_0}(f_{\text{MATCH}}) = 4b - 1$$

and

$$\lceil \log_2(4b - 2) \rceil \leq D_{\Omega_0}(f_{\text{COMP}}) \leq 5.17 \log_2(4b - 2)$$

$$\lceil \log_2 2b \rceil \leq D_{\Omega_0}(f_{\text{MATCH}}) \leq \lceil \log_2 2b \rceil + 1$$

Over the basis $\Omega_1 = P_{1,2}^{(2)}$, $C_{\Omega_1}^*(f_{\text{MATCH}}) = 2b - 1$ and the lower bound on its delay complexity is achieved.

6.3.4. Delay Complexity of Overflow Tests

In the next four sections, we examine the four arithmetic operations and bound their combinational and delay complexities when the integers are given the standard binary representation. This choice of representation is very important since use of a representation can have a significant impact on the complexities of an arithmetic operation. In particular, multiplication has a much smaller delay complexity when the integers $\{1, 2, \ldots, N\}$ are represented by their exponents in their prime number decomposition because multiplication can be accomplished by adding corresponding exponents and because the largest exponent has size $\lceil \log_2 N \rceil$.

In this section, we derive representation independent lower bounds on the delay complexity of two important tests associated with arithmetic operations, detection of overflow under addition and multiplication. Overflow occurs when the product or sum of two integers falls outside a given range.

Let $\phi: U \times V \to W$ be a function of two variables with domain $U \times V$ and range W. It has value $\phi(u, v) = w$, $w \in W$, on the pair (u, v) where $u \in U$ and $v \in V$.

Example 6.3.4.1. Let $Z_N = \{0, 1, 2, \ldots, N - 1\}$. Then

$$\phi_+: Z_N \times Z_N \to \{0, 1\} \qquad \text{and} \qquad \phi_\times: Z_N \times Z_N \to \{0, 1\}$$

are overflow functions defined by

$$\phi_+(u, v) = \begin{cases} 1, & u + v \geq N \\ 0, & \text{otherwise} \end{cases}$$

$$\phi_\times(u, v) = \begin{cases} 1, & u \cdot v \geq N \\ 0, & \text{otherwise} \end{cases}$$

where $+$ and $\cdot$ denote integer addition and multiplication.

The function $\phi: U \times V \to W$ is to be realized by a chain over some basis. For this purpose, we allow arbitrary binary encodings of the sets U, V, and W in order to obtain an encoding ϕ^* of ϕ with the smallest possible delay complexity. Let $e_U: U \to \{0, 1\}^m$, $e_V: V \to \{0, 1\}^n$, and $e_W: W \to \{0, 1\}^p$ be such encodings with the property that e_W is 1–1; that is, $e_W(w_1) \neq e_W(w_2)$ if $w_1 \neq w_2$. This is required so that the encoded value of ϕ is unambiguous. Then $\phi^*: \{0, 1\}^{m+n} \to \{0, 1\}^p$, the encoded version of ϕ, satisfies

$$e_W(\phi(u, v)) = \phi^*(e_U(u), e_V(v))$$

for all $u \in U$ and $v \in V$.

Definition 6.3.4.1. The delay complexity of $\phi\colon U \times V \to W$ is the minimal value of the delay complexity of ϕ^* under all possible encodings of U, V, and W with the stated properties.

A few more definitions are necessary before we can state the lower bound to delay complexity. We let $e_{W,j}\colon W \to \{0, 1\}$ be the function associated with the jth digit of $e_W\colon W \to \{0, 1\}^p$ for $1 \leq j \leq p$. Also, we let $|S|$ denote the cardinality of the set S.

Definition 6.3.4.2. Let $\phi\colon U \times V \to W$ be given and let $\phi^*\colon \{0, 1\}^{m+n} \to \{0, 1\}^p$ be the binary function obtained from ϕ by the encoding e_U, e_V, and e_W. Let β be a straight-line algorithm for ϕ^*. Then a subset $\mathfrak{U}_j$ of U ($\mathfrak{V}_j$ of V) is called a *j-separable set* for β in the first (second) variable of ϕ if for any two elements u_1 and u_2 of $\mathfrak{U}_j$ (v_1 and v_2 of $\mathfrak{V}_j$) there exists an element v of V (u of U) such that

$$e_{W,j}(\phi(u_1, v)) \neq e_{W,j}(\phi(u_2, v))$$

$$\left(e_{W,j}(\phi(u, v_1)) \neq e_{W,j}(\phi(u, v_2))\right)$$

Therefore, each element of $\mathfrak{U}_j$ and $\mathfrak{V}_j$ must be given a distinct binary encoding if ϕ^* is to be a proper encoding of ϕ.

Theorem 6.3.4.1. The delay complexity of $\phi\colon U \times V \to W$ with respect to the basis Ω of fan-in r, $D_\Omega(\phi)$, must satisfy the inequality

$$D_\Omega(\phi) \geq \min_{e_W} \max_j \lceil \log_r\{\lceil \log_2|\mathfrak{U}_j|\rceil + \lceil \log_2|\mathfrak{V}_j|\rceil\}\rceil$$

Proof. Since each element of both $\mathfrak{U}_j$ and $\mathfrak{V}_j$ must be given a distinct binary encoding, at least

$$\lceil \log_2|\mathfrak{U}_j|\rceil + \lceil \log_2|\mathfrak{V}_j|\rceil$$

binary digits are necessary to represent these elements. Furthermore, $e_{W,j}(\phi)$, the jth digit of ϕ^*, is a Boolean function that is essentially dependent on at least this many variables. Also, since at most r^d inputs can be reached by a chain of depth d over a basis of fan-in r, the lower bound follows immediately. □

This theorem can be generalized to functions of more than two variables and is the basic theorem employed by Winograd in his development of bounds on the time to add and multiply (Winograd, 1965, 1967; see also Spira, 1969). We now apply it to the two overflow functions defined above. These results were obtained by Winograd (1967).

Theorem 6.3.4.2. Let Ω be a basis of fan-in r. Then, for $N \geq 4$,

$$D_\Omega(\phi_+) \geq \lceil \log_r 2 \lceil \log_2 N \rceil \rceil, \qquad D_\Omega(\phi_\times) \geq \lceil \log_r 2 \lceil \log_2 \lfloor \sqrt{N} \rfloor \rceil \rceil$$

Proof. The lower bound for ϕ_+ is developed first. For every encoding function $e_W \colon W \to \{0, 1\}^p$, there must exist a $1 \leq j \leq p$, such that $e_{W,j}(0) \neq e_{W,j}(1)$. We show that $\mathfrak{U}_j = \mathfrak{V}_j = Z_N$. Let $s_1, s_2 \in Z_N$ and $s_1 < s_2$. Then, with $z = N - s_2$,

$$\phi_+(s_1, z) \neq \phi_+(s_2, z) \qquad \text{and} \qquad \phi_+(z, s_1) \neq \phi_+(z, s_2)$$

Since this result is true for any two elements of Z_N, the first lower bound holds.

The lower bound for $\phi_\times$ uses the observation made above for the encoding function e_W. We claim that $\mathfrak{U}_j$ and $\mathfrak{V}_j$ contain $\{1, 2, \ldots, q\}$ where $q = \lfloor \sqrt{N} \rfloor$. Let $s_1, s_2 \in \{1, 2, \ldots, q\}$, $s_1 < s_2$. Then let $z \in Z_N$ be the smallest integer such that $s_2 \cdot z \geq N$. (Clearly, such exists since $s_2 \geq 2$.) Then

$$s_2 \cdot (z - 1) < N \qquad \text{or} \qquad z < \frac{N}{s_2} + 1$$

and

$$s_1 \cdot z \leq (s_2 - 1) \cdot z < N - 1 + s_2 - \frac{N}{s_2} \leq N - 1$$

since

$$s_2 - \frac{N}{s_2} \leq 0 \qquad \text{for } s_2 \leq \lfloor \sqrt{N} \rfloor$$

Therefore,

$$\phi_\times(s_1, z) \neq \phi_\times(s_2, z), \quad \phi_\times(z, s_1) \neq \phi_\times(z, s_2)$$

and the desired conclusion follows. $\qquad \square$

If $N = 2^k$ and $r = 2$, we have that $D_\Omega(\phi_+ \geq \lceil \log_2(2k) \rceil$ and $D_\Omega(\phi_\times) \geq \lceil \log_2 k \rceil$. The lower bound for addition can be approached, as we demonstrate in the next section, using the standard binary representation for integers. The lower bound for multiplication is more difficult to achieve but can also be approached.

6.3.5. Addition

The binary function defining addition of integers represented in standard binary notation is one of the first functions to be examined in this book (see Figure 2.2.2 and Section 3.1.1). In this section, we discuss a straight-line algorithm for it due to Krapchenko (1967) which is presented in the Appendix and which has small combinational complexity and asymptotically optimum delay complexity. Sklansky (1960a, b) and Ofman (1962) exhibited chains for addition that achieved the lower bound to delay complexity up to a constant multiplier, and Ofman also demonstrated that it is possible to simultaneously realize an adder with a number of logic elements linear in the number of input digits.

We recall that integers in the set $\{0, 1, 2, \ldots, 2^n - 1\}$ can each be represented by a binary n-tuple $\mathbf{x} = (x_0, x_1, \ldots, x_{n-1})$ which denotes the integer

$$|\mathbf{x}| = x_0 + x_1 \cdot 2 + x_2 \cdot 2^2 + \cdots + x_{n-1} 2^{n-1}$$

The *addition function* $f_A^{(2n)}$: $\{0, 1\}^{2n} \to \{0, 1\}^{n+1}$ is defined by

$$f_A^{(2n)}(x_0, x_1, \ldots, x_{n-1}, y_0, \ldots, y_{n-1}) = (s_0, s_1, \ldots, s_n)$$

where $\mathbf{x}$, $\mathbf{y}$, and $\mathbf{s}$ are the indicated tuples,

$$|\mathbf{s}| = |\mathbf{x}| + |\mathbf{y}|$$

and $+$ denotes integer addition. Here $s_n = 1$ when the sum exceeds $2^n - 1$.

As indicated earlier in this book, $f_A^{(2n)}$ can be realized by a chain of Full Adders in which carries $c_0, c_1, c_2, \ldots, c_{n-1}$ are generated as well as sums $s_0, s_1, \ldots, s_{n-1}$ where $s_n = c_{n-1}$, and for $0 \leq j \leq n - 1$,

$$s_j = x_j \oplus y_j \oplus c_{j-1}$$

$$c_j = x_j \cdot y_j + (x_j \oplus y_j) \cdot c_{j-1}$$

Here the convention is that $c_{-1} = 0$. These equations are the basis for the Krapchenko realization which is given in the Appendix. We show here that a delay complexity asymptotically equal to $\log_2 n$ can be achieved.

For $0 \leq j \leq n - 1$, let

$$u_j = x_j \cdot y_j, \qquad v_j = x_j \oplus y_j$$

Then the equation for c_j can be applied recursively to show that

$$c_j = u_j + v_j \cdot u_{j-1} + v_j \cdot v_{j-1} \cdot u_{j-2} + \cdots + v_j \cdot \cdots \cdot v_1 \cdot u_0$$

since $c_{-1} = 0$. In studying c_j, it is useful to define the following function.

Let

$$g_{b-a+1}(u_b, v_b, \ldots, u_a) = u_b + v_b \cdot u_{b-1} + \cdots + v_b \cdot v_{b-1} \cdot \cdots \cdot v_{a+1} \cdot u_a$$

Then g_k has k products (including the trivial one) and

$$c_j = g_{j+1}(u_j, v_j, \ldots, u_0)$$

Furthermore, if $2^{m-1} < n \le 2^m$, any c_j, $0 \le j \le n - 1$ can be realized from $g_{2^m}(u_{2^m-1}, \ldots, u_0)$ by choosing

$$u_{2^m-1} = \cdots = u_{j+1} = 0$$

$$v_{2^m-1} = \cdots = v_{j+1} = 1$$

Therefore, every carry digit c_j can be obtained with a delay of at most one more than that of $g_{2^m}(u_j$ and v_j, $0 \le j \le n - 1$, must be computed), and a sum digit s_j requires at most one more unit of delay. Consequently,

$$D_\Omega(f_A^{(2n)}) \le D_\Omega(g_{2^m}) + 2$$

and we now concentrate on bounding the delay complexity of g_{2^m}.

Observe that for $a < b < c$,

$$g_{c-a+1}(u_c, v_c, \ldots, u_a) = g_{c-b+1}(u_c, v_c, \ldots, u_b)$$

$$+ v_c \cdot v_{c-1} \cdot \cdots \cdot v_{b+1} \cdot g_{b-a+1}(u_b, v_b, \ldots, u_a)$$

When this is applied recursively, it follows that g_{2^m} can be written as

$$g_{2^m}(u_{2^m-1}, \ldots, u_0) = g_{2^r}(u_{2^m-1}, \ldots, u_{2^m-2^r})$$

$$+ v_{2^m-1} \cdot \cdots \cdot v_{2^m-2^r} \cdot g_{2^r}(u_{2^m-2^r-1}, \ldots, u_{2^m-2\cdot2^r})$$

$$+ \cdots + v_{2^m-1} \cdot \cdots \cdot v_{2^r} \cdot g_{2^r}(u_{2^r-1}, \ldots, u_0)$$

that is, it is written as a sum (OR) of 2^{m-r} terms. It follows that the delay complexity is bounded above by the depth of the circuit to form that sum (i.e., $m - r$) plus the delay associated with the worst term.

$$D_\Omega(g_{2^m}) \le m - r + 1 + \max(D_\Omega(g_{2^r}), D_\Omega(v_{2^m} \cdot \cdots \cdot v_{2^r}))$$

We now show by induction that $D_\Omega(g_{2^m})$ is bounded above by $m_{l+1} = (l + 1)l/2$ when $m = m_l$. The bound clearly holds for $l = 1$ since $m_1 = 0$, $m_2 = 1$, and $g_1(u_0) = u_0$. Suppose the result is true for $l = i$. We show that it is true for $l = i + 1$ as follows: Set $r = m_i$, $m = m_{i+1}$. Then

$$D_\Omega(v_{2^m} \cdot \cdots \cdot v_{2^r}) \le m = m_{i+1}$$

and

$$D_\Omega(g_{2^m}) \leq m_{i+1} - m_i + 1 + m_{i+1}$$

since

$$D_\Omega(g_{2^r}) \leq m_{i+1}$$

Because $m_{i+1} - m_i = i$ and $m_{i+1} + i + 1 = m_{i+2}$, we have

$$D_\Omega(g_{2^{m_{i+1}}}) \leq m_{i+2}$$

which is the desired conclusion.

If $m \neq m_l$ for some l, choose t such that $m_{t-1} < m \leq m_t$, and in the original inequality for $D_\Omega(g_{2^m})$, set $r = m_{t-1}$. It follows that

$$D_\Omega(g_{2^m}) \leq m - m_{t-1} + 1 + \max(m_t, m)$$

$$\leq m + m_t - m_{t-1} + 1 = m + t$$

but

$$m_{t-1} = \frac{(t-1)(t-2)}{2} < m$$

and this inequality is further weakened by replacing $t - 1$ by $t - 2$. It follows that

$$t < \sqrt{2m} + 2$$

and observing that $2^{m-1} < n \leq 2^m$, we conclude that

Theorem 6.3.5.1.   Over the basis $\Omega = \{+, \cdot, \oplus, ^-\}$, the delay complexity of the addition function $f_A^{(2n)} : \{0, 1\}^{2n} \to \{0, 1\}^{n+1}$ satisfies

$$m + 1 \leq D_\Omega(f_A^{(2n)}) \leq m + \sqrt{2m} + 4$$

where $m = \lceil \log_2 n \rceil$.

Proof.   The lower bound is an immediate consequence of Theorem 6.3.4.2 and the fact that s_n realizes ϕ_+ on the set $\{0, 1, 2, \ldots, 2^n - 1\}$. The upper bound follows directly from the above derivation and the two facts that $m = \lceil \log_2 n \rceil$ and that one unit of delay is involved in computing u_j and v_j and another in computing s_j from u_j, v_j, and c_{j-1}. $\square$

These bounds are derived by assuming that the carries are derived by independent circuits. This results in a large adder. Krapchenko (1967) has presented a rather involved straight-line algorithm with large overlap between the circuits for computing carries, and this algorithm is developed in the Appendix to this chapter. The algorithm is a very good one, as indicated by the numbers shown in Table 6.3.5.1. They are obtained from an exact accounting of the delay and number of elements used by the algorithm when the design parameter τ has value 1.

Table 6.3.5.1. Comparison of Two Addition Algorithms

# bits / word	Krapchenko Algorithm		Full Adder chain	
	delay	# elements	delay	# elements
16	12	143	31	77
32	14	311	63	157

In the Appendix, upper bounds are derived to the delay and number of elements used by the Krapchenko algorithm. These bounds are stated in the following theorem.

Theorem 6.3.5.2. Over the basis $\Omega = \{ +, \cdot, \oplus, ^- \}$, the addition function $f_A^{(2n)} : \{0, 1\}^{2n} \to \{0, 1\}^{n+1}$ can be computed by a chain that simultaneously achieves a delay of at most

$$m + 7\sqrt{2m} + 14$$

and has a number of computation steps (logic elements) bounded above by

$$3n + 6 \cdot 2^m$$

where $m = \lceil \log_2 n \rceil$.

These bounds demonstrate that for large n an asymptotically optimal delay can be achieved with a circuit containing a number of logic elements that is linear in the number of inputs. Also, when n is a power of 2 and $n \geq 6$, the number of elements used is no more than twice the number of elements used in a Full Adder chain.

6.3.6. Subtraction

Addition is considered in the preceding section only for the case of nonnegative integers. In this section, we again consider addition but we now let either one or both of the two integers be negative. When one of the integers is nonnegative and the other is negative, the addition is called subtraction.

We begin by considering three representations for integers which explicitly permit the representation of negative integers. They are the sign-and-magnitude, 1's complement, and 2's complement notations. The first

two are representations for integers in the set $\{-(2^n-1), -(2^n-2),$
$\ldots, -1, -0, +0, +1, \ldots, (2^n-1)\}$ while the third is a representation
for integers in the set $\{-2^n, -(2^n-1), \ldots, -1, 0, +1, \ldots, (2^n-1)\}$.
In each case, a number is represented by a pair $(\sigma, \text{rep}(p))$ where $\text{rep}(p)$
has a different meaning for each notation. The sign is also denoted by σ
where

$$\sigma = \begin{cases} 0, & p \geq 0 \\ 1, & p \leq 0 \end{cases}$$

(Note that 0 can be both positive and negative.) Let $\mathbf{p} = (p_0, p_1, \ldots, p_{n-1})$
be the standard binary representation for the integer

$$|\mathbf{p}| = p_0 + p_1 \cdot 2 + p_2 \cdot 2^2 + \cdots + p_{n-1} 2^{n-1}$$

and for $q \geq 0$ let $\beta_n(q)$ be the binary n-tuple representing the integer q
modulo 2^n in this notation. Then $\beta_n(q)$ is the set of n least significant digits
in the binary expansion of q.

In the *sign-and-magnitude* (SAM) notation,

$$\text{rep}(p) = \begin{cases} \beta_n(p), & p \geq 0 \\ \beta_n(-p), & p \leq 0 \end{cases}$$

In the *1's complement* (OC) notation,

$$\text{rep}(p) = \begin{cases} \beta_n(p), & p \geq 0 \\ \beta_n(2^n - 1 + p), & p \leq 0 \end{cases}$$

and in the *2's complement* (*TC*) notation,

$$\text{rep}(p) = \begin{cases} \beta_n(p), & p \geq 0 \\ \beta_n(2^n + p), & -2^n \leq p < 0 \end{cases}$$

The three notations are shown in Table 6.3.6.1 for $n = 2$ and with vectors
$\mathbf{p} = (p_0, \ldots, p_{n-1})$ written in the conventional order $(p_{n-1}, \ldots, p_0)$.

The 1's complement of a positive number represented by $\mathbf{p}$ is obtained
by inverting every digit in $\mathbf{p}$. This follows because $\beta_n(2^n - 1) =$
$(1, 1, 1, \ldots, 1)$, and $\beta_n(2^n - 1 - p)$ is obtained by subtracting $\mathbf{p}$ from this
binary number. The 2's complement of a positive number represented by $\mathbf{p}$
is obtained by adding 1 to the 1's complement of $\mathbf{p}$. These facts are
corroborated by Table 6.3.6.1.

The actual realization of addition and subtraction inside a machine will
be dependent on the assumed representation for positive and negative

Table 6.3.6.1. Representations for Numbers

p	SAM	OC	TC
3	011	011	011
2	010	010	010
1	001	001	001
+ 0	000	000	000
− 0	100	111	000
− 1	101	110	111
− 2	110	101	110
− 3	111	100	101
− 4	—	—	100

numbers within that machine. For the purpose of illustration, we assume that SAM notation is used.

Consider the addition of two numbers p and q, that is, $p + q$. There are four cases to examine:

1. $p \geq 0, \quad q \geq 0$.
2. $p \geq 0, \quad q \leq 0$.
3. $p \leq 0, \quad q \geq 0$.
4. $p \leq 0, \quad q \leq 0$.

which are determined by the sign digits of the two numbers σ_p and σ_q. In the first and fourth cases, the signs of the sums are 0 and 1, respectively, and the magnitudes are the sums of the magnitudes. Such sums can be performed on a conventional adder for positive integers. In the remaining two cases, a subtraction is necessary.

Consider the case of $p \geq 0, \quad q \leq 0$. The 2's complement of q can be formed, $\beta_n(2^n + q)$, and the result added to p. This can be done with a conventional adder since $\beta_n(2^n + q)$ represents a positive integer. The n-digit sum $(s_0, s_1, \ldots, s_{n-1})$ that appears at the adder output represents $\beta_n(p + 2^n + q)$. The remaining output s_n, the overflow bit, has the following values:

$$s_n = \begin{cases} 1 & p + q \geq 0 \\ 0, & p + q < 0 \end{cases}$$

Since $\beta_n(q) = \beta_n((q \bmod 2^n))$

$$\beta_n(2^n + p + q) = \begin{cases} \beta_n(p + q), & p + q \geq 0 \\ \beta_n(2^n + (p + q)), & p + q < 0 \end{cases}$$

that is, the output $(s_0, s_1, \ldots, s_{n-1})$ represents $(p + q)$ when nonnegative, and the 2's complement of the negative integer $p + q$ otherwise. In the latter case, $0 < 2^n + (p + q) \leq 2^n - 1$ and the 2's complement of $2^n + (p + q)$ is

$$\beta_n(2^n - (2^n + (p + q))) = \beta_n(-(p + q))$$

which is the magnitude of $p + q$.

Addition of integers p, q from $\{-(2^n - 1), \ldots, 1, -0, +0, 1, \ldots, 2^n - 1\}$ can then be accomplished as follows:

1. Represent p, q by the SAM notation
2. If p and q have the same sign, that is, $\sigma_p \oplus \sigma_q = 0$, add their magnitudes in a conventional adder (for positive integers). Overflows may occur (i.e., $s_n = 1$).
3. If p and q have different signs, that is, $\sigma_p \oplus \sigma_q = 1$, form the 2's complement of the magnitude of the negative number and add in a conventional adder to the magnitude of the other number. Overflows never occur here. If $s_n = 0$, form the true complement of the result. This is the magnitude of the sum. Its sign is s_n.

In the SAM notation, a function $f_s : \{0, 1\}^{2n+2} \rightarrow \{0, 1\}^{n+2}$ has been defined on the representations for p and q that returns the representation for $p + q$ plus an overflow bit of 1 if $|p + q| \geq 2^n$. It is easy to demonstrate that the combinational complexity of f_s is linear in n, that its delay complexity is logarithmic in n, and that both rates of growth can be achieved simultaneously. Subtraction can also be accomplished in the 1's complement notation and leads to a slightly different algorithm.

Addition of two integers from the set $\{-2^n, -(2^n - 1), \ldots, -1, 0, 1, \ldots, (2^n - 1)\}$ can also be done using the 2's complement notation as the internal representation of integers. The reader is encouraged to show that the sum of two numbers in this system can be correctly computed, including the sign bit, by treating the numbers and their sign bits as nonnegative integers and adding them in an adder for such integers. Overflows are easy to determine, as the reader can verify (see Problem 6-11).

6.3.7. Multiplication

Integer multiplication is the familiar binary operation $\times : \{0, 1, 2, \ldots, N - 1\}^2 \rightarrow \{0, 1, 2, \ldots, (N - 1)^2\}$ which maps two arbitrary integers $a, b \in \{0, 1, 2, \ldots, N - 1\}$ into their product $\times(a, b)$ which is defined either as a added to itself b times or b added to itself a times. The multiplication problem is that of finding a binary encoding of the integers such that the multiplication function can be realized by a straight-line algorithm with a small number of computation steps and a small delay.

There are no known encodings and straight-line algorithms for multiplication for which the number steps is linear in n and simultaneously the delay is at most logarithmic in n where $n = \lceil \log_2 N \rceil$. It is possible to multiply with a delay on the order of $\log(\log n)$ with a straight-line algorithm which assumes that integers are represented by their exponents in their unique prime factorizations (Winograd, 1965, 1967; Spira, 1969). This is the best possible delay complexity, but the circuit that achieves it has a number of logic elements that is exponential in n. Also, the circuit cannot be used to detect overflow because the delay complexity of the function that tests for overflow under multiplication grows as $\log n$, as shown in Section 6.3.4. Since circuits or straight-line algorithms based on the standard binary representation for integers do intrinsically test for overflow, we limit our attention to such circuits in the sequel.

Consider the function $f_M^{(2n)}$: $\{0, 1\}^{2n} \to \{0, 1\}^{2n}$ obtained from $\times$: $\{0, 1, \ldots, N-1\}^2 \to \{0, 1, \ldots, (N-1)^2\}$ by encoding the integers with the standard binary encoding when $N = 2^n$. Let $\mathbf{x} = (x_0, x_1, \ldots, x_{n-1})$ and $\mathbf{y} = (y_0, y_1, \ldots, y_{n-1})$ represent two integers $|\mathbf{x}|$ and $|\mathbf{y}|$ in this notation. Then we can write

$$f_M^{(2n)}(x_0, \ldots, x_{n-1}, y_0, \ldots, y_{n-1}) = \beta_{2n}(|\mathbf{x}| \cdot |\mathbf{y}|)$$

$$= \beta_{2n}\left(\sum_{j=0}^{n-1} x_j \cdot 2^j \cdot |\mathbf{y}|\right)$$

where Σ and $\cdot$ denote integer addition and multiplication and $\beta_{2n}(q)$ is the binary expansion of the integer q as a $2n$-tuple. Since $2^j \cdot |\mathbf{y}|$ represents the integer $|\mathbf{y}|$ shifted by j places, multiplication can be realized by successively shifting $\mathbf{y}$ and adding to the accumulated total if the corresponding digit x_j is 1.

Example 6.3.7.1. Multiply $|(1, 0, 1)| = 5$ by $|(0, 1, 1)| = 6$ in binary.

$$f_M^{(6)}(1, 0, 1, 0, 1, 1) = \beta_6\left(1 \cdot |(0, 1, 1)| + 0 \cdot 2|(0, 1, 1)| + 1 \cdot 2^2|(0, 1, 1)|\right)$$

$$= \beta_6\left(|(0, 1, 1, 0, 0, 0)| + |(0, 0, 0, 1, 1, 0)|\right) = (0, 1, 1, 1, 1, 0)$$

which corresponds to the decimal number 30.

The preceding realization of multiplication can be implemented by an algorithm described as follows:

1. Form the $(2n - 1)$-tuples:

$$(x_0 {\cdot} y_0, x_0 {\cdot} y_1, \ldots, x_0 {\cdot} y_{n-1}, 0, \ldots, 0)$$
$$(0, x_1 {\cdot} y_0, \ldots, x_1 {\cdot} y_{n-2}, x_1 {\cdot} y_{n-1}, 0, \ldots, 0)$$

$$\vdots$$

$$(0, 0, \ldots, 0, x_{n-1} {\cdot} y_0, \ldots, x_{n-1} {\cdot} y_{n-1})$$

by AND'ing x_i and y_j for all $0 \le i, \; j \le n - 1$.

2. Add the n binary numbers.

This scheme, known as *multiplication by shifting and adding*, is frequently implemented in central processing units by carrying out the successive shifts and additions in successive computation cycles.

If this scheme is realized by a logic circuit, the number of elements employed will be proportional to n^2 and the delay will be proportional to $(\log n)^2$, at best, because at least $\lceil \log_2 n \rceil$ levels of additions are necessary and each introduces a delay that is at least proportional to $\log n$. A simple method introduced by Ofman (1962) and Wallace (1964) for reducing the sum of three binary numbers to the sum of two can be used to decrease the delay to the order of $\log n$ without significantly affecting the number of logic elements.

Lemma 6.3.7.1. There exists a binary function $f_{TR}^{(k)} : \{0, 1\}^{3k} \to \{0, 1\}^{2(k+1)}$ that maps three binary k-tuples $\mathbf{a}, \mathbf{b}, \mathbf{c}$ onto two binary $(k + 1)$-tuples $\mathbf{u}, \mathbf{v}$ with the property that the corresponding integers satisfy the relationship

$$|\mathbf{a}| + |\mathbf{b}| + |\mathbf{c}| = |\mathbf{u}| + |\mathbf{v}|$$

that is, the last two are the sum of the first three. Furthermore, over the basis $\Omega = \{+, \cdot, \oplus, ^-\}$,

$$C\Omega(f_{TR}^{(k)}) \le 5k$$

$$D_\Omega(f_{TR}^{(k)}) \le 3$$

NOTE. This is known as a *carry-save adder*.

Proof. Let $v_0 = 0$, $u_{k+1} = 0$. Then define u_i and v_{i+1} in $\{0, 1\}$ for $0 \le i \le k - 1$ by the equation

$$a_i + b_i + c_i = u_i + 2 {\cdot} v_{i+1}$$

wherein $+$ and $\cdot$ denote normal integer addition and multiplication.

Multiplying both sides by 2^i and summing clearly shows that the desired identity holds. Also, u_i and v_{i+1} are the sum and carry digits, respectively, at the output of a Full Adder with inputs a_i, b_i, and c_i. From this and Figure 2.2.2 concerning the Full Adder, the upper bounds follow. $\square$

Ofman and Wallace proposed that the n numbers generated in the first step of the above algorithm for multiplication be added using the method of this lemma. For simplicity, consider each of these numbers as a $(2n - 1)$-tuple. Collect as many numbers together as possible in groups of three and reduce each group to two $2n$-tuples. Collect these tuples and those not grouped together at the first step and repeat. Do this until exactly two words remain and add them together using any method.

At the initial (or zeroth) stage of this procedure, there are $n_0 = n$ numbers of length $2n - 1$. If there are n_{j-1} numbers at the $(j - 1)$th stage, at the next stage there are $\lfloor n_{j-1}/3 \rfloor$ groups of three numbers and $2\lfloor n_{j-1}/3 \rfloor$ resulting words of $2n - 1 + j$ bits apiece. Another $n_{j-1} - 3\lfloor n_{j-1}/3 \rfloor$ words are not part of any group. Thus, there are n_j numbers each of $2n - 1 + j$ bits at the jth stage where

$$n_j = 2 \left\lfloor \frac{n_{j-1}}{3} \right\rfloor + n_{j-1} - 3 \left\lfloor \frac{n_{j-1}}{3} \right\rfloor = n_{j-1} - \left\lfloor \frac{n_{j-1}}{3} \right\rfloor$$

Since $(x - 2)/3 \le \lfloor x/3 \rfloor \le x/3$, the reader can verify that (see Problem 6-16)

$$\left(\tfrac{2}{3}\right)^j \cdot n \le n_j \le \left(\tfrac{2}{3}\right)^j \cdot n + 2$$

Let k be the number of stages after which $n_k = 2$. Then $n_{k-1} \ge 3$, and from these inequalities,

$$\frac{\log_2 n/2}{\log_2\left(\tfrac{3}{2}\right)} \le k \le \frac{\log_2 n}{\log_2\left(\tfrac{3}{2}\right)} + 1$$

Since each stage introduces a delay of 3, this scheme has a total delay of $3k$. At the jth stage, $5(2n - 2 + j)$ logic elements are used for each of the $\lfloor n_{j-1}/3 \rfloor$ groups. The number of elements is then bounded by

$$\sum_{j=1}^{k} 5(2n - 2 + j) \left\lfloor \frac{n_{j-1}}{3} \right\rfloor \le 5(2n - 2 + k) \sum_{j=1}^{k} \frac{\left(\tfrac{2}{3}\right)^{j-1} \cdot n + 2}{3}$$

$$\le \frac{5(2n - 2 + k)(3n + 2k)}{3}$$

which is of the order of n^2.

Theorem 6.3.7.1. There is a straight-line algorithm over $\Omega = \{+, \cdot, \oplus, ^-\}$ for the function $f_M^{(2n)}$ that has delay bounded above by

$$3k + m + 7\sqrt{2m} + 14$$

and a number of logic elements proportional to n^2 where

$$k \leq \frac{\log_2 n}{\log_2(\frac{3}{2})} + 1$$

and $m = \lceil \log_2(2n + k - 1) \rceil$.

Proof. At the last step of the procedure, make use of the straight-line algorithm given in Section 6.3.5 to add the two $(2n + k - 1)$-tuples. $\square$

The next procedure we present for multiplication is due to Karatsuba (in Karatsuba and Ofman, 1962). It requires many fewer logic elements and has a delay proportional to $(\log n)^2$.

Let $\mathbf{x}$ and $\mathbf{y}$ be two binary n-digit numbers. Let n be even and write

$$\mathbf{x} = (\mathbf{x}_1, \mathbf{x}_2), \qquad \mathbf{y} = (\mathbf{y}_1, \mathbf{y}_2)$$

where $\mathbf{x}_1, \mathbf{x}_2, \mathbf{y}_1$ and $\mathbf{y}_2$ are each $(n/2)$-bit numbers. Then

$$|\mathbf{x}| = |\mathbf{x}_1| + 2^{n/2} \cdot |\mathbf{x}_2|, |\mathbf{y}| = |\mathbf{y}_1| + 2^{n/2} \cdot |\mathbf{y}_2|$$

and

$$|\mathbf{x}| \cdot |\mathbf{y}| = |\mathbf{x}_1| \cdot |\mathbf{y}_1| + 2^n \cdot |\mathbf{x}_2| \cdot |\mathbf{y}_2|$$
$$+ 2^{n/2}(|\mathbf{x}_1| \cdot |\mathbf{y}_1| + (|\mathbf{x}_2| - |\mathbf{x}_1|) \cdot (|\mathbf{y}_1| - |\mathbf{y}_2|) + |\mathbf{x}_2| \cdot |\mathbf{y}_2|)$$

where $+$, $-$ and $\cdot$ denote integer addition, subtraction, and multiplication. The interesting thing to observe about this expansion is that only three integer multiplications are necessary because multiplication by a fixed power of 2 in this notation amounts to a shift by a fixed number of places. Thus, multiplication of two n-bit numbers can be done with three multiplications of $(n/2)$-bit numbers and six additions or subtractions. The obvious expansion uses four multiplications and three additions. Since multiplications are more costly than additions, the reduction in the number of multiplications and the recursive application of this algorithm leads to the improved straight-line algorithm.

As is evident from the last two sections, addition and subtraction of n-bit numbers can be done in the sign-and-magnitude notation with a number of elements proportional to n and with a delay proportional to

$\log_2 n$. Since the two subtractions result in $(n/2)$-bit numbers in this notation (not including the sign bit), if we define $D(n)$ and $C(n)$ to be the delay and number of logic elements used by this multiplication algorithm on n-bit numbers, we have

$$D(n) \leq D\left(\frac{n}{2}\right) + d\log_2 n$$

$$C(n) \leq 3C\left(\frac{n}{2}\right) + cn$$

where d and c are two nonnegative constants. Also, $D(1) = 1$, $C(1) = 2$. Then, if $n = 2^k$ and $d \geq 1$, $c \geq 2$,

$$D(n) \leq d(k + k - 1 + \cdots + 2 + 1) = d\frac{k(k + 1)}{2}$$

$$C(n) \leq c2^k\left(1 + \left(\frac{3}{2}\right) + \left(\frac{3}{2}\right)^2 + \cdots + \left(\frac{3}{2}\right)^k\right) \leq 3c3^k$$

We summarize these results in the following theorem.

Theorem 6.3.7.2. There exists a straight-line algorithm over $\Omega = \{+, \cdot, \oplus, ^-\}$ for the function $f_M^{(2n)}$ that has delay proportional to $(\log_2 n)^2$ and a number of computation steps proportional to $n^{\log_2 3}$, where $\log_2 3 \cong 1.59$.

Proof. The theorem is an immediate consequence of the fact that $3^k = n^{\log_2 3}$ when $n = 2^k$. □

The Karatsuba algorithm is not the last word on integer multiplication using the standard binary encoding. Schönhage and Strassen (1971) have presented a straight-line algorithm that uses on the order of $n(\log_2 n)$ × $(\log_2 \log_2 n)$ steps and has delay proportional to $(\log_2 n)$. Their algorithm makes use of the Fast Fourier Transform.

6.3.8. Division

Division of one integer by another results in a number that is not always an integer, and frequently the result cannot be expressed by a finite number of digits in radix notation. This is illustrated by the division of the decimal number 7 by 3 which produces the result 2.333 .... . We are moved then to consider approximations to the quotient of two numbers. Since the quotient A/B for two integers A and B can be represented as the product of A with the reciprocal of B, that is, $A \times (1/B)$, we further consider only the computation of reciprocals.

There are many methods for computing reciprocals, the most common being long division. When implemented in a logic circuit to compute the n-place reciprocal of an integer, it uses on the order of n^2 elements and has a delay proportional to $n \log_2 n$. Delay is important in the design of central processing units, so it is important to note that all known methods for division have delay that is at least proportional to $(\log_2 n)^2$. By the measure of delay complexity, division appears to be much more complex than any of the three other arithmetic operations.

The method that we present in this section for computing reciprocals is described in Anderson et al. (1967) and is similar to that suggested by S. A. Cook (see Knuth, 1969, Section 4.3.3). Our development of the method uses more operations than those given by Knuth (1969) or Aho et al. (1974), but is somewhat simpler and does permit a delay as small as on the order of $(\log_2 n)^2$.

Let $\mathbf{y} = (y_{n-1}, y_{n-2}, \ldots, y_0)$ represent the integer

$$|\mathbf{y}| = y_{n-1}2^{n-1} + y_{n-2}2^{n-2} + \cdots + y_0$$

and let $y_{n-1} = 1$. The reciprocal $|\mathbf{r}|$ of $|\mathbf{y}|$ is represented by $\mathbf{r} = (r_{-1}, r_{-2}, r_{-3}, \ldots)$ where

$$|\mathbf{r}| = r_{-1} \cdot 2^{-1} + r_{-2} \cdot 2^{-2} + r_{-3} \cdot 2^{-3} + \cdots$$

Clearly, the first $n - 2$ digits of $\mathbf{r}$ are zero. If $|\mathbf{r}|$ is to be computed to within n digits, we compute $r_{-(n-1)}, \ldots, r_{-(2n-1)}$. It follows that by shifting $\mathbf{r}$ left by $2n - 1$ places, we are computing

$$\left\lfloor \frac{2^{2n-1}}{|\mathbf{y}|} \right\rfloor$$

when we discard the remaining digits of $\mathbf{r}$.

Let

$$z = 2^{-n}|\mathbf{y}|$$

and observe that $\frac{1}{2} \leq z < 1$. We wish to compute the n-digit approximation to $2^{n-1}/z$. Let

$$z = 1 - x$$

and observe that

$$\frac{1}{1-x} = \frac{1}{1-x} \cdot \frac{1+x}{1+x} \cdot \frac{1+x^2}{1+x^2} \cdot \ldots \cdot \frac{1+x^{2^{j-1}}}{1+x^{2^{j-1}}} = \frac{P_j(x)}{1-x^{2^j}}$$

where $0 < x \leq \frac{1}{2}$ and

$$P_j(x) = (1 + x)(1 + x^2)(1 + x^4) \cdots (1 + x^{2^{j-1}}) = \frac{1-x^{2^j}}{1-x}$$

Thus, if j is large, $P_j(x)$ is a good approximation to the reciprocal of $1 - x$. In fact,

$$0 \leq \left| P_k(x) - \frac{1}{1 - x} \right| \leq \frac{x^{2^k}}{1 - x} \leq 2 \cdot 2^{-2^k} \; .$$

since $0 < x \leq \frac{1}{2}$. Here k is a parameter that will be fixed later.

The algorithm that we employ to compute $1/(1 - x)$ is based on the following procedure:

1. Compute approximations to $x^{2^{j-1}}$ for $2 \leq j \leq k$.
2. Form the sums $1 + x^{2^{j-1}}$ for $1 \leq j \leq k$.
3. Form approximations to $P_j(x)$ for $1 \leq j \leq k$.

Let $\hat{x}$ be an approximation to x obtained by retaining only the s most significant digits, $(a_{-1}, a_{-2}, \ldots, a_{-s})$, in the binary expansion of x. (Note that $a_{-1} = 0$.) Then

$$x - \delta \leq \hat{x} \leq x$$

where $\delta = 2^{-s}$. We inductively define $(\hat{x})^{2^{j-1}}$ to be the square of $(\hat{x})^{2^{j-2}}$ truncated to its s most significant digits. We claim (see Problem 6-17) that

$$x^{2^{j-1}} - 2\delta \leq (\hat{x})^{2^{j-1}} \leq x^{2^{j-1}}$$

which is true for $j = 1$, as shown, and can be verified for $2 \leq j \leq k$ by induction. Each of the squaring operations is a multiplication of s-bit binary numbers and can be done with any binary multiplier.

Let

$$t_j(x) = 1 + (\hat{x})^{2^{j-1}}$$

for $1 \leq j \leq k$. This is represented by an $(s + 1)$-tuple with 1 positioned to the left of the radix point while the digits to the right represent $(\hat{x})^{2^{j-1}}$. Let $\hat{P}_j(x)$, $1 \leq j \leq k - 1$, be approximations to $P_j(x)$ formed as follows:

1. $\hat{P}_1(x) = t_1(x)$.
2. $\hat{P}_j(x)$ is $\hat{P}_{j-1}(x) \cdot t_j(x)$ truncated to its s most significant digits.

Clearly, each $\hat{P}_j(x)$ is computed by multiplying two $(s + 1)$-bit numbers and truncating.

We claim that

$$P_j(x) - \varepsilon_j(x) \leq \hat{P}_j(x) \leq P_j(x)$$

for $1 \leq j \leq k - 1$, where

$$\varepsilon_j(x) = (3j - 2) \frac{(1 - x^{2^{j-1}})}{1 - x} \delta$$

The upper bound clearly holds. We establish the lower bound by induction. For $j = 1$, $\varepsilon_j(x) = \delta$, which is obviously correct, and the basis for induction is verified. Assume the claim is true for $j = l$. Then

$$\hat{P}_l(x) \cdot t_{l+1}(x) \geq (P_l(x) - \varepsilon_l(x))(1 + x^{2^l} - 2\delta)$$

$$\geq P_{l+1}(x) - \varepsilon_l(x)(1 + x^{2^l}) - 2\delta P_l(x)$$

and since $x^{2^l} < x^{2^{l-1}}$

$$\varepsilon_l(x)(1 + x^{2^l}) + 2\delta P_l(x) < (3l - 2)\frac{(1 - x^{2^{l-1}})}{1 - x}\delta(1 + x^{2^{l-1}})$$

$$+ 2\delta\frac{(1 - x^{2^l})}{1 - x}$$

$$= 3l\frac{(1 - x^{2^l})}{1 - x}\delta$$

Furthermore, the product $\hat{P}_l(x) \cdot t_{l+1}(x)$ is truncated by deleting coefficients of $2^{-(s+1)}$, $2^{-(s+2)}$, and so forth, that is by decreasing the product by at most $2^{-s} = \delta$. Subtracting δ from the product and observing that $\delta < \delta(1 - x^{2^l})/(1 - x)$, we conclude that

$$\hat{P}_{l+1}(x) \geq P_l(x) - \varepsilon_{l+1}(x)$$

with $\varepsilon_{l+1}(x)$ given by the claim. The claim is thus verified.

Combining the various results, we conclude that

$$\left|\frac{1}{1 - x} - \hat{P}_k(x)\right| = \left|\frac{1}{1 - x} - P_k(x) + P_k(x) - \hat{P}_k(x)\right|$$

$$\leq \left|\frac{1}{1 - x} - P_k(x)\right| + \left|P_k(x) - \hat{P}_k(x)\right|$$

$$\leq 2 \cdot 2^{-2^k} + \varepsilon_k(x)$$

$$\leq 2 \cdot 2^{-2^k} + (3k - 2) \cdot 2 \cdot 2^{-s}$$

since $0 < x \leq \frac{1}{2}$. For $\hat{P}_k(x)$ to approximate the reciprocal of $1 - x$ to within n digits (one to the left of the radix point and $n - 1$ to the right), they must not differ by more than 2^{-n+1}. Therefore, choose s and k to satisfy

$$2 \cdot \left(2^{-2^k} + (3k - 2) \cdot 2^{-s}\right) \leq 2^{-n+1}$$

It is sufficient to choose

$$k = \lceil \log_2 n \rceil + 1, \qquad s = n + 3 + \lceil \log_2 k \rceil$$

We summarize these results in the following theorem.

Theorem 6.3.8.1. The reciprocal of an n-bit integer $\mathbf{y} = (y_{n-1}, y_{n-2}, \ldots, y_0)$, with $y_{n-1} = 1$, can be computed to n significant places with a straight-line algorithm that has

$$2(k - 1)M(s + 1)$$

computation steps and delay

$$2(k - 1)D(s + 1)$$

in addition to the number of steps and delay needed to form the 2's complement of $\mathbf{y}$. Here $M(r)$ and $D(r)$ are the number of steps and delay in any particular algorithm for multiplying two r-bit numbers and

$$k = \lceil \log_2 n \rceil + 1, \qquad s = n + 3 + \lceil \log_2 k \rceil$$

Proof. Observe that x is computed from $|\mathbf{y}|$ by $x = 2^{-n}(2^n - |\mathbf{y}|)$, that is, by taking the 2's complement. Then the $k - 1$ terms $(\hat{x})^{2^{j-1}}$, $2 \leq j \leq k$, are formed by $k - 1$ multiplications of s-bit numbers, and the $k - 1$ terms $\hat{P}_j(x)$, $2 \leq j \leq k$ are obtained from $k - 1$ multiplications of $(s + 1)$-bit numbers. We assume that $M(r)$ and $D(r)$ are nondecreasing functions of r. $\qquad \square$

The bound on the number of computation steps can be improved to $M(Kn)$ for some constant K by other algorithms (see Knuth, 1969, Section 4.3.3, and Aho et al., 1974, Section 8.2). The delay complexity with our procedure grows at best as $(\log_2 n)^2$, and no asymptotically better algorithm is known.

6.3.9. Floating-Point Arithmetic

The standard binary representation for integers in the set $\{0, 1, 2, \ldots, 2^n - 1\}$ is a set of binary n-tuples. It is one example of a *fixed-point representation* for numbers. Others are the sign-and-magnitude, 1's complement, and 2's complement notations for signed integers. If $\mathbf{x} = (x_{n-1}, x_{n-2}, \ldots, x_0)$, $x_i \in \{0, 1\}$ represents the integer

$$|\mathbf{x}| = x_{n-1} \cdot 2^{n-1} + x_{n-2} \cdot 2^{n-2} + \cdots + x_0$$

then the radix point is to the right of x_0 and $\mathbf{x}$ is alternately written as

$x_{n-1}, x_{n-2}, \ldots, x_1, x_0$. with the radix point as shown. If the radix point is moved left k places (with 0's introduced to the left of x_{n-1}, if necessary), the result represents the number $2^{-k}|x|$ which in general is not an integer. The effect of placement of the radix point on each of the above mentioned notations for signed numbers is simple and obvious. Its effect on the algorithms presented above for the four arithmetic operations is straightforward and easy to comprehend.

Fixed-point representations have a major shortcoming. They do not permit the representation of very large or very small numbers with a modest number of binary digits. For example, Planck's constant, $h = 6.626 \times 10^{-34}$ Joule-seconds, requires at least 111 bits to represent it in a fixed-point binary notation. However, it is given above in the compact form $F10^E$, which is a *floating-point representation* where F is the *fraction* 6.626 and E is the exponent (-34). Floating-point representations are useful for denoting large and small numbers with a precision limited to the number of significant digits in the fraction part.

Consider base-2 floating-point numbers of the form $F2^E$ represented by the pair (F, E). We let the fraction F be a signed number with magnitude $|F|$ of at most 1 represented by p binary digits, that is, $(\sigma, F_{-1}, \ldots, F_{-p})$ where $\sigma \in \{0, 1\}$ denotes the sign and

$$|F| = F_{-1} \cdot 2^{-1} + F_{-2} \cdot 2^{-2} + \cdots + F_{-p} 2^{-p}$$

Also, we let

$$E = e - 2^{q-1}$$

where e is an integer represented in binary as $(e_{q-1}, e_{q-2}, \ldots, e_0)$ and

$$e = e_{q-1} 2^{q-1} + e_{q-2} 2^{q-2} + \cdots + e_0$$

Therefore, $-2^{q-1} \le E \le 2^{q-1} - 1$.

Multiplication and division of floating-point numbers is quite straight forward and realized by multiplying or dividing fractions and adding or subtracting exponents. Addition and subtraction are done after adjusting exponents and scaling fractions so that only fractions of numbers with equal exponents are added or subtracted. These rules are defined as follows:

Multiplication

$$(F_1, E_1) * (F_2, E_2) = (F_1 * F_2, E_1 + E_2)$$

Division

$$(F_1, E_1) / (F_2, E_2) = (F_1 / F_2, E_1 - E_2)$$

Addition and Subtraction

$$(F_1, E_1) \pm (F_2, E_2) = \left\{ \begin{array}{ll} (F_1 \pm F_2 2^{-(E_1 - E_2)}, E_1), & E_1 \geq E_2 \\ (F_1 2^{-(E_2 - E_1)} \pm F_2, E_2), & E_1 < E_2 \end{array} \right\}$$

Circuits for multiplying or dividing floating-point numbers are easy to realize from circuits for addition, subtraction, multiplication, and division of fixed-point numbers. Addition and subtraction require comparison of exponents and shifting of fractions by amounts determined by the difference of exponents. Given the background developed in this section, it is also quite easy to construct circuits for these operations.

To get the full benefit of floating-point representations, every number (F, E) should be *normalized* by choosing the exponent so that the most significant digit in the fraction is 1, that is, $|F| \geq \frac{1}{2}$. Otherwise, the fraction loses some of its significance. If we assume that the arithmetic operations are on normalized numbers, we observe that a result of an operation may need to be normalized. Also, if two identical numbers are subtracted, the resulting fraction is 0 and cannot be normalized.

If accuracy is not to be lost in the fractions resulting from the arithmetic operations, more than p binary digits will have to be retained. This is also true because normalization will sometimes cause a shifting of the digits in the fraction parts.

Another problem arises in floating-point arithmetic. Overflow or underflow of exponents may occur because two large or two small exponents have been added during multiplication. It may also result from the normalization process. When this happens, an error indication is warranted.

We do not construct circuits and derive bounds to the combinational and delay complexities of floating-point arithmetic operations. This is left as an exercise for the reader.

For a more detailed treatment of floating-point arithmetic, the reader is referred to Knuth (1969) for algorithms meant to be implemented in software and to Hill and Peterson (1973) for algorithms meant to be implemented in hardware.

6.4. CENTRAL PROCESSING UNIT

A central processing unit (CPU) is a sequential machine that receives, transmits, and processes instructions and data and as such maintains control over the many devices and storage units that, in aggregate, constitute a general-purpose computer. In this section, we give a brief introduction to the typical organization of a CPU. We show its principal components and a basic method for exercising control over these components.

Our purpose here is twofold. First, we attempt to give the reader adequate information to comprehend the leap from logic circuits or straight-line algorithms to machine language programs. Second, we build the foundation that is necessary to derive the theorems of the following chapter concerning limits on the performance of general-purpose computers. We begin by describing the types of register that are found in CPUs and then describe "microprogramming," which is a method for translating instructions in machine language into operations on registers and devices. Our treatment of microprogramming owes much to the survey article of Rosin (1969). The term *microprogramming* was coined by Wilkes in 1951 (see Wilkes, (1969).

6.4.1. Microinstructions for a Simple CPU

A simple, incomplete central processing unit is shown in Figure 6.4.1.1. It serves to illustrate the principal features of a CPU including (1) the storage and transfer of instructions and data, (2) the execution of logical and arithmetical functions, (3) register operations and commands, and (4) branching of both the conditional and the unconditional variety. It is incomplete because we do not explicitly handle sign computations and overflow.

The simple CPU has 10 registers outside of the control. The memory address register (MAR) and the memory data register (MDR) are used to address the random access memory (RAM). Words in the RAM are numbered sequentially, and the location counter (LOC CTR) holds an address that is one more than the address of the instruction currently being executed. The instruction register (IR) holds a word that defines the instruction currently being executed, and the word has two parts, the operation code (OP CODE) and the address part (AP). The OP CODE is examined by the CONTROL, which then carries out a sequence of microinstructions (given in Tables 6.4.1.1 to 6.4.1.4). The accumulator (AC) is the principal data register in the CPU. All but a few data operations of the logical or arithmetical variety use the AC. The multiplier-quotient register (MQ) is used for multiplication and division when they are done by successive additions and shifts, subtractions and shifts, respectively (as assumed here). MQ is an extension of AC.

Input and output are handled in this simple model by an input/output address register (I/OAR), an input/output buffer (I/OBFR), and an input/output status register (FI/O). They serve functions similar to those of the RAM except that FI/O is needed to record the status of auxiliary storage devices such as disks, drums, and tapes.

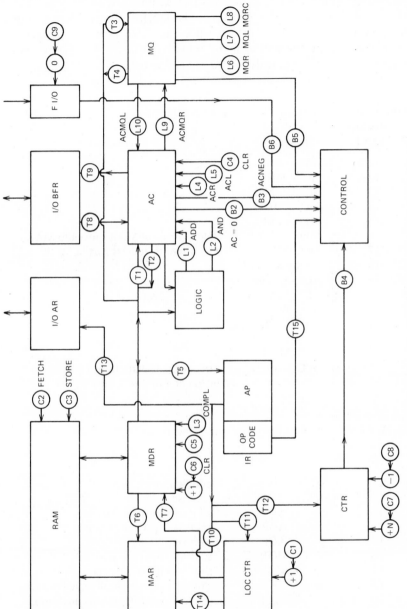

Figure 6.4.1.1. Organization of a simple central processing unit.

The CPU has 15 data paths, which are labeled in Figure 6.4.1.1 and described in Table 6.4.1.1. Data and instructions are gated along these paths by activation of the appropriately labeled signal. For example, activation of T11 (by setting it to the Boolean value 1) causes the address part of the current instruction to be transferred to the location counter. Circuitry for such gatings is described in Section 6.2.1.

Table 6.4.1.1. Register-to-Register Transfer Operations

Instruction Label	Mnemonic	Comments
T1	MDR → AC	
T2	AC → MDR	
T3	MDR → MQ	
T4	MQ → MDR	
T5	MDR → IR	
T6	MDR → MAR	Address part of MDR moved to MAR
T7	LC → MDR	LC moved to address part of MDR
T8	I/OBFR → AC	
T9	AC → I/OBFR	
T10	AP → MAR	
T11	AP → LC	
T12	AP → CTR	
T13	AP → I/OAR	
T14	LC → MAR	
T15	OPCD → MIR	Decode OP CODE, transfer to instruction ring of control

Table 6.4.1.2. Arithmetical and Logical Operations

Instruction Label	Mnemonic	Comments
L1	MDR + AC → AC	addition, result in AC
L2	(MDR) $\land$ (AC) → AC	bit-wise AND, result in AC
L3	− MDR	2's complement of MDR
L4	ACR	shift AC right one position
L5	ACL	shift AC left one position
L6	MQR	shift MQ right one position
L7	MQL	shift MQ left one position
L8	MQRC	shift MQ right cyclically one position
L9	ACMQR	shift AC and MQ right as one word (ignore signs)
L10	ACMQL	shift AC and MQ left as one word (ignore signs)

Our model also contains 10 different logical and arithmetical functions (shown in Table 6.4.1.2), the most important of which are addition (of the numbers in the MDR and the AC), logical AND, and 2's complement of the contents of the MDR. The first two operations are shown in Figure 6.4.1.1 as being realized by a logical cicuit. At this point in the CPU, other logical and arithmetical functions, such as vector functions and floating-point arithmetic functions, could also be computed. The seven other operations given in Table 6.4.1.2 are shifting operations. They include ACMQR and ACMQL, which are important in the realization of multiplication and division using shifting and addition, and shifting and subtraction, respectively.

A number of additional operations on individual registers or commands are needed, and 10 of these are given in Table 6.4.1.3. They include incrementing the location counter, decrementing the counter, storing and fetching from the RAM, and clearing the accumulator and the memory data register. Of particular importance is the command RMCR, which sets a ring counter in the CONTROL so that the CONTROL can begin another instruction sequence.

Table 6.4.1.3. Register Operations

Instruction Label	Mnemonic	Comments
C1	LC + 1 → LC	increment LC
C2	MFETCH	read into MDR from RAM
C3	MSTORE	store MDR into RAM at location MAR
C4	CLR AC	set AC to "zero"
C5	CLR MDR	set MDR to "zero"
C6	MDR + 1 → MDR	increment MDR as an integer
C7	N → CTR	assumes $N + 1$ bits/word
C8	CTR − 1 → CTR	decrement counter
C9	0 → FI/O	set I/O flag to "zero"
C10	RMCR	reset minor cycle ring in CONTROL

The last set of instructions used in Figure 6.4.1.1 are branching instructions which are shown in Table 6.4.1.4. There are one unconditional branching instruction and five conditional branching instructions. The latter are dependent on whether the number in the accumulator is zero (AC = 0) or negative (AC NEG), and whether the number in the counter is nonzero (CTR $\neq$ 0), the low order bit in the MQ register is 1(MQL = 1), or the I/O flag is 1(FI/O = 1). In an unconditional branch, the indicated microinstruction or microprogram (sequence of microinstructions) is

Table 6.4.1.4. Branching Instructions

Instruction Label	Mnemonic	Comments
B1	$\rightarrow X$	go to microprogram or microinstruction X
B2	IF(AC = 0) $\rightarrow X$	go to X if AC zero
B3	IF(AC NEG) $\rightarrow X$	go to X if AC negative
B4	IF(CTR $\neq$ 0) $\rightarrow X$	go to X if CTR nonzero
B5	IF(MQL = 1) $\rightarrow X$	go to X if low order MQ bit is 1
B6	IF(FI/O = 1) $\rightarrow X$	go to X if I/O flag is 1

carried out, while in the conditional case it is carried out only if the stated condition is met.

All the microinstructions described can be implemented in hardware (logic circuits) with a number of logic elements proportional to the storage capacities of the registers and with a delay that is at worst logarithmic in these capacities. This can be verified by examining the results of preceding sections, and in particular, those of Section 6.2.1. If we add a multiplier or divider circuit to that for addition, these linear and logarithmic bounds may no longer hold.

6.4.2. Microprograms

A microprogram is a sequence of microinstructions. We present a representative set of 15 microprograms that serve as a basis for a machine language. The microprograms that are needed to complete the machine language are easily patterned on those that are presented.

A micropgogram that is not a machine language instruction but that is used by every other microprogram is called IFETCH and described in Table 6.4.2.1. It fetches the next instruction from the RAM, transfers it from the MDR to the IR, increments the location counter, transfers the OP CODE to the CONTROL, and restarts the CONTROL. (Note that LOC CTR always contains a number that is one more than the address of the current instruction.) Also shown in Table 6.4.2.1 are microprograms to load the accumulator (LAC) with a word from location AP, to check the input/output buffer flag (CIOF), which causes the next instruction to be skipped if the flag is 1, and to read the I/O buffer into AC and zero the flag (RIOB). These three microprograms are labeled M2, M3, and M4, respectively, and will be used as machine language instructions.

Table 6.4.2.1 also contains microprogram M5 (SHAC), which shifts the contents of the accumulator right a number of places equal to the number in AP. It makes use of two other microprograms (M6 and M7) to which it

Table 6.4.2.1. Seven Microprograms

Label	Mnemonic	Microprograms	Instruction Sequence	Comments
M1	IFETCH	LC → MAR	T14	Fetch instruction from
		MFETCH	C2	location LC and transfer
		⌈ MDR → IR	T5	toIR; increment LC
		⌊ LC + 1 → LC	C1	and execute instruction.
		⌈ OPCD → MIR	T15	
		⌊ RMCR	C10	
M2	LAC	AP → MAR	T10	Transfer word at location
		MFETCH	C2	AP into AC. Fetch next
		⌈ MDR → AC	T1	instruction (FNI).
		→ M1	B1	
		⌊ RMCR	C10	
M3	CIOF	IF(FI/O = 1) → C1	B6	If FI/O is 1, increment
		⌈ → M1	B1	LC. FNI.
		⌊ RMCR	C10	
M4	RIOB	⌈ I/OBFR → AC	T8	Transfer I/O buffer to
		0 → FI/O	C9	AC, set FI/O to zero,
		→ M1	B1	FNI.
		⌊ RMCR	C10	
M5	SHAC	⌈ AP → CTR	T12	Transfer AP to CTR, with
		→ M6	B1	M6 and M7, shift AC right
		⌊ RMCR	C10	by this amount.
M6	RSLPA	⌈ IF(CTR ≠ 0) → M7	B4	If CTR ≠ 0, go to RSLP.
		IF(CTR ≠ 0) → C10	B4	Else FNI.
		⌈ → M1	B1	
		⌊ RMCR	C10	
M7	RSLP	⌈ ACR	L4	Shift AC right once,
		CTR − 1 → CTR	C8	decrement CTR, go
		→ M6(RSLPA)	B1	to RSLPA.
		⌊ RMCR	C10	

branches. While the counter is nonzero, AC is shifted right and the counter decremented. It is clear that the time required to execute this instruction can vary widely, since it depends on the value of AP, and may be much larger than the time to execute any of the four preceding microprograms.

Table 6.4.2.2 contains eight more microprograms. The action of M8 (ADD) is to add the contents of location AP to that of the accumulator with the result left in the accumulator. It is assumed that addition is done

Table 6.4.2.2. Eight Additional Microprograms

Label	Mnemonic	Microprograms	Instruction Sequence	Comments
M8	ADD	AP → MAR	T10	Add word at location AP
		MFETCH	C2	to AC, FNI
		⌈ MDR + AC → AC	L1	
		| → M1	B1	
		⌊ RMCR	C10	
M9	JMS	⌈ AP → MAR	T10	Store AP at location LC,
		⌊ LC → MDR	T7	FNI at location AP + 1
		MSTORE	C3	
		AP → LC	T11	
		⌈ LC + 1 → LC	C1	
		| → M1	B1	
		⌊ RMCR	C10	
M10	ISZ	AP → MAR	T10	Increment word at location
		MFETCH	C2	AP and if 0, skip following
		MDR + 1 → MDR	C6	instruction; otherwise
		⌈ MSTORE	C3	execute following instruc-
		⌊ MDR → AC	T1	tion
		IF(AC = 0) → C1	B2	
		→ M1	B1	
		RMCR	C10	
M11	JMP	⌈ AP → LC	T11	Jump to address at location
		| → M1	B1	AP. FNI
		⌊ RMCR	C10	
M12	MPY	⌈ N → CTR	C7	Multiply contents of AC
		⌊ AC → MDR	T2	with word at location AP
		⌈ MDR → MQ	T3	
		| CLR → AC	C4	
		⌊ AP → MAR	T10	
		MFETCH	C2	
		→ M13	B1	
M13	MLP	⌈ IF(MQL = 1) → M15	B5	If MQL = 1, go to MADD.
		⌊ IF(MQL = 1) → C10	B5	Else go to MLPA
		⌈ → M14	B1	
		⌊ RMCR	C10	
M14	MLPA	⌈ CTR − 1 → CTR	C8	Decrement CTR, shift AC
		⌊ ACMQR	L9	and MQ right once. If
		⌈ IF(CTR ≠ 0) → M13	B4	CTR ≠ 0, go to MLP.
		⌊ IF(CTR ≠ 0) → C10	B4	Else FNI
		⌈ → M1	B1	
		⌊ RMCR	C10	
M15	MADD	⌈ MDR + AC → AC	L1	Add contents of MDR to AC
		| → M14	B1	Go to MLPA
		⌊ RMCR	C10	

using 2's complement as the internal representation, as discussed in Section 6.3.6. The microprogram M9 (JMS) is used to jump to a subroutine. It transfers the contents of the location counter (which is one more than the address of the current instruction and which is the return address) to location AP. It then advances to location AP + 1 and continues (see Section 6.4.4). Microprogram M10 (ISZ) increments the number in location AP and skips the instruction following ISZ if the incremented number is 0. Microprogram M11 (JMP) is a simple jump instruction that causes the program to jump to location AP.

The remaining microprograms of Table 6.4.2.2 implement multiplication by shifting and adding. The multiplier, which is originally in AC, is transferred to MQ and AC is cleared. The multiplicand is found at location AP and brought to MDR. The low order bit of the multiplier is in MQ (it is MQL), and if 1, it causes the multiplicand to be added to the contents of AC. The result is shifted, the next least significant bit of the multiplier now becomes MQL, and the process is repeated until all bits of the multiplier have been examined. The product is a double length word that resides in AC and MQ.

In each table, microinstructions that can be executed in parallel are grouped together.

6.4.3. Microprogrammed Control

A microprogrammed control is a sequential machine that decodes an OP CODE and then executes one or more microprograms. There are many ways to realize such a control of which the most attractive from a pedagogical point of view is the type of hardwired control shown in Figure 6.4.3.1. It has an instruction register (MIR) that holds the identity of the microprogram under execution. The effect is to activate one of the horizontal lines by application of the Boolean value 1. The minor cycle ring is advanced once per clock cycle so that only one vertical line is activated at a time (by application of the Boolean value 1). Vertical lines are activated from left to right. At the intersection of vertical and horizontal lines are AND gates which generate an output of 1 only when the corresponding lines are activated. The output of an AND gate is connected at one or more points of the CPU and, when activated, results in the execution of one or more microinstructions. Some of these microinstructions cause a resetting of MIR and of the minor cycle ring, thus changing the state of the control itself.

Some of the outputs of the AND gates pass through an additional AND gate, the other input to which is a test signal. When the test signal is 1, the microinstructions indicated are carried out. It is by this means that conditional branching is realized.

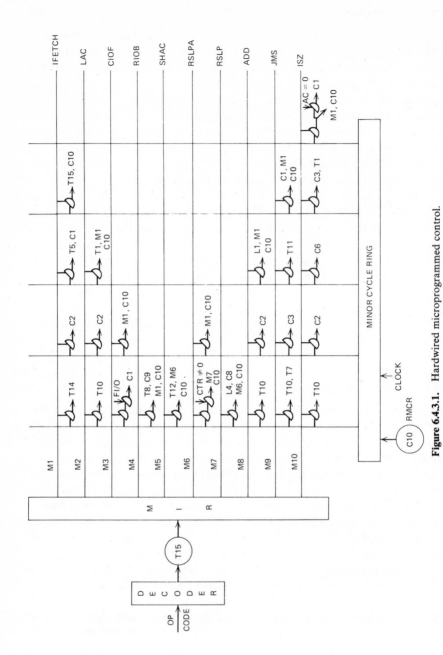

Figure 6.4.3.1. Hardwired microprogrammed control.

In Tables 6.4.2.1 and 6.4.2.2 a number of microinstructions in each microprogram are grouped together. These are instructions that can be executed in parallel, and the same groupings are used in the hardwired microprogrammed control.

A microprogrammed control can also be constructed from a read-only (random access) memory (ROM). In this case, the OP CODE points to a location from which a word is fetched. This word contains one or more subwords (describing microinstructions) that point to lines in the CPU to be activated. A sequence of such words is generally read before the control branches back to the reading of another OP CODE.

6.4.4. Machine Language Programming

A machine language is a low level programming language whose instructions are immediately interpreted by a CPU. For example, the microprograms LAC, CIOF, RIOB, ISZ, SHAC, ADD, MPY, JMP, and JMS are a subset of a machine language for the CPU described above. Each of these instructions is immediately decoded by this CPU, and they result in the execution of one or more microprograms.

Table 6.4.4.1 contains an instruction set for a sample machine language that could be run on the CPU described above. The instructions that have not been encountered yet are similar to those we have seen. The memory access instruction LMQ loads the MQ register from the address in AP while STAC and STMQ store the AC and MQ at locations in AP. The I/O instruction SIOB transfers AC to the I/O buffer and AP to I/OAR, the I/O address register. Of the arithmetic and logical instructions, CLAC clears the accumulator, and SUB and DIV subtract and divide the number

Table 6.4.4.1. Instructions for a Machine Language

Memory Access Instructions	Arithmetic and Logical Instructions	
LAC	ISZ	SUB
LMQ	CLAC	MPY
STAC	SHAC	DIV
STMQ	ADD	
I/O Instructions	Jump Instructions	
CIOF	JMP	
RIOB	JMS	
SIOB	JMAN	
	JMAZ	
	HALT	

in location AP from and into the number in the accumulator. The new jump instructions, JMAN and JMAZ, cause a jump to address AP if the accumulator is negative or zero, respectively, while HALT stops the execution of all microinstructions by deactivating all horizontal lines of the microprogrammed control.

Each of these instructions, with the exception of CIOF, RIOB, SIOB, CLAC, and HALT, is called a *direct address instruction* because the address to which it refers is that in AP. The locations to which CIOF, RIOB, SIOB, and CLAC refer are *implied*. As we see in the sample program given in the next paragraph, it is sometimes useful to have *indirect addressing*. In this case, AP is not the address to which the instruction refers but is the location where that address can be found. For example, JMPI is a new instruction that is exactly like JMP except that the address to which it causes a jump is found in location AP. A microprogram for JMPI transfers AP to the MAR, fetches, transfers the address in MDR to MAR, and does another fetch. The result is transferred to IR, since a jump is being executed. In general, an instruction mnemonic given in Table 6.4.4.1 to which has been affixed the suffix I is to be intrepreted as the given instruction in which addressing is indirect.

We now present a sample machine language program that illustrates the use of the various instructions. Our program computes the polynomial

$$A(N)X^N + A(N-1)X^{N-1} + \cdots + A(1)X + A(0)$$

using Horner's rule when $N, X, A(N), A(N-1), \ldots, A(0)$ are each treated as variables. Horner's rule evaluates the polynomial by computing $A(N) \cdot X + A(N-1)$, multiplying the result by X, adding $A(N-2)$, and so on, as indicated by the following formula:

$$(\ldots ((A(N)X + A(N-1))X + A(N-2))X + \ldots)X + A(0)$$

Our sample program is more readily understood if we describe it in a higher level language akin to ALGOL (see Dijkstra, 1962):

> Read X
> Read N
> $N \rightarrow T$
> **while** $T \geq 0$ **do** Read $A(T)$, $T - 1 \rightarrow T$ **od**
> $N \rightarrow T$
> $0 \rightarrow S$
> **while** $T \geq 0$ **do** $S \cdot X + A(T) \rightarrow S$, $T - 1 \rightarrow T$ **od**

Here "Read X" means read X from the I/O buffer, "$N \rightarrow T$" means give

T the value N and "**while** $T \geq 0$ **do** . . . **od**" means do the operations between **do** and **od** repeatedly while $T \geq 0$.

The reader can verify that this program defines a procedure for implementing Horner's rule. The machine language program we give is essentially a direct translation of this program.

The read instruction is applied to the I/O buffer and can be executed only if the I/O flag is 1. The following *subroutine* continuously polls the I/O flag until it is 1, at which point the contents of the buffer are transferred to the AC and the machine returns to the address at location P, which is called the *subroutine return address*. This is but one (highly inefficient) way in which to handle I/O.

Subroutine to Read I/O Buffer

Location	Mnemonic	Address Part	Comment
P	—	—	contains return address
P + 1	CIOF	—	check FI/O
P + 2	JMP	P + 1	if FI/O = 0, repeat
P + 3	RIOB	—	if FI/O = 1, transfer I/OBFR to AC
P + 4	JMPI	P	return to address at location P

Note the use of indirect addressing to return to the address located in the address part of location P. The dashes denote "don't care" entries whose values are irrelevant.

Using this subroutine, the instructions Read X, Read N, and $N \rightarrow T$ are given in our machine language as follows:

Location	Mnemonic	Address Part	Comment
Q	JMS	P	read X into AC
Q + 1	STAC	L	store X at location L
Q + 2	JMS	P	read N into AC
Q + 3	STAC	L + 1	store N at location L + 1
Q + 4	STAC	L + 2	N → T (T at location L + 2)

The instruction JMS stores the address of the location following it (in the first use of JMS this is Q + 1) into location P of the subroutine, and it is to this address that the subroutine returns. It transfers the contents of the I/O buffer into AC. We caution the reader that it is not considered good programming practice to leave the results of subroutine computations in programmer-accessible registers of a CPU. Rather they should be left in certain prespecified locations in memory, with the general registers restored to the values they contained before the subroutine was entered. This practice avoids costly programming errors.

The next section of code implements the first **"while do"** loop. The variables $A(N), A(N-1), \ldots, A(0)$ are stored at locations L + 3, L + 4, ..., L + N + 3, respectively, and before entering instruction Q + 5, the AC contains N. Location A initially contains the number L + 3 and location A + 2 contains 1.

Location	Mnemonic	Address Part	Comment
Q + 5	ADD	A	location A contains L + 3
Q + 6	STAC	A	location A now contains L + N + 3
Q + 7	LAC	L + 2	read T into AC
Q + 8	JMPAN	Q + 17	while T $\geqslant$ 0 continue, else exit
Q + 9	LAC	A	AC contains L + N + 3
Q + 10	SUB	L + 2	AC contains L + N + 3 − T
Q + 10	STAC	A + 1	location A + 1 contains L + N + 3 − T
Q + 11	JMS	P	read A(T) into AC
Q + 12	STACI	A + 1	store A(T) (indirectly) into location L + N + 3 − T
Q + 13	LAC	L + 2	read T into AC
Q + 14	SUB	A + 2	T − 1 → T in AC
Q + 15	STAC	L + 2	T − 1 stored into L + 2
Q + 16	JMP	Q + 7	return to test T.

The next and last section of code sets $N \to T$, $0 \to S$ and realizes the second **"while do"** loop. The result S is in location A + 3. We begin by restoring the indirect address A + 1 to L + N + 3 and clearing S.

Location	Mnemonic	Address Part	Comment
Q + 17	LAC	A	read L + N + 3 into AC
Q + 18	STAC	A + 1	store L + N + 3 at location A + 1
Q + 19	CLAC	—	zero accumulator
Q + 20	STAC	A + 3	set 0 → S
Q + 21	LAC	L + 1	read N into AC
Q + 22	STAC	L + 2	set N → T
Q + 23	LAC	L + 2	read T into AC
Q + 24	JMPAN	Q + 36	while T $\geqslant$ 0 continue, else exit
Q + 25	LAC	A + 1	AC contains L + N + 3
Q + 26	SUB	L + 2	AC contains L + N + 3 − T
Q + 27	STAC	A + 1	location A + 1 contains L + N + 3 − T
Q + 28	LAC	A + 3	read S into AC

Location	Mnemonic	Address Part	Comment
Q + 29	MPY	L	AC contains S · X
Q + 30	ADDI	A + 1	AC contains S · X + A(T)
Q + 31	STAC	A + 3	set S · X + A(T) → S
Q + 32	LAC	L + 2	read T into AC
Q + 33	SUB	A + 2	set T − 1 → T
Q + 34	STAC	L + 2	store T
Q + 35	JMP	Q + 23	return to test T
Q + 36	HALT		result S is in location A + 3

The program uses locations Q, Q + 1, . . . , Q + 36, L, L + 1, . . . , L + N + 3, P, P + 1, . . . , P + 4 and A, A + 1, A + 2, A + 3, which must not overlap but which need not be contiguous. The total number of locations used is $n + 47$ where $n = N + 3$ is the number of variables of the problem.

6.4.5. Other Features of General-Purpose Computers

The General-Purpose computer (GPC) that has the CPU described above is characterized as a stored-program, word-organized, single-address machine with no general or index registers. Many machines are *byte oriented*, that is, organized around eight-bit subwords, and instructions can point to and use one or more bytes.

A number of the instructions listed in our sample machine language are implied address instructions (such as CLAC), while others are single-address instructions (such as JMP). However, a few are binary operations that take two operands one of whose address is specified and the other implied (it is the AC). For such operations, it may be desirable to use *multiaddress instructions*. They explicitly contain a two-part address that contains the locations (including the AC) from which the operands are to be fetched. In some machines, instructions contain a third address part which is the location into which the result is to be stored.

Many machines have *index registers*, useful in subroutines, which hold increments that can be added to base addresses in instructions so that a sequence of instructions can be applied to an array of elements. *General registers* are registers that can serve as index registers or auxiliary accumulators or that can be used in logical operations.

The handling of input and output to a CPU was done in our simple model by repeatedly checking the I/O flag. The other principal method for dealing with I/O is through the use of *interrupts*. An interrupt is a signal from an external device that causes a program to be interrupted and results in a new sequence of microinstructions responding to the source of the interrupt. In many machines, the interrupt could have come from one of many different sources, and the control must first identify the source. After completing a response to an interrupt, a microprogrammed control resumes the interrupted program. This requires that the MIR and the minor cycle ring have backup registers from which to return the interrupted states.

Appendix

The Krapchenko (1967) straight-line algorithm consists of five subcircuits, B_1, B_2, B_3, B_4 and B_5. A given subcircuit may use the results in any prior subcircuit. We let $D(B_1)$ and $C(B_1)$ be the delay and number of logic elements introduced in B_1 and we assume that the available basis is $\Omega = \{ +, \cdot, \oplus, ^- \}$. Also, we define m by

$$m = \lceil \log_2 n \rceil$$

B_1 Compute $u_j = x_j \cdot y_j$, $v_j = x_j \oplus y_j$, $0 \leq j \leq n - 1$:

$$D(B_1) = 1, \qquad C(B_1) = 2n$$

B_2 Let $V_{b,a} = v_b \cdot v_{b-1} \cdot \cdots \cdot v_a$, $G_{b,a} = g_{b-a+1}(u_b, v_b, \ldots, u_a)$. Let τ be an integer to be determined later. Then B_2 has τ levels labeled $1 \leq l \leq \tau$. At level l compute

$$V_{(j+1)2^l - 1, j \cdot 2^l} = V_{(2j+2)2^{l-1} - 1, (2j+1)2^{l-1}} \cdot V_{(2j+1)2^{l-1} - 1, 2j \cdot 2^{l-1}}$$

$$\begin{aligned} G_{(j+1)2^l - 1, j \cdot 2^l} &= G_{(2j+2)2^{l-1} - 1, (2j+1)2^{l-1}} \\ &+ V_{(2j+2)2^{l-1} - 1, (2j+1)2^{l-1}} \cdot G_{(2j+1)2^{l-1} - 1, 2j \cdot 2^{l-1}} \end{aligned}$$

for all values of $0 \leq j \leq (2^m/2^l) - 1$. The terms on the right-hand side of each equation are computed at level $l - 1$ since $2j + 1 \leq (2^m/2^{l-1}) - 1$ for $j \leq (2^m/2^l) - 1$. (See Figure 6.A.1 for an illustration of B_2.) It follows that

$$D(B_2) = 2\tau, \qquad C(B_2) = 3 \sum_{l=1}^{\tau} 2^{m-l} = 3 \cdot 2^m (1 - 2^{-\tau})$$

These equations show the possibility of a tradeoff of delay for combinational complexity by changing τ. This will also be true for the entire circuit, and τ will be chosen to give a favorable tradeoff.

B_3 The inputs to subcircuit B_3 are the outputs at level τ of B_2 that are renamed as

$$v'_j = V_{(j+1)2^\tau - 1, j \cdot 2^\tau}$$

$$u'_j = G_{(j+1)2^\tau - 1, j \cdot 2^\tau}$$

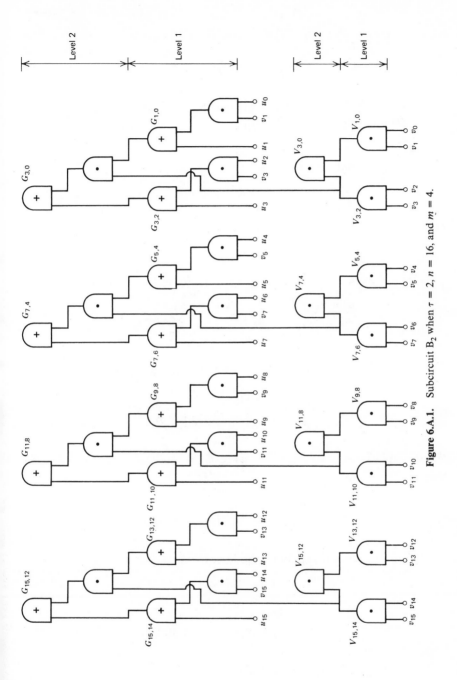

Figure 6.A.1. Subcircuit B_2 when $\tau = 2$, $n = 16$, and $m = 4$.

for $0 \leq j \leq (2^m/2^\tau) - 1$. B_3 computes the functions

$$G'_{j,0} = g_j(u'_j, v'_j, \ldots, u'_0)$$

in the new variables using a construction that is essentially that of Theorem 6.3.5.1 but that eliminates duplication of subcircuits.

The development of B_3 requires a number of auxiliary parameters. Let

$$m' = m - \tau$$

Recalling that

$$m_l = \frac{l(l-1)}{2}$$

we choose the integer t to satisfy

$$m_{t-1} < m' \leq m_t$$

B_3 will have t levels labeled $1 \leq l \leq t$. We introduce

$$d_l(j) = \begin{cases} \left\lfloor \dfrac{j}{2^{m_l}} \right\rfloor 2^{m_l} & 1 \leq l \leq t-1 \\ 0 & l = t \end{cases}$$

which is defined for $0 \leq j \leq 2^{m'} - 1$. For integers j and N,

$$\frac{(j - (N-1))}{N} \leq \left\lfloor \frac{j}{N} \right\rfloor \leq \frac{j}{N}$$

Consequently,

$$j - (2^{m_l} - 1) \leq d_l(j) \leq j$$

For $2 \leq l \leq t$, and $0 \leq j \leq 2^{m'} - 1$, define $e_l(j)$ by

$$e_l(j) = \frac{\left[d_{l-1}(j) - d_l(j)\right]}{2^{m_{l-1}}}$$

Then it follows by applying the bounds to $d_l(j)$ that

$$e_l(j) \leq \frac{\left[j - d_l(j)\right]}{2^{m_{l-1}}} < 2^{l-1}$$

for $2 \leq l \leq t-1$ since $m_l - m_{l-1} = l - 1$ and for $l = t$

$$e_t(j) \leq \frac{j}{2^{m_{t-1}}} < 2^{m' - m_{t-1}} \leq 2^{t-1}$$

since $d_t(j) = 0$ and $m' \leq m_t$.

The values of these parameters when $n = 16$, $m = 4$, $\tau = 2$, $m' = 2$, and $t = 3$ are shown in Table 6.A.1. Note that $m_1 = 0$, $m_2 = 1$, and $m_3 = 3$.

Table 6.A.1. Values of Parameters in Construction of Adder

j	$d_1(j)$	$d_2(j)$	$e_2(j)$	$e_3(j)$
0	0	0	0	0
1	1	0	1	0
2	2	2	0	1
3	3	2	1	1

Define the new functions

$$V'_{b,a} = v'_b \cdot \cdots \cdot v'_a, \qquad G'_{b,a} = g_{b-a+1}(u'_b, v'_b, \ldots, u'_a)$$

At level l of B_3, $1 \leq l \leq t - 1$, compute

$$V'_{j,\,d_l(j)-k2^{m_l}} = V'_{j,\,d_l(j)} \cdot \prod_{r=1}^{k} V'_{d_l(j)-(r-1)2^{m_l}-1,\,d_l(j)-r2^{m_l}}$$

for each $1 \leq k \leq e_{l+1}(j)$ and $0 \leq j \leq 2^{m'} - 1$. (If $e_{l+1}(j) = 0$, the term is not computed.) Here $\prod$ denotes repeated AND.

When $k = e_{l+1}(j)$, $d_l(j) - k2^{m_l} = d_{l+1}(j)$, and $V'_{j,\,d_{l+1}(j)}$ is computed at level l. Therefore, the first term on the right-hand side of this equation is computed at level $l - 1$. This is also true of the other terms because $d_l(j) = k \cdot 2^{m_l}$ for some integer $k(\geq r)$ and

$$d_l(k \cdot 2^{m_l} - (r - 1)2^{m_l} - 1) = k2^{m_l} - r2^{m_l}$$

$$= d_l(j) - r2^{m_l}$$

that is, these other terms are of the form $V'_{j',\,d_l(j')}$ for $j' = d_l(j) - (r-1)2^{m_l} - 1$ and are computed at level $l - 1$.

Also at level l of B_3, with $2 \leq l \leq t$, for $0 \leq j \leq 2^{m'} - 1$ compute

$$G'_{j,\,d_l(j)} = G'_{j,\,d_{l-1}(j)} + \sum_{r=1}^{e_l(j)} V'_{j,\,d_{l-1}(j)-(r-1)2^{m_{l-1}}}$$

$$\cdot\, G'_{d_{l-1}(j)-(r-1)2^{m_{l-1}}-1,\,d_{l-1}(j)-r2^{m_{l-1}}}$$

where Σ denotes repeated OR. Observe that $G'_{j,j} = u'_j$ and $V'_{j,j} = v'_j$. That the two sides are equal follows from the identities for the function g.

The terms on the right-hand side are computed at level $l - 1$. This is obvious by induction for $G'_{j, d_{l-1}(j)}$. The V' terms are by definition computed at level $l - 1$. The remaining G' terms are of the form $G'_{j', d_{l-1}(j')}$ where $j' = d_{l-1}(j) - (r - 1)2^{m_{l}-1} - 1$, as demonstrated.

A graph of B_3 for $n = 16$, $\tau = 2$, $m = 4$, $m' = 2$, and $t = 3$ is shown in Figure 6.A.2.

The delay introduced at level l of the V' portion of B_3 is $\max_j \lceil \log_2 (e_{l+1}(j) + 1) \rceil \leq l$ for $1 \leq l \leq t - 1$. The delay introduced by the G'

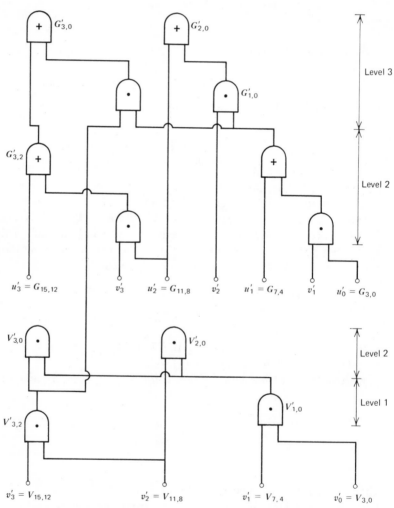

Figure 6.A.2. Subcircuit B_3 when $n = 16$, $\tau = 2$, $m = 4$, $m' = 2$ and $t = 3$.

portion is $\max_j \lceil \log_2(e_l(j) + 1) \rceil + 1$, which is no more than l for $2 \le l \le t - 1$, and $m' - m_{t-1} + 1$ for $l = t$. Consequently,

$$D(B_3) \le \left(\sum_{l=1}^{t-1} l \right) + m' - m_{t-1} + 1$$

$$= m' + t$$

Following the analysis leading to Theorem 6.3.5.1, we see that

$$t < \sqrt{2m'} + 2$$

where

$$m' = m - \tau$$

Therefore,

$$D(B_3) \le m' + \sqrt{2m'} + 2$$

The number of binary logic elements used in the V' portion of B_3 is

$$\sum_{l=1}^{t-1} \sum_{j=0}^{2^{m'}-1} \sum_{k=1}^{e_{l+1}(j)} k = \sum_{l=1}^{t-1} \sum_{j=0}^{2^{m'}-1} \frac{e_{l+1}(j)(e_{l+1}(j) + 1)}{2}$$

and in the G' portion is

$$\sum_{l=2}^{t} \sum_{j=0}^{2^{m'}-1} 2e_l(j)$$

Since $e_l(j) \le 2^{l-1} - 1$ for all $1 \le l \le t$, a straightforward counting argument shows that

$$C(B_3) \le 2^{m'} \left(\frac{2^{2t} - 10}{6} + 3 \cdot 2^{t-1} \right) \le 2^{m'} 2^{2t-1}$$

for $t \ge 1$.

The G' portion of B_3 computes the functions $G'_{j, d_t(j)} = G'_{j, 0}$, $0 \le j \le 2^{m'} - 1$. The reader can readily demonstrate that

$$G'_{j, 0} = G_{(j+1)2^\tau - 1, 0} = c_{(j+1)2^\tau - 1} = c_{k \cdot 2^\tau - 1}$$

for $k = j + 1$ and $1 \le k \le 2^{m'} = 2^m / 2^\tau$.

B₄ At level l, $1 \le l \le \tau$, of B_4 and for each $0 \le j \le 2^m / 2^{\tau - l + 1} - 1$, compute

$$c_{(2j+1)2^{\tau-l} - 1} = G_{(2j+1)2^{\tau-l} - 1, (2j)2^{\tau-l}} + V_{(2j+1)2^{\tau-l} - 1, (2j)2^{\tau-l}} \cdot c_{(2j)2^{\tau-l} - 1}$$

(If $j = 0$, the Vc term is zero.) Clearly, the G and V terms are computed at level $\tau - l$ of B_2 because $2j \leq 2((2^m/2^{\tau-l+1}) - 1) < (2^m/2^{\tau-l}) - 1$ so that $2j$ is in the range of subscripts of B_2 at level $\tau - l$.

We show by induction that $c_{k \cdot 2^{\tau-l}-1}$ is available at level l of B_4 for all $1 \leq k \leq 2^m/2^{\tau-l}$ and for each $1 \leq l \leq \tau$. At the input of B_4 (level 0), this is true. Assume that it is true for level $l - 1$ and demonstrate that it is also true for level l. By assumption, $c_{(2j)2^{\tau-l}-1} = c_{j \cdot 2^{\tau-l+1}-1}$ is available at level l since the second term is available at level $l - 1$ for $1 \leq j \leq 2^m/2^{\tau-l+1}$. That is, $c_{(2j)2^{\tau-l}-1}$ is available at level l for $2 \leq 2j \leq 2^m/2^{\tau-l}$. The preceding equation then implies that $c_{(2j+1)2^{\tau-l}-1}$ is computed at level l for all $0 \leq j \leq (2^m/2^{\tau-l+1}) - 1$ or for $1 \leq 2j + 1 \leq (2^m/2^{\tau-l}) - 1$. Therefore, $c_{k \cdot 2^{\tau-l}-1}$ is available at level l for all $1 \leq k \leq 2^m/2^{\tau-l}$ and the induction hypothesis is established.

When $l = \tau$, c_{k-1} is computed by B_4 for all $1 \leq k \leq n$; that is, all carries $c_0, c_1, \ldots, c_{n-1}$ are available at the output of B_4. Figure 6.A.3 shows this subcircuit when $n = 16$, $m = 4$, $\tau = 2$.

Clearly,

$$D(B_4) = 2\tau, \qquad C(B_4) = 2\sum_{l=1}^{\tau} 2^{m-\tau+l-1} = 2^{m+1}(1 - 2^{-\tau})$$

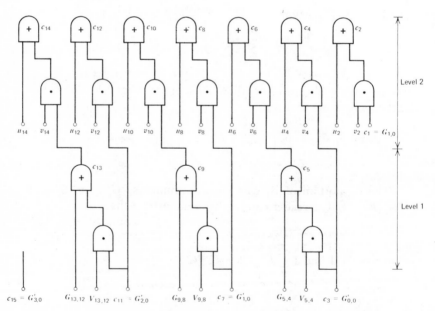

Figure 6.A.3. Subcircuit B_4 when $n = 16$, $m = 4$, $\tau = 2$.

B₅ For $1 \le j \le n - 1$, compute

$$s_j = v_j \oplus c_{j-1}$$

and observe that $s_0 = v_0$. Obviously,

$$D(B_5) = 1, \qquad C(B_5) = n - 1$$

Combining the results for the five subcircuits, we conclude that the total delay is

$$\sum_{i=1}^{5} D(B_i) \le m' + \sqrt{2m'} + 4\tau + 4$$

and the total number of elements used is

$$\sum_{i=1}^{5} C(B_i) \le 3n + 5 \cdot 2^m(1 - 2^{-\tau}) + 2^{m'+2t-1}$$

where $m = \lceil \log_2 n \rceil$, t is an integer satisfying

$$t < \sqrt{2m'} + 2$$

and $m' = m - \tau$ where τ is an integer whose value is yet to be decided.

Theorem 6.3.5.2. Over the basis $\Omega = \{+, \cdot, \oplus, ^-\}$, the addition function $f_A^{(2n)} \colon \{0, 1\}^{2n} \to \{0, 1\}^{n+1}$ can be computed by a chain that simultaneously achieves a delay of at most

$$m + 7\sqrt{2m} + 14$$

and has a number of computation steps (logic elements) bounded above by

$$3n + 6 \cdot 2^m$$

where $m = \lceil \log_2 n \rceil$.

Proof. Choose $\tau = \lceil 2\sqrt{2m} \rceil + 3$ and observe that

$$2t - 1 - \tau \le 2\sqrt{2m} + 4 - 1 - (2\sqrt{2m} + 3) = 0$$

Also, note that $\sqrt{2m'} < \sqrt{2m}$. $\qquad\qquad\square$

Problems

6-1. Show that the transition function for a J-K flip-flop is in $P_{2,3}^{(3)}$.

6-2. Design a decrementing modulo 2^k counter, a counter that is decremented by each application of the clock pulse and that resets to $2^k - 1$ when decrementing from 0. Use master-slave flip-flops in your design.

6-3. Design a ring counter.

6-4. Design a counter that counts modulo 13.

6-5. Define a RAM that has two input ports with two separate sets of inputs and commands. Resolve the conflict when both ports attempt to write into the same location by giving control to the first port. Derive good upper and lower bounds to the combinational and delay complexities of the transition and output functions of this memory unit.

6-6. Define a memory that can be accessed either as a RAM or a CAM but not both simultaneously. Derive good upper and lower bounds to the combinational and delay complexities of the transition and output function of this memory unit.

6-7. Using the construction of Section 6.3.2, give a circuit for the shifting function f_{SR} that improves on the bound of Theorem 6.3.2.1.

6-8. Use the method of Section 6.3.4 to derive a lower bound to the delay complexity of the comparison function ϕ_{MATCH}: $Z_N \times Z_N \to \{0, 1\}$ where $Z_N = \{0, 1, \ldots, N - 1\}$ and $\phi_{MATCH}(u, v) = 1$ if $u = v$ and is 0 otherwise.

6-9. Repeat Problem 8 for the function ϕ_{COMP}: $Z_N \times Z_N \to \{0, 1\}$ where $\phi_{COMP}(u, v) = 1$ if $u < v$ and is 0 otherwise.

6-10. Represent the integers in $\{1, 2, \ldots, N - 1\}$ by their exponents in the prime number decomposition. Show that two integers can be multiplied with a delay complexity that is much smaller than the delay complexity of the overflow test for multiplication.

6-11. Give procedures for adding signed numbers when the numbers are represented in each of the following notations:
(a) 1's complement.
(b) 2's complement.

6-12. Design an analog of a Full Adder chain for subtracting two positive n-bit numbers. Show that the subtraction function has a delay complexity logarithmic in n.
Hint. Replace "carries" in a Full Adder chain by "deficits."

6-13. Residue arithmetic is another useful method for doing arithmetic. Given positive integers $p_1, p_2, \ldots, p_k$ that are relatively prime (no common factors), we can represent integers in the range $0 \leq n \leq N - 1$ where $N = p_1 \cdot p_2 \cdot \ldots \cdot p_k$ as $\mathbf{n} = (n_1, n_2, \ldots, n_k)$ where $n_i = n \bmod p_i$.

(a) Show that if $n \neq m$, $0 \leq n$, $m \leq N - 1$, then $\mathbf{n} \neq \mathbf{m}$.

(b) Given n and m, $0 \leq n$, $m \leq N - 1$, form $\mathbf{n} + \mathbf{m}$ by adding the ith components of $\mathbf{n}$ and $\mathbf{m}$ modulo p_i. Show that $\mathbf{n} + \mathbf{m}$ is the (unique) representation for $(n + m)$ modulo N in this notation.

(c) Form $\mathbf{n} \times \mathbf{m}$ by multiplying the ith components of $\mathbf{n}$ and $\mathbf{m}$ modulo p_i. Show that $\mathbf{n} \times \mathbf{m}$ is the (unique) representation for $(n \times m)$ modulo N in this notation.

6-14. Let $N = (2^{10} + 3)(2^{11} + 1)(2^{12} + 1)(2^{13} + 5)(2^{14} + 1)$ and write N as a product of five relatively prime integers. Represent integers in residue form using these integers and design an adder and multiplier that have much smaller delay than the Full Adder chain and the standard multiplier that multiplies by shifting and adding. Is there a simple test on the outputs for determining whether the sum or product equals or exceeds N?

6-15. Given that integers in the set $\{0, 1, 2, \ldots, 2^n - 1\}$ are represented by the standard binary notation, determine whether or not the squaring function has a much larger combinational complexity than the multiplication function.

6-16. Show that the following identities imply the existence of an integer k such that $n_k = 2$:

$$n_0 = n$$

$$n_j = n_{j-1} - \left\lfloor \frac{n_{j-1}}{3} \right\rfloor, \quad j \geq 1$$

Furthermore, demonstrate that

$$\left(\tfrac{2}{3}\right)^j n \leq n_j \leq \left(\tfrac{2}{3}\right)^j n + 2$$

6-17. Extend the carry-save method used in the Ofman integer multiplication algorithm by grouping $2^r - 1$ binary m-tuples and replacing them by r binary tuples where the sum of the $2^r - 1$ integers is equal to the sum of the r new integers. Apply this scheme to integer multiplication and evaluate the delay of the corresponding circuit.

6-18. Let $0 \leq x < \tfrac{1}{2}$ and let $\hat{x}$ be an approximation to x obtained by truncating x to its s most significant digits in the binary expansion of fractional numbers. That is, $\hat{x} = (a_{-1}, a_{-2}, \ldots, a_{-s})$, $a_{-1} = 0$, and

$$|\hat{x}| = a_{-1} \cdot 2^{-1} + a_{-2} \cdot 2^{-2} + \cdots + a_{-s} 2^{-s}$$

$$\hat{x} = |\hat{x}| = 2^{-s} \lfloor 2^s x \rfloor$$

Let $\delta = 2^{-s}$.

(a) Show that $x - \delta \leq \hat{x} \leq x$.

(b) Let $(\hat{x})^{2^{j-1}}$ be defined inductively to be the square of $(\hat{x})^{2^{j-2}}$ truncated to its s most significant places. Show that

$$x^{2^{j-1}} - 2\delta \leq (\hat{x})^{2^{j-1}} \leq x^{2^{j-1}}$$

6-19. Write microprograms for the machine language instructions STAC, CLAC, SUB, and JMAN, which are defined in Section 6.4.4.

6-20. Show how the microprograms for ADD, JMS, and JMP are modified when indirect addressing is used.

6-21. Assume that interrupts may arrive from several sources and that each source has a 1-bit register that records the interrupt. How can the microprogrammed control be modified to respond to interrupts?

6-22. Describe modifications that could be made to the simple CPU of Section 6.4 to facilitate the sorting of items when items are represented as binary b-tuples $\mathbf{x}$, $\mathbf{y}$, and $\mathbf{x} \leq \mathbf{y}$ if and only if corresponding components x_i and y_i satisfy $x_i \leq y_i$.

6-23. Describe modicifactions that could be made to the simple CPU of Section 6.4 to implement the "carry-save adder" which is the basis for the Ofman integer multiplication algorithm of Section 6.3.7.

6-24. Evaluate the combinational complexity of the simple CPU of Section 6.4 as a function of b, the size of data registers, and $\log_2 M$, the size of address registers. What effect do the modifications of Problems 22 and 23 have on this number?

Chapter 7

Storage-Time Tradeoffs

In this chapter, we examine computation on general-purpose computers at a macroscopic level. At this level, we are primarily concerned with gross parameters of machines and programs, such as space and time, and with relationships between these parameters. As a result, we acquire a new kind of understanding of computers and computing. This move to a high level of abstraction is a response to the complexity of computing.

We derive computational inequalities of the first and second kind for general-purpose computers that are based on combinational complexity and program complexity, respectively. These inequalities state lower limits on exchanges of space, time, and other parameters of machines and programs. We show that under some circumstances we can come close to achieving the inequalities and we use them as a basis for discussing computational efficiency.

7.1. PROBLEMS, MACHINES, PROGRAMS, AND COMPUTATIONS

In this chapter, we derive lower limits on space–time tradeoffs in terms of the complexity of a task as measured in several ways. To derive these results, we need an unambiguous definition for a task. For example, it is insufficient to describe a task as the calculation of the square root of a real number because neither the representation of real numbers nor their range is specified. Furthermore, if the stated representation of numbers is not that used to represent numbers internally in a machine or if numbers can be represented internally in several ways, such as integer or floating point, ambiguity may still exist and the task may not be completely defined relative to the machine. To avoid such problems, we define a task by a binary function $f : \{0, 1\}^n \rightarrow \{0, 1\}^m$ that defines the input–output mapping that must be realized by the binary machine on which the task is to be executed.

287

The information necessary to compute a function $f : \{0, 1\}^n \to \{0, 1\}$ is called a *program*, and at two preceding points in this book we have given definitions for programs. In Section 4.5 programs for sequential machines are defined, and in Section 5.7 programs for Turing machines are given. A program for a function f on a given machine is a string containing constants (0 and 1 for binary machines) and the variables of f that, when variables are given values, specifies all inputs and initial conditions on a machine so that the machine computes f. (One can also allow "don't cares," inputs or constants whose value is immaterial.)

The machines examined in this chapter are general-purpose computers consisting of a CPU and either one or two memories, as indicated in Figure 7.1.1. The one-memory machine is allowed to have either a random access (RAM), tape (TAM), drum (or disk) (DRUM) or content-addressable memory (CAM). The two-memory machine has a RAM and a DRUM. Each of these memories is defined and described is Section 6.2.

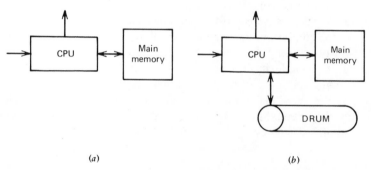

(a)   (b)

Figure 7.1.1.   Two types of general-purpose computer: (a) one-memory; (b) two-memory.

We explicitly assume that all input to and output from these machines is through the CPU. We also explicitly assume that the CPU is not connected to any other computing element. For example, we disallow a connection to an outside storage device that results in outputs from the CPU affecting subsequent inputs to the CPU in any way. This does not eliminate the use of an outside storage device for pure generation of input or for pure reception of output. If an outside computing element is attached to the CPU of one of these machines (including human computing elements), it must be shown explicitly and included in the derivation of computational inequalities.

The models of computers that we have chosen to analyze here are fairly simple but representative of important components of many existing machines. The study of these machines gives us new insight into the limitations on the performance of computers.

7.2. COMPUTATIONAL INEQUALITIES OF THE FIRST KIND

Computational inequalities are derived in Section 4.5 for collections of sequential machines. They state relationships that must hold between the complexities of a function and the size of machines and execution times. For example, if a single sequential machine S is used to compute f in T cycles (T fixed for each point in the domain of f) and the positions of valid outputs (see page 164) are data independent, then

$$C_\Omega(f) \le C_\Omega(\delta, \lambda)T$$

where δ and λ are the transition and output functions of S. Thus, if S has a small equivalent size, $C_\Omega(\delta, \lambda)$, relative to $C_\Omega(f)$, then T must be large to compute f. Such inequalities clearly delimit size–time tradeoffs but explicitly permit larger machines and execution times than are necessary.

The inequalities discussed in this section are extensions and applications of those derived in Section 4.5. All are based on the construction of computational chains or straight-line algorithms (equivalently logic circuits) that simulate the computations carried out in time by machines with memory, namely, sequential machines. They are called *computational inequalities of the first kind*. Those discussed in the next section are based on the construction of programs in a universal language to simulate such computations.

Inequalities are derived for GPCs first. Consider five representative types, M_{RAM}, M_{TAM}, M_{DRUM}, M_{CAM}, and M_{DUAL}, each of which has one CPU with cycle length τ_{CPU}, in seconds, and one or more memories as indicated below:

1. M_{RAM} one (M, b) RAM, $\tau_{RAM} = \tau_{CPU}$
2. M_{TAM} one (M, b) TAM, $\tau_{TAM} = \tau_{CPU}$
3. M_{DRUM} one (K, L, b) DRUM, $\tau_{DRUM} = \tau_{CPU}$
4. M_{CAM} one (M, b, r)CAM, $\tau_{CAM} = \tau_{CPU}$
5. M_{DUAL} one (M, b) RAM, $\tau_{RAM} = \tau_{CPU}$
      one (K, L, b) DRUM, $\tau_{DRUM} = 4\tau_{CPU}$

The four basic types of memory are defined as in Sections 6.2.2 through 6.2.5, and it is assumed that M, K, and L are powers of 2. The RAM and TAM have M b-bit words, as does the CAM, and the latter is accessed by the content of an r-bit word. Each of these has a storage capacity of $S = Mb$ bits. The DRUM has K b-bit words per track, L tracks, and a storage capacity of $S = KLb$ bits. For simplicity and without significant loss of generality, we assume that the cycle lengths of the CPU and the memory in each of the first four machines are equal. Similarly, for the machine M_{DUAL} with two memories we let the CPU and the RAM have the same cycle length and let that of the DRUM be 4 times this number. The CPU that is used with each machine may differ. We say more about these machines later, but at the moment we assume that they can address the assumed number and type of memory.

We now state computational inequalities for these machines. They follow as a direct application of Theorem 4.5.1 and were first derived by Savage (1972).

Theorem 7.2.1.1.   Let $f : \{0, 1\}^n \to \{0, 1\}^m$ be computed by each of the four machines described above and let T_{CPU}, T_{RAM}, T_{TAM}, T_{DRUM}, and T_{CAM} be the maximum numbers of cycles (maximized over all points in the domain of f) executed by the component sequential machines. Then the following relations must hold where combinational complexity is measured with respect to $\Omega = P_{1,2}^{(2)}$:

$$M_{RAM}: \quad C_\Omega(f) \leq (C_{CPU} + 5m)T_{CPU} + \left(5S\left(1 + \frac{1}{b}\right) + 2(b-1)\right)T_{RAM}$$

$$M_{TAM}: \quad C_\Omega(f) \leq (C_{CPU} + 5m)T_{CPU}$$

$$+ \left(5S\left(1 + \frac{1}{b}\right) + 5b + 23(\log_2 M) - 1\right)T_{TAM}$$

$$M_{DRUM}: \quad C_\Omega(f) \leq (C_{CPU} + 5m)T_{CPU}$$

$$+ \left(5\frac{S}{K}\left(1 + \frac{1}{b}\right) + 5b + 3(\log_2 L) + 7(\log_2 K) + 2\right)T_{DRUM}$$

$$M_{CAM}: \quad C_\Omega(f) \leq (C_{CPU} + 5m)T_{CPU} + \left(5S\left(1 + \frac{(2r)}{5b}\right) + 2b\right)T_{CAM}$$

$$M_{DUAL}: \quad C_\Omega(f) \leq (C_{CPU} + 5m)T_{CPU} + \left(5S_1\left(1 + \frac{1}{b}\right) + 2(b-1)\right)T_{RAM}$$

$$+ \left(5\frac{S_2}{K}\left(1 + \frac{1}{b}\right) + 5b + 3(\log_2 L) + 7(\log_2 K) + 2\right)T_{DRUM}$$

Here S is the storage capacity in bits on each of the first four machines, and S_1 and S_2 are the capacities of the RAM and DRUM, respectively, in the fifth machine. Also, $C_{CPU} = C_\Omega(\delta_{CPU})$ since it is assumed that λ_{CPU} is a projection operator of zero combinational complexity.

These inequalities are examined closely in Section 7.4 for the implications that they hold for efficient computation on general-purpose computers. Some appreciation for them here can be had by letting $T_{CPU} = T_{RAM} = T$ in the first inequality for a GPC with one CPU and one RAM. This is a reasonable assumption which, for $b \cong 16$, say, implies that f can be computed with storage capacity S in T cycles only if

$$C_\Omega(f) \lesssim (C_{CPU} + 5m + 5S)T$$

If S is large by comparison to m and C_{CPU}, which is often true, then

$$C_\Omega(f) \lesssim 5ST$$

Thus, if there are several programs on the GPC that compute f with various values of S and T, they must all satisfy this inequality. Furthermore, complex functions require a large space–time product. What is striking about this inequality is that *it relates parameters, S, T, of programs* (of an *unrestricted* nature) *to the length of the shortest-length straight-line program for the function that is to be computed.*

The second inequality applies to a machine with tape storage. The composite machine is close to but a bit different from a 1-tape Turing machine because our model assumes that the position of the head is available as an output of the TAM. Despite this difference, our procedure readily yields an upper bound of approximately

$$C_\Omega(f) \lesssim (C_{CPU} + 5S)T$$

for multitape Turing machines. It is conventional to assume that the heads on each tape of a multitape Turing machine have prechosen initial positions at the start of every computation. Using this fact and the special structure of the storage medium; we derive a computational inequality in Section 5.8 that improves on that given in the preceding. It has the form

$$C_\Omega(f) \le (C_{CONT} + Kp \log_2 S)T$$

Here $K > 0$ is a constant, p is the number of tapes, and C_{CONT} is the combinational complexity of the transition and output function of the Control.

Synchronous combinational complexity, defined in Section 3.5, is a measure of the number of logic elements and unit delay elements in a logic circuit in which delay elements have been introduced so that signals applied simultaneously at the input arrive simultaneously at each logic element and at the output. Thus, the logic circuit is synchronous. The synchronous combinational complexity of $f : \{0, 1\}^n \to \{0, 1\}^m$ over the basis Ω, $C_\Omega^s(f)$ is the minimum number of logic and delay elements in synchronous logic circuits for f.

Computational inequalities can also be derived by using synchronous combinational complexity, as we now demonstrate for M_{RAM}. To do so, we upper bound $C_\Omega^s(\delta_{\text{RAM}})$ and then unwind the sequential machine consisting of CPU and RAM, as indicated in Sections 4.4 and 4.5. In Figure 6.2.2.1 we show a portion of a circuit that realizes δ_{RAM}; shown is the depth of a circuit for the binary to positional transformer $f_T^{(m)}$. The reader can readily verify by reference to that figure that

$$ C_\Omega^s (\delta_{\text{RAM}}) \leq KS \log_2\!\left(\frac{S}{b} \right) $$

for some constant $K > 0$ where $\Omega = P_{1,2}^{(2)}$. When S is large, it follows that to compute f on M_{RAM} requires that the following computational inequality be satisfied:

$$ C_\Omega^s (f) \leq K'ST \log_2\!\left(\frac{S}{b} \right) $$

Here $K' > 0$ is a constant. This implies that ST is large when $C_\Omega^s(f)$ is large. From the previously derived inequality, which uses combinational complexity, a similar conclusion follows. Thus, standard combinational complexity and synchronous combinational complexity are both useful in deriving lower bounds on space–time tradeoffs.

7.3. COMPUTATIONAL INEQUALITIES OF THE SECOND KIND

The inequalities derived in the preceding section involve two simple ideas, simulation and measurement of the complexity of the simulating program. The programs that are used are straight-line, and their complexity is measured with combinational complexity, the number of computation steps. As indicated in Section 4.5, a different set of inequalities results when delay complexity is chosen as the measure of the complexity of straight-line programs.

In this section, we continue the derivation of computational inequalities by using a "universal" language for programs and using the total length of the program as the complexity measure. The inequalities again relate the complexity of a function f [this time the measure is called *program complexity*, $I_U(f)$] to parameters of computation. For example, if f is computed in T cycles on a GPC with one CPU and one RAM of storage capacity S bits, then

$$I_U(f) \lesssim 2(S + Tb)$$

where b is the size in bits of input words to the CPU. This should be contrasted with the inequality

$$C_\Omega(f) \lesssim 5ST$$

which we derived. The dependence on space and time is quite different, and the new inequality dominates the earlier one for all values of S and T except small S or large T, or vice versa, when $(I_U(f))^2 \gg C_\Omega(f)$. This point is discussed in the next section, but we observe here that this condition is satisfied by many functions of interest.

The derivation of computational inequalities of the second kind is patterned after that for those of the first kind. Given a sequential machine S that executes a maximum of T cycles, we associate with it a descriptor function $G_{S,T}: S \times I^T \to O^{T+1}$ which maps the initial state and T inputs onto $T + 1$ outputs. Descriptor functions can also be associated with collections of interconnected sequential machines. The machines with which we are concerned are the five defined Section 7.2.

A collection of machines is used to compute a function $f : \{0, 1\}^n \to \{0, 1\}^m$. Thus, inputs and the initial states of these machines must be specified by what is called a *program* in Section 7.1. One machine in the collection (the CPU in the five general-purpose computers) produces a set of external outputs in which is imbedded the value of f. We have adopted the output convention which identifies certain output words as valid words, and we are asssuming that the concatenation of valid words forms the value of f.

The equalities of the second kind are derived with respect to some 1-tape universal Turing machine U (see Section 5.4). If G is the descriptor of an interconnected set of sequential machines and F is the mapping defined by the inputs and outputs of the set when it is programmed to compute f, then F is a restriction of G. By Theorem 5.7.3, the *program complexity* of F with respect to U, $I_U(F)$, satisfies

$$I_U(F) \leq I_U(G)$$

However, f is easily computed from F by deleting all but the valid output words and concatenating the results. If the value of F (which is a set of

T_{CPU} b-bit words) is represented by a string

$$\$v_1\$v_2\$ \cdots \$v_{T_{CPU}}\$$$

where v_i is a binary b-tuple, then the reader can readily construct (see Problem (7-2) a Turing machine of fairly small size that deletes $'s and all binary digits except the last b-1 in (valid) words whose first bit is 1. These are the ideas used to derive computational inequalities of the second kind.

Consider the five general-purpose computers defined in Section 7.2. Each has one CPU, and for concreteness we let it be of the type discussed in Section 6.4 except that certain obvious but simple extensions are allowed. The CPU of that section has five (5) b-bit registers, three (3) address registers of $\log_2 M$ bits apiece, one (1) $\lceil \log_2 b \rceil$–bit counter which counts down from $N = b - 1$, and one (1) 1-bit I/O status register. We modify that CPU so that external outputs are generated during each computation cycle. One way to do this is to add a b-bit *output buffer* OBFR and a *status flip-flop* SFF. We would also add microinstructions to permit transfers to OBFR and SFF. If a valid word is to be generated in a given cycle, the word is transferred to the output buffer and the status flip-flop is set to 1. The Control is redesigned so that, at the start of every cycle, SFF is set to 0 to prevent an output word from being interpreted as a valid word more than once. Other modifications that could be made to the CPU include the following:

(a) The addition of a finite number of b-bit registers.
(b) The addition of a finite number of I/O ports.
(c) The addition of output status signals indicating the internal state of the CPU.
(d) The modification of the Control to permit interrupts to be processed at the end of every execution cycle.
(e) Inclusion of multiplication hardware and floating-point arithmetic hardware.

The b-bit registers mentioned in (a) can serve many functions. For example, they can hold subroutine return addresses (resulting in a modification of the JMS instruction), they can hold indices to facilitate the accessing of arrays, and in groups of one or more, they can serve as I/O address registers. In the later case they would grant access to a very large number of externally stored words. Modification (b) may be desirable in a GPC that has more than one I/O device.

Suppose that a CPU, modified as indicated above, is to be simulated by a Turing machine. We claim that a 1-tape Turing machine M_{CPU} with a control of fixed size can be constructed that simulates the CPU and uses a number of tape squares linear in $b + \log_2 M$. We sketch the construction of such a machine for the CPU of Section 6.4 modified as indicated in the preceding to permit output.

On the tape of M_{CPU} we reserve space for the six (6) b-bit registers MDR, IR, AC, MQ, I/OBFR, and OBFR; the three (3) $(\log_2 M)$–bit registers MAR, LOC CTR, and I/O AR; the $\lceil \log_2 b \rceil$–bit CTR; the 1-bit FI/O register; and the 1-bit SFF register. The Control of M_{CPU} in one "cycle" examines IR and carries out a sequence of microinstructions that may include a fetch or store from the main memory (shown as a RAM in Figure 6.4.1.1). When a fetch or store is required, we assume that magic genie is available to execute the command. Later we sketch the construction of a complete Turing machine to simulate a GPC, and the magic genie is then replaced by a transfer to the appropriate submachine.

If REG is the name of a register, let **REG** be contents of that register in binary. Let the twelve registers be separated on the tape of M_{CPU} with 12 markers $M_i = B2^iB$ where 2^i denotes the i-fold repetition of $\cdot 2$ and $1 \leq i \leq 12$. For concreteness, let the registers be arranged in the following order:

$$s_{CPU} = \text{CTR } 2M_1 \text{ LOC CTR } 2M_2 \text{ IR } 2M_3 \text{ AC } 2M_4 \text{ MQ } 2M_5 \text{ MAR } 2M_6$$

$$\text{MDR } 2M_7 \text{I/OAR } 2M_8 \text{ I/OBFR } 2M_9 \text{ FI/O } 2M_{10} \text{ OBFR } 2M_{11} \text{ SFF } 2M_{12}$$

The leftmost 2 in $2M_i$ is used to mark a position in a word, and it is moved about within that word to the left of M_i. This is useful in exectuting the register-to-register transfer operations of Table 6.4.1.1. For example, to transfer the address part **AP** or **IR** to **LOC CTR**, which is microinstruction T11, M_3 is found by moving the head right until three (3) 2's are encountered with B's on either side. Then the rightmost bit of IR is recorded in the Control; interchanged with the adjacent 2, and the head is moved left until M_2 is found. The digit to the left of the 2 in the section of the tape bordered by M_1 and M_2 is replaced by the digit found in **IR** and this digit and the 2 on its right are interchanged. The Control cycles between **LOC CTR** and **IR** until the character to the left of 2 in the section between M_1 and M_2 is B. This indicates that the transfer of **AP** to **LOC CTR** is complete and the 2's are returned to their original positions. It should be clear that each of the register-to-register transfer operations can be carried out (if in a clumsy manner) by a Control that does *not* know the sizes of the various registers.

The microinstructions of our CPU are divided into four categories. They are the transfer operations described above, arithmetical and logical operations (Table 6.4.1.2), register operations (Table 6.4.1.3), and branching instructions (Table 6.4.1.4). The reader should have no trouble convincing him or herself that each of these instructions, except possibly $N \to \text{CTR}$, can be executed by a Control that has no knowledge of b or of $\log_2 M$. The instruction C7, namely $N \rightarrow \text{CTR}$ where $N = b - 1$, also can be executed without explicit knowledge of b in the Control if $b = 2^l$ because $b - 1$ is represented in binary by a string of l 1's and l is specified by the separation between characters on the tape. We assume that b is a power of 2. If it is not, the value of b could be recorded on another portion of the tape.

The machine M_{CPU} whose construction has been sketched has a tape alphabet $\Sigma = \{0, 1, 2, B\}$ and makes use of $6b + 3\log_2 M + \log_2 b + 114$ tape squares. If the CPU is modified in any of the ways indicated above, the number of tape squares used will again be linear in $b + \log_2 M$.

Now consider the first machine defined in Section 7.2. It has a RAM and a CPU. We sketch the construction of a 1-tape (basic) Turing machine $M^{(1)}$ that simulates a maximum of T_{CPU} cycles of the CPU of this GPC. Machine $M^{(1)}$ is given the initial state and the T_{CPU} inputs given to the GPC, and at the completion of the computation it leaves the tape blank except for a binary string that is the concatenation of the valid words in the output. This string is placed left-adjusted on the semiinfinite tape. Thus, if $M^{(1)}$ is initialized with a program for f, the value of f will remain on the tape of $M^{(1)}$ at the completion of the computation. That is, $M^{(1)}$ can be used to compute f. We write a program for $M^{(1)}$ on U, which includes the initial string on the tape of $M^{(1)}$. With suitable initialization, this is a program for f and its length is greater than or equal to $I_U(f)$, which gives us the type of inequality we want.

On the tape of $M^{(1)}$ place the string s_{CPU} followed to the right by the strings s_{RAM} and s_{IN}:

$$s_{\text{RAM}} = s M_{13} a 2 M_{14} \omega^* 2 M_{15} t 2 M_{16} 2 \omega_0 \omega_1 \cdots \omega_{M-1} M_{17}$$

$$s_{\text{IN}} = 2 u_1 u_2 \cdots u_{T_{\text{CPU}}} M_{18}$$

Here (s, a, ω^*) is the input triple to a RAM where $s \in \{0, 1\}^2$, $a \in \{0, 1\}^{\log_2 M}$, and $\omega^* \in \{0, 1\}^b$. Also, $\omega_0, \omega_1, \ldots, \omega_{M-1}$ are in $\{0, 1\}^b$ and $t \in \{0, 1\}^{\log_2 b}$ is initialized at 0 and used to measure the size of binary b-tuples. And s_{IN} contains the inputs $u_1, u_2, \ldots, u_{T_{\text{CPU}}}$, where $u_i \in \{0, 1\}^b$.

With $s_{\text{CPU}} s_{\text{RAM}} s_{\text{IN}}$ left-adjusted on its otherwise blank tape, $M^{(1)}$ simulates the GPC in question as follows:

1. It enters the initial state of M_{CPU} with the head located over the leftmost square.
2. The OP CODE part of IR (which is a fixed number of bits independent of b and $\log_2 M$) is examined, and a sequence of microinstructions is carried out on the registers of the CPU.
3. If a microprogram has a memory access, the command, s, address a,

and word ω^* (if a store operation is required) are transferred to the region between M_{12} and M_{15}.

4. $M^{(1)}$ then enters the first state of a submachine M_{RAM} which moves the 2 following M_{16} right until it is to the immediate right of $\omega_{|a|}$, the word that is to be accessed. The space reserved by **t** is used to count in units of b, and by counting down from $|a|$ using **a**, the 2 can be so positioned.

5. If the command is a "fetch," $\omega_{|a|}$ is transferred to **MDR**, while if a "store," ω^* is transferred to $\omega_{|a|}$. The 2 in the section bordered by M_{16} and M_{17} is then returned to its initial position.

6. After the execution of each instruction, the 2 following M_{17} in s_{IN} is moved right b places so that it is to the immediate left of the input which could be read in the next cycle. The space reserved by **t** is used to count to b.

7. If an input is required, the b-bit word to the immediate right of the 2 between M_{17} and M_{18} is transferred to **I/OBFR**.

8. If the 2 between M_{17} and M_{18} has a B to its immediate right, T_{CPU} cycles have been executed and $M^{(1)}$ enters a "cleanup state."

9. If the CPU generates a valid output word, that word is placed to the immediate right of the rightmost nonblank symbol to the right of M_{18}.

10. If the CPU enters a halt state, either because it is instructed to do so or because T_{CPU} cycles have been completed, let $M^{(1)}$ enter a cleanup state in which M_{18} and all characters to its left are replaced by B (blank) and the remaining binary digits (the concatenation of valid words) are left-adjusted on the otherwise blank tape.

The purpose of this lengthy development is to demonstrate that a Turing machine $M^{(1)}$ can be constructed that has a Control whose size is independent of b and $\log_2 M$ and that can simulate a simple GPC with one CPU and one RAM. Such a lengthy development is not attempted for the remaining four GPCs.

The machine $M^{(1)}$ has a finite Control, and its initial nonblank tape string $s^{(1)} = s_{CPU}s_{RAM}s_{IN}$ has length $l(s^{(1)})$ where

$$l(s_{CPU}) = 6b + 3 \log_2 M + \log_2 b + 114$$

$$l(s_{RAM}) = Mb + b + \log_2(Mb) + 91$$

$$l(s_{IN}) = T_{CPU}b + 21$$

and

$$l(s^{(1)}) = S + T_{CPU}b + 7b + 4 \log_2 S + 226$$

Here $S = Mb$ is the storage capacity in bits of the RAM and $T_{CPU}\,b$ is the maximum amount of input, in bits, that the CPU can receive. The reader can verify that the effect on $l(s^{(1)})$ of any of the modifications of the CPU permitted in the preceding is to change the coefficients of the terms b and $\log_2 S$ and to change the additive constant. Thus, no significant change in the size of $s^{(1)}$ results unless M and/or T_{CPU} is small.

We can now state the first major result of this section.

Theorem 7.3.1. Let U be a universal Turing machine of the type described in Section 5.4. Let $f : \{0, 1\}^n \to \{0, 1\}^m$ be computed by the GPC M_{RAM} consisting of a CPU and a RAM, as described above. Then the program complexity of f relative to U, $I_U(f)$, must satisfy the inequality

$$M_{RAM}: \qquad I_U(f) \le 2(S + T_{CPU}b) + \alpha_{11}(b + \log_2 S) + \alpha_{12}$$

where $\alpha_{11}, \alpha_{12} \ge 0$ are constants. Here S is the storage capacity of the RAM in bits and T_{CPU} is the maximum number of cycles executed by the CPU of the GPC to compute f.

Proof. $M^{(1)}$ computes f when $s^{(1)}$ is initialized with a program for f. The tape alphabet of $M^{(1)}$ is quaternary whereas the universal machines of Section 5.4 simulate only machines with binary tape alphabets. We translate $M^{(1)}$ into a binary machine, in the obvious manner, and $s^{(1)}$ maps into a string of twice the length. The rest follows from the nature of the universal machine and our bound to $l(s^{(1)})$.   ☐

This is the result we have been expecting. We now outline similar results for the four other GPCs on our list. Let $M^{(i)}$, $2 \le i \le 5$, be 1-tape Turing machines that simulate the GPCs M_{TAM}, M_{DRUM}, M_{CAM}, and M_{DUAL}. Let $s^{(i)}$, $2 \le i \le 5$, be the strings with which we initialize $M^{(i)}$ to simulate each. Then, following the preceding development, we can write

$$s^{(2)} = s_{CPU}\, s_{TAM}\, s_{IN}$$

$$s^{(3)} = s_{CPU}\, s_{DRUM}\, s_{IN}$$

$$s^{(4)} = s_{CPU}\, s_{CAM}\, s_{IN}$$

$$s^{(5)} = s_{CPU}\, s_{RAM}\, s_{DRUM}\, s_{IN}$$

As we have seen, the inequalities are determined principally by the lengths of these strings. The markers in the strings s_{IN} that suffix each $s^{(i)}$ may vary and cause $l(s_{IN})$ to vary by a constant amount. We concentrate on the lengths of s_{TAM}, s_{DRUM}, and s_{CAM}.

The (M, b) tape memory (TAM) is described in Section 6.2.3, and the data it needs to function consist of M b-bit words $\omega_0, \omega_1, \ldots, \omega_{M-1}$, a

$\log_2 M$-bit head position vector **p**, and the $(2 + \log_2 M + b)$-bit input **s**, **a**, ω^*. From this information, it computes its status β and the output word ω_M. Thus, $l(\mathbf{s}_{\text{TAM}}) = S + b + 2 \log_2 M + \alpha$ for $\alpha \geq 0$, a constant, where $S = MB$ is the storage capacity of the TAM.

The (K, L, b) drum memory (DRUM) is described in Section 6.2.4, and the data it needs to function consist of $K(Lb)$-bit words $\mathbf{W}_0, \mathbf{W}_1, \ldots, \mathbf{W}_{K-1}$, the $\log_2 K$–bit head position **p**, and the $(2 + \log_2 L + \log_2 K + b)$–bit input **s**, $\mathbf{a}_1$, $\mathbf{a}_2$, ω^*. It follows that $l(\mathbf{s}_{\text{DRUM}}) = S + b + \log_2 L + 2 \log_2 K + \alpha$ where $\alpha \geq 0$ is a constant and $S = KLb$ is the storage capacity of the DRUM.

Similarly, the (M, b, r) content-addressable memory (CAM) with $r \leq b$ is described in Section 6.2.5, and the data it needs to function consist of M b-bit words $\omega_0, \omega_1, \ldots, \omega_{M-1}$ and a $(2 + r + b)$–bit input(**s**, **c**, ω^*). Thus, $l(\mathbf{s}_{\text{CAM}}) = S + b + r + \alpha$ where $\alpha \geq 0$ is a constant and $S = Mb$ is the storage capacity of the CAM.

We are now in a position to state computational inequalities of the second kind for the four other machines of Section 7.2.

Theorem 7.3.2. Let U be a universal machine of the type described in Section 5.4. Let $f : \{0, 1\}^n \to \{0, 1\}^m$ be a function with program complexity $I_U(f)$. Let f be computed by M_{TAM}, M_{DRUM}, M_{CAM}, or M_{DUAL} of Section 7.2. Then the following inequalities must be satisfied:

M_{TAM}: $I_U(f) \leq 2(S + T_{\text{CPU}}b) + \alpha_{21}(b + \log_2 S) + \alpha_{22}$

M_{DRUM}: $I_U(f) \leq 2(S + T_{\text{CPU}}b) + \alpha_{31}(b + \log_2 S) + \alpha_{32}$

M_{CAM}: $I_U(f) \leq 2(S + T_{\text{CPU}}b) + \alpha_{41}(b + \log_2 S) + \alpha_{42}$

M_{DUAL}: $I_U(f) \leq 2(S_R + S_D + T_{\text{CPU}}b) + \alpha_{51}(b + \log_2 S_R S_D) + \alpha_{52}$

Here $\alpha_{i1}, \alpha_{i2} \geq 0$ are constants that are machine dependent. Also, S is the storage capacity in bits of the machines with one memory while S_R and S_D are the storage capacities of the RAM and DRUM of the machine M_{DUAL} which has one CPU and two memories; T_{CPU} is the number of cycles executed by the CPU of each machine.

The inequalities of the last two theorems have the following immediate interpretation: $I_U(f)$ *is the minimum amount of information that must be given to U so that it may compute f.* It is less than or equal to the righthand side of each inequality, which is approximately $2(S + T_{\text{CPU}}b)$ (S = total storage capacity) and is the actual amount of information, measured relative to U, given to a GPC so that it may compute f. Thus, these inequalities relate quantities of information. The right-hand side of each inequality is dominated by the number of variables of the descriptor function G for the corresponding GPC. When the GPC is programmed to compute f, some of these variables are assigned fixed values that are independent of the values assigned to variables of f. This demonstrates the importance of fixing on a measure of program complexity that combines the fixed and variable parts of a program.

We might ask whether we can improve on these inequalities. The answer is positive if the storage device (devices) is (are) initially empty (say filled with 0's) or if the CPU is physically incapable of accepting inputs in every cycle. In the first case, it is unnecessary to specify each of the initial words of the device (devices) because a more compact description is possible whose length is proportional to $\log_2 S$. (We need only state the size of the memory.) A similar argument applies to the input. However, if no restrictions as to the initial state of the memory (memories) are specified and if inputs can be received and acted on by the CPU in every cycle, then, at least in principle, the outputs from the GPC can depend on all T_{CPU} inputs and all S bits initially in memory; that is, the descriptor G depends on all $S + T_{CPU}b$ of its binary variables. By Theorem 5.7.4, $I_U(G) \geq S + T_{CPU}b$, indicating that no substantial improvement in any of the inequalities is possible in general.

This completes our derivation of computational inequalities of the second kind. These inequalities are presented in Savage (1973). We now turn to the application and interpretation of the two types of inequality.

7.4. LIMITS ON THE PERFORMANCE OF COMPUTERS

The computational inequalities of the preceding sections can be viewed in two significantly different ways. On the one hand, they provide upper bounds to the complexities of functions in terms of parameters of computation, while, on the other, they define lower limits on possible tradeoffs between these parameters. It is the latter view that prevails in this section since it is our purpose to develop the type of information that is relevant to the efficient use of computers.

We begin the section with a review of the computational inequalities and the conditions under which they apply. We then limit our attention to M_{RAM}, M_{CAM}, and M_{DUAL} and demonstrate that the lower limits on space–time tradeoffs the inequalities define can be approached for functions that are very complex and for some that are simple. Then, working with various cost measures, including the space–time product, and assuming that the lower limits can be approached, we exhibit those operating points of M_{RAM} and M_{CAM}, that is, values of space and time, at which the cost of computing is minimized. This provides us with an opportunity to introduce the definition of the "computing power" of a machine and to discuss the importance of balancing the computational load in a computing system. Finally, we examine our observations and conclusions when the general-purpose computer is M_{DUAL}, a machine with a main and a peripheral memory.

7.4.1. Summary of Computational Inequalities

Five different general-purpose computers are described in Section 7.2: M_{RAM}, M_{TAM}, M_{DRUM}, M_{CAM}, and M_{DUAL}. Each has one CPU, and the first four have one memory, of the type indicated by the subscripts. The fifth GPC has two memories, a RAM and a DRUM. The CPU is taken to be that of Section 6.4, modified as suggested in Section 7.3. Because M_{RAM}, M_{CAM}, and M_{DUAL} are the three most realistic models of GPCs, we limit our discussion here to them.

The computational inequalities of the first and second kind are derived for these three machines in Sections 7.2 and 7.3. In these sections we do not explicitly state a relationship between the number of cycles executed by the CPU and that executed by the memories. However, it is reasonable to assert that $T_{RAM} = T_{CPU}$ for M_{RAM}, and $T_{CAM} = T_{CPU}$ for M_{CAM}. On M_{DUAL}, we assume that a DRUM access produces a block of K words consisting of one full track (called a *page*) of the DRUM. We also assume that the start of a block is randomly placed on a track relative to the time that an access is made. This means that on the average $K/2$ cycles are necessary to locate the start of a page, and K additional cycles are needed to read a page. If there are maximum of η accesses during the computation of f, then $T_{DRUM} = \eta(3K/2)$. Let the CPU be involved as a channel for transfer of data from the DRUM to the RAM. Then T_{CPU} consists of two parts, the time (in cycles) it acts as a channel, $4\eta K$ (we have assumed that $\tau_{DRUM} = 4\tau_{RAM}$,) and the time it spends accessing the RAM, exclusive of the role it plays as a channel, $T_{RAM} - 4\eta K$. Therefore, $T_{CPU} = T_{RAM} - 4\eta K + 4\eta K = T_{RAM}$ and $T_{RAM} \geq 4\eta K$.

We summarize these constraints as follows:

$$M_{RAM}: \quad T = T_{CPU} = T_{RAM}$$

$$M_{CAM}: \quad T = T_{CPU} = T_{CAM}$$

$$M_{DUAL}: \quad T = T_{CPU} = T_{RAM}, \qquad T_{DRUM} = \eta\,\frac{3K}{2}, \qquad T_{RAM} \geq 4\eta K$$

$$\eta = \#\ \text{DRUM accesses}$$

$$K = \#\ \text{words/DRUM access} = \#\ \text{words/track} = 1\ \text{page}$$

We now state the computational inequalities of the two kinds in which we absorb small terms into ε's. The inequalities are stated for functions $f : \{0, 1\}^n \rightarrow \{0, 1\}^m$ and $\Omega = p_{1,2}^{(2)}$ and a universal machine U of the type described in Section 5.4.

$$M_{\text{RAM}}: \quad C_\Omega(f) \leq (C_{\text{CPU}} + 5S(1 + \varepsilon) + 5m)T$$

$$I_U(f) \leq 2(S + Tb)(1 + \varepsilon^*) + \alpha_{\text{RAM}}$$

$$M_{\text{CAM}}: \quad C_\Omega(f) \leq (C_{\text{CPU}} + 7S(1 + \varepsilon) + 5m)T$$

$$I_U(f) \leq 2(S + Tb)(1 + \varepsilon^*) + \alpha_{\text{CAM}}$$

$$M_{\text{DUAL}}: \quad C_\Omega(f) \leq (C_{\text{CPU}} + 5S_R(1 + \varepsilon))T$$

$$+ \tfrac{15}{2}\eta S_D(1 + \varepsilon)$$

$$I_U(f) \leq 2(S_R + S_D + Tb)(1 + \varepsilon^*) + \alpha_{\text{DUAL}}$$

Here S is the storage capacity in bits of the first two machines, and S_R and S_D are storage capacities of the RAM and the DRUM, respectively, in M_{DUAL}. Also, α_{RAM}, α_{CAM}, and α_{DUAL} are nonnegative constants. We have assumed that $r \leq b$ for the CAM and $\log_2 K \ll Lb = S_D / K$, as it would be in a typical DRUM with $L = 200$ tracks, $b = 32$ bits/word, and $K = 5 \times 10^3$ words/track.

To derive these inequalities, we have assumed that the initialization of the memories and the values of the T inputs are specified by programs. A program for $f : \{0, 1\}^n \rightarrow \{0, 1\}^m$ is a string over $\{x_1, \ldots, x_n, 0, 1\}$, where $x_1, \ldots, x_n$ denote the variables of f. In the inequalities of the first kind, S is the maximum total storage capacity used to compute f, and T is the maximum total number of CPU cycles executed, where S and T are maximized over all points in the domain of f. In the inequalities of the second kind, S, S_R, S_D, and T have a different meaning. They represent the capacities and number of inputs that carry information relevant to the computation of f. To be concrete, if substantial portions of a memory are initially blank or many inputs are not explicitly used, this can be specified for U in a much more compact manner than by explicitly listing blank inputs. This could result in a considerable reduction in the right-hand side of inequalities of the second kind.

7.4.2. Space–Time Boundaries for M_{RAM} and M_{CAM}

Inequalities of the first and second kind determine lower limits on space–time tradeoffs. Observe that for M_{RAM} and M_{CAM}, their inequalities define lower limits specified by the following equations:

$$C_\Omega(f) = (\mu + \beta S)T$$

$$I^* = S + Tb$$

where

$$\mu = C_{CPU} + 5m$$

$$I^* = \frac{I_U(f) - \alpha}{2(1 + \varepsilon^*)}, \qquad \alpha \in \{\alpha_{RAM}, \alpha_{CAM}\}$$

and

$$\beta = \begin{cases} 5(1 + \varepsilon), & M_{RAM} \\ 7(1 + \varepsilon), & M_{CAM} \end{cases}$$

The boundaries defined by these equations are shown in Figure 7.4.2.1. The region of space and time below either boundary is inaccessible because f cannot be computed at such operating points.

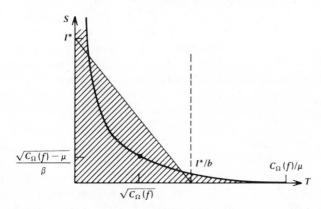

Figure 7.4.2.1. Boundaries defined by computational inequalities.

Several additional observations are in order concerning these boundaries. First, the inequality of the first kind defines a hyperbola whose asymptotes are the ordinate and a line parallel to the abscissa at $S = -(C_{CPU} + 5m)/\beta$. Second, both the hyperbolic and linear boundaries move away from the origin as the function increases in complexity. Third, the boundaries overlap as shown if the simultaneous solution of the two defining equations yields real solutions. The reader can verify that substitution of S from the second equation into the first yields the following quadratic equation in T:

$$T^2 \beta b - (\mu + \beta I^*)T + C_\Omega(f) = 0$$

The solutions to this equation are

$$T = \frac{(\mu + \beta I^*) \pm \sqrt{(\mu + \beta I^*)^2 - 4C_\Omega(f)\beta b}}{2\beta b}$$

and they are real under the following condition:

C1. $\left[C_{\text{CPU}} + 5m + \dfrac{\beta}{2(1 + \varepsilon^*)} (I_U(f) - \alpha) \right]^2 \geq 4C_\Omega(f)\beta b$

Furthermore, if the left-hand side is much larger than the right, the solutions are far apart and the overlap of the two boundaries is substantial.

Finally, note that the intercepts of the two boundaries on the abscissa are in the order shown in Figure 7.4.2.1 if the following condition holds:

C2. $C_\Omega(f)b \geq (C_{\text{CPU}} + 5m)(I_U(f) - \alpha)/2(1 + \varepsilon^*)$

In this case, the hyperbolic boundary dominates the linear boundary for large values of T. Also, if the memory is initially "blank," that is, if any useful data in the memory must be read in, then the computational inequalities of the second kind for M_{RAM} and M_{CAM} reduce to

$$T \geq \frac{I^*}{b}$$

This boundary is shown in Figure 7.4.2.1. For the hyperbolic boundary to dominate this constraint for a substantial range of values for T, the gap between the left-and right-hand sides of C2 should be large. It cannot be too large if both $C_\Omega(f)$ and $I_U(f)$ are linear in n. However, if for all $n \geq 1$, $f_n : \{0, 1\}^n \to \{0, 1\}^{m_n}$ is the restriction of $F : \{0, 1\}^* \to \{0, 1\}^*$, a total recursive function, to strings of length n, then $I_U(f_n)$ is linear in n. But there are many important recursive problems such as sorting and matrix-matrix multiplication for which the corresponding functions are thought to have combinational complexity that grows faster than linearly with n.

7.4.3. Realizable Storage–Time Tradeoffs

Having stated lower limits on storage–time tradeoffs, we now turn to the task of exhibiting algorithms that come close to achieving these lower limits. We use formulas or circuits of fan-out 1 to show that a constant $K > 0$ exists for an M_{RAM} such that all $f : \{0, 1\}^n \rightarrow \{0, 1\}^m$ can be computed at many values of S and T that all satisfy

$$S + Tb \leq KL_\Omega(f)\log_2 \log_2 L_\Omega(f)$$

where $L_\Omega(f)$ is the formula size of f. For many simple functions and for the very complex functions, this result indicates that we can come very close to achieving the inequality of the second kind for M_{RAM} (and M_{DUAL} when the DRUM is not used).

The development of our upper bounds to space–time tradeoffs proceeds as follows:

1. We compute a Boolean function from a formula over $P_{1,2}^{(2)}$ using a traversal of the corresponding binary tree (see Section 5.7).
2. We demonstrate that the number of auxiliary storage locations needed for such an evaluation is at most $\lceil \log_2(N + 1) \rceil$ if the binary tree has N internal nodes.
3. We demonstrate that $f : \{0, 1\}^n \rightarrow \{0, 1\}^m$ can be computed on M_{RAM} from formulas by dividing the computation into two pieces: the computation of subformulas from storage, and the simultaneous computation of the rest of the formulas from the input to the CPU.

We begin by deriving the bound of 2.

Consider the function $f : \{0, 1\}^n \rightarrow \{0, 1\}$ whose fan-out 1 circuit is shown in Figure 7.4.3.1. Here f is associated with node d. Suppose that this function is to be computed by a GPC that has one data register (an

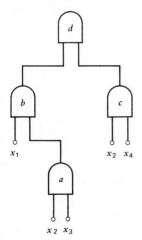

Figure 7.4.3.1. A fan-out 1 circuit.

accumulator, say). We compute f by computing the values of the functions associated with nodes a, b, c, d, in that order. Read x_2 into storage location $L1$; read x_3 into the data register; read an instruction which commands that the function associated with node a be computed on the entry in $L1$ and the entry in the data register; store the result in $L1$; read x_1 into the data register; compute b on the contents of $L1$ and the data register; store in $L1$; read x_2 into location $L2$; read x_4 into the data register; compute c on $L2$ and the data register; store the result in the data register; compute d on $L1$ and the data register; store the result in the data register.

The set of steps described above can be described in a simple language that has the following types of instructions:

1. Storage instruction: $[00; x; L]$ − "Store x at location L."
   Here $x \in \{0, 1\}$ is a variable and, L is a memory address where $L = 0$ denotes the data register.
2. Transfer instruction: $[01; L]$ − "Transfer data register to Location L."
   Here L is a memory address, $L > 1$.
3. Computational instruction: $[10; OP; L]$ − "Compute OP on contents of L and data register."
   Here OP denotes a Boolean function in $P_{1,2}^{(2)}$ and takes the contents of L as its left argument and the contents of the data register as its right argument.

Certainly, a simple CPU could be devised to execute a sequence of such instructions. The instructions could be fetched in sequence from a memory such as a RAM or a CAM (by augmenting the length of words) or they could be provided to the external input of a CPU. A sequence of such instructions is called "straight-line code" because no branching or looping is done.

It is obvious that if f has a fan-out 1 circuit consisting of one computation node, then at most one auxiliary storage location is necessary in a machine with one data register. (If the instructions for f are in a memory, memory locations can be reused, whereas if the instructions arrive as external inputs, one new location is necessary.) We have the basis for a proof by induction of the fact that at most $\lceil \log_2(N + 1) \rceil$ auxiliary locations are necessary to compute a Boolean function that has N computation nodes in its fan-out 1 circuit. We assume that this statement is true for $N \leq k - 1$ and show that it is true for $N = k$.

Let a fan-out 1 circuit for f be as shown in Figure 7.4.3.2 where the left subtree has n_1 nodes, the right subtree has n_2 nodes, and $n_1 + n_2 + 1 = k$. We can compute f by computing g, the function associated with the left subtree and then h and combining the result, or vice versa, so without loss of generality, assume that $n_2 \leq n_1$. Then compute f by computing g, using

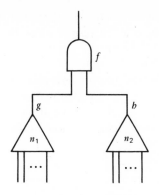

Figure 7.4.3.2. Schematic drawing of a tree for f.

at most $\lceil \log_2(n_1 + 1) \rceil$ auxiliary locations, holding g in one location, and then computing h using at most $\lceil \log_2(n_2 + 1) \rceil$ additional auxiliary locations. The number of auxiliary locations is at most

$$\max(\lceil \log_2(n_1 + 1) \rceil, 1 + \lceil \log_2(n_2 + 1) \rceil)$$

Since $n_1 + n_2 + 1 = k$ and $0 \leq n_2 \leq n_1$, we have

$$n_1 + 1 \leq k$$

$$n_2 + 1 \leq \frac{k + 1}{2} \quad \text{and} \quad \log_2(n_2 + 1) \leq \lceil \log_2(k + 1) \rceil - 1$$

Consequently, the maximum of these two quantities is at most $\lceil \log_2(k + 1) \rceil$, which is the desired conclusion.

Returning to programs for Boolean functions $f : \{0, 1\}^n \to \{0, 1\}$, observe that one instruction is required for each occurrence of a variable, and either one or two instructions for each computation node, depending on whether the result can be left in the data register or not. Thus, if a Boolean function has a fan-out 1 circuit with N computation nodes and $N + 1$ source nodes, then between $2N + 1$ and $3N + 1$ instructions are needed to compute it in the language sketched. Each of these instructions may carry an address of one of the at most $\lceil \log_2(N + 1) \rceil$ auxiliary locations. Thus, for some $\alpha, \beta \geq 0$, the length of each instruction in bits is bounded above by $\alpha \lceil \log_2 \lceil \log_2(N + 1) \rceil \rceil + \beta$.

Given a function $f : \{0, 1\}^n \to \{0, 1\}$, we could store the program in a RAM and execute it using the program locations as auxiliary locations. This method uses large storage and large time. Alternately, we could read the program from an external source (which serves as a source of pure input) and use at most $\lceil \log_2(N + 1) \rceil$ 1-bit storage locations in an RAM.

This method uses small storage and large time and is a fairly good method because it has ST proportional to $N \log N$ and $S + Tb$ proportional to $N \log \log N$ where we can take N to be $L_\Omega(f)$. There are many intermediate solutions, however, as we now demonstrate.

In a tree for $f : \{0, 1\}^n \to \{0, 1\}$ over $\Omega = P_{1,2}^{(2)}$, find the smallest subtree of at least k computation nodes. Let h be the function associated with this subtree. Then, since the left and right subtrees of this subtree have at most $k - 1$ nodes, the subtree associated with h has N_h computation nodes where

$$k \leq N_h \leq 2k - 1$$

Let $f^* : \{0, 1\}^{n+1} \to \{0, 1\}$ be the Boolean function that results from f by replacing h by the new variable x_{n+1}. Then we can write

$$f(x_1, \ldots, x_n) = f^*(x_1, \ldots, x_n, h)$$

which suggests that f can be computed by computing h, $f^*(x_1, \ldots, 0)$, and $f^*(x_1, \ldots, 1)$ in parallel and choosing one of the latter two values as the value of f, as determined by the value of h. This is exactly the procedure we follow, and it allows for a favorable tradeoff between space and time.

To compute $f^*(x_1, \ldots, 0)$ and $f^*(x_1, \ldots, 1)$, modify the instructions so that each operation and each variable (especially x_{n+1}) of f^* can have two values. Then the data register and each auxiliary location hold two bits, and an operator acts on the first bit of the data register and of an auxiliary location to produce one result and on the second bits to produce a second result. The effect on the number of bits in an instruction is minuscule while the number of instructions is unchanged.

Consider next a collection of Boolean functions denoted $f : \{0, 1\}^n \to \{0, 1\}^m$. Its fan-out 1 circuit consists of m trees. Let them have $N_1, N_2, \ldots, N_m$ computation nodes, respectively, and order them according to these numbers so that $N_1 \leq N_2 \leq \cdots \leq N_m$. Let $N = N_1 + \cdots + N_m$ be the total number of computation nodes in all trees. Given $k \geq 0$, choose the largest l such that $N_1 + \cdots + N_l < k$ and then choose the smallest subtree from the next tree so that $N_1 + \cdots + N_l$ plus the number of computation nodes in this subtree is $\geq k$. Let this total be N^*. From a preceding argument, we know that

$$k \leq N^* \leq 2k - 1$$

Let g be the function associated with the $(l + 1)$st tree and let h be the function associated with its selected subtree. Also, let g^* be the function obtained from g by replacing h by a new variable.

We now sketch the construction of a program for $f : \{0, 1\}^n \to \{0, 1\}^m$ that can be run on an M_{RAM} with a suitable simple CPU. Construct programs for the first l Boolean functions of f as well as for the subfunction h of the $(l + 1)$st Boolean function. Read these programs into the external input of the CPU and execute instructions as they arrive. Introduce special instructions that specify certain words in the data register as output words and that allow the value of h to select from $g^*(x_1, \ldots, 0)$ and $g^*(x_1, \ldots, 1)$. Store programs for g^* and the remaining functions in an RAM. Assume that the CPU has two data registers so that it can execute two program sequences simultaneously, the one supplied externally and the one stored in the RAM.

The number of cycles, T^*, spent executing the first l trees and the subtree of the $(l + 1)$st satisfies

$$\sum_{j=1}^{l} (2N_j + 1) + 2\left(N^* - \sum_{j=1}^{l} N_j\right) + 1$$

$$\leq T^* \leq \sum_{j=1}^{l} (3N_j + 1) + 3\left(N^* - \sum_{j=1}^{l} N_j\right) + 1$$

$$2N^* + l + 1 \leq T^* \leq 3N^* + l + 1$$

while the number of cycles, T^{**}, spent executing the rest of the circuit for f satisfies

$$\sum_{j=l+2}^{m} (2N_j + 1) + 2\left(\left(\sum_{j=1}^{l+1} N_j\right) - N^*\right) + 1$$

$$\leq T^{**} \leq \sum_{j=l+2}^{m} (3N_j + 1) + 3\left(\left(\sum_{j=1}^{l+1} N_j\right) - N^*\right) + 1$$

$$2(N - N^*) + m - l \leq T^{**} \leq 3(N - N^*) + m - l$$

The running time T, in cycles, of the two program sequences running in parallel is the maximum of the two, that is,

$$T = \max(T^*, T^{**})$$

Let N be large by comparison to m so that we can conclude that

$$2(N - N^*) + m - l \leq T \leq 3(N - N^*) + m - l$$

when

$$N^* \leq \frac{N}{2}$$

and

$$2N^* + l + 1 \leq T \leq 3N^* + l + 1$$

when

$$N^* \geq \frac{N}{2}$$

The proposed segmentation of the computation of $f : \{0, 1\}^n \to \{0, 1\}^m$ into parallel computations uses storage capacity S (in bits) which is bounded above by

$$T^{**}\left(\alpha\lceil \log_2\lceil \log_2(N + 1)\rceil\rceil + \beta\right) + \lceil \log_2(N + 1)\rceil$$

for constants $\alpha, \beta \geq 0$ because space for the T^{**} instructions of the second half of the program must be provided as well as space for the auxiliary locations of the first half.

Consider the case of $N^* \geq N/2$. Then

$$S + Tb \leq KN \log_2 \log_2 N$$

for some constant $K > 0$ because b, the size of input words in bits, is also bounded above by $\alpha[\log_2(N + 1)] + \beta$. When $N = L_\Omega(f)$, the formula size of f, we have the following theorem.

Theorem 7.4.3.1. Let $\Omega = P_{1,2}^{(2)}$. Let $f : \{0, 1\}^n \to \{0, 1\}^m$ be such that $m \ll L_\Omega(f)$. Then there exists an M_{RAM} that satisfies the computational inequality of the second kind such that f can be computed on M_{RAM} with storage capacity S (in bits) in T cycles and input words of b bits, where

$$S + Tb \leq KL_\Omega(f) \log_2 \log_2 L_\Omega(f)$$

and $K > 0$ is a constant independent of f. For any $(N + 2)/4 \leq k \leq N$, this inequality is satisfied by a value of T in the interval

$$2k + 1 \leq T \leq 6k + m - 3$$

Proof. The upper bound to $S + Tb$ has been derived in the preceding. We note that $N^* \geq N/2$, $k \leq N^* \leq 2k - 1$, and $2N^* + l + 1 \leq T \leq 3N^* + l + 1$, from which the bounds on T follow when we note in addition that $0 \leq l \leq m - 1$. □

To further extend, that is, lower, the range of values of T for which this inequality holds, we can further divide the program sequence stored in the RAM into two pieces of equal length and further augment the CPU so that it can handle three program sequences in parallel, two stored in two RAM's and a third supplied as input. Thus, as the degree of parallelism increases, the range of validity of the upper bound to $S + Tb$ can be extended to smaller values of T. Also, such realizable space–time tradeoffs apply to any "general-purpose" CPU, with sufficient parallelism, because each instruction in our prototype language can be replaced by a finite number of instructions in some standard "general-purpose" language.

As discussed in Theorem 5.7.6, for most functions $f : \{0, 1\}^n \rightarrow \{0, 1\}^m$ with n large, $I_U(f)$ is on the order of $(m2^n)/(\log_2 n)$, while $L_\Omega(f)$ is of about the same size. Thus, for such (random) functions, the bound on $S + Tb$ has to be regarded as quite tight. On the other hand, if $L_\Omega(f)$ is linear in n, then so is $I_U(f)$ (assuming that f depends on each of its variables) and the bound is again tight. Also, in the case of simple functions, the upper bound to $S + Tb$ can often be improved to $L_\Omega(f)$ or $C_\Omega(f)$.

There are two observations we wish to make here:

1. For some functions f, $C_\Omega(f) \ll L_\Omega(f)$, although for most functions $f : \{0, 1\}^n \rightarrow \{0, 1\}^m$, $m \ll 2^n$, $C_\Omega(f) \log C_\Omega(f)$ is comparable to $L_\Omega(f)$ $\log \log L_\Omega(f)$.
2. Theorem 7.4.3.1 is derived under the assumption that instructions and data can be stored initially in the RAM at no cost.

The first observation leads us to search for another upper bound to $S + Tb$ stated in terms of combinational complexity $C_\Omega(f)$. This we undertake in the next paragraph. The second can be answered as follows:

(a) If a program is to be run many times in succession, the cost of initialization can be distributed over the many runs.
(b) In some memories, several ports are available so that data storage can be done in parallel with computation in a disjoint section of memory.
(c) An operating system may always initialize every word in a portion of memory, even if only with 0's, in which case initialization is free.

These comments suggest that initialization of memory may be feasible and/or desirable at little or no cost.

Given a chain for a function $f : \{0, 1\}^n \rightarrow \{0, 1\}^m$, a chain with no restriction on the fan-out, we can construct a set of instructions in straight-line code that would cause an M_{RAM} to compute f. Such a straight-line code is described in the proof of Theorem 5.7.5. It could be executed on an M_{RAM} with $Tb \leq KC_\Omega(f) \log_2 C_\Omega(f)$ for some constant

$K > 0$ and it could use as many as $C_\Omega(f)$ 1-bit temporary storage locations. This gives one operating point (S, T) such that

$$S + Tb \leq K^* C_\Omega(f)\log_2 C_\Omega(f)$$

As stated in the preceding, $C_\Omega(f) \log_2 C_\Omega(f)$ is on the same order of magnitude as $L_\Omega(f) \log_2 \log_2 L_\Omega(f)$ for very complex functions, but it may offer an improvement for functions of intermediate complexity.

Before we leave the subject of this section, we note that a weaker set of realizable space–time tradeoffs applies to M_{CAM} then is exhibited for M_{RAM} in Theorem 7.4.3.1. As the reader can demonstrate (Problem 7-4), the bound that applies to $S + Tb$, which follows from the construction leading to Theorem 7.4.3.1, is proportional to $L_\Omega(f) \log_2 L_\Omega(f)$. This is a consequence of the fact that M_{CAM} accesses memory by content, which requires that each word in memory contain its address as a subword. The upper bound of $KC_\Omega(f) \log_2 C_\Omega(f)$ on $S + Tb$ exhibited in the preceding paragraph for M_{RAM} also applies to M_{CAM}, however (see Problem 7-5).

This completes our presentation of methods for computing functions at operating points near those defined by our computational inequalities.

7.4.4. Computational Efficiency

In this section, we examine the implications that the computational inequalities of the first and second kind have for the efficient use of M_{RAM} and M_{CAM} when certain realistic cost measures are assumed. Our observations are relevant primarily to problems that require large space or time or both, not to small problems.

As demonstrated in the preceding section, functions $f : \{0, 1\}^n \rightarrow \{0, 1\}^m$ can be computed at values of space S and time T that lie on or inside a locus defined by

$$S + Tb = KL_\Omega(f) \log_2 \log_2 L_\Omega(f)$$

that is, a locus that is parallel to that defined by the computational inequality of the second kind, namely,

$$\frac{I_U(f) - \alpha}{2} \leq S + Tb$$

Also, in Section 7.4.2. we state a condition, namely, C1, on functions such that this inequality dominates the inequality of the first kind for some values of S and T. If $I_U(f)$ and $C_\Omega(f)$ are large, the condition for the linear inequality to dominate the hyperbolic inequality for most values of S and

T is

$$[I_U(f)]^2 \gg C_\Omega(f)b$$

This condition holds for most functions $f : \{0, 1\}^n \to \{0, 1\}^m$, that is, the "random" functions, and it applies to simple functions with many variables, that is, functions for which $I_U(f)$ is linear in n and $C_\Omega(f)$ grows less rapidly than n^2. Sorting and matrix multiplication are problems of this type (see Problem 7-6) as are many other important problems.

To illustrate the use of the computational inequalities, we make three assumptions:

A1. The computational inequalities can be achieved on M_{RAM} and M_{CAM}.
A2. The inequality of the second kind dominates that of the first kind except for S small, T large and S large, T small.
A3. The functions in question have large program and combinational complexities.

The type of analysis that we are about to do would ideally be done on the realizable $S-T$ locus for a particular problem. Such loci are difficult to discover at present, so we content ourselves with these assumptions as a basis for illustration of the methods of analysis.

Figure 7.4.4.1 shows the locus on which it is assumed that a function f can be computed. We now evaluate the cost of various operating points on this locus using several different cost measures.

As our first cost measure, we propose computational work W, which, as defined in Section 4.5, is the right-hand side of a computational inequality

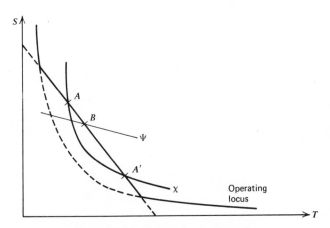

Figure 7.4.4.1. Assumed operating points.

of the first kind, as shown for M_{RAM} (see Section 7.4.1):

$$C_\Omega(f) \leq (C_{\text{CPU}} + 5S(1 + \varepsilon) + 5m)T = W$$

Here ε is assumed to be small. This cost measure could be justified as follows:

1. (a) The cost of a CPU should be proportional to the number of its logic elements, which should be a small multiple of its equivalent complexity C_{CPU}.
   (b) The cost of a RAM or CAM should be proportional to its storage capacity.
   (c) If a machine has a fixed lifetime, the cost of using it should be proportional to its cost and to the time it is used or to the product of cost and time.
2. A main memory is of central importance in a GPC, and its use could be discouraged with a user cost proportional to ST.

The first argument is applicable to many machines and the second probably is applicable to those where the first is not. In fact, there are many computer installations where a measure close to ST is a component of a user's cost. These arguments would justify any cost measure χ that is a weighting of C_{CPU} and S, multiplied by T, such as

$$\chi = (\alpha_1 C_{\text{CPU}} + \alpha_2 S)T$$

This second cost measure defines a hyperbola, as does computational work W, as discussed in Section 7.4.2.

A cost measure that defines a hyperbola is shown in Figure 7.4.4.1. The operating points A, A' on the assumed realizable locus are the points achieving the cost χ associated with the hyperbola shown. As the cost χ increases, A and A' approach each other. Thus, with a hyperbolic space–time cost measure, the operating points with minimal cost lie in the region of small space, large time, or large space, small time. When the cost measure χ is computational work W, the minimal cost operating points lie on the hyperbola defined by the inequality of the first kind.

As a second type of cost measure consider the following, which is linear in both space and time:

$$\Psi = \alpha_1 S + \alpha_2 T, \qquad \alpha_1, \alpha_2 \geq 0$$

This measure could apply to a computer facility in which the cost of computing is divided into a storage cost, which is proportional to space, and a CPU cost, which is proportional to computation time. This cost measure defines a straight line of negative slope $-\alpha_2/\alpha_1$, as shown in

Figure 7.4.4.1. Its slope could be more or less, in magnitude, than b, the slope defined by the inequality of the second kind. If $\alpha_2/\alpha_1 < b$, as shown, the cost of computing is decreased by moving the operating point B in the direction of small S and large T. The reverse is true for $\alpha_2/\alpha_1 > b$.

We conclude that under the assumptions A1, A2, and A3 and either linear or quadratic space–time costs, the minimal cost operating points on M_{RAM} and M_{CAM} are those of small space, large time or large space, small time.

It is interesting to observe that the operating points in the region of small space, large time are those that are approached by minicomputers and by modern operating systems that put many programs into a large memory, giving each program a small portion of that memory. We note at this point that experience teaches us that programs generally need some small but modest amount of storage space in the main memory. This storage space is called the minimal "working set" (Denning, 1968), and the existence of such a set suggests that it may be possible to operate near but not on the boundaries defined by the computational inequalities in the region of small space and large time.

There are few problems of interest that can be computed in small time (and therefore large space) at points near the locus defined by the computational inequalities. One that can is characterized by the "table look up" function $f_{\mathrm{TL}}: \{0, 1\}^{nb + \lceil \log_2 n \rceil} \to \{0, 1\}^b$ defined by

$$f_{\mathrm{TL}}(\mathbf{a}, \mathbf{w}_0, \ldots, \mathbf{w}_{n-1}) = \mathbf{w}_{|\mathbf{a}|}$$

where $\mathbf{w}_i \in \{0, 1\}^b$, $\mathbf{a} \in \{0, 1\}^{\lceil \log_2 n \rceil}$, and $|\mathbf{a}|$ is the number represented by the binary tuple $\mathbf{a}$. If $\mathbf{w}_0, \ldots, \mathbf{w}_{n-1}$ are stored in an RAM of capacity nb bits, f_{TL} can be computed in one cycle by using $\mathbf{a}$ as the address of $\mathbf{w}_{|\mathbf{a}|}$. Thus, only one word of the program and data for f_{TL} is accessed. In general, one should expect that a substantial fraction of a program for a function must be accessed, in which case, one should *not* expect that a function can be computed efficiently in the region of large storage and small time. This leaves the region of small storage and large time as the only potential region for efficient computation.

When an important and suggestive conclusion like this is drawn (albeit under certain generally untested assumptions), an intuitive explanation is desired. We develop the basis for such an explanation by introducing the notion of the *computing power* of a machine and the notion of *mismatch of computing powers of machines*.

We define the *computing power* P of a sequential machine S (with transition and output functions δ and λ) as the time rate at which S does computational work. Let $C_\Omega(\delta, \lambda)T$ be the work done, $\Omega = P_{1,2}^{(2)}$, by S in T cycles. If S has a cycle length τ, in seconds, T cycles occupies $t = T\tau$

seconds, and the time rate P at which S does work is given by

$$P = \frac{C_\Omega(\delta, \lambda) T}{T\tau} = \frac{C_\Omega(\delta, \lambda)}{\tau}$$

Thus, in M_{RAM} and M_{CAM}, the computing power of the memory with cycle length τ_m is proportional to S/τ_m while that of the CPU is $C_{\text{CPU}}/\tau_{\text{CPU}}$.

If the memory can do work at a much greater rate than can the CPU, that is, if $S \gg C_{\text{CPU}}$ and $\tau_m = \tau_{\text{CPU}}$, and if the two are in constant interaction, then we could argue that the memory is not fully utilized or a mismatch exists. Such a mismatch occurs in M_{RAM} and M_{CAM} unless S is quite small (and T large) and may explain why this is the operating region of highest apparent efficiency. We note that a mismatch can be reduced by reducing S *or* by increasing the size or number of CPUs. Thus,

parallel computation and relatively small main memories seem to provide the necessary conditions for efficient computation with respect to the linear and quadratic cost measures.

Before closing this section, we note parenthetically that our measure of the computing power of a memory is almost exactly the same as the figure of merit (of the same name) used by Knight (1966, 1968) in his study of the relation between cost and performance of computers. He chose this figure of merit after consulting 43 knowledgeable people and indicated that the computing power P of machines is in proportion to C^α, where C is their cost and $2 < \alpha < 3$. This relation is called Grosch's Law.

7.4.5. Limits on the Performance of a Two-Memory Machine

Until this point, we have focused primarily on one-memory general-purpose computers. We close this chapter with a brief examination of the limits on the performance of a typical two-memory machine, namely, M_{DUAL}, a GPC with one CPU, one RAM, and one DRUM.

Computational inequalities of the first and second kind are stated for M_{DUAL} in Section 7.4.1 and are restated as follows:

$$C_\Omega(f) \leq (C_{\text{CPU}} + 5S_R(1 + \varepsilon))T + \tfrac{15}{2}\eta S_D(1 + \varepsilon)$$

$$I_U(f) \leq 2(S_R + S_D + Tb)(1 + \varepsilon^*) + \alpha_{\text{DUAL}}$$

Here S_R and S_D are the storage capacities of the RAM and the DRUM, T is the number of cycles executed by the CPU and the RAM, and η is the number of accesses to the DRUM. Each access is assumed to provide the contents of one track (called a *page*) consisting of K b-bit words. For this reason, $T \geq 4\eta K$ because each DRUM transfer requires the assistance of the CPU and the RAM which are assumed to be four times faster than the DRUM.

The two computational inequalities define boundaries in a three-dimensional space that is best visualized by fixing S_D. In this case, the boundaries defined by the inequalities are those given in Figure 7.4.2.1 except that $C_\Omega(f)$ is reduced by $\frac{15}{2}\eta S_D(1 + \varepsilon)$ and $I_U(f)$ is reduced by $2S_D(1 + \varepsilon^*)$. The condition C1 for the domination of the hyperbolic boundary by the linear boundary becomes

$$\text{C1'.} \left[C_{\text{CPU}} + 5m + \frac{5(1 + \varepsilon)}{2(1 + \varepsilon^*)} \left(I_U(f) - 2S_D(1 + \varepsilon^*) - \alpha \right) \right]^2$$

$$\geq 4\left[C_\Omega(f) - \tfrac{15}{2}\eta S_D(1 + \varepsilon) \right] 5b(1 + \varepsilon)$$

The linear boundary dominates the hyperbolic boundary for most values of S and T if the left-hand side is much larger than the right-hand side.

Inspection of C1' indicates that when S_D and ηS_D are small by comparison to $I_U(f)$ and $C_\Omega(f)$ and when the latter are large, then the condition

$$\left[I_U(f) \right]^2 \gg C_\Omega(f)$$

implies that the linear boundary dominates the hyperbolic for most values of S_R and T. However, that dominance could be expected to be lost as S_D becomes comparable to $I_U(f)$.

A reasonable cost measure for computation on M_{DUAL} is

$$\phi = \alpha_1(C_{\text{CPU}} + 5S_R)T + \alpha_2\eta S_D$$

for the following reasons:

1. $(C_{\text{CPU}} + 5S_R)T$ is a reasonable cost measure for the CPU and RAM.
2. The cost of each access to the DRUM (of which there are η) should be proportional to the selection power of the drum, L (the number of tracks), and the the volume of data transmitted per access, Kb, or to the product $KLb = S_D$.

If S_D is fixed, by our earlier argument, ϕ defines a hyperbola.

Suppose that we can operate on the boundaries and that S_D is not too large so that C1' holds. Then ϕ is smallest when S_R is small and T large or when S_R is large and T small. But $T \geq 4\eta S_D$, so only the small S_R, large T region is accessible. If S_D is comparable to $I_U(f) - \alpha_{\text{DUAL}}$ but ηS_D is small by comparison to $C_\Omega(f)$, C1' is violated and the hyperbola is the dominant boundary. In this case, any value of S_R gives small cost. However, if S_D being large means that $I_U(f) - \alpha_{\text{DUAL}} - 2S_D(1 + \varepsilon^*)$ and $C_\Omega(f) - \frac{15}{2}\eta S_D(1 + \varepsilon)$ are small, then again S_R should be chosen small and T large.

From these observations, it appears that if the boundaries can be approached, then a good *rule of thumb* for M_{DUAL} is the following:

> Operate each program with as small an amount of main memory as is practicable.

We mentioned the need to have an acceptable working set of a program in main memory above, and subject to this proviso, we see that our rule of thumb coincides with current practice.

One last observation, obtained from the use of the computing powers of machines and the notion of mismatch of computing powers, is germane. The computing powers of the CPU, RAM, and DRUM are proportional to $C_{\text{CPU}}/\tau_{\text{CPU}}$, S_R/τ_{CPU}, and Lb/τ_{DRUM}, respectively. (For the last, see Section 6.2.4 and the preceding section. Here L is the number of tracks and b is the number of bits per word. We assume that $\tau_{\text{CPU}} = 4\tau_{\text{DRUM}}$.) For a typical DRUM, $L = 200$ and $b = 32$ so that a balanced system, that is, one without major mismatches in computing power, is one in which S_R is comparable to C_{CPU} and Lb, that is, S_R is small (and T large). This agrees with the conclusions derived.

This completes our discussion of the limits on performance of computers.

Problems

7-1. Using results of Section 4.5, derive computational inequalities of the first kind for the five general-purpose computers of Section 7.2 using delay complexity instead of combinational complexity. Also make use of the results of Problem 4-12.

7-2. Design a Turing machine that, given a string

$$\$v_1\$v_2\$ \cdots \$v_T\$$$

with $v_i \in \{0, 1\}^b$, $b \geq 2$, processes that string by deleting all characters except the bits in words v_i whose first component is 1 and that concatenates the remaining bits to form a string.

7-3. Describe the effect on the computational inequalities of the first and second kind when the RAM in M_{RAM} is replaced by a two-port RAM of the type described in Problem 6-5.

7-4. Use the method of Section 7.4.3 to derive an upper bound to $S + Tb$ for the computation of Boolean functions from formulas on M_{CAM}. Show that the bound applies for many values of S and T and compare the upper bound to the lower bound specified by the computational inequality of the second kind.

7-5. Demonstrate that $f : \{0, 1\}^n \rightarrow \{0, 1\}^m$ can be computed on M_{CAM} from an encoding of an optimal straight-line program with $S + Tb \leq KC_{\Omega}(f) \log_2 C_{\Omega}(f)$ for some constant $K > 0$.

7-6. Derive upper bounds to the combinational complexity and lower bounds to the program complexity of each of the following problems and show that condition C1 of Section 7.4.2 is satisfied for each when the number of variables in each problem is large.

(a) Sorting of n integers represented as binary b-tuples (see Section 8.1).

(b) Multiplication of Boolean $n \times n$ matrices when multiplication is AND and addition is EXCLUSIVE OR.

(c) Calculation of the determinant of an $n \times n$ Boolean matrix with addition and multiplication as defined in (b) (see Section 3.1.3).

7-7. Devise a computational inequality of the first kind using synchronous combinational complexity for M_{DUAL}. Do the conclusions of Section 7.4.5 change in any major way when this complexity measure is used?

7-8. Consider the item-recognition function $f_{IR}: \{0, 1\}^{(n+1)b} \rightarrow \{0, 1\}$ defined by

$$f(\mathbf{x}_1, \mathbf{x}_2, \dots, \mathbf{x}_n, \mathbf{y}) = \begin{cases} 1, & \mathbf{x}_i = \mathbf{y} \text{ for some } 1 \leq i \leq n \\ 0, & \text{otherwise} \end{cases}$$

where $\mathbf{x}_i, \mathbf{y} \in \{0, 1\}^b$ and $\mathbf{x}_i = \mathbf{y}$ if and only if they agree in every position. Show that f can be computed on an M_{RAM} with $S + Tb \leq KI_U(f)$ for some constant $K > 0$ and for many values of S and T.

7-9. Repeat Problem 8 for M_{CAM}.

7-10. Show that an M_{RAM} exists with fixed storage capacity that can compute an arbitrary Boolean function $f : \{0, 1\}^n \rightarrow \{0, 1\}$ for arbitrary $n \geq 1$. What is the minimum time in which the most complex such function can be computed on the given machine?

Chapter 8

Combinatorial and Algebraic Problems

Three topics are treated in this chapter: sorting, matrix multiplication, and *NP*-complete problems. Under the heading of sorting, we examine (non-adaptive) comparator networks as well as some algorithms based on (adaptive) decision trees. The section on matrix multiplication covers many topics including Strassen's algorithm for matrix-matrix multiplication and the Fast Fourier Transform. The third major section examines a large number of combinatorial problems, including 0-1 integer programming and the Traveling Salesman Problem, and demonstrates that they are *NP*-complete. This implies that for every such problem a best universal algorithm (an algorithm that applies to every instance of the problem) is either exponential or polynomial. It remains unknown whether all *NP*-complete problems are exponential or polynomial.

8.1. SORTING

Given a set of items, such as files indexed by family name, it is often necessary to order the items. The ordering of such items is called *sorting*. In this section, we examine a few adaptive and nonadaptive sorting algorithms. *Nonadaptive* sorting algorithms process lists of items in a data-independent manner, and the algorithms that we consider are described as networks of comparators. These are devices that accept two inputs and put them into "order." *Adaptive* sorting algorithms execute a sequence of data-dependent instructions. We consider algorithms that make inter-item comparisons and one that does not, and we develop a lower bound on the number of comparisons needed for the first type of algorithm.

8.1.1. Sorting Networks

Shown in Figure 8.1.1.1 are two schematic diagrams of a comparator module. We let the lower output of a comparator carry the maximum of the two inputs. The nature of the items x, y is unspecified except to say that they can be ordered. Examples of items and orderings on them are

1. Family names and lexicographical ordering.
2. Real numbers and the natural ordering.
3. n-Tuples of reals where $\mathbf{x} \leq \mathbf{y}$ if corresponding components x_i and y_i are in the relation $x_i \leq y_i$.

Networks of comparators will be formed for sorting.

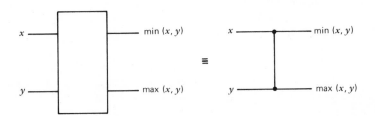

Figure 8.1.1.1. A comparator element.

The comparator networks that we consider are of the type shown in Figure 8.1.1.2. The network has n lines and between any two lines is placed a comparator. Thus, the fan-out from each output of a comparator is 1.

The network given in Figure 8.1.1.2 is a particularly simple type of sorting network which implements *insertion sorting*. This method is better understood by reference to Figure 8.1.1.3, in which the parallelism has

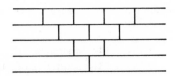

Figure 8.1.1.2. Typical comparator network.

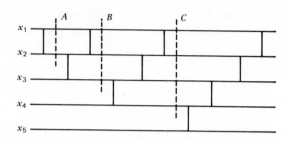

Figure 8.1.1.3. Insertion sorting network.

been eliminated. At point A, x_1 and x_2 are sorted. Into this sorted list, x_3 is inserted and it trickles up until its proper place is found. This procedure is repeated for each additional input. Insertion sorting networks with n lines have $n(n-1)/2$ comparators.

Other n-sorters exist that have many fewer comparators. The one we present here is due to Batcher (1968) and is based upon a scheme he introduced for merging two sorted lists of s and t items, $s + t = n$, into one sorted list of n items. His scheme is known as the *odd-even merge* and is applied recursively to sort n items.

Let $\mathbf{x} = (x_1, x_2, \ldots, x_s)$ and $\mathbf{y} = (y_1, y_2, \ldots, y_t)$ be two sorted sequences with $x_i \leq x_{i+1}$ and $y_i \leq y_{i+1}$. An (s, t)-*merging network* accepts $\mathbf{x}$ and $\mathbf{y}$ as input and produces a sorted n-sequence containing the elements of $\mathbf{x}$ and $\mathbf{y}$. If $s = t = 1$, such a network consists of a single comparator. Thus, assume that $st \geq 2$.

An (s, t)-merging network based on the odd-even merge is shown in Figure 8.1.1.4 for $s = 4, t = 5$. The odd-merging network accepts the odd-numbered inputs from $\mathbf{x}$ and $\mathbf{y}$ and merges them while the even-merging network merges the even-numbered inputs from $\mathbf{x}$ and $\mathbf{y}$. (Dashed lines indicate that a line is unaltered as it passes through the indicated network.) The outputs of the two merging networks are compared in pairs, as shown, to complete the merging network. We prove that the network does indeed merge sorted s- and t-sequences after we introduce the *zero-one principle* (Knuth, 1973).

Theorem 8.1.1.1. (Zero-one principle). A comparator network with n lines fails to sort an n-sequence only if there is a 0-1 n-sequence that it fails to sort.

Proof. Let $(a_1, \ldots, a_n)$ be the sequence of inputs applied to the network and let $(a'_1, \ldots, a'_n)$ be the sequence of outputs, where a_n and a'_n are associated with the bottom line of the network. Let f be a monotonic

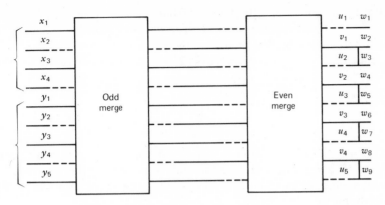

Figure 8.1.1.4. Odd-even merging network.

function with the property that $f(x) \leq f(y)$ if $x \leq y$. It is easy to demonstrate by induction on the size of the network that input n-sequence $(f(a_1), \ldots, f(a_n))$ is transformed into $(f(a'_1), \ldots, f(a'_n))$ by the network. Now suppose that $(a'_1, \ldots, a'_n)$ is not sorted into ascending order and in particular that $a'_i > a'_{i+1}$. Then choose the function f defined by

$$f(x) = \begin{cases} 0, & x \leq a'_{i+1} \\ 1, & x > a'_{i+1} \end{cases}$$

Then the 0-1 input sequence $(f(a_1), \ldots, f(a_n))$ is transformed into the 0-1 sequence $(f(a'_1), \ldots, f(a'_n))$ which is not sorted. $\qquad\square$

If a comparator network is designed to accept an arbitrary n-sequence and to sort that sequence, then it correctly sorts all n-sequences if and only if it correctly sorts each of the 2^n binary n-tuples. If the inputs to a sorting network are all distinct, this reduces the number of inputs on which the network has to be tested from $n!$ to 2^n.

The odd-even merging network merges s- and t-sequences, each of which has been previously sorted, into a sorted $(s + t)$-sequence. To prove that it correctly merges, assume that a correct s-sorter and t-sorter exist that together with the merging network form an $(s + t)$-sorter. It follows that the $(s + t)$-sorter is correct if and only if the (s, t) merging network correctly merges nondecreasing 0-1 s- and t-sequences. Let $(x_1, \ldots, x_s)$ be a nondecreasing 0-1 sequence containing k 0's and $s - k$ 1's. Similarly let $(y_1, \ldots, y_t)$ contain l 0's and $t - l$ 1's. Then, the odd-merge network of

Figure 8.1.1.4 selects exactly $\lceil k/2 \rceil$ 0's from $(x_1, \ldots, x_s)$ and $\lceil l/2 \rceil$ 0's from $(y_1, \ldots, y_t)$ to produce a sequence $(u_1, u_2, \cdots)$ consisting of $\lceil k/2 \rceil + \lceil l/2 \rceil$ 0's followed by 1's. Similarly, the even-merge network produces a sequence $(v_1, v_2, \cdots)$ containing $\lfloor k/2 \rfloor + \lfloor l/2 \rfloor$ 0's followed by 1's. Since $\lceil x \rceil - \lfloor x \rfloor$ is 0 or 1,

$$\Delta = \left\lceil \frac{k}{2} \right\rceil + \left\lceil \frac{l}{2} \right\rceil - \left(\left\lfloor \frac{k}{2} \right\rfloor + \left\lfloor \frac{l}{2} \right\rfloor \right) = 0, 1, 2$$

If $\Delta = 0$ or 1, the sequence $(u_1, v_1, u_2, v_2, \cdots)$ is already sorted, whereas if $\Delta = 2$, the last level of comparators puts the sequence into nondecreasing order. Thus, Batcher's odd-even merging network does correctly merge sequences.

A complete (4, 4) merging network is shown in Figure 8.1.1.5 and is obtained from that of Figure 8.1.1.4 by applying the odd-even merge scheme recursively to each merging network and noting that a (1, 1) merging network is a comparator.

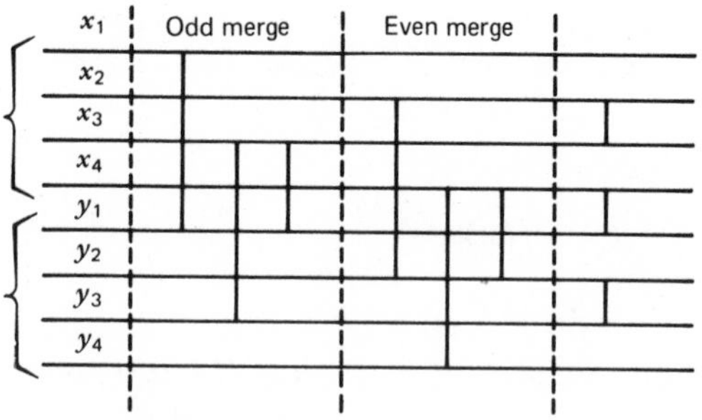

Figure 8.1.1.5. A (4, 4) merging network.

Now consider a $(2^k, 2^k)$-merging network based on odd-even merge and let $\lambda(2^k)$ be the number of comparators that it contains. From the definition of odd-even merging, the network contains two $(2^{k-1}, 2^{k-1})$-merging networks plus $2^k - 1$ additional comparators. Thus, we can write

$$\lambda(2^k) = 2\lambda(2^{k-1}) + 2^k - 1$$

Since $\lambda(1) = 1$, it is easy to show by induction that

$$\lambda(2^k) = k \cdot 2^k + 1$$

A sorting network can now be designed using merging networks. Given $n = 2^l$ inputs, group them into $n/2$ pairs and merge the pairs using $(n/2)\lambda(2^0)$ comparators. This produces $n/2$ sorted sequences of length two grouped into $n/4$ pairs and merged using $(n/4)\lambda(2^1)$ additional comparators. This process is continued until two sorted sequences remain of length 2^{l-1} merged in one $(2^{l-1}, 2^{l-1})$–merging network with $\lambda(2^{l-1})$ comparators. The total number of comparators in this sorting network is $s(n)$ where

$$s(n) = \sum_{j=0}^{l-1} 2^j \lambda(2^{l-j-1})$$

and $n = 2^l$. An 8-sorter based on this method of construction is shown in Figure 8.1.1.6.

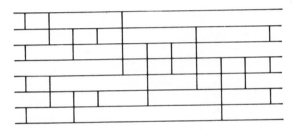

Figure 8.1.1.6. An 8-sorter based on odd-even merging.

Theorem 8.1.1.2. Let n be a power of 2. Then, Batcher's n-sorter based on odd-even merging has $s(n)$ comparators where

$$s(n) = \frac{n}{4}\left[(\log_2 n)(\log_2 n - 1) + 4\right] - 1$$

The proof of this theorem involves a simple summation of a series for which the reader may wish to make use of the result of Problem 3-1.

We now develop a lower bound (due to Van Voorhis, 1972) on the number of comparators needed in any n-sorter. Consider the bottom (or largest) output in an n-sorter. With it we associate a binary tree defined as follows. Associate the root of the tree with the comparator that is connected directly to the output. Let this root have two descending edges to two distinct nodes corresponding to the (possibly identical) comparators or network inputs that are input to the root comparator. If one of these nodes is associated with a comparator, on this node repeat the process that has been applied to the root. In the end, a binary tree is constructed in which comparators and inputs may correspond to more than one node. Nevertheless, the tree has at least n leaves because each input could be potentially the largest and each must be connected to the bottom output by some path. As we have seen many times above, any binary tree with at least n leaves has some path of length at least $\lceil \log_2 n \rceil$.

In the above binary tree, if the ith input line is the terminus for the longest path, apply an input to it that is larger than any other input. By so doing, the outputs of each comparator on the path from this input to the bottom output are predetermined, and these comparators can be eliminated. This procedure eliminates at least $\lceil \log_2 n \rceil$ comparators and results in an $(n-1)$–sorter for the remaining elements. Thus, if $s(n)$ is the minimum number of comparators in any n-sorter, we have $s(2) = 1$ and

$$s(n) \geq s(n-1) + \lceil \log_2 n \rceil$$

This inequality is solved in the proof of Theorem 3.2.2.1, and its solution is given in the following theorem.

Theorem 8.1.1.3.   Any n-sorter has at least

$$s(n) \geq n\lceil \log_2 n \rceil - 2^{\lceil \log_2 n \rceil} + 1$$

comparators.

A comparison of this bound with the size of Batcher's sorter demonstrates that $s(n) = s(n)$ for $n = 2, 4$ and $s(8) = 17$ while $s(8) = 19$. Thus, for small n, Batcher's n-sorter has nearly optimal size, although the gap between the bounds increases with n. No type of n-sorter is known whose size grows more slowly than $n(\log n)^2$, and thus, up to a constant multiple, Butcher's algorithm is the best known.

8.1.2.   Adaptive Sorting

The sorting networks of the preceding section are examples of nonadaptive sorting algorithms because the set of operations they perform and the sequence in which they perform them are data independent. Adaptive sorting algorithms are in much wider use because they offer flexibility and a performance advantage over nonadaptive algorithms.

How many comparisons between items are needed to sort a list of n items? Surprisingly, the answer is zero, as we now demonstrate. *Radix sorting* is commonly used in puched card readers and is the principal example of adaptive sorting that uses no comparisons between items. To illustrate the method, consider the problem suggested by Knuth (1973), the sorting of a 52-card deck of playing cards by suit and by face value within each suit. Let

$$A < 2 < 3 < \cdots < 10 < J < Q < K$$

be the ordering of face values and let

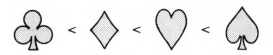

be the ordering of suits. The deck can be sorted by creating one pile for each suit and then ordering piles according to face value. However, it is more efficient to use radix sorting—that is, to create 13 piles corresponding to face values first and then create 4 piles according to suit by distributing the cards in the A pile, followed by those in the 1 pile, and so forth. Clearly, the bottom card in each of the four piles will be A, followed by 1, and so on, and the deck will have been ordered.

In the playing card example, cards were not compared to one another, but they were compared with respect to face values and with suits. Radix sorting of multidigit numbers is done by classifying them according to their least significant digits and reading from this list in digit order to classify them according to their second least significant digits, and so forth, until digits of every significance have been seen. To radix sort n k-digit numbers, nk memory accesses are sufficient.

While interitem comparisons are not necessary to sort, very many sorting algorithms do make use of only such comparisons. Such algorithms can be described by *decision trees*, one of which is shown in Figure 8.1.2.1. Internal nodes in such binary trees are labeled $i : j$, which means item x_i is to be compared to x_j and the left branch taken if $x_i \leq x_j$. Otherwise, the right branch is taken. The leaves of the tree are labeled with the correct order of the items. Thus, if $x_1 > x_2$, $x_1 > x_3$, and $x_2 \leq x_3$, then $x_2 \leq x_3 \leq x_1$. Furthermore, every set of three items can be sorted with at most three comparisons. Even when the only comparisons used in sorting are interitem comparisons, many other operations are necessary to access and organize the data to be sorted. For an exhaustive treatment of sorting, including a realistic assessment of the cost of all operations, the reader is referred to Knuth (1973). It is interesting, nonetheless, to examine just the number of comparisons necessary in decision trees for sorting.

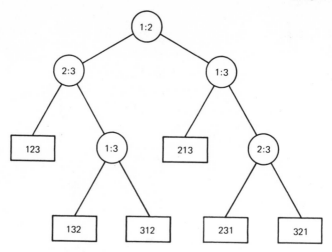

Figure 8.1.2.1. A decision tree for sorting three items.

Theorem 8.1.2.1.   The minimum number of comparisons necessary to sort n distinct items with a decision tree is at least $\lceil \log_2(n!) \rceil \geq \lceil n\log_2 n - n\log_2 e + \log_2 e \rceil$

Proof.   The number of distinct permutations of n distinct items is $n! = n(n-1)(n-2) \cdots 2 \cdot 1$. This many distinct leaves are necessary in any decision tree, and, since it is binary, it must have a longest path of length l where $2^l \geq n!$; otherwise, not all leaves can be reached. Thus, at least $\log_2(n!)$ comparisons are necessary to sort some set of n items in every decision tree for this task.

The lower bound to $\log_2(n!)$ follows from the expansion for $n!$ and the observation that

$$\ln k \geq \int_{k-1}^{k} \ln x \, dx$$

Then

$$\ln n! \geq \int_{1}^{n} \ln x \, dx = n(\ln(n) - 1) + 1$$

Multiplying by $\log_2 e$, we have the desired result.   □

There are a number of sorting algorithms that come close to achieving this lower bound. One is *binary insertion sort*, which is described as follows for a list of *n* items:

1. If $n = 2$, compare and rearrange the two items. If $n > 2$, go to 2.
2. Sort the first $n - 1$ items using binary insertion sort. Insert the *n*th item into the sorted list using the following *binary insertion algorithm*:
   (a) In a sorted list of size *k*, find the $\lceil k/2 \rceil$th element.
   (b) Compare this element to the item to be inserted. If it is strictly smaller than the new item, the new item is to be inserted in the list of $k - \lceil k/2 \rceil$ largest items; otherwise, it is to be inserted in the list of $\lceil k/2 \rceil - 1$ smallest items.
   (c) If the new list is empty, insert the new item and HALT. Otherwise, return to (a) with *k* equal to the size of the new list.

A decision tree for binary insertion sort is shown in Figure 8.1.2.2 for $n = 3$. It is constructed from a tree for sorting of two elements, and every node added to that tree contains a comparison of the new item to the first or second item.

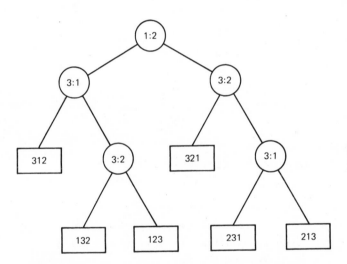

Figure 8.1.2.2. A sorting tree based upon insertion sort.

We now show that the binary insertion algorithm described in (a), (b) and (c) uses a maximum of $\lceil \log_2(k + 1) \rceil$ comparisons to insert an item into a sorted list of *k* items. This result is then employed to compute the maximum number of comparisons necessary for insertion sort. Clearly, if $k = 1$, one comparison is used by the binary insertion algorithm and the claim is true in this case. Suppose now that the claim is true for $k \leq m - 1$. Consider insertion into a sorted list of m items. After the first comparison, the item is inserted into a list of size $\lceil m/2 \rceil - 1$ or one of size $m - \lceil m/2 \rceil$. Since the latter is greater than or equal to the former, insertion into the list of size $m - \lceil m/2 \rceil$ requires the most comparisons. By our induction hypothesis, this is $\lceil \log_2(m - \lceil m/2 \rceil + 1) \rceil$. Our claim is proved if we can show that

$$\lceil \log_2(m + 1) \rceil = \left\lceil \log_2 \left(m - \left\lceil \frac{m}{2} \right\rceil + 1 \right) \right\rceil + 1$$

for all $m \geq 2$. When m is odd, $\lceil m/2 \rceil = (m + 1)/2$ and equality is obvious. When m is even, $\lceil m/2 \rceil = m/2$ and

$$\left\lceil \log_2 \left(m - \left\lceil \frac{m}{2} \right\rceil + 1 \right) \right\rceil + 1 = \lceil (\log_2(m + 2)) - 1 \rceil + 1 = \lceil \log_2(m + 2) \rceil$$

Now let

$$l = \lceil \log_2(m + 1) \rceil$$

so that m satisfies

$$2^{l-1} < m + 1 \leq 2^l$$

However, m is even, which implies that

$$2^{l-1} < m + 2 \leq 2^l$$

or

$$\lceil \log_2(m + 2) \rceil = l$$

and we have equality.

Theorem 8.1.2.2. The adaptive binary insertion sorting algorithm sorts a list of n items with a maxium of $s_I(n)$ comparisons where

$$s_I(n) = n \lceil \log_2 n \rceil - 2^{\lceil \log_2 n \rceil} + 1$$

Proof. By the definition of the algorithm,

$$s_I(n) = s_I(n - 1) + \lceil \log_2 n \rceil$$

because the insertion is into a list of size $n - 1$. Since $s_I(2) = 1$, The proof of Theorem 8.1.1.3 is applicable. $\qquad \square$

Two other types of adaptive sorting algorithms are *tree selection* and adaptive *odd-even merging*, which is an adaptive version of the algorithm described in the preceding section. An example of a tree selection algorithm is *heapsort*, an algorithm that uses a number of comparisons that is a small multiple of the minimum and that uses no more storage capacity than that required to store the list to be sorted.

An important first step in the description of heapsort is the presentation of a simple numbering system for the nodes of a binary tree. Shown in Figure 8.1.2.3 is a full binary tree of depth 4. The root is labeled "1" and the successive integers are assigned from left to right at successive levels of the tree. This numbering makes it easy to determine the descendants of the node numbered i (they are $2i$ and $2i + 1$) and the antecendent of node i (it is $\lceil i/2 \rceil$ if $i \geq 2$). Heapsort is described in terms of such a numbering of binary trees. (The reader should not confuse these trees with decision trees.)

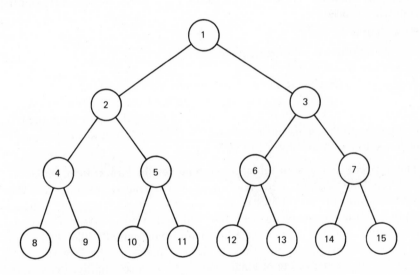

Figure 8.1.2.3. A numbering of nodes in a binary tree.

Heapsort is based on the idea of a *heap*. A set of n items is placed at the first n nodes of a binary tree, as numbered above, and the structure forms a heap if the item at each nonleaf node is the maximum of all of its descendants and itself. An example of a heap is shown in Figure 8.1.2.4. To show that a binary tree is a heap, it is sufficient to demonstrate that no node has a larger value than its antecedent.

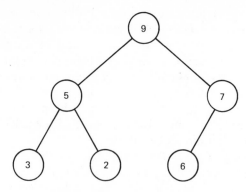

Figure 8.1.2.4. Example of a heap.

If a set of items is arranged in the form of a heap, the largest item is at the top of the heap. Thus, to sort a list of $n \geq 2$ items, we can carry out the following procedure:

HEAPSORT

1. Put the original set of n items into a heap.
2. Set $k = n$.
3. If $k = 2$, interchange items at locations 1 and 2 and HALT.
4. Given a heap with k nodes, interchange the item at the root of the tree with the item at location k of the tree and delete this node from the tree.
5. Rearrange the items in the tree of $k - 1$ nodes into a heap.
6. Set k to $k - 1$ and return to step 3.

This procedure forms an initial heap, removes the largest item, replaces it with the "most distant" item, rearranges the elements into a heap, and then repeats until only two nodes remain which are in inverse order. Furthermore, the interchange of the root item and that at position k in a heap of k nodes makes it possible to reuse all of the space initially allocated to the list of items. At the completion of the computation, the largest item is stored at location n of the original binary tree with consecutive items in the ordered list falling into consecutive decreasingly numbered locations of the tree.

We now describe a procedure for putting the original list into a heap (called NEWHEAP) and a procedure for rearranging the elements of a heap after a root exchange or replacement (REHEAP). We describe REHEAP first and use it to define NEWHEAP.

REHEAP

1. If the given subtree has one node, HALT.

2. Compare the root item R with its two immediate descendants (one if the tree has two nodes) and let M be the node of these three with the largest value.
3. If $R \neq M$, interchange R and M and apply REHEAP to the subtree with R as its new root.

This procedure is always applied to trees where every root of every subtree, except possibly the tree itself, contains the maximum element of the subtree. After one application of REHEAP, the root of the tree contains the maximum element of the tree, and the original element, if not maximal, sifts down until it becomes a leaf or a root of a subtree of which it is a maximal element. Thus, REHEAP halts with the tree in the form of a heap.

NEWHEAP

1. Set $k = n$.
2. If $k = 0$, HALT
3. Insert the $(n - k + 1)$st item into node k of the tree.
4. If this node is not a leaf, apply REHEAP to the subtree with this as its root.
5. Replace k by $k - 1$ and go to step 2.

The procedure NEWHEAP fills positions $n, n - 1, n - 2, \ldots, 1$ of the binary tree in this order, that is, from the bottom level on up and after each application of step 4. the subtrees that have been created are all heaps. Thus, at step 3, if node $n - k + 1$ is not a leaf, a subtree is created that would be a heap if its root item were large enough. The application of REHEAP makes that subtree into a heap.

In step 1 of HEAPSORT, we apply NEWHEAP while in step 5, we apply REHEAP. These are the only steps of HEAPSORT that involve comparisons. If REHEAP is applied to a tree of depth d, that is, a tree whose longest path has d nodes, at most $d - 1$ applications fo step 2 are necessary. Since each application involves at most two comparisons, RE-HEAP on a tree of depth d uses at most $2(d - 1)$ comparisons. NEW-HEAP invokes REHEAP at each nonleaf node of the tree of n nodes. This tree has depth h where

$$h = \lceil \log_2(n + 1) \rceil$$

because n satisfies

$$2^{h-1} - 1 < n \leq 2^h - 1$$

The nodes at the bottom level of the tree, that is, at depth h, are leaf nodes. All others could be nonleaf nodes. Those at depth l, of which there are

2^{l-1}, are roots of trees of depth at most $h - l + 1$. Thus, NEWHEAP will invoke REHEAP at most 2^{l-1} times at level l, $1 \leq l \leq h - 1$, and each invocation will necessitate at most $2(h - l)$ comparisons for a total of χ_N comparisons, where

$$\chi_N \leq \sum_{l=1}^{h-1} 2^{l-1} 2(h - l) = 2(2^h - h - 1)$$

as the reader can show by induction.

We have now bounded the number of comparisons involved in step 1 of HEAPSORT, that is, as a result of applying NEWHEAP. At step 5 of HEAPSORT, REHEAP is applied to trees of size $n - 1, n - 2, \ldots, 2$, in that order. The number of comparisons involved here, χ_R, is bounded by

$$\chi_R \leq 2 \sum_{k=2}^{n-1} \left(\lceil \log_2(k + 1) \rceil - 1 \right)$$

$$= 2 \left[n(\lceil \log_2 n \rceil - 1) - 2^{\lceil \log_2 n \rceil} + 2 \right]$$

because a tree with k nodes has depth $\lceil \log_2(k + 1) \rceil$.

Theorem 8.1.2.3. HEAPSORT sorts a list of n items with a maximum of at most $s_H(n)$ comparisons where

$$s_H(n) \leq 2(n - 1)(\lceil \log_2(n + 1) \rceil - 1)$$

Proof. $s_H(n) = \chi_N + \chi_R$, and by considering the two cases $\lceil \log_2 n \rceil = \lceil \log_2(n + 1) \rceil$ and $\lceil \log_2 n \rceil = \lceil \log_2(n + 1) \rceil - 1$, it is easy to show that Theorem 8.1.2.3 gives the resulting bound. □

The bound to $s_H(n)$, the number of comparisons used by HEAPSORT, is about twice that for binary insertion sorting and the lower bound to Theorem 8.1.2.1. However, we caution the reader not to assume that binary insertion sorting is generally superior to HEAPSORT just because it requires fewer comparisons. In fact binary insertion sorting is much less attractive than HEAPSORT because it generally requires many cycles of computation to restructure the data after each insertion.

8.2. MATRIX MULTIPLICATION

In this section, we examine a number of important topics concerning matrix multiplication. We present Strassen's algorithm for multiplying two matrices which offers a considerable asymptotic advantage over the standard algorithm, and we derive the Fast Fourier Transform (FFT) algorithm. The FFT permits a marked improvement on the standard algorithm for the convolution of sequences.

8.2.1. The Multiplication Problem

Given two matrices, an $m \times n$ matrix **A** and an $n \times p$ matrix **B**, the *matrix multiplication problem* is to find an "efficient" algorithm for computing the $m \times p$ product matrix **C**, denoted

$$C = AB$$

where an entry c_{ij} of **C** is defined in terms of entries a_{ik} and b_{kj} of **A** and **B**, respectively, by

$$c_{ij} = \sum_{k=1}^{n} a_{ik} \cdot b_{kj}, \qquad 1 \leq i \leq m, \quad 1 \leq j \leq p$$

This definition of **C** gives the *standard algorithm* for matrix multiplication, and it uses mnp binary multiplications and $m(n-1)p$ binary additions. As we see in the next section, there are more efficient algorithms.

In the preceding, we have not specified the domain of definition of the variables or the properties of the operators. To do this, we invoke the notion of a ring.

Definition 8.2.1. A *ring* is an algebraic structure $(S, +, \cdot, 0, 1)$ where S is a set of elements, 0 and 1 are distinguished elements of S and $+ : S \times S \to S$ and $\cdot : S \times S \to S$ are binary operations on S. These two binary operators have the following properties for all a, b, and c in S:

1. $(a + b) + c = a + (b + c)$ $+$ is associative
2. $(a \cdot b) \cdot c = a \cdot (b \cdot c)$ $\cdot$ is associative
3. $(a + b) \cdot c = a \cdot c + b \cdot c$ $\cdot$ distributes over $+$ on the right
4. $a \cdot (b + c) = a \cdot b + a \cdot c$ $\cdot$ distributes over $+$ on the left
5. $a + b = b + a$ $+$ is commutative
6. $a + 0 = 0 + a = a$ 0 is the additive identity
7. $a \cdot 1 = 1 \cdot a = a$ 1 is the multiplicative identity
8. $\exists - a \in S$ such that a has an additive inverse
   $a + (-a) = (-a) + a = 0$

A ring is *commutative* if the operator $\cdot$ is commutative.

There are many common examples of rings, including the integers (positive, negative, and 0), the real numbers, and the complex numbers, where $+$ and $\cdot$ denote the standard addition and multiplication operators for these sets. Each of these three rings is commutative. The following defines a common noncomutative ring.

Example 8.2.1.1. Let $R = (S, +, \cdot, 0, 1)$ be a ring. Consider the set M_n of $n \times n$ matrices with entries from R. Let $\mathbf{0}_n$ be the $n \times n$ matrix all of whose entries are $0 \in S$ and let $\mathbf{I}_n$ be a similar matrix except that it has $1 \in S$ as every entry on its main diagonal. For $\mathbf{A}$ and $\mathbf{B}$ in M_n, $\mathbf{A} +_n \mathbf{B}$ is the matrix $\mathbf{C}$ with ij entry $c_{ij} = a_{ij} + b_{ij}$, and $\mathbf{A} \cdot_n \mathbf{B}$ is the matrix $\mathbf{C}$ with ij entry $c_{ij} = \sum_{k=1}^{n} a_{ik} \cdot b_{kj}$.

Lemma 8.2.1.1. $(M_n, +_n, \cdot_n, \mathbf{0}_n, \mathbf{I}_n)$ is a noncommutative ring.

The proof of this result is left as an exercise for the reader.

In Section 8.2, we assume that the entries of every matrix are defined over some ring. Thus, addition and multiplication of entries satisfy the associate and distributive laws, addition is commutative, additive inverses exist, and the ring has an additive identity and a multiplicative identity. The entries may be defined over rings that satisfy more conditions. For example, multiplication may be commutative and every nonzero element may have a multiplicative inverse. In this case, the algebraic structure is a field.

On the face of it, matrix-matrix multiplication of an $m \times n$ matrix $\mathbf{A}$ by an $n \times p$ matrix $\mathbf{B}$ may appear to be more general than matrix-vector multiplication. This is not so because the entries in $\mathbf{AB}$ are exactly the entries resulting from the following matrix-vector product:

$$
\beta = \begin{bmatrix} \mathbf{A} & & \mathbf{0} \\ & \mathbf{A} & \\ \mathbf{0} & & \mathbf{A} \end{bmatrix}
\begin{bmatrix} b_{11} \\ b_{12} \\ \vdots \\ b_{n1} \\ b_{12} \\ \vdots \\ b_{n2} \\ \vdots \\ b_{np} \end{bmatrix}
$$

Here the matrix β has the matrix $\mathbf{A}$ on its main diagonal and 0 is elsewhere; the vector consists of the concatenation of the columns of $\mathbf{B}$.

We know from Problem 3-17 that when matrix-matrix multiplication is done with chains over a monotone mappable algebraic system, such as the integers $\{0, 1, 2, 3, \cdots \}$ with standard addition and multiplication, the standard algorithm is optimal. This means that n^3 multiplications and $n^2(n - 1)$ additions are necessary and sufficient to multiply two $n \times n$ matrices under these conditions. As the result of the next section demonstrates, the availability of additive inverses, that is, negation, can considerably simplify the matrix-matrix multiplication problem.

8.2.2. Strassen's Matrix Multiplication Algorithm

The standard algorithm for the multiplication of two 2×2 matrices uses 8 multiplications and 4 additions. Strassen (1969) has introduced an algorithm for this purpose that uses only 7 multiplications but requires 18 additions. An important feature of the algorithm is that it does not assume that the multiplication rule is commutative. For this reason, the algorithm could be applied to multiply two 2×2 matrices whose entries are also matrices. Thus, if A and B are two $n \times n$ matrices where n is even, then we can write A, B, and the product matrix $C = AB$ as 2×2 matrices whose entries are $(n/2) \times (n/2)$ matrices:

$$C = \begin{bmatrix} C_{11} & C_{12} \\ C_{21} & C_{22} \end{bmatrix} = \begin{bmatrix} A_{11} & A_{12} \\ A_{21} & A_{22} \end{bmatrix} \begin{bmatrix} B_{11} & B_{12} \\ B_{21} & B_{22} \end{bmatrix}$$

It is important to observe that this algorithm exchanges 1 multiplication for 14 additions, and when applied to multiplication of $n \times n$ matrices, 1 multiplication of two $(n/2) \times (n/2)$ matrices is exchanged for 14 additions of such matrices. Since matrix multiplication seems to require many more basic operations than does addition, this is a most favorable trade.

We now describe the Strassen algorithm for the multiplication of matrices whose elements are from a ring R. Consider the product $C = AB$ defined in the preceding. Its entries can be computed by forming the following seven products:

$$P_1 = (A_{11} + A_{22})(B_{11} + B_{22})$$

$$P_2 = (A_{21} + A_{22})B_{11}$$

$$P_3 = A_{11}(B_{12} - B_{22})$$

$$P_4 = A_{22}(-B_{11} + B_{21})$$

$$P_5 = (A_{11} + A_{12})B_{22}$$

$$P_6 = (-A_{11} + A_{21})(B_{11} + B_{12})$$

$$P_7 = (A_{12} - A_{22})(B_{21} + B_{22})$$

and then combining them:

$$C_{11} = P_1 + P_4 - P_5 + P_7$$

$$C_{12} = P_3 + P_5$$

$$C_{21} = P_2 + P_4$$

$$C_{22} = P_1 + P_3 - P_2 + P_6$$

The application of this algorithm to the multiplication on $n \times n$ matrices whose elements are members of a ring is obvious. Consider as an example matrices for which $n = 2^k$. Since addition of $m \times m$ matrices requires m^2 elementary operations on entries of the matrices, for the total number of elementary operations on $n \times n$ matrices, $M(n)$, we can write

$$M(n) \leq 7M\left(\frac{n}{2}\right) + 18\left(\frac{n}{2}\right)^2$$

If we write

$$\lambda(k) = M(2^k)$$

we have

$$\lambda(k) \leq 7\lambda(k-1) + \tfrac{9}{2} \cdot 2^{2k}$$

whose solution satisfies

$$\lambda(k) \leq 7^{k+1} - 6 \cdot 4^k = 7n^{\log_2 7} - 6n^2$$

since $\lambda(0) = 1$.

Theorem 8.2.2.1. Two $n \times n$ matrices can be multiplied with at most $kn^{\log_2 7}$ arithmetic operations for some constant $k > 0$.

It is now clear that the standard algorithm is not an asymptotically optimum algorithm. We emphasize the word "asymptotically" because the Strassen algorithm has hidden costs associated with it that make it more time consuming to run than the standard algorithm when the matrices are small. These are caused primarily by the difficulty associated with accessing elements of the matrix.

The coefficient k of Theorem 8.2.2.1 can be improved by applying the algorithm to matrices for which $n = p2^k$ and subdividing the problem until $p \times p$ matrices are reached, where p is small, and then applying the standard algorithm. By such means, the coefficient k can be reduced to 4.7 (see Problem 8-12).

8.2.3 Matrix-Vector Multiplication

As we have seen, matrix-matrix multiplication corresponds to matrix-vector multiplication where the matrix has a special structure. In this section we take a brief look at matrix-vector multiplication when the matrix has arbitrary entries and when it has some special form. (Fiduccia, 1973b)

Consider the multiplication of an $m \times n$ matrix $\mathbf{A}$ by a column n-vector $\mathbf{b}$ to produce a column m-vector $\mathbf{c}$. We write this as

$$
\begin{bmatrix} c_1 \\ c_2 \\ \vdots \\ c_m \end{bmatrix} = \begin{bmatrix} a_{11} & a_{12} & \cdots & a_{1n} \\ a_{21} & & \cdots & a_{2n} \\ & & \vdots & \\ a_{m1} & & \cdots & a_{mn} \end{bmatrix} \begin{bmatrix} b_1 \\ b_2 \\ \vdots \\ b_n \end{bmatrix}
$$

The standard algorithm for this problem uses mn multiplications and $m(n-1)$ additions.

Methods for obtaining lower bounds to the number of operations required in matrix-vector multiplication have been derived under the assumption that the algorithms are straight-line or are what are called chains in Chapter 2. (For a survey of these results, see Borodin, 1973.) These lower bounding methods invoke properties of the algebraic system from which the entries are drawn. However, a simple lower bound can be derived by using ideas developed in Chapter 2. Extend the definition of chains to functions over nonbinary sets realized by a sequence of operations, such as addition, multiplication, and negation, which are defined over nonbinary sets. Then Theorem 2.4.1.1 holds and, when applied to $c_1 + c_2 + \cdots + c_m$, gives a lower bound of $mn + n - 1$ for a basis of fan-in 2 since this sum depends on every entry of $\mathbf{A}$ and $\mathbf{b}$. Since $c_1 + c_2 + \cdots + c_m$ is realized from $c_1, c_2, \ldots, c_m$ with $m - 1$ additional operations, this provides a lower bound of $mn + n - m$ on the total number of operations. Under the appropriate conditions on the entries of the matrix and the vector, this can be improved by about a factor of 2 to show that the standard algorithm is optimal.

If the matrix $\mathbf{A}$ is special in some sense, then we would expect to improve on the standard algorithm for matrix multiplication. Consider an $n \times n$ *Toeplitz matrix* $\mathbf{T}$ whose entry set is $\{a_1, a_2, \ldots, a_{2n-1}\}$:

$$
\mathbf{T} = \begin{bmatrix} a_n & & \cdots & a_3 & a_2 & a_1 \\ a_{n+1} & a_n & \cdots & \cdots & a_3 & a_2 \\ \vdots & & & & & \\ \vdots & & & & & \\ a_{2n-1} & & \cdots & \cdots & a_{n+1} & a_n \end{bmatrix}
$$

All the elements on a diagonal of a Toeplitz matrix are the same.

If n is even, a Toeplitz matrix $\mathbf{T}$ can be written as a 2×2 matrix whose entries are $(n/2) \times (n/2)$ matrices (see Problem 8-13):

$$\mathbf{T} = \begin{bmatrix} \mathbf{T}_1 & \mathbf{T}_2 \\ \mathbf{T}_3 & \mathbf{T}_1 \end{bmatrix} = \begin{bmatrix} \mathbf{0} & \mathbf{T}_2 - \mathbf{T}_1 \\ \mathbf{T}_3 - \mathbf{T}_1 & \mathbf{0} \end{bmatrix} + \begin{bmatrix} \mathbf{T}_1 & \mathbf{T}_1 \\ \mathbf{T}_1 & \mathbf{T}_1 \end{bmatrix}$$

Furthermore, $\mathbf{T}_1$, $\mathbf{T}_2$, and $\mathbf{T}_3$ are also Toeplitz. If we write $\mathbf{T}$ as the sum of these two matrices, then multiplication of $\mathbf{T}$ by $\mathbf{b}$, a column n-vector, can be written as

$$\mathbf{Tb} = \begin{bmatrix} \mathbf{T}_1(\mathbf{b}_1 + \mathbf{b}_2) + (\mathbf{T}_2 - \mathbf{T}_1)\mathbf{b}_2 \\ (\mathbf{T}_3 - \mathbf{T}_1)\mathbf{b}_1 + \mathbf{T}_1(\mathbf{b}_1 + \mathbf{b}_2) \end{bmatrix}$$

where $\mathbf{b}$ is written as a 2-vector whose components are $(n/2)$-vectors $\mathbf{b}_1$ and $\mathbf{b}_2$, that is,

$$\mathbf{b} = \begin{bmatrix} \mathbf{b}_1 \\ \mathbf{b}_2 \end{bmatrix}$$

This algorithm for multiplication by $\mathbf{T}$ involves two additions (subtractions) of $(n/2) \times (n/2)$ Toeplitz matrices [which can be done by adding the $n - 1$ distinct entries in each with this many elementary operations for a total of $2(n - 1)$ operations] and three additions of $(n/2)$-vectors (using $3n/2$ elementary operations). If we call $T(n)$ the number of elementary operations necessary to multiply a Toeplitz $n \times n$ matrix by an n-vector when n is even, then we have the following bound:

$$T(n) \leq 3T\left(\frac{n}{2}\right) + \tfrac{7}{2}n - 2$$

Since

$$T(1) = 1 \qquad \text{if } n = 2^k$$

we have

$$T(2^k) \leq 7[3^k - 2^k] + 1 = 7[n^{\log_2 3} - n] + 1$$

where $\log_2 3 = 1.59$. Furthermore, since any $n \times n$ Toeplitz matrix can be imbedded in an $m \times m$ Toeplitz matrix, where $m = 2^{\lceil \log_2 n \rceil}$, it follows that multiplication of a vector by such a matrix requires a number of arithmetics that grows at worst as $n^{1.59}$. As shown in Problem 8-17, this rate of growth can be reduced to the order of $n \log n$.

Another special type of matrix is the *Kronecker product matrix*. The Kronecker product $\mathbf{A} \times \mathbf{B} = (a_{ij}\mathbf{B})$ is obtained by replacing the entry a_{ij} in $\mathbf{A}$ by the matrix $a_{ij}\mathbf{B}$. If $\mathbf{A}$ is $m \times n$ and $\mathbf{B}$ is $p \times q$, then $\mathbf{A} \times \mathbf{B}$ is $mp \times nq$. Furthermore, multiplication of $\mathbf{A} \times \mathbf{B}$ by an nq-vector $\mathbf{b}$ can be represented as

$$\mathbf{A} \times \mathbf{B}\, \mathbf{b} = (a_{ij}\mathbf{B}) \begin{bmatrix} \mathbf{b}_1 \\ \vdots \\ \mathbf{b}_n \end{bmatrix}$$

where $\mathbf{b}_i$ is a q-vector. Therefore, the product is obtained by forming $\mathbf{Bb}_i$ for $1 \le i \le n$ and then multiplying $\mathbf{A}$ by the p n-vectors consisting of the jth entries of $\mathbf{Bb}_1, \ldots, \mathbf{Bb}_n$ for $1 \le j \le p$. If $M_{\mathbf{A}}$ operations are necessary for matrix-vector multiplication by the matrix $\mathbf{A}$, then we have

$$M_{\mathbf{A} \times \mathbf{B}} \le pM_{\mathbf{A}} + nM_{\mathbf{B}}$$

for a bound on the number of operations to multiply by the Kronecker product of two matrices.

Consider a matrix $\mathbf{A}^{[k]}$ that is the kth *Kronecker power* of the $m \times m$ matrix $\mathbf{A}$, that is,

$$\mathbf{A}^{[1]} = \mathbf{A}$$
$$\mathbf{A}^{[k]} = \mathbf{A}^{[k-1]} \times \mathbf{A}, \qquad k \ge 2$$

Then the preceding inequality implies that

$$M_{\mathbf{A}^{[k]}} \le mM_{\mathbf{A}^{[k-1]}} + m^{k-1} \cdot m$$

since $\mathbf{A}^{[k]}$ is an $m^k \times m^k$ matrix. If $n = m^k$, it follows that

$$M_{\mathbf{A}^{[k]}} \le (k + 2(m-1))m^k = n(\log_m n + 2(m-1))$$

since $M_{\mathbf{A}} \le 2m^2 - m$. A particularly important Kronecker product matrix is the *Hadamard matrix* for which

$$\mathbf{A} = \begin{bmatrix} 1 & 1 \\ 1 & -1 \end{bmatrix}$$

For this matrix $M_{\mathbf{A}} = 2$, since multiplications are unnecessary, and the bound becomes

$$M_{\mathbf{H}_k} \le n \log_2 n$$

where $\mathbf{H}_k = \mathbf{A}^{[k]}$ and $n = 2^k$. The Hadamard matrix plays an important role in the *Walsh Transform* (see Walsh, 1923).

Another example of a special matrix is one whose entries are variables drawn from a set of s variables. If the matrix is $n \times n$, then procedures exist to multiply a vector by such a matrix with on the order of $n^2/\log_s n$ operations (see Savage, 1974). Thus, restricting the number of different entries in a matrix, even if they are all variables, can lead to an improvement on the standard algorithm. Such an algorithm can be used for multiplication of $n \times n$ matrices. Careful analysis of such an algorithm, which uses on the order of $n^3/\log_2 n$ operations for $s = 2$, shows that it is superior to Strassen's algorithm for $n \leq 10^{10}$!!!

8.2.4. The Fast Fourier Transform

The discrete Fourier Transform is a very important tool in signal processing that also has many other applications. The Fast Fourier Transform (FFT) algorithm is a method for computing the transform of a sequence of length n that uses on the order of $n \log n$ arithmetic operations as opposed to on the order of n^2 for the obvious algorithm. The improvement is substantial for strings of moderate length, and the FFT has made tractable what otherwise would be too costly or time consuming. The FFT has a long history and has been rediscovered many times. The paper by Cooley and Tukey (1965) led to its widespread use, but for a history of the subject, the reader is referred to Cooley, Lewis, and Welch (1967).

The discrete (complex) Fourier Transform is defined in terms of the principal nth root of unity $w = e^{i2\pi/n}$ in the ring of the complex numbers. (Here $i = \sqrt{-1}$ and n is an integer.) It has the following properties:

1. $w^n = 1$
2. $\displaystyle\sum_{k=0}^{n-1} w^{kl} = 0$ for $1 \leq |l| \leq n - 1$

Given a sequence $\mathbf{a} = (a_0, a_1, \ldots, a_{n-1})$ of n complex numbers, the *Fourier Transform* of $\mathbf{a}$, $F(\mathbf{a})$, is a sequence of n complex numbers

$$F(\mathbf{a}) = (f_0, f_1, \ldots, f_{n-1})$$

where

$$f_l = \sum_{k=0}^{n-1} a_k w^{kl}$$

We can write f_l as the value of the polynomial $p(x)$,

$$p(x) = a_0 + a_1 x + a_2 x^2 + \cdots + a_{n-1} x^{n-1}$$

at the point $x = w^l$, that is,

$$f_l = p(w^l)$$

We use this representation to derive the FFT.

Our task is to compute $p(w^l)$ for $0 \leq l \leq n - 1$. To do this, we separate out the odd- and even-numbered terms in $p(x)$ to form two polynomials $p_o(x)$ and $p_e(x)$ in terms of which we can write $p(x)$. This development is given in the following, in which we have assumed that n is even. It is due to Borodin and Munro (1975).

$$p(x) = a_0 + a_1 x + a_2 x^2 + \cdots + a_{n-1} x^{n-1}$$

$$= \left(a_0 + a_2 x^2 + \cdots + a_{n-2} x^{n-2} \right)$$

$$+ x\left(a_1 + a_3 x^2 + \cdots + a_{n-1} x^{n-2} \right)$$

$$= p_e(x^2) + x p_o(x^2)$$

Here

$$p_e(y) = a_0 + a_2 y + a_4 y^2 + \cdots + a_{n-2} y^{n/2-1}$$

and

$$p_o(y) = a_1 + a_3 y + a_5 y^2 + \cdots + a_{n-1} y^{n/2-1}$$

We observe that the evaluation of $p(x)$ at w^l, $0 \leq l \leq n - 1$, leads to the evaluation of $p_e(y)$ and $p_o(y)$ at $(w^l)^2$, $0 \leq l \leq n - 1$. But the distinct elements in $\{(w^l)^2 | 0 \leq l \leq n - 1\}$ are the elements in the set $\{\theta^{l'} | 0 \leq l' \leq n/2 - 1\}$, where $\theta = w^2 = e^{i2\pi/(n/2)}$ is the $(n/2)$th principal root of unity. Thus, the evaluation of $p(x)$ on $\{w^l | 0 \leq l \leq n - 1\}$ is equivalent to the evaluation of $p_e(x)$ and $p_o(x)$ on $\{\theta^l | 0 \leq l \leq n/2 - 1\}$ followed by one addition for each point in $\{w^l | 0 \leq l \leq n - 1\}$, that is, n additions, and one fewer multiplication, that is, $n - 1$ multiplications (because $w^0 = 1$).

Let $\Psi(n)$ be the number of (complex) arithmetic operations used by the preceding procedure to compute the discrete Fourier Transform of an n-sequence. Then

$$\psi(n) = 2\psi\left(\frac{n}{2} \right) + 2n - 1$$

and since $\psi(1) = 0$, it follows that for $n = 2^k$,

$$\psi(2^k) = (2k - 1)2^k + 1 = n(2 \log_2 n - 1) + 1$$

We summarize this result in a theorem taking into account the fact that if n is not a power of 2, an n-sequence can be padded with 0's so that its length is a power of 2.

Theorem 8.2.4.1. A straight-line algorithm exists for computing the complex Fourier Transform of an n-sequence that uses at most

$$(2k - 1)2^k + 1$$

additions, multiplications, and subtractions for $k = \lceil \log_2 n \rceil$.

It is interesting to examine the sequences whose Fourier Transforms are combined to form the Fourier Transform of the n-sequence. The subscripts of $a_0, a_1, \ldots, a_{n-1}$ for $n = 16$ and the successive groupings of odd and even-numbered coefficients that result from this algorithm are

0	1	2	3	4	5	6	7	8	9	10	11	12	13	14	15

0	2	4	6	8	10	12	14	1	3	5	7	9	11	13	15

0	4	8	12	2	6	10	14	1	5	9	13	3	7	11	15

0	8	4	12	2	10	6	14	1	9	5	13	3	11	7	15

0	8	4	12	2	10	6	14	1	9	5	13	3	11	7	15

The polynomial $p(x) = a_0 + a_1 x + \cdots + a_{15} x^{15}$ has an even polynomial $a_0 + a_2 x + a_4 x^2 + \cdots + a_{14} x^7$, and this in turn has an odd polynomial $a_0 + a_4 x + a_8 x^2 + a_{12} x^3$, and so on. To evaluate $p(x)$ at $w^0, w^1, \ldots, w^{15}$, where $w = e^{i2\pi/16}$, we evaluate its even and odd polynomials at θ^0, $\theta^1, \ldots, \theta^7$, where $\theta = e^{i2\pi/8}$, and the even and odd polynomials of these at $\psi^0, \psi^1, \psi^2, \psi^3$, where $\psi = e^{i2\pi/4}$, and so on.

The Fourier Transform of the n-sequence $\mathbf{a}$, $F(\mathbf{a}) = (f_0, f_1, \ldots, f_{n-1})$, has a corresponding *inverse transform* $F^{-1}(\mathbf{b})$, where $\mathbf{b}$ is also an n-sequence. If we associate the polynomial $q(x)$ with $F(\mathbf{a})$, that is,

$$q(x) = f_0 + f_1 x + f_2 x^2 + \cdots + f_{n-1} x^{n-1}$$

then we define F^{-1} by

$$F^{-1}(f_0, f_1, \ldots, f_{n-1}) = \left(\frac{1}{n} q(w^0), \frac{1}{n} q(w^{-1}), \ldots, \frac{1}{n} q(w^{-(n-1)}) \right)$$

and have

$$F^{-1}(F(\mathbf{a})) = \mathbf{a}$$

as we now show. This result follows from the already stated properties of a principal nth root of unity. We write

$$\frac{1}{n} q(w^{-l}) = \frac{1}{n} \left(f_0 + f_1 w^{-l} + \cdots + f_r(w^{-l})^r + \cdots + f_{n-1}(w^{-l})^{n-1} \right)$$

$$= \frac{1}{n} \sum_{r=0}^{n-1} \left(\sum_{k=0}^{n-1} a_k (w^r)^k \right) w^{-lr}$$

$$= \frac{1}{n} \sum_{k=0}^{n-1} a_k \left(\sum_{r=0}^{n-1} w^{r(k-l)} \right)$$

and the last inner sum on r is 0 unless $k = l$ when it has value n. Therefore, we have

$$\frac{1}{n} q(w^{-l}) = a_l$$

which is the desired conclusion.

Clearly, the same algorithm that has been given for computing the Fourier Transform can be applied to compute its inverse after replacing w by w^{-1}. Thus, both the Fourier Transform and its inverse can be computed using on the order of $n \log n$ arithmetic operations.

The FFT finds important application in the computation of the convolution of two sequences. The *convolution* of sequences $\mathbf{a} = (a_0, a_1, \ldots, a_{n-1})$ and $\mathbf{b} = (b_0, b_1, \ldots, b_{n-1})$, denoted $\mathbf{a} \otimes \mathbf{b}$, is a $2n$-sequence:

$$\mathbf{a} \otimes \mathbf{b} = (c_0, c_1, \ldots, c_{2n-1})$$

where

$$c_r = \sum_{\substack{0 \le k, l \le n-1 \\ k+l=r}} a_k b_l$$

Thus,

$$c_0 = a_0 b_0, \qquad c_1 = a_0 b_1 + a_1 b_0, \qquad c_2 = a_0 b_2 + a_1 b_1 + a_2 b_0$$

Actually, $c_{2n-1} = 0$, but we include it for simplicity. The following theorem demonstrates the role the Fourier Transform plays in the computation of the convolution of two sequences.

Theorem 8.2.4.2. Let F and F^{-1} denote the complex Fourier Transform and its inverse for $(2n)$-sequences. Let $\mathbf{a}$ and $\mathbf{b}$ be the following two $(2n)$-sequences:

$$\mathbf{a} = (a_0, a_1, \ldots, a_{n-1}, 0, \ldots, 0), \qquad \mathbf{b} = (b_0, b_1, \ldots, b_{n-1}, 0, \ldots, 0)$$

with transforms

$$F(\mathbf{a}) = (f_0, f_1, \ldots, f_{2n-1}), \qquad F(\mathbf{b}) = (g_0, g_1, \ldots, g_{2n-1})$$

The convolution $\mathbf{a} \otimes \mathbf{b}$ is a $(2n)$-sequence satisfying

$$\mathbf{a} \otimes \mathbf{b} = F^{-1}(F(\mathbf{a}) \times F(\mathbf{b}))$$

where

$$F(\mathbf{a}) \times F(\mathbf{b}) = (f_0 g_0, f_1 g_1, \ldots, f_{2n-1} g_{2n-1})$$

Proof. The convolution $\mathbf{a} \otimes \mathbf{b}$ is actually a $(4n)$-sequence whose rightmost $2n$ digits are 0, and we have taken the liberty of deleting these in the identity given for $\mathbf{a} \otimes \mathbf{b}$.

We have

$$f_r = \sum_{k=0}^{n-1} a_k (w^r)^k, \qquad g_r = \sum_{k=0}^{n-1} b_l (w^r)^l$$

since $a_j = b_j = 0$ for $j \geq n$. We have that

$$F^{-1}(F(\mathbf{a}) \times F(\mathbf{b})) = (h_0, h_1, \ldots, h_{2n-1})$$

where

$$h_t = \frac{1}{2n} \sum_{r=0}^{2n-1} f_r g_r (w^{-t})^r$$

$$= \frac{1}{2n} \sum_{r=0}^{2n-1} \sum_{k=0}^{n-1} \sum_{l=0}^{n-1} a_k b_l w^{r(k+l-t)}$$

$$= \sum_{k=0}^{n-1} \sum_{l=0}^{n-1} a_k b_l \left(\frac{1}{2n} \sum_{r=0}^{2n-1} w^{r(k+l-t)} \right)$$

By the two properties on the $(2n)$th root of unity, w, the inner sum is 0 except for $t = k + l$ when it is 1. Therefore,

$$h_t = \sum_{\substack{0 \leq k, l \leq n-1 \\ k+l=t}} a_k b_l = c_t$$

which establishes the desired result. $\square$

An immediate consequence of this, the *convolution theorem*, is that two n-sequences can be convolved with on the order of $n \log_2 n$ arithmetic operations. This is to be compared with the direct algorithm, which uses on the order of n^2 operations.

8.3. DIFFICULT COMBINATORIAL PROBLEMS

The traveling salesman problem (find the shortest route for a salesman who must visit n cities), the k-clique problem (does an undirected graph on n nodes contain a complete subgraph on k nodes?), and the 0-1 integer programming problem (does a set of linear equations possess a 0-1 solution?) are examples of problems that have been studied for decades by combinatorial mathematicians and computer scientists and for which all known algorithms have a running time that is exponential in the length of the input. Exponential growth is something to be avoided, if possible, because it can quickly put a problem beyond practical computational limits. It is important, then, to know whether or not these three problems, and many others for which only exponential-time algorithms are known, are truly exponential.

Ideally such problems are shown to be exponential by deriving exponential lower bounds to the running time of their best algorithms, or they are shown to be polynomial by constructing polynomial-time algorithms. In the absence of such strong results, we do the next best thing and show that a large class of problems exists with the property that every problem is transformable to every other problem in a time that is polynomial in the length of the input. From this, we conclude that all problems in the class are simultaneously polynomial or nonpolynomial, and answering the question for one problem is sufficient to answer it for the class.

There is a special class of great importance for which such polynomial transformations apply: the set of *NP*-complete problems. They contain the three problems and are so named because any problem that can be solved in polynomial time on a nondeterministic Turing machine (a machine that can "guess" a solution) is polynomially tranformable to them. Nondeterminism is a useful tool for establishing polynomial transformations, as we see.

Many *NP*-complete problems have been identified, and it seems that such problems are very difficult and probably exponential. If so, solutions are still needed, and we turn naturally to algorithms that provide approximate solutions. We show that some *NP*-complete problems have approximating algorithms that run in polynomial time while others have the property that all closely approximating algorithms are also *NP*-complete. For the latter problems, all known polynomial-time approximating algorithms yield results that are not arbitrarily close to the exact solutions.

The identification of the class of *NP*-complete problems and the first extensive enumeration of its members were done by Cook (1971) and Karp (1972).

8.3.1. Nondeterministic Turing Machines

A (basic) 1-tape Turing machine $T = \langle S, \Sigma, \delta, F, q_1 \rangle$ with a semiinfinite tape, state set S, tape alphabet Σ, final state set F (on which T halts), initial state q_1, and transition function δ (see Section 5.1) is *nondeterministic* if δ is a mapping from $S \times \Sigma$ to subsets of $S \times \Sigma \times \{L, N, R\}$. Thus, if T is in state q and reading tape symbol u, $\delta(q, u)$, the value of the transition function is a set of triples $\{(q', u', M)\}$ where q' is a successor state, u' is a new tape symbol, and M denotes head movement (L for left, N for none, and R for right). If the value of $\delta(q, u)$ is a single triple, the Turing machine is *deterministic* since each move is unambiguously defined. [There are called deterministic Turing machines (DTMs).]

There are several interpretations that can be given to a computation by a nondeterministic Turing machine (NDTM). If the value of $\delta(q, u)$ consists of more than one triple, a new copy of the machine could be created for each triple and the action indicated by the triple carried out, or some one triple could be chosen (by some arbitrary means) as the next move of the machine. In the first case, the number of copies of the machine that is created could grow exponentially with time, while in the second the next move is not predetermined, given q and u. The second interpretation invites the appellation *guessing* and clearly is nondeterministic in nature.

Let $B \in \Sigma$ be the blank tape symbol of the MDTM T. Then a nonblank string $\mathbf{w} \in (\Sigma - B)^*$ is *accepted* by T if, when placed left-adjusted on the otherwise blank tape of T, T can execute a series of moves, under the second interpretation given above, and end in a final state. The *language accepted by T*, $L(T)$, is the set of strings accepted by T. It is important to emphasize that $\mathbf{w}$ is accepted by T if there exists *some* sequence of moves ending in a halting state.

Example 8.3.1.1. Let $a_1, \ldots, a_r, b$ be positive integers. Then the *knapsack problem* is to determine whether or not there exists a subset of $\{a_1, \ldots, a_r\}$ that sums to b. If $a_1, \ldots, a_r, b$ are each represented in binary with a special marker # separating them, then the knapsack problem can be solved nondeterministically. One such machine scans the string from left to right and at each a_i decides whether or not to include that number in a sum it is forming (by marking a_i in some fashion). The sum is formed and compared with b, and the string is accepted if they are equal. If there is a subset of $\{a_1, \ldots, a_r\}$ that sums to b, one of the sequences of choices will find it, so the string w representing the knapsack problem is accepted by an NDTM if and only if the problem has a solution.

We can say more about this nondeterministic solution to the knapsack problem. The decisions on whether to include an a_i can be made in one scan, taking time n, where n is the length of the string. The items included in the sum can then be added deterministically in on the order of n^2 cycles and the comparison with b completed deterministically in on the order of n^2 or fewer cycles. Thus, the knapsack problem can be solved nondeterministically in polynomial time. This observation is useful later.

The languages defined above are those accepted by NDTMs that have a single semiinfinite tape. We might ask whether the set of languages changes any if the single tape is allowed to be doubly infinite or if more than one tape is allowed. Reference to the arguments of Section 5.2 will show that the answer is negative. Clearly the same is true for DTMs.

8.3.2. The Classes *P* and *NP*

We are now about to recognize two classes of languages: those that are accepted in polynomial time on DTMs, *P*, and those accepted in polynomial time on NDTMs, *NP*. For these definitions to be complete, we need to define polynomial-time acceptance.

Definition 8.3.2.1. A language $L \subset \Sigma^*$, Σ finite, is accepted in polynomial time by an NDTM T if $L(T) = L$ and if there exists a polynomial p such that if $w \in L$ is a string of length n, then T accepts w in at most $p(n)$ moves. If T is a DTM, L is accepted in polynomial time if, in addition, T rejects all strings of length n in $\Sigma^* - L$ in at most $p(n)$ moves.

The classes *P* and *NP* are now clearly defined. From the discussion of the preceding section, we see that the knapsack problem is in *NP*. If $P = NP$, then this problem has a polynomial solution, which is most interesting since all known algorithms for this problem require exponential time.

There are certain languages in *NP* that are prototypical in the sense that if any of these languages is in *P* then all languages in *NP* are in *P*. These are the *NP*-complete languages. To define them we introduce the notion of *polynomial transformability*.

Definition 8.3.2.2. A language L is *polynomially transformable* to a language L' if there is a deterministic Turing machine T that will convert each string w over the alphabet of L into a string w' over the alphabet of L' in a time that is bounded by a polynomial in the length of w, such that $w \in L$ if and only if $w' \in L'$.

Clearly, if L is polynomially transformable to L' and L' is accepted in polynomial time by a DTM, then we can determine membership in L deterministically in polynomial time. We are now prepared to define NP-complete languages.

Definition 8.3.2.3.   A language L is NP-complete if

1. $L \in NP$.
2. Every language in NP is polynomially transformable to L.

With these definitions, the following theorem is obvious.

Theorem 8.3.2.1.   Either all NP-complete languages are in P or none of them are. In the former case, $P = NP$.

In the next section, we demonstrate that the satisfiability problem is NP-complete. Armed with this fact, we show in the following section that a small sample of languages is NP-complete by demonstrating (1) that each is in NP and (2) that the satisfiability problem is polynomially transformable to each of them. Since every language in NP is polynomially tranformable to the satisfiability problem, it follows that the same is true for each of the sample languages and each is NP-complete.

Up to this point we have been speaking about two classes of *languages*, P and NP, and have been asking questions about the time to determine membership in these classes. This implies that we are looking for Yes–No answers to questions. However, there are many problems that not naturally have such answers, as indicated below.

Example 8.3.2.1.   An *undirected graph* G on n nodes is a pair $G = (N, E)$ where $N = \{1, 2, \ldots, n\}$ represents the nodes and $E \subseteq N \times N$ is a set of pairs denoting edges where $(i, j) \in E$ if there is an edge between nodes i and j. Clearly $(i, j) \in E$ if an only if $(j, i) \in E$, since G is undirected, although this condition does not hold in general for *directed graphs*. In the latter case, $(i, j) \in E$ means that G has an edge from node i to node j. An undirected graph G has a *k-clique* if there are k nodes in G such that all edges between these nodes are edges of G. (The subgraph defined by these k nodes is *complete*.) The *clique problem* is to find the size of the largest clique in a graph and the *k-clique problem* is to determine whether the graph has a k-clique. The graph of Figure 8.3.2.1 has a 3-clique and a 4-clique but no 5-clique.

Clearly the clique problem does not have a Yes–No answer as does the k-clique problem, but the latter can be solved for $2 \leq k \leq n$ to find the answer to the former. Consequently, they are both polynomial-time or both exponential-time problems.

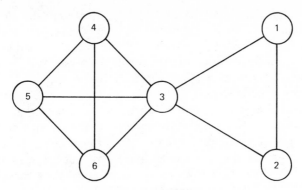

Figure 8.3.2.1. An undirected graph.

A few words must be said concerning the representation of Yes–No problems with languages. Given the k-clique problem, we need a natural statement of it that reflects the way it is normally computed and that provides all the information needed to solve it. The k-clique problem for $G = (N, E)$ could be described by a string of the form

$$k, (p_1, q_1), (p_2, q_2), \ldots, (p_r, q_r)$$

where $(p_i, q_i) \in E$ and $r \le n(n - 1)/2$, the maximum number of edges that G could have when $|N| = n$. For the graph shown in Figure 8.3.2.1, the 5-clique problem would be stated as

$$5, (1, 2), (1, 3), (2, 3), (3, 4), (3, 5), (3, 6), (4, 5), (4, 6), (5, 6)$$

At this point, however, the encoding of the problem is not complete because we have not specified how the integers are to be represented.

It is natural to give integers the standard binary representation, as we assume, but other less natural encodings can change the character of the problem. For example, if integer m is represented as $0^{2^m}1$, then the preceding string will have a length that is exponential in n, the number of nodes. Since the largest clique can be found by examining all sets of n or fewer nodes to see if they form a clique, there being 2^n such sets, it is easy to show that the problem can be solved in a number of steps that is polynomial in the length of the (exponential length) input. If the integers are encoded in binary, however, the input has length of at most $Kn^2\log_2 n$ for some constant $K > 0$, and this algorithm becomes an exponential-time algorithm.

Since most problems of interest to us will have their input specified in binary, decimal, or other radix notation, we assume that the standard binary notation is used, to which other radix notations can be transformed in polynomial time. We also assume that graphs are represented by edges (a, b) where a and b are node labels that we assume take values from 1 to n when the graphs have n nodes. Where Boolean variables are used, as in the satisfiability problem, we represent them by integers in a context where their meaning is understood.

We make one last major point before going on to show that satisfiability is NP-complete. The language representation of the k-clique problem gives a string for each k, each n, and each graph of $n(n - 1)/2$ or fewer edges, and the question asked is whether the graph on n nodes specified by such a string has a k-clique. The question is to be settled by a machine that is programmed to handle all values of k and n and all graphs on n nodes. Thus, the machine implements a *universal algorithm*. However, if for each n we use the algorithm that minimizes time (a potentially nonuniversal algorithm), we find that *time is polynomial in n* because the machine (such as Turing machine or M_{RAM} of Chapter 7) can use the input string as an address of a storage location (in the Control of the Turing machine or in the RAM of M_{RAM}) that is preprogrammed to contain the answer. Thus, a potentially nonuniversal algorithm exists (table look-up) that solves the k-clique problem in polynomial time. Because the space used in table look-up, however, is exponential in the input, we are moved to ask whether space can be made polynomial in the input. It can, but the time required seems to be exponential. With these thoughts in mind, we recall the computational inequalities of the first and second kind of Chapter 7 and recognize that they could be useful in bounding the space–time tradeoffs that hold for nonuniversal algoithms. These arguments apply to all the NP-complete problems discussed.

8.3.3. The Satisfiability Problem is *NP*-complete

A formula of the form $(x_1 + \bar{x}_2)(\bar{x}_3 + x_2)(\bar{x}_1)$, which is the product (AND) of sums (OR) of literals (Boolean variables with or without complementation) is said to be in *product of sums* (POS) *form*. A formula in POS form is said to be *satisfiable* if there is an assignment of values to variables so that the formula has value 1. The preceding formula is satisfiable when $x_1 = 0$, $x_2 = 0$, and $x_3 = 0$.

Definition 8.3.3.1. The *satisfiability problem* is to determine whether or not a formula in POS form is satisfiable. We call this *POS-satisfiability*.

An example of a formula in POS form that is satisfiable has been given. One that is not satisfiable is $(x_1 + \bar{x}_2)(\bar{x}_1 + x_3)(\bar{x}_1 + \bar{x}_3)(x_1 + x_2)$, as the reader can show.

Our task in this section is to demonstrate that every language in NP is polynomially transformable to POS-satisfiability and that POS-satisfiability is also in *NP*. By the definition of the preceding section, any (reasonable) language, SAT, that characterizes this problem is *NP*-complete. One such reasonable language represents variable x_i by the integer i in binary and uses brackets (,), operators •, + for AND and OR, and ⌐ to denote Boolean complementation. If **i** denotes the integer i in binary with leading 0's deleted, then we can write $(x_1 + \bar{x}_2)(\bar{x}_3 + x_2)(\bar{x}_1)$ as $(1 + ⌐\ 2)•(⌐\ 3 + 2)•(⌐\ 1)$. At the risk of some loss of precision, we identify the language SAT with POS-satisfiability.

Any other reasonable language for POS-satisfiability is polynomially transformable to SAT, and vice versa. We now show that any language in *NP* is polynomially transformable to SAT.

Let $L \in NP$ and let L be accepted by an NDTM $T = \langle S, \Sigma, \delta, F, q_1 \rangle$ in polynomial time $p(n)$. Let the state set $S = \{q_1, \ldots, q_s\}$ and the tape alphabet $\Sigma = \{\sigma_1, \ldots, \sigma_r\}$ where, without loss of generality, we let σ_r denote the blank B. We number the squares of the semiinfinite tape from left to right with square 1 being the first, 2 the second, and so forth. For each string **w** of length n over $\Sigma - \{\sigma_r\}$, we construct a formula that is satisfiable if and only if $\mathbf{w} \in L$. This formula is constructed using the following Boolean variables:

1. $SQ(i, j, t)$, which is 1 if and only if square i of the tape contains symbol σ_j at time t, $1 \le i \le p(n)$, $1 \le j \le r$, and $0 \le t \le p(n)$.
2. $Q(k, t)$, which is 1 if and only if T is in state q_k at time t, $1 \le k \le s$ and $0 \le t \le p(n)$.
3. $H(i, t)$, which is 1 if and only if the head of T is over square i at time t, $1 \le i \le p(n)$ and $0 \le t \le p(n)$.

We have introduced variables for tape squares numbered i and time t for $1 \le i \le p(n)$ and $0 \le t \le p(n)$ because it is possible that $p(n)$ squares can be visited by T while processing a string **w** of length n. The number of variables introduced here is $(p(n) + 1)[s + (r + 1)p(n)]$, which is polynomial in n since r and s are fixed.

We use these variables to construct seven formulas, $A, B, \ldots, G$, which are satisfiable if and only if the following seven conditions are met, and these hold if and only if T accepts a string **w** of length n, that is, if and only if $\mathbf{w} \in L$.

1. The tape head is scanning one tape square at each instant of time t, $0 \le t \le p(n)$.
2. Each tape square contains exactly one symbol at each instant of time t, $0 \le t \le p(n)$.
3. T is in exactly one state at each instant of time t, $0 \le t \le p(n)$.
4. T is in state q_1 initially, that is, at $t = 0$, the head is over square 1, the

first n squares of the tape contain **w** of length n, and the remaining $p(n) - n$ squares are blank.

5. At most one tape square, the one under the head, has its contents changed in any one cycle.

6. The change of state, head position, and contents of the square under the head are those allowed by the transition function δ of T.

7. Since T halts in a final state, the state of T at time $p(n)$ must be a final state.

To construct the formulas associated with these seven conditions, we make use of the first elementary symmetric function $\sigma_1 : \{0, 1\}^p \to \{0, 1\}$ of Section 3.1.2, which, to avoid confusion with tape symbols, we call $u_p : \{0, 1\}^p \to \{0, 1\}$. We write the following formula for u_p which is 1 if and only if exactly one of its variables is 1:

$$u_p(x_1, \ldots, x_p) = (x_1 + \cdots + x_p)\left[\prod_{\substack{i,j \\ 1 \le i < j \le p}} (\bar{x}_i + \bar{x}_j)\right]$$

Here $\prod$ denotes AND and the product is 0 if two or more variables are 1. Since the sum is 0 if all variables are 0, the formula is 1 exactly when one variable is 1. This formula has $p(p + 1)/2$ occurrences of variables.

We now derive the formulas $A, B, \ldots, G$ that describe the seven conditions:

1. $A_t = u_{p(n)}(H(1, t), H(2, t), \ldots, H(p(n), t))$

$$A = A_0 \cdot A_1 \cdot \cdots \cdot A_{p(n)}$$

2. $B_{it} = u_r(SQ(i, 1, t), SQ(i, 2, t), \ldots, SQ(i, r, t))$

$$B = \prod_{0 \le t \le p(n)} \prod_{1 \le i \le p(n)} B_{it}$$

3. $C_t = u_s(Q(1, t), Q(2, t), \ldots, Q(s, t))$

$$C = \prod_{0 \le t \le p(n)} C_t$$

4. $D = Q(1, 0)H(1, 0) \prod_{1 \le i \le n} SQ(i, j_i, 0) \prod_{n < i \le p(n)} SQ(i, r, 0)$

Here j_i is the index of the ith tape symbol in the string $\mathbf{w} = (w_1, w_2, \ldots, w_n)$, that is, $w_i = \sigma_{j_i}$. Also, σ_r denotes the blank B.

5. $E_{ijt} = (\overline{SQ(i,j,t) \oplus SQ(i,j,t+1)}) + H(i,t)$

$$E = \prod_{0 \le t \le p(n)-1} \prod_{1 \le i \le p(n)} \prod_{1 \le j \le r} E_{ijt}$$

Here E_{ijt} is 1 if square i contains σ_j at time t and $t+1$ or if the head is over this square at time t. It follows that condition 5 is satisfied if ABE is 1 because then the head is over at most one square, a square contains at most one symbol, and at most one square can have its contents changed in one cycle, the square under the head.

6. For each value of $i, j, k,$ and $t,$
   (a) the tape head is not over square i at time t
   or
   (b) the machine T is not in state q_k at time t.
   or
   (c) the ith square does not contain σ_j at time t
   or
   (d) the converse of each of the preceding holds, and T makes one of the allowed transitions from state q_k with tape symbol σ_j at square i and time t.

We capture these conditions with the formula F_{ijkt}:

$$F_{ijkt} = \overline{H(i,t)} + \overline{Q(k,t)} + \overline{SQ(i,j,t)}$$

$$+ \sum_l SQ(i,j_l,t+1)Q(k_l,t+1)H(i_l,t+1)$$

$$F = \prod_{0 \le t \le p(n)-1} \prod_{1 \le i \le p(n)} \prod_{1 \le j \le r} \prod_{1 \le k \le s} F_{ijkt}$$

Here Σ denotes OR, and the sum is over all triples (j_l, k_l, i_l) that could result from a transition $\delta(q_k, \sigma_j)$. Note that $i_l = i - 1$, i, or $i + 1$ depending on whether the head movement allowed by $\delta(q_k, \sigma_j)$ is L, N, or R. Also, condition 6 holds if $ABCEF$ is 1.

7. $G = Q(k_1, p(n)) + Q(k_2, p(n)) + \cdots + Q(k_z, p(n))$. Here $q_{k_1}, \ldots, q_{k_z}$ are the final states of T, and G is 1 only if T is in a final state at time $t = p(n)$.

The formula $ABCDEFG$ is clearly 1 only when T makes a sequence of at most $p(n)$ moves allowed by δ, which results in acceptance of **w** of length

n. We are almost done because u_p is in product of sums form, as are A_t and A, B_{it} and B, C_t and C, and D and G. The formulas E_{ijt} and F_{ijkt} are not in this form, but, since they both have a bounded number of variables, they are transformable to formulas in this form in a fixed number of steps. This could be done by computing the conjunctive normal form for each, as described in Section 2.1.

The last observations that are required are that the variables denoting the status of squares, the head, and the state can each be represented by binary numbers of length at most $K \log_2 n$ for some $K > 0$ and that they occur a polynomial number of times in the formula $ABCDEFG$. Therefore, the length of this formula is polynomial in n and the question of acceptance of **w**, a string of length n, by T, is polynomially transformable to a Boolean expression in POS form that is satisfiable if and only if **w** is accepted by T, that is, if **w** $\in L$. We have proved the following.

Theorem 8.3.3.1. The satisfiability of Boolean expressions in product of sums form is NP-complete.

We now exhibit a number of important problems that are also NP-complete.

8.3.4. Some NP-Complete Problems

We are now prepared to list a number of interesting NP-complete problems. We give the name of each problem, specify the input that is given, and define the property that must hold on the input.

1. POS-SATISFIABILITY
   INPUT: Clauses $S_1, S_2, \ldots, S_n$ where $S_i \subseteq \{x_1, \ldots, x_p, \bar{x}_1, \ldots, \bar{x}_p\}$
   for some p and S_i does not contain x_j and $\bar{x}_j$ for any
   $1 \leq j \leq p$.
   PROPERTY: There exist $c_1, c_2, \ldots, c_p \in \{0, 1\}$ such that with $x_j = c_j$, all S_i are satisfiable; that is, at least one element of S_i
   is 1 for $1 \leq i \leq n$.

2. CLIQUE
   INPUT: Undirected graph G, positive integer k.
   PROPERTY: G has a set of k mutually adjacent nodes, a k-clique.

3. 3-SATISFIABILITY
   INPUT: Clauses $S_1, S_2, \ldots, S_n$ where
   $S_i \subseteq \{x_1, \ldots, x_p, \bar{x}_1, \ldots, \bar{x}_p\}$ for some p and $|S_i| \leq 3$.
   PROPERTY: All S_i are satisfiable.

4. 0-1 INTEGER PROGRAMMING
   INPUT: Integer matrix **C** and integer vector **b**.
   PROPERTY: There exists a 0-1 vector **v** such that $\mathbf{Cv} = \mathbf{b}$.

5. CHROMATIC NUMBER
   INPUT:　Undirected graph G, positive integer k.
   PROPERTY: There is an assignment of k colors to nodes of G such
   　　　　　　that no two adjacent nodes have the same color.
6. EXACT COVER
   INPUT: Family $\{S_j\}$ of subsets of S,　$S_j \subseteq S = \{u_1, \ldots, u_p\}$.
   PROPERTY: There exist $S_{j_1}, S_{j_2}, \ldots, S_{j_t}$ for some $t \geq 1$ such that
   　　　　　　these subsets are disjoint and $\bigcup_{1 \leq l \leq t} S_{j_l} = S$.
7. KNAPSACK
   INPUT:　Positive integers $a_1, a_2, \ldots, a_n, d$
   PROPERTY: $\sum_j a_j x_j = d$ has a 0-1 solution.
8. TASK SEQUENCING
   INPUT:　Positive integers $T_1, T_2, \ldots, T_p$, which are execution times;
   　　　　　$D_1, D_2, \ldots, D_p$, which are deadlines; $P_1, P_2, \ldots, P_p$, which
   　　　　　are penalties; and positive integer k.
   PROPERTY: There is a permutation π of $\{1, 2, \ldots, p\}$ such that

$$\left(\sum_{j=1}^{p} \left[\text{if } T_{\pi(1)} + \cdots + T_{\pi(j)} > D_{\pi(j)} \text{ then } P_{\pi(j)} \text{ else } 0 \right] \right) \leq k$$

9. DIRECTED TRAVELING SALESMAN
   INPUT:　Directed graph $G = (N, E)$, nonnegative integers $d(i, j)$ (the
   　　　　　distance from node i to node j), $i, j \in N$, and positive
   　　　　　integer k.
   PROPERTY: There is a permutation π of $N = \{1, 2, \ldots, n\}$ such
   　　　　　that

$$d(\pi(1), \pi(2)) + d(\pi(2), \pi(3)) + \cdots + d(\pi(n), \pi(1)) = k$$

10. UNDIRECTED TRAVELING SALESMAN
    Same as the preceding except that $G = (N', E')$ is undirected.
11. APPROXIMATE TRAVELING SALESMAN
    INPUT:　Undirected graph $G = (N, E)$, nonnegative integers $d(i, j)$,
    　　　　　$i, j \in N$, and positive integers l, e.
    PROPERTY: There is a permutation π of $N = \{1, 2, \ldots, n\}$ such
    　　　　　that

$$l \leq d(\pi(1), \pi(2)) + d(\pi(2), \pi(3)) + \cdots + d(\pi(n), \pi(1)) \leq l\left(1 + \frac{1}{e}\right)$$

The first two problems have been discussed. The third, 3-SATISFIA-
BILITY, is POS-SATISFIABILITY, in which each sum has at most three
literals. The next four problems, 0-1 INTEGER PROGRAMMING,
CHROMATIC NUMBER, EXACT COVER, and KNAPSACK are easy

to understand whereas the next, TASK SEQUENCING, needs a few words of explanation. The problem here is to find an ordering of the tasks that minimizes the sum of the penalties assigned if the tasks are not completed within the specified deadlines. The DIRECTED TRAVELING SALESMAN problem and its undirected version are to find a closed path that visits *n* cities (a *tour*) and that has minimum cost. In the first case, the tour must respect the direction of edges. The APPROXIMATE TRAVEL-ING SALESMAN problem is to find a tour on an undirected graph whose length is within a factor of $(1 + 1/e)$ times the length of the minimum tour.

Theorem 8.3.4.1. Each of the 11 problems defined above is NP-complete.

To show that a language is NP-complete, we must show that it is in NP and that every language in NP is polynomially transformable to it. To show the latter, it is sufficient to show that *any* NP-complete language is polynomially transformable to it because the composition of two poly-nomial transformations is a polynomial transformation. Figure 8.3.4.1

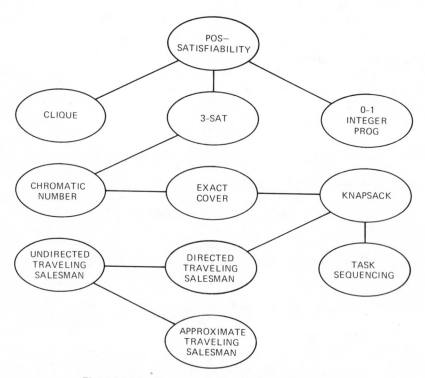

Figure 8.3.4.1. Sequence of polynomial transformations.

shows the sequence of polynomial transformations that we make from POS-SATISFIABILITY to each of our remaining 10 problems. Since it is easy to show that each of these 10 languages is in *NP*, we will have demonstrated that each of them is *NP*-complete.

We now state in compact form the polynomial transformations that are indicated in Figure 8.3.4.1. They are followed by a few explanatory comments. The reader should note that a transformation maps the input of one problem onto that of another such that the property of the second is satisfied if and only if that of the first is. Furthermore, the transformation must be one that can be completed by a Turing machine in a number of cycles that is polynomial in the length of the input to the first problem. We use the notation **PROBLEM 1** → **PROBLEM 2** to indicate that the first problem is being transformed to the second.

POS-SATISFIABILITY → 0-1 INTEGER PROGRAMMING

$$
c_{ij} = \begin{cases}
1, & \text{if } x_j \in S_i, \quad 1 \le j \le p \\
-1, & \text{if } \bar{x}_j \in S_i, \quad 1 \le j \le p \\
-1, & ip + 1 \le j \le (i+1)p \\
0, & \text{otherwise}
\end{cases}
$$

$$b_i = 1 - q_i$$

q_i = number of complemented variables in S_i

$\mathbf{C} = [c_{ij}]$ is $n \times m$ where $m = (n+1)p$.

COMMENT. Write $\mathbf{C}$ and $\mathbf{v}$ as

$$
\mathbf{C} = \begin{bmatrix}
& -1 & -1 & \cdots & -1 & 0 & \cdots & 0 & 0 & \cdots & 0 \\
& 0 & 0 & & 0 & -1 & \cdots & -1 & & \vdots & \\
\mathbf{B} & \vdots & & & & \vdots & & & 0 & \cdots & 0 \\
& 0 & 0 & \cdots & 0 & 0 & \cdots & 0 & -1 & \cdots & -1
\end{bmatrix},
$$

$$
\mathbf{v} = \begin{bmatrix} \mathbf{y} \\ \mathbf{z} \end{bmatrix}
$$

where $\mathbf{B}$ is $n \times p$ and there are an additional p entries in each row that are -1. Also, $\mathbf{y}$ is a p-vector and $\mathbf{z}$ is an (np)-vector, both of which are 0-1. Furthermore, $\mathbf{Cv} = \mathbf{b}$ if and only if $\mathbf{By} \geq \mathbf{b}$. Consider the ith component in $\mathbf{By}$ and let $\mathbf{y}$ select u_i uncomplemented variables and k_i complemented variables from the ith row of $\mathbf{B}$. Then $u_i - k_i \geq b_i = 1 - q_i$ or $u_i + (q_i - k_i) \geq 1$. Let $\mathbf{y}$ specify the values given to the variables $x_1, x_2, \ldots, x_p$. Then u_i is the number of uncomplemented variables of S_i set to 1 and $q_i - k_i$ is the number of complemented variables set to 0 and $u_i + (q_i - k_i) \geq 1$ if and only if S_i is satisfied. Thus, the clauses $S_1, \ldots, S_n$ are simultaneously satisfied if and only if $\mathbf{Cv} = \mathbf{b}$.

POS-SATISFIABILITY $\rightarrow$ CLIQUE

$$N = \{\langle y, i\rangle | y \text{ is a literal in } S_i\}$$

$$E = \{\langle y, i\rangle, \langle z, j\rangle | i \neq j \text{ and } y \neq \bar{z}\}$$

$$k = n, \text{ the number of clauses}$$

COMMENT   For each literal (x_j or $\bar{x}_j$) in S_i, for each i, there is a node in the graph $G = (N, E)$. The nodes $\langle y, i\rangle$ for $y \in S_i$ have no edges between them, and $\langle y, i\rangle$ and $\langle z, j\rangle$ are adjacent for $i \neq j$ if and only if $y \neq \bar{z}$. If G has an n-clique, the clique contains exactly one node from each set $\{\langle y, i\rangle | y \in S_i\}$, $1 \leq i \leq n$. Let $\langle y_1, 1\rangle, \langle y_2, 2\rangle, \ldots, \langle y_n, n\rangle$ be these n nodes. This set is a clique if and only if there does not exist r and s such that $y_r = \bar{y}_s$. Consequently, $y_1, y_2, \ldots, y_n$ can be given values independently to satisfy all clauses. Therefore, all clauses are satisfiable if and only if the stated graph has an n-clique.

POS-SATISFIABILITY $\rightarrow$ 3-SATISFIABILITY

Replace each clause S_i of the form $y_1 + y_2 + \cdots + y_k$, $k \geq 4$, with the following product of sums:

$$(y_1 + y_2 + z_1)(y_3 + \bar{z}_1 + z_2)(y_4 + \bar{z}_2 + z_3)$$

$$\cdots (y_{k-2} + \bar{z}_{k-4} + z_{k-3})(y_{k-1} + y_k + \bar{z}_{k-3})$$

Here $z_1, z_2, \ldots, z_{k-3}$ are new Boolean variables.

3-SATISFIABILITY → CHROMATIC NUMBER

$$N = \{x_1, \ldots, x_p\} \cup \{\bar{x}_1, \ldots, \bar{x}_p\} \cup \{v_1, \ldots, v_p\} \cup \{s_1, \ldots, s_n\}$$

$$E = \{(v_i, v_j) | i \neq j\} \cup \{(x_i, \bar{x}_i) | 1 \leq i \leq p\}$$

$$\cup \{(v_i, x_j), (v_i, \bar{x}_j) | i \neq j\}$$

$$\cup \{(s_i, x_j) | x_j \notin S_i\} \cup \{(s_i, \bar{x}_j) | \bar{x}_j \notin S_i\}$$

$G = (N, E)$ is undirected

$k = p + 1$

Assume that $p \geq 4$ because otherwise 3-SATISFIABILITY is in P.

COMMENT. The subgraph with nodes $\{v_1, \ldots, v_p\}$ is complete and requires p colors since all nodes are adjacent. But nodes x_i and $\bar{x}_i$ are adjacent to each other and to v_j for $j \neq i$. Therefore, at least $p + 1$ colors are necessary. If $p + 1$ colors are used, either x_i and v_i (which are not adjacent) have the same color or $\bar{x}_i$ and v_i do. But one or the other of nodes x_i and $\bar{x}_i$ has a $(p + 1)$st color which we call RED. If z_i is the one of $\{x_i, \bar{x}_i\}$ that is not RED, then, since it has the same color as v_i, the nodes $\{z_1, \ldots, z_p\}$ have p different colors.

The nodes $s_1, s_2, \ldots, s_n$ have to be assigned colors. Each s_i is adjacent to at least $2n - 3$ of the nodes $\{x_1, \ldots, x_p, \bar{x}_1, \ldots, \bar{x}_p\}$. Since $2n - 3 \geq n + 1$ for $n \geq 4$, each s_i is adjacent to both x_j and $\bar{x}_j$ for some $1 \leq j \leq p$. Therefore, s_i cannot be RED. If the graph has a $(p + 1)$-coloring, s_i has one of the other p colors.

We claim that for each i, there exists a literal $y \in S_i$ such that node y is not RED. If not, then all $y \in S_i$ are colored RED and s_i is adjacent to the nodes $\{z_1, \ldots, z_p\}$ of all p colors plus RED nodes, or more than $p + 1$ colors are necessary. Thus, the given graph is $(p + 1)$-colorable if and only if there exists a literal $y \in S_i$ that is not RED. Now assign value 0 to RED nodes and 1 to the others. Then the n clauses are all satisfied (since $\bar{y} = 0$ or $y = 1$ for some $y \in S_i$) if and only if the given graph has a $(p + 1)$-coloring.

CHROMATIC NUMBER → EXACT COVER

Given $G = (N, E)$, let $S = N \cup \{\langle e, i \rangle | e \in E, 1 \leq i \leq k\}$ with a family of subsets $\{S_{vi}, R_{ei}\}$ for $v \in N$, $e \in E$, and $1 \leq i \leq k$, where

$$S_{vi} = \{v\} \cup \{\langle e, i \rangle | e \text{ is incident upon } v \in N\}$$

$$R_{ei} = \{\langle e, i \rangle\}$$

COMMENT. Let G have a k-coloring with color c_v (an integer) attached to node v for $1 \leq c_v \leq k$. The family of subsets S_{vc_v} for $v \in N$, together with R_{ei} for $\langle e, i \rangle \notin S_{vc_v}$ for any v, is an exact cover, as we show. If $e = (v, w)$ is an edge of G, then $c_v \neq c_w$, and S_{vc_v} and S_{wc_w} are disjoint. If v and w are not adjacent, they are also disjoint. Furthermore, every element of S is in one of these subsets.

If S has an exact cover, then for each $v \in N \subseteq S$, there is a unique c_v such that $v \in S_{vc_v}$. Furthermore, $1 \leq c_v \leq k$. If G does not have a k-coloring, then there exists $e = (v, w)$ such that $c_v = c_w$. But this implies that S_{vc_v} and S_{wc_w} both contain $\langle e, c_v \rangle$, which contradicts the assumption that S has an exact cover. Therefore, G has a k-coloring if and only if the set S has an exact cover.

EXACT COVER → KNAPSACK

Let $n = |\{S_j\}|$, $\beta = |\{S_j\}| + 1$, $d = (\beta^p - 1)/(\beta - 1)$. Then

$$\varepsilon_{ji} = \begin{cases} 1, & u_i \in S_j \\ 0, & \text{otherwise} \end{cases}, \qquad a_j = \sum_{i=0}^{p-1} \varepsilon_{ji} \beta^{i-1}$$

COMMENT. If $a_{j_1} + a_{j_2} + \cdots + a_{j_t} = d$, then

$$\sum_{r=1}^{t} a_{j_r} = \sum_{i=0}^{p-1} \left(\sum_{r=1}^{t} \varepsilon_{j_r, i} \right) \beta^{i-1} = d = 1 + \beta + \beta^2 + \cdots + \beta^{p-1}$$

However, $\sum_{r=1}^{t} \varepsilon_{j_r, i} \leq \beta - 1$, so for each $0 \leq i \leq p - 1$,

$$\sum_{r=1}^{t} \varepsilon_{j_r, i} = 1$$

Therefore, for each i, u_i is in exactly one subset S_{j_r}, and the subsets S_{j_1}, $S_{j_2}, \ldots, S_{j_t}$ form an exact cover. The converse argument is almost identical.

KNAPSACK → DIRECTED TRAVELING SALESMAN

$$N = \{0, 1, 2, \ldots, n + 1\}$$

$$E = \{(i, j) | i, j \in N\}$$

$$d(i, j) = \begin{cases} a_j, & i \leq j \leq n \\ 0, & \text{otherwise} \end{cases}$$

$$k = d$$

COMMENT. All edges entering node j, $1 \leq j \leq n$, have weight a_j except those from nodes $i > j$. All edges entering and exiting node $n + 1$ have weight 0. Let $\pi(0)$, $\pi(1)$, ..., $\pi(n + 1)$ be a cycle of weight $k = d$ where π is a permutation of N. Then

$$d(\pi(j-1), \pi(j)) = \begin{cases} a_j, & \pi(j-1) < \pi(j) \leq n \\ 0, & \text{otherwise} \end{cases}$$

and there exist $a_{j_1}, \ldots, a_{j_t}$ whose sum is d. On the other hand, given $a_{j_1}, \ldots, a_{j_t}$ whose sum is d, order the indices so that $j_1 < j_2 < \cdots < j_t$ and construct a permutation where $\pi(0) = 0$, $\pi(1) = j_1$, $\pi(2) = j_2$, ..., $\pi(t) = j_t$, $\pi(t + 1) = n + 1$, and $\pi(l)$, $t + 2 \leq l \leq n + 1$ visits the remaining indices in N in decreasing order. The weight of this cycle is precisely $a_{j_1} + \cdots + a_{j_t}$.

DIRECTED TRAVELING SALESMAN $\rightarrow$ UNDIRECTED TRAVELING SALESMAN

$$N' = \{\langle v, 0 \rangle, \langle v, 1 \rangle, \langle v, 2 \rangle | v \in N\}$$

$$E' = \{(\langle v, 0 \rangle, \langle v, 1 \rangle), (\langle v, 1 \rangle, \langle v, 2 \rangle) | v \in N\}$$

$$\cup \{(\langle v, 2 \rangle, \langle w, 0 \rangle) | (v, w) \in E\}$$

$$d'(\langle v, i \rangle, \langle v, i + 1 \rangle) = 0, \qquad i = 0, 1, \quad v \in N$$

$$d'(\langle v, 2 \rangle, \langle w, 0 \rangle) = d(v, w), \qquad v, w \in N$$

COMMENT. $G' = (N', E')$ is undirected and contains three nodes, $\langle v, 0 \rangle$, $\langle v, 1 \rangle$, and $\langle v, 2 \rangle$, for every node of $G = (N, E)$. Node $\langle v, 1 \rangle$ is adjacent to $\langle v, 0 \rangle$ and $\langle v, 2 \rangle$ and no other nodes of G'. Node $\langle v, 2 \rangle$ and $\langle w, 0 \rangle$ are adjacent if and only if there is an edge in G from v to w. Any cycle of G' must visit nodes whose second component varies in the order 0, 1, 2, 0, 1, ..., or 2, 1, 0, 2, 1 .... Since G' is undirected, there is no loss of generality in assuming that the first order applies. But this represents a directed cycle in the original graph of the same length since the directed edge (v, w) in G corresponds to the path $\langle v, 0 \rangle$, $\langle v, 1 \rangle$, $\langle v, 2 \rangle$, $\langle w, 0 \rangle$ in G'.

UNDIRECTED TRAVELING SALESMAN $\rightarrow$ APPROXIMATE TRAVELING SALESMAN

Same graph

$$d'(i, j) = 1 + d(i, j)$$

$$l = k + |N|, \qquad e = k + |N| + 1$$

COMMENT. $d'(i, j) \geq 1$ for all $i, j \in N$, and the length of a cycle in this problem is $|N|$ plus the length of the same cycle in the original problem. The difference between the upper and lower bounds on cycle length for cycles satisfying the condition is $l/e = (k + |N|)/(k + |N| + 1) < 1$. It follows from $d'(i, j) \geq 1$ that any such cycle has length $l = k + |N|$, or its length in the original graph is exactly k. Thus, it is just about as difficult to get a very good approximation to the traveling salesman problem as to solve the problem directly.

KNAPSACK → TASK SEQUENCING

$$n = p, \qquad T_i = P_i = a_i, \qquad D_i = d, \qquad k = \left(\sum_i a_i \right) - d$$

COMMENT. The property that must be satisfied is

$$\sum_{j=1}^{n} \left[\text{if } a_{\pi(1)} + \cdots + a_{\pi(j)} > d \text{ then } a_{\pi(j)} \text{ else } 0 \right] \leq k$$

for some permutation π of $\{1, 2, \ldots, n\}$. The sum is the sum of the penalties $a_{\pi(l+1)}, \ldots, a_{\pi(n)}$ where l is such that $s = a_{\pi(1)} + \cdots + a_{\pi(l)} \leq d$ and $s + a_{\pi(l+1)} > d$. Thus, the sum of the sum of the penalties is $\geq \sum_i a_i - d$ and if the sum is $\leq k$, then the sum of the first l terms is exactly d or the KNAPSACK problem has a solution.

This completes our proof of Theorem 8.3.4.1. There are many other *NP*-complete problems, and for these the reader is referred to Karp (1972, 1975). The polynomial transformations that have been used in the preceding found in Karp (1972), except for the reduction of KNAPSACK to DIRECTED TRAVELING SALESMAN, which is due to L. H. Harper (personal communication), and the transformation of UNDIRECTED TRAVELING SALESMAN to APPROXIMATE TRAVELING SALESMAN, which is due to Sahni and Gonzales (1974).

8.3.5. Polynomial-Time Approximations to *NP*-Complete Problems

In this section, we present polynomial-time algorithms for the (undirected) traveling salesman (TS) problem and a version of the knapsack problem. The algorithm for the TS problem gives a cycle whose length is at most twice that of the minimum length cycle, and there exist graphs for which it does about this poorly. The second problem has input $a_1, \ldots, a_n, d$ which are positive integers, and the object is to find a subset of $\{a_1, \ldots, a_n\}$ whose sum is largest of those whose sum is less than or equal to d. We call this the *knapsack problem* since it is a maximization problem related to

KNAPSACK given in the preceding section. The TS problem is a minimization problem.

Definition 8.3.5.1. In a minimization or maximization problem let F be the positive real function to be minimized or maximized and let F^* be its extreme value. Let $\hat{F}$ be the value of F given by an approximating algorithm. Then $\hat{F}$ is an ε-*approximation*, for $\varepsilon > 0$, if $|(F^* - \hat{F})/F^*| \leq \varepsilon$.

As we have seen, the APPROXIMATE TRAVELING SALESMAN problem is a language that is NP-complete. It can be converted to a minimization problem in polynomial time and, as the reader can verify, gives an ε-approximation to the TS problem for $\varepsilon = 1/e$. The approximating algorithm that we give here is called NEARINSERT and gives an ε-approximation for $\varepsilon = 1$. It is due to Rosenkrantz, Stearns, and Lewis (1974) and applies to graphs that satisfy the triangle inequality. This states that the distance between nodes i and j, $d(i, j)$, satisfies

$$d(i, j) \leq d(i, k) + d(k, j)$$

for all nodes i, j, k. The authors of NEARINSERT argue that any graph that does not satisfy this condition can be converted to one that does by adding a constant to each distance.

The algorithm NEARINSERT constructs a cycle for the complete graph by stages. It begins with one node and adds one node at every step by inserting the new node between two nodes on the cycle of the smaller graph.

NEARINSERT

1. Start with a subgraph of one node $\{i\}$ and no edges.
2. Find a node k for which $d(i, k)$ is minimal and, in the subgraph with nodes $\{i, k\}$, form the cycle consisting of two copies of the edge (i, k).
3. Given a cycle on a subset of the nodes, find an uncontained node k closest to a contained node.
4. Given k, find an edge (i, j) of the cycle for which the cost

$$C(i, j, k) = d(i, k) + d(k, j) - d(i, j)$$

of inserting k between i and j, $i \neq j$, is minimal.
5. Insert k between i and j by deleting (i, j) from the cycle and adding (i, k) and (k, j).
6. If all of the nodes of the original graph are not on the new cycle, go to step 3. Otherwise, HALT.

Theorem 8.3.5.1. Let D_o and $\hat{D}$ be the lengths of the shortest cycle and the cycle selected by NEARINSERT, respectively. Then

$$\hat{D} < 2D_o$$

or

$$|(D_o - \hat{D})/D_o| < 1.$$

Proof. The cost at step 2 of inserting k into the one-node graph is

$$C(i, j, k) = 2d(i, k)$$

For graphs of more than two nodes, the cost of inserting k between i and j, $i \neq j$, $C(i, j, k)$, is given in step 4.

To bound $\hat{D}$, we consider an arbitrary tree T that contains all the nodes of the graph. The weights assigned to edges of T are the distances defined on the graph. If TREE is the sum of these weights, then we show that

$$\hat{D} \leq 2 \cdot \text{TREE}$$

This inequality holds for any tree T and, in particular, holds for a tree consisting of the optimal (smallest length) cycle with one edge deleted. In this case, TREE $< D_o$, and we have the desired result.

Given the tree T and the node i of step 1, there is a unique path in T from i to node k of step 2. Remove the edge (i, x) on this path, separating T into two trees each of which contains exactly one node from the new cycle. From the definition of k, $d(i, k) \leq d(i, x)$ and

$$C(i, i, k) \leq 2d(i, x)$$

We have associated the cost of inserting k into the graph of one node with the distance between two nodes of T. Furthermore, the corresponding edge has been eliminated when T is divided into two trees.

We now describe a procedure that begins with a cycle of r nodes and r trees formed from T and creates a set of $r + 1$ trees when the $(r + 1)$st node is added to the cycle. At every step, all of the nodes of T are in one of the trees formed from T, and each of the r trees contains exactly one of the r nodes on the cycle that exists at this point. These conditions clearly hold when $r = 2$, as seen in the preceding.

At step 3 of NEARINSERT, node k is selected. Let the cycle at this point contain r nodes. Then k is in one of the r subtrees, call it T_k. Also, T_k contains one node of the existing cycle, say, node p. There is a unique path from p to k in T_k, and let edge (p, x) be on this path. This implies that x is not in the cycle. Remove (p, x) to split T_k into two trees. At this point, the $r + 1$ trees satisfy the stated condition on trees.

Let node m of the cycle be the node of the cycle to which k is closest and let edge (m, m') be the edge that is deleted to insert k. Then the cost of insertion is

$$C(m, m', k) = d(m, k) + d(k, m') - d(m, m')$$

From the triangle inequality,

$$d(k, m') \leq d(k, m) + d(m, m')$$

so

$$C(m, m', k) \leq 2d(k, m)$$

The deleted edge (p, x) contains node p of the cycle and node x which is not on the cycle. Since k is the node closest to a node of the cycle (node m), $d(k, m) \leq d(p, x)$. It follows that

$$C(m, m', k) \leq 2d(p, x)$$

Thus, at every application of step 3, we further split T, and the cost of inserting a new node is at most twice the length of the edge of T that is deleted to further split it. It follows that $\hat{D} \leq 2 \cdot \text{TREE}$. $\qquad\square$

Rosenkrantz, Stearns, and Lewis (1974) have given an example of a graph on n nodes, $n \geq 6$, for which $\hat{D} = 2(1 - 1/n)D_o$. Therefore, the upper bound just derived is about the best possible for their algorithm.

The knapsack problem, as defined earlier, is to find a subset of the positive integers $\{a_1, \ldots, a_n\}$ whose sum is largest of those whose sum is $\leq d$. We present a sequence of algorithms due to Johnson (1973) that run in polynomial time and give ε-approximations to this problem. The "size" of the polynomial increases as $\varepsilon \to 0$. Sahni (1975) obtained similar results, and Ibarra and Kim (1975) offer ε-approximating algorithms that have a much weaker dependence on ε and, for fixed ε, require a running time that grows as $n \log_2 n$ for graphs with n nodes.

We now define an algorithm **A**k for k an integer, $k \geq 1$, that gives an ε-approximation to the knapsack problem for $\varepsilon = 1/(k + 1)$. Let $I = \{1, 2, \ldots, n\}$.

Ak

1. Let SUB $\subseteq \{i \in I | a_i > d/(k + 1)\}$ be the subset whose sum $(\Sigma_{j \in \text{SUB}} a_j)$ is closest to, without exceeding d. Let SUM be the sum and let LEFT $= I - \text{SUB}$.
2. If for all $i \in \text{LEFT}$, $a_i + \text{SUM} > d$, HALT.
3. Let $j \in \text{LEFT}$ be such that $a_j + \text{SUM}$ is closest to, without exceeding d.
4. Set LEFT $= \text{LEFT} - \{j\}$, SUB $= \text{SUB} - \{j\}$, SUM $= \text{SUM} + a_j$.
5. Go to step 2.

The set $\{i \in I/a_i > d/(k + 1)\}$ can be constructed in polynomial time and has at most k elements. Thus, there are at most 2^k subsets, and the sums associated with each can be formed in time proportional to m^2, where m is the size of the input. Thus, the work of step 1 requires time polynomial in m for fixed k. The same is true of the remaining steps, as the reader can show.

Theorem 8.3.5.2. Let $\hat{s}$ and s_o be the size of the subset sum of $\{a_1, \ldots, a_n\}$ given by **Ak** and the largest size $\leq d$, respectively. Then

$$\hat{s} \geq s_o \frac{k}{k+1}$$

or $|(\hat{s} - s_o)/s_o| < 1/(k+1)$.

Proof. Let $T_o \subseteq I$ be an optimal subset whose sum is s_o. Let $T_1 \subseteq I$ be a subset generated by **Ak** whose sum is $\hat{s}$. Partition T_o and T_1 into disjoint sets T_i^{BIG}, T_i^{SMALL}, $i \in \{0, 1\}$:

$$T_i^{\text{BIG}} = \left\{ j \in T_i \,|\, a_j > \frac{d}{k+1} \right\}, \qquad T_i^{\text{SMALL}} = T_i - T_i^{\text{BIG}}$$

Let $s(T_i^{\text{BIG}})$ and $s(T_i^{\text{SMALL}})$ be the corresponding subset sums. Then, we have

$$s_o = s\left(T_o^{\text{BIG}}\right) + s\left(T_o^{\text{SMALL}}\right) \geq \hat{s} = s\left(T_1^{\text{BIG}}\right) + s\left(T_1^{\text{SMALL}}\right)$$

By step 1, $s(T_1^{\text{BIG}}) \geq s(T_o^{\text{BIG}})$. If $T_o^{\text{SMALL}} \subseteq T_1^{\text{SMALL}}$, then $s(T_1^{\text{SMALL}}) \geq s(T_o^{\text{SMALL}})$, and we have $s_o = \hat{s}$. If this containment does not occur, there exists $i \in T_o^{\text{SMALL}}$ that is not in T_1^{SMALL}. But this implies that $a_i + \hat{s} > d$ (otherwise i would not be excluded from T_1^{SMALL}) and $a_i \leq d/(k+1)$ (since $i \in T_o^{\text{SMALL}}$). Consequently,

$$\hat{s} > d - a_i \geq d \frac{k}{k+1} \geq s_o \frac{k}{k+1}$$

and this is the desired result. $\square$

When the algorithm **Ak** is applied to the knapsack problem with $n = k + 2$, $d = k + 1$ and $a_1 = 1 + \varepsilon, a_j = 1$, $2 \leq j \leq k + 2$, and $0 < \varepsilon < 1$, then $s = k + \varepsilon$, while $s_o = k + 1$. Therefore, by making ε arbitrarily small, we have $\hat{s} \cong [k/(k+1)]s_o$ which indicates that no significant improvement on the lower bound of the above theorem can be expected.

Problems

8-1. In a comparator network, some comparisons can be done simultaneously, that is, in parallel. Those that can be performed simultaneously are grouped together in one level of the network. The number of levels is called the *delay* of the network, and the minimum delay of all networks performing a given task is called the *delay complexity* of that task.

(a) Determine the delay associated with an insertion sorting comparator network.

(b) Determine the delay associated with a $(2^k, 2^k)$ odd-even merging network.

(c) Derive an expression for the delay of a 2^l-sorter that is based on odd-even merging.

(d) Derive a lower bound to the delay complexity of n-sorters.

8-2. Determine whether the following comparator network sorts all inputs.

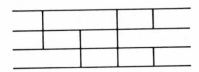

8-3. Let $s(n)$ be the lower bound of Theorem 8.1.1.3 on the number of comparators in an n-sorter. Show that for each $2 \le n \le 8$ there exists an n-sorter with $s(n)$ comparators for which $0 \le s(n) - s(n) \le 2$.

8-4. (Levy and Paull, 1969) Let the max and min operators of a comparator be relabeled as

$$x + y \equiv \max(x, y), \qquad x \cdot y \equiv \min(x, y)$$

If x and y are 0-1 valued, max corresponds to OR and min corresponds to AND.

(a) Show that these operators are associative and commutative.

(b) Show that a formula over $\{+, \cdot\}$ in the variables x_1, x_2, x_3, and x_4 can be associated with each output of a 4-sorter.

(c) Demonstrate that formulas associated with outputs of an n-sorter in the manner indicated in (b) are the threshold functions of Section 3.1.1.

8-5. (Batcher, 1968) A sequence $(z_1, z_2, \ldots, z_p)$ is *bitonic* if there exists an integer $1 \le k \le p$ such that $z_1 \ge \cdots \ge z_k \le \cdots \le z_p$.

(a) Show that a bitonic sorting network can be constructed by sorting $(z_1, z_3, z_5, \ldots)$ and $(z_2, z_4, z_6, \ldots)$ and then comparing and interchanging z_1' and z_2', z_3', and z_4', and so on, where z_i' is the item on the ith line after the first sorting stage.

(b) Show that two ordered lists can be merged with a bitonic sorter and that an n-sorter can be constructed from bitonic sorters.

(c) Determine the number of comparators in a 2^l-sorter that is based on merging with bitonic sorters.

8-6. Show that the binary insertion sorting algorithm of Section 8.2.1 eventually halts and correctly sorts a list of n items, even when identical items are on the list.

8-7. Construct a decision tree for binary insertion sorting of a list of four items.

8-8. Carry out the sequence of comparisons and interchanges required by HEAPSORT when the list of items to be sorted is 9, 8, 7, 6, 5, 4, 3, 2, 1 in that order.

8-9. Let S be the set $\{ \pm k | k = 0, 1, 2, 3, \cdots \}$, let $+$ be integer addition, and let multiplication be defined $x \cdot y = \max(x, y)$. Show that $(S, +, \cdot, 0, 1)$ is not a ring.

8-10. Show that the ring of $n \times n$ matrices is noncommutative.

8-11. Show that an arbitrary $n \times n$ Toeplitz matrix, n even, has the representation as a 2×2 matrix that is given in Section 8.2.3.

8-12. Generalize Strassen's matrix multiplication algorithm to matrices that are $m \times m$ where $m = p2^k$ for integers p and k. Bound the number of arithmetic operations needed. Given an arbitrary positive integer n, show, by imbedding $n \times n$ matrices into $m \times m$ matrices, $m = p \cdot 2^k$, and by choosing the appropriate values for p and k, that at most $4.7 \, n^{\log_2 7}$ arithmetic operations are necessary to multiply $n \times n$ matrices over a ring.
Hint. Choose $k = \lfloor \log_2 n - 4 \rfloor$ and $p = \lfloor n2^{-k} \rfloor + 1$.

8-13. Demonstrate for n even that an arbitrary $n \times n$ Toeplitz matrix and be written as a 2×2 matrix of $(n/2) \times (n/2)$ matrices:

$$\mathbf{T} = \begin{bmatrix} \mathbf{T}_1 & \mathbf{T}_2 \\ \mathbf{T}_3 & \mathbf{T}_1 \end{bmatrix}$$

8-14. An $n \times n$ circulant matrix C has entries $\{c_{ij} | 1 \leq i, j \leq n\}$ where

$$c_{ij} = a_{(i+j-2)\bmod n}$$

Show that matrix-vector multiplication by an $n \times n$ circulant can be done with on the order of $n^{\log_2 3}$ elementary arithmetic operations.

8-15. Let $a + ib$ and $c + id$ be complex numbers. Show that the complex multiplication of these two numbers can be written as a matrix-vector product and deduce that three real multiplications are sufficient to compute the complex product.

8-16. Show that the convolution of two equal length sequences can be written as a matrix-vector product with either a circulant or a Toeplitz matrix. Use this fact to derive upper bounds on the number of arithmetic operations necessary to convolve two n-sequences.

8-17. Demonstrate that the result of matrix-vector multiplication with an $n \times n$ Toeplitz matrix can be obtained from an appropriately defined convolution. As a result, show that this matrix-vector multiplication over the reals can be done with on the order of $n \log n$ arithmetic operations.

8-18. Consider two polynomials $p(x)$ and $q(x)$ of real coefficients and degree n and m, respectively. Show that the product can be computed with on the order of $(n + m) \log(n + m)$ arithmetic operations.

8-19. Do a complete design of an NDTM for the k-clique problem.

8-20. Show that for every NDTM T there is a DTM T^* that accepts the same language. Let T accept L in polynomial time. Bound the number of moves made by T^*.

8-21. Let C and $\mathbf{b}$ be $m \times n$ and $m \times 1$ matrices with integer entries. Show that the question of the solvability of the linear equation $C\mathbf{v} = \mathbf{b}$, where $\mathbf{v}$ is an $n \times 1$ matrix with real entries, is in P. Contrast this problem with the 0-1 integer programming problem.

8-22. (Karp, 1972) Show that the following problem is in NP.
PARTITION
INPUT: Positive integers $c_1, c_2, \ldots, c_s$
PROPERTY:There is a set $I \subset \{1, 2, \ldots, s\}$ such that

$$\sum_{h \in I} c_h = \sum_{h \notin I} c_h$$

8-23. (Sahni, 1972) Show that the following problem is in NP.
MINIMAL LENGTH FORMULA
INPUT: Formula over $\{+, \cdot, \bar{\ }, (,), 0, 1\}$ for a Boolean function. Positive integer k.
PROPERTY: There exists a formula for the same function with $\leq k$ characters.
Hint. Make use of the Boolean complement of POS-SATISFIA-BILITY (called DNF-TAUTOLOGY) in proving that the problem is in NP.

8-24. Consider the DIRECTED TRAVELING SALESMAN and UNDI-RECTED TRAVELING SALESMAN problems in which the property has been modified to read

PROPERTY: There is a permutation π of $N = \{1, 2, \ldots, n\}$ such that

$$d(\pi(1), \pi(2)) + d(\pi(2), \pi(3)) + \cdots + d(\pi(n), \pi(1)) \leq k$$

Show that these new problems are *NP*-complete. Show also that these problems and their associated minimization problems are both of exponential or polynomial running time.

Bibliography

This bibliography contains an extensive list of items on *combinational complexity* and related topics, denoted by an *asterisk* (*) located next to the year of publication. Many of these items have appeared in the Russian literature. The source of the English translation is shown for those that have been translated.

Aho, A. V., J. E. Hopcroft, and J. D. Ullman
(1974)   *The Design and Analysis of Computer Algorithms*, Addison-Wesley, Reading, Mass.

Alekseev, V. B.
(1973)*   On the Number of k-Valued Monotonic Functions, Engl. transl. in *Sov. Math.—Dokl.*, Vol. 14, No. 1 (1973), pp. 87–91; orig. in *Dokl. Akad. Nauk SSSR*, Vol. 208, No. 3, pp. 505–508.

Anderson, S. F., J. G. Earle, R. E. Goldschmidt, and D. M. Powers
(1967)*   The IBM System/360 Model 91: Floating-Point Execution Unit, *IBM J. Res. Dev.*, Vol. 11, No. 1, pp. 34–53.

Avizienis, A.
(1961)*   Signed-Digit Number Representations for Fast Parallel Arithmetic, *IRE Trans. Electron. Comput.*, Vol. EC-10, No. 9, pp. 389–400.

Batcher, K. E.
(1968)*   Sorting Networks and Their Applications, *Proceedings AFIPS Spring Joint Computer Conference*, Vol. 32, pp. 307–314.

Bell, C. Gordon and Allen Newell
(1971)   *Computer Structures: Readings and Examples*, McGraw-Hill, New York.

Booth, Taylor L.
(1967)   *Sequential Machines and Automata Theory*, Wiley, New York.

Booth, Taylor L.
(1971)   *Digital Networks and Computer Systems*, Wiley, New York.

Born, Richard C. and Allan K. Scidmore
(1968)*   Transformation of Switching Functions to Completely Symmetric Switching Functions, *IEEE Trans. Comput.*, Vol. C-17, No. 6, pp. 596–599.

Borodin, A. and I. Munroe
(1975)   *The Computational Complexity of Algebraic and Numeric Problems*, American Elsevier, New York, London, Amsterdam.

Borodin, A.
(1973)   Computational Complexity: Theory and Practice, *Currents in the Theory of Computing*, edited by A. V. Aho, Prentice Hall, pp. 35–89.

Breitbart, Yu. Ya.
(1968)*   Comparison of the Complexities of Realization of Boolean Functions by Automata and Turing Machines, Engl. transl. in *Sov. Phys.—Dokl.*, Vol. 13, No. 6 (1968), pp. 524–526; orig. in *Dokl. Akad. Nauk SSSR*, Vol. 180, No. 5, pp. 1053–1055.

Brzozowski, Janusz A.
(1964)   Derivatives of Regular Expressions, *JACM*, Vol. 11, No. 4, pp. 481–494

Carlson, Walter M.
(1971)   Reflections on Ljubljana, ACM President's Letter, *CACM*, Vol. 14, No. 10, p. 615.

Chaitin, G. J.
(1966)   On the Length of Programs for Computing Finite Binary Sequences, *JACM*, Vol. 13, No. 4, pp. 547–569.

Cobham, Alan
(1966)   The Recognition Problem for the Set of Perfect Squares, *IEEE Conference Record of the 1966 Seventh Annual Symposium on Switching and Automata Theory*, Oct. 26–28, pp. 78–87.

Cook, Stephen A.
(1966)*   "On the Minimum Computation Time of Functions," Ph.D. Thesis, Harvard University.

Cook, Stephen A.
(1971)   The Complexity of Theorem-Proving Procedures, *Proceedings of the Third ACM Symposium on Theory of Computing*, pp. 151–158.

Cooley, J. M., P. A. Lewis, and P. D. Welch
(1967)   History of the Fast Fourier Transform, *Proc. IEEE*, Vol. 55, pp. 1675–1677.

Cooley, J. M. and J. W. Tukey
(1965)   An Algorithm for the Machine Calculation of Complex Fourier Series, *Math. Comput.*, Vol. 19, pp. 297–301.

Dahl, O.-J., E. W. Dijkstra and C. A. R. Hoare
(1972)   *Structured Programming*, Academic Press, London.

Denning, P. J.
(1968)   The Working Set Model for Program Behavior, *CACM*, Vol. 11, No. 5, pp. 323–333.

Dijkstra, E. W.
(1962)   *A Primer on ALGOL 60 Programming*, Academic Press, London, New York.

Ehrenfeucht, A.
(1972)*   Practical Decidability, *Report CU-CS-008-72*, Department of Computer Science, University of Colorado.

Even, S., I. Kohavi, and A. Paz
(1967)*   On Minimal Modulo 2 Sums of Products for Switching Functions, *IEEE Trans. Electron. Comput.*, Vol. 16, No. 10, pp. 671–674.

Fiduccia, C. M.
(1971)   Fast Matrix Multiplication, *Proceedings of Third Annual ACM Symposium on Theory of Computing*, pp. 45–49.

(1973a)   On Obtaining Upper Bounds on the Complexity of Matrix Multiplication, *Complexity of Computer Computations*, edited by R. E. Miller and J. W. Thatcher, Plenum, New York, pp. 31–40.

(1973b)   On the Algebraic Complexity of Matrix Multiplication, Ph.D. Thesis, Brown University.

Finikov, B. I.
(1957)*   On a Family of Classes of Functions in the Logic Algebra and Their Realization in the Class of π-Schemes, *Dokl. Akad. Nauk SSSR*, Vol. 115, No. 2, pp. 247–248.

Fischer, M. J. and A. R. Meyer
(1971)   Boolean Matrix Multiplication and Transitive Closure, *IEEE Conference Record of the Twelfth Annual Symposium on Switching and Automata Theory*, pp. 129–131.

Fischer, M. J., A. R. Meyer, and M. S. Paterson
(1975)*   Lower Bounds on the Size of Boolean Formulas, *Proceedings of the Seventh Annual ACM Symposium on Theory of Computing*, Albuquerque, New Mexico, May 5–7, pp. 37–44.

Fischer, M. and N. Pippenger
(1973)*   Personal communication.

Garey, M. R., D. S. Johnson, and L. Stockmeyer
(1974)   Some Simplified *NP*-Complete Problems, *Proceedings of the Sixth Annual ACM Symposium on Theory of Computing*, Seattle, pp. 47–63.

Gavrilov, M. A., O. P. Kuznetsov, and V. E. Khazotskii
(1969)*   Description and Analysis of Switching Circuits with Large Numbers of Input Variables, Engl. transl. in *Autom. Remote Control* No. 16 (1969), pp. 1643–1650; orig. in *Avtom. i Telemekh.*, No. 16, pp. 108–115.

Gershkovich, Yu. B. and V. M. Poltervich
(1967)*   Nonrepeating Superpositions of Boolean Functions of Two Variables, Engl. transl. in *Autom. Remote Control*, No. 5 (1967), pp. 753–760; orig. in *Avtom. i Telemekh.*, No. 5, pp. 109–152.

Gilbert, E. N.
(1954)*   Lattice Theoretic Properties of Frontal Switching Functions, *J. Math. Phys.*, Vol. 33, No. 1, pp. 57–97.

Hansel, G.
(1964)*   Nombre Minimal de Contacts de Fermeture Nécessaires pour Réalisser une Fonction Booléenne Symetrique de *n* Variables, *C. R. Acad. Sci.*, Paris, Groupe 1, pp. 6037–6040.

(1966a)*   Sur le Nombre des Fonctions Booléennes Monotones de *n* Variables, *C. R. Acad. Sci.*, Paris, Vol. 262, Série A, pp. 1088–1090.

(1966b)*   Construction d'un Schéma de Contacts Bipolaire pour une Fonction Booléenne Isotone Arbitrarie de *n* Variables, *C. R. Acad. Sci.*, Paris, Vol. 263, Série A, pp. 651–654.

Harper, L. H.
(1975A)*   A Note on Some Classes of Boolean Functions, *Stud. Appl. Math.*, Vol. 54, No. 2, pp. 161–164.

(1975B)*   An *n* log *n* Lower Bound on Synchronous Combinational Complexity, to appear in *Trans. Am. Math. Soc.*

Harper, L. H. and J. E. Savage
(1972)*   On the Complexity of the Marriage Problem, *Adv. Math.*, Vol. 9, No. 3, pp. 299–312.

(1973)*   Complexity Made Simple, *Proceedings of the International Symposium on Combinatorial Theory*, Rome, September 2–15.

(1976)*   Non-Linear Lower Bounds on the Complexity of Integer and Matrix Multiplication, in preparation.

Harper, L. H., W. N. Hsieh, and J. E. Savage
(1975)*   A Class of Boolean Functions with Linear Combinational Complexity, *Theor. Comput. Sci.*, Vol. 1, No. 2, pp. 161–183.

Harrison, M. A.
(1965)*   *Introduction to Switching and Automata Theory*, McGraw-Hill, New York.

Hennie, F. C.
(1965)   One-tape Off-line Turing Machine Computations, *Inf. Control*, Vol. 8, No. 6, pp. 553–578.

(1968)   *Finite-State Models for Logical Machines*, Wiley, New York.

Herstein, I. N.
(1964)   *Topics in Algebra*, Blaisdell, New York, p. 283.

Hill, F. H. and G. R. Peterson
(1973)   *Digital Systems: Hardware Organization and Design*, Wiley, New York.

Hodes, L.
(1970)*   The Logical Complexity of Geometric Properties in the Plane, *JACM*, Vol. 17, pp. 339–347.

Hopcroft, J.
(1971)   An *n* log *n* Algorithm for Minimizing States in a Finite Automaton, in *Theory of Machines and Computations*, edited by Zvi Kohavi and Azaria Paz, Academic Press, New York, pp. 189–196.

Hsieh, W. N.
(1974)*   Intersection Theorems for Systems of Finite Vector Spaces and Other Combinatorial Results, Ph.D. Thesis, Department of Mathematics, MIT, Cambridge, Mass.

Huffman, D. A.
(1954)   The Synthesis of Sequential Switching Circuits, *J. Franklin Inst.*, Vol. 257, pp. 161–190, 275–303.

Ibarra, O. H. and C. E. Kim
(1975)   Fast Approximation Algorithms for the Knapsack and Sum of Subset Problems, *JACM*, Vol. 22, No. 4, pp. 463–468.

Johnson, D.
(1973)   Private communication.

Johnson, D. S.
(1973)   Approximation Algorithms for Combinatorial Problems, *Proceedings of the Fifth Annual ACM Symposium on Theory of Computing*, Austin, Texas, pp. 38–49.

Johnson, D., J. E. Savage, and L. R. Welch
(1972)*   Combinational Complexity Measures as a Function of Fan-Out, J.P.L. Technical Report 32-1526, Vol. 5, October, pp. 79–81.

Karatsuba, A. and Yu. Ofman
(1962)*   Multiplication of Multidigit Numbers on Automata, Engl. transl. in *Sov. Phys.—Dokl.*, Vol. 7, No. 7 (1963), pp. 595–596; orig. in *Dokl. Akad. Nauk SSSR*, Vol. 145, No. 2, pp. 293–294.

Karp, Richard
(1972)   Reducibility among Combinatorial Problems, in *Complexity of Computer Computations*, edited by R. E. Miller and J. Thatcher, Pelnum, New York, pp. 85–104.
(1975)   On the Computational Complexity of Combinatorial Problems, *Networks*, Vol. 5, No. 1, Wiley, New York, pp. 45–68.

Karpovskii, M. G. and E. S. Moskalev
(1967)*   Realization of a System of Logical Functions by Means of an Expansion in Orthogonal Series, Engl. transl. in *Autom. Remote Control*, No. 12 (1967), pp. 1921–1931; orig. in *Avtom. i Telemekh.*, No. 12, pp. 119–129.

Kautz, William H.
(1966)*   A Survey and Assessment of Progress in Switching Theory and Logical Design in the Soviet Union, *IEEE Trans. Electron. Compute.*, Vol. EC-15, No. 2, pp. 164–204.

Khasin, L. S.
(1969a)*   Complexity Bounds for the Realization of Monotone Symmetrical Functions by Means of Formulas in the Basis $+, \cdot, ^-$, Engl. transl. in *Sov. Phys.—Dokl.*, Vol. 14, No. 12 (1970), pp. 1149–1151; orig. in *Dokl. Akad. Nauk SSSR*, Vol. 189, No. 4, pp. 752–755.

(1969b)*   On Realizations of Monotonic Symmetric Functions by Formulas in the Basis $+, \cdot, ^-$, Engl. transl. in *Syst. Theory Res.*, Vol. 21 (1971), pp. 254–259; orig. in *Probl. Kibern.*, Vol. 21, pp. 253–257.

Kirkpatrick, David
(1972)   On the Additions Necessary to Compute Certain Functions, *Proceedings of the Fourth Annual ACM Symposium on Theory of Computing*, Denver, pp. 94–101.

Kleene, S. C.
(1956)   Representation of Events in Nerve Nets and Finite Automata, *Automata Studies* (*Annals of Math Studies*, No. 34), Princeton University Press, Princeton, New Jersey, pp. 3–42.

Kleitman, D.
(1973)*   The Number of Sperner Families of Subsets of an n Element Set, *Colloq. Math. Soc. János Bolyai*, Vol. 10, Infinite and Finite Sets, Keszthely, Hungary, pp. 989–1001.

Kloss, B. M.
(1966)*   Estimates of the Complexity of Solutions of Systems of Linear Equations, Engl. transl. in *Sov. Math.—Dokl.*, Vol. 7, No. 6 (1966), pp. 1537–1540; orig. in *Dokl. Akad. Nauk SSSR*, Vol. 171, No. 4, pp. 781–783.

Knight, Kenneth E.
(1966)   Changes in Computer Performance, *Datamation*, September, pp. 40–54.
(1968)   Evolving Computer Performance 1963–1967, *Datamation*, January, pp. 31–35.

Knuth, Donald E.
(1969)   *The Art of Computer Programming—Seminumerical Algorithms*, Vol. 2, Addison-Wesley, Reading, Mass.

(1973)   *The Art of Computer Programming—Sorting and Searching*, Vol. 3, Addison-Wesley, Reading, Mass.

Kobrinskii, N. E. and B. A. Trakhtenbrot
(1965)*   *Introduction to the Theory of Finite Automata*, North-Holland, Amsterdam.

Kolmogorov, A. N.
(1965)   Three Approaches to the Quantitative Definition of Information, *Probl. Peredachi Inf.*, Vol. 1, No. 1, pp. 3–11.

Krapchenko, V. M.
(1963)*   On a Method of Transforming a Multiserial Code into a Uniserial One, Engl. transl. in *Sov. Phys.—Dokl.*, Vol. 8, No. 1 (1963), pp. 8–10; orig. in *Dokl. Akad. Nauk SSSR*, Vol. 148, No. 2, pp. 296–299.

(1967)*   Asymptotic Estimation of Addition Time of a Parallel Adder, Engl. transl. in *Syst. Theory Res.*, Vol. 19 (1970), pp. 105–122; orig. in *Probl. Kibern.*, Vol. 19, pp. 107–122.

(1971a)* Complexity of the Realization of a Linear Function in the Class of Π-Circuits, Engl. transl. in *Math. Notes Acad. Sci. USSR* (1971), pp. 21–23; orig. in *Mat. Zamet.*, Vol. 9, No. 1, pp. 35–40.

(1971b)* A Method of Obtaining Lower Bounds for the Complexity of Π-Schemes, Engl. transl. in *Math. Notes Acad. Sci. USSR* (1972), pp. 474–479; orig. in *Mat. Zamet.*, Vol. 10, No. 1, pp. 83–92.

(1972)*   The Complexity of the Realization of Symmetrical Functions by Formulae, Engl. transl. in *Math. Notes Acad. Sci. USSR* (1972), pp. 70–76; orig. in *Mat. Zamet.*, Vol. 11, No. 1, pp. 109–120.

Krichevskii, R. E.
(1959)*   Realizations of Functions by Superpositions, Engl. transl. in *Probl. Cybern.*, Vol. 2 (1961), pp. 458–477; orig. in *Probl. Kibern.*, Vol. 2, pp. 123–138.

(1963)*   Complexity of Contact Circuits Realizing a Function of Logical Algebra, Engl. transl. in *Sov. Phys.—Dokl.*, Vol. 8, No. 8 (1964), pp. 770–772; orig. in *Dokl. Akad. Nauk SSSR*, Vol. 151, No. 4, pp. 803–806.

Kung, H. T.
(1974)   New Algorithms and Lower Bounds for the Parallel Evaluation of Certain Rational Expressions, *Proceedings of the Sixth Annual ACM Symposium on Theory of Computing*, Seattle, Washington, April 30–May 2, pp. 323–333.

Lamagna, E. A.
(1973)*   On the Computational Complexity of Certain Finite Functions, Brown University Technical Report, February.

(1975)*   The Complexity of Monotone Functions, Ph.D. Thesis, Computer Science Program, Brown University.

Lamagna, E. A. and J. E. Savage
(1973)*   On the Logical Complexity of Symmetric Switching Functions in Monotone and Complete Bases, Brown University Technical Report, July.

(1974)*   Combinational Complexity of Some Monotone Functions, *Proceedings of the Fifteenth Annual Symposium on Switching and Automata Theory*, New Orleans, October 14–16, pp. 140–144.

Lee, C. Y.
(1959)   Representation of Switching Circuits by Binary Decision Programs, *BSTJ*, Vol. 38, pp. 985–998.

Levy, S. Y. and M. C. Paull
(1969)*   An Algebra with Application to Sorting Algorithms, *Proceedings of the Princeton Conference on Information Sciences and Systems*, pp. 285–291.

Lewis, P. M. II, R. E. Stearns, and J. Hartmanis
(1965)   Memory Bounds for Recognition of Context-Free and Context-Sensitive Languages, *IEEE Conference Record on Switching and Automata Theory*, Ann Arbor, Michigan, pp. 191–202.

Lupanov, O. B.
(1958)*   A Method of Circuit Synthesis, *Izv. V.U.Z. Radiofiz.*, Vol. 1, No. 1, pp. 120–140.

(1959)*   On the Asymptotic Bounds of the Complexities of Formulas Which Realize Logic Algebra Functions, Engl. transl. in *Autom. Expr.*, Vol. 2, No. 6 (1960), pp. 12–14; orig. in *Dokl. Akad. Nauk SSSR*, Vol. 128, No. 3, pp. 464–467.

(1960a)*   The Complexity of Realizing Functions of Logical Algebra by Means of Formulas, Engl. transl. in *Autom. Expr.*, Vol. 3, No. 6 (1961), p. 30; orig. in *Probl. Kibern.*, Vol. 3, pp. 61–80.

(1960b)*   Complexity of Formula Realization of Functions of Logical Algebra, Engl. transl. in *Probl. Cybern.*, Vol. 3 (1962), pp. 782–811; orig. in *Probl. Kibern.*, Vol. 3, pp. 61–80.

(1961a)*   Implementing the Algebra of Logic Functions in Terms of Bounded Depth Formulas in the Basis +, ·, ⁻, Engl. transl. in *Sov. Phys.—Dokl.*, Vol. 6, No. 2 (1961), pp. 107–108; orig. in *Dokl. Akad. Nauk SSSR*, Vol. 136, No. 5, pp. 1041–1042.

(1961b)*   On the Principle of Local Coding and the Realization of Functions of Certain Classes of Networks Composed of Functional Elements, Engl. transl. in *Sov. Phys.—Dokl.*, Vol. 6, No. 6 (1962), pp. 750–752; orig. in *Dokl. Akad. Nauk SSSR*, Vol. 140, No. 2, pp. 322–325.

(1961c)*   On the Realization of Functions of Logical Algebra by Formulae of Finite Classes (Formulae of Limited Depth) in the Basis ·, +, ⁻, Engl. Transl. in *Probl. Cybern.*, Vol. 6 (1965), pp. 1–14; orig. in *Probl. Kibern.*, Vol. 6, pp. 5–14.

(1962a)*   On Comparing the Complexity of the Realizations of Monotonic Functions by Contact Networks Containing Only Closing Contacts and by Arbitrary Contact Networks, Engl. transl. in *Sov. Phys.—Dokl.*, Vol. 7, No. 6 (1962), pp. 486–489; orig. in *Dokl. Akad. Nauk SSSR*, Vol. 144, No. 6, pp. 1245–1248.

(1962b)*   A Class of Circuits of Functional Elements, *Probl. Kibern.*, Vol. 7, pp. 61–114.

(1965a)*   The Problem of Realizing Symmetric Functions in the Algebra of Logic by Contact Schemes, *Probl. Kibern.*, No. 15, pp. 85–99.

(1965b)*   An Approach to Systems Synthesis—A Local Coding Principle, *Probl. Kibern.*, Vol. 14, pp. 31–110.

(1970)*   Effect of the Depth of Formulas on Their Complexity, Engl. transl. in *Cybernetics*, Vol. 1, No. 2 (1973), pp. 123–130; orig. in *Kibernetika*, No. 2, pp. 46–49.

(1972)*   Circuits Using Threshold Elements, Engl. transl. in *Sov. Phys.—Dokl.*, Vol. 17, No. 2 (1972), pp. 91–93; orig. in *Dokl. Akad. Nauk SSSR*, Vol. 202, No. 6, pp. 1282–1291.

McCarthy, John
(1963)   A Basis for a Mathematical Theory of Computation, in *Computer Programming and Formal Systems*, edited by Braffort and Hirschberg, North-Holland, Amsterdam.

MacLane, S. and G. Birkhoff
(1967)   *Algebra*, Macmillan, New York.

MacSorley, O. L.
(1961)*   High-Speed Arithmetic in Binary Computers, *Proc. IRE*, Vol. 49, No. 1, pp. 67–91.

Malyshev, V. A.
(1967)*   The Class of "Almost All" Functions with Nonlinear Complexity in the Realization of Π-Networks, Engl. transl. in *Sys. Theory Res.*, Vol. 19 (1970), pp. 305–312; orig. in *Probl. Kibern.*, Vol. 19, pp. 299–306.

Manna, Z. and J. McCarthy
(1970)   Properties of Programs and Partial Function Logic, in *Machine Intelligence*, American Elsevier, New York, pp. 27–38.

Manna, Z., S. Ness, and J. Vuillemin
(1973)   Inductive Methods for Proving Properties of Programs, *CACM*, Vol. 16, No. 8, pp. 491–502.

Markov, A. A.
(1957)*   On the Inversion Complexity of a System of Functions, Engl. transl. in *JACM*, Vol. 5, No. 4 (1958), pp. 331–334; orig. in *Dokl. Akad. Nauk SSSR*, Vol. 116, pp. 917–919.

McNaughton, R. and H. Yamada
(1960)   Regular Expressions and State Graphs for Automata, *IRE Trans. Electron. Comput.*, Vol. EC-9, No. 1, pp. 39–47.

Mealey, G. H.
(1955)   A Method of Synthesizing Sequential Circuits, *BSTJ*, Vol. 34, pp. 1045–1079.

Melhorn, Kurt
(1974)*   On the Complexity of Monotone Realizations of Matrix Multiplication, Technical Report, A74-11, Fachbereich Angewandte Mathematik und Informatik, Universität des Saarlandes, September.

Meyer, A.
(1974)*   6.853 Lecture Notes, Department of Electrical Engineering, MIT, Cambridge, Mass.

Miller, R. E.
(1965)*   *Switching Theory*, Vols. I and II, Wiley, New York.

Minsky, Marvin L.
(1967)   *Computation: Finite and Infinite Machines*, Prentice-Hall, Englewood Cliffs, New Jersey.

(1970)   Form and Content in Computer Science, *JACM*, Vol. 17, No. 2, pp. 197–215.

Minsky, Marvin and Seymour Papert
(1972)   *Perceptrons: An Introduction to Computational Geometry*, MIT Press, Cambridge, Mass., second printing, pp. 215–221.

Moore, E. F.
(1956)   Gedanken-Experiments on Sequential Machines, *Automata Studies* (*Annals of Mathematics Studies*, No. 34), Princeton University Press, Princeton, N. J., pp. 129–153.

Muchnick, B. A.
(1970)*   Bound on Complexity of Realization of a Linear Function by Formulas in Certain Bases, Engl. transl. in *Cybernetics*, No. 4 (1973), pp. 395–406; orig. in *Kibernetika*, No. 4, pp. 29–38.

Mukhopadhyay, Amar (Ed.)
(1971)*   *Recent Developments in Switching Theory*, Academic Press, New York, London.

Muller, D. E.
(1956)*   Complexity in Electronic Switching Circuits, *IRE Trans. Comput.*, Vol. EC-5, pp. 15–19.

Muller, D. E. and F. P. Preparata
(1975)*   Bounds to Complexities of Networks for Sorting and Switching, *JACM*, Vol. 22, No. 2, pp. 195–201.

Naur, P. (Ed.)
(1963)   Revised Report on the Algorithmic Language ALGOL 60, *CACM*, Vol. 6, No. 1, pp. 1–17.

Nechiporuk, E. I.
(1960)*   On the Complexity of Superpositions in Bases that Contain Nontrivial Linear Formulas with Zero Weight, Engl. transl. in *Sov. Phys.—Dokl.*, Vol. 6, No. 1 (1961), pp. 6–9; orig. in *Dokl. Akad. Nauk. SSSR*, Vol. 136, No. 3, pp. 560–563.

(1961)*   Complexity of Networks in Certain Bases Containing Nontrivial Elements with Zero Weights, Engl. transl. in *Sov. Math.—Dokl.*, Vol. 2, No. 4 (1961), pp. 1087–1088; orig. in *Dokl. Akad. Nauk SSSR*, Vol. 139, No. 6, pp. 1302–1303.

(1962)*   On the Complexity of Networks in Certain Bases Containing Nontrivial Elements with Zero Weights, *Probl. Kibern.*, No. 8, pp. 123–160.

(1963)*   On the Synthesis of Logical Nets in Incomplete and Degenerate Bases, Engl. transl. in *Sov. Phys.—Dokl.*, Vol. 9, No. 3 (1964), pp. 207–208; orig. in *Dokl. Akad. Nauk SSSR*, Vol. 155, No. 2, pp. 299–301.

(1964a)*   Synthesis of Circuits from Threshold Elements, Engl. transl. in *Sov. Math.—Dokl.*, Vol. 5, No. 1 (1964), pp. 163–166; orig. in *Dokl. Akad. Nauk SSSR*, Vol. 154, No. 4, pp. 763–766.

(1964b)*   On the Synthesis of Logical Networks in Incomplete and Degenerate Bases, *Dokl. Akad. Nauk. SSSR*, Vol. 155, pp. 299–301.

(1964c)*   On Self-Correcting Gating Circuits, *Dokl. Akad. Anuk SSSR*, Vol. 156, pp. 1045–1048.

(1964d)*   The Synthesis of Networks from Threshold Elements, Engl. transl. in *Autom. Expr.*, Vol. 7, No. 1, pp. 35–39, and No. 2, pp. 27–32 (1964); orig. in *Probl. Kibern.*, No. 11, pp. 49–62.

(1965)*   Complexity of Gating Circuits Which Are Realized by Boolean Matrices with Undetermined Elements, Engl. transl. in *Sov. Phys.—Dokl.*, Vol. 10, No. 7 (1966), pp. 591–593; orig. in *Dokl. Akad. Nauk SSSR*, Vol. 163, No. 1, pp. 40–42.

(1966)*   A Boolean Function, Engl. transl. in *Sov. Math.—Dokl.*, Vol. 7, No. 4 (1966), pp. 999–1000; orig. in *Dokl. Akad. Nauk SSSR*, Vol. 169, No. 4, pp. 765–766.

(1969)*   On a Boolean Matrix, Engl. transl. in *Syst. Theory Res.*, Vol. 21 (1971), pp. 236–239; orig. in *Probl. Kibern.*, Vol. 21, pp. 237–240.

(1970)*   Realizations of Disjunctions and Conjunctions in Monotone Bases, Engl. transl. in *Syst. Theory Res.*, Vol. 23 (1973), pp. 305–307; orig. in *Probl. Kibern.*, Vol. 23, pp. 291–293.

Ofman, Yu.
(1962)*   On the Algorithmic Complexity of Discrete Functions, Engl. transl. in *Sov. Phys. —Dokl.*, Vol. 7, No. 7 (1963), pp. 589–591; orig. in *Dokl. Akad. Nauk SSSR*, Vol. 145, No. 1, pp. 48–51.

(1963)*   Approximate Realization of Continuous Functions by Automata, Engl. Transl. in *Sov. Math.—Dokl.*, Vol. 4, No. 5 (1963), pp. 1439–1443; orig. in *Dokl. Akad. Nauk SSSR*, Vol. 152, pp. 823–826.

Orlov, V. A.
(1971)*   The Algorithmic Unsolvability of the Problem of Finding the Asymptotic Behavior of the Shannon Function in the Realization of Boundedly Deterministic
Operators Using Networks in an Arbitrary Basis, Engl. transl. in *Sov. Phys.—
Dokl.*, Vol. 16, No. 2 (1971), pp. 81–83; orig. in *Dokl. Akad. Nauk SSSR*, Vol.
196, No. 5, p. 1036.

Paterson, Michael S.
(1975)*   Complexity of Monotone Networks for Boolean Matrix Product, *Theor. Comput.
Sci.*, Vol. 1, No. 1, pp. 13–20.

Paul, Wolfgang
(1975)*   A 2.5*N* Lower Bound for the Combinational Complexity of Boolean Functions,
Proceedings of the Seventh Annual ACM Symposium on Theory of Computing,
Albuquerque, New Mexico, May 5–7, pp. 27–36.

Pippenger, Nicholas
(1974)*   Short Formulae for Symmetric Functions, IBM Report RC 5143, November 20.
(1975)*   Short Monotone Formulae for Threshold Functions, short paper.

Pratt, V. R.
(1975)*   The Power of Negative Thinking in Multiplying Boolean Matrices, *SIAM J.
Comput.*, Vol. 4, No. 3, pp. 326–329.

Preparata, F. P. and D. E. Muller
(1970)*   Generation of Near-Optimal Universal Boolean Functions, *J. Comput. Syst. Sci.*,
Vol. 4 (1970), pp. 93–102.

(1971)*   On the Delay Required to Realize Boolean Functions, *IEEE Trans. Comput.*, Vol.
C-20, No. 4, pp. 459–461.

(1975)*   Efficient Parallel Evaluation of Boolean Expressions, IEEE Computer Society
Repository, Report R75-247, 3 pages.

Rabin, M. O. and D. Scott
(1959)   Finite Automata and Their Decision Problems, *IBM J.*, Vol. 3, No. 2, pp.
114–125.

Red'kin, N. P.
(1969a)*   Synthesis of Two-Layer Threshold-Element Circuits, Engl. transl. in *Autom.
Remot Control*, No. 2 (1969), pp. 233–241; orig. in *Avtom. i Telemekh.*, No. 2, pp.
82–91.

(1969b)*   Complexity of Realization of Incompletely Defined Boolean Functions, Engl.
transl. in *Autom. Remote Control* (1970), pp. 1474–1477; orig. in *Avtom. i
Telemekh.*, No. 9, pp. 118–122.

(1970)*   Decompositional Approach to Circuit Synthesis, Engl. transl. in *Autom. Remote
Control* (1970), pp. 1273–1277; orig. in *Avtom. i Telemekh.*, No. 8, pp. 84–88.

(1971)*   Realization of Boolean Functions in a Certain Class of Threshold Element
Circuits, Engl. transl. in *Autom. Remote Control* (1972), pp. 1252–1256; orig. in
Avtom. i Telemekh., No. 8, pp. 102–107.

(1973)*   Proof of Minimality of Circuits Consisting of Functional Elements, *Syst. Theory
Research*, Vol. 23 (1973), pp. 85–103; orig. in *Probl. Kibern.*, Vol. 23, pp. 83–102.

Reznik, V. I.
(1961)*   The Realization of Monotonic Functions by Means of Networks Consisting of
Functional Elements, Engl. transl. in *Sov. Phys.—Dokl.*, Vol. 6, No. 7 (1962), pp.
558–561; orig. in *Dokl. Akad. Nauk SSSR*, Vol. 139, No. 3, pp. 566–569.

(1962)* The Realization of Monotonic Functions by Means of Networks Consisting of Functional Elements, *Sov. Phys.—Dokl.*, Vol. 6, No. 7, pp. 558–561.

Riordan, J. and C. E. Shannon
(1942)* The Number of Two-Terminal Series-Parallel Networks, *J. Math. Phys.*, Vol. 21, pp. 83–93.

Rosenkrantz, D. J., R. E. Stearns, and P. M. Lewis
(1974) Approximate Algorithms for the Traveling Salesperson Problem, *Proceedings of the 15th Annual Symposium on Switching and Automata Theory*, New Orleans, pp. 33–42.

Rosin, Robert F.
(1969) Contemporary Concepts of Microprogramming and Emulation, *Comput. Surv.*, Vol. 1, No. 4, pp. 197–212.

Sahni, Sartaj
(1972) Some Related Problems from Network Flows, Game Theory and Integer Programming, *Proceedings of the 13th Annual Symposium on Switching and Automa Theory*, October, pp. 130–138.

(1975) Approximate Algorithms for the 0/1 Knapsack Problem, *JACM*, Vol. 22, No. 1, pp. 115–124.

Sahni, Sartaj and Teofila Gonzales
(1974) *P*-Complete Problems and Approximate Solutions, *Proceedings of the 15th Annual Symposium on Switching and Automata Theory*, New Orleans, pp. 28–32.

Sapozhenko, A. A.
(1968)* On the Greatest Length of a Dead-end Disjunctive Normal Form for Almost All Boolean Functions, Engl. transl. in *Math. Notes Acad. Sci. USSR* (1968), pp. 881–886; orig. in *Mat. Zamet.*, Vol. 4, No. 6, pp. 649–658.

Savage, J. E.
(1971)* The Complexity of Decoders—Part II: Computational Work and Decoding Time, *IEEE Trans. Inf. Theory*, Vol. IT-17, No. 1, pp. 77–84.

(1972)* Computational Work and Time on Finite Machines, *JACM*, Vol. 19, No. 4, pp. 660–674.

(1973) Bounds on the Performance of Computing Systems, *Proceedings of Computer Science and Statistics: Seventh Annual Symposium on the Interface*, Iowa State University, October 18–19, pp. 79–85.

(1974)* An Algorithm for the Computation of Linear Forms, *SIAM J. Comput.*, Vol. 3, No. 2, pp. 150–158.

Schmookler, M. S.
(1969)* On Mod-2 Sums of Products, *IEEE Trans. Comput.*, Vol. C-18, p. 957.

Schnorr, C. D.
(1973) Lower Bounds for the Product of Time and Space Requirements of Turing Machine Computations, *Proceedings of MFCS*, High Tatras, pp. 153–163, September 3–8.

(1974)* Zwei Lineare Untere Schranken für die Komplexität Boolescher Funktionen, *Computing*, Vol. 13, pp. 155–171.

(1975)* The Network Complexity and the Turing Machine Complexity of Finite Functions, to appear in *Acta Inf.*

Schonhage, A. and V. Strassen
(1971)* Schnelle Multiplikation Grosser Zahlen, *Computing*, Vol. 7, pp. 281–292.

Shannon, C. E.

(1938)* A Symbolic Analysis of Relay and Switching Circuits, *Trans. AIEE*, Vol. 57, pp. 713–723.

(1949)* The Synthesis of Two-Terminal Switching Circuits, *BSTJ*, Vol. 28, pp. 59–98.

Shepherdson, J. C.

(1959) The Reduction of Two-Way Automata to One-Way Automata, *IBM J. Res. Dev.*, Vol. 3, No. 2, pp. 198–200.

Sholomov, L. A.

(1967)* On Functionals Characterizing the Complexity of a System of Undetermined Boolean Functions, Engl. transl. in *Syst. Theory Res.*, Vol. 19 (1970), pp. 123–141; orig. in *Probl. Kibern.*, Vol. 19, pp. 123–140.

(1970)* On Calculating the Complexity of Boolean Functions on Turing Machines, Engl. transl. in *Syst. Theory Res.*, Vol. 22 (1972), pp. 51–65; orig. in *Probl. Kibern.*, Vol. 22, pp. 53–66.

(1971)* Information Complexity of Problems Associated with Minimal Realization of Boolean Functions by Networks, Engl. transl. in *Sov. Phys.—Dokl.*, Vol. 16, No. 9 (1972), pp. 714–717; orig. in *Dokl. Akad. Nauk SSSR*, Vol. 200, No. 3, pp. 556–559.

Simon, Herbert

(1969) *The Sciences of the Artificial*, MIT Press, Cambridge, Mass.

Sklansky, J.

(1960A)* An Evaluation of Several Two-Sum and Binary Adders, *IRE Trans. Electron. Comput.*, Vol. EC-9, No. 2, pp. 213–226.

(1960B)* Conditional-Sum Addition Logic, *IRE Trans. Electron. Comput.*, Vol. EC-9, No. 2, pp. 226–231.

Solomonoff, R. J.

(1964) A Formal Theory of Inductive Inference, *Inf. Control*, Vol. 7, pp. 1–22, 224–254.

Soprunenko, E. P.

(1965)* Minimal Realizations of Functions by Circuits Using Functional Elements, *Probl. Kibern.*, Vol. 15, pp. 117–134.

Specker, E.

(1967) Elimination von Quantoren und Lange von Formeln [Abstract], *J. Symb. Logic*, Vol. 32, pp. 567–568.

Spira, P. M.

(1969)* The Time Required for Group Multiplication, *JACM*, Vol. 16, No. 2, pp. 235–243.

(1971)* On Time–Hardware Complexity Tradeoffs for Boolean Functions, *Proceedings of Fourth Hawaii International Symposium on System Sciences*, pp. 525–527.

(1973)* Computation Times of Arithmetic and Boolean Functions in (d, r) Circuits, *IEEE Trans. Comput.*, Vol. C-22, No. 6, pp. 552–555.

Stockmeyer, L.

(1974)* The Complexity of Decision Problems in Automata and Logic, Technical Report MAC TR-133, Project MAC, MIT, Cambridge, Mass.

Strassen, V.

(1969) Gaussian Elimination Is Not Optimal, *Numer. Math.*, Vol. 13, pp. 354–356.

Subbotovskaya, B. A.

(1961)*   Realizations of Linear Functions by Formulas Using +, ·, ‾, Engl. transl. in *Sov. Math.—Dokl.*, Vol. 2 (1961), pp. 110–112; orig. in *Dokl. Akad. Nauk SSSR*, Vol. 136, No. 3, pp. 553–555.

(1963)*   Comparison of Bases in the Realization by Formulas of Functions of the Algebra of Logic, Engl. transl. in *Sov. Math.—Dokl.*, Vol. 4, No. 2 (1963), pp. 478–481; orig. in *Dokl. Akad. Nauk SSSR*, Vol. 149, No. 4, pp. 784–787.

Symes, D. M.

(1972)   The Computation of Finite Functions, *Proceedings of the Fourth Annual ACM Symposium on Theory of Computing*, Denver, May 1–3, pp. 177–182.

Toom, A. L.

(1963)*   The Complexity of a Scheme of Functional Elements Realizing the Multiplication of Integers, Engl. transl. in *Sov. Math.—Dokl.*, Vol. 3 (1963), pp. 714–716; orig. in *Dokl. Akad. Nauk SSSR*, Vol. 150, No. 3, pp. 496–498.

(1967)*   Complexity of Realization of Binary Functions with Small Subfunctions, Engl. transl. in *Syst. Theory Res.*, Vol. 18 (1968), pp. 77–84; orig. in *Probl. Kibern.*, Vol. 18, pp. 83–90.

Trakhtenbrot, B. A.

(1959)*   Asymptotic Evaluation of the Complexity of Logic Nets with Memory, Engl. transl. in *Autom. Expr.*, Vol. 2, No. 2 (1959), pp. 13–14; orig. in *Dokl. Akad. Nauk SSSR*, Vol. 127, No. 2, pp. 281–284.

Turing, A. M.

(1936)   On Computable Numbers with an Application to the Entscheidungsproblem, *Proc. Lond. Math. Soc.*, Vol. 42, pp. 230–265; correction in Vol. 43, pp. 544–546.

Van Voorhis, C. C.

(1972)*   An Improved Lower Bound for Sorting Networks, *IEEE Trans. Comput.*, Vol. C-21, No. 6, pp. 612–613.

Wallace, C. S.

(1964)*   A Suggestion for a Fast Multiplier, *IEEE Trans. Comput.*, Vol. EC-13, No. 1, pp. 14–17.

Walsh, J. L.

(1923)   A Closed Set of Normal Orthogonal Functions, *Am. J. Math.*, Vol. 45, pp. 5–24.

Wilkes, M. V.

(1969)   The Growth of Interest in Microprogramming—A Literature Survey, *Comput. Surv.*, Vol. 1, No. 3, pp. 139–145.

Winograd, S.

(1965)*   On the Time Required to Perform Addition, *JACM*, Vol. 12, No. 2, pp. 277–285.

(1967)*   On the Time Required to Perform Multiplication, *JACM*, Vol. 14, No. 4, pp. 793–802.

(1968)   A New Algorithm for Inner Product, *IEEE Trans. Comput.*, Vol. C-17, No. 7, pp. 693–694.

(1970)*   On the Number of Multiplications Necessary to Compute Certain Functions, *Comm. Pure Appl. Math.*, Vol. 23, pp. 165–179.

Yablonskii, C. V.

(1954)*   Realization of Linear Functions in the Class of Π-Schemes, *Dokl. Akad. Nauk SSSR*, Vol. 94, No. 5, pp. 804–806.

(1959)*   On the Impossibility of Eliminating the Trials of All Functions in P_2 in Solving Certain Problems in the Theory of Networks, Engl. transl. in *Autom. Expr.*, Vol. 1 (1959), pp. 32–34; orig. in *Dokl. Akad. Nauk SSSR*, Vol. 124, pp. 44–47.

Zakharova, E. Yu.

(1972)*   The Realization of Functions of the P_k by Formulae ($k \geq 3$), Engl. transl. in *Math. Notes Acad. Sci. USSR*, (1972), pp. 64–69; orig. in *Mat. Zamet.*, Vol. 11, No. 1, pp. 99–108.

Index